Brazil
Amazon and Pantanal
The Ecotravellers' Wildlife Guide

Other Ecotravellers' Wildlife Guides
Alaska *by Dennis Paulson and Les Beletsky*
Belize and Northern Guatemala *by Les Beletsky*
Costa Rica *by Les Beletsky*
Ecuador and Its Galápagos Islands *by David L. Pearson and Les Beletsky*
Florida *by Fiona Sunquist, Mel Sunquist and Les Beletsky*
Hawaii *by Les Beletsky*
Perú *by David L. Pearson and Les Beletsky*
Tropical Mexico *by Les Beletsky*

Forthcoming guides
The Caribbean Islands *by H. Raffaele, J. Wiley and L. Beletsky*
East Africa *by C. FitzGibbon, J. Fanshawe and W. Branch*
Eastern Australia *by Les Beletsky*
Malaysia and Singapore *by David L. Pearson and Les Beletsky*
New Zealand *by Paddy Ryan and Les Beletsky*
Northern Mexico and Baja *by D.E. Brown, C.A. Lopez-Gonzalez and L. Beletsky*
Southern Africa *by W. Branch, W. Tarboton and C & T Stuart*
Thailand *by David L. Pearson and Les Beletsky*
Western Canada *by Dennis Paulson and Les Beletsky*

series editor Les Beletsky

Brazil
Amazon and Pantanal
The Ecotravellers' Wildlife Guide

David L. Pearson and Les Beletsky

Illustrated by:
Priscilla Barrett
David Beadle
David Dennis
Dan Lane
John Myers
Colin Newman
David Nurney
John O'Neill
John Sill

Contributors:
Martha L. Crump
Stacey Combes
Richard Francis

ACADEMIC PRESS
SAN DIEGO   SAN FRANCISCO   NEW YORK
BOSTON   LONDON   SYDNEY   TOKYO

This book is printed on acid-free paper.

Academic Press
A division of Harcourt, Inc.
Harcourt Place, 32 Jamestown Road, London NW1 7BY, UK
http://www.academicpress.com

AP Natural World is published by
A division of Harcourt, Inc.
525 B Street, Suite 1900, San Diego
California 92101–4495, USA
http://www.academicpress.com

ISBN: 0–12–548052–0

Library of Congress Catalog Card Number: 2001090242

A catalogue record for this book is available from the British Library

Typeset by J&L Composition Ltd, Filey, North Yorkshire
Colour Separation by Tenon & Polert Colour Scanning Ltd, Hong Kong
Printed in Hong Kong by Midas Printing Ltd
02 03 04 05 06 07 MD 9 8 7 6 5 4 3 2 1

Contents

Foreword

Throughout the world, wild places and wildlife are dwindling. Their conservation will require ever more intense protection, care, and management. We always value things more when we stand to lose them, and it is perhaps no coincidence that people are increasingly eager to experience unspoiled nature, and to see the great wildlife spectacles. Tourists are increasingly forsaking the package tour and the crowded beach, to wade through jungle streams, to dive on coral reefs, and to track elusive wildlife. But despite its increasing popularity, nature tourism is nothing new, and the attraction to the tourist is self evident – so why should a conservation organization like the Wildlife Conservation Society encourage it?

The answer is that nature tourism, if properly conducted, can contribute directly to the conservation of wild places and wildlife. If it does that, such tourism earns the sobriquet *ecotourism*. A defining quality of ecotourism is that people are actively encouraged to appreciate nature. If people experience wild areas, they can grow to appreciate their beauty, stability and integrity. And only if they do so, will people care about conserving these places. Before you can save nature, people need to know that it exists.

Another characteristic of ecotourism is that people tread lightly on the natural fabric of wild places. By their very definition, these are places with minimal human impact, so people must not destroy or degrade what they come to experience. Tourists need to take only photographs, leave only footprints – and ideally not even that. Wastes and pollution need to be minimized. Potential disturbance to animals and damage to vegetation must always be considered.

The third characteristic, and that which most clearly separates ecotourism from other forms of tourism, is that tourists actively participate in the conservation of the area. That participation can be direct. For instance, people or tour companies might pay fees or make contributions that support local conservation efforts, or tourists might volunteer to work on a project. More likely, the participation is indirect, with the revenues generated by the tourism entering the local economy. In this way, tourism provides an economic incentive to local communities to continue to conserve the area.

Ecotourists thus are likely to be relatively well informed about nature, and able to appreciate the exceptional nature of wild places. They are more likely to travel by canoe than cruise ship. They will be found staying at locally owned lodges rather than huge multi-national hotels. They will tend to travel to national parks and protected areas rather than to resorts. And they are more likely to contribute to conservation than detract from it.

The Wildlife Conservation Society was involved in promoting ecotourism since before the term was generally accepted. In the early 1960s, the Society (then known as the New York Zoological Society) studied how to use tourism to provide revenues for national park protection in Tanzania (then known as Tanganyika).

By the 1970s, the Society was actively involved in using tourism as a conservation strategy, focusing especially on Amboseli National Park in Kenya. The Mountain Gorilla Project in the Virunga mountains of Rwanda, a project started in the late 1970s, still remains one of the classic efforts to promote conservation through tourism. Today the Society continues to encourage tourism as a strategy from the lowland Amazonian forests to the savannas of East Africa.

We at the Wildlife Conservation Society believe that you will find these Ecotravellers' Wildlife Guides to be useful, educational introductions to the wildlife of many of the world's most spectacular ecotourism destinations.

John G. Robinson
Vice President and
Director of International Conservation
Wildlife Conservation Society

WCS

WILDLIFE CONSERVATION SOCIETY

● to sustain wildlife   ● to teach ecology   ● to inspire care for nature

The mission of the Wildlife Conservation Society, since its founding in 1895 as the New York Zoological Society, has been to save wildlife and inspire people to care about our nature heritage. Today, that mission is achieved through the world's leading international conservation program working in 53 nations to save endangered species and ecosystems, as well as through pioneering environmental education programs that reach more than two million schoolchildren in the New York metropolitan area and are used in 49 states and several nations, and through the nation's largest system of urban zoological facilities including the world famous Bronx Zoo. WCS is working to make future generations inheritors, not just survivors.

With 60 staff scientists and more than 100 research fellows, WCS has the largest professional field staff of any US-based international conservation organization. WCS's field programs benefit from the technical support of specialists based at WCS's Bronx Zoo headquarters in New York. The Field Veterinarian Program sends experts around the globe to assess wildlife health, develop monitoring techniques, and train local veterinarians. WCS's curatorial staff provides expertise in breeding endangered species in captivity. The Science Resource Center helps researchers assess data through computer mapping, statistical treatments, and cutting-edge genetic analysis. The Education Department writes primary and secondary school curricula that address conservation issues and hosts teacher-training workshops around the world.

WCS's strategy is to conduct comprehensive field studies to gather information on wildlife needs, train local conservation professionals to protect and manage wildlife and wild areas for the future, and advise on protected area creation, expansion, and management. Because WCS scientists are familiar with local conditions, they can effectively translate field data into conservation action and policies, and develop locally sustainable solutions to conflicts between humans and wildlife. An acknowledged leader in the field, the Wildlife Conservation Society forges productive relationships with governments, international agencies and local organizations.

To learn more about WCS's regional programs and membership opportunities, please see our pages in the back of this book. And please visit our website at **www.wcs.org**.

Preface

This book and others in the series are aimed at environmentally conscious travellers for whom some of the best parts of any trip are glimpses of wildlife in natural settings; at people who, when speaking of a journey, often remember days and locations by the wildlife they saw: "That was where we watched the monkeys," and "That was the day we saw the hawk catch a snake." The purpose of this book is to heighten enjoyment of a trip and enrich wildlife sightings by providing you with information to identify several hundred of the most frequently encountered animals and plants of Brazil, along with up-to-date information on their natural history, behavior, and conservation. Your skills at recognizing many of the species you see on your travels through Brazil will be greatly enhanced with this book's color illustrations of 31 species of insects and arthropods, 95 amphibians and reptiles, 288 birds, 70 mammals, 35 fish, and 37 species of common plants characteristic of each major habitat type.

The idea to write this book grew out of our own travel experiences and frustrations. First and foremost, we found that we could not find a single book to take along on a trip that would help identify all the types of animals and plants that interested us. There are bird and mammal field guides and plant identification handbooks, but their number and weight quickly accumulate until you need an extra suitcase just to carry them. Thus, the idea: create a single guide-book that travellers could carry to help them identify and learn about the different kinds of animals and plants they were most likely to see. Also, in our experience with guided tours, we've found that guides vary tremendously in their knowledge of nature and wildlife. Many, of course, are fantastic sources of information on the ecology and behavior of animals and plants. Some, however, know only about certain kinds of animals, birds, for instance. And many others, we found, knew precious little about any animals or plants, and what information they did tell their groups was often incorrect.

Last, like most ecotravellers, we are concerned about the threats to many species as their natural habitats are damaged or destroyed by people; when we travelled, we wanted current information on the conservation statuses of species we encountered. This book provides the traveller with conservation information on many of the species pictured or discussed in the book.

A few administrative notes: because this book has an international audience, we present measurements in both metric and English system units. The scientific classification of common species by now, you might think, would be pretty much established and unchanging; but you would be wrong. These days, what with molecular methods to compare species, classifications of various groups that were first worked out during the 1800s and early 1900s are undergoing radical changes. Many bird groups, for instance, are being reclassified after comparative studies of their DNA. The research is so new that many biologists are still arguing about the results. We cannot guarantee that all the classifications that we use in the book are absolutely the last word on the subject, or that we have been wholly consistent in the classifications we used. However, for most users of this book, such minor transgressions are probably too esoteric to be of much significance.

Finally, we have tried to make the style of writing interesting and readable, but at the same time challenging and precise. We have tried to avoid terse, dry, textbook prose, sometimes with narratives that include anthropomorphisms – providing plants and animals with human characteristics. We do this for fun; hopefully, in so doing, we have not offended our professional colleagues. Plants and animals do not, of course, reason and think like humans. If you do not appreciate our sense of humor, please ignore those sections; you should still have remaining a solid natural history guide to the Amazonian and Pantanal regions of Brazil.

We need to acknowledge the help of a large number of people in producing this book. First, much of the information we use is gleaned from published sources, and we owe the authors of these books and scientific papers a great deal of credit; their names and the titles of their publications are listed in the References and Additional Reading section on page 246. We are especially indebted to Martha Crump (Northern Arizona University) for her writing of the amphibian chapter and for editing the reptile chapter (and M. Crump thanks Teresa Avila-Pires, John E. Cadle, William E. Duellman, Celio F. B. Haddad, Ronald W. Heyer, Cynthia Prado, and Laurie J. Vitt for their expert help with information on Brazilian amphibians and reptiles), to Stacey Combes for writing the conservation chapter, and to Richard Francis for the chapter on Amazon fish. In addition, most book sections were read and critiqued by at least one outside expert in that field, and their comments and corrections greatly increased the accuracy of the book. These experts included: Bill Lamar (University of Texas at Tyler), reptiles; Kevin Zimmer (Victor Emanuel Nature Tours, Austin, Texas), birds; Andrew Smith (Arizona State University, ASU) and Ted Flemming (University of Miami), mammals; Phil DeVries (Milwaukee Museum, Wisconsin), Ian Kitching (British Museum, London), and Célio Magalhães (INPA, Manaus), arthropods; Gary Hartshorn (Duke University) and Ghillean Prance (Kew Gardens, London), plants. John and Karen Shrader (Centerville, Ohio) shared extensive notes on their trips to the Pantanal with us. Over the last 15 years several friends and colleagues in Brazil helped us with logistics, research permits and insight into the natural history of the Amazon and Pantanal: Bill Overal and Dave Oren (Goeldi Museum, Belém); Claudio Rui Fonseca (INPA, Manaus) and Joachim Adis (Max Planck Institute, Plön, Germany). Cátia Nunes da Cunha, Marinêz Isaac Marques, and Dalci M. M. de Oliveira took time from their busy schedules at the Federal University of Mato Grosso in Cuiabá to join us in the field and share their extensive knowledge of the natural history of the Pantanal. Nancy Pearson suffered extended periods of neglect during the writing process of this book, but she cheerfully supported us at every step. Ghillean Prance and Visuals Unlimited provided the excellent habitat photos. We wish also to thank our editor at Academic Press, Andrew Richford, and assistant editor, Samantha Fallon, and the artists who produced the marvelous illustrations: Priscilla Barrett (mammals), David Beadle (birds), David Dennis (amphibians and reptiles), Dan Lane (birds), John Myers (plants), Colin Newman (amphibians, reptiles, fish and arthropods), Dave Nurney (birds), John O'Neill (birds) and John Sill (birds).

Please let us know of any errors, opinions on the book, and suggestions for future editions. We are interested in hearing of your wildlife travel experiences. Write care of the publisher or e-mail: ECOTRAVEL8@aol.com

Chapter 1

Ecotourism: Travel for the Environmentally Concerned

- What Ecotourism Is and Why It's Important
- How Ecotourism Helps; Ecotravel Ethics
- Brazil: Biodiversity and Ecotourism
- Brazil: Environmental Problems and Changing Attitudes

What Ecotourism Is and Why It's Important

Ecotourism or *ecotravel* is travel to (usually exotic) destinations specifically to admire and enjoy wildlife and undeveloped, relatively undisturbed natural areas, as well as indigenous cultures. The development and increasing popularity of eco-tourism is a clear outgrowth of escalating concern for conservation of the world's natural resources and *biodiversity* (the different types of animals, plants, and other life forms found within a region). Owing mainly to peoples' actions, animal species and wild habitats are disappearing or deteriorating at an alarming rate. Because of the increasing emphasis on the importance of the natural environment by schools at all levels and the media's continuing exposure of environmental issues, people now have an enhanced appreciation of the natural world and an increased awareness of environmental problems globally. They also have the very human desire to want to see undisturbed habitats and wild animals before they are gone, and those with the time and resources increasingly are doing so.

But that is not the entire story. The purpose of ecotravel is actually twofold. Yes, people want to undertake exciting, challenging, educational trips to exotic locales – wet tropical forests, wind-blown deserts, high mountain passes, mid-ocean coral reefs – to enjoy the scenery, the animals, and the nearby local cultures. But the second major goal of ecotourism is often as important: travellers want to help conserve the very places – habitats and wildlife – that they visit. That is, through a portion of their tour cost and spending into the local economy of destination countries – paying for park admissions, engaging local guides, staying at local hotels, eating at local restaurants, using local transportation services, etc. – ecotourists help to preserve natural areas. Ecotourism helps because local people benefit economically as much or more by preserving habitats and wildlife for continuing use by ecotravellers than they could by "harvesting" the habitats for short-term gain. Put another way, local people can sustain themselves better economically by participating in ecotourism than by, for instance, cutting down rainforests for lumber or hunting animals for meat or the pet trade.

Preservation of some of the Earth's remaining wild areas is important for a number of reasons. Aside from moral arguments – the acknowledgment that we share the planet with millions of other species and have some obligation not to be the continuing agent of their decline and extinction – increasingly we understand that conservation is in our own best interests. The example most often cited is that botanists and pharmaceutical researchers each year discover another wonder drug or two whose base chemicals come from plants that live, for instance, only in tropical rainforest. Fully one-fourth of all drugs sold in the USA come from natural sources – plants and animals. About 50 important drugs now manufactured come from flowering plants found in rainforests, and, based on the number of plants that have yet to be cataloged and screened for their drug potential, it is estimated that at least 300 more major drugs remain to be discovered. The implication is that if the globe's rainforests are soon destroyed, we will never discover these future wonder drugs, and so will never enjoy their benefits. Also, the developing concept of *biophilia*, if true, dictates that, for our own mental health, we had better preserve much of the wildness that remains in the world. Biophilia, the word coined by Harvard biologist E. O. Wilson, suggests that because people evolved amid rich and constant interactions with other species and in natural habitats, we have deeply ingrained, innate tendencies to affiliate with other species and actual physical need to experience, at some level, natural habitats. This instinctive, emotional attachment to wildness means that if we eliminate species and habitats, we will harm ourselves because we will lose things essential to our mental well-being.

If ecotourism contributes in a significant way to conservation, then it is an especially fitting reprieve for rainforests and other natural habitats, because it is the very characteristic of the habitats that conservationists want to save, wildness, that provides the incentive for travellers to visit and for local people to preserve.

How Ecotourism Helps; Ecotravel Ethics

To the traveller, the benefits of ecotourism are substantial (exciting, adventurous trips to stunning wild areas; viewing never-before-seen wildlife); the disadvantages are minor (sometimes, less-than-deluxe transportation and accommodations that, to many ecotravellers, are actually an essential part of the experience). But what are the actual benefits of ecotourism to local economies and to helping preserve habitats and wildlife?

The pluses of ecotourism, in theory, are considerable:

1 Ecotourism benefits visited sites in a number of ways. Most importantly from the visitor's point of view, through park admission fees, guide fees, etc., ecotourism generates money locally that can be used directly to manage and protect wild areas. Ecotourism allows local people to earn livings from areas they live in or near that have been set aside for ecological protection. Allowing local participation is important because people will not want to protect the

sites, and may even be hostile toward them, if the people formerly used the now-protected site (for farming or hunting, for instance) to support themselves, but are no longer allowed such use. Finally, most ecotour destinations are in rural areas, regions that ordinarily would not warrant much attention, much less development money, from central governments for services such as road building and maintenance. But all governments realize that a popular tourist site is a valuable commodity, one that it is smart to cater to and protect.

2   Ecotourism benefits education and research. As people, both local and foreign, visit wild areas, they learn more about the sites – from books, from guides, from exhibits, and from their own observations. They should come away with an enhanced appreciation of nature and ecology, an increased understanding of the need for preservation, and perhaps a greater likelihood of supporting conservation measures. Also, in many cases, a percentage of ecotourist dollars are funneled into research in ecology and conservation, work that will in the future lead to more and better conservation solutions.

3   Ecotourism can also be an attractive development option for developing countries. Investment costs to develop small, relatively rustic ecotourist facilities are minor compared with the costs involved in trying to develop traditional tourist facilities, such as beach resorts. Also, it has been estimated that, at least in some regions, ecotourists spend more per person in the destination countries than any other kind of tourists.

A conscientious ecotraveller can take several steps to maximize his or her positive impact on visited areas. First and foremost, if travelling with a tour group, is to select an ecologically committed tour company. Basic guidelines for ecotourism have been established by various international conservation organizations. These are a set of ethics that tour operators should follow if they are truly concerned with conservation. Travellers wishing to adhere to ecotour ethics should ascertain whether tour operators conform to the guidelines (or at least to some of them), and choose a company accordingly. Some tour operators conspicuously trumpet their ecotour credentials and commitments in their brochures and sales pitches. A large, glossy brochure that fails to mention how a company fulfills some of the ecotour ethics may indicate an operator that is not especially environmentally concerned. Resorts, lodges, and travel agencies that specialize in ecotourism likewise can be evaluated for their dedication to eco-ethics.

Basic ecotour guidelines, as put forth by the United Nations Environmental Programme (UNEP), the International Union for Conservation of Nature (IUCN), and the World Resources Institute (WRI), are that tours and tour operators should:

1   Provide significant benefits for local residents; involve local communities in tour planning and implementation.
2   Contribute to the sustainable management of natural resources.
3   Incorporate environmental education for tourists and residents.
4   Manage tours to minimize negative impacts on the environment and local culture.

For example, tour companies could:

1   Make contributions to the parks or areas visited; support or sponsor small, local environmental projects.
2   Provide employment to local residents as tour assistants, local guides, or local naturalists.

3   Whenever possible, use local products, transportation, food, and locally owned lodging and other services.

4   Keep tour groups small to minimize negative impacts on visited sites; educate ecotourists about local cultures as well as habitats and wildlife.

5   When possible, cooperate with researchers; for instance, Costa Rican researchers are now making good use of the elevated canopy walkways in tropical forests that several ecotour facility operators erected on their properties for the enjoyment and education of their guests.

Committed ecotravellers can also adhere to the ecotourism ethic by disturbing habitats and wildlife as little as possible, by staying on trails, by being informed about the historical and present conservation concerns of destination countries, by respecting local cultures and rules, and even by actions as simple as picking up litter on trails.

Ecotourism, of course, is not a perfect remedy for threatened habitats and wildlife. Some negatives have been noticed, such as overuse of trails and the disruption of the natural behavior of wildlife when ecotourists intrude upon the animals' domains. On balance, however, most experts agree that in many situations, in most parts of the world, responsible ecotourism can have a positive role in conservation.

Brazil: Biodiversity and Ecotourism

Brazil is considered by conservation groups to be one of 10 or so "mega-diversity" countries, harboring huge numbers of animal and plant species. It contains about a third of the Earth's remaining tropical forest. About 1600 species of birds occur in Brazil, more species than are found in all but two other countries, and more than 10% of them are endemic (occur only in Brazil) or nearly endemic. More than 500 mammal species, 460 reptiles and 500 amphibians occur in Brazil (see Table 1, p. 119).

Most ecotravellers to Brazil head to two main areas, the Amazon and Pantanal (see Map 1, p. 9), and both are covered in this book.

Amazon

For wildlife watchers, naturalists, and adventurers, few places on the planet match the allure of Brazil's Amazon region. Along with the African savannah, the Galápagos Islands, the Great Barrier Reef, and few other sites, the Amazon is on the "must-visit" lists of most ecotravellers. The Amazon is both a giant river system and an associated vast lowland forest area that covers about half of Brazil (and a large portion of South America, particularly when the Amazon sections of adjacent countries are included). The Amazon River itself is huge, very broad in some areas, 2 km (1.2 miles) wide at its narrowest, and every day spewing, so they say, enough fresh water into the Atlantic Ocean to satisfy New York City's needs for 10 years. The forest surrounding the Amazon River and its myriad meandering tributaries and their associated floodplains covers an area of millions of square kilometers, and is the Earth's largest remaining tract of continuous forest (tropical or otherwise).

Where do tourists go in the Amazon region and how do they get there? Most ecotourists to the Amazon visit the region by boat. They fly to Belém (on the North Atlantic coast at the mouth of the river) or to Manaus (more than 1100 km (700 miles) upriver, where the Río Negro joins the Amazon) and board boats of various sizes. Large boats ply the major rivers, smaller boats explore small tributaries, and motorized canoes carry tourists up small rivers and large streams (where the best wildlife-viewing occurs). The main destinations for ecotourists (in descending order of popularity) are:

1   Manaus and the Río Negro area.
2   Cruises of one to two weeks on the Amazon between Belém and Manaus, or between Belém (or Manaus) and Iquitos (Perú); these stop frequently at sites along the Amazon.
3   The Belém area, which is the mouth of the Amazon, west to the Río Xingu.
4   The Río Tapajos area (including Santarem to Itaituba).
5   Tabatinga, on the Perú and Colombia border.

Some travellers, however, shun boats and instead head for jungle lodges where they can hike and bird-watch on forest trails, spend time in the forest canopy using aerial walkways, partake of piranha fishing, and be taken in canoes along small channels through the forest. More adventurous types even take camping tours of the region.

Pantanal

The Pantanal region of Brazil lies in the southwestern part of the country, nestled against Paraguay. It is a relatively small realm when compared with the enormous Amazon region, with which it is contiguous (Map 1, p. 9). But it is actually a vast area that contains one of the world's great wetland ecosystems – huge expanses of sub-tropical wetland forests and wet grasslands, and a hundred or more major and minor rivers.

Wildlife is the main ecotourism attraction of the Pantanal. The diversity, abundance, and conspicuousness of animal life here is sometimes compared favorably with the renowned Okavango Delta of southern Africa. A major reason that visitors see so much wildlife is that the region is a highly seasonal wetland (the planet's largest). It rains for many months (p. 9), inundating the Pantanal, flooding the grasslands and forests, but then, during the dry season, the floodwaters slowly recede until water is restricted to ponds in low-lying areas and to rivers. During the wet season, when the lowland forest and grassland areas flood, many terrestrial animals are forced to relocate to scattered patches of slightly-higher-elevation scrub, where many species can be easily seen. In the dry season, some wildlife that was spread out during the rainy season congregates around the few remaining water sources, and so is easily seen at this time. Caiman, crocodile relatives, concentrate at these ponds and small rivers in enormous numbers. Pig-like Capybara, the world's largest rodents, are seen easily along roads and waterways. And a particular prize for birders, the endangered Hyacinth Macaw, the world's largest parrot, is seen in small flocks in trees near water. Also, rare mammals such as Giant Anteater, Marsh Deer, and even Jaguar, are often spotted.

The Pantanal was little-visited until the 1970s (roads first went into the region in the late 1960s), and it was mostly an unknown, lightly visited natural site until the 1980s, when it started showing up on ecotour itineraries. It is now one of the world's wildlife-viewing "hot-spots," a profitable destination for most large wildlife tour companies.

Where do tourists go in the Pantanal and how do they get there? Most visitors to the Pantanal fly (or take very long car or bus rides from Rio de Janeiro or São Paulo) to the town of Cuiabà at the northern end of the Pantanal or to Campo Grande at the southern end, and then take organized tours into the wetlands. There are several lodges in the Pantanal that travellers overnight at, after taking day-trips in vans, open trucks, and boats. Because of the wetland nature of the area, roads (except for one main road that bisects the Pantanal, north to south) and trails are few, making independent exploration on foot difficult.

Brazil: Environmental Problems and Changing Attitudes

Brazil, as you might expect, with a population estimated to be about 180 million and a poverty rate hovering between 30% and 40%, faces a host of environmental problems. The list includes high rates of deforestation and overgrazing to accommodate hungry colonists in search of new agricultural fields and cattle pastures, logging companies interested in quick profits but not in conservation, introduction of domestic animals and plants that compete with native species, and short-sighted government environmental policies – such as plans to drain the Pantanal to increase farmland or channelize rivers to increase barge traffic year-round. Mining currently dominates many political decisions; its economic power usually has its way. Pollution of inland rivers and coastal waters from mine tailings and chemical runoff is rampant. If these human-caused problems aren't bad enough, their impact on Brazil is multiplied by what seems to be a constant parade of natural disasters – floods from heavy rains, droughts, and extensive forest fires that during the day can block out the sun for weeks. With these overwhelming natural and human-made problems, it's easy to consider environmental protection a low priority and conservation measures a luxury.

Behind all this pessimism, however, there is hope. Numerous non-government organizations (NGOs), largely staffed by energetic, young Brazilians with a dream, are in many areas holding their own against environmental destruction. Environmental awareness is increasingly being taught in local schools and discussed on television and in newspapers. Large mining companies have discovered the advantages of positive public relations and are introducing better methods of discarding used chemicals and tailings. Politicians are slowly being pressured into at least proclaiming their advocacy for *green* (environment-enhancing) policies and programs. It is now less unusual to hear that they have taken a stand that benefits the environment. One of the strongest and most rapidly growing forces to benefit the environment in Brazil is ecotourism. As its economic weight and effect on the country's GDP become more obvious, ecotourism's voice is being heard and its needs and desires heeded – sometimes even when they run counter to those of mining companies and plantation owners. Groups of NGOs, tourist agencies, and indigenous peoples are working together to solidify their power and convince the government that ecotourism is an important part of Brazil's future. Your trip to Brazil to experience its natural wonders is a statement in itself that will benefit Brazil's environment. If you want to be more than passively involved, however, use your influence to actively help Brazil and its environment. If you see tour agencies, lodge operators, or officials following procedures or policies that run counter to the principle of ecotourism as a sustainable use of resources, say something to them. Also, seek out Brazilian and international non-profit NGOs that run on donations and make contributions.

Environmental threats and conservation in Brazil are explored in more detail in Chapter 4.

Chapter 2

Geography and Habitats

Geography and Climate

Brazil (Map 1, p. 9) is a huge country (8,547,403 sq km, 3,300,000 sq miles). Only slightly smaller than the USA, it is the fifth largest country in the world and has the world's ninth largest economy. It is the largest country in South America and includes almost half of the continent's land area. It straddles the equator and shares common boundaries with every South American country except Chile and Ecuador. In terms of topographic variety, it is mostly flat to rolling lowlands with some hills and low mountains in the extreme north and along a narrow coastal belt.

Both the Amazonian and Pantanal regions of Brazil show distinct seasonality in rainfall, and, to some extent, temperatures. In general this seasonality becomes

Map I   Brazil, showing main cities, towns, rivers, roads, and Amazon and Pantanal regions.

more and more marked the farther south you go. Some average annual rainfall values are as follows (see Map 1 for locations): for the town of Manaus, average annual rainfall = 1811 mm (72 in) and driest months are June to September; for Belém, average annual rainfall = 2439 mm (98 in) and driest months are August to November; for Cuiabá, average rainfall = 1390 mm (55 in) and driest months are May to September. In the dry, winter months (June to October) the Pantanal and southern portions of the Amazon are far enough south to occasionally receive cold weather fronts moving up from the Antarctic. These fronts, called *frente fria* or *friagem,* often bring extended periods of cloud cover and rain in addition to drops in temperature (sometimes down to 8 °C, 46 °F).

The Greater Amazon Basin covers 6 million sq km (2,316,000 sq miles) and includes parts of nine countries: from the Atlantic Ocean west to the base of the Andes mountains in Bolivia, Perú, Ecuador and Colombia, and from Venezuela, Guyana, Surinam and French Guiana south into central Brazil. The Brazilian part alone contains more than half this area. The Amazon forest makes up nearly one-third of the tropical lowland rainforests of the world and is the largest tract of continuous forest remaining in the world.

Connected to the Amazon forest's most southerly extension and sharing much of its wetland flora and fauna, is the Pantanal (Map 1; Map 2, p. 10), an immense geological depression in the Earth's surface through which flows the Paraguai River. One of the world's largest wetland ecosystems, the Pantanal at the height of its annual flood season makes up more than 140,000 sq km (55,000 sq miles), an area the size of Scotland and Ireland together or the USA state of Georgia. Nestled primarily in the southwestern part of Brazil, a small portion of it spills over into neighboring Bolivia and Paraguay. The Pantanal serves as a breeding ground for enormous rookeries of waterfowl, many large mammals and numerous reptile species. In addition, numerous vertebrate and invertebrate species are restricted to this area. This savannah-grassland area receives its maximum inundation levels as early as February in the north and as late as June in the south, but the extent of flooding varies greatly from year to year. This great marshy basin soaks up millions of cubic meters (yards) of water each year during the rainy season, and it thus helps regulate flooding in rivers downstream.

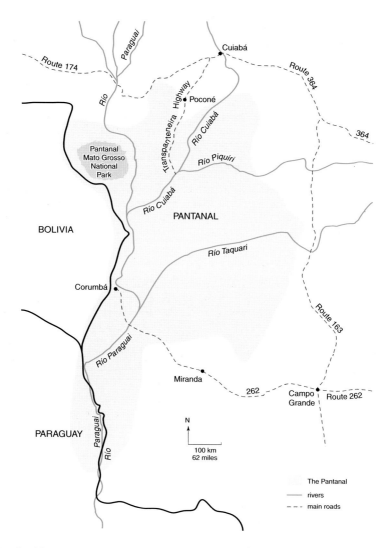

Map 2   Main towns, rivers, and roads of the Pantanal region of southern Brazil.

During the dry season, it reverts to a grassland savannah, in appearance, not unlike that of eastern Africa. The Pantanal's extraordinary diversity and abundance of wildlife are under great threat from deforestation, expanding agriculture (mainly from cattle-ranching – there are 1100 cattle ranches in the Pantanal and a total of 3 million cattle – and soy bean cultivation), illegal hunting and fishing, uncontrolled tourism, and pollution from pesticides and chemical pollutants from mining (see Chapter 4).

Vegetation Patterns

The most striking thing about tropical habitats is their high degree of species diversity. Temperate forests in Europe or North America often consist of only a few tree species. The norm in tropical forests is to find between 100 and 300 tree species within an area of a few hectares or acres. Sometimes after appreciating a specific tree and then looking around for another of the same species, you have to walk several kilometers before finding the next one. Ecologists say tropical areas have a much higher *species richness* than temperate regions – for plant life, as well as for some animals such as insects and birds. Brazil has one of the richest floras in the world, with more than 55,000 species of plants. Some 17,000, nearly one-third, of these plants are *endemic* to Brazil (that is, they occur nowhere else in the world; see Close-up, p. 117).

During first visits to tropical forests, people from Europe, North America, and other temperate-zone areas are usually impressed with the richly varied plant forms, many of which are not found in temperate regions. Although not every kind of tropical forest includes all of them, you will usually see a number of highly typical plant forms and shapes.

Tree Shape and Forest Layering

Many tropical trees grow to great heights, straight trunks rising many meters (yards) before branching. Tropical forests often appear layered, or *stratified,* and several more or less distinct layers of vegetation can sometimes be seen. A typical tropical forest has a surface herb layer (ground cover), a low layer of low shrubs and immature trees, one or more lower levels of shorter trees, and a higher, or *canopy,* tree layer (Figure 1). In reality, there are no formal layers – just various species of trees that grow to different, characteristic, maximum heights. Lone, very tall trees that soar high above their neighbors are sometimes referred to as *emergents* and are characteristic of tropical forests. Trees whose *crowns,* or high leafy sections, are in the often continuous upper layer are part of the *canopy.* Many of the crowns of tropical trees in the canopy are characteristically shaped and look like umbrellas (Figure 1). Those in the next highest layers form the *sub-canopy.* Shrubs, bushes and short or baby trees make up the *understory* (Figure 1). The *leaf litter* on the forest floor is a variable layer that during the dry season accumulates many dry leaves, uneaten fruits and fallen branches. However, it becomes very thin during the rainy season when warm temperatures and moist humidity permit fungi, insects and bacteria to quickly break down this organic material into chemicals and nutrients. They in turn are taken up immediately by the shallow root systems and fungal associates of the trees and shrubs.

Figure 2 Interior view of a typical tropical forest.

Figure 1 Exterior view of a typical tropical forest.

Large-leaved Understory Plants

Tropical forests often have dense concentrations of large-leaved understory herbs (Figure 2). Several plant families are usually represented:

1   Aroids, family Araceae, include plants such as *Dieffenbachia*, or Dumb Cane, and climbers such as *Monstera, Philodendron* (Plate D), and *Syngonium*.
2   Marantas, family Marantaceae, including *Calantha insignis*, the Rattlesnake plant, which is an herb whose flattened yellow flowers resemble a snake's rattle.
3   *Heliconia* (Plate E), family Heliconiaceae, which are large-leaved perennial herbs.

The large leaves of these understory plants at least partially function to help gather the meager sunlight that makes its way though the canopy and subcanopy, so that adequate photosynthesis can take place to maintain the plant.

Tree Bases and Roots

Any northerner visiting a tropical forest for the first time quickly stops in his or her tracks and stares at the bottoms of trees. The trunks of temperate zone trees may widen a bit at the base but they more or less descend straight into the ground. Not so in the tropics, where many trees are *buttressed* – huge ridges emerge and descend from the lower section of the trunk and spread out around the tree before entering the ground (Figure 2). The buttresses appear as narrow vertical ridges attached to the sides of a trunk. In older trees they are big and deep enough to hide a person (or a coiled snake!). The function of buttresses is believed to be tree support and, indeed, buttressed trees are highly wind resistant and difficult to blow down. But whether increased support is the primary reason that buttressing evolved is an open question, one that plant biologists study and argue over (the "hypotenuse theory" of shorter distances between the major roots and the crown is another hotly argued possible explanation). Another unusual root structure associated with the tropics is *stilt*, or *prop*, *roots*. These are roots that seem to raise the trunk of a tree off the ground. They come off the tree some distance from the bottom of the trunk and grow out and down, entering the ground at various distances from the trunk (Figure 2). Stilt roots are characteristic of trees, such as mangroves, that occur in habitats that are covered with water during parts of the year, and many palms. Aside from anchoring a tree, functions of stilt roots are controversial.

Climbers and Vines

Tropical trees are often conspicuously loaded with climbing vines (Figures 1 and 2). Vines, also called *climbers, lianas*, and *bush-ropes*, are species from a number of plant families that spend their lives associated with trees. Some ascend or descend along a tree's trunk, perhaps loosely attached; others spread out within a tree's leafy canopy before descending toward the ground, free, from a branch. Vines are surprisingly strong and difficult to break; many older ones grow less flexible and more woody, sometimes reaching the diameter of small trees. Common vines that climb trees from the ground up are Philodendrons and those of the genus *Monstera*.

Epiphytes

Epiphytes are plants that grow on other plants (usually trees) but do not harm their "hosts" (Figure 2). They are not parasites – they do not burrow into the trees to suck out nutrients; they simply take up space on trunks and branches. Ecologically, we would call the relationship between a tree and its epiphytes *commensal*: one party to the arrangement, the epiphyte, benefits – it gains growing space and access to sunlight – and the other party, the tree, is unaffected. Epiphytes harm trees probably only when an epiphyte load becomes so heavy that the branch bearing it breaks off. How do epiphytes grow if they are not rooted in the host tree or the ground? Epiphyte roots that grow along the tree's surface capture nutrients from the air – bits of dust, soil, and plant parts that breeze by. Eventually, by collecting debris, each epiphyte develops its own bit of soil, into which it is rooted. Epiphytes are especially numerous and diverse in middle and higher-elevation rainforests, where persistent cloud cover and mist provide them ideal growing conditions. *Orchids*, with their striking flowers that attract bees and wasps for pollination, are among the most famous kinds of epiphytes. *Bromeliads*, restricted to the Americas, are common epiphytes with sharply pointed leaves that grow in a circular pattern, creating a central tank, or *cistern*, in which collects rain water, dust, soil, and plant materials. Recent studies of bromeliads and other water-holding plants (called *phytotelmata*) show that these cisterns function as small aquatic ecosystems, with a number of different animals – insects, worms, snails, among others – making use of them. Several groups of amphibians are known to spend parts of their life cycles in these small pools (p. 91), and a number of species of tiny birds nest in bromeliads. (Not all bromeliads are epiphytes; some grow on the ground as largish, spiny plants, such as the pineapple – a native of Brazil.) Other plants that grow as epiphytes are mosses and ferns.

Palms

The trees most closely associated with the tropics worldwide are *palms*. Being greeted by palm trees upon exiting a jet is a sure sign that you have arrived in a warm climate. In fact, it is temperature that probably limits palms mainly to tropical and subtropical regions. They grow from a single point at the top of their stems, and so are very sensitive to frost; if that part of the plant freezes, the plant dies. Almost everyone recognizes palms because, for trees, they have unusual forms: they have no branches, but all leaves (which are quite large and called *fronds*) emerge from the top of the single trunk; and their trunks are usually of the same diameter from base to top. Many taller palms have stilt roots propping them up. Some palms have no trunks, but grow as small understory plants. More than 40 species of palms can be found in the Amazon and Pantanal.

Major Ecosystems and Habitats; Common Plants

Using associations of particular plant species, several broad ecosystems and habitats can be distinguished in Brazil's Amazon and Pantanal regions. Each ecosystem consists of large numbers of unique plant species that characterize and make it different from other ecosystems. Often, some animal species are also associated with each of these ecosystems. Below are brief descriptions of Brazil's major ecosystems and listings of some of the more abundant and recognizable types of vegetation that visitors are almost sure to see. Note that many plants occur in more than one ecosystem type, so although a tree like *Cecropia* (Plate C), for instance, occurs throughout Brazil's Amazon lowland forests, it and related species are also found up to middle elevations on the Eastern Andean slopes. Some common plants do not have English names. Forests that are pristine and have not been cut down by humans are called *primary* or *old growth forests*. Forests that have grown up in areas where humans earlier cut down the primary forest are called *secondary forests*.

Amazonian Forest

Brazil's lowland wet forests in the Amazon are classic tropical rainforests with emergent trees and deciduous or evergreen canopy trees reaching 40 to 55 m (130 to 180 ft) in height. Canopy trees have broad crowns and sub-canopy trees have smaller and deeper crowns. Tree buttresses are very common and often extend high up on trunks. Palms are abundant, often with stilt roots. The ground in these forests is either mostly bare or sparsely covered with an herb layer. Vines and epiphytes are usually abundant. Biologically, these kinds of forests are probably the richest ecosystems on Earth – supporting the most species of both plants and animals per unit area (more plant species probably support greater animal richness). This forest is made up of numerous patches of forest habitat types, many habitats often occurring within a small area. Tall, cathedral-like tree species grow on higher ground that is never flooded by rising rivers, called *terra firme*. Closer to rivers and swamps, the forests are flooded more regularly, and the vegetation is made up of species quite different from that found in terra firme. Forest that is flooded, sometimes up to depths of 12 m (40 ft), by nutrient-poor "blackwater" rivers (see Close-up, page 37) has a unique set of plants that creates a habitat called *igapó*. The nutrient-poor deposits here mean that igapó plants often have to find alternative ways to access the nutrients they need to grow and fruit. A high percentage of trees in this habitat have associations with ants that bring in detritus and food particles to store in nests in the tree. This "garbage" breaks down and the tree can absorb many of these materials and use them as food. Forests flooded by more nutrient- and sediment-rich "white water" rivers have yet another set of plant species that together are called *varzea*. Flooding along the Amazon is caused by high rainfall during certain seasons. There is also daily tidal flooding that backs up the flow of fresh water down the Amazon and has an impact up to 450 km (275 miles) inland.

Some common, recognizable trees and plants of Brazil's Amazon forests are:

Ceiba (*Ceiba pentandra*): Ceiba (also called Cotton Kapok or Giant Kapok; Plate D) are massive, often epiphyte-laden, trees, large enough to be emergents, with broad, flat crowns. Frequently they are the only trees left standing when pastures are cleared. Fibrous kapok from fruiting pods is used to stuff cushions and furniture. Canopy towers and canopy walkways constructed at some ecotravel lodges are usually built on massive Ceibas that emerge above the rest of the canopy.

Bacabá Palm (*Oenocarpus bacaba*): These tall (7 to 22 m, 23 to 73 ft) thin-trunked palms (Plate A) are obvious and have huge fronds. The trees are usually found

b Bacabá Palm,
Oenocarpus bacaba

a Mauritia Palm,
Mauritia flexuosa

d Rubber tree,
Hevea brasiliensis

c Tucumã Palm,
Astrocaryum tucuma

Plate A

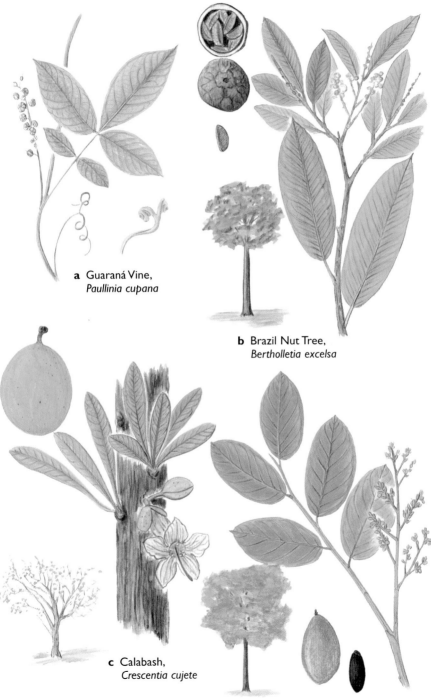

a Guaraná Vine,
Paullinia cupana

b Brazil Nut Tree,
Bertholletia excelsa

c Calabash,
Crescentia cujete

d Tonka Bean Tree,
Dipteryx odorata

Plate B

a Swamp Aroid,
Montrichardia sp.

b Amazonian Cecropia,
Cecropia sp.

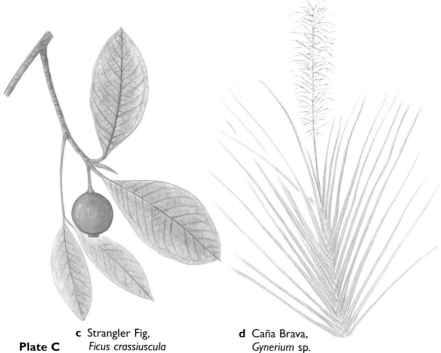

Plate C

c Strangler Fig,
Ficus crassiuscula

d Caña Brava,
Gynerium sp.

a Willow,
   Salix humboldtiana

b Giant Kapok, or Ceiba, Tree,
   Ceiba pentandra

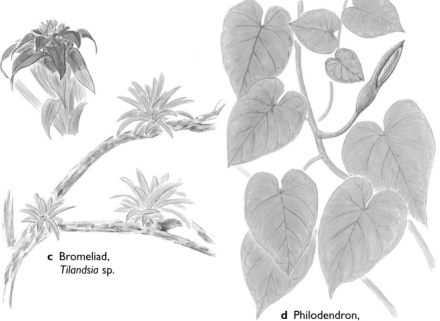

c Bromeliad,
   Tilandsia sp.

d Philodendron,
   Philodendron sp.

Plate D

a Ginger,
  Costus sp.

b Ant-associated Melastome,
  Maieta sp.

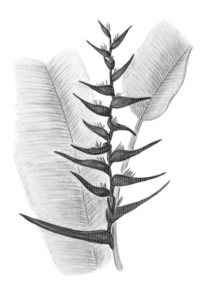

c Piper,
  Piper sp.

d Heliconia,
  Heliconia sp.

Plate E

a Bamboo,
   Chusquea sp.

b Bocaiuva Palm,
   Acrocomia sclerocarpa

c Carunda Palm,
   Copernicia alba

Plate F

d Bacurí Palm,
   Scheelia phalerata

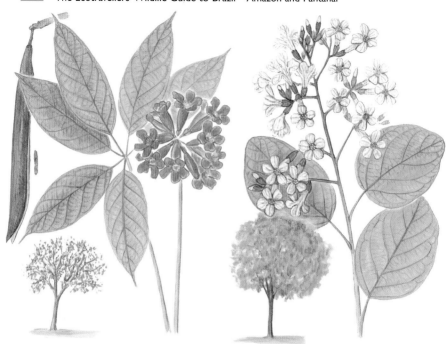

a Tabebuia,
Tabebuia impetiginosa

b Louro,
Cordia glabrata

c Jatobá,
Hymenaea courbaril

d Chico Magra,
Guazuma sp.

Plate G

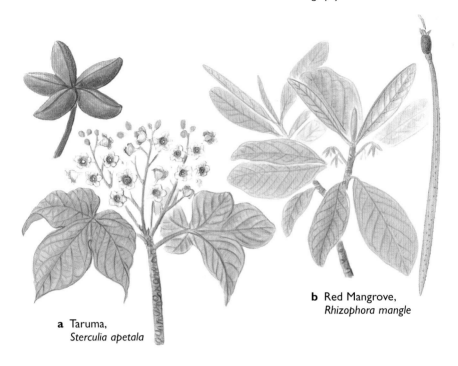

b Red Mangrove,
  Rhizophora mangle

a Taruma,
  Sterculia apetala

d Banana Tree,
  Musa x paradisiaca

c Black Mangrove,
Plate H *Avicennia germinans*

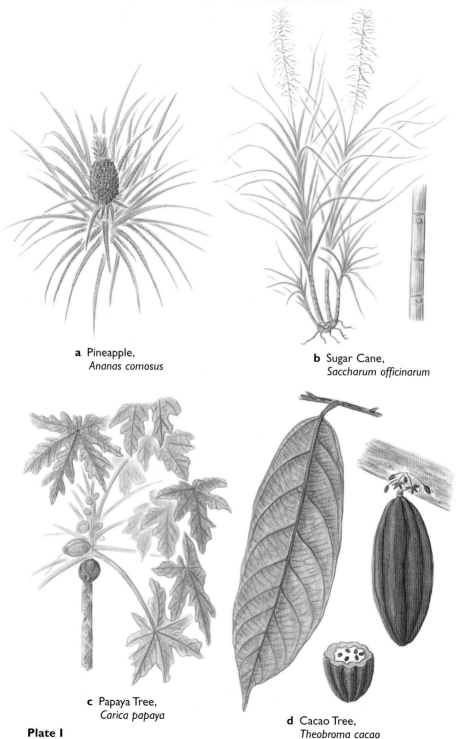

a Pineapple,
Ananas comosus

b Sugar Cane,
Saccharum officinarum

c Papaya Tree,
Carica papaya

d Cacao Tree,
Theobroma cacao

Plate 1

solitarily or in small groups on terra firme. The flowers and fruits hang in a cluster from a short, thick base. Its fruits are used to make a drink by some indigenous people.

Tucumã Palm (*Astrocaryum tucuma*): Sometimes considered a variety of the species *A. aculeatum*, the trunks of these tall (8 to 20 m, 26 to 66 ft), solitary palms (Plate A) are covered with long black spines, and the fronds are relatively small. They often grow in disturbed areas and at the forest edge. Their fruits are highly prized and sold commonly in markets.

Rubber Tree (*Hevea brasiliensis*): Famous as the traditional source of rubber, these trees (Plate A) typically rise to the subcanopy. They are in the euphorb family and are found naturally only in the Amazon. The latex, from which commercial rubber is produced, is released as a sticky yellowish-white substance at injury sites. It oozes out and physically impedes animals trying to eat leaves and branches. The rubber tree often grows in poorly drained areas of terra firme forest, but individuals are usually great distances apart from each other. Their fruits "explode" when mature and shoot the seed out for long distances away from the tree. Several attempts have been made to clear portions of Amazonian forest and establish plantations of rubber trees so that their latex can be harvested more economically. But all attempts do so in South America have failed because of diseases and insects that attack the trees. However, in the 1800s, rubber plantations were begun in Southeast Asia from "stolen" Brazilian rubber tree seeds, and the trees grew and thrived there in extensive plantations, so much so that the "rubber" boom in Brazil crashed.

Guaraná Vine (*Paullinia cupana*): The fruits if this liana (vine) (Plate B) have been used by native peoples for centuries. Historically they would make a paste of the fruits and seeds and combine it with manioc meal and water. The resultant mixture was then dried and later eaten as a stimulant. Modern day entrepreneurs have marketed this fruit as a popular soft drink called *guaraná*. It is sold throughout Brazil in its carbonated form, and its unique flavor is finding a market now in Europe and North America. Laboratory studies on mice show that chemicals in this drink increase physical capacity, increase learning ability and reduce anti-oxidants (aging factors). In nature, the seeds are dispersed by large birds such as toucans and guans. One of the major chemicals inside the seeds, however, is caffeine. The concentrations of the caffeine are so high (part of what makes them a stimulant to humans) that they are likely toxic to birds that eat them. How can the birds swallow the seeds to disperse them without becoming sick or dying? The answer is that as long as the birds don't crack the seeds and only digest away the sugars and carbohydrates surrounding the seed, there is no release of the caffeine. A cracked seed would likely not survive and germinate, so apparently having toxic substances inside its seeds is the plant's way of making sure that birds, such as macaws, that crack and kill the seeds, aren't attracted to its fruits. Only birds that eat the fruits whole and permit the seeds to pass unharmed through the digestive system to be deposited later away from the mother tree can successfully eat these seeds.

Bromeliads: These pineapple relatives (Plate D) usually grow as epiphytes high up in the canopy, perched on top of the larger branches of trees. The base of the long, narrow but thick leaves interconnect to form a tank which holds up to 5 liters (a gallon) of water. The beautiful flowers of bromeliads are often showy and bright red or pink.

Brazil Nut Tree (*Bertholletia excelsa*): These immense trees (to 40 m, 130 ft, high; Plate B), often rise solitarily well above the canopy of both terra firme and flood plain forest. The fruit of this tree is like a huge cannon ball (to 2 kg, 4.5 lb), and almost as hard. When it falls during the fruiting season, you might want to be wearing a hard hat. The 15 to 20 large seeds inside are extracted only with considerable work – even by machete wielding humans. Forest floor rodents such as agoutis (p. 230), however, by persistent gnawing can gain access to the delicious seeds inside. Each seed is 70% fat by weight, so after eating one or two, the rodent is full. It often takes the rest of the uneaten seeds and buries them in a cache far from the tree for a later day's hunger (if it can remember where the cache is). Brazil Nut Trees are pollinated by orchid bees (Plate 5), which have to find alternative sources of nectar during the 11 months when Brazil Nut Trees are not in flower. The country's name is derived from the French word, *brésil*, which originally referred to the reddish color dye traditionally extracted from the Brazil Nut.

Calabash (*Crescentia cujete*): These small trees produce huge round fruits (Plate B) that are either harvested from the wild or cultivated. The dried gourds serve many purposes for indigenous people, such as storing articles or carrying water.

Tonka Bean Tree (*Dipteryx odorata*): This huge legume (pea family) tree (Plate B) often rises above the forest canopy. Its smooth, reddish bark, contorted trunk and large buttresses are distinctive. During the flowering season, its massive display of magenta to purple flowers is very conspicuous.

Strangler Fig (*Ficus crassiuscula*): Seed remains of a strangler fig fruit are defecated by a bird or mammal high in the branches of another tree. Here the seed sprouts, the fig tree (Plate C) starting out as an epiphyte. Its leaves grow out to photosynthesize the sun's energy and quickly produce its own canopy. Then it sends its roots down the trunk of the host until they form the scaffolding of a trunk and eventually reach the ground and burrow in. As it continues to grow, the fig eventually out-competes the host tree for sunlight and nutrients, and so kills the host, which it no longer needs for support.

Philodendron: The large, heart-shaped leaves of this semi-epiphytic climber/vine (Plate D) on trees are unmistakable.
    Some common plants of the forest floor:

Ginger (*Costus* sp.): Ginger (Plate E) is unique. It grows in a spiral-staircase stem, often a meter (yard) or more high. It is common in moister areas on the forest floor, and its flowers are bright and conspicuous, growing from a tiny pineapple-like base. Because its flowers bloom one at a time over several weeks, hummingbirds and insects can rely upon the presence of the nectar and pollen at the same place, so they can form daily routes of flower visitation, or "traplines" (see p. 161). The fruits that form from pollinated flowers also ripen sequentially so that tinamous and rodents, which eat the fruits, learn to return to the site every day for another prize.

Ant-associated Melastome (*Maieta* sp.): The species of the family of melastomes are among the most common in the undergrowth and easiest to recognize. The pattern of parallel cross veins on the leaves running perpendicular to long veins is unique (Plate E). Species of the genus *Maieta* have distinctive hollow swellings at the base of each leaf that are covered with thick white hairs. Ants use these hollow areas as homes and apparently protect the leaves of the plant from being eaten by herbivorous insects.

Piper: A very common and widespread genus of tropical forest understory shrubs, with more than 120 species represented in Brazil. The erect, candle-like, flowering structures (Plate E) make them easy to identify. Bats (p. 210), instead of insects or birds, act as pollinators on many of these shrubs. Short-tailed Fruit Bats (Plate 85) are the main disperser of its fruits. Usually 2 to 3 m (6 to 10 ft) high; occurs at elevations up to 2000 m (6500 ft). Black pepper is harvested from a species in this family.

Heliconia: A genus of striking flowering plants (Plate E) that is characteristic of tropical forests in the Americas; about 70 species occur in Brazil. They grow within forests along streams and in sunny gaps, around clearings, and in disturbed areas such as roadsides and overgrown agricultural fields. *Heliconia* have very large, banana-tree-like leaves and their flowering structures are red, orange and yellow, large and flat, resembling nothing so much as lobster claws. *Heliconia* are pollinated by hummingbirds.

Bamboo (*Chusquea* sp.): These tall woody grasses (Plate F) grow in dense stands and are often 5 m (16 ft) tall. You are most likely to see them in lowland forest areas with poor drainage. Bamboos produce their seed-like fruits at long intervals of 10 or more years, and the entire population chooses the same year to flower. Then they die. It is unknown how they synchronize their flowering over wide areas. Many species of insects, birds and mammals are tightly associated with these bamboo stands. When the stand dies, these animals must quickly disperse and find another stand in which to live – not an easy undertaking if all the stands in a wide area have died at the same time.

Varzea and Oxbow Lakes

Near the edge of rivers in Amazonian Brazil grows a forest type (*varzea*) that is flooded frequently and that is adapted to maturing quickly in clearings created by the water's scouring action (this forest type in some regions is also called *riverine forest*). The fast-growing plants include the hollow *Cecropia*, 5-m (16-ft) high grasses (*caña brava*) and willows. These plants also predominate on islands in the larger rivers. Other types of forest vegetation are associated with the meandering river systems that are more common in eastern parts of Brazil. As a meander forms, the momentum of the water continuously cuts out the banks on the outside of the curve. Eventually, the meander becomes U-shaped. Then, as the water continues to undercut the banks, the two tails of the "U" come closer and closer until, in a surge, the river cuts through the top of the "U". The meander is completely cut off from the river except at highest flood levels. In Brazil, these cut-off meanders form lakes called *oxbows*. An oxbow no longer has a constant current to scour out accumulated tree trunks, sand, and floating vegetation. The oxbow slowly fills in, and a series of forest types replace each other in an often predictable sequence. Floating lily pads and grasses die and accumulate to form soils that give more terrestrial plant species a toehold. *Cecropia* gives way to semi-terrestrial species such as Mauritia Palm and Chonta Palm, which in turn give way to flood-forest species.

Some common, recognizable trees and shrubs of Brazil's varzea and oxbows are:

Mauritia Palm (*Mauritia* sp.): These large palms (5 to 25 m, 17 to 82 ft) have fan-shaped leaves (Plate A) and grow in pure stands along the edges of oxbows (called buritales in Portuguese) and in low moist areas of the forest. Many birds, such as macaws, depend heavily on the fruits in these trees for food. Fallen fruits are major food sources for more than 20 species of fish, turtles, agoutis, peccaries, deer, pacas, and iguanas. This tree is one of the most widely used by humans in South America. The leaves are used for thatching, fibers from the leaves are woven into artifacts, the fruits and stem starch are eaten, and an oil is extracted from the fruit pulp.

Swamp aroid (*Montrichardia* sp.): Related to *Philodendron*, this tall, almost tree-like plant (Plate C) forms dense stands in swampy areas and along small rivers. It is a favorite food of the Hoatzin (p. 322), and apparently this bird gets its highly distasteful flesh from chemicals found in this plant.

Amazonian Cecropia (*Cecropia* sp.): These conspicuous trees (Plate C) are among the first species to grow in recently cleared areas (*pioneer* species) with lots of sun. Generally they are thinnish trees with very large, umbrella-like leaves. Most Cecropias harbor teeming colonies of stinging ants in their hollow trunks, and these ants end up protecting the tree from herbivores (or ecotravellers foolish enough to lean a hand on the Cecropia's trunk) by defending their nest site and food source. Various species of *Cecropia* grow over much of Brazil.

Caña Brava (*Gynerium* sp.): An early succession cane-grass (Plate C) 5 to 6 m (to 20 ft) high, it grows in dense stands along Amazonian river banks and low river islands recently scoured by floods. The caña brava on these river islands often forms the bulk of a unique habitat to which more than ten species of birds are restricted.

Willow (*Salix humboldtiana*): This small species of willow (Plate D) occurs along white-water rivers in the mid-elevations of the Andes but also descends to the Amazon lowlands. Here it is common in pure stands on sand bars and low islands of larger rivers.

Pantanal

Although we have referred to the Pantanal as a relatively distinct ecosystem, it is actually made up of many different types of habitats. Botanists have defined these habitats based on the dominant plants of each, and they include: Tabebuia parkland, palm savannah, gallery forest (tall trees often grow along rivers and streams, and this forest type is also called *riparian forest*), forest islands on raised soil mounds, thorn scrub, swamps, scrub grassland, and flooded grassland. You will find many plant and animal species restricted to one or two of these habitats, but other species will occur across many of them.

Some common trees of the Pantanal:

Bocaiuva Palm (*Acrocomia sclerocarpa*): Often considered a variety of the widespread species *A. aculeata*, these medium height (4 to 12 m, 13 to 40 ft) palms (Plate F) have thin trunks occasionally swollen near the middle and are often solitary in drier areas. Their frond tips are usually very frayed, and the leaves of the fronds go off in many directions, giving the green leafy top of the tree a spherical shape. The fruits are edible and an oil is often extracted from the pulp. Its roots are used to make a tea to cure hepatitis.

Carunda Palm (*Copernicia alba*): This is the dominant tree (Plate F) in the palm savannah areas of the Pantanal. They are often surrounded by extensive grassy areas.

Bacurí Palm (*Attalea (Scheelia) phalerta*): These short to tall palms (Plate F) have relatively thick trunks and long feather-like fronds. They grow in sandy soil at the forest edge and in open areas. The seeds are edible.

Tabebuia (*Tabebuia impetignosa*): Large trees (Plate G), they lose their leaves during the dry season but late in the dry season an individual will suddenly produce an overwhelming mass of maroon flowers (called "big bang" flowering) for about a week (other species of Tabebuia have bright yellow flowers). This strategy of flowering over a short period of a few days but with a massive display is thought to serve as a "flag" to attract pollinating insects, mainly a variety of bees. An individual tree can sometimes have two or three of these mass flowering episodes within a dry season. The seeds have "wings" and are dispersed primarily by the wind. These trees have some of the heaviest and hardest wood in the Neotropics – so heavy that it cannot float on top of water.

Louro (*Cordia glabrata*): These tall trees (Plate G) usually have a tall slender trunk that is greyish-white. The crown is relatively small and rounded. The white flowers are very fragrant, and are visited by moths in the early morning and by butterflies, bees and beetles during the day. Because this tree is so fast-growing, it has been suggested as an ideal native species for reforestation projects.

Jatobá (*Hymenaea courbaril*): A member of the legume (pea) family, this huge tree (Plate G) is "evergreen" (leaves are dropped once a year simultaneously and replaced quickly over a 10-day period) and often reaches heights of 40 m (132 ft). An individual has flowers for 4 to 6 weeks but only ten or so white flowers are produced at a time and they last only one night. Bats are attracted to these flowers and serve as the principal pollinator. Because a few flowers are available every night over a long period, these bats can depend on this tree being a source of nectar and form a "trapline" of trees that are visited sequentially in a night. The huge flat pods are 15 cm by 7 cm (6 by 2.8 in) and contain 4 to 6 seeds surrounded by a starchy and sweet pulp. The seeds are dispersed by large rodents. A sticky resin is produced by the tree, and it often oozes from the wood and leaves where they have been cut or injured. If this resin becomes fossilized over tens of thousands of years it produces *amber*. Sometimes an insect was trapped in the sticky resin and became preserved in the amber. Jatobá is the most common source of fossil amber in the Neotropics and occasionally a source of well-preserved ancient insects.

Chico Magra (*Guazuma* sp.): A tree of sunny disturbed areas and open fields, Chico Magra (Plate G) rarely reaches more than 10 m (33 ft) in height. You can easily identify it by the saw-tooth (serrate) edges of the oblong leaves. Most other trees in the area have smooth-edged leaves. It loses its leaves during the dry season, but then you identify it by the trunk, which is usually twisted and deeply grooved. Because this tree resprouts so readily from even a cut stump, and the leaves and fruits are readily eaten by livestock, it is an economically valuable resource in the Pantanal.

Taruma (*Sterculia apetala*): These large "evergreen" trees (Plate H) are common on rich soil along water courses (*gallery forests*) of the Pantanal. The fruits are unique, each made up of a cluster of five small rounded chambers containing small seeds.

Mangrove and Coastal Vegetation

Along the coast of extreme northeastern Brazil where fresh or brackish water is predictable, such as along estuaries, mangroves are common and form another floral region with distinct plants and animals. Mangroves are relatively short tree species of several unrelated plant families. They have in common the fact that they grow in areas exposed to salt water, usually around bays, lagoons, and other protected coastal infoldings. Common mangrove species are the Red Mangrove, *Rhizophora mangle* (Plate H) and the Black Mangrove, *Avicennia germinans* (Plate H).

Pastures, Farms, and Plantations

Agriculture in Brazil is split between traditional small family farms of, usually, 5 to 10 hectares (12 to 25 acres), which are still plentiful, and large corporate plantations. Family farms generally grow several crops, and plantations, single crops. The biggest export crops are coffee, cotton, and sugar. Some chocolate (from cacao; Plate I), bananas (Plate H), poultry, beef, and dairy products are also important. Banana trees, with their large leaves and distinctive fruit, have an Asian origin. They occur in gardens, throughout the tropical lowlands. Sugar cane (Plate I), grown in several regions of Brazil but particularly in the warmer lowlands, is a perennial grass that may have originated in the New Guinea region. Pineapple plants (Plate I) are bromeliads, and are Neotropical in origin. They are grown mainly in the moist lowlands. Other common crops are corn (maize), rice, and papaya (Plate I).

Environmental Close-up 1
Why is Farming so Difficult in the Tropics?

An experienced farmer from the temperate zone, such as one who worked in Iowa or France, gazing for the first time at a tropical rainforest, could be excused if he (or she) thought he saw a farming bonanza before him. It would be natural for him to exclaim: "Just cut down the forest and plant the cleared fields with a more useful crop, a cash crop. If those dense, tall trees can grow there so luxuriantly, surely a field of alfalfa, corn, cotton or soy beans should also grow wonderfully there! Why, with the perpetual warm weather and regular rain, you could even have three or four harvests a year!" But it is not as easy as that; indeed, this type of thinking has led many hopeful farmers in the tropics into an economic and ecological disaster.

The main problem is that tropical soils, in contrast to most temperate soils, are often very nutrient-poor. In fact, tropical rainforests themselves, and the soil in which they are rooted, are of such different designs when compared with temperate forests and soils, that many of the agricultural rules a farmer would have learned in North America and Europe don't even apply. For instance, in temperate zones, soils accumulate organic material in the form of dead leaves, fallen branches, dead animals and so on – they are essentially a natural compost heap. This accumulation of organic chemicals, including many of the basic nutrients that plants need to grow (such as nitrogen-containing compounds and phosphates), is possible because there is only a relatively short period each year when it is warm and moist enough for fallen plant and animal material to decompose completely. The bacteria, fungi and other soil organisms that make decomposition possible can't be active and break down dead tissues if it is too cold or dry. Thus, over time, organic materials build up in the soil and produce *humus* (rich black soil) and a large reservoir of nutrients sometimes 30 cm (a foot) or more deep. But this is not the case in tropical forests. Here the forest floor is generally so warm and humid throughout the year that any organic material falling to the forest floor is quickly broken down completely by the abundant *decomposer* termites, fungi and bacteria. There is little chance for a build-up of organic humus. The average depth of organic material below the floor of moist tropical forests is measured in millimeters (tenths of an inch) instead of centimeters (inches). In addition, most tropical soils are composed largely of old clay with a high content of aluminum and iron (causing the reddish soil visible in cleared areas); minerals in these soils useful to plants have long ago been weathered away.

How does the lush tropical vegetation of these forests exist if soils are so nutrient-poor? Actually, the plants do have access to nutrients, they just have to be ready to capture the nitrogen, phosphates and other nutrients almost as soon as they become available via the action of the soil decomposers. Instead of having root systems that penetrate deep down into the soil, tropical trees tend to produce roots that grow sideways, close to the soil surface. Most roots in tropical forests are within 30 cm (1 ft) of the soil surface. Together with symbiotic fungi, called *mycorrhizae*, living in the roots, these trees (and other plants) with shallow roots are able to efficiently and quickly capture the nutrients as they become available – that is, the tree roots, being near the forest floor, are able to quickly capture and absorb organic nutrients and minerals just as they are made available at the soil surface by the action of soil decomposers. Unlike temperate zone habitats, in which more than half of an area's nutrients are in the soil, tropical forest habitats often have only 1% of their nutrients in the soil at any one time. So where are the rest of the habitat's nutrients? They are stored in the cells of living plants. That means up to 99% of the nutrients in tropical forests are in the plants themselves. So if you cut tropical forest and burn off the dead vegetation, you lose much the habitat's nutrients – they disappear by logging truck and/or into the air with the smoke. When the rains begin, the few remaining nutrients are eroded (leached) out of the soil by the runoff of the water.

The main consequence of tropical forest clearing and burning for agriculture is obvious. After one or two crops of corn planted to replace the luxuriant tropical forest, the few nutrients left in the soil are used up. Because commercial fertilizer is too expensive for most farmers in the tropics, the sad alternative is to move to the next patch of forest, cut or burn it down, and squeeze out another couple of years of crops before the soil there is also exhausted. This wasteful, destructive procedure is known as *slash-and-burn agriculture* – moving every 2 or 3 years to a new patch of forest and cutting and/or burning it to provide temporarily productive fields.

Even selective timber removal from tropical forests is a limited economic option. This is because the shallow root systems, seeds in the soil, and the decomposer community are easily disrupted or killed with the compacting action of heavy tractors and equipment. Also, if too many trees are removed for timber, the total amounts of nutrients in the system may fall below a critical minimum to maintain the rest of the uncut forest. In addition, large cleared areas (called *light gaps*) permit high levels of sunshine to strike the soil surface, and if the clay is of just the right composition, it can be baked into a stone-like adobe called *laterite*. Seeds and roots cannot penetrate the laterite, and the forest can only regenerate itself in these areas with great difficulty. If that weren't bad enough, it turns out that these trees with shallow root systems depend on dense stands of trees to protect themselves from high-wind storms. Large light gaps, however, remove this protection on the edge of a gap, and so the trees there are easy victims of the next storm. When they fall, their neighbors become unprotected, and so on.

Beyond these nutrient cycling problems of farming, precipitation cycles also have different rules in tropical rainforests. Although rainfall is generally high compared with that in most temperate zone forests, cutting tropical forest to produce agricultural fields actually reduces rainfall that crops need. Through a process that moves water and nutrients up from the roots to the leaves (called *evapotranspiration*), water vapor escapes from leaf surfaces in tropical rainforests and builds up over the canopy. As this vapor rises it eventually cools and condenses. Tropical rainforests produce up to 70% of their own rainfall in this manner. Thus, if extensive areas of tropical forest are cleared and then burned off to create cattle pastures or for crop farming, most of the local nutrients and much rainfall are removed in one fell swoop.

What then are the alternatives for agriculture in rainforests? Theoretically, one plan would be to follow traditional agricultural practices. Indigenous peoples long ago developed a system that mimics natural processes, maintains soil nutrients, and so allows for continual use of the same fields (that is, permits "sustainable" agriculture). They clear only small areas of the forest and then plant a mixed cultivation of fast-growing food crops, such as corn and beans, interplanted with slower growing pepper and passion fruit, which are vines that grow up trees such as cacao, rubber, and fruit palms. They also plant crops with high numbers of mycorrhizae in their roots, which pump nutrients into the soil, enriching it, and help recycle nutrients locally. Furthermore, rotation and succession of these crops help reduce the occurrence of plant pests and diseases. But this kind of sustainable agricultural system is obviously labor intensive and involves careful, thoughtful planting. Tropical agriculture can work, but only with great care and substantial training.

New farmers and new settlers who push into Neotropical rainforests to claim land and homestead, usually do not have such skillful knowledge. With high hopes they burn and plant, only to discover after a few years that their fields' productivity has declined; they move and start over again. Large-scale commercial ranching and farming operations prefer to continually grow single crops over large areas (that is, *monocultures*), which quickly deplete soil nutrients and require ever-increasing amounts of artificial fertilizers and pesticides to maintain the crop. These agricultural forces – essentially mistreatment of tropical forests and soils for ill-informed farming – in combination have created what most consider to be an ecological disaster (disappearing tropical forests; increasingly poor soils for farming; increasing fertilizer and pesticide use, which eventually enter local waterways to pollute them and downstream areas). Remedies, such as encouraging ecologically sustainable farming practices on large scales, are only beginning to be proposed. But until such practices are widely adopted, much farming in the tropics will continue to be difficult and ecologically damaging.

Chapter 3

Parks and Reserves: Brief Descriptions

- Northeastern Amazon (NEA) and Coastal Mangrove Forest (CMF)
- Northwestern Amazon (NWA)
- Southern Amazon (SAM)
- Pantanal (PAN)
- *Environmental Close-up 2*: Blackwater Rivers and Whitewater Rivers: Water Colors in the Amazon and Pantanal

Officially Brazil has protected less than 4% of its Amazon and Pantanal areas as national parks, biological reserves, and ecological stations. (The Brazilian government agency directly in charge of these protected areas is called by its acronym, IBAMA.) Of these, only the national parks are officially open to the public, and even then to visit some of them you need prior permission from IBAMA. The reserves and ecological stations generally are available solely for scientific research. In many areas, private ecotourism companies have purchased land or made arrangements with the government to manage additional areas specifically for ecotourism.

We selected the parks and natural areas described below for two reasons. Some of these areas are the ones most often visited by ecotravellers in Brazil – by people who come on organized tours and also those who travel independently. Others are more remote, and to see them takes additional planning and effort. But because they are so remote, it is also less likely that illegal colonization, poaching and mining have altered or severely affected the quality of these habitats and their natural inhabitants. See Map 3 (p. 34) for park locations. The animals profiled in the color plates are keyed to parks and reserves in the following way: the profiles list the Brazilian regions, Northeastern Amazon (NEA), Coastal Mangrove Forests (CMF), Northwestern Amazon (NWA), Southern Amazon (SAM), and Pantanal (PAN), in which each species is most likely to be found, and the parks and reserves listed below are arranged by the regions. Visitors who stay at lodges or resorts in the same regions as the parks listed below can expect to encounter similar types of habitats and wildlife as described for these parks and preserves. Tips on increasing the likelihood of seeing mammals, birds, reptiles, amphibians or flashy insects are given in the introductions to each of those chapters. For more particulars on planning your trip to the Brazilian Amazon or Pantanal, choosing

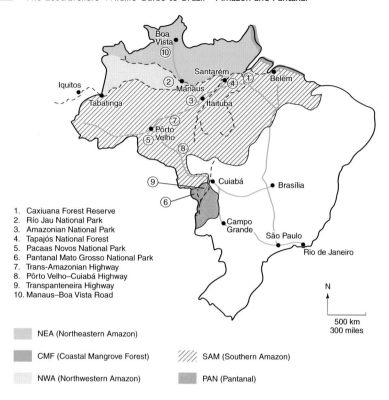

1. Caxiuana Forest Reserve
2. Río Jau National Park
3. Amazonian National Park
4. Tapajós National Forest
5. Pacaas Novos National Park
6. Pantanal Mato Grosso National Park
7. Trans-Amazonian Highway
8. Pôrto Velho–Cuiabá Highway
9. Transpanteneira Highway
10. Manaus–Boa Vista Road

NEA (Northeastern Amazon)

CMF (Coastal Mangrove Forest)

NWA (Northwestern Amazon)

SAM (Southern Amazon)

PAN (Pantanal)

Map 3   Brazil, showing locations of parks and reserves, some main roads, and the five regions used in the book to specify species ranges.

which areas to visit, places to stay, and transportation, we suggest you consult one of several ecotravel-friendly guides available at bookstores, such as *Brazil: A Lonely Planet Travel Survival Kit*, by Nick Selby and others, and *Insight Guide: Brazil*, edited by Pam Barrett.

Northeastern Amazon (NEA) and Coastal Mangrove Forest (CMF)

Belém

Belém is a port city near the mouth of the Río Amazonas and is the center of eco-tourist activity for the northeastern part of Amazonian Brazil. The *Guama Ecological Research Area*, on the east side of the city, is a large patch of primary forest that can be visited with permission from EMBRAPA, a government agricultural office. Small planes, ferries and motor boats make day trips to the savannah, forest and mangroves of the immense island, *Ilha de Marajó* (the size of Switzerland), that lies on the other side of the river from Belém. Many beaches and small isolated islands with forest are also accessible by bus or car north and northeast of Belém.

Kalamazoo Valley Community College

Texas Township Campus Library

Title: Brazil : Amazon and Pantanal : the ecotravellers' wildlife guide / David L. Pearson and Les Beletsky ; illustrated by Priscilla Barrett ... [et al.] ; contributors, Martha L. Crump, Stacey Combes, Richard Francis.

ID: 32972001570300
Due: Thursday, April 28, 2011

Total items: 1
4/7/2011 6:32 PM

Reminders and Notices are e-mailed to your KVCC e-mail address. Overdue fines are assessed for late returns. Please renew or return by the due date.   Thank you!

TTC Library Circulation: 269-488-4328
         or renew online: valleycat.kvcc.edu

Here, areas, such as Ilha de Mosqueiro and Salinópolis, offer natural habitats with tourist accommodations.

Caxiuana Forest Reserve

West of Belém 350 km (220 miles) and just east of the Río Xingu, is this beautiful forest reserve with a new field station that will accept ecotourists (Ferreira Penna Scientific Station). This site has comfortable accommodations, many forest trails and a canopy tower. Contact the Museu Paraense Emilio Goeldi in Belém for reservations and information.

Northwestern Amazon (NWA)

Manaus

Manaus, located at the confluence of the black water of the Río Negro and the brown, muddy water of the Río Solimões (Amazon), is the center of much of the country's ecotourism industry. Private lodges to the north along the Río Negro (*Anavilhanas Archipelago*) and to the south provide comfortable access to extensive marshes, flooded forest, campina (white sand), and terra firme forest habitats. The *Ducke Biological Reserve* in the north part of the city has a large remnant of primary forest and can be visited with permission of INPA (Instituto Nacional de Pesquisa da Amazônia). Twenty km (12 miles) farther north of the city, on the Manaus–Boa Vista Road, there are many patches of forest along the highway. With a mean annual rainfall of nearly 3 m (10 ft), the rainy season in this area runs from June through September and the rainier season is the rest of the year.

Río Jau National Park

With 2,272,000 hectares (5,611,840 acres), Río Jau is the largest national park in Brazil. It was set aside in 1980 and is located between the Río Negro and the Río Solimões northwest of Manaus. Most tourists explore this area by motorized boat from the Río Negro or small airplane from Manaus.

Southern Amazon (SAM)

Amazonian National Park

Established in 1975, this park has 994,000 hectares (2,455,180 acres). It is located between the Río Tapajos and the Río Amazonas, 53 km (32 miles) southwest of the city of Itaituba. The park occupies a large plain dissected by the Río Tapajos, which is mainly covered with rainforest, but there are also extensive areas of marshes and seasonally flooded grasslands. Access during the dry season is from the little-used Trans-Amazonian Highway, which runs along the north shore of the Río Tapajos. Camping and primitive cabins are available on the southern border of the park.

Santarém

Santarém is a pleasant city of 25,000 inhabitants with daily flights from Manaus and Belém and good tourist accommodations. Its beautiful white sand beaches and isolation (connecting highways have deteriorated to the point of being abandoned during the rainy season) have helped keep its dry forest habitats relatively untrammeled. The *Tapajós National Forest (Floresta Nacional do Tapajós)* (contact IBAMA in Santarém for permission and arrangements) and the resort town of Alter do Chão offer nearby areas that are excellent for observing wildlife.

Alta Floresta

The town of Alta Floresta lies just west of Brazil's geographic center, near the border of the states of Mato Grosso and Pará. This habitat lies on the southern edge of the Amazonian forest area. Comfortable hotels are available in the town. An ecotourist lodge on privately owned land has been constructed east of the town and east of the Río Tapajos along a small tributary, the Río Cristalino. Access is by small plane from Cuiabá, 625 km (390 miles) to the south.

Pôrto Velho

Pôrto Velho is a modern city with many tourist accommodations. It is a gateway for visiting ecotourist sites in the state of Rondônia on the Bolivian border. Most of these sites, such as *Pacaas Novos National Park,* are along or accessed from the Pôrto Velho–Cuiabá Highway. Other areas, such as the border town of Guajará-Mirim and its many Amazon forest areas, are southwest of Pôrto Velho.

Pantanal (PAN)

Pantanal – There are two main approaches to visiting this immense area. The north entrance is from the city of Cuiabá, along the only road to penetrate this part of the Pantanal, the *Transpantaneira*. The wildlife viewing along this road at any season is nothing less than spectacular, although the dry season (April to October) is the best because the lakes and wet areas become more restricted and concentrate birds, mammals and reptiles in large numbers. Avoid the height of the rainy season (February to March), as all but the highest areas become flooded, and the road can become impassable. Accommodations are available in Cuiabá and at ranches (*fazendas*) along the road. The south entrance to the Pantanal is from Campo Grande and Corumbá on the Bolivian border. The southern areas, however, have more cattle ranching and human activity than in the north, and you are less likely to see big mammals. In addition to hotels in Corumbá, accommodations are available in the smaller towns of Aquidauana and Miranda. Tours into the Pantanal can be arranged with travel agencies in Cuiabá or Campo Grande. Only a small part of the immense Pantanal region is officially protected within a small national park near the Bolivian border (*Pantanal Matogrosso National Park*). This park can be visited by motor boat or small plane as roads are only passable in the short dry season, May to August.

Environmental Close-up 2
Blackwater Rivers and Whitewater Rivers: Water Colors in the Amazon and Pantanal

As you first fly over the Amazon or Pantanal regions of Brazil, your impression of a flat forest of green vegetation extending from horizon to horizon will probably be a highlight. After gaping at all that vegetation, try looking at the other dominant feature of the landscape, its rivers. They are almost everywhere meandering back and forth – some wide and obvious, others hard to see for the tree canopy obscuring their path of movement. Another prominent distinction is that some are dark-colored and clear while others are milky-brown and opaque.

The dark rivers look like over-brewed tea and are called *blackwater rivers*. The milky-brown rivers are called *whitewater rivers* (but should be distinguished from the clear rushing mountain streams that rafters and kayakers also call whitewater rivers). The milky color of whitewater rivers is caused by the load of fine-grained silt eroded far to the west from relatively young, nutrient-rich soils in the Andes and their foothills. As the water in these rivers moves down the steep mountain inclines, gravity keeps the current moving fast and its high energy can carry large volumes of suspended material long distances. As these rivers abruptly hit the flat lowlands in the Amazon, they slow down, lose their ability to maintain much of the suspended soil, and the soil drops out of suspension to produce extensive flood plains. Because this fine-grained sediment is so light and unstable, local flooding can again easily pick it up into suspension and move it farther down the river bed until the current again slows down and drops its load of rich nutrients at yet another point. The abundant vegetation along these rivers grows quickly and profusely to produce a flooded forest community of species called *varzea*.

Blackwater rivers, on the other hand, have their origins not in the Andes, but in the nutrient-poor soils of the lowlands themselves. Geological changes such as movements of continental plates and uplifting of the Earth's crust have exposed some areas to long bouts of weathering and erosion. Many of the soils of these headwater areas are now so old and weathered that they have had most nutrients, such as phosphorous, nitrogen and potassium, long ago eroded away (leached). All that remains in many of these areas is white sand. The forests flooded by these blackwater rivers are called *igapó*. Few sediments of any kind are left to become suspended in the rivers flowing through them. Some of these old areas are small and isolated, out of which a few rivers originate and flow next to whitewater rivers originating in the mountains. Other old and weathered areas are large, such as the Guiana Shield. This region of poor, sandy soil covers a vast part of eastern Brazil north of the Río Amazonas, and it is one of the oldest geological formations anywhere on Earth. Many rivers, including the huge Río Negro, have their headwaters in its sterile soil.

However, the silt-free water flowing in them does not stay crystal clear long – it quickly becomes blackish. Why? The shrubs and trees in these areas lack the natural fertilizers that the whitewater rivers provide their forests. As a result, food is so scarce in areas influenced by blackwater rivers that the plants there can only produce leaf material at half the rate of their whitewater cousins. Thus, if an herbivorous insect eats a leaf of a blackwater-associated plant, this plant is in serious trouble. The destroyed leaf means the plant has that much less photosynthetic surface and it cannot be replaced quickly. If the plant is to survive in such a hostile environment, grow, and produce seeds to germinate, it must be able to convert sufficient sunlight energy into plant material through photosynthesis and be able to protect such material. One result is that plants here need extra defenses not seen in most other areas. A commonly used defense against herbivore damage is the plant's production of toxic chemicals so that herbivores taking a bite out of them get sick or cannot digest the plant material very efficiently. Plants in whitewater areas also produce toxins but not in such high concentrations. These toxins, mainly tannins and phenols, are eventually leached out of the fallen leaves and flow into the rivers, turning them to the color of dark tea as well as making the water more acidic than that in the whitewater rivers. Tea plants themselves have these chemicals, as do coniferous bogs in North America and Eurasia where blackwater swamps and rivers are also common.

Blackwater and whitewater rivers flowing into one another are an exciting sight in many parts of the Amazon and Pantanal. The mother of all black- and whitewater meldings, however, is at Manaus. Here the latte coffee-colored Río Solimões flows side by side with the dark tea-stained Río Negro for many kilometers until they reluctantly mix to form the Río Amazonas. This homogenization obscures the geologically and biologically distinct origins of these rivers. It also obscures the often different species communities of plants and animals that have become adapted to such distinct habitats. On a large scale, then, the mosaic of blackwater and whitewater areas with their specialized floras and faunas overlays and enhances the many other factors that contribute to the area's extremely high diversity of species.

Chapter 4

Environmental Threats and Conservation

by Stacey Combes
Department of Zoology
University of Washington

Environmental Threats

Amazon

The Amazon basin contains the Earth's largest remaining continuous tract of tropical forest, and is home to a mind-boggling array of creatures. The total number of species in the Amazon is difficult to estimate because new species are still being discovered. Even mammals and birds, for which new discoveries are rare worldwide, continue to pop up in the Amazon; at least nine new species of primates have been discovered in the Amazon since 1990. Estimates of the total number of species here range from 800,000 to 30 million, including a known

30,000 species of plants, 2000 species of fish, 1600 species of birds, and 75 species of primates. Many of these animals are endemic to the Amazon area. While the vast rivers and diverse animals that inhabit the region are an integral part of the ecosystem, in many ways it is the forest that is the heart of the Amazon – sheltering, protecting, and sustaining the creatures, and even helping to produce the weather upon which the entire system depends (see Close-up, p. 30). Unfortunately, Amazon forests are increasingly under threat.

Deforestation

In light of all the roles the forest plays in Amazonian ecology, it is not surprising that deforestation in the Amazon has serious and often irreversible consequences, even beyond the loss of habitat for animals. When the forest is cleared by burning (which is most often the case), rain carries away the few centimeters of soil that are present. The frequency of rain declines and the temperature rises. Lush, moist forest is rapidly transformed into a desert, and owing to the permanent loss of nutrients and biomass, the forest cannot re-grow. Large areas of the northeastern Amazon that have been cleared show almost no regeneration of vegetation; great tracts of land cleared 50 years ago in the state of Pará still contain only scrub and bush. The increased temperature and reduced precipitation in cleared areas make the remaining forest more susceptible to forest fires. Areas that have been cleared also affect the nearby forest in more subtle ways. For over 20 years, the Biological Dynamics of Forest Fragments Project (administered by Brazil's National Institute for Amazonian Research and the USA's Smithsonian Institution) has been studying species richness and persistence in forest fragments that are created when land on all sides is cleared. The project has shown that the survival of species in forest fragments is negatively affected not only by fragment size (the smaller the forest patch, the fewer species it can support), but also by interactions between the forest patch and the vegetation in the surrounding clearing, as well as by the physical and biological processes that occur at forest edges.

Despite such knowledge, deforestation in the Amazon continues at alarming rates. Satellite data from the Brazilian government indicate that an average of 21,000 sq km (8000 sq miles) of the Amazon was deforested each year between 1978 and 1988. This figure dropped to 11,000 sq km (4300 sq miles) in 1991 (after intense international pressure in the late 1980s), but rose again to a high of 28,500 sq km (11,000 sq miles) in 1995. Independent estimates of deforestation rates are up to twice as high as these figures. It is estimated that 12% to 15% of the original forest is gone; at current rates, a third of the forest will be gone by 2030, and two-thirds will be lost by 2090.

There are many causes of this deforestation; the "taming of nature" has been a part of Brazilian culture for so long that the majority of significant economic activities in the Amazon involve deforestation. In the Amazon, the forest is often cut just to clear land for other activities; the wood is not even extracted, but simply burned. Before being set on fire, areas of the forest are sometimes dried with toxic chemical defoliants, which remove leaves and allow the forest to be burnt more easily. In Jaú, Pará, defoliants have even included the incredibly destructive Agent Orange, a poison that quickly blinds animals and dooms them to a period of intense suffering before being engulfed by flames.

Land in the Amazon is generally cleared either for large-scale agriculture and ranching or for subsistence agriculture by poor family farmers. Both large-scale agriculture and cattle ranching are businesses that generally make little economic sense in the Amazon. Current methods are completely unsustainable – in most parts of the Amazon, soil remains fertile for only 2 to 3 years for agriculture, and only 5 to 8 years for ranching. In pastures, phosphorus content declines rapidly, and soil erosion and compaction prevent continued vegetation growth. The cattle industry in the Amazon, which is responsible for a large portion of the deforestation, is unproductive overall, and critics complain that the industry is driven more by government incentives and subsidies than by true economic value.

Many large-scale agricultural operations in the Amazon have made the mistake of clearing the forest and planting huge areas with a single crop plant (a "monoculture"), which often fails. One notable example is that of Brazil nut monocultures. Brazil nuts are pollinated by a single species of bee, which depends on other trees in the forest for food during the months when Brazil nut trees are not blooming. In monoculture plantations of Brazil nut trees, the bees cannot survive these periods without the alternative food sources, and they abandon the stands. Farmers are left with fields of thriving trees that do not produce nuts because there are no bees to fertilize the flowers.

Burning

Some large landowners in the Amazon own tracts of land that are far larger than they can reasonably manage. Extremely harmful laws that were in place until the late 1990s defined clearing land an "improvement," and considered this a sign of active occupancy. This encouraged landowners to burn and clear much of the land that they weren't using in order to claim it before landless peasants could become the legal owners (which they sometimes can by occupying "un-used" land for a long period). The issue of land ownership has not only caused increased deforestation but has also led to decades of violence. In Brazil, 45% of the land is owned by only 1% of the population, and clashes between police and landless peasants protesting for agrarian reform led to over 200 deaths in the 1990s alone. President Fernando Henrique Cardoso, who took office in 1995, pledged to settle hundreds of thousands of landless families. Unfortunately, many of these families have been settled on newly cleared land along the sides of roads in remote, unproductive areas of the Amazon. The settlers subsist on slash-and-burn agriculture (clearing and burning small plots of land), and because of the low soil fertility, they generally must move on and clear more forest every few years.

Another serious threat to the Amazon is the growing iron industry. After iron ore is mined, it must be heated and converted to a usable form, pig iron, before being sold. In Brazil, charcoal is used for the heating process, and huge areas of the forest are cut just to produce charcoal. Numerous other projects in the Amazon, such as cement factories, also require charcoal for their operation.

Often, activities that involve burning the forest can lead to uncontrolled forest fires. While the moist root system and dense vegetation of virgin tropical forest would normally make it virtually impossible to burn, continued deforestation in the Amazon seems to have brought the forest to a critical level of dryness at which many areas are now susceptible to burning out of control. The added drying effect of the 1997–1998 El Niño may have contributed to an enormous forest fire in Roraima that burned 6200 sq km (2400 sq miles) of rainforest in March of 1998.

The overall effects of the combined fires (intentional and unintentional) on the Amazon are severe. In addition to permanent deforestation, loss of species, and alteration of the climate, smoke from the fires causes serious air pollution.

In 1986, a satellite detected a compact smoke screen over the Amazon that was 65,000 sq km (25,000 sq miles) in area. In parts of the Amazon (such as Rondônia), airports and schools are frequently closed during the burning season. In Manaus, the sun remains hidden for days on end. Along with the obvious health problems this causes for humans and animals, this "dry fog" inhibits dew production; dew, which forms only on clear nights, is often the only water available to plants and animals at this dry time of year. On a more global scale, the massive amount of carbon dioxide that these burnings release to the atmosphere is thought to contribute significantly to the *greenhouse effect*, which leads to global warming.

Logging

While burning to clear land accounts for a large share of the deforestation in the Amazon, logging for valuable tropical hardwoods is also a serious threat. The Amazon region of Brazil is the world's largest producer of tropical hardwood, yielding 30 million cubic meters (1 billion cubic ft) each year. However, it is estimated that 80% of the total wood cut in the Amazon is done illegally, so the true figure may be much higher. In most cases, 60% to 70% of the timber is wasted by inefficient harvesting methods. At least 22 illegal foreign mills are known to be operating in the Amazon, along with countless local illegal loggers. These loggers are nearly impossible to catch in the vast, remote stretches of the Amazon. Many even build their own bridges or airstrips to gain access to the most remote areas. Thankfully, the paltry $2500 fine for unauthorized deforestation has recently been raised to a maximum fine of $25 million, and illegal logging has been classified as an offense punishable with jail; of course, these punishments can only be applied if the loggers are actually caught.

Some of the areas hardest hit by illegal logging are in territory belonging to indigenous groups. These areas are often among the most inaccessible stretches of land, and thus are difficult for government inspectors to patrol. Loggers sometimes buy off tribal leaders with token gifts or small sums of money and then strip the land. Similar problems exist with illegal gold mining on indigenous lands. Miners leave gaping craters, rivers filled with silt, and mercury contamination in the water downstream of their operations.

Pet Trade

Another illegal activity that is big business in the Amazon is the trafficking of live animals for the pet trade. Although birds are among the most frequent victims of this trade, trafficking in monkeys, reptiles, butterflies, and even spiders is common. The smuggling of live animals out of Brazil is a business estimated to be worth $1 billion annually; some traffickers have reported making up to $100,000 in a month (in a country with a per capita income of $6300 per year). International trade represents only 30% of the animals captured in Brazil; 70% of the animals captured are sold domestically – many of these are birds destined for cages, a cultural icon present in all classes of Brazilian society. Unfortunately, the rarest birds are inevitably the ones most sought after by pet owners – thus the last two Spix's Macaws known in the wild were captured and sold for a fortune in 1988.

Dams

A final serious concern for the Amazon is the push for further development of hydroelectric energy sources. Brazil currently gains about 90% of its energy from hydroelectric power, and the government considers this to be a "clean energy source" that does minimal damage to the environment. In 1985, a plan was announced to build 76 dams in the Amazon by 2010. Although this is unlikely to happen, 16 large dams have been proposed and are currently under consideration.

The devastating effects of dams on tropical forests are illustrated by the Balbina Hydroelectric Plant in the Amazon north of Manaus. This dam flooded over 2000 sq km (800 sq miles) of forest, extending for 150 km (93 miles) upriver. Planners argued that the dam would not harm local wildlife because the nearly 1500 islands in the submerged area would serve as refuges. Instead, these islands became "killing grounds" of fierce competition and predation, because they were far too small to support the number of animals that remained. After all of this, the Balbina dam turned out to provide an extremely low ratio of power generation to flooded area, and has been held up internationally as an example of economic and ecological failure.

Although publicity about the plight of the Amazon has died down since the late 1980s, the problems have by no means done the same. While the Amazon is often thought of as being a stable ecosystem because of the profuse growth of plants and multitude of animals that it contains, the forest is in many ways quite fragile. The escalation of its abuse from machete to fire and bulldozer has pushed the Amazon to the brink of disaster, and many of its inhabitants towards extinction.

Pantanal

Unlike the lush forests that define the Amazon, the heart of the Pantanal lies in its waterways. The Pantanal is the largest freshwater wetland in the world, covering an area of 140,000 sq km (54,000 sq miles) in Brazil alone. Each year, nearly two-thirds of this region is covered with water, which gradually dries until all that is left is a vast plain dotted with shallow watering holes and sliced by thin rivers. The plants and animals that live in the Pantanal have adapted to this dual existence to such an extent that many of them could not survive without the seasonal changes in water level that define the Pantanal wetlands. Thus it becomes obvious that the major threats to the Pantanal are activities that pollute or interfere with the natural movement of water.

Cattle ranching is the main industry in the Pantanal, and it has co-existed with the native plants and animals for more than 200 years. Ranching is so well established that cattle and cowboys are dominant components of the local culture and landscape. The only direct effect of the presence of cattle is that the herds (as well as feral cattle) compete with native animals, such as deer, for grasses. More serious than the presence of cattle are the practices of the ranchers themselves. In the last few decades, many ranchers have planted exotic (non-native) grasses that they hoped would be more productive in their pastures. Most of these grasses are now considered noxious weeds, which spread rapidly and interfere with native vegetation. Ironically, the cattle will not eat many of these introduced species, and these weeds take over as the cattle selectively eat native grasses. Eventually, the fields must be burned to rid them of the weeds.

Clearing fields by burning them is a common practice in the Pantanal, and does not pose a serious environmental threat if fields are burned in the right season. Natural fires occur in the Pantanal at the end of the dry season (August to September). Most plants and animals are adapted to these fires – animals take shelter in the waterways and many plants sprout in the ashy, mineral-enriched soils that result. However, the practice of setting large areas on fire all at once and setting fires in the wrong season has led to increased mortality among nesting birds and slower-moving animals, such as Giant Anteaters and tortoises, which cannot outrun the flames.

Another common ranching practice that threatens the Pantanal is the hunting of animals that are thought to endanger cattle. Capybaras, the world's largest rodents (weighing up to 65 kg, 140 lb), are hunted in the Pantanal for both their coats and their meat, but hundreds of these animals are also slaughtered by ranchers for supposed "sanitary" reasons (capybaras suffer from many parasites, and are thought to carry the parasitic agent of brucellosis, a disease which could potentially be passed on to cattle). Ranchers have also historically had their ranch hands hunt any cats, such as Jaguars, Ocelots, and Pumas, that might attack cattle or cause other damage. The skins of these animals are valuable, and increased poaching now endangers many of the Pantanal's cats.

Poachers pose an even greater threat to caiman, which are relatives of crocodiles. Massive poaching of caiman (Spectacled Caiman, mostly; Plate 16) for their skins (for use in handbags, shoes, etc.) began in the late 1960s. Gangs of armed caiman poachers (*coureiros*) ruled the swamps of the Pantanal in the 1960s and 1970s, and by 1980 an estimated 30,000 caiman were killed each month for their skins. While caiman pose no threat to humans, other, more harmful, species thrive when caiman are not present to control their populations – species such as aquatic snails that pass diseases on to cattle that eat them, and huge schools of piranhas (a favorite food of caiman). Thankfully, the poaching of caiman for their skin has decreased since the 1980s. The trade in caiman skins is controlled by CITES (p. 57), and many repentant coureiros are now tourist guides and unofficial wardens, protecting the local wildlife with as much vigor as they once hunted caiman.

Unfortunately, although caiman poaching has lessened in recent years, pollution and alteration of the waterways that are so vital to the Pantanal have increased. Deforestation and large-scale agriculture on the Planalto headwaters above the Pantanal have led to massive erosion and silting of the rivers. The Río Taquari now carries so much sand that it is no longer navigable. The silting of rivers poses a serious threat to the spectacular *piracemas*, or annual fish migrations, that are an integral part of the Pantanal ecosystem. The hundreds of kilometers of dikes and dams built after severe floods in the 1970s also interfere with these piracemas, and promote the survival of a few non-migratory fish, as well as the creation of "badwaters," where low oxygen content leads to fish mortality.

Another threat to the natural flow of water was proposed in the 1980s. The Hidrovia, a 3400-km (2100-mile) network of water "highways" linking Brazil with Paraguay, Uruguay, Bolivia, and Argentina, was touted as being an environmentally friendly development project that would lower transportation costs and promote trade and development in the five countries involved. However, to allow large ships to navigate the shallow, winding waterways of the Pantanal would have required massive dredging, channel straightening, and the blasting of rock outcroppings. A large, deep channel such as the Hidrovia would collect much of the floodwater that normally covers large areas of the Pantanal, and drastically alter the natural cycle of flooding. Wisely, Brazil withdrew from the project in 1998, and is pursuing less destructive options for improving navigation, such as updated signaling equipment.

A final serious threat to the Pantanal ecosystem is contamination of its water. Herbicides are used heavily to combat unwanted vegetation in pastures and agricultural stands, and pesticide use in the region is increasing rapidly. Organic waste discharged into the waterways from soybean agriculture and fuel alcohol distilleries located above the Pantanal lowers the pH of the water and alters the nutrient balance in the wetlands. Mercury pollution from gold mining also shows signs of becoming a serious problem. This heavy metal is toxic to birds and mammals, and concentrates as it moves up the food chain; so while levels of mercury in the sediment may not be dangerously high, as the metal travels from invertebrates to the fish that eat them, and to the birds that eat the fish, levels of mercury become higher and higher and more dangerous.

In comparison with the Amazon, the environmental degradation currently observable in the Pantanal seems minor. This marshy ecosystem appears to be resilient to a certain level of disturbance, perhaps because of the destructive natural cycles of flooding and fire that it endures, and the fact that this ecosystem has attracted the most rugged species from surrounding regions. However, the lack of monitoring of the effects of a wave of recent human disturbances, as well as the fact that the Pantanal is essentially a giant "settling pond," where pollution and disturbances from surrounding regions will gradually build up, is worrisome. In the Pantanal, the threat is perhaps not so much of losing large numbers of undiscovered species, as in the Amazon, but more of losing the amazing spectacle of the huge populations of animals that thrive in this land of water and cowboys.

Conservation

In Brazil, the system of protected areas and laws intended to protect the environment are reasonably good, at least on paper. A bill recently passed in Congress (1998) gave the federal environmental agency the power to levy fines for damaging the environment, prosecute polluters, and order companies to correct the damage they have caused. While some of the tougher parts of this legislation were omitted at the last minute, it still represents a vast improvement over the previous system, in which 94% of the environmental fines levied by the government were thrown out by the courts, and the environmental agency had no real power to enforce laws. In addition, Brazil has created a large system of federally protected lands. There are five major types of federal conservation areas in Brazil, which vary in the degree to which they are protected. In addition, conservation units can be declared by state or local governments, and the federal government recognizes "private refuges," on which the owners choose to prohibit hunting and other activities that harm the environment.

Overall, the five types of federal conservation areas protect more than 170,000 sq km (66,000 sq miles) of land in Brazil (about 2% of the country's total area). Unfortunately, very few of these protected areas are within the Pantanal; the main Pantanal national park (Pantanal Matogrosso National Park) is very small (only 1350 sq km, 500 sq miles), and protects relatively few species and types of habitat, as 90% of it is under water during the rainy season. There have been some management efforts in the region aimed at protecting the more famous animal residents, such as caiman and Jaguars. However, our knowledge of the many unique habitats within the Pantanal is so limited that it is not even clear which of its areas are most in need of protecting. A project addressing this question is currently underway, with participation from the Brazilian Ministry of the Environment, the World Wide Fund for Nature, local landowners, universities, and local NGOs (non-governmental organizations). The goal of this project is to identify priority areas for biodiversity conservation, and to establish a network of conservation areas that is representative of the Pantanal's diverse plants, animals, and habitats.

Unlike the Pantanal, the Amazon has been actively studied by scientists from Brazil and throughout the world for decades, and the need for its protection is clear. More than 130,000 sq km (50,000 sq miles) of land in the Amazon is protected in the five types of federal conservation areas (about 2.5% of the Amazon's area), including three national parks that each cover 10,000 sq km (4000 sq miles) or more. This relatively large amount of protected area would seem to bode well for conservation in the Amazon. Unfortunately, the reality is that the majority of these "protected" areas receive little, if any, true protection. A large portion of these areas have been decreed on paper, but not yet established – borders have not been set, there is no staff to oversee the land, and many are still in private hands where logging, mining, burning, commercial fishing, and poaching are rampant. The fate of these areas seems to be ultimately dictated more by economics than by conservation; two established national parks have been completely destroyed by hydroelectric dams, and one was bisected by a road built to provide access to a cattle ranch. Many protected areas are repeatedly reduced in size by official decrees.

IBAMA (the Brazilian Institute of the Environment and Renewable Natural Resources), which is responsible for protecting the environment, as well as these conservation areas, is underfunded and understaffed. IBAMA's budget was cut from $20 million in 1989 to only $3 million in 1999. Most of the hundreds of millions of dollars that are donated by other countries and international organizations to protect the environment in Brazil remain tied up in red tape and are seldom seen by those directly involved with conservation. As of 1999, IBAMA had a total of 1168 environmental officers to oversee the entire country of 8.5 million sq km (3.3 million sq miles). Only 400 of these are assigned to protect the 5.3 million sq km (2 million sq miles) of the Amazon, where much of the worst environmental damage is being done. The Pantanal has only 20 IBAMA agents, and one airplane.

Even if there were funding to hire more IBAMA agents, the job is less than attractive. In the Amazon, an average of two agents are lost per year (and not in accidents). In 1999, three agents were held hostage for three days by Kayapo Indians who were in league with the illegal loggers that the agents were attempting to shut down. The director of the Amazonia National Park regularly leaves his phone off the hook because of the number of death threats he receives. And all of this is tolerated for little respect and a salary of perhaps $500 per month.

Extractive Reserves

The situation in the federally protected areas leads one to a somewhat paradoxical idea: that the key to truly protecting the Amazon from man's destruction may lie, ironically, in having people occupy the areas that are to be protected. These people can act as witnesses and bring about their own economic pressures to preserve the forest, combating the economic pressures to destroy it. One remarkable example of this idea in action is the recent development of a new kind of protected area in Brazil: *extractive reserves*.

The extractive reserve owes its existence to the *seringueiros*, or rubber tappers of the Amazon. Since the rubber boom at the beginning of the 1900s, generations of rubber tappers have made daily rounds of the natural forest, collecting the rubber that drips slowly from trees into their collecting buckets. This extraction of rubber is sustainable, and traditional populations of seringueiros make their living from the forest without cutting it down.

In the 1970s and 1980s, however, more and more ranchers and farmers from the south moved into the Amazon, clearing the forest and displacing the seringueiros. Chico Mendes, a rubber tapper and leader of a local union in Acre, began seeking international aid for the rubber tappers. He and anthropologist Mary Allegretti formed the idea of extractive reserves, forest reserves held in trust and managed by local populations that use the forest without destroying it.

In 1988, Mendes was assassinated by cattle ranchers. His death drew international attention to the plight of rubber tappers and the destruction of the Amazon, and led to the creation of nine extractive reserves (including one marine extractive reserve). The total of all state and federal extractive programs now covers more than 30,000 sq km (11,500 sq miles) and involves more than 50,000 people, making these reserves a critical experiment in sustainable development.

While rubber tapping was the origin of extractive reserves, many other products can be sustainably extracted from the forest. Nuts, fruits, oils, honey, and even husks and bark are being extracted and transformed into products ranging from shampoos and massage oils to soft drinks and ice cream. It is estimated that sustainable extraction yields more profit per acre than crop agriculture, livestock, or timber harvesting. Some groups of extracters have formed associations, such as the Rural Workers' Union (whose members harvest Brazil nuts, among other products), to pool their resources and create communal facilities for transporting, processing, and storing their products. Non-profit agencies, such as Cultural Survival, Inc., are also helping these forest extracters increase their profits by facilitating the sale of extracted products directly to buyers. Cultural Survival, Inc. alone oversees orders that have increased from $4.5 million in the first year to an estimated $1 billion in 2000.

Sustainable Agriculture

While sustainable extraction has great potential for preserving traditional lifestyles and areas of the forest that traditional populations inhabit, much of the destruction in the Amazon occurs in areas where government incentives have brought in massive numbers of settlers from other parts of the country. These colonists are generally unfamiliar with the forest and subsist on slash-and-burn agriculture. As discussed earlier, non-native crops such as rice, beans, and corn (which make up the majority of the crops planted in Brazil) can grow for only a few years after the forest is burned, and cattle can be grazed for only a few years more. In less than ten years, settlers must move on and clear a new area of the forest. This cycle benefits no one; the forest is rapidly destroyed and the settlers must endure a life of wandering poverty.

A possible solution to this problem may lie in the development of sustainable agriculture in the Amazon. Sustainable agriculture avoids depleting the soil, as traditional crops do, by mixing different types of crops of varying heights within a plot. Farmers shelter their plots with tall trees, such as rubber, mango, and Brazil nut, and grow shade-tolerant plants (such as coffee, cacao, or guarana) and small plots of annual crops (such as rice, corn, beans, sugar, and manioc) below. The benefit of this system is that the trees, from which products can be extracted, help prevent leaching, erosion, and soil compaction. They have a higher tolerance to the soil acidity and high levels of aluminum present in the Amazon, and cycle nutrients efficiently.

While this type of agriculture is relatively new and must be custom tailored for each soil type, it is believed that this kind of land use could be sustained indefinitely, slowing the destruction of the forest and allowing slash-and-burn farmers to settle permanently. In the Ouro Preto do Oeste region of Rondônia, sustainable agriculture is being promoted to help combat the destruction brought about by massive settlement that resulted from government free land programs (28% of the state is already deforested). Local NGOs and labor unions provide educational programs and free seedlings. Unfortunately, disseminating information in remote areas can be challenging; only 21% of farmers recently surveyed in this region knew anything about sustainable agriculture. However, of those that had heard of sustainable agriculture, 83% had adopted the practices, and a study done in 1990 showed that farmers in Rondônia who switched to sustainable methods made, on average, twice the income of traditional farmers.

One common thread ties together many of the most successful conservation programs in Brazil: local involvement. Local unions and NGOs play a critical role, from passing on the word about the benefits of sustainable agriculture to pooling their resources to form cooperative marketing networks. Communities that come together and organize can succeed in protecting the land that they depend on, from the extractive reserves of the seringueiros to the newly declared Sustainable Development Reserve of Mamirauá, where community members patrol the forests and rivers for illegal activities and meet regularly to decide on their own local hunting, fishing, and logging regulations. These kinds of locally administered conservation programs are proving to be more efficient, and clearly much more effective, than simply declaring areas to be protected on paper from thousands of miles away.

Ecotourism

For Brazil, ecotourism represents a vast, untapped resource with the potential to solve some of the country's conservation problems. In its best form, ecotourism not only exposes visitors to the natural beauty of an area, but also contributes to the management of conservation areas and improves the local quality of life by training and employing people who live nearby. Unfortunately, the tourism industry in Brazil appears far too often to be mis-using the label of ecotourism to promote any tourist activity that comes in contact with nature – from convention centers with shopping malls, bars, and restaurants that happen to be located within a nature reserve, to hotels with hundreds of rooms and manicured tropical gardens for guests to stroll through.

In the Amazon, tour operators specializing in nature tourism abound, but true ecotourism destinations are hard to find. Most tourists to the Amazon fly either to Belém, at the mouth of the Amazon River, or to Manaus, 1100 km (700 miles) upstream. Immediately, they are besieged by hordes of salesmen offering nature tours. Few of these tour operators mention how the money spent on the tour will benefit local conservation efforts, and many of the people involved are from larger cities or other countries, where much of the revenue flows.

A notable exception to this confusing array of opportunists is the Silves community ecotourism project. This project was started by local fishermen who had been battling for 20 years with the depletion of fish stocks due to large-scale commercial fishing and habitat destruction. The fishermen of this island community 300 km (180 miles) east of Manaus banded together and pressured the government to declare a series of lakes and rivers surrounding their community as an Environmental Protection Area, to preserve both the fish stocks and their traditional way of life. This plan allowed the local people to control fishing in the lakes, and the community decided that ecotourism was the best way to provide funds for the monitoring, patrolling, and research that was necessary to ensure the survival of the fish.

With the help of the World Wide Fund for Nature, Silves has become the first community-based ecotourism program in the Brazilian Amazon. A simple 12-room lodge, the Aldeia dos Lagos Hotel, was built on the island of Silves, and community members were trained to operate the hotel. A selection of tours was developed, including wildlife viewing by canoe or foot, and cultural tours with visits to local indigenous populations. Five communities in the Silves area are involved in the ecotourism program, and a system has been set up to monitor the environmental and cultural impacts of the visitation. All lakes in the region have been classified based on how much (if any) fishing is to be allowed, and the lakes are policed by community members. Revenue from the ecotourism program also goes towards ranger patrols, community education, and habitat restoration. The Aldeia dos Lagos Hotel opened its doors in September of 1997, and serves as a model of what ecotourism could be for the rest of the Amazon.

Ecotourism in the Pantanal differs dramatically from that in the Amazon, owing mainly to the differences in land ownership and population in the two regions. The Pantanal remained an obscure and little-known corner of Brazil until the telenovela "Pantanal" in 1990 made the area a popular destination for Brazilians. The Rondon family, upon whom the TV soap opera was loosely based, turned their ranch house into a tourist hotel, the Fazenda Río Negro, and began offering nature tours. Other ranchers followed suit, and within a decade, hundreds of thousands of tourists visited this no-longer obscure corner of Brazil. Now, more than 100 ranches have opened tourist hotels, offering wildlife viewing – by foot, horseback, truck, or boat – as well as sport fishing.

Ecotourism has undoubtedly had a positive influence on conservation in the Pantanal. Many of the ranchers have created substantial private nature reserves on parts of their land. Ecotourism has placed pressure on everyone in the Pantanal to conserve wildlife, and ranch hands that formerly doubled as poachers have now become private game wardens. One of the main goals of ecotourism, an improvement in the local quality of life, seems to be realized in parts of the Pantanal, where new revenues have reached almost everyone – from ranch owners to migrant farm hands.

There are also some encouraging signs that the government recognizes the potential of ecotourism, and the problems with how the ecotourism label is being mis-used by some of the tourist industry in Brazil. The tourism ministry has initiated a series of workshops (mostly in Amazonian states) to train groups of people in ecotourism practices and ethics. However, without some basic improvements in the tourism infrastructure, many attempts at ecotourism are likely to fail. One of the main problems in linking ecotourism with conservation in Brazil is that very few of the protected areas have tourist facilities nearby. With the lack of money available for rangers and wardens, it is essential for these areas to be visited and to generate funds to help pay for their own protection.

The government is currently dabbling in setting up some unique ecotourism programs in various protected areas. For example, programs of "eco-scientific tourism" have been suggested for Brazil's genetic reserves, areas that have been set aside to protect some of the country's vast genetic biodiversity. Ten different indigenous groups have proposed ecotourism programs, and five of these have been accepted by the tourism ministry for further development. The government is also holding ecotourism workshops in nine of the country's extractive reserves.

While there are instances of glaring abuse of the ecotourism label, there are also positive signs that many people in Brazil see the potential value of developing true ecotourism throughout the country. The single most important thing that visitors to Brazil can do to encourage this trend is to choose their tour operators carefully – being vigilant in searching out organizations that strive to improve conservation and quality of life in the local area, and not just increase the contents of their wallets.

Chapter 5

How to Use This Book: Ecology and Natural History

- What is Natural History?
- What is Ecology and What Are Ecological Interactions?
- How to Use This Book
  Information in the Family Profiles
  Information in the Color Plate Sections

What is Natural History?

The purpose of this book is to provide ecotravellers with sufficient information to identify many common plant and animal species and to learn about them and the families to which they belong. Information on the lives of plants and animals is known generally as *natural history*. More specifically, we can define natural history as the study of plants' and animals' natural habits, including especially their ecology, distribution, classification, and behavior. This kind of information is important for a variety of reasons: researchers need to know natural history as background on the species they study, and wildlife managers and conservationists need natural history information because their decisions about managing animal populations must be partially based on it. More relevant for the ecotraveller, natural history is simply interesting. People who appreciate plants and animals typically like to watch them, touch them when appropriate, and know as much about them as they can.

What is Ecology and What Are Ecological Interactions?

Ecology is the branch of the biological sciences that studies the interactions between living things (animals and plants) and their physical environment and with each other. Broadly interpreted, these interactions take into account most everything we find fascinating about plants and animals – what nutrients they need and how they get them, how and when they breed, how they survive the rigors of extreme climates, why they are large or small, or dully or brightly colored, and many other facets of their lives.

A plant or animal's life, in some ways, is the sum of its interactions with other plants and animals – members of its own species and others – and with its environment. Of particular interest are the numerous and diverse ecological interactions that occur between different species. Most can be placed into one of several general categories, based on how two species affect each other when they interact; they can have positive, negative, or neutral (that is, no) effects on each other. The relationship terms below are used in the book to describe the natural history of various plants and animals.

Competition is an ecological relationship in which neither of the interacting species benefits. Competition occurs when individuals of the same or different species use the same resource – a certain type of food, nesting holes in trees, etc. – and that resource is in insufficient supply (*limiting resource*) to meet all their needs. As a result, both species are less successful than they could be in the absence of the interaction (that is, if the other were not present).

Predation is an ecological interaction in which one species, the *predator*, benefits, and the other species, the *prey*, is harmed. Most people think of predation as something like a mountain lion eating a deer, and they are correct; but predation also includes such things as a wasp killing a caterpillar or an insect eating a seed.

Parasitism, like predation, is a relationship between two species in which one benefits and one is harmed. The difference is that in a predatory relationship, one animal kills and eats the other, but in a parasitic one, the parasite feeds slowly on the *host* species and usually does not kill it. There are internal parasites, like protozoans and many kinds of worms, and external parasites, such as leeches, ticks, and mosquitos. Even a deer munching on the leaves of a bush can be considered a type of parasitism.

Mutualisms are some of the most intriguing ecological relationships – interactions in which both participants benefit. Plants and their pollinators engage in mutualistic interactions. A bee species, for instance, obtains a food resource, nectar or pollen, from a plant's flower; the plant it visits benefits because it is able to complete its reproductive cycle when the bee transports pollen to another plant. In Brazil, numerous plants, such as the undergrowth bush *Maieta* (Plate E), exhibit mutualism with the ants that live in them: the ants obtain food (the plants produce fat and sugar for them) and shelter from the plant and in return, the ants defend the plants from plant-eating insects. Sometimes the species have interacted so long that they now cannot live without each other; theirs is an *obligate* mutualism. For instance, termites (Plate 1) cannot by themselves digest wood. Rather, it is the single-celled animals, protozoans, that live in their gut that produce the digestive enzymes that digest wood. At this point in their evolutionary histories, neither the termites nor their internal helpers can live alone.

Commensalism is a relationship in which one species benefits but the other is not affected in any obvious way. For example, epiphytes (p. 14), such as orchids and bromeliads, that grow on tree trunks and branches obtain from trees some shelf space to grow on, but, as far as anyone knows, neither hurt nor help the trees. A classic example of a commensal animal is the Remora, a fish that attaches itself with a suction cup on its head to a shark, then feeds on scraps of food the shark leaves behind. Remora are *commensals*, not parasites – they neither harm nor help sharks, but they benefit greatly by associating with sharks. Cattle Egrets

(Plate 27) are commensals – these birds follow cattle, eating insects and other small animals that flush from cover as the cattle move about their pastures; the cattle, as far as we know, couldn't care one way or the other (unless they are concerned about that certain loss of dignity that occurs when the egrets perch not only near them, but on them as well).

A term many people know that covers some of these ecological interactions is *symbiosis*, which means living together. Usually this term suggests that the two interacting species do not harm one another; therefore, mutualisms and commensalisms are the symbiotic relationships discussed here.

How to Use This Book

The information here on animals is divided into two sections: the *plates*, which include artists' color renderings of various species together with brief identifying and location information; and the *family profiles*, with natural history information on the families to which the pictured animals belong. The best way to identify and learn about Brazilian animals may be to scan the illustrations before a trip to become familiar with the kinds of animals you are likely to encounter. Then when you spot an animal, you may recognize its general type or family, and can find the appropriate pictures and profiles quickly. In other words, it is more efficient, upon spotting a bird, to be thinking, "Gee, that looks like a flycatcher," and be able to flip to that part of the book, than to be thinking, "Gee, that bird is partly yellow" and then, to identify it, flipping through all the animal pictures, searching for yellow birds.

Information in the Family Profiles

Classification, Distribution, Morphology

The first paragraphs of each profile generally provide information on the family's classification (or *taxonomy*), geographic distribution, and *morphology* (shape, size, and coloring). Classification information is provided because it is how scientists separate plants and animals into related groups, and often it enhances our appreciation of various species to know these relationships. You may have been exposed to classification levels sometime during your education, but if you are a bit rusty, a quick review may help: *Kingdom* Animalia: all the animal species detailed in the book are members of the animal kingdom. *Phylum* Chordata, *Subphylum* Vertebrata: all the species in the book with backbones and an internal skeleton are vertebrates. The arthropods, including insects, spiders, and crabs, lack a backbone or internal skeleton, and they are placed in the broad category of Invertebrata. *Class*: the book covers several vertebrate classes: Amphibia (amphibians), Reptilia (reptiles), Aves (birds), and Mammalia (mammals); and invertebrate classes: Insecta (insects), Arachnida (spiders), Decapoda (crabs). *Order*: each class is divided into several orders, the members of each order sharing many characteristics. For example, one of the mammal orders is Carnivora, the carnivores, which includes mammals with teeth specialized for meat-eating – dogs, cats, bears, raccoons, weasels. *Family*: families of animals are subdivisions of each order that contain closely related species that are very similar in form, ecology, and behavior. The family Canidae, for instance, contains all the dog-like mammals – coyote, wolf, fox, dog. Animal family names end in *-dae*; subfamilies, subdivisions of families, end in *-nae*. *Genus*: further subdivisions; within each genus are grouped species that are very closely related – they are all considered to have evolved from a common ancestor. *Species*: the lowest classification level; all members of a species are similar enough to be able to breed and produce living, fertile offspring.

Example	Classification of the Toco Toucan (Plate 54):
Kingdom	Animalia, with more than a million species
Phylum	Chordata, Subphylum Vertebrata, with about 40,000 species
Class	Aves (birds), with about 9000 species
Order	Piciformes, with about 350 species; includes honeyguides, woodpeckers, barbets, and toucans
Family	Ramphastidae, with about 40 species; all the toucans (some newer classifications add the barbets into this group)
Genus	*Ramphastos*, with 13 species; one group of toucans
Species	*Ramphastos toco*, known to its friends as Toco Toucan.

Some of the family profiles in the book cover animal orders, while others describe families or subfamilies.

Species' distributions vary tremendously. Some species are found only in very limited areas, whereas others range over several continents. Distributions can be described in a number of ways. An animal can be said to be *Old World* or *New World*; the former refers to the regions of the globe that Europeans knew of before Columbus – Europe, Asia, Africa; and the latter refers to the Western Hemisphere – North, Central, and South America. Brazil falls within the part of the world called the *Neotropics* by biogeographers – scientists who study the geographic distributions of living things. A Neotropical species is one that occurs within southern Mexico, Central America, South America, and/or the Caribbean Islands. The terms *tropical*, *temperate*, and *arctic* refer to climate regions of the Earth; the boundaries of these zones are determined by lines of latitude (and ultimately, by the position of the sun with respect to the Earth's surface). The tropics, always warm, are the regions of the world that fall within the belt from 23.5 degrees North latitude (the Tropic of Cancer) to 23.5 degrees South latitude (the Tropic of Capricorn). The world's temperate zones, with more seasonal climates, extend from 23.5 degrees North and South latitude to the Arctic and Antarctic Circles, at 66.5 degrees North and South. Arctic regions, more or less always cold, extend from 66.5 degrees North and South to the poles. The position of Brazil with respect to these zones is shown in Map 4.

Several terms help define a species' distribution and describe how it attained its distribution:

Range. The particular geographic area occupied by a species.

Native or *Indigenous.* Occurring naturally in a particular place.

Introduced. Occurring in a particular place owing to people's intentional or unintentional assistance with transportation, usually from one continent to another; the opposite of native. For instance, pheasants were initially brought to North America from Europe/Asia for hunting, Europeans brought rabbits and foxes to Australia for sport, and the British brought European Starlings and House Sparrows to North America.

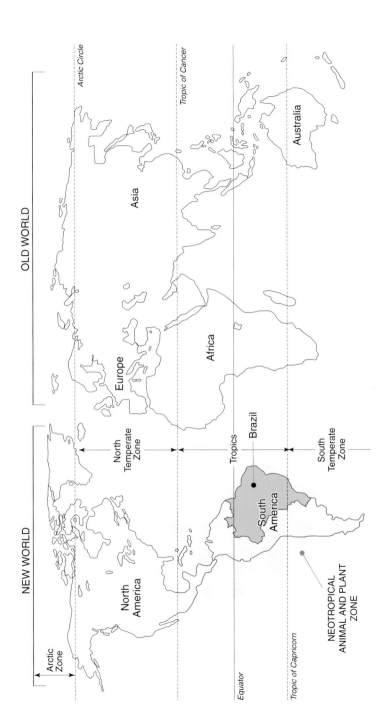

Map 4 Map of the Earth showing the position of Brazil; Old World and New World zones; tropical, temperate, and arctic regions; and the Neotropical animal and plant life zone.

Endemic. A species, a genus, an entire family, etc., that is found in a particular place and nowhere else. A small monkey, the Brazilian Bare-faced Tamarin, occurs only in Brazil along the north side of the Río Amazonas east of Manaus. Galápagos Finches are endemic to the Galápagos Islands; nearly all the reptile and mammal species of Madagascar are endemics; all species are endemic to Earth (as far as we know).

Cosmopolitan. A species that is widely distributed throughout the world.

Ecology and Behavior

In these sections, we describe some of what is known about the basic activities pursued by each group. Much of the information relates to when and where animals are usually active, what they eat, and how they forage.

Activity Location – *Terrestrial* animals pursue life and food on the ground. *Arboreal* animals pursue life and food in trees or shrubs. Many arboreal animals have *prehensile* tails, long and muscular, which they can wrap around tree branches to support themselves as they hang to feed or to move about more efficiently. *Cursorial* refers to animals that are adapted for running along the ground. *Fossorial* means living and moving underground.

Activity Time – *Nocturnal* means active at night. *Diurnal* means active during the day. *Crepuscular* refers to animals that are active at dusk and/or dawn.

Food Preferences – Although animal species can usually be assigned to one of the feeding categories below, most eat more than one type of food. Most frugivorous birds, for instance, also nibble on the occasional insect, and carnivorous mammals occasionally eat plant materials.

Herbivores are predators that prey on plants.
Carnivores are predators that prey on animals.
Insectivores eat insects.
Granivores eat seeds.
Frugivores eat fruit.
Nectarivores eat nectar.
Piscivores eat fish.
Omnivores eat a variety of things.
Detritivores, such as vultures, eat dead stuff.

Breeding

In these sections, we present basics on each group's breeding particulars, including type of mating system, special breeding behaviors, durations of egg incubation or *gestation* (pregnancy), as well as information on nests, eggs, and young.

Mating Systems – A *monogamous* mating system is one in which one male and one female establish a pair-bond and contribute fairly evenly to each breeding effort. In *polygamous* systems, individuals of one of the sexes have more than one mate (that is, they have harems): in *polygynous* systems, one male mates with several females, and in *polyandrous* systems, one female mates with several males.

Condition of Young at Birth – *Altricial* young are born in a relatively undeveloped state, usually naked of fur or feathers, eyes closed, and unable to feed themselves, walk, or run from predators. *Precocial* young are born in a more developed state, eyes open, and soon able to walk and perhaps feed themselves.

Notes

These sections provide interesting bits and pieces of information that do not fit elsewhere in the account, including associated folklore.

Status

These sections comment on the conservation status of each group, including information on relative rarity or abundance, factors contributing to population declines, and special conservation measures that have been implemented. Because this book concentrates on animals that ecotravellers are most likely to see – that is, on more common ones – few of the profiled species are immediately threatened with extinction. The definitions of the terms that we use to describe degrees of threat to various species are these: *Endangered* species are known to be in imminent danger of extinction throughout their range, and are highly unlikely to survive unless strong conservation measures are taken; populations of endangered species generally are very small, so they are rarely seen. *Threatened* species are known to be undergoing rapid declines in the sizes of their populations; unless conservation measures are enacted, and the causes of the population declines identified and halted, these species are likely to move to endangered status in the near future. *Vulnerable to threat*, or *near-threatened*, are species that, owing to their habitat requirements or limited distributions, and based on known patterns of habitat destruction, are highly likely to be threatened in the near future. Several organizations publish lists of threatened and endangered species, but agreement among the lists is not absolute.

Where appropriate, we also include threat classifications from the Convention on International Trade in Endangered Species (CITES) and the United States Endangered Species Act (ESA) classifications. CITES is a global cooperative agreement to protect threatened species on a worldwide scale by regulating international trade in wild animals and plants among the 130 or so participating countries. Regulated species are listed in CITES Appendices, with trade in those species being strictly regulated by required licenses and documents. CITES Appendix I lists endangered species; all trade in them is prohibited. Appendix II lists threatened/vulnerable species, those that are not yet endangered but may soon be; trade in them is strictly regulated. Appendix III lists species that are protected by laws of individual countries that have signed the CITES agreements. The USA's Endangered Species Act works in a similar way – by listing endangered and threatened species, and, among other provisions, strictly regulating trade in those animals. The International Union for Conservation of Nature (IUCN) maintains a "Red List" of threatened and endangered species that often is more broad-based and inclusive than these other lists, and we refer to the Red List in some of the accounts.

Information in the Color Plate Sections

Pictures. Among amphibians, reptiles, and mammals, males and females of a species usually look alike, although often there are size differences. For many species of birds, however, the sexes differ in color pattern and even anatomical features. If only one individual is pictured, you may assume that male and female of that species look exactly or almost alike; when there are major sex differences, both male and female are depicted. The animals shown on an individual plate, in most cases, have been drawn to the correct scale relative to each other.

Name. We provide the common English name for each profiled species and the scientific, or Latin, name. Often, in Brazil, the local name for a given species varies regionally. For some species, there is no agreed-upon Portuguese name; for a few, there is no English name.

ID. Here we provide brief descriptive information that, together with the pictures, will enable you to identify most of the animals you see. The lengths of amphibians given in this book are usually their snout–vent lengths (SVLs), unless we mention that the tail is included. The vent is the opening on amphibian and reptile bellies that lies approximately where the rear limbs join the body, and through which sex occurs and wastes exit. Therefore, frogs' long legs are not included in their reported length measurements. Unless otherwise indicated, reptile body lengths are given as total lengths (tail included). For the lizards, however, lengths reported are SVLs. For mammals, size measures given are generally the lengths of the head and body, but do not include tails. Birds are measured from tip of bill to end of tail. For birds commonly seen flying, such as seabirds and hawks, we provide wingspan (wingtip to wingtip) measurements, if known. For most birds, we describe their sizes in terms of their overall body length: *very large* (more than 1 m, 3.3 ft); *large* (49 cm to 1 m, 1.6 to 3.3 ft); *mid-sized* (20 to 48 cm, 8 in to 1.5 ft); *small* (10 to 19 cm, 3.5 to 7 in); and *tiny* (less than 10 cm, 3.5 in).

Habitat/Region. In these sections we list the regions (see Map 3, p. 34) and habitat types in which each species occurs and provide symbols for the habitat types each species prefers.

Explanation of habitat symbols:

= Terra firme lowland forest (p. 15).

= Varzea forest (also called flooded or riverine forest; p. 27).

= Igapó forest (also called white sand forest; p. 15).

= Forest edge and streamside. Some species typically are found along forest edges or near or along streams; these species prefer semi-open areas rather than dense, closed, interior parts of forests. Also included here: open woodlands, tree plantations, and shady gardens.

= Pastureland, non-tree plantations, savannah (grassland with scattered trees and shrubs), gardens without shade trees, roadside. Species found in these habitats prefer very open areas.

= Freshwater. For species typically found in or near lakes, streams, rivers, marshes, swamps.

= Saltwater/marine. For species found in or near the ocean, ocean beaches, or mangroves.

REGIONS (see Map 3, p. 34):

NEA   Northeastern Amazon
CMF   Coastal Mangrove Forest
NWA   Northwestern Amazon
SAM   Southern Amazon
PAN   Pantanal

Example

Plate 54a

Toco Toucan
Ramphastos toco
ID: Large (66 cm, 2.2 ft); black body with white throat and lower back; huge yellow-orange bill with black spot on tip.

HABITAT: Forest edge, palm savannah and gardens.

REGION: NEA, SAM, PAN

Chapter 6

Insects and Other Arthropods

Introduction

All of the *insects*, together with *spiders*, *scorpions*, *centipedes*, *crabs*, *shrimps* and *barnacles* are placed together in the megagroup Arthropoda. By some estimates, the *arthropods* of the world make up more than four of every five organisms known and occupy every habitat in the world, including the bottom of the deepest oceans and the ice cap of Antarctica. On the basis of their species numbers, diversity of habitats they inhabit, and the absolute number of individuals, the arthropods must be the most successful group of animals ever to live on Earth.

Among the arthropods, by sheer numbers insects are the dominant group and the one which we emphasize here. They make up over 75% of all the species of animals in the world (by some estimates that means more than 10 million species), and we guarantee that this is one group of animals that you will see, hear and experience no matter where you go in Brazil. With the word "insect," however, your first reaction may be to conjure up images of scurrying cockroaches, clouds of mosquitos, and childhood memories of disgusting small things with buzzy wings and too many legs. But these stereotypes and prejudices are belied by the facts. Insects and their relatives are a beneficial and integral part of virtually all habitats in Brazil. Scientists who study insects (*entomologists*) estimate that less than 5% of all insect species are actually harmful to humans, and most of the rest are directly or indirectly beneficial. To name just a few direct benefits: as pollinators of fruit orchards and grain-crop fields, they help supply a large proportion of the food eaten in North America and Europe; as efficient predators, they keep plague species, such as white flies and cotton bole weevils in check (*biological control*); and as sensitive barometers of pollution, they provide warning of changes in the environment long before we could see them ourselves (acting as *bioindicators*). Even the herbivorous (plant-eating) insects have become essential to the quality and health of our lives. They often force plants to produce defense chemicals, many of which end up, by coincidence, having a physiological effect on humans – so are the source for many of the medicines we use today. If we want to be honest about it, we should be thanking insects rather than squashing them.

Because of insects' often restricted ranges and high degree of habitat specialization, some scientists suggest that with habitat destruction and forest clearing, it is almost certain that many species of insects in Brazil and other regions are probably becoming extinct every year – most never having been discovered or described by scientists before their demise. In fact, we know so little about the biology and distribution of most insect species in Brazil that it is difficult to judge how many are endangered or threatened. Some species, such as the PEANUT BUG (Plate 1), have extensive geographical ranges throughout the forests of Central America and northern South America. Many others, perhaps the majority of Neotropical insects, however, have incredibly small ranges that may include a single mountain valley or particular type of river island. What causes some species to become restricted to small endemic ranges and permits others to have wide ranges is a focus of many ecological, physiological and biogeographical studies, many of them using insects as test organisms.

The majority of ecotravellers to Brazil are most excited about seeing the big hairy and feathered animals. However, the effects of charismatic Jaguars, macaws, and others of their ilk, on the habitats they inhabit, while important, are nowhere as significant as those of the humble arthropods. Without the pollination, seed dispersal, insect control, and decomposing of organic material undertaken largely if not uniquely by insects, the habitats we "ooh" and "ahh" over would be much simpler, less diverse, and much less interesting. Some scientists studying fossil evidence of plant evolution have suggested that a major rise of insects in the Cretaceous period (120 million years before present) is directly linked to the abrupt rise of flowering plants at that time through pollination specialization and co-dependence of the plants and insects. Thus, the flowering plants are linked inextricably both in their origin and survival with insects.

For the ecotraveller, many arthropods, especially insects, will provide an additional esthetic quality to enhance a trip to Brazil. The beautiful butterflies, the dragonflies and beetles, and the bizarre insects to which you can't even begin to put a name, will pique your curiosity and raise your appreciation of Brazil's wonderful wildlife. The dreaded insects, such as mosquitos, that you might have anticipated with anxiety, will underwhelm you. In comparison to the clouds of mosquitos people become accustomed to in the summer in many parts of the USA or Europe, you will be pleasantly surprised at how few there are on a path in the middle of the Amazon jungle. Except for a few marshy areas, these pests are insignificant for most of the year.

General Characteristics and Classification of Arthropods

All arthropods share the characteristics of having a hard outer skeleton, or exoskeleton (*cuticle*), and multi-jointed legs. These legs are variously modified for walking, swimming, feeding, defense, mating and for sensing the environment. The *lobsters*, *crayfish*, and *shrimp* (Class Crustacea) are found primarily in the ocean (but some are in freshwater and a few are on land). They have two pairs of antennae and ten or more pairs of legs. The *spiders*, *ticks*, and *scorpions* (Class Arachnida) are found primarily on land. They have four pairs of walking legs and claw-like mouth parts. Their bodies are divided into a head (*cephalothorax*) and large rear segment (*abdomen*). The *insects* (Class Insecta) are found primarily on land and in freshwater and have two pairs of wings, three pairs of legs (reduced to two in the butterfly subfamily, Nymphalinae) and usually jaw-like mandibles. Their bodies are divided into three distinct parts, a head, *thorax* (which bears the legs and wings), and an abdomen. The class is made up of about 26 orders, such as *beetles*, *flies*, *butterflies*, *wasps*, *true bugs*, and *termites*.

Features of Tropical Arthropods

As with most other groups, arthropods, especially insects, are much more diverse in the tropics than in North America or Europe. What we don't know about these insects is overwhelming. On one 5-km (3-mile) path in the western Amazon, specialists in butterflies (*lepidopterists*) found almost 1200 species of butterflies (this doesn't count any of the night-flying moths), many more than are found in all of North America. From a single tree in the Amazon, another biologist found more species of ants than occur in all of England. From the canopy of another tree a researcher collected 1 kg (2.2 lb) of insects and spiders, which contained almost 2000 species, but only about 100 of these species were known before or had scientific names; the rest were completely new to science.

Arthropods in Brazil eat a wide variety of food including leaves, nectar, plant juices, other insects, and blood, but few can eat wood. The major component of the tough cell walls that surround plant cells is a sugar-starch called *cellulose*, which is held together like a cable by very strong chemical bonds. Every year plants produce 100 billion tons of cellulose worldwide, and it is the most abundant organic compound on Earth. Most herbivorous insects cannot digest these tough cell walls made of cellulose and instead consume the more easily digested ingredients contained inside the plant cells. It turns out that among the few organisms that can actually digest cellulose, especially in its densest form, wood, are termites. In partnership (*mutualism*) with specialized one-celled organisms that occur only in their guts and produce unique enzymes to break down wood, termites have access to an abundant food source with little competition from other organisms. They break otherwise indigestible wood into shorter-chained sugar products that they and other organisms can use and break down further until eventually the chemical chains are so fragmented that they can be taken up through the roots of nearby plants. As a nutrient, these chemicals are then used to make, among other things, cellulose and wood, and the cycle starts all over again. Termites, therefore, help recycle dead wood that otherwise would accumulate and go unused for many years or even centuries as it weathered slowly away.

Reproductive strategies of arthropods are so diverse and remarkable that they often make bird and mammal mating systems seem simple. Some species have *asexual reproduction*, in which only females are present and eggs mature without the influence of sperm. Other species alternate between asexual and sexual reproduction, but many rely fully on sexual reproduction. Mating behavior includes promiscuity, monogamy, and polyandry, but the most common mating system among arthropods, and insects in particular, is polygyny. Among some insects, such as the OWL BUTTERFLY (Plate 4) and MERIAN'S ORCHID BEE (Plate 5), males form lecs and gather in open areas of the forests to attract females. Like in the birds, mammals and frogs, female arthropods tend to have most of the say in selecting potential mates, and males are often left then with the problem of communicating to a female just how superior their genes are, so she can choose the best one to father her young. The result is a complex of courtship behavior, spectacular male colors and behavior, territoriality, and a plethora of other characters – enough to satisfy the programming demands of TV's Discovery and Animal Planet Channels for the next thousand years.

Among some insects, the young are like small wingless forms of the adult and are called *nymphs*. They get progressively bigger until they have full wings and reach adult size. In other insect groups, however, the young are completely different from the adults. This young insect is called a *larva*, and it eventually undergoes a sudden transformation (*metamorphosis*) into the adult form. In butterflies, larvae are known as *caterpillars*; in flies, *maggots*; in beetles, *grubs*. Most insects spend far more of their lives in these immature stages than as adults, and the change into the adult stage (*emergence*) is often cued for many species simultaneously by the right combination of rain and temperature. For the most part, adults are active during parts of the year that are rainy and warm. Don't worry, however, if your trip to Brazil doesn't conform to one of these rainy, warm periods; there will be at least a few arthropods active in any habitat during any month of the year.

Seeing Arthropods in Brazil

It may sound ludicrous to provide advice on how to see arthropods, but most species do not seek out humans or come to them uninvited. Many nocturnal species are attracted to lights at night, and it can be rewarding to study the little beasts flapping around the light outside your cabin or at a fluorescent light at a rural petrol station. From a canoe or along a trail at night, shine your flashlight on the vegetation, and you will often see small white reflections that are the eyes of *jumping spiders* and *wolf spiders* stalking their insect prey. During the day, look for these night-active spiders on the underside of leaves and the surface of tree trunks, where they spend the day motionless, depending for protection on their abilities to match the background color. Many day-active species concentrate around flowers, rotting fruit and dung. Other species are active only on sandy beaches or rock faces. Some arthropod species such as *cicadas* make their presence known more by sound than sight, and at dusk the sounds of a forest full of cicadas can make sensitive ears ring. Many other insects, however, make more subtle sounds. Listen for *crickets* and *katydids* making their different clicks and churring notes all night long. Because many insects are so small, it is easy to pass them up as uninteresting. But even if you don't have a microscope or magnifying glass, try looking at these interesting, tiny animals. If you have binoculars, reverse them and carefully look through them backwards. As you get within about 2 cm (1 in) from an insect or spider, it will come into focus and be sufficiently enlarged so you can see lots of detail. You will be amazed at the variety of shapes, forms, and colors you see and at the behaviors you can watch.

Order and Family Profiles

Tens of thousands of species of arthropods occur in Brazil. Brazil's leading entomologists estimate that there are more than 3600 species of butterflies alone in Brazil, of which at least 250 species are endemic. Entire guide-books could be written on any of the orders and most of the families of Brazil's insects, but there is no room for such detail in a book of this size. Here we focus on 31 species that both represent the range of the common arthropod groups you are likely to see on your trip to Brazil and whose natural history is fairly well-studied.

I. Dragonflies and Damselflies

Relatively large, often colorful, and actively flying during the day, adult *dragonflies* and *damselflies* (Order Odonata) are easy to recognize. Their four elongate wings are folded back at rest in most damselflies and spread out to the side in dragonflies. The large eyes bulge out from the sides of the head, and are widely separated in the front in damselflies, but approach or actually touch each other in the front in dragonflies. The antennae are very short and bristlelike. The abdomen is long and slender with finger-like structures at the end, used by the male to clasp the female in copulation. Present-day *odonates* vary in length from 2 to 18 cm (1 to 7 in), but a species that lived 250 million years ago and known only from fossils had a wing spread of 64 cm (2.5 ft)! Adults catch small insects in the air using their legs like a basket. Unlike all other insects, which have their copulatory organs at the end of their abdomen, male odonates have theirs at the front of the abdomen. The two sexes spend considerable time flying together in "tandem" with the male clasping the female. The female may lay her eggs while in tandem with the male or alone, depending on the species, but she always deposits her eggs in or near water. Some species show considerable territoriality, with the male guarding the female while she deposits eggs in his territory. The nymphs live underwater using gills at the end of the abdomen to breathe. They use modified mouth parts to grab small prey items such as tadpoles, small fish, and larvae of other insects. When they eventually grow large enough, the last nymphal stage crawls out of the water on a blade of grass or detritus. The adult, winged form breaks out of the husk of hard exoskeleton that surrounded the nymph and sits quietly just above the surface of the water. Here its soft brown outer surface slowly hardens and takes on color. During this hardening stage, the young adult is especially vulnerable to predation because it cannot fly well.

You will see many dragonflies and damselflies in virtually every habitat in Brazil, and most will look and behave like ones you might have seen in North America or Europe. As a purely Neotropical representative, however, no odonate is more spectacular and different than the huge HELICOPTER DAMSELFLY (Plate 1). There are 19 species of these peculiar damselflies (Family Pseudostigmatidae), and they are all restricted to the tropical lowland forests of South and Central America. On a sunny day in rainforest, especially following a rainy day, these long (15 cm, 6 in), thin damselflies flutter like some small-scale helicopter through the lower and mid levels of vegetation. The four long wings often beat slowly and independently, and their bright yellow or white tips make them obvious and seemingly easy prey for any hungry bird. These damselflies, however, are very maneuverable and almost like magic easily avoid being caught as they rise into the canopy. They search for insects and spiders sitting on leaves, but they also often hover in front of spider webs and pluck out the resident spider when it makes itself obvious. The long abdomen is used to put eggs into hollow bamboo, tree holes, or pineapple-like bromeliads that hold reservoirs of water. Here the nymphs hatch out into the water and feed on mosquito larvae, small frog tadpoles and other odonate nymphs, until they finally emerge from the water as adults. Males of some species defend this larval site for several months, breeding with females that visit them.

Profile
Helicopter Damselfly, *Mecistogaster ornata*, Plate 1a

2. Grasshoppers, Crickets, and Cockroaches

Most of the species of this order (Orthoptera) are large, from 2 to 18 cm (0.8 to 7 in) long. They have front wings that are elongated and thickened like leather. At rest, these thickened wings cover the membranous hind wings. The body is elongated and the antennae are very short to relatively long. Young develop gradually into adults. Some of the best songsters in the insect world are found in this order – especially *grasshoppers* and *crickets*. Sounds are produced by *stridulation*: rubbing a scraper over a filelike ridge that is variously placed on the legs, wings or other body parts. Each species produces a different song. Along with this sound-producing ability, most species have a large ear (*tympanum*) along the side of the thorax or abdomen. It is used to detect the sounds and distinguish specific rhythms in songs that are used, for instance, for mate attraction or to signal species identity. In some species many males will sing together in a synchronized chorus. Most species feed on plant material like leaves and seeds, but a few eat other insects, and others, such as many cockroaches, are scavengers.

Many of the species of LEAF-MIMICKING KATYDIDS (Plate 1) have wings that so resemble leaves, that you must look twice to see it is an insect and not part of the plant on which it is resting. These herbivorous insects are night-active and eat leaves mainly from vegetation in the understory of forests. Quite often adults are attracted to lights at night. To make sounds at night, they have little bumps on the insides of their wings that they rub over each other by moving the closed wings back and forth. Usually males make most of these sounds to attract females, and the song of each species is different. The young nymphs also eat leaves. During the day you can find katydids sitting in among the leaves of undergrowth shrubs.

Profile

Leaf-mimicking Katydid, *Cycloptera speculata*, Plate 1b

3. Termites

The small insects in the Order Isoptera, known as *termites*, are the oldest of all social insects and have the most complex societies in the insect world. *Termite* colonies usually have two or three different-sized and shaped individuals (*castes*) within a single species, each having different jobs such as workers, soldiers, or reproductives (Plate 1). Within the same colony, there can be individuals with wings (four and held flat) and those without wings. More subtly, there can be further specialization within each caste so that some workers do only one task and other workers a different task. Some colonies have "wild-card" nymphs, which, as they grow, perform a variety of tasks but transform into workers, soldiers or reproductives depending on the colony's needs. Males and females also are different castes.

Most, but not all, termites are light-colored, with soft bodies, long and threadlike antennae, and a broad connection between the abdomen and thorax. They look somewhat like white ants, but are quite different. Ants have hard, dark bodies, short and bent antennae and usually a narrow waist connecting the abdomen to the thorax. In ants, the castes are exclusively female except for a few male drones, and the young are white grubs that do not work. In termites, the various body forms or castes within a colony are made up of both sexes, and young nymphs are usually workers. Termites must eat the droppings of each other to pass on one-celled organisms that live in their guts and carry the enzymes for breaking down wood (p. 63) – the main food of most termites. Without these helpers, termites would starve. Nests of termites can be completely underground (subterranean), sit on the ground in the form of a hard mud-like cone (termitarium), or be off the ground and attached to the trunk or large branch of a tree (arboreal). The covered tunnels or runways running from these nests to feeding areas are constructed of termite feces; they function to protect the termites from predators and temperature fluctuations.

The common arboreal termite nest in Brazil is made by the NASUTE TERMITE (Plate 1), named after the soldier caste, which is often called a "nozzle head" for the unique shape of its head. Soldiers and workers may be either males or females, but they are sterile. Fertile queen and king castes carry on reproduction. The soldier of this type of termite squirts a smelly, sticky turpentine-like chemical from the nozzle on its head to cover enemies. This chemical makes it hard for other arthropods, especially enemy ants, to walk or fly and may even be irritating to large predators like anteaters and birds. The workers are more typical in shape and have mandibles. Because the soldiers lack mandibles, the workers must feed them as well as undertake all their other tasks.

The large (1 to 2 m, 3 to 7 ft), round or oval-shaped termite nests are dark brown. They are made from a paste of chewed wood glued together with termite feces. This paste quickly toughens into a hard exterior protecting the interior filled with tunnels and chambers. Long, thin tunnels, made of the same paste, extend from the nest to feeding sites. These tunnels protect the movements of termites from predators, rainfall, and high temperatures. These characteristic tunnels also distinguish termite nests from the often similar-looking nests made by some ants and wasps. Some birds such as trogons and puffbirds often hollow out arboreal termite nests and use them as a cavity nest for their own young. Spectacular mass flights of dispersing winged termites often follow a heavy rainfall. At this time they are easy pickings for many birds. Evidently, however, the explosion of dispersing termites is so dense and short-lived that the predators in the area are never abundant enough to eat all of them, no matter how easy they are to catch; many survive to start new colonies. These termites frequently live with a wide variety of ants (one or more species) in the same nest. Whether this togetherness is equally beneficial to both termites and ants is not yet known for sure.

Profile
Nasute Termite, *Nasutitermes* sp., Plate 1c

4. Cicadas and Relatives

This order of insects (Homoptera) includes minute species such as *aphids* less than 1 mm (0.04 in) long to *cicadas* more than 5 cm (2 in) long. All are distinguished by mouth parts that have been modified for a piercing-sucking function; in fact, they cannot chew. They insert their beak into plants and suck juices from them. The wings at rest are held roof-like over the back.

The EVENING CICADA (Plate 1), as is typical of all cicadas, lives as an adult for only a month or so. Most of its life is spent as a nymph underground sucking plant juices from roots. Nymphs of some species construct large, 25-cm (6-in) high chimneys of red clay that extend up from the moist floor of Amazonian forests. Nymphs develop gradually into adult forms, and the left-over brownish and hollow skin (*exuviae*) of the last stage before the adult is often left hanging on the side of a tree trunk or some other vertical surface. Because adult cicadas are mainly found in the canopy of the forest, you are most likely to see them only when they are attracted to lights at night. Most likely, however, your encounter with adult cicadas will be auditory. Male cicadas produce sounds, often painfully loud, and each species gives sounds at its own characteristic pitch, intensity and timing. Some species sing in all-male choirs that can become very intense. The sound-producing organs are called *tymbals*, which are thin plates on the side of the abdomen; they are depressed inwards by a pair of large muscles attached to them and then spring back to make a noise. They are depressed and released with extreme rapidity to make the various sounds and pitches, much like the old metal clicker or "cricket" toys that mature ecotravellers will remember from their childhood. Strangely, these sound producers are located right at the opening of the ears on the side of the abdomen – how can you hear anything with such a noise next to your ear? Most species make their sounds in the late afternoon and early evening.

The PEANUT BUG, or LANTERN BUG (Plate 1), is a regular inhabitant of Brazil's Amazonian forests. Throughout Central and South America, local legends assert that it is poisonous, but no scientist has ever been able to substantiate anything more than that it looks dangerous. It is quite large (10 cm,

4 in), but during the day hides camouflaged on the trunks of large trees, sometimes in small groups. If a predator is smart enough to recognize it despite the camouflage, the bug has a whole repertoire of additional anti-predator strategies. It can intimidate would-be predators by flashing open its wings to reveal large eye spots that resemble the eyes of an owl or large bird. If that doesn't work, its snake-like head is marked with apparent eyes, mouth and teeth to alarm the predator – never mind that this entire front part of the "head" is a hollow sham. The bug's real eyes and mouth are hidden back at the base of the wings. Finally, if worse comes to worst, there are reports that it can release a foul-smelling defense chemical. The adults apparently suck plant juices in the canopy, but little is known of the nymph stages.

Profiles

Evening Cicada, *Fidicina mannifera*, Plate 1d
Peanut Bug, *Fulgora laternaria*, Plate 1e

5. Antlions

As adults, all the members of this order (Neuroptera) have soft bodies, four membranous wings and long antennae. They are relatively weak fliers. Most are predators on other insects, but some species do not feed at all as adults. Larvae of most species live in the ground, but a few live underwater. The representative of this order that you are most likely to see in Brazil is the *antlion*. The adults look like dragonflies but have long antennae with knobs on the end (Plate 1). They sometimes come to lights at night. It is the larval form, however, that you will see most commonly. The short, flat larva has enormous mandibles. It excavates a funnel-shaped pit in dry sand and lies in wait at the bottom, often completely buried except for its mandibles. When an insect comes strolling along and accidentally stumbles at the precipitous edge, the antlion flicks sand grains out of the bottom to produce a constant avalanche of sand giving out under the hapless insect. This causes the insect to slide down into the waiting mandibles of the antlion. Crunch!

Profile

Antlion, *Myrmeleon* sp., Plate 1f

6. Beetles

The beetle order (Coleoptera) has more species in it than any other insect order – some estimate more than a million. These species occur in virtually all habitats on land and freshwater, but not in the ocean or in Antarctica. The trait shared by all these species is a front pair of wings hardened into shields (*elytra*) that when the insect is at rest cover the second pair of membranous flight wings and the top of the abdomen. The mandibles of the adults are usually large and variously used for catching small insect prey, crushing seeds, or chewing wood. The grub larvae often occur in habitats different from those of the adults or have very different behavior. Many beetle species are attracted to lights at night.

On a warm, humid night near a forest edge, you may be surprised by the approach of two small and round "headlights." The intense glow of these blue-green lights, much brighter and more persistent than the otherwise similar glow of *fireflies* (another family of beetles) can be dazzling if not mystifying. The lights are the luminescence (cold light) of organs on the body of a large (4 cm, 1.5 in, long) beetle called the HEADLIGHT CLICK BEETLE (Plate 2). As the beetle flies by, you may be able to hear the clacking of its wings. Before the era of batteries and flashlights, a dozen of these beetles placed in a perforated gourd produced enough light for reading. If you pick up one of these beetles, hold it upside down in the palm of your hand. They have a "spring-loaded" spine on the underside that when quickly released causes the beetle to jerk suddenly and catapult itself off your hand and into the air – probably a defense against predators. The adults eat plant material, and the larvae, which live in the soil and also glow, are predators on larvae of other beetle larvae. The chemical reactions producing this cold light have considerable economic potential and are thus a research focus for many chemical companies.

Along muddy and sandy river banks, the NOCTURNAL RIVERINE TIGER BEETLE (Plate 2) runs actively at the water's edge or in the moist grassy upper beaches. On cloudy or foggy days, you can see a few of these medium-sized (16.5 mm, 0.7 in), metallic maroon-green beetles running among cracks in the mud. On sunny days they burrow into the sand and remain immobile until night falls. Although they have wings, they rarely fly. They are predators on other arthropods and search for them using their large eyes. With their long legs, they run the prey down, grab them in their monstrous and sharp mandibles, then puree them. If you catch one, watch out for the mandibles; the bite, together with an enzyme they spit up, can really sting. They lay their eggs in moist sand and mud, and when the larvae hatch they immediately burrow vertically down into the soil. Then from this tunnel, the larva waits, its head just perfectly filling the mouth of the tunnel, for an ant or some other arthropod to come within striking distance. The larva, aided by hooks on its back, stretches quickly out of the tunnel backwards to grab the prey in its large mandibles. If successful, the larva pulls the prey to the bottom of the tunnel and dismembers it, eventually tossing the inedible parts from the mouth of the tunnel. More than 200 species of tiger beetle have been found in Brazil, some of them on sandy river banks like the Nocturnal Riverine Beetle, but most of them are active during the day on moist soil surfaces, grassy fields and on the forest floor.

The GREEN DUNG BEETLE (Plate 2) is attractive to the eye, but its habits may at first be off-putting to more squeamish ecotravellers. The members of this part of the Family Scarabaeidae (most of which are black) are some of the most intensely studied insects in Brazil. They are crucial in passing nutrients and vital chemicals to the rest of the ecosystem by helping decompose dung. They are also unusual among insects because so many of these species have complex behavior when it comes to constructing nests and caring for their young. Some dung beetles, called *dwellers*, merely eat their way through dung and deposit their eggs below a dung pat in a superficial nest. Other species, the *tunnelers*, dig a vertical tunnel below the dung pat and carry, push and drag dung down into the bottom of the tunnel to avoid competitors and predators. Here the dung is either used as food by the adults or stored as food for eggs laid here. Finally, a large number of dung beetles are *rollers*. Making a ball of dung, they stand on their fore legs, use their hind legs to push and steer the ball, and transport this resource away from the dung pat area before burying it in a suitable location. The female sometimes helps roll this ball, but more often than not she just rides on top of the ball, walking as the world turns under her. At some distance from the original site of the pat, the pair stops and buries the ball. They mate, and the female lays eggs on the section of dung they buried. When the eggs hatch, the larvae are protected underground from predators and competitors and have a dung banquet upon which they can feed and grow.

Males of many species have a prominent horn on the tip of their snout that curves back over the head. The horn is used to battle other males over the dung, as well as to impress the females that wait to see who wins the dung fight.

Dung is located mainly by smell, and the beetles' feather-shaped antennae act as super sniffers. Particular types of dung, however, are so prized by some beetle species that they also apparently use their eyes to quickly locate this resource as it falls from the canopy. The beetles use a circling flight with ever tighter loops to home in on the prize. Some species of dung beetles will use almost any type of dung they encounter, while others are highly specialized on bird dung, monkey dung, cat dung, and even snail and millipede dung. One highly specialized dung beetle rides around near the anus of sloths (p. 207) and waits for a sloth to climb down from the canopy and defecate. The dung of herbivorous animals tends to be rich in carbohydrates whereas dung of carnivorous animals tends to be rich in nitrogen; and the different needs of various dung beetle species (during larval growth as well as for energy in adult phases) influence their choice of repast.

The spectacular and large (6 cm, 2.4 in) HARLEQUIN LONG-HORNED BEETLE (Plate 2) is a member of the long-horned beetle family (Cerambycidae), which is characterized by extremely long antennae and a propensity to bore into dead or living tree trunks and branches. Some members of this family are unusual in that they directly produce enzymes that break down plant cellulose. Unlike termites (p. 66) and other cellulose-eating insects, they do not rely on one-celled organisms in their gut to provide the proper enzymes. The bright orange, gray and black coloring of the Harlequin Beetle may function to break up its shape visually, so predators do not notice it easily. The front legs of the male are much longer than those of the female and are used both when copulating and for reaching across gaps to walk from branch to branch. The adults are primarily active during the day. After mating, the female chews a gash in the bark of a tree and places her eggs in it. The young hatch out and tunnel deeper into the tree, producing a maze, or *gallery*, of tunnels. Sometimes their damage can be so extensive that they kill the tree. These beetles carry around a mini-ecosystem on their backs: small herbivorous mites graze on the algae and fungi that grow over the body surface of large adults; tiny predaceous pseudoscorpions, in turn, feed on the mites.

A huge and fantastically-colored insect, the GIANT METALLIC WOOD-BORING BEETLE (Plate 2) is over 7 cm (2.8 in) long. Its brilliant metallic green and red colors in the sunlight are incomparable. This coloring, however, is often covered by a yellowish powder that wipes off easily. You are most likely to see this species in a slow and noisy flight through mid-stories of the forest. The larvae burrow into the wood of large soft-wood trees such as the Ceiba (p. 15). Both adults and larvae are roasted by indigenous people and eaten like popcorn. The hard wing coverings (elytra) of the adults are often strung together as adornments.

Weevils are bizarre-looking beetles. Their mouth parts are modified into long snouts with small but powerful mandibles at the tips that are used to drill into hard seeds, nuts and wood. There are more than 50,000 species worldwide and 12,000 in Latin America. Of the weevils in Brazil, the one you are most likely to notice is the PALM WEEVIL (Plate 2). At 5 cm (2 in), it is one of the largest weevils in the world. This huge black species is usually seen on palm trees, where it makes a deep incision at the base of the palm fronds and deposits its eggs. The larvae hatch out and bore deeper into the tree, usually a dead tree but sometimes live trees. They are a major economic pest in coconut palm and African oil palm plantations. The large larvae are often extracted and eaten by local people.

Profiles

Headlight Click Beetle, *Pyrophorus* sp., Plate 2a
Nocturnal Riverine Tiger Beetle, *Tetracha sobrina*, Plate 2b
Harlequin Long-horned Beetle, *Acrocinus longimanus*, Plate 2c
Giant Metallic Wood-boring Beetle, *Euchroma gigantea*, Plate 2d
Green Dung Beetle, *Oxysternon conspicillatum*, Plate 2e
Palm Weevil, *Rhynchophorus palmarum*, Plate 2f

7. Butterflies and Moths

The *butterflies* and *moths* (Order Lepidoptera) are perhaps the most easily recognized insect groups in the world. They have four wings, but the hind- and forewing on each side often have a coupling mechanism that makes them look and act like a single huge wing. The characteristic shared by all members of this group, however, is the layer of tiny scales covering the wings. They come off easily, and if you handle the wings of a butterfly, look for the scales on your finger (the scales will look like dust). The adults either do not feed at all or feed on nectar, feces, or rotting fruit juices. Their mouth parts are shaped into a long thin proboscis that can be rolled up when not extended for feeding. This proboscis can be longer than the insect's body, such as in the SPHINX MOTHS (Plate 4), and is used to access nectar at the base of long flowers. While partaking of the flower's sweet reward, pollen falls onto the insect's body or head and is passed on to the next flower visited. Males often need extra sodium and other salts for producing sperm, and so it is not unusual to see clouds of male butterflies fluttering near and landing on dung, urine, rotting fruit, or even the nose of a basking turtle, to suck up excretions containing these chemicals. Along beaches of Amazonian watercourses, clouds of SULPHUR BUTTERFLIES (Plate 3), GLAUCOUS KITE SWALLOWTAILS (Plate 3) and URANIA MOTHS (Plate 3) often assemble where large mammals have recently urinated or defecated. Even salt-laden human sweat can attract beautiful butterflies, so don't swat all the insects that come flying around you. However, if you attract butterflies day after day, it may be time to take a shower.

In general, adult butterflies are active during the day and have thread-like antennae with knobs on the end. Butterflies usually rest with their wings folded together, vertically, over their backs. Moths are usually active at night and rest with their wings held horizontally. They have either thread-like antennae without knobs or large feather-shaped antennae. These feather-like antennae are usually found in the males, and they can contain more than 60,000 minute structures called *sensilla*. These structures are used to detect molecules of a perfume (*pheromone*) released by a female ready to mate. Each female moth species releases a different scent, and the pheromone plume is carried by the wind. The male follows the plume upwind by zig-zagging back and forth, and moving toward higher concentrations of the molecules until he finds the female. Experiments have shown that males can follow this scent plume for more than 10 km (6 miles).

Larval *lepidopterans* are almost all plant-eating, using their large mandibles to chew holes out of the edges of leaves. Many of the major agricultural pests in the world are larval moths. Some lepidopteran species have their own specific food plant species on which they lay eggs and on which their caterpillars feed when they emerge. The ornate and often colorful chamber in which the larval butterfly metamorphoses into an adult is called a *chrysalis*. The brown silken chamber of the larval moth is called a *cocoon*. The protein (*fibroin*), used by many moth species to construct these cocoons, is the product we weave into silk cloth. However, species of only four moth families are used for commercial production of silk, all of them in Asia. The larva of the SNAKE-MIMICKING SPHINX MOTH (Plate 4) has coloring on the back end of its body that looks like snake eyes and a snout with a small forked tongue. When disturbed by a potential enemy, the larva swings its rear-end out from the branch on which it was hiding and twitches its snake-like derrière from side to side – looking for all the world like a small and dangerous snake hanging from a branch.

The intense, almost neon-like blue of the first male BRAZILIAN MORPHO BUTTERFLY (Plate 3) you see will be a sight you will never forget. There are many species of morphos in Brazil. Some are duller blue to black, some have females that are very dull, and others, like the one we have illustrated here, have females almost as brilliant as the males. These huge butterflies flap lazily along river edges and forest trails with an up and down movement of the whole body. Apparently entire populations in an area will use the same flight path day after day, so if you see one using a path, just wait and others will eventually fly along the same route. Often you will come across several adults on the ground "puddling" at a muddy area or sucking rotted fruit or feces. With their wings folded, the highly camouflaged undersides make them very difficult to see until suddenly they fly up, flashing the blue uppersides of the wings. Their major enemies are jacamars (p. 166) and other flycatching birds, and the slow flapping of the wings may help them escape these birds. By making themselves alternately obvious and camouflaged as their wings open and close in flight, and randomly changing directions between wingbeats, they apparently confuse pursuing birds trying to anticipate which direction the morphos will be going when next their wings open up. The large larvae (9 cm, 3.5 in) are red and yellow, and the head is covered with specialized hairs that sting like nettles when broken off by a naive predator.

One of the most common butterfly species you will see low on forest paths in Brazil is the AURORINA CLEAR-WINGED SATYR (Plate 4). Except for the black spots and reddish color at the tail-end of the wings, this butterfly has no scales on its wings, and they are thus transparent. At rest, the red rear ends of the wings together with the black spots give the impression of a head, and this confusion is probably a way of diverting a predator's attention from the real head and direction of escape.

Another common forest butterfly in Brazil has bold orange and black stripes and is called the *Tiger Butterfly*. In reality this butterfly is not a single species but instead is a jumble of 20 or more confusingly and amazingly similar species of butterflies and moths. This color pattern is common throughout the forests of Brazil and represents a "mimicry complex." Within this mimicry complex, the MAZAEUS MECHANITIS BUTTERFLY (Plate 3) larvae are able to harmlessly absorb and store the nasty chemicals from the specific food plant they eat (deadly Nightshade). When they metamorphose into adults, they keep these chemicals in their body and wings. This species represents a distasteful and poisonous species in the tropical subfamily Ithomiinae that serves as an evolutionary *model*. Its bright color pattern and high population levels ensure that naive predators will quickly learn and unambiguously remember that bright orange and black stripes mean a terrible taste, causing vomiting or even worse. Another species, the AMPHIONE DISMORPHA BUTTERFLY (Plate 3), shares a similar color pattern and size. It, however, is much rarer and in the cabbage butterfly family, Pieridae, most species of which are the familiar white or yellow species (such as the SULPHUR BUTTERLY, Plate 3) we see in our gardens in North America and Europe. This species is not protected by poisons or distastefulness, but instead cheats as a *mimic* of the distasteful species. Because the distasteful model species is more common, the predators have most likely learned to associate any orange-and-black striped butterfly with a very bad gustatory experience, so the rarer but tasty mimic is mistaken for the model species and also avoided. In many cases the males of mimic species are not as similar to the model species as are the females. Perhaps so that females will choose them as mates, the males have to prove their gene superiority by showing they can survive even as imperfect mimics. Alternatively, the males may have different wing patterns because they have to show more clearly just which species they are, so the females don't waste time trying to mate with a confusingly similar male of another species.

Easily mistaken for a swallow-tailed butterfly, the bright metallic green and black LELIUS' URANIA MOTH (Plate 3) is actually a day-flying moth. Conspicuous in its spectacular colors, this species is also common, often seen puddling along the river's edge of rainforest. It is most famous, however, for its massive migrations, when thousands pass over a river or forest site in a day. The explanation for these massive movements of adults may lie in their food plant, a genus (*Omphalea*) of vine related to the rubber plant. As the larvae of these specialized moths munch away at the leaves of this vine, they apparently "induce" the plant to respond by increasing the levels of toxic chemicals in its leaves. After three or four generations of attack from Urania larvae, the levels of plant toxins become so high that the next generation of moths will not be able to handle them, no matter how specialized they are at detoxifying them normally. At this point the adults somehow recognize the futility of laying their eggs on vines in this area, and they all get up and fly hundreds of kilometers to another area that has not had a concentration of Urania moths feeding on these vines for a long time. To save energy, the plants reduce the level of production of toxins when they are not under attack. The eruptive migrations of Urania occur at a low level every year, but about every 4 to 8 years a super movement occurs that lasts only a few weeks. The adults feed on nectar of leguminous trees and are important pollinators.

Profiles

Brazilian Morpho Butterfly, *Morpho deidamia*, Plate 3a
Mazaeus Mechanitis Butterfly, *Mechanitis mazaeus*, Plate 3b
Amphione Dismorpha Butterfly, *Dismorphia amphione*, Plate 3c
Sulphur Butterfly, *Phoebis* sp., Plate 3d
Lelius' Urania Moth, *Urania lelius*, Plate 3e
Glaucous Kite Swallowtail, *Eurytides glaucolaus*, Plate 3f

Window-winged Atlas Moth, *Rothschildi* sp., Plate 4a
Snake-mimicking Sphinx Moth, *Hemeroplanes tritolemus*, Plate 4b
Claudina's Red-winged Agrias, *Agrias claudina*, Plate 4c
Green Long-winged Butterfly, *Philaethria dido*, Plate 4d
Owl Butterfly, *Caligo* sp., Plate 4e
Aurorina Clear-winged Satyr, *Cithaerias aurorina*, Plate 4f

8. Flies

Another very large group of insects is the *flies* (Order Diptera). Their identifying character is the presence of only the front pair of wings. The rear wings have been reduced to small knobs (*halteres*) used for balance in flight. Most adults are small and soft-bodied, and they include many of the biting insects we stereotype as "bad," such as mosquitos, horseflies, "no-seeums," and black flies; only the females bite. Because of their roles in the spread of disease as well as in agricultural plagues, representatives of this group surely rank high as pests. However, many species of flies are critical for such functions as cleaning up rotted bodies, killing other insects and pollinating flowers. Larvae are grub-like and most live in water, where they feed on dead vegetation, decaying animal matter or other larvae.

One of the largest (2.5 cm, 1 in) and most intriguing flies in Brazil is the ROBBER FLY (Plate 5). Its long body and big eyes are diagnostic. The many species of this fly are all predators and hunt flying insects with a spectacular flight from a perch on the ground or low vegetation. Using its long thin wings for quick acceleration and maneuverability, the robber fly pursues and grabs an insect in the air with its long legs. Then, quickly inserting its pointed mouth parts into a body joint of the prey, it injects a venom to quickly dispatch it. The fly then returns to its perch and sucks the body juices from the dead insect. These robber flies are so tough that they often kill wasps and bees larger than themselves. The long, relatively inflexible wings make a lot of noise when they fly, and with a little practice you can hear a robber fly before you see it. Evidently the extreme acceleration needed to move from rest to fast flight requires long and noisy wings. The high amount of energy these flights need requires fairly warm temperatures, so some species of robber flies are active in very hot environments, such as around river sand bars. Some species are also active in the forest understory, but only on warm and sunny days; on cloudy days and at night they remain inactive. The grub-like larvae live in the ground or in leaf litter and are predators on the larvae of other insects.

Profile
Chestnut-colored Robber Fly, *Diomites castaneus*, Plate 5a

9. Ants, Wasps, and Bees

Although this group (Order Hymenoptera) is perhaps best known for its stinging females, it contains some of the most beneficial insect species in the world. *Ants* help turn over and aerate soil as well as disperse seeds. Many species of *wasps* are predators on herbivorous insects and function as a major biological control of numerous pest species. *Bees* are important pollinators of many native and agricultural plants. In Brazil, a steadily rising market for honey has made bees even more economically important. The species with wings have four membranous wings, in which the fore- and hind-wings on each side are fastened together with tiny hooks. The mouth parts are either strong mandibles for chewing or modified into a long tongue for sucking up nectar and other liquid food. In most species the abdomen is attached to the thorax by a narrow waist. The larvae are grub-like and usually cared for in hives or nests. Many species are highly colonial. Sex of an egg is determined by whether or not it has been fertilized by male sperm. If it has been fertilized, it develops into a female, but if not, it develops into a male.

The underground nests of LEAF-CUTTER ANTS (Plate 5) are obvious in moist forests. The up to 0.2 hectare (half-acre) of exposed clay and mud is completely devoid of undergrowth plants. Up to 5 million individuals live in a single colony. All day, columns of ants carrying small pieces of leaves or flowers enter holes in the ground while others exit. The columns of ants extend from the colony via cleared paths to the trees under attack. Their activity usually ceases at nightfall and during extended rainy periods during the day. The leaf pieces are cut with the sharp mandibles of the large worker caste and carried by them like an umbrella back to the nest. Many of these workers are susceptible to attack by flies and wasps trying to lay eggs on them that will later emerge and consume the worker. With her mandibles occupied carrying the leaf load, she cannot protect herself without dropping the leaf. Instead, small caste ants (*minima*) often ride on top of the leaf, where they can challenge approaching danger and keep it at bay. In the nest, special galleries are set aside where the leaf bits are received by other workers. These leaves are not food, but instead they are cleaned, scraped and then added to underground gardens. Here a specialized fungus grows on the leaves and produces a spongy layer that is eaten by the entire ant colony and fed to developing larvae. If a queen ant leaves the nest to start a new colony, she must take a mouthful of the fungus to use as a starter for food in the new colony. This farming behavior is important for the forest because it quickly moves immense amounts of nutrients through the system. The ants are very choosy about which plant species they incorporate into their underground gardens. Apparently the chemicals contained in the leaves of some plant species inhibit fungal growth and are thus avoided by the ants.

There are many species of *army ants*, but the most obvious and well-studied species is BURCHELL'S ARMY ANT (Plate 5). A single colony of this ant can contain more than a million individuals of several castes. Even though they lack eyes, they forage in immense but coordinated *raiding columns* 3 to 15 m (10 to 50 ft) wide. They swarm across the forest floor, driving escaping animals in front of them, and pouncing on slower insects, spiders and occasionally small lizards; they overpower the prey by sheer numbers and incessant stings. This immense colony is always only temporarily "bivouacked" because they must move on every month or so as their raids reduce the number of prey in the vicinity of the bivouac. The framework of the bivouac nest is actually made up of an immense cluster of ants holding on to each other with their mandibles, usually in the hollow of a tree or base of a buttress root. The eggs, larvae, and single queen are all guarded within this unique structure and carry on their normal functions until the colony moves to its next location. You can tell if the army ant column is raiding or moving by what the workers are carrying. If they are carrying white larvae and not dead insect parts, you know it is a *relocation column*. Males, with wings and large eyes, are produced in very small numbers, and you are most likely to see them attracted to night lights at the beginning of the rainy season. It is always a good idea to glance down at the ground every once in a while as you walk or stand in the forest, to make sure you are not standing in an army ant column. Otherwise, if you haven't tucked your pants' legs inside your socks, you will soon find out by their stings that the ants are there. Although their stings can be painful, army ants, unlike their Hollywood movie portrayal, do not attack and carry off large vertebrates such as humans. The worst thing you can do, however, is to stomp your feet and crush these ants. They use chemicals rather than sight to coordinate their movements, and a crushed ant gives off a chemical that elicits defensive behavior by the rest of the column. You don't want that. Just calmly but quickly walk away from the column and brush off your pants' legs and shoes (you have, of course, by now already tucked your pants' cuffs into the tops of your socks). One good way to find a raiding column is to listen for the growling calls of antbirds (p. 177) around the ants. A large flock of these noisy and obvious birds usually assembles at the head of the raiding column to catch large flying insects trying to escape the ants, but the birds do not eat the ants.

The large (16 to 22 mm, 0.5 to 1 in), all-dark reddish brown GIANT HUNTING ANT (Plate 5) is probably the most dangerous animal you will encounter during your trip to the rainforests in Brazil. In Portuguese it is called *tocandiras, tocandeiras* or *tocangueras*. There is just one species in the genus. If all you do is see it, count yourself lucky, because the sting of this animal is considered one of the most painful in the entire world – it may even cause hallucinations in some people. In some parts of Brazil it is sometimes referred to as the "24 hours" ant (*formigas vinte e quatro horas*) because the pain from the sting often lasts for a day. Its effect varies considerably from person to person, and we have seen big, husky and macho men crying unashamedly in pain from its sting, while some smaller people, male and female, only felt some pain for a minute or so. Never place your hand on a tree while you rest along a trail, because this is the surest way to encounter the Giant Hunting Ant. As a warning for potential enemies, these ants make a noise by scraping body parts together, a sound called *stridulating* that you should learn to listen for. Because they are so well protected from predators, several other insect species have evolved similar body shapes to mimic these ants. One, an arboreal tiger beetle, not only looks and walks like a Giant Hunting Ant but also stridulates using the same sound frequencies as the ant. The nests of this ant are usually in the ground at the base of a tree, and they usually contain fewer than two hundred individuals, one queen and the rest a single caste of workers. They forage, often singly, from the forest floor and undergrowth vegetation all the way up into the canopy. They are active during the daytime in the rainy season and at night during the dry season. Besides hunting live prey, including other insects and occasionally small lizards and birds, they also scavenge dead animals and eat nectar from flowers.

As you walk through a rainforest in Brazil, you often can hear the low but distinct humming of a large bumblebee-like insect flying lazily through the undergrowth or along the trail. As it gets closer, you will see a large, colorful bee, MERIAN'S ORCHID BEE (Plate 5), investigating nooks and crannies of trees and plants or landing in a wet section of the path to gather mud. If it flies close to you, it is probably only investigating some new smell that has attracted its attention. These bees are docile and do not sting unless severely provoked. They pollinate a wide range of flowers, the males being especially attracted to orchids. Instead of nectar, each orchid species offers a different chemical reward that can smell like wintergreen, vanilla, bubble gum, eucalyptus oil or cinnamon. Evidently the males need this chemical to combine into a particular smell that attracts females. When the male enters the orchid flower to get to the chemical, it has to lean against a part of the interior of the blossom that has a sticky packet of pollen (*pollinarium*), and, depending on the orchid species, it becomes attached to the bee's chest, back or abdomen. When this bee visits the next blossom of the same species of orchid, an even stickier part of the flower strips the pollinarium off the bee to deposit it on the female part of the flower for pollination. Many smaller species of orchid bees are common in the forest, and they are often bright metallic green or blue. You can identify them as they hover in front of a flower or tree trunk, rubbing their hind legs together.

Profiles

Leaf-cutter Ant, *Atta* sp., Plate 5b
Burchell's Army Ant, *Eciton burchelli*, Plate 5c
Giant Hunting Ant, *Paraponera clavata*, Plate 5d
Merian's Orchid Bee, *Eulaema meriana*, Plate 5e

10. Spiders

Probably the most maligned arthropods are the *spiders*. Although almost all the 35,000 species in the world have venom glands that they use together with their fangs to kill prey, only a very few species are dangerous to humans. The benefits spiders provide by controlling populations of insects more than outweigh the problems of a few bites and extra duties for fastidious house-cleaners. Most spiders are on land, but a few hunt underwater. Many spiders build webs to catch flying insects. These webs can be sticky, ornate orbs, flat sheets, funnel-shaped, or combinations thereof. Some spiders even use webbing like nets to throw onto prey. Most spiders catch small- to medium-sized insect prey, but some species are large enough to catch small birds in their webs. Waiting in a retreat at the side of the web, the spider detects a struggling prey by the vibrations transmitted along the strands of webbing. It then rushes out to inject the prey with poison and often wraps it in a cocoon of silk. Several large groups of spiders, however, do not use webs to catch prey but instead rely on ambush, stealth or stalking. All produce silk, however, which is a protein produced in the abdomen. It is released from the abdomen through finger-like projections with holes in their ends, called *spinnerets*. Young spiders often go to a high point in the habitat, spin out a line of silk and then let the wind take them, the silk serving as a balloon or parachute. This method of transportation can disperse spiders over long distances. Eggs are laid in a silk pouch near the web, on the female, or in a crevice. The young hatch out looking like miniature spiders, and they grow gradually.

Because they are all predators and cannibalism is common, most spiders are solitary. Only during courtship and mating do they socialize, and then often to the detriment of the smaller male. Strangely, however, the spider you are most likely to see in the moist forests of Brazil is one of 50 species in the world that is colonial or, more accurately, cooperative. The NEOTROPICAL COLONIAL SPIDER (Plate 5) builds communal webs that can be several meters (yards) long, the largest web of any spider in the world. The colony can range in numbers from one female and her offspring to more than 20,000 individuals. The immense webs follow the contour of vegetation along river and forest edges or in the understory of the forest itself. New colonies arise by a number of females moving some distance away from the parent colony and spinning their webs at a fresh site. Because these colonial spiders show no physical caste differences and have no subdivision of labor, their colonies are quite different from the highly organized ant and termite societies. In many ways the colonial spider social organization is more similar to that of communally breeding birds like anis (p. 152). Each male and each female spider builds and maintains its own orb web within the colony. This web is defended from other spiders, and prey captured in a web are not shared (at least voluntarily) with other spiders in the same colony.

One advantage to this colonial existence is that, together, the webs produce a more efficient trap for insects flying in the area. Each spider captures more prey in the colonial web than it would elsewhere by itself, with only its own small web. Another advantage is that by using the support of other webs, each spider uses less silk to make its orb. Although predators and parasites can more easily locate the immense webs and the spiders living in them, the complex labyrinth of webs often makes it harder for enemies to enter. These immense webs have a disadvantage, however, in that disease, fungi and other microbes, can easily be spread throughout the colony. More than 20% of these colonies become extinct every generation because of factors like this that are associated with crowding. Also, the complex arrangement of webs in a colony provides many hiding places for other species of spiders that make their living by stealing prey. They are called *kleptoparasites* and can have drastic effects on the amount of food the owners of the webs actually eat.

Profile

Neotropical Colonial Spider, *Anelosimus eximus*, Plate 5f

11. Crustaceans

The members of this group (Crustacea) include over 40,000 species of *crabs, crayfish, lobsters,* and *barnacles.* They include some that are predators, others that are herbivores or parasites, and some that eat dead organisms. Many have the first leg modified into a claw or pincher (*cheliped*). A number of these species, such as the *shrimps*, are important commercially as food. The young larval forms of crustaceans are tiny, swimming organisms called *zoea.* They are important because they can disperse great distances on river and ocean currents. Although most crustaceans are found in oceans, several shrimp species are found in freshwater, and a few crabs are common on the floor of moist forests. The most common crabs in the Amazonian and Pantanal areas are a group of poorly known species of FOREST CRAB (Plate 5). During the rainy season you can find them on the floor of almost any moist forest. They are often nocturnal, but if you encounter one during the day, it will back up and challenge you with its very seriously big chelipeds. These forest crabs retreat to streams, lakes and rivers during the dry season.

Profile

Forest Crab, *Fredius* sp., Plate 5g

Chapter 7

Amphibians

by Martha L. Crump

Introduction

We know from the fossil record that during the middle of the Paleozoic Era (the Devonian period, about 380 million years ago), fish with lungs that could breathe air were common in freshwater lakes. These lunged fish had fins in the shape of stubby lobes. They probably used these fins to support themselves on the bottoms of their ponds while waiting for prey to swim by, and to waddle about on land during times when their ponds dried. Both of these characteristics, lungs and lobed fins, allowed the fish to survive for brief periods on land. About 365 million years ago, these fish evolved into the first *tetrapods* (terrestrial vertebrates) – the amphibians. As you would expect, this evolution involved drastic changes in support and locomotor systems, feeding mechanisms, and breathing organs, to name but a few modifications.

The word amphibian comes from the Greek *amphibios,* meaning "living a double life," in reference to the fact that most amphibians spend part of their lives in water and part on land. Approximately 4700 species of living amphibians are known today. Biologists separate amphibians into three main groups. The largest group, with about 4100 species, is the *frogs* (order Anura, "without tails," which includes *toads*), followed by the *salamanders* (order Caudata, the "tailed" amphibians) with about 430 species, and a little-known group, the *caecilians* (suh-SEAL-ians, order Gymnophiona), with approximately 170 species.

General Characteristics and Classification of Amphibians

Most amphibians retain the reproductive pattern of their fish ancestors and return to water to breed because their eggs dry out easily. Most frogs and toads have *external fertilization*; that is, as the female releases her eggs, the male releases sperm onto them – outside the body. Only a few species have *internal fertilization*. In contrast, most salamanders and all caecilians have internal fertilization. Most amphibians pass through the aquatic phase of their "two-world" lifestyle only as eggs and free-swimming larvae (larval frogs and toads are called *tadpoles*; larval salamanders and caecilians are just called *larvae*). Some amphibians, however, are fully aquatic as adults. Still other species lay their eggs in moist areas on land and never enter standing water. Water is essential for all amphibians because, in addition to using lungs, they breathe through their skin. In order to do this, their skin must be kept moist. Thus, even species that are fully terrestrial in all phases of their lives require a humid environment.

Most *salamanders* look like lizards, with four limbs and a long tail. They are easily distinguished from lizards, however, by their skin. Salamanders have skin that is kept moist by mucus, whereas lizards have scales. A few aquatic species of salamanders have four tiny legs, and several have only the two front legs. Salamanders range in size from among the smallest known terrestrial vertebrates, with body lengths of less than 1.5 cm (0.6 in), to a giant Asian species that grows to 2 m (6.5 ft). Because their skin is susceptible to drying out, salamanders inhabit moist environments. Familiar salamanders of North America and Europe typically live on the ground, hidden under logs when they're not active. They forage for invertebrate prey such as insects, worms, and spiders in the leaf litter and under rocks or decaying logs. Many live near streams in moist forests. Some species, however, are completely aquatic, spending their entire lives in swamps, ponds, lakes, and rivers. Others live in trees (*arboreal*) or underground (*fossorial*). Most salamanders secrete poisons from glands in the skin as a defense against predators. Some of the most toxic species are brightly colored to warn potential predators of their toxicity. About 90% of all salamanders have internal fertilization. In these species, males produce packets of sperm called *spermatophores*. In most species, during courtship, males deposit spermatophores onto the substrate. They lead the females over the spermatophores, at which point they are picked up into the females' bodies.

Salamanders are found mostly in North America and in northern Eurasia. One family, however, the Plethodontidae, is common and diverse in Central America, and a few species of this family occur in South America. Salamanders are not known from tropical regions of the Old World. Plethodontidae, the *lungless salamanders*, is the largest salamander family, with nearly 270 species in North, Central and South America; oddly, one genus also occurs in southern Europe and Sardinia. In the absence of lungs, all respiration in plethodontid salamanders takes place through the skin. AMAZONIAN SALAMANDERS (Plate 6) range in color from dark gray to reddish brown and have heavily webbed front and hind feet. They are active at night, moving around on leaves up to 2 m (6.5 ft) above the ground; they forage in the leaves for insects and other small, moving prey. During the day they sleep in moist leaf litter on the ground. Fertilization is internal via spermatophores. The eggs are deposited on land, and the females guard the eggs, which develop directly into tiny salamanders. Individuals reach lengths (including tail) of 9 cm (3.6 in), though most are smaller.

Most people have never heard of caecilians, and fewer still have ever seen a live one. *Caecilians* resemble large earthworms with rings around their bodies. They lack limbs throughout their lives, and they either have short tails or none at all. Their bodies feel slimy because they are covered with mucus. In fact, it is very difficult to hold onto one! Caecilians are poorly known because they live only in tropical regions (in Africa, Asia, and Central and South America) and because they are difficult to find. Caecilians live either underground or in water. The only time you are likely to see the underground ones is following heavy rain, when the soil becomes saturated and they move to the surface. Because their eyes are covered with skin or bone, caecilians are essentially blind. They have sensory organs called *tentacles*, small fleshy projections located between the eyes and nostrils. The tentacles function in picking up chemical stimuli and thus help in locating insects, worms, and other ground-dwelling prey. Of the species for which the mode of reproduction is known, about 75% have internal fertilization of eggs that undergo development inside the mother's body; the young are born as tiny but fully formed baby caecilians. Although the other 25% of the species for which their reproductive pattern is known also have internal fertilization, they have aquatic larvae. The SOUTH AMERICAN CAECILIAN (Plate 6), a terrestrial burrower, reaches 50 cm (20 in) in length and about 1.5 cm (0.6 in) in diameter; the body is blue with lighter blue rings. The eyes are visible through the thin skin, and are slightly raised at the surface.

Frogs and *toads* are found just about everywhere in the world except in extremely dry deserts, on some islands, and near the North and South poles. All frogs and toads have four limbs as adults; their rear limbs are much larger than their front ones. Most of them are strong jumpers and can cover long distances. Some brightly colored species have poisonous skin secretions that protect them from predators. Others have toxins, but are dull in color. Males use mating calls to attract females during the breeding season; each species has its own particular call, and females respond only to that one type of call. Almost all adult frogs and toads eat insects, spiders, and other invertebrates; a few species eat other frogs and even small lizards, snakes, birds, and mammals. Presumably all Brazilian species breed via external fertilization. During mating, the male mounts the back of the female and holds on to her tightly with his front legs either around the waist or in her armpits. This position is called *amplexus*. As she releases her eggs, he releases sperm over them. Although most species abandon their eggs, some have elaborate forms of parental care. Most species have aquatic tadpoles. In some species, however, the eggs develop directly into tiny froglets. The frogs and toads known from the Amazon and Pantanal regions of Brazil are diverse in body shape, size, color, and habits (see Family Profiles).

Seeing Amphibians in Brazil

With luck and perseverance, you could see more than 30 species of amphibians in a few weeks during your visit to the Brazilian Amazon and Pantanal regions. The specific examples discussed and profiled in this chapter should allow you to identify any amphibian you find, at least to its family or genus. One of the reasons ecotourists enjoy learning about amphibians is that, unlike with birds and mammals, it is often possible to watch and photograph the animals up close. In fact, because many species are small, you need to get close to be able to identify them.

Finding amphibians is relatively easy. One way is simply to search the ground in the forest during the day, especially near streams, ponds, or other moist areas, and look for frogs and toads hopping about. A second way is potentially more rewarding and a lot of fun: with a flashlight, carefully search the tops of leaves at night up to 2 m (6.5 ft) above the ground. With some patience, you are likely to encounter at least a few nocturnal, arboreal frogs and perhaps some salamanders. You'll also find some bizarre-looking insects! Good places to try this include road edges, along forest trails, or in any forest edge area. By far the best way to see a high diversity of frogs at night is to locate small temporary ponds or puddles along forest edges, in swampy areas, along the edges of roads, or near rivers. Up to a dozen species might be calling at one time at some temporary ponds. Many species call from leaves or branches over the water, others while floating in the water, others from the ground next to the water. When large numbers of frogs are calling, such *breeding aggregations* make a loud racket that can be heard from some distance away. If you find a shallow pond during the day, the frogs will be sleeping – some on leaves over the water, others on the ground. Search for eggs and tadpoles in the water, and then return with a flashlight after dark to look for adults. Look carefully, for even at a pond crawling with frogs, many will blend in with their surroundings and be difficult to locate.

Family Profiles

1. Toads

Although many people think of frogs and *toads* as two distinct groups, all toads are frogs just as all poodles are dogs. The common name "toad" is used for species in several families of frogs, but the main family of toads is the Bufonidae, a worldwide group of about 380 species. Most bufonid toads, especially those in the genus *Bufo*, have thick, dry skin that enables them to live in dry habitats. Toads typically have short, squat, heavy bodies with relatively short limbs, and broad rounded snouts. Many species have distinct bony crests between the eyes. *Bufonids* lack teeth, an unusual condition among frogs. The majority are colored dull olive to dark brown, although there are exceptions, such as the Day-Glo orange GOLDEN TOAD, *Bufo periglenes*, found only in Costa Rica (but now thought to be extinct). Most toads have scattered wart-like bumps on the skin of the upper surface of the body. Most also have a pair of prominent, large *parotoid glands* on the shoulder area, one behind each eye. Toads range from tiny species less than 2 cm (0.8 in) in length as adults, to the COLOMBIAN GIANT TOAD, *Bufo blombergi*, which grows to 25 cm (10 in).

Natural History
Ecology and Behavior

Most toads of the genus *Bufo* are nocturnal (although some are primarily active by day) and terrestrial, spending much of their time foraging for invertebrate prey on the ground. Because of their thick dry skin, many species of toads are able to live away from water and often in very dry places. Their parotoid glands secrete a noxious, milky poison that serves as a defense against would-be predators. The dark tan or brown colors typical of most toads allow them to blend in with the soil and dead leaves on the forest floor. The MARINE TOAD (Plate 7) inhabits open areas such as clearings, forest edges, and around human habitation, although juveniles are also found in forests. You will most likely encounter this species as it sits near lights at night, attracted by the insects flying into the light.

The CURURU TOAD (Plate 7) is a master at defending itself from would-be predators. When harassed, it puffs up by inflating its lungs with air. It also secretes a milky poison from its huge parotoid glands. When this substance is absorbed through an animal's mucous membranes, nausea and vomiting often result. In larger quantities, paralysis and death may occur. Because the poison is not absorbed through your skin, it's safe to handle these large toads as long as you don't have open cuts on your hands. But don't rub your eyes or put your fingers in your mouth or nose! And wash your hands thoroughly afterward.

Breeding

Most bufonid toads lay their eggs in water, and the eggs hatch into tadpoles. Males call from in or near the water to attract females. The male grasps the female (amplexus) and deposits sperm over the eggs she releases into the water. Bufonids are unique in their habit of laying eggs in two long strings, one from each ovary, as opposed to the clumps of eggs produced by most frogs. Each egg is connected to the one before and after it, like beads in a necklace. Sometimes the strings of eggs sink to the bottom of the pond, but usually they get entwined around vegetation. The MARINE TOAD breeds in a wide variety of temporary and permanent bodies of water, each female producing 8000 to 20,000 eggs and then abandoning them. Needless to say, there is considerable predation on the tadpoles … otherwise Brazil would be overrun with toads in no time!

Notes

People from many different cultures in the world use toads as medicines. Eighteenth-century physicians used powder made from dried toads to lower a patient's fever. The Chinese make a powder from *Bufo* parotoid secretion. Called Ch'an Su, this powder is used in treating heart ailments, for drying boils and abscesses, and for healing ulcers. It seems odd that *Bufo* secretion is so widely used as medicine – until you learn that the secretion contains epinephrine and norepinephrine, chemicals known to stimulate the human heart and to help the human body deal with stress.

Other uses for parotoid secretions have been invented as well. The parotoid secretions of the MARINE TOAD are often one of the ingredients of a complex soup concocted by Haitian witch doctors to induce near-death comas and to create "zombies." The secretions of COLORADO RIVER TOADS, *Bufo alvarius*, contain powerful hallucinogenic chemicals. Smoking dried parotoid secretions has become a popular pastime among some foolhardy people in Arizona and California! Anthropologists have speculated that the ancient cultures of Mesoamerica may have used toad parotoid secretion as hallucinogens during religious ceremonies, as abundant images of toads with prominent parotoid glands have been found on sculptures and engravings at archaeological sites.

Status

Unfortunately, we know little about the population status of most toads in Brazil. Several species of *Bufo* from Chile, Mexico, Puerto Rico, Costa Rica, and the USA mainland are considered threatened or endangered. On the other hand, the MARINE TOAD has become a pest when it has been introduced into areas where it is not native. For example, the toad has been widely introduced into sugarcane-growing areas around the world to control insect pests (thus the alternate common name, Cane Toad). But the toads don't just feed on sugarcane pests. They eat beneficial insects and other frogs. Among other places, it has become established in parts of Australia, New Guinea, and southern Florida (USA), where it is abundant and threatens native amphibians both due to competition and direct predation. In addition, these large toads cause the death of pet dogs and cats, which, when they attack the toads, can receive a fatal mouthful of parotoid secretion.

Profiles

Common Lesser Toad, *Bufo granulosus*, Plate 6c
South American Common Toad, *Bufo typhonius*, Plate 6d
Marine Toad, *Bufo marinus*, Plate 7a
Cururu Toad, *Bufo paracnemis,* Plate 7b

2. Rainfrogs

The common name for frogs in the Family Leptodactylidae is *rainfrogs*. The name stems from the fact that breeding activity is most intense following heavy rains. (This points out how relatively useless common names are, because *most* frogs are more reproductively active following heavy rains!) Leptodactylids occur in Mexico, Central and South America, and the Caribbean; a few species are found as far north as the southern USA. With about 900 species, and new ones being discovered each year, rainfrogs make up the largest family of frogs. As a group, they have the same wide range of body sizes that bufonid toads (p. 82) have. Species range from 1.2 cm to 25 cm (0.5 to 10 in). Rainfrogs found in the areas of Brazil covered in this book belong to three main groups, or subfamilies, distinguished by body size, shape, and lifestyle.

The AMAZON HORNED FROG (Plate 7), a fascinating and rather bizarre frog, is a member of the first subfamily. This frog resembles a hopping mouth, with a huge head relative to its body. The large head and wide mouth allow this frog to eat other frogs, lizards, and even, when they get the chance, baby birds and small rodents. These robust, tan or green frogs reach lengths up to 12 cm (4.8 in).

Members of a second subfamily have the unusual form of reproduction of constructing foam nests (see Breeding, below). One example is the BASIN WHITE-LIPPED FROG (Plate 8), often found calling from shallow water in clearings and in swampy areas in the forest. This terrestrial frog is medium in size, reaching lengths of about 6 cm (2.4 in). The robust SMOKY JUNGLE FROG (Plate 7) can reach 17 cm (6.8 in) in length. Both of these species are members of the genus *Leptodactylus*, frogs that superficially resemble common North American frogs such as *bullfrogs* or *leopard frogs*. Most *Leptodactylus* frogs are tan or brown, with varying patterns of large spots or bands on a stout body. Their limbs are relatively short, the head is broad and rounded, and most species have prominent folds of skin on each side of the upper part of the body. The tips of the toes lack expanded discs; the front feet lack webbing, and the hind feet are only slightly webbed. Other members of this subfamily include PETER'S DWARF FROG (Plate 9), a small toad-like frog with a pointed snout, and its relative the CUYABA DWARF FROG (Plate 9), a frog with an unusual anti-predator defense (see Ecology and Behavior, below).

The frogs you are most likely to see belonging to the third subfamily are members of the genus *Eleutherodactylus*, for example the RIO MAMORE ROBBER FROG (Plate 9) and the CARABAYA ROBBER FROG (Plate 9). *Eleutherodactylus* frogs are generally small (2 to 7 cm, 0.8 to 2.8 in), and most are arboreal. Many species are patterned with various shades of yellow, tan, gray, brown, or black. Some have contrasting yellow, cream, orange, or red spots on the thighs or in the groin; often you can see the spots only when the frog extends its legs. Many species have color patterns that vary greatly among individuals, making identification difficult. Most *Eleutherodactylus* frogs have distinctly expanded discs on toes of both the front and hind feet; these discs provide a firm grip on leaves and branches. The toes generally lack webbing and are slender and delicate. The genus *Eleutherodactylus* contains well over 550 of the 900 species of rainfrogs. It is the most species-rich genus of vertebrates in the world.

Natural History
Ecology and Behavior
AMAZON HORNED FROGS spend much of the time partially buried in leaf litter. They are classic *sit-and-wait predators* (that is, they sit and wait for something to move rather than actively searching for prey). Hunkered in the leaf litter, they remain still until an unsuspecting prey moves nearby, at which point they lunge for the catch.

The *Leptodactylus* rainfrogs in Brazil occur mainly in forests and in open areas, where they frequent low-lying marshy areas and temporary ponds. All species are nocturnal and terrestrial. They are opportunistic feeders that eat just about any animal that they can catch and swallow, including many types of invertebrates and small amphibians and reptiles. Many *Leptodactylus* have noxious skin secretions (for defense), which they exude when handled. If you pick up one of these frogs, be sure to wash your hands afterwards. And don't rub your eyes! SMOKY JUNGLE FROGS often sleep by day in large holes in the ground. They emerge at night and, sitting next to their cavities for a quick retreat if needed, give their loud "whoooop" calls.

One of everyone's favorite Brazilian amphibians is the CUYABA DWARF FROG, a charming little animal with an unusual defensive behavior. These frogs have a large pair of circular glands (inguinal glands) on their rumps; the glands are jet black outlined in white. When threatened by a potential predator, a frog turns away from the threat, lowers its head and extends its back legs, presenting the attacker with its rump and two prominent huge black eyes, giving the impression of being a much larger animal than it really is. A common name for this frog in Brazil is *sapo-de-quatro-olhos* (four-eyed toad).

Although some *Eleutherodactylus* frogs are active in the leaf litter by day, most species are nocturnal. At night they usually perch on leaves between 1 and 3 m (3 to 10 ft) above the ground, where they feed on insects and spiders. These small frogs are themselves preyed upon by birds, bats and other small mammals, as well as by a variety of tree snakes, some large frogs, and even by large invertebrates such as tarantulas.

Breeding

AMAZON HORNED FROGS lay their eggs scattered about on the bottom of shallow ponds. This unusual pattern of egg-laying probably improves survivorship of the young, as the tadpoles readily eat eggs and hatchlings of their own species. If the eggs are spread out, there's less chance that all the offspring from one clutch will be eaten.

Many leptodactylids, including *Leptodactylus* and *Physalaemus*, suspend their eggs in a foam nest made by the male while the pair is mating. While the male holds on to the female tightly with his front legs, he kicks his feet and stirs a mixture of water and air with the eggs, mucus, and sperm. This white froth (the consistency of whipped-up egg whites), in which the eggs are suspended, floats on the surface of the water and helps protect the developing eggs from predators and from drying out. After hatching, the tadpoles swim out of the foam and complete their development in the water. Each female produces hundreds or thousands of eggs per clutch. A variation on this pattern of reproduction is exhibited by frogs of the genus *Adenomera*, for example the NAPO TROPICAL BULLFROG (Plate 8). These frogs excavate flask-shaped cavities in the ground and then lay their eggs suspended in a foam nest in the cavity. The tadpoles hatch with large quantities of yolk, which they digest until metamorphosing into froglets. Thus, they never experience a free-swimming larval stage.

In contrast, *Eleutherodactylus* rainfrogs typically produce only a few large eggs (usually 5 to 60), but each has a high energy investment. These frogs breed on land in the absence of standing water. Males of most species call from low vegetation to attract the larger females. At least two species of *Eleutherodactylus* have internal fertilization (extremely rare for frogs), but as far as we know, all Brazilian species have external fertilization. The fertilized eggs are deposited in a moist, secluded place such as in a cavity of a decaying log, beneath leaf litter, or tucked between the leaves of a bromeliad plant. The eggs require about 30 to 60 days to develop, depending on the species. Eventually they hatch as tiny but fully formed froglets. This type of development is called *direct*, because all development occurs within the egg capsule.

Notes

Rainfrogs, like most amphibians, have glands in their skin that secrete milky substances of varying degrees of toxicity and offensive smell. When the frog is molested by a predator, it secretes the noxious fluid and in many cases the predator backs off, allowing the amphibian to escape. SMOKY JUNGLE FROGS secrete a potent substance called "leptodactylin," named after the genus name, *Leptodactylus*. The effects of leptodactylin on a predator are drastic, including blocking neuromuscular activity and over-stimulating parts of the nervous system. Some people experience sneezing fits after handling these frogs. Interestingly, in some parts of the species' range, native peoples eat these frogs after removing the skin under running water. Purportedly the meat tastes like chicken.

A favorite field biologist's trick to play on the uninitiated is to say that you'll shine your flashlight in a Smoky Jungle Frog's eyes and your companion should circle around behind and grab the large frog with both hands. When your companion grabs the unsuspecting frog, it gives out a loud yelp reminiscent of a cat whose tail has been stepped on. Shocked, your companion will drop the frog and be left with slime all over his or her hands – two ways Smoky Jungle Frogs have of defending themselves.

AMAZON HORNED FROGS and others in the genus *Ceratophrys* have become popular as pets, especially in the USA and in Europe. In the pet trade they are often called "pac-man frogs," in reference to the popular video arcade game in which hungry blobs with huge mouths cruise through a maze looking for food. These frogs make interesting pets in large part because of their voracious appetites. It's fascinating to watch a frog eat a mouse, an unusual twist of the normal feeding hierarchy. Fortunately, most of the animals for sale are captive-bred, thus wild populations are not being depleted.

Status
We don't know what constitutes normal, healthy population sizes and distributions for most species of rainfrogs. Some species are known from only a few specimens collected from one place. Many have been discovered recently, so we have no historical records for comparison of population sizes. Although no Brazilian rainfrog is officially classified as threatened or endangered, given the extensive deforestation that has happened in some areas of the country and the very limited ranges of some species, it is likely that declines are occurring.

Profiles
Amazon Horned Frog, *Ceratophrys cornuta*, Plate 7c
Knudsen's Frog, *Leptodactylus knudseni*, Plate 7d
Smoky Jungle Frog, *Leptodactylus pentadactylus*, Plate 7e
Rufous Frog, *Leptodactylus fuscus*, Plate 8a
Basin White-lipped Frog, *Leptodactylus mystaceus*, Plate 8b
Pointed-belly Frog, *Leptodactylus podicipinus*, Plate 8c
Cei's White-lipped Frog, *Leptodactylus chaquensis*, Plate 8d
Napo Tropical Bullfrog, *Adenomera hylaedactyla*, Plate 8e
Cuyaba Dwarf Frog, *Physalaemus nattereri*, Plate 9a
Peter's Dwarf Frog, *Physalaemus petersi*, Plate 9b
Río Mamore Robber Frog, *Eleutherodactylus fenestratus*, Plate 9c
Carabaya Robber Frog, *Eleutherodactylus ockendeni*, Plate 9d

3. Treefrogs

The *treefrogs*, family Hylidae, are a large group of about 740 species, with a nearly worldwide distribution. More than 500 species occur in the New World, where they are most abundant and diverse in the tropics. Because many species have bright colors and large eyes, they have joined animals such as parrots, monkeys, and the Jaguar, as popular icons associated with rainforests. Relatively stable moisture and temperature conditions prevalent in tropical forests allow treefrogs to inhabit at least the lower levels of the forest.

Most treefrogs are small and have long, slender limbs relative to their body size, and large feet with varying amounts of webbing. The toes usually end in expanded "discs" that have pads on the bottom; these toe pads provide a firm grip as the frogs move about on leaves and branches. Treefrogs typically have a slender waist and a large, broad head and snout. Although most of the species you are likely to encounter in Brazil are between 2.5 and 5 cm (1 and 2 in) long, adults of various species range in length from 1.7 cm (0.7 in) to 15 cm (6 in). Some species are green or brown, with or without patterns of darker green or dark brown. Other species are brightly colored, often in shades of yellow or orange. One group of treefrogs, the *leaf frogs* (genus *Phyllomedusa*), have exceedingly long limbs and opposed thumbs and first toes (usually without webbing); they often walk slowly and deliberately instead of jumping.

Natural History
Ecology and Behavior
As their name suggests, most treefrogs spend much of their time among leaves and branches of shrubs and trees. Most live in lower vegetation 1 to 3 m (3 to 10 ft) above the ground. They forage at night for invertebrate prey, and they sleep during the day in the vegetation. There are exceptions, however. Some species are terrestrial, some are fossorial (burrowing), and others are semi-aquatic. Many treefrogs can change colors with respect to time of day; they are often lighter when they are sleeping and darker at night when they are active. These changes are generally associated with light and moisture conditions.

The VEINED TREEFROG (Plate 10) has well-developed glands throughout the skin. Some of these are mucous glands, others are poison glands. These glands secrete copious amounts of fluid, which probably have a dual function. The noxious secretions no doubt deter predators, and the mucous secretions help prevent the body from losing water. In fact, it is probably the presence of the thick mucous glands that allow this frog to occur in very dry habitats where you normally would not expect to find frogs.

Breeding
One of the more fascinating aspects of treefrogs is the diversity of the ways they reproduce. In fact, treefrogs have the widest array of reproductive patterns of any single family of frogs. These patterns range from the "standard" mode of laying eggs directly in water (eggs that hatch into tadpoles) to remarkable species that brood their eggs in a protective pouch on the mother's back. Most of the unusual modes of reproduction are restricted to the tropics. Some Brazilian treefrogs lay their eggs on leaves above standing water. For example, in the WHITE-LINED LEAF FROG (Plate 10), males call (a harsh "cluck") from perches over temporary ponds. The female deposits from 600 to 1000 eggs on a leaf overhanging the water. The eggs hatch into tadpoles within 10 days or so and drop into the water below (if they're lucky and there still is water below), where they complete their development until metamorphosis into frogs. Other treefrogs, such as the UPPER AMAZON TREEFROG (Plate 12), COMMON CLOWN TREEFROG (Plate 12), and TRIANGLE TREEFROG (Plate 12), deposit smaller clutches of smaller eggs on leaves over water.

Although many species of treefrogs in the wet tropics have evolved reproductive independence of standing water, there are still many species that lay their eggs directly in water. Most of these avoid permanent bodies of water, presumably because of the danger of predation on eggs and tadpoles by fish. An exception is the MAP TREEFROG (Plate 13), which usually breeds in permanent bodies of water such as lakes. Curiously, the tadpoles form large schools, often composed of more than 1000 individuals. By swimming around in these large aggregations, the tadpoles may be better able to escape the jaws of hungry fish. Many treefrog species, such as the COMMON FLAT TREEFROG (Plate 10), the RED-SKIRTED TREEFROG (Plate 11), and the POLKADOT TREEFROG (Plate 12), breed only in temporary ponds. These ponds are formed when low-lying areas fill with rainwater. Because these ponds dry out quickly, fish cannot survive in them. The frogs still must contend with abundant aquatic insect predators, however, which exact a large toll on their numbers. A few species of treefrogs lay their eggs in small pools of water that accumulate in the central parts, or *cisterns*, of bromeliad plants, or in depressions and cavities of tree limbs and trunks. Another unusual mode of reproduction is exhibited by the GIANT GLADIATOR FROG (Plate 13), which breeds along the edges of rivers. The male uses his feet to scoop out a depression up to 40 cm (16 in) in diameter in the mud or sand. After water seeps in and fills his depression, he calls and, if lucky, attracts a female, which lays up to several thousand eggs in the nest.

Clutch size (the number of eggs produced during a breeding bout) is highly variable among species. Some, particularly those that lay their eggs directly in water, produce large numbers (up to 2000 or more per clutch). Generally the fewest eggs per clutch are found in species that have parental care (often fewer than 50 eggs). Intermediate numbers are typical of species that lay their eggs on leaves over water. In areas with distinct wet and dry seasons, most treefrogs breed during the wet season when ponds are available. In less seasonal environments, treefrogs breed sporadically year-round; most breeding activity occurs after heavy rains, again when aquatic sites are most numerous. In contrast, the Giant Gladiator Frog breeds during the dry season, when the level of the rivers is lower.

The fact that each species has its own preferred time and place for breeding helps to reduce competition for breeding sites. Furthermore, because some species deposit their eggs directly in water, some on leaves above water, and others are independent of water for reproduction, there is less demand on the available sites than there would be without this reproductive diversity. If all the frogs lay their eggs in temporary ponds, all at the same time, food would likely be severely limited for the tadpoles.

Notes

Adult treefrogs avoid or escape predators by rapid jumping, cryptic coloring that allows them to blend into their environment, loud, startling screams or squawks given when grabbed by predators, curling up and playing dead, and by poisons in their skin. Many treefrogs (and other types of frogs) have contrasting color patterns (such as bands of dark purple on an orange background) on surfaces of the limbs and the body that are usually hidden. These colors are only visible when the limbs are extended. When a frog jumps to escape danger, these contrasting color patches, called *flash coloration*, attract the predator's attention. Then when the frog assumes a sitting position the predator has lost the image because the frog is now cryptic once again. Leaf frogs have especially pronounced flash coloration. The flanks of the White-lined Leaf Frog are green above and red below a row of cream spots. The TIGER-STRIPED LEAF FROG (Plate 10) has orange flanks with purplish brown bars.

One of the more infamous Brazilian leaf frogs is the GIANT MONKEY FROG, *Phyllomedusa bicolor*. Men from the Mayoruna indigenous tribe along the Brazil/Peru border use this frog's skin secretion as a drug for "hunting magic." Captive frogs are harassed until they release their defensive secretions. The secretions are collected and dried into a powder. Prior to a hunting expedition, the men inflict burns on their arms or chest and introduce the powder into these open wounds. The chemicals rapidly enter the bloodstream and cause intense vomiting, elevated pulse rate, and incontinence for the next hour. The person lapses into a state of listlessness that lasts up to several days. Eventually the person wakes and feels "godlike" in strength and confident of a successful hunt because his senses are sharpened.

Status

We have so little information on populations of Brazilian treefrogs that it is impossible to determine the status of most species. Given the present high rate of forest clearing and disturbance, some species undoubtedly are declining, particularly those with restricted ranges, specialized habitat requirements, or small populations.

Profiles

Common Laughing Frog, *Osteocephalus taurinus*, Plate 9e
Tiger-striped Leaf Frog, *Phyllomedusa tomopterna*, Plate 10a
White-lined Leaf Frog, *Phyllomedusa vaillanti*, Plate 10b
Veined Treefrog, *Phrynohyas venulosa*, Plate 10c
Common Flat Treefrog, *Scinax rubra*, Plate 10d
Mato Grosso Snouted Treefrog, *Scinax acuminatus*, Plate 10e
Short-legged Treefrog, *Hyla leali*, Plate 11a
Lesser Treefrog, *Hyla minuta*, Plate 11b
Dwarf Treefrog, *Hyla nana*, Plate 11c
Sarayacu Treefrog, *Hyla parviceps*, Plate 11d
Red-skirted Treefrog, *Hyla rhodopepla*, Plate 11e

Upper Amazon Treefrog, *Hyla bifurca*, Plate 12a
Common Clown Treefrog, *Hyla leucophyllata*, Plate 12b
Triangle Treefrog, *Hyla triangulum*, Plate 12c
Jade Treefrog, *Hyla granosa*, Plate 12d
Polkadot Treefrog, *Hyla punctata*, Plate 12e
Marbled Treefrog, *Hyla marmorata*, Plate 13a
Quacking Treefrog, *Hyla lanciformis*, Plate 13b
Giant Gladiator Frog, *Hyla boans*, Plate 13c
Troschel's Treefrog, *Hyla calcarata*, Plate 13d
Map Treefrog, *Hyla geographica*, Plate 13e

4. Poison-dart Frogs

Poison-dart frogs, family Dendrobatidae, are popular as rainforest poster animals. They are also commonly pictured on note cards, T-shirts, and even ties and boxer shorts. Much of the charm of these frogs is that many species have bright colors that warn predators of their extraordinary toxicity. The 175 species in the family are restricted to the warm tropical climates of Central and South America. Poison-dart frogs typically have very restricted ranges. Some of the species found in Brazil are found nowhere else. New species are still being discovered as previously unexplored areas are being surveyed.

Poison-dart frogs are small; adults range from little more than 1.5 cm (0.6 in) to about 5 cm (2 in). Most species have large eyes and a short head and snout. The body and limbs are fairly short and stout, and the toes end with expanded tips that are usually rectangular. Toes of the front feet lack webbing; although most species have no webbing on the back feet, some are partially webbed.

The most striking characteristic of many poison-dart frogs is their spectacularly bright coloration, often with a metallic shine. Colors range from red, orange, and yellow to blue, purple, and green. Often these bright colors are combined with black, in contrasting patterns of stripes, spots, or mottling. Some species have only one color on the upper surface of the body, but some, such as the

RIO MADEIRA POISON-DART FROG (Plate 14), have two or more colors. Some species, such as the SPOT-LEGGED POISON-DART FROG (Plate 14) have bright colors restricted to their limbs or in the armpits or groin. The bellies of some species are mottled blue and black or blue and white. Fully half the species in the family, however, are not brightly colored. These are frogs in the genus *Colostethus*, such as the AMAZON ROCKET FROG (Plate 14). Their colors range from dull tan to dark brown, allowing the frogs to blend in with their surroundings. Frogs of this genus often have pale cream to yellowish stripes along the upper and/or lower sides of the head and body. The undersides are often cream, pale yellow, or tan; some have a spotted pattern on a darker background. *Colostethus*, although similar in habits to others in the family, do not produce highly toxic skin secretions.

Natural History
Ecology and Behavior
Poison-dart frogs are terrestrial. By day they hop about in the leaf litter foraging for invertebrates such as insects and spiders. Although they eat a wide variety of prey, ants and termites make up at least two-thirds of their diet. Some species sleep at night on leaves, usually less than a meter (3 ft) above the ground. Some of the drab species are also active at night, although to a lesser extent. One characteristic of poison-dart frogs is that they move rapidly, taking short jumps and often darting about in irregular paths. They can be extremely difficult to catch. Some of the brightly colored species are abundant in primary forest near small streams; others prefer secondary forest or swampy areas. Many of the drab species are poorly known, partially because they are wary and secretive (not surprising considering their lack of potent skin toxins and warning colors). Nearly all poison-dart frogs live near streams or bromeliad plants, sites where their tadpoles develop (see Breeding, below).

The bright colors of the toxic species of poison-dart frogs send a warning to potential predators: Danger! Don't eat me! Poison-dart frogs have some of the strongest poisons of any frogs. The poisons, secreted by glands in the skin, are fat-soluble alkaloids that affect nerves and muscles, causing paralysis. Biologists speculate that the source of the poisons may come from the frogs' food because when poison-dart frogs are removed from their native habitat and fed on fruit flies and baby crickets, instead of their natural diet of ants, they lose their toxicity. Something in their natural diet of ants may be necessary for the frogs to be able to produce their own poisons.

Breeding
Reproduction in poison-dart frogs is unlike that of most other frogs. Eggs are deposited on land, and then a parent transports the tadpoles to water for further development. Each species has its own particular set of courtship behaviors. In general, the behavior involves the male calling from his territory to attract a female. When a receptive female appears, he leads her to an appropriate egg-laying spot. After mating, one or the other of the parents (depending on the species) stays with the eggs, and in some species the parent empties fluid from its bladder onto the eggs to keep them moist. After the eggs hatch into tadpoles, the guarding parent straddles the tadpoles. They climb onto the parent's back and are then transported to a nearby stream or water-filled plant. The Río Madeira Poison-dart Frog frequently deposits its tadpoles in fallen rain-filled fruit capsules of the Brazil nut tree. Most poison-dart frogs care for their young only until they deposit

the tadpoles in water. A few species that deposit their tadpoles in water-filled bromeliads, however, go one step further. The female lays infertile eggs into the water for the tadpoles to eat. Based on observations of a few well-studied species, poison-dart frogs produce small numbers (usually 6 to 20) of relatively large eggs. Some species in environments without strong seasonality may breed throughout the year.

Brazil is home to an unusual species of rocket frog, STEPHEN'S ROCKET FROG, *Colostethus stepheni*. Around the area of Manaus, this rocket frog lives in the same places as the AMAZON ROCKET FROG and the BRILLIANT-THIGHED POISON-DART FROG (Plate 14). But unlike these two species, and indeed unlike the vast majority of other poison-dart frogs, Stephen's Rocket Frogs do not transport their tadpoles to water. Instead, the male guards the "nest" (usually a cup-shaped leaf with a second leaf acting as a roof) where the 3 to 5 eggs have been deposited, and after the tadpoles hatch they stay on the leaf where they develop until they metamorphose into tiny froglets. Thus, they never experience an aquatic stage. Development within a terrestrial nest site is unique among the rocket frogs, although in at least one other species, the tadpoles ride on the back of the parent until they transform into tiny froglets.

Notes

The name "poison-dart frog" refers to the fact that some species are used by indigenous peoples in South America to poison blowgun darts for hunting. Only three species, all in the genus *Phyllobates*, are known to be used to poison blowgun darts. For this reason, some herpetologists argue that only frogs in the genus *Phyllobates* should be called poison-dart frogs and that species in other toxic groups in the family are more appropriately called poison frogs; many refer to frogs in the genus *Colostethus* as *rocket frogs*.

In the northern Chocó of Colombia, hunters poison their darts with secretions of two different species of *Phyllobates* by impaling hapless frogs on sharp sticks, and then slowly roasting them over a flame to gather the secretions. The poison, spread on the sharp ends of the darts, is strong enough to rapidly debilitate even large prey such as monkeys. The most poisonous species of dart-frog was discovered only about 20 years ago in Colombia, and was named *Phyllobates terribilis* (the TERRIBLE YELLOW POISON-DART FROG) in reference to the extraordinary toxicity of its poison. In the southern Chocó, the Indians use *P. terribilis* to poison darts, but unlike the two species to the north, the bright yellow or orange frog is spared death. This species is so toxic that the person only needs to rub his dart tip briefly on the back of a frog. The frogs are then released unharmed. The poison from this frog is in fact one of the most potent natural toxins found on Earth. Indirect estimations suggest that each frog has enough poison to kill ten people or about 20,000 mice! The hunters handle these frogs with leaves, avoiding direct contact with their skin. There is no effective antidote known for the toxin.

Status

Very little is known about the populations of most species of poison-dart frogs. Since many species have restricted ranges, poison-dart frogs are especially susceptible to habitat destruction and over-collecting. For this reason, and because of their beauty and popular appeal in the pet trade, all poison-dart frogs are listed on CITES Appendix II.

Profiles

Amazon Rocket Frog, *Colostethus marchesianus*, Plate 14a
Río Madeira Poison-dart Frog, *Dendrobates quinquevittatus*, Plate 14b
Brilliant-thighed Poison-dart Frog, *Epipedobates femoralis*, Plate 14c
Spot-Legged Poison-dart Frog, *Epipedobates pictus*, Plate 14d

5. Other Frogs

Although the family Ranidae, or *true frogs*, has a nearly worldwide distribution (and over 700 species), the family's only representative in Brazil is the AMAZON RIVER FROG (Plate 15). These frogs, which resemble North American bullfrogs and can grow to 13 cm (5.2 in) in length, are medium to dark green, with fully webbed hind feet, no webbing on the front feet, prominent external ear discs, and distinct folds of skin on the upper sides of the body. The largest frog in the world belongs to the family Ranidae, the GIANT SLIPPERY FROG, *Conraua goliath*, from west Africa, at 30 cm (12 in).

Narrowmouthed toads, family Microhylidae, contrary to what the family name suggests, are neither tiny treefrogs nor toads. There are about 315 species in the family, distributed nearly worldwide. Most narrowmouthed toads look ridiculous with their rotund bodies, short stubby limbs, and tiny pointed heads. Life-style is highly variable, including terrestrial, fossorial (burrowing), and arboreal. Microhylids live in arid deserts, in wet rainforests, and in just about all habitats in between these extremes. They range in size from tiny (1 cm, 0.4 in) to medium sized frogs (10 cm, 4 in). If you spot a small (usually less than 5 cm, 2 in), dull gray to dark brown, smooth-skinned frog that resembles a mud-covered golf ball with legs and a pointed head, hopping about on the ground, you probably have found a narrowmouthed toad. In some places, the BOLIVIAN BLEATING FROG (Plate 15), a microhylid, is the most abundant terrestrial frog active at night.

Another frog family represented in Brazil is one of the most bizarre on Earth. The SURINAM TOAD (Plate 15), family Pipidae, looks like it has been run over by a truck and had its head smashed into a triangular mass. Small, beady eyes and nostrils are perched on top of this unusual-looking head. This completely aquatic frog has an extremely flattened, dark brown body (about 17 cm, 6.8 in, long) with flattened limbs. The hind feet are completely webbed, but the long fingers of the front feet are not. These frogs live in permanent ponds and swamps in the Amazon Basin. They are virtually helpless on land. There are 30 species in the family, most of which occur in sub-Saharan Africa.

The family Pseudidae is composed of only four species. They have a disjunct distribution, occuring only in the Magdalena Valley of Colombia and in tropical South America east of the Andes Mountains. They have robust hindlimbs, fully webbed feet, and large eyes. All four species are fully aquatic. One, the SWIMMING FROG (Plate 15), is renowned for its giant tadpole (see Ecology, Behavior, and Breeding below).

Natural History
Ecology, Behavior, and Breeding

The AMAZON RIVER FROG is found in lowland forest, and is active mostly at night in or near ponds, lakes, streams, and swamps. These frogs are often found in association with *treefrogs* and *rainfrogs* at temporary ponds. They are more aquatic than are most forest frogs, usually seen within 5 m (16 ft) of water. Amazon River Frogs lay 5000 to 7000 eggs directly in the water. Like other frogs in the genus *Rana*, Amazon River Frogs are strong jumpers with powerful hind limbs.

Narrowmouthed toads are usually nocturnal, and most are terrestrial. Many are burrowers. Most species prefer primary forest, but some are also found in secondary forest and along forest edges. Although many species feed almost exclusively on ants and/or termites, other invertebrate prey, such as beetles, are also eaten. Narrowmouthed toads congregate to breed at small forest ponds, especially during or immediately following heavy rain. Males call from the edge or the surface of the water. If you hear what sounds like a sheep "baaaahing" from the edge of a pond, you're probably hearing a BOLIVIAN BLEATING FROG. Mating occurs in the water and females deposit 100 to 600 eggs, which hatch into tadpoles. One group of narrowmouthed toads deposits a small number of eggs (5 to 10) in water-filled bromeliad plants. Instead of feeding on an external source of food, the tadpoles develop into frogs by digesting their large supplies of yolk. Worldwide, narrowmouthed toads exhibit a wide variety of breeding strategies, including terrestrial eggs with direct development and parental care.

SURINAM TOADS do not have tongues, so they capture their food in a different way from most frogs. They rest motionless in the water with their arms outstretched. As soon as they sense any food-sized moving creature within range, they bring their arms together and scoop the object into their mouths. Surinam Toads feed mainly on fish and invertebrates. The reproductive behavior of this genus is unique. The pair somersaults through the water, in a series of elaborate acrobatics, with the female releasing eggs, the male fertilizing them, and then the fertilized eggs falling onto the back of the female. Pressure of the male during amplexus ensures that the eggs (about 80 per clutch) are pressed into the soft skin on the back of the female, after which the skin swells rapidly around the eggs. Safely embedded in the mother's back, the eggs travel with her until fully formed froglets pop out of her skin a few months later.

The SWIMMING FROG is a fascinating paradox. The tadpole grows to about 23 cm (9.2 in), reaching its full size in about 4 months. Then, during metamorphosis it shrinks to a fraction of its larval length. Adult frogs reach a maximum body length of only 7.3 cm (2.9 in).

Status

Although no species of these four frog families is considered to be threatened or endangered in Brazil, most of the species are too poorly known to make informed recommendations concerning population status.

Profiles

Amazon River Frog, *Rana palmipes*, Plate 15a
Bolivian Bleating Frog, *Hamptophryne boliviana*, Plate 15b
Swimming Frog, *Pseudis paradoxa*, Plate 15c
Surinam Toad, *Pipa pipa*, Plate 15d

Environmental Close-up 3
Frog Population Declines

The Problem

For over a decade, scientists have reported that many populations of frogs, toads, and salamanders are declining in numbers. Some populations, and in fact entire species, have disappeared entirely. Several major questions are being asked: (1) How widespread is the problem? (2) Are amphibian population declines a special case, happening for reasons unrelated to the general loss of biodiversity? and (3) If there is a generalized worldwide amphibian decline, what are the causes?

The available data indicate a widespread pattern of amphibian declines. There are reports from low elevations and high elevations, from the USA, Central America, the Amazon Basin, the Andes, Europe, and Australia. Habitat loss almost certainly contributes to general declines in population sizes of amphibians, and in this sense, amphibian declines are part of the worldwide loss of biodiversity. But what is going on with amphibians seems to be more extreme than the declines seen in other animals. Why would amphibians be more vulnerable? One reason is that because amphibians have thin, moist skin that they use for breathing, chemical pollutants found in the water, soil, and air are able to enter their bodies easily. Secondly, many amphibians are exposed to double jeopardy: because they live both on land (usually in the adult stage) and in the water (usually the egg and larval stages), they are exposed to environmental contaminants, vagaries of the weather, and other potential factors affecting survivorship in both habitats.

So what could be causing the observed declines of amphibians? One possible cause is environmental pollution, for example *acid rain* – rain that is acidified by various atmospheric pollutants, leading to lake and river water being more acidic. Acidic water is known to decrease fertilization success because sperm become less active and often disintegrate. The eggs that are fertilized often develop abnormally. Another suggestion is that the increased level of ultraviolet (UV) radiation, due to the thinning of the protective atmospheric ozone layer, might be damaging. Frogs often lay their eggs in shallow water directly exposed to the sun's rays, tadpoles often seek shallow water where the temperatures are warmer, and some juvenile and adult frogs bask for warmth. Studies have shown that increased levels of UV light kill some species of frog eggs and can interact chemically with diseases and acid rain to increase amphibian mortality rates. Another possible cause is global warming. Some species of amphibians may not be able to adapt to the warmer, drier climate the world is currently experiencing. For example, drought during a severe El Niño year in 1986–1987 has been implicated in the declines and disappearances of 40% (20 of 50 species) of the frog species (including the now likely extinct Golden Toad) that lived in the vicinity of Monteverde, Costa Rica. The frogs may have died directly from desiccation (drying out), or they may have been so stressed that they became more vulnerable to disease, fungus, or windborne environmental contaminants. Another cause of some population declines is a parasitic chytrid fungus that has been identified from Central and South America, the United States, Europe, and Australia. The fungus seems to infest especially the victims' bellies – the area where frogs take up water through the skin. Thus, one speculation is that the frogs may be suffocating and drying out.

Another possibility is that the fungus may release toxins that are lethal to the frogs when they are resorbed into the skin. Scientists are wondering where the killer fungus will show up next, and what is stressing amphibians to make them more vulnerable to pathogens such as fungus. They're also wondering if people (including researchers and ecotourists) could inadvertently be spreading the fungus on their shoes and boots. Perhaps non-human animals, such as insects, are spreading the fungus as well.

The Controversy

Not all biologists agree that amphibian declines are a phenomenon over and above the worldwide decline in biodiversity. Scientists who study natural fluctuations in size of animal populations point out that populations of many animals cycle between scarcity and abundance. Many insects are known for their wildly fluctuating population sizes. Population levels of vertebrates also fluctuate with environmental conditions such as food availability and density of prey. For example, voles and lemmings, small rodents of the arctic tundra, are well known for one year being at low population densities (a few per acre or hectare) but several years later, being at very high densities (thousands per acre or hectare). Skeptics point out that, unless those sounding the alarm of amphibian declines can show that the declines are not part of natural cycles, it is too early to panic. They emphasize that the only way to document natural population cycles is to monitor amphibian populations during long-term field studies. Unfortunately, few such studies have been done.

Those scientists who believe that widespread amphibian declines are more than merely natural fluctuations argue that we need to act *now*. Although they agree that we need to initiate long-term studies, they believe we can't wait for the conclusions of such studies 10 or 20 years down the road before we try to reverse the situation. At that point, they argue, it will be too late to do anything but record extinctions.

The Future

The controversy will continue. The important consequence of the debate is that many investigators are working on the problem, considering many different possible causes, from climatic change to a parasitic fungus. A major problem is that even if the scientific consensus right now were that disease, fungi, pollution, climate change, increased level of UV radiation, or some combination, were causing worldwide amphibian declines, the interest and resources are currently lacking to do anything about it on the massive scale required. Because amphibians and reptiles are not uniformly liked and respected, preservation efforts for these animals, except for special cases like sea turtles, will always lag behind conservation efforts made on behalf of birds and mammals. Fortunately, however, because the current conservation emphasis is on preserving entire ecosystems, rather than particular species, amphibians will benefit even if they don't have feathers or fur.

Chapter 8

Reptiles

Edited by Martha L. Crump

Introduction

The fascinating colors, shapes and behaviors of *reptiles* pique the interest of biologists and non-biologists alike. To see many species of reptiles in the wild, however, you need to walk slowly and quietly and look closely. The reason is that, to avoid predation, most reptiles are inconspicuous and often flee from the approach of humans. There are some exceptions. For example, crocodilians and iguanas are *not* inconspicuous and *do not* readily flee from humans. Small lizards can be quite common along forest trails. And geckos are often common in the lodges where ecotourists stay.

General Characteristics and Classification of Reptiles

Reptiles have been around for a long time, arising during the late Paleozoic Era, some 300 million years ago. Today more than 7000 species live in almost all regions of the Earth, with a healthy contingent in the American tropics. Reptile skin is covered with tough scales, which cuts down significantly on water loss from their body surface. The development of this trait permitted vertebrates to remain for extended periods on dry land. Most of today's reptiles are completely terrestrial. In contrast, most amphibians lack a tough skin and must remain in or near water or moist places. Reptiles have much more efficient heart and blood systems than those of amphibians. This increased efficiency allows for a high blood pressure and the sustained muscular activity required for living on land. The crocodilians even have a completely four-chambered heart that is otherwise found only in birds and mammals. A reptile egg is covered with a shell that provides mechanical protection, but at the same time allows movement of respiratory gases and water vapor. One of the major differences between a reptile egg and an amphibian egg is that the reptile embryo is surrounded by a membrane called the *amnion*. This membrane provides the developing embryo with a fluid environment, and thus, unlike most amphibians, reptiles do not have to return to the water to deposit their eggs. In addition, the developing young in reptile eggs are much better protected against predators and the elements.

Biologists recognize four major living groups of reptiles. The *turtles* and *tortoises* (land turtles) constitute one group, with about 260 species worldwide. Some turtles live on land throughout their lives. The *sea turtles* live in the oceans, coming ashore only to lay eggs. Most turtles live in lakes and ponds. Some eat plants, some are carnivorous, and others eat both plants and animals. Turtles are easily distinguished by their unique body armor of tough plates that cover their back and belly, creating wrap-around shells into which head and limbs are retracted when danger looms. The *crocodiles* and their relatives, large predatory carnivores that live along the shores of swamps, rivers, and estuaries, constitute a small second group of 22 species. The third group is represented by two lizard-like species of *tuataras*, found only on small islands off the coast of New Zealand. The fourth group consists of the *squamates*, the 3300 *lizard* species and 3500 *snakes*. Lizards and snakes have very similar skeletal traits, indicating that they are closely related.

Lizards walk on all four limbs, except for a few that are legless. Many live on the ground, but a fair number spend much of their lives in trees. Almost all are capable of moving rapidly. Most lizards are insectivorous, but some, especially larger ones, eat plants, and several prey on amphibians, other lizards, mammals, birds, and even fish. The ecological success of lizards is likely due primarily to a combination of their efficient predation on insects and other small animals as well as their low daily energy requirements. Lizards rely primarily on external sources of heat such as the sun to raise their internal temperature enough to be active. When it gets too hot they use behavior such as seeking shade to lower their internal temperature so they can again be active. However, when the external temperature falls too much, instead of burning up stored energy to maintain their body temperature, they just let their internal temperature drop and become inactive. Their cooled bodies go into a resting state that needs little energy. In some ways, this can be considered an advantage over birds and mammals, which must continually seek food to maintain constant body temperatures.

Most Brazilian lizards eat insects, spiders, and mites. Lizards use two main foraging strategies. Some, such as the small microteid lizards (p. 115), are *active searchers*. They move continually while looking for prey, nosing about in the leaf litter of the forest floor. *Sit-and-wait* predators are usually highly camouflaged; they remain motionless on the ground or on tree trunks or branches, waiting for prey to happen by. When they see a likely meal, they snatch it if it is close enough or dart out to chase it down. Many lizards are territorial, defending territories from other members of their species with displays, such as bobbing up and down on their front legs, spreading out their *dewlaps* (throat fans), and raising their head crests. Lizards are especially common in deserts and semi-deserts, but they are numerous in other habitats as well. They are active primarily during the day, except for many of the gecko species, which are nocturnal.

Snakes probably evolved from burrowing lizards, and all are limbless. Although all snakes are carnivores, their methods of capturing prey differ. Several groups of species have evolved glands that manufacture toxic venom that is injected into prey through the teeth. The venom immobilizes and kills the prey, which is then swallowed whole. Other snakes strike out at and then wrap themselves around their prey, constricting the prey until it suffocates. Most snakes are nonvenomous; they seize prey with their mouths and rely on their size and strong jaws to subdue it. Snakes have no eardrums for hearing, but they can detect ground vibrations through their bodies. They generally rely most on vision and smell to locate prey, although members of two families have thermal sensor organs on their heads that detect the heat of prey animals.

The success of snakes is at least partially attributable to their ability to devour prey that is larger than their heads. (Their jaw bones are highly mobile and can be moved easily out of their socket joints on the cranium to accommodate large prey as it is swallowed). Because they eat large items, they need to search for and capture prey only infrequently. For this reason, they can spend long periods hidden and secluded, safe from predators. Snakes use either active searching or sit-and-wait foraging strategies.

As is true for lizards, temperature regulates a snake's life, and is the key to understanding their ecology. Unlike birds and mammals, snakes' body temperatures are determined primarily by how much heat they obtain from the physical environment. Many can only be active when they gather sufficient warmth from the sun. They have some control over their body temperature, but it is behavioral rather than physiological. Snakes can lie in the sun or retreat to shade to raise or lower their internal temperatures to within a good operating range, but only up to a point. They must "sit out" hours or days in which the air temperature is either too high or too low. This dependence on air temperature affects most aspects of snakes' lives, from date of birth, to food requirements, to the rapidity with which they can strike at prey.

Snakes are themselves prey for hawks and other predatory birds, other snakes, as well as for some mammals. Many snakes are quite conspicuous against a solid color, with their bold and colorful skin patterns. Against their normal backdrops, however, such as a leaf-strewn forest floor, they are highly camouflaged. They rely on their cryptic coloration, and sometimes on speed, to evade predators. Within a species male and female snakes usually look alike, although in some there are minor differences between the sexes in color patterns or the sizes of their scales.

Seeing Reptiles in Brazil

Most species of reptiles in Brazil are shy and often difficult to observe. They spend most of their time concealed or still. Few vocalize like birds or frogs, so you cannot use sound to find them. The superb cryptic coloration of many snakes means that snakes probably will see more of you than you will of them. Because of the difficulty people have seeing snakes before getting very close to them, the rule for exploring any area known to have venomous snakes or any area for which you are unsure, is NEVER to place your hand or foot anywhere that you cannot see first. Do not climb rocks or trees; do not clamber over rocks where your hands or feet sink into holes or crevices; do not reach into bushes or trees. Walk carefully along trails and try to watch your feet and where you are going. Don't be frightened, but be respectful.

If you want to see reptiles, there are a few ways to increase the chances. Knowing about activity periods helps. Lizards and many snakes are active during the day, but some snakes are active at night. Thus, a night walk with flashlights that is organized to find amphibians will also yield reptile sightings. For instance, many small lizards and some snakes sleep on leaves and branches above the ground, in the same places where treefrogs are active. In rainforest, many lizards are active by day on tree trunks, and also in sunny areas near forest edges. Snakes and lizards are often more active in sunny, warm weather. If all else fails, look for small snakes and lizards by CAREFULLY moving aside rocks and logs with a robust stick or with your boots. Because there are some venomous snakes that are difficult to identify correctly, all snakes are best observed from a safe distance unless you are accompanied by someone who is very familiar with the animals.

Unfortunately, common names of reptiles are not standardized, as they are for birds. Common names for many South American reptiles are especially troublesome. For example, some people call *Ameiva ameiva* (Plate 25) the Amazon Racerunner, others call it the Giant Ameiva. How are the uninitiated supposed to know it's the same species? Many other species have no generally accepted common names. For the sake of consistency, where possible we use here the common names adopted by Lamar (1997; see p. 247) and those that appear in previous Ecotravellers' Wildlife Guides.

Unless otherwise indicated, reptile body lengths are given as total lengths (tail included). For the lizards, however, lengths reported in the plate information section are from the tip of the snout to the vent (i.e., excluding the tail). The reason is that lizards often drop their tails when attacked by predators (p. 117). When the tail regenerates, it is shorter than normal.

Family Profiles

1. Crocodilians

Remnants of the age when reptiles ruled the world, today's 22 species of crocodilians (*alligators*, *caimans*, and *crocodiles*), generally inspire awe, respect, a bit of fear, and a great deal of curiosity. Crocodilians are distributed over most tropical and sub-tropical areas of the world. The crocodilian most likely to be seen in the areas of Brazil covered in this book is the SPECTACLED CAIMAN (Plate 16), probably the most abundant crocodilian in the New World. This species is medium-sized, reaching a length of about 2 m (6.5 ft). The much larger BLACK CAIMAN (Plate 16), the largest crocodilian in South America, can reach a length of 6 m (19.5 ft). In contrast to these larger caimans, the SMOOTH-FRONTED CAIMAN (Plate 16) is a forest-dwelling species that grows to only about 1.5 m (4.9 ft) in length. Brazil's caimans occupy inland rivers, streams, ponds, and lakes.

Natural History
Ecology and Behavior
Although crocodilians usually move slowly over land, they can cover ground rapidly in short bursts. They are easiest to see as they bask in the sunshine along banks of rivers, streams, lakes, and ponds. Most of their time is spent in the water, however. Crocodilians in the water are largely hidden, resembling floating logs. This unassuming appearance allows them to move close to shore and seize animals that come to the water to drink. Crocodilians are meat-eaters, but they also eat carrion. Juvenile caiman eat primarily aquatic insects; adults often prey on fish and amphibians, and on birds and small mammals when they have the opportunity. Large adult BLACK CAIMAN eat turtles and fish, but also deer and large rodents such as Capybara. Given the chance, they'll eat domestic animals such as dogs and pigs as well. Black Caiman and SPECTACLED CAIMAN often forage at night, when they can be seen on the surface of the water; their eyes reflect red when you shine a flashlight on them. In contrast, the smaller SMOOTH-FRONTED CAIMAN often hunts for birds and small mammals on land near forest streams.

Caiman sometimes excavate burrows along waterways, into which they retreat to escape predators and, when water levels fall too low, to *aestivate* (sleep until water conditions improve). Young, very small caiman are eaten by a number of predators, including larger caiman, birds such as herons, storks, egrets and Anhingas, and a variety of mammals such as Jaguars. Large adults apparently have only two enemies: people and large anacondas.

Crocodilians have some of the most developed parental care behaviors of any reptile. Nests are guarded, and one or both parents often help hatchlings free themselves from the nest. In some species, parents carry hatchlings to water. Females may remain with and protect the young for up to two years. Juveniles give alarm calls when threatened, and parents respond by coming quickly to their rescue. This complex parental care in crocodilians is sometimes used by scientists who study dinosaurs to support the idea that dinosaurs may have exhibited complex social and parental behaviors. Crocodilians are long-lived animals, many surviving 60+ years in the wild.

One of the most commonly seen reptiles in the Pantanal is a subspecies of the Spectacled Caiman, the Jacaré Caiman, *Caiman crocodilus yacare*. They live in rivers, where they feed on snails, fishes, reptiles, birds, and mammals. During the dry season, these caiman aggregate in and around the remaining pools and lakes. During the wet season one can watch females building and attending their nests.

Breeding
During courtship, male crocodilians often defend aquatic territories, giving displays with their tails – up-and-down and side-to-side movements – that probably serve both to defend the territory from other males and to court females. Typically the female makes the nest by scraping together grass, leaves, twigs, and sand or soil, into a pile near the water's edge. She then buries 20 to 30 eggs in the pile

that she, and sometimes the male, guard for about 70 days until hatching. Nests of the SMOOTH-FRONTED CAIMAN are sometimes located near termite mounds in the forest. As in the turtles and some lizards, the sex of developing crocodilians is determined largely by the temperature of the ground around the eggs (see p. 104); males develop at relatively high temperatures, females at lower ones. Caiman young from a single brood may remain together in the nest area for up to 18 months.

Notes

Although larger caiman are potentially dangerous to people, they are not particularly aggressive and most are not large enough to eat large land mammals. Local people sometimes swim near SPECTACLED CAIMAN and SMOOTH-FRONTED CAIMAN without concern. The same is NOT true of the larger BLACK CAIMAN!

Because of their predatory nature and large size, crocodilians play important roles – both positive and negative – in the history and folklore of many cultures, going back at least to ancient Egypt and a crocodile-headed god known as Sebek. Egyptians even built and named the holy city of Crocodilopolis in honor of crocodiles. The Egyptians apparently welcomed crocodiles into their canals, possibly as a defense from human invaders. However, perhaps because of the reptile's association with darkness, Egyptians and other African peoples believed that crocodiles caused blindness. Blindness was a very real fear for these people because of the prevalence of a disease called *river blindness*, caused by a river-borne parasitic roundworm. To appease the crocodiles during canal construction, a virgin was sacrificed to the reptiles. Indeed, providing crocodiles with virgins seems to have been a fairly common practice among several cultures, showing a preoccupation with these animals (and with virgins). Crocodilians were important in the cultures of many early Central American peoples also. For example, the ancient Olmecs of eastern Mexico had a crocodile deity. The Mayans had a god, a symbol of death, shaped like a crocodile. The Aztecs had a crocodilian image that symbolized agricultural fertility and another that brought the rain. Potions made from crocodilians were, and still are, used in both the Old and New Worlds as cures for various ailments and diseases.

Status

Most crocodilian species worldwide were severely reduced in numbers during the 20th century. Several were hunted almost to extinction for their skins. In the USA, hunting almost caused AMERICAN ALLIGATORS to go extinct. In 1961 hunting alligators was declared illegal, but poaching continued. Thanks to the 1973 Endangered Species Act, which gave protection to alligators, they have returned to most of the areas from which they were eliminated. Crocodile and alligator farms (with captive-bred stock) and ranches (wild-caught stock) in many areas of the world now provide skins, leaving wild populations relatively unmolested. Many of the Latin American crocodilians were hunted heavily during the first half of the 20th century. Today, only the SPECTACLED CAIMAN is hunted in large numbers, particularly in the Pantanal region of Brazil. All crocodilians are listed by the international CITES agreements, preventing or highly regulating trade, and their numbers have been steadily rising during the past 20 years. Nevertheless, most of the 22 crocodilian species are still threatened or endangered.

Profiles

Spectacled Caiman, *Caiman crocodilus*, Plate 16a
Black Caiman, *Caiman niger*, Plate 16b
Smooth-fronted Caiman, *Paleosuchus trigonatus*, Plate 16c

2. Turtles

It is a shame that *turtles* are rarely encountered in the wild at close range because they are intriguing to watch. It is always a pleasant surprise stumbling across a turtle on land, perhaps laying eggs, or discovering a group of them basking in the sunshine on rocks or logs along a river's edge or in the middle of a pond. The 260 living turtle species are grouped into 12 families that can be divided into three types by their typical habits and body forms. There are two families of *sea turtles*, ocean-going animals whose females come to shore only to lay eggs. The members of nine families, containing most of the turtle species, live in freshwater habitats – lakes and ponds – except for the *box turtles*, which live on land (*terrestrial*). Finally, one family contains the *land tortoises*, which, as their name suggests, are all terrestrial.

Turtles all have the same basic body plan: bodies encased in tough shells (made up of two layers – an inner layer of bone and an outer layer of scale-like plates); four limbs, sometimes modified into flippers; highly mobile necks; toothless jaws; and small tails. This body plan must be among nature's best, because it has survived unchanged for a long time; turtles have looked more or less the same for at least 200 million years. Enclosing the body in heavy armor above and below apparently was an early solution to the problems vertebrates faced when they moved onto land. It provides rigid support when outside of buoyant water and protection from predators and desiccation (drying out).

Turtles range in color from brown to black to green, with many being olive-green. They range in size from tiny terrapins 11.5 cm (4.6 in) long to giant LEATHERBACK SEA TURTLES that can grow to more than 2 m (6.5 ft) long, 3.6 m (11.7 ft) across (flipper to flipper), and that weigh 600+ kg (1300+ lb). Leatherbacks are the heaviest turtles. In many turtle species, females are larger than males.

Natural History

Ecology and Behavior

The diet of freshwater turtles changes as they develop. Early in life they are carnivorous, eating almost anything they can get their jaws on – snails, insects, fish, frogs, salamanders, reptiles. As they grow, the diet of many species changes to herbivory. Turtles are slow-moving on land, but they can retract their heads, tails, and limbs into their shells, rendering them almost impregnable to predators – unless they are swallowed whole, such as by crocodilians. Long-lived animals, individuals of many turtle species typically live 25 to 60 years in the wild. As is typical of most, if not all, reptiles, a turtle grows throughout its life.

The turtles of Brazil occupy a variety of habitats. Sea turtles live in the open oceans off the coast of Brazil, except when females come onto land to lay their eggs. Some of the aquatic freshwater species spend most of their time in lakes and ponds, but a few leave the water to forage on land. The YELLOW-SPOTTED RIVER TURTLE (Plate 16) is most often seen sunning itself on logs in the water or on muddy beaches of rivers in remote and undisturbed parts of the Amazon Basin. One of nature's most bizarre turtles is the MATAMATA (Plate 17) – bizarre because of the fleshy proboscis that extends from its snout and because its mouth seemingly is in a perpetual grin. Matamatas live in rivers, where they spend much of their time resting in one position on the bottom, waiting for an unsuspecting meal to come by, at which point they lunge at the fish or invertebrate. The freshwater TWIST-NECKED TURTLE (Plate 17) is a type of sideneck turtle, so-called because when one withdraws its head, it bends its neck to one side of the body between the gap in its upper and lower shells; they are unable to fully retreat the neck and head within the shell as can many other turtles and tortoises. Although the SCORPION MUD TURTLE (Plate 17) is largely aquatic, during the rainy season it travels over land in search of temporary puddles and ponds. The YELLOWFOOT TORTOISE (Plate 16) is found on moist ground in forests.

If turtles can survive the dangerous juvenile stage, when they are small and soft enough for a variety of predators to eat them, they enjoy very high year-to-year survival; up to 80% or more of an adult population usually survives from one year to the next. However, there is very high mortality in the egg and juvenile stages. Nests are not guarded, and many kinds of predators, such as crocodiles, lizards, and armadillos, dig up turtle eggs or eat the hatchlings.

Breeding

Courtship in turtles can be quite complex. In some, the male swims backward in front of the female, stroking her face with his clawed feet. The male SCORPION MUD TURTLE nibbles at the edge of the female's upper shell. When he's ready to copulate, he climbs aboard and grabs the rim of her shell with all four feet. He uses the sharp claw at the tip of his tail to hook onto the female's shell, further reinforcing his hold. Courtship in tortoises often involves butting and nipping. All turtles lay their leathery eggs on land. The female digs a hole in the earth or sand, deposits the eggs into the hole, then covers them and leaves. It is up to the hatchlings to dig their way out of the nest and navigate to water. Many tropical turtles breed at any time of year.

Although the numbers of eggs laid per nest varies extensively among Brazilian freshwater turtles (from one to about 100), in general these turtles lay small clutches. The reason seems to be that, because of the continuous warm weather, they need not breed in haste like their northern cousins, putting all their eggs in one nest. The danger with a single nest is that if a predator finds it, a year's breeding is lost. Tropical turtles, by placing only one or a few eggs in each of several nests spread throughout the year, are less likely to have predators destroy their total annual breeding production. Also, it may pay to lay a few big eggs rather than many small ones because bigger hatchlings may be less vulnerable to predators.

Notes

There is an intriguing relationship between turtle reproduction and temperature that nicely illustrates the intimate connection between animals and the physical environment. For many vertebrates, the sex of an individual is determined by the kinds of sex chromosomes it has. In people, if each cell has an X and a Y chromosome, the person is male, and if two Xs, female. In birds, it is the opposite. But in most turtles, it is not the chromosomes that matter, but the temperature at which an egg develops. In most turtles studied to date, eggs incubated at constant temperatures above 30 °C (86 °F) all develop as females, whereas those incubated at 24 to 28 °C (75 to 82 °F) become males. At 28 to 30 °C (82 to 86 °F), both males and females are produced. In some species, a second temperature threshold exists –

eggs that develop below 24 °C (75 °F) again become females. (In the crocodiles and lizards, the situation reverses, with males developing at relatively high temperatures and females at low temperatures.) The exact way that temperature determines sex is not clear although it is suspected that temperature directly influences a turtle's developing brain. Scientists haven't yet figured out *why* this system of sex determination exists. Is there some advantage of this system to the animals that we as yet fail to appreciate? Or is it simply a consequence of reptile structure and function, some fundamental constraint of their biology?

Status

The ecology and status of populations of most freshwater and land turtles are poorly known, making it difficult to determine whether population numbers are stable or changing. Several species of large river turtles have virtually disappeared from all but the most remote streams and lakes. This rapid decline is due largely to over-harvesting of their eggs, which are buried in sandy river bars. These nests are easily found by local people who then sell them to food markets in regional cities. The YELLOW-SPOTTED RIVER TURTLE and the YELLOWFOOT TORTOISE are considered threatened and are included on the IUCN Red List. Worldwide, sea turtles are heavily exploited by people, and almost all of them are threatened. Sea turtle eggs are harvested illegally for food in many parts of the world, including Brazil, and adults of some species are taken for meat and for their shells.

Profiles

Yellowfoot Tortoise, *Geochelone denticulata*, Plate 16d
Yellow-spotted River Turtle, *Podocnemis unifilis*, Plate 16e
Twist-necked Turtle, *Platemys platycephala*, Plate 17a
Matamata, *Chelus fimbriatus*, Plate 17b
Scorpion Mud Turtle, *Kinosternon scorpioides*, Plate 17c

3. Colubrids: Your Regular, Everyday Snakes

Many people think that all *snakes*, particularly tropical species, are venomous, and hence, must be avoided. Unfortunately, this "reptile anxiety" prevents some people from enjoying tropical forests. In Brazil the vast majority of snakes are NOT venomous. Venomous snakes in the American tropics tend to be nocturnal, secretive, and hard to find, even if you are looking for them. Therefore, with caution, you can enjoy your days in Brazil without worrying unduly about venomous snakes. If you do find one, you will likely discover that it is a beautiful animal and worth a look.

The largest group of snakes is the family Colubridae – the *colubrid* snakes. Most of these are non-venomous or, if venomous, dangerous only to small prey such as lizards and rodents. This is a worldwide group comprising more than 1700 species, including about three-quarters of the New World snakes. Most of the snakes with which people are familiar, such as *water, brown, garter, whip, green, rat,* and *king snakes*, are colubrids, a family that has a wide variety of habits and lifestyles. It is not possible to provide a general physical description of all colubrid snakes because of the great variety of shapes and colors associated with their respective lifestyles. Most people will not get close enough to notice, but an expert could identify colubrids by their anatomy. Colubrids have rows of teeth on the upper and lower jaws but they do not have hollow, venom-injecting fangs in front on the upper jaw.

Natural History
Ecology and Behavior
Because colubrids vary so much in their natural history, we will concentrate on the habits of the species profiled here: arboreal, terrestrial, and aquatic. Arboreal snakes spend most of their time in trees and shrubs. The STRIPED SHARPNOSE SNAKE (Plate 18), for example, is a slender arboreal snake that feeds on lizards and frogs. Their thin, long bodies resemble vines and if not moving, these snakes are very difficult to see. They rely on camouflage for both hunting and protection: they freeze in place when alerted to danger. BLUNT-HEADED TREESNAKES (Plate 18), also arboreal, have broad and squarish heads, long, thin bodies, and large, bulging eyes. They forage at night for small frogs and lizards. Another group of slender nocturnal-arboreal tree snakes are the *thirst snakes*, or *snail-eaters* (Plate 17), which, as you might expect, feed on snails (and slugs but apparently little else). Both blunt-headed snakes and thirst snakes are lightweight tree snakes that are slightly flattened sideways, and can move from branch to branch over open gaps that are half the length of their bodies. Thin-bodied COMMON CAT-EYED SNAKES (Plate 18) cruise through the vegetation around ponds at night, looking for frogs or leaf frog eggs to eat. (Leaf frogs lay their eggs on leaves above the water; see p. 88.)

The COMMON MUSSURANA (Plate 19) is a terrestrial snake with a broad range in the Neotropics in wet and semi-dry lowland areas. Hunting by day or night, mussuranas have a varied diet, including rodents, lizards, and other snakes. In fact, they even capture and eat venomous pit-vipers, and are appreciated for this habit by knowledgeable local people who protect the snakes. Ironically, however, because the juveniles are patterned red, black, and yellow, they are often mistaken for venomous *coral snakes* (p. 108) and are therefore killed. The OLIVE WHIPSNAKE (Plate 18) and TROPICAL RATSNAKE (Plate 19), though partially terrestrial, sleep coiled in vegetation at night. Another terrestrial snake, the COMMON FALSE VIPER (Plate 19), closely resembles the very venomous FER-DE-LANCE (Plate 21), thus gaining a certain amount of protection.

The many varieties of *false coral snakes*, for example the COMMON FALSE CORALSNAKE (Plate 19), are terrestrial forest dwellers that inhabit the leaf litter and rotting logs. These brightly colored snakes visually mimic venomous coral snakes, and thus gain protection from predators. Many people assume that false coral snakes have no fangs or venom, but in fact many species have fangs in the rear of the mouth associated with venom glands (but these snakes do not produce venom strong enough to harm people).

The SOUTH AMERICAN WATER SNAKE (Plate 19) is widespread throughout the Amazon Basin, where it lives in rivers, streams, and pools of water. These snakes have nasty dispositions and given half a chance, will bite you viciously. The heavy-bodied BRAZILIAN FALSE WATER COBRA (Plate 20) lives in shallow still water of the flooded Pantanal. This semi-aquatic snake feeds on frogs and fish, including eels. When threatened, a Brazilian False Water Cobra flattens itself and expands its neck, reminiscent of an African or Asian cobra; hence the common name. When grabbed, these snakes readily bite, causing bleeding, pain, and swelling.

Breeding
Relatively little is known of the breeding patterns of Brazilian colubrids. The typical number of eggs per clutch varies from species to species, but some, such as

the BLUNT-HEADED TREESNAKE, lay small clutches of 1 to 3 eggs. Most snakes that lay eggs deposit them in a suitable location and depart; the parents provide no care of the eggs or young.

Notes

Snakes' limbless condition, their manner of movement, and the venomous nature of some of them, have engendered for these intriguing reptiles fear from people, stretching back thousands of years. Myths about the evil power and intentions of snakes are ubiquitous. But one need go no farther than the Old Testament, in which the snake plays the pivotal role as Eve's corrupt enticer, responsible for people's expulsion from the Garden of Eden. Because these myths cross so many cultures around the world, sociobiologists have hypothesized that fear of snakes may be instinctive. Some studies of monkey behavior seem to support this possibility. Whether or not this fear is instinctive behavior or learned is controversial. We lean toward the learned behavior argument, based primarily on our visits to grade schools with live snakes in hand. Most grade school kids seem to lack the irrational fear often exhibited by their parents.

Although snakes are feared by many people, they are also a source of fascination for those same people. Snakes are despised, but they are also worshipped; they symbolize disease, but also health. No doubt because of their ability to throw off their old skins and acquire fresh ones, snakes represent rejuvenation and immortality in diverse cultures around the world.

Status

Two of Brazil's colubrid snakes are regulated for conservation purposes: the COMMON MUSSURANA and the BRAZILIAN FALSE WATER COBRA. Both are CITES Appendix II listed. Little is known about the biology and population sizes of most colubrids. Long-term studies are necessary to determine if population sizes are stable or changing. Because individual species normally are not found in great numbers, it is difficult to tell when they are threatened. Worldwide, about 30 colubrids are listed as vulnerable, threatened, or endangered. The leading threats are habitat destruction and the introduction by people of exotic animals that prey on snakes at some point in their life cycles, such as Giant Toads, Cattle Egrets, armadillos, and fire ants.

Profiles

Ornate Thirst Snake, *Dipsas catesbyi*, Plate 17d
Big-headed Thirst Snake, *Dipsas indica*, Plate 17e
Striped Sharpnose Snake, *Xenoxybelis argenteus*, Plate 18a
Brown Vinesnake, *Oxybelis aeneus*, Plate 18b
Common Cat-eyed Snake, *Leptodeira annulata*, Plate 18c
Blunt-headed Treesnake, *Imantodes cenchoa*, Plate 18d
Olive Whipsnake, *Chironius fuscus*, Plate 18e
Common Mussurana, *Clelia clelia*, Plate 19a
Tropical Ratsnake, *Spilotes pullatus*, Plate 19b
Common False Viper, *Xenodon rabdocephalus*, Plate 19c
Common False Coralsnake, *Erythrolamprus aesculapii*, Plate 19d
South American Water Snake, *Helicops angulatus*, Plate 19e
Brazilian False Water Cobra, *Hydrodynastes gigas*, Plate 20a

4. Dangerous Snakes and Boas

For convenience, we group together in this section what are usually considered the more dangerous snakes, those that are highly venomous and large ones that kill by squeezing their prey – *anacondas* and *boas*. Anacondas are a kind of boa, and of the entire group, only the anacondas are considered potentially dangerous to adult humans (and then only if you were very much in the wrong place at the wrong time). Most of the venomous snakes and constrictors are well camouflaged, secretive in their habits, and/or nocturnal. (For more information on venomous snakes in Latin America, see *The Venomous Reptiles of Latin America*, by J. A. Campbell and W. W. Lamar.)

Vipers, of the Family Viperidae, comprise most of the New World's venomous snakes. If you are trying to capture and eat a large animal without the benefit of legs and feet, any way of quickly stopping the prey from wriggling free of your grasp would be advantageous. These snakes have evolved just such a method – a venom-injection mechanism: long, hollow fangs that introduce poison into the prey. Snake venoms are complex substances that contain a variety of proteins designed to destroy specific targets, such as nerves or blood. Therefore, generalities about the effects from a certain type of snake's venom are often misleading. From a practical standpoint, what is important for treatment of snakebite is that if at all possible, the snake involved should be correctly identified. Typically vipers coil prior to striking. They vary considerably in size, shape, color pattern, and lifestyle. Many of the vipers are referred to as *pit-vipers* because they have thermal-sensitive "pits," or depressions, between their nostrils and eyes that are sensory organs. Pit-vipers occur from southern Canada to Argentina, as well as in the Old World. The familiar venomous snakes of North America – *rattlesnakes*, *copperheads*, and *water moccasins* – are pit-vipers, as are many of Brazil's venomous snakes.

The deadly FER-DE-LANCE (Plate 21) is abundant in wet forests and along watercourses in drier areas. Most are shorter than the maximum length of 2 m (6.5 ft). They are slender snakes with lance- or spear-shaped heads (hence the name, which means "iron spear"). NEUWIED'S LANCEHEAD (Plate 21), a medium-sized viper, occurs in the Pantanal and in isolated areas of the southern Amazon. This snake is often found in high densities around water-filled ditches, suggesting that they feed on frogs. AMAZON BUSHMASTERS (Plate 21), the largest venomous snakes of the Western Hemisphere, inhabit lowland wet forest areas. They are the large-headed giants of the pit-vipers, reaching lengths of 2.5 to 3.6 m (8 to 12 ft).

The Family Elapidae contains what are regarded as the world's deadliest snakes, the Old World *cobras* and *mambas*. In the Western Hemisphere, the group is represented by *coral snakes* – slender snakes that are usually quite gaily attired in rings of red, yellow and black. They have a very powerful venom. An example of a coral snake that occurs in the Amazon region of Brazil is the SOUTH AMERICAN CORALSNAKE (Plate 21). Coral snakes rarely grow longer than a meter (3.3 ft). Fortunately, all *elapids* in Brazil, although having highly toxic venom, have small fangs, making it difficult for them to bite humans effectively.

Members of the Family Boidae kill their prey by constriction. This family encompasses 63 species that are distributed throughout the world's tropical and sub-tropical regions. They include the Old World *pythons* and the New World boas and anacondas. Pythons and anacondas are the world's largest snakes. The

RED-TAILED BOA (Plate 20) reaches lengths of about 4 m (13 ft), but typically individuals are only 1.5 to 2.5 m (5 to 8 ft) long. These snakes have shiny, smooth scales and a pattern of dark, squarish shapes that provides good camouflage against an array of backgrounds. In general body form the COMMON ANACONDA (Plate 20) is similar to the Red-tailed Boa, but the anaconda is a more massive snake. Other boas in Brazil, such as the AMAZON TREE BOA (Plate 20) and the RAINBOW BOA (Plate 20) are more slender and much smaller, only reaching about 2 m (6.5 ft) in length.

Natural History
Ecology and Behavior
FER-DE-LANCE are primarily terrestrial, although both adults and more commonly juveniles sometimes sleep and rest in vegetation. They inhabit moist forests but also some drier areas. These snakes eat birds and mammals such as opossums. Like other pit-vipers (and some other snakes), they can sense the heat radiated by prey animals, which assists their foraging. Searching by heat detection probably works for both warm-blooded prey (birds, mammals) as well as cold-blooded (lizards, frogs), as long as the prey is at a higher temperature than its surroundings. BUSHMASTERS are terrestrial snakes that feed chiefly on mammals. They are mainly nocturnal and therefore, even where fairly common, are infrequently seen. In a recent Costa Rican study during which these snakes could be followed closely because they were outfitted with radio transmitters, biologists learned that the bushmaster diet consisted almost entirely of rather large forest rats. Typically, a bushmaster would lie in wait for days or even weeks at the same spot on the ground, usually beneath a tree; after capturing a rat, the snake moved to a new site. This lazy, low-energy lifestyle has its advantages; the same study calculated that a single snake would need to eat only about six rats per year to survive!

Coral snakes are usually secretive and difficult to observe; consequently relatively little is known about their ecology and behavior in the wild. They apparently forage by crawling along slowly on the ground, intermittently poking their heads into the leaf litter. They eat lizards, caecilians (Plate 6), and small snakes, which they kill with their powerful venom. They are often found under rocks and logs, and many probably burrow into the soil for protection, and while foraging. They can be day- or night-active.

A number of non-venomous or mildly venomous colubrid snakes, as well as at least one caterpillar species, mimic the bright, striking coral snake color scheme: alternating rings of red, yellow (or white), and black. The function of this *mimicry* apparently is to take advantage of the avoidance behavior many predatory animals show toward the lethal coral snakes. Ever since this idea was first proposed more than a hundred years ago, the main argument against it has been that it implied either that the predators had to be first bitten by a coral snake to learn of its toxicity and then survive to generalize the experience to all snakes that look like coral snakes, or that the predators had to be born with an innate fear of the coral snake color pattern. It has now been demonstrated experimentally that several bird predators on snakes (motmots, kiskadees, herons, and egrets) need not learn that a coral snake is dangerous by being bitten. They avoid these snakes instinctively from birth. Thus, many snakes have evolved as defensive mechanisms color schemes that mimic that of coral snakes.

All Brazilian boas are mainly nocturnal. Some are terrestrial, but do sometimes climb into the vegetation; others are primarily arboreal. The COMMON

ANACONDA, however, is mostly aquatic, foraging in or very near large bodies of water such as in the backwaters of rivers or swamps. Diets of boas include reptiles, birds, and mammals. Prey, recognized by visual, chemical (smell), or heat senses, is seized with the teeth after a rapid, open-mouth lunge. As it strikes, a boa or anaconda also coils around the prey, lifting it from the ground, and then constricts, squeezing the prey. The prey cannot breathe and suffocates. When the prey stops moving, the snake swallows it whole, usually starting with the head.

Breeding

Details of the breeding in the wild of most tropical vipers are not well known. Many may follow the general system of North American rattlesnakes, which have been much studied. Female rattlesnakes attract males when they are ready to mate by releasing *pheromones* (odor chemicals) into the air and also, through the skin of their sides and back, onto the ground. Males search for females. When one is located, the male accompanies and courts her for several days before mating occurs. Although North American rattlers have distinct breeding periods, many tropical vipers may breed at almost any time of year.

Unlike the colubrids, most of the vipers give birth to live young. The FER-DE-LANCE has a reputation as a prolific breeder; females give birth to between 20 and 70 young at a time. Each is about 18 cm (7.2 in) long at birth, fully fanged with active poison glands. And dangerous. The BUSHMASTER, the only egg-laying viperid of the New World, usually produces small clutches of 10 or fewer eggs. Coral snakes lay up to 10 eggs per clutch. All boas in Brazil, including the COMMON ANACONDA, give birth to live young. Litters range from 12 to 60.

Notes

All of the venomous snakes discussed in this section, if encountered, should be given a wide berth. Watch them only from a distance. Very few visitors to the tropics, even those that spend their days tramping through forests, are bitten by venomous snakes. Remember that their venom-delivery system is a highly evolved prey-capture strategy, and only secondarily a defensive mechanism. Venom is energetically costly to produce, and venomous snakes can bite without injecting any venom. They can also vary the amount of venom injected. Even if venom is injected, one does not necessarily receive a fatal dose. Within the same species, the toxicity of a snake's venom can vary geographically, seasonally, and from individual to individual.

The brightly colored coral snakes are rarely seen by people because of their secretive habits. Most are usually quite docile. However, if threatened, some give a frightening defensive display: they erratically snap their body back and forth, swing their head from side to side with the mouth open, and bite any object that is contacted. Although their mouths and fangs are small, their venom is very powerful. Be advised not to adhere to rules learned for hiking or camping in North America about how to distinguish, based on coloring, coral snakes from non-venomous mimic snakes. The snakes in South America don't follow the rules.

Boa personalities vary; some are docile, others are very willing to defend themselves. Boas may hiss loudly at people, draw their heads back with mouths open in a threat posture, and bite. They have large sharp teeth that can cause deep puncture wounds. Therefore, even though boas present no threat to people, keeping a respectful distance is advised.

Status

None of Brazil's vipers or coral snakes is officially considered threatened or endangered. Both the RED-TAILED BOA and the RAINBOW BOA are regulated for conservation purposes; they are both listed on CITES Appendix II. Some of the other boas may be threatened in some areas of the country by habitat destruction and by capture for the pet trade; otherwise boas seem to do well living near people and are still common in many parts of Brazil and the rest of the New World tropics.

Profiles

Red-tailed Boa, *Boa constrictor*, Plate 20b
Amazon Tree Boa, *Corallus hortulanus,* Plate 20c
Rainbow Boa, *Epicrates cenchria*, Plate 20d
Common Anaconda, *Eunectes murinus,* Plate 20e
South American Coralsnake, *Micrurus lemniscatus*, Plate 21a
Neuwied's Lancehead, *Bothrops neuwiedi*, Plate 21b
Fer-de-Lance, *Bothrops atrox*, Plate 21c
Amazon Bushmaster, *Lachesis muta*, Plate 21d

5. Amphisbaenians

Amphisbaenians, often called *worm lizards*, are specialized burrowing lizards that occur in tropical areas around the world. Of the 142 species, only 3 have legs. All worm lizards burrow, but some species also venture onto the surface, especially after heavy rains. Amphisbaenians range in size from about 10 cm (4 in) to about 80 cm (32 in). They live in diverse habitats, from extremely arid deserts to wet and humid lowland rain forests.

Natural History

Ecology and Behavior

Worm lizards burrow by driving their heads through the soil. Their bodies are well-adapted to this lifestyle: solid skull, no external ear openings, blunt head, short tail, elongated body, and, in most, no limbs. They resemble giant earthworms with scales. Amphisbaenians feed on earthworms, termites, ants, crickets, beetle larvae, and other small invertebrates.

The SPECKLED WORM LIZARD (Plate 22) is widespread in the Amazon Basin, but infrequently encountered because of its secretive habits. Your best bet of seeing one is to sift through the leaf litter after a heavy rain. If you find one, handle it carefully because these seemingly innocuous creatures can inflict painful bites with their sharp teeth and powerful jaws. When a Speckled Worm Lizard is disturbed, it often raises both its head and tail off the ground – confusing to a person and perhaps to other predators as well.

Breeding

Very little is known concerning reproduction and life history patterns in worm lizards. Like other lizards, amphisbaenians have internal fertilization. Most species lay eggs, though a few give birth to live young.

Status

The status of amphisbaenians is unknown, in large part because they are so difficult to observe. No species is included on the IUCN Red List.

Profiles

Speckled Worm Lizard, *Amphisbaena fuliginosa*, Plate 22a

6. Geckos

Geckos are fascinating organisms because, of their own volition, they have become "house lizards." The family, Gekkonidae, is spread throughout tropical and subtropical areas of the world, with about 870 species. In many regions, geckos have invaded houses and buildings, becoming ubiquitous adornments of walls and ceilings. Ignored by human residents, they move around dwellings chiefly at night, munching insects.

Brazilian geckos are fairly small lizards, usually gray or brown, with large eyes. They have thin, soft skin, usually covered with small, granular scales that produce a slightly lumpy appearance. Many have large fingers and toes with well-developed claws and broad specialized pads that allow them to cling to vertical surfaces and even upside-down on ceilings. The way geckos manage these feats has engendered a fair amount of scientific detective work. Various forces have been implicated in explaining the gecko's anti-gravity performance, from the ability of their claws to dig into tiny irregularities on man-made surfaces, to their large toes acting as suction cups, to an adhesive quality of friction. The real explanation appears to lie in the series of minuscule hair-like structures on the bottoms of the finger and toe pads, which provide attachment to walls and ceilings by something akin to surface tension – the same property that allows some insects to walk on water. Not all Brazilian geckos have these toe pads, however; for example, the toes of the AMAZON STREAK LIZARD (Plate 22) lack pads. Most adult geckos are only 5 to 10 cm (2 to 4 in) in length, tail excluded; tails can double the length. Because lizard tails frequently break off and regenerate (p. 117), their length varies tremendously; gecko tails are particularly fragile.

Natural History
Ecology and Behavior

Although most lizards are active during the day and inactive at night, many gecko species, such as the COMMON HOUSE GECKO (Plate 22) and the TURNIP-TAILED GECKO (Plate 22) are nocturnal. In natural settings, Common House Geckos are primarily ground dwellers, but, as their behavior in buildings suggests, they are also excellent climbers. It is often easy to watch these geckos forage for insects around lights at night, both in and outside of houses. Turnip-tailed Geckos are abundant in forest situations as well as in houses. When disturbed, these lizards often jump, gliding through space with the webbing between their toes expanded. In contrast, both the Amazon Streak Lizard and the AMAZON DWARF GECKO (Plate 22) are active by day. Amazon Streak Lizards, one of the most common lizards in the Amazon Basin, are often seen basking in sunny spots in the forest. The tiny Amazon Dwarf Geckos are most commonly seen in the leaf litter on the ground in forest.

Unlike most lizards, which do not vocalize, geckos at night are avid little chirpers and squeakers. They communicate with each other with loud calls – surprisingly loud for such small animals. Various species sound differently. The word "gecko" approximates the sound of calls from some of the Asian species.

Geckos feed chiefly on insects. In fact, it is their ravenous appetite for cockroaches and other insect undesirables that render them welcome house guests in many parts of the world. Geckos are *sit-and-wait* predators. Instead of wasting energy actively searching for prey that is usually highly alert and able to flee, they sit still for long periods, waiting for unsuspecting insects that venture a bit too near, then lunge, grab, and swallow. Geckos rely chiefly on their *cryptic coloration* and their ability to flee rapidly for escape from predators, which include snakes and birds during the day and snakes, owls, and bats at night. When cornered, geckos give threat displays; when seized, they give loud calls to distract predators, and they bite. Should the gecko be seized by its tail, it breaks off as a last resort, allowing the gecko time to escape, albeit tail-less. Although this action causes considerable stress to the animal, the tail usually regenerates. Some geckos when seized also secrete thick, noxious fluids from their tails; these secretions presumably discourage predators.

Breeding
Almost all geckos are egg-layers. Mating occurs after courtship, which involves a male displaying to a female by waving his tail around, followed by some mutual nosing and nibbling. Clutches usually contain only one to a few eggs, but a female may lay several clutches per year. There is no parental care; after eggs are deposited, they and the tiny geckos that hatch from them are on their own.

Status
More than 25 gecko species are listed as rare, vulnerable, threatened, or endangered, but they are almost all restricted to the Old World. None of Brazil's geckos is officially considered threatened, but the status of most is very poorly known.

Profiles
Amazon Streak Lizard, *Gonatodes humeralis*, Plate 22b
Amazon Dwarf Gecko, *Pseudogonatodes guianensis*, Plate 22c
Common House Gecko, *Hemidactylus mabouia*, Plate 22d
Turnip-tailed Gecko, *Thecadactylus rapicauda*, Plate 22e

7. Iguanas and Relatives

The Iguanidae is a large group of lizards that is considered a single family by some experts but divided into several separate families by others. For convenience's sake, we will consider all of the 750 species in this group as *iguanoids*. They are found only in the New World. Many of the lizards commonly encountered by ecotravellers, or that are on their viewing wish-lists, are members of this group. The family includes the very abundant *anolis lizards*, for example, the SLENDER ANOLE (Plate 23), GOLDENSCALE ANOLE (Plate 23), and BARK ANOLE (Plate 23); the spectacular GREEN IGUANA (Plate 23); the COLLARED TREE LIZARD (Plate 24); and the BLUE-LIPPED TREE LIZARD (Plate 24).

The iguanoids are a rich and varied group exhibiting diverse habits. Many in the family are brightly colored and have adornments such as crests, spines, or throat fans (*dewlaps*). They range in size from tiny anolis lizards, or *anoles*, only a few centimeters in total length and a few grams in weight, to Green Iguanas, which are up to 2 m (6.5 ft) long. Some species of small iguanoids (especially anoles) are very common in natural areas in Brazil and also around human habitations.

Natural History
Ecology and Behavior
You can't mistake the GREEN IGUANA. It's the large one resembling a dragon sitting in the tree near the river. They are common inhabitants of many Neotropical

rain forests, in moist areas at low to middle elevations. They are often common in town squares and city parks along the coast. These lizards spend most of their time in trees, usually along waterways, and they don't move much. When they do move it's often in slow-motion, though they can move very quickly when surprised or threatened. They are herbivores as adults, eating mainly leaves, twigs, and fruit; insects are eaten by juveniles. When threatened, an iguana sitting on a branch out over a river will drop from its perch into the water, making its escape underwater. Green Iguanas are good swimmers. During their breeding season, males establish and defend mating territories on which live one to four females.

Anoles are small, diurnal, often arboreal lizards with streamlined bodies. Many species are represented in Brazil and many are frequently encountered; others, such as those that live in the high canopy, are rarely seen. Some are ground dwellers, and others spend most of their time on tree trunks perched head toward the ground, visually searching for insect prey. Many sleep at night on leaves. Anoles are well-known for their territorial behavior. Males defend territories on which one to three females may live. In some species males with territories spend up to half of each day defending their territories from males looking to establish new territories. The defender will roam his territory, perhaps 30 sq m (325 sq ft), occasionally giving territorial advertisements – repeatedly displaying his extended throat fan, or *dewlap*, and performing *push-ups*, bobbing his head and body up and down. Trespassers that do not leave the territory are chased and even bitten. Anoles are chiefly *sit-and-wait* predators on insects and other small invertebrates. Anoles themselves are frequent prey for many birds (motmots, trogons, and others) and snakes.

The COLLARED TREE LIZARD and the BLUE-LIPPED TREE LIZARD are active by day, often found on tree trunks in the forest. They are sit-and-wait predators, and feed principally on ants. At night they sleep pressed against vines and are very difficult to see. Snakes, including vipers, are major predators on these lizards. True to its name, the Blue-lipped Tree Lizard has blue lips and mouth lining, a feature that makes it easily identifiable.

Breeding
Breeding in Green Iguanas usually occurs during the early part of the dry season. These large lizards lay clutches that average about 40 eggs. They are laid in sandy soil, in burrows that are 1 to 2 m (3.3 to 6.5 ft) long, dug by the females. After laying her clutch, a female iguana fills the burrow with dirt, giving the site a final packing down with her nose. After the young hatch, they eat the feces of adult Green Iguanas. The most plausible explanation for this odd behavior is that by eating feces, they inoculate their guts with bacteria that help in digesting cellulose from the plants they eat. Anoles are also egg-layers. Most species lay a single egg at a time, although some of the larger species lay up to 3 eggs. Anoles may produce eggs every few weeks and breed throughout the year. Tree lizards lay from 2 to 5 eggs in a clutch, often depositing them in a cluster in decaying logs.

Notes
Iguanoids are not poisonous, and they will not bite unless given no other choice. Large iguanas are hunted by local people for food. Many people say iguanas are delicious, the meat tasting like chicken.

Via interactions between the external environment and their nervous and hormonal systems, many iguanoids can change their body color. Such color changes may be adaptations that allow them to be more *cryptic*, to blend into their surroundings, and hence, to be less detectable to predators. Alterations in color throughout the day may also aid in temperature regulation. Lizards must obtain their body heat from the sun, and darker colors absorb more heat. The feat is accomplished by moving pigment granules within individual skin cells either to a central clump (causing that color to diminish) or spreading them evenly about the cell (enhancing the color). It is now thought that the stimulus to change colors arises with the physiology of the animal rather than with the color of its surroundings.

Status

GREEN IGUANAS are regulated for conservation purposes; they are listed on CITES Appendix II. Because they are hunted for meat, they are scarce in some localities. None of Brazil's other iguanoids is currently considered threatened or endangered.

Profiles

Green Iguana, *Iguana iguana*, Plate 23a
Slender Anole, *Norops fuscoauratus*, Plate 23b
Goldenscale Anole, *Norops chrysolepis,* Plate 23c
Bark Anole, *Norops ortonii*, Plate 23d
Collared Tree Lizard, *Tropidurus plica*, Plate 24a
Blue-lipped Tree Lizard, *Tropidurus umbra ochrocollaris*, Plate 24b

8. Other Lizards: Teids, Microteids, and Skinks

The family Gymnophthalmidae, often called *microteids*, is composed of about 140 species. Many of these are 10 to 15 cm (4 to 6 in) in length, including tail. Examples profiled here include the BLACK-STRIPED SHADE LIZARD (Plate 24), LARGE-SCALED SHADE LIZARD (Plate 24), and the ELEGANT EYED LIZARD (Plate 24). You'll find these lizards mostly in forest leaf litter, but they are secretive and hard to see. The Large-scaled Shade Lizard is usually found near water.

Family Teiidae, known as *teids*, are a New World group of about 105 species, distributed throughout the Americas. Most are tropical residents, inhabiting most areas below 1500 m (5000 ft) in elevation. Many species, such as the GOLDEN TEGU (Plate 25) and the AMAZON RACERUNNER (Plate 25), are diurnal sun-baskers, and are often quite abundant and conspicuous along trails, roads, beaches, and in forest clearings. Known for their alert behavior and fast movements, they are often easily spotted but difficult to approach closely. The Golden Tegu can reach a total length of more than 1 m (3.3+ ft). If you surprise one along a trail, it can startle you by making a lot of noise as it crashes through the vegetation to escape. Teids have slender bodies, angular, pointed heads and long, slender, whip-like tails (usually much longer than the body). The scales of the larger conspicuous species are very small, giving them a velvety or shiny appearance. Some teids are striped, others are striped and spotted, or irregularly blotched.

The *skinks* are a large family (Scincidae, with nearly 1100 species) of small and medium-sized lizards with a worldwide distribution. Skinks are easily recognized because they look different from other lizards, being slim-bodied with relatively short limbs, and having smooth, shiny scales that produce a satiny look. Many skinks are in the 5 to 9 cm (2 to 3.6 in) long range, not including the tail, which can easily double an adult's length.

Natural History
Ecology and Behavior

The small microteiids inhabit leaf litter in shaded areas and forage for invertebrate prey such as roaches, grasshoppers, crickets, and spiders. Teids such as the AMAZON RACERUNNER and SPIX'S KENTROPYX (Plate 25) actively search for their food, which includes just about any animal small enough to eat. Typically they forage by moving slowly along the ground, poking their noses into the leaf litter and under sticks and rocks. Although mostly terrestrial, they also climb into lower vegetation to hunt. Teids have a characteristic gait, moving jerkily forward while rapidly turning their head from side to side. The PARAGUAY CAIMAN LIZARD (Plate 25), a teid named for its caiman-like tail, is a large (total length to 1.2 m – 3.9 ft) semi-aquatic lizard that feeds almost exclusively on aquatic snails. The lizards submerge themselves in the water and walk slowly along the bottom, poking their snouts beneath the decaying leaves. When a snail is found, the lizard brings it to the surface to eat. It crushes the shell with its strong teeth, discards the shell fragments with its tongue, and then swallows the snail.

Many terrestrial skinks are found in moist habitats such as near streams and springs or under wet leaf litter. A few species are arboreal, and some are burrowers. Skinks use their limbs to walk but when the need arises for speed, they move by making rapid wriggling movements with their bodies, snake-fashion, with little leg assistance. Through evolutionary change, in fact, some species have lost limbs entirely, all movement being handled snake-fashion. Skinks are day-active lizards, and in the tropics they are most active in the morning hours; they spend the heat of midday in sheltered, insulated hiding places, such as deep beneath the leaf litter. Some skinks are sit-and-wait foragers, whereas others actively seek their food. They consume many kinds of insects, which they grab, crush with their jaws or beat against the ground, then swallow whole. Predators on Brazilian skinks include snakes, larger lizards, birds, and mammals such as coati, armadillo, and opossum. Skinks generally are not seen unless searched for. Most species are quite secretive, spending most of their time hidden under rocks, vegetation, or leaf litter. The BLACK-SPOTTED SKINK (Plate 25) is diurnal and terrestrial, and is most commonly seen in semi-open forests and forest edges, where it suns itself.

Breeding

Microteids lay very few eggs per clutch, but usually more than one clutch per year. Female LARGE-SCALED SHADE LIZARDS generally produce only 2 eggs per clutch, and female ELEGANT EYED LIZARDS lay only 1 or 2 eggs per clutch. Females of many species of Brazilian teids produce small clutches that average 3 to 5 eggs, and individuals produce two or more clutches per year. The AMAZON RACERUNNER lays 2 to 6 eggs, buried in the sand or loose soil. The GOLDEN TEGU often lays its eggs in termite nests. Nests containing up to 32 tegu eggs have been found, but these presumably represent communal nests. Skinks are either egg-layers or live-bearers. The BLACK-SPOTTED SKINK gives birth to 3 to 8 live young; the eggs are protected within the mother's body throughout development. They breed sporadically all year.

Among the teids and microteids, some species exhibit what for vertebrates is an odd method of reproduction. All individuals in these species are female. They breed by *parthenogenesis*. Females lay unfertilized eggs, which all develop as females that, barring mutations, are all genetically identical to mom. (A few species of fish and many insects also reproduce this way.) It is likely that parthenogenetic species arise when individuals of two different but closely related, sexually reproducing, "parent" species mate and, instead of having hybrid young that are sterile (a usual result, as when horses and donkeys mate to produce sterile mules), have young whose eggs result in viable females.

Notes

Many lizards, including the skinks, teids, microteids, and geckos, have a drastic predator escape mechanism: they leave their tails behind for the predator to attack and eat while they make their escape. The process is known as *tail autotomy* – "self removal." Owing to unusual anatomical features of the tail vertebrae, the tail is only tenuously attached to the rest of the body; when the animal is grasped forcefully by its tail, the tail breaks off. The shed tail then wriggles vigorously for a while, diverting a predator's attention for the instant it takes the lizard to find shelter. A new tail can grow to replace the lost one, but regeneration requires a lot of energy that could be used for growth or reproduction.

Is autotomy successful as a lifesaving tactic? Some snakes that have been dissected have had nothing but lizard tails in their stomachs. Also, a very common finding when a field biologist surveys any population of small lizards (catching as many as possible in a given area to count and examine) is that often 50% or more have regenerating tails. This indicates that tail autotomy is common and successful in preventing predation.

Status

Both the GOLDEN TEGU and the PARAGUAY CAIMAN LIZARD are regulated for conservation purposes; they are listed on CITES Appendix II. Unfortunately for these lizards, they have beautiful undersides that are highly valued for making cowboy boots, belts, and purses. For this reason, in past years large numbers of tegus and caiman lizards have been caught, killed, and exported, and the lizards are still hunted illegally. No other of Brazil's teids, microteids, or skinks is known to be threatened or endangered. As is the case for many reptiles and amphibians, however, many species have not been sufficiently monitored to determine the true status of populations.

Profiles

Black-striped Shade Lizard, *Cercosaura ocellata*, Plate 24c
Large-scaled Shade Lizard, *Alopoglossus angulatus*, Plate 24d
Elegant Eyed Lizard, *Prionodactylus argulus*, Plate 24e
Amazon Racerunner, *Ameiva ameiva*, Plate 25a
Spix's Kentropyx, *Kentropyx calcarata*, Plate 25b
Golden Tegu, *Tupinambus teguixin*, Plate 25c
Paraguay Caiman Lizard, *Dracaena paraguayensis*, Plate 25d
Black-spotted Skink, *Mabuya nigropunctata*, Plate 25e

Environmental Close-up 4
Endemism and High Species Diversity: Why Brazil?

An organism is *endemic* to a place when it is found only in that place. But the size or type of place referred to is variable: a given species of frog, say, may be endemic to the Western Hemisphere, to a single continent such as South America, to a small mountainous region of Brazil, or to a speck of an island off Brazil's coast.

A species' history dictates its present distribution. When it's confined to a certain or small area, the reason is that:

1 There are one or more barriers to stop further spread (an ocean, a mountain range, a thousand kilometers or miles of tropical rainforest in the way);
2 The species evolved only recently and has not yet had time to spread; or
3 The species evolved long ago, spread long ago, and now has become extinct over all but a remnant part of its prior range.

A history of isolation also matters: the longer a group of animals and plants is isolated from their close relatives, the more time they have to evolve by themselves and to change into new, different, and unique groups. The best examples are on islands. Some islands once were attached to mainland areas but continental drift and/or changing sea levels led to their isolation in the middle of the ocean; other islands arose suddenly via volcanic activity beneath the seas. Take the island of Madagascar. Once attached to Africa and India, the organisms stranded on its shores when it became an island had probably 100 million years in isolation to develop into the highly endemic fauna and flora we see today. It's thought that about 80% of the island's plants and animals are endemic – half the bird species, about 800 butterflies, 8000 flowering plants, and essentially all the mammals and reptiles. Most of the species of lemurs of the world – small, primitive but cute primates – occur only on Madagascar, and an entire nature tourism industry has been built there around the idea of endemism: if you want to see wild lemurs, you must go there. Other examples of islands with high concentrations of endemic animals abound: Indonesia, where about 15% of the world's bird species occur, a quarter of them endemic; Papua New Guinea, where half the birds are endemic; the Philippines, where half the mammals are endemic; and the Galápagos Islands, where 42% of the resident bird species occur nowhere else in the world.

Recent biological surveys of Brazil show that this country supports a surprising number of species (some of which are endemic but most of which are not). Brazil is, in fact, considered one of 10 or so "mega-diversity" countries in the world. It has more species of animals and plants than almost any other country in the world (Table 1, below). Brazil's high biodiversity is due to several factors:

1 Virtually all groups of animals and plants, such as lizards, insects, trees, and birds, show a pattern of species number related to latitude. The higher latitudes (the north and south poles are at 90 degrees latitude and the equator is at zero degrees latitude) have few species and as you sample at lower and lower latitudes toward the equator the number of species increases. This pattern is called a *latitudinal gradient in species diversity* and is likely caused by an increasing availability of sunlight energy, photosynthetic rates and food availability as you move toward the equator. Brazil straddles the equator, where the world's greatest species diversity occurs.
2 Owing to Brazil's great size, it has a multitude of habitat types, and also some highly isolated habitats that act as "biological islands" (for example, inland highland areas surrounded by lower-lying regions – such as forest habitats around the isolated highlands of Rondônia, Mato Grosso and the Pico da Neblina on the southern Venezuela border). These isolated areas support large numbers of endemics, and the wide range of habitat types, espe-

cially at different altitudes, makes room for lots of species, endemic and non-endemic, to exist in a relatively small area. The forest of Brazil's Atlantic coast is isolated from other forests by extensive savannah and grasslands. Most of Brazil's endemic and endangered species are from this narrow strip of fast-disappearing habitat.

3   The Amazon area of Brazil is part of the most species-rich area in the world. But to understand the area's current diversity, we have to look at its geological history. Over the last 100,000 years or so there apparently have been ten-thousand-year cycles of drought and heavy rainfall. These cycles may have changed some parts of this immense forest region by contraction and expansion of the geographical ranges of different species of animals and plants. Some species less tolerant to climatic changes may have become isolated, other species more tolerant may have been widespread. Because of the Andes Mountains and the shape of the continental coastline, rainfall across the Amazon Basin is not, and probably never has been, uniform. Even today, in the middle of a high rainfall part of the cycle, small pockets of forest with 3 to 4 m (10 to 13 ft) of annual rainfall can be surrounded by forest areas with less than 1.5 m (5 ft) of annual rainfall. During the most severe drought epochs, annual rainfall totals were probably cut by a third or more. Some or maybe even many species of plants and animals became isolated from their kin in contracting ranges. Isolated for tens of thousands of years, these populations of plants and animals changed (evolved) into different species and no longer were capable of breeding with members of their former species in other isolated areas. When the drought cycle shifted back to high rainfall, the isolated populations were again able to expand and reclaim areas in which they could now occur. Eventually the expansion of these species brought them into contact again with their long-separated kin. At the zones of contact, where the expanding species populations met, some of these populations had been separated so long that they could no longer breed together. The new species formed during the period of isolation spread and mixed, thus greatly enriching the diversity of species. Scientists are struggling with interpretations of data that show conflicting timing and positioning of these climatic events, and there is little agreement on the details. However, most scientists

Table 1. Number of species of selected animal groups in Brazil (8,547,403 sq km, 3.3 million sq miles, in area) and in the USA (9.4 million sq km, 3.6 million sq miles), the number of those that are endemic to Brazil, and a comparison to the worldwide number of species.

Group	Total no. of species in USA	Total no. of species in Brazil	Number of species endemic to Brazil (% endemic)	Approximate no. of species worldwide (% in Brazil)
Mammals	428	524	131 (25)	4629 (11)
Birds	768	1622	198 (12)	9040 (18)
Reptiles	261	468	172 (37)	7000 (7)
Amphibians	194	517	294 (57)	4700 (11)
Butterflies	678	3680	267 (7)	24,000 (15)
Tiger Beetles	111	184	122 (66)	2250 (8)

will agree that the forests of Brazil have not been static, and that changes, subtle and not so subtle, have occurred over the last several hundred thousand years that have affected the present distribution of species and helped increase their number.

Chapter 9

Birds

- Introduction
- General Characteristics and Classification of Birds
- Features of Tropical Birds
- Seeing Birds in Brazil
- Family Profiles
    1. Pelicans, Cormorants, and Anhingas
    2. Terns
    3. Herons and Egrets
    4. Marsh and Stream Birds
    5. Ducks
    6. Shorebirds
    7. Tinamous and Rhea
    8. Guans and Trumpeter
    9. Vultures
    10. Hawks, Eagles, and Kites
    11. Falcons and Osprey
    12. Pigeons and Doves
    13. Parrots
    14. Cuckoos and Anis
    15. Owls
    16. Nightjars and Potoos
    17. Swifts and Swallows
    18. Hummingbirds
    19. Trogons
    20. Kingfishers

Introduction

By far the most common vertebrate animals you will see on a visit to Brazil are birds. Unlike many other terrestrial vertebrates, birds are most often active during the day, visually conspicuous and usually quite vocal as they pursue their daily activities. But why are birds so much more conspicuous than other vertebrates? The reason goes to the essential nature of birds: they fly. The ability to fly is one of nature's premier anti-predator escape mechanisms, and animals that can fly well are released from the danger of being stalked by a large proportion of the predators in an area. Most mortality from predators among tropical birds comes while they are eggs or helpless young in the nest. Once they reach adulthood, their mortality rate by predation falls to very low levels. By being able to escape most predation, they are released from much of the tyranny of natural selection that places a premium on camouflage, unobtrusiveness and shyness. Thus they can be both reasonably conspicuous in their behavior and also reasonably certain of daily survival. Most flightless land vertebrates, tied by gravity to moving in or over the ground or on plants, are easy prey unless they are quiet, concealed, and careful or, alternatively, very large or fierce; many smaller ones, in fact, have evolved special defense mechanisms, such as poisons or nocturnal behavior.

Not only are birds among the easiest animals to watch, but they are among the most beautiful. Experiences with Brazil's birds will almost certainly provide some of your trip's most memorable naturalistic moments. Your first view of a flock of huge and noisy Blue-and-yellow Macaws flying over the forest tops in the Amazon or a flock of thousands of Whistling Ducks in the Pantanal will be highlights you will want to share with everyone.

General Characteristics and Classification of Birds

Birds have one trait that they share with no other vertebrates – they have *feathers*. Feathers evidently evolved from reptilian scales, and they, together with most everything else in and on the bird body, serve to lighten the load and provide the power to make flight possible. The feathers provide an ultra light but durable protective covering. The hollow bones of the skeleton provide a light but sturdy framework to attach powerful flight muscles, especially on the breast. The teeth are replaced by an expanded part of the digestive tract, the *gizzard*, which along with the reduction and rearrangement of many internal organs makes the center of gravity more aerodynamically positioned. A four-chambered heart together with warm-bloodedness and a super-efficient lung system make possible an accelerated use of energy to sustain the physiologically expensive costs of flight. Finally, the forelimbs have evolved to become sublime wings, with spoilers to overcome wing-tip air turbulence, ailerons for maneuvering, and such a host of detailed adaptations for flight control that engineers at the Boeing Company can only marvel with envy.

Birds began evolving from reptiles during the Jurassic Period of the Mesozoic Era, perhaps 150 million years ago, and then there was an explosive development of new species during the last 50 million years or so. The development of flight is the key factor behind birds' evolution, their historical spread throughout the globe, and their current ecological success. Flight, as mentioned above, is a fantastic predator evasion technique, but it also permits birds to move over long distances in search of particular foods or habitats, and its development opened up for vertebrate exploration and exploitation an entirely new and vast theater of operations – the atmosphere.

At first glance, birds appear to be highly variable beasts, ranging in size from 135-kg (300-lb) Ostriches to 4-kg (9-lb) eagles to 3-g (a tenth of an ounce) hummingbirds. However, when compared with other types of vertebrates, birds are remarkably standardized physically. The reason is that, whereas mammals or reptiles can be quite diverse in form and still function as mammals or reptiles (think how different in form are lizards, snakes, and turtles), if birds are going to fly, the physics of aerodynamics narrowly dictates which shape and form will most efficiently stay in the air. Thus, all flying birds have a similar gestalt, or body plan.

(The flying mammals, bats, also follow these dictates.) Only birds such as Ostriches, which lost their ability to fly, developed very unbird-like body shapes.

Bird classification is one of those areas of science that continually undergoes revision. Currently more than 9000 separate species are recognized worldwide, and they are placed in 2040 genera. These genera are grouped into 170 families, which in turn are grouped into 28 to 30 orders, depending on whose classification scheme you want to follow. The orders are roughly divided into two major groups, the usually small perching species such as robins, sparrows and jays (Passerines, or "dickie birds") and all the rest (Non-passerines), which includes everything from penguins, ducks and herons to parrots, kingfishers and hawks. For purposes in this book we divide birds into various groups: those that are unrelated but occur together in broad habitat types; those that are similar in appearance and might be confused easily; and finally, those that are closely related (and thus often found in similar habitats and also often similar in appearance).

Features of Tropical Birds

The first thing to know about tropical birds is that they are exceedingly diverse. There are many more species of birds in the tropics than in temperate or arctic regions (see Close-up, p. 117). For instance, somewhat fewer than 700 bird species occur regularly in North America north of Mexico, and about 3300 species occur in the Neotropics (Central and South America). But more than 1600 species are found in Brazil – nearly half of the species of the Neotropics and nearly 17% of all the species in the world!

Tropical birds, like their temperate zone brethren, eat insects, seeds, nectar, fruits and, for the predaceous species, meat. A big difference, however, is the degree of specialization in tropical species. In temperate areas fruit is such a temporary resource that few species can afford to make their living as confirmed *frugivores*, but in many tropical areas fruit is available throughout much of the year, so bird species have evolved bills, digestive systems and behavior that make them experts on finding and eating fruits. Similarly, species that eat insects (*insectivores*), seeds (*granivores*), flower nectar (*nectarivores*) and, to some degree, even the meat-eaters (*carnivores*), have high degrees of specialization.

Mating systems of birds show a pattern of inequality between the sexes. Females generally have the most power to choose mates. Each male is thus left with the task of convincing these picky females that he and he alone is the most appropriate one to father her young. A male can scream this message with louder or prettier songs, longer and more colorful tail feathers, or a combination of sounds, colors and behavioral antics that increase his chances of convincing the female of his gene superiority.

Mating systems range from single territorial males with one female (*monogamy*) to one male having numerous female mates (*polygyny*) and even some cases of a female having numerous male mates (*polyandry*). Among tropical birds, monogamy apparently is the most common form of mating, although we now know that there is a lot of extracurricular sneaking around. Monogamous mating is perhaps made most obvious when the males sing on the boundaries of their territories to declare to all the world, but especially to other males of the same species, "Stay out. This is my home and you are not welcome to tarry here."

Polygyny is less common but often made obvious by the many bizarre behaviors associated with this mating system. Among polygynous species, males often have to congregate together, each strutting his gene superiority so that a female can compare them side by side and make her choice – a kind of beauty contest. This type of congregated male courting is called a *lec* (often spelled *lek*, the original Swedish form). Females in this type of society are usually single working mothers because the father, after mating, has no further contact with his mate or his eventual offspring. Polyandry is the rarest type of mating system, and it is practiced primarily by only three groups of birds in the Brazilian Amazon and Pantanal: the rheas, tinamous and jacanas. In these cases males guard nests and females dump eggs in each of several males' nests after mating with them.

Breeding seasons in the tropics tend to be longer than in temperate areas but are usually closely tied to the wet season and the abundance of food associated with it, especially heavy concentrations of insect life and ripening fruit. In Brazil, birds in the Pantanal breed primarily from November to April. In the Amazon the breeding season is more ambiguous, with some species breeding almost every month of the year, but the majority of species nest during the early rainy season, in November to January in the south and from February to May in the north. One notable aspect of bird breeding in the tropics that has long puzzled biologists is that clutches of the small land birds (Passerines) are usually small, most species typically laying only two eggs per nest. Similar birds that breed in temperate zone areas usually have clutches of three to five eggs. Possible explanations are that (1) small broods attract fewer nest predators; (2) because such a high percentage of nests in the tropics are destroyed by predators, it is not worth putting too much energy and effort into any one nest; and (3) with the increased hours of daylight during the summer breeding season in northern areas, temperate zone birds have more time each day to gather enough food for extra nestlings.

Finally, tropical birds include some of the most gorgeously attired birds in the world. Many have bright, flashy colors and vivid plumage patterns, with some of Brazil's parrots, toucans, trogons, cotingas, and tanagers, claiming top honors. Why so many tropical birds possess highly colored plumages is unknown, but it may be at least partially explained by the presence of a large number of species in which males are under natural selection pressures by female mating choices to have gaudy plumage. Also, although people take more notice of birds with bright, striking plumage colors and patterns, we should point out that, actually, most species in the tropics are dull-colored and visually unremarkable.

Seeing Birds in Brazil

We chose for illustration and profiling below 288 species that are among Brazil's most frequently seen birds, or, in a few cases, rare species that are representative of Brazil's Amazon and Pantanal regions. The best way to spot these birds is to follow three easy steps: (1) Look for them at the correct time. You can see birds at any time of the day, but your best chance of seeing them is when they are most active and singing frequently, during early morning and late afternoon. Some species of owls, potoos and nightjars are strictly nocturnal, and the best way to see them is to follow their calls at night and find them in the beam of your flashlight. (2) Be quiet as you walk along trails or roads, and stop periodically to look around carefully. Not all birds are noisy, and some, even brightly colored ones, can be quite inconspicuous when they are skulking through thick grass or directly above you in the forest canopy. Trogons, for instance, beautiful medium-sized birds with green backs and bright red or yellow bellies, are notoriously difficult to see among branches and leaves. Sometimes sitting or standing quietly, especially along a stream, is the best way to see otherwise shy denizens. (3) BRING BINOC-ULARS on your trip. You would be surprised at the number of people who visit tropical areas with the purpose of viewing wildlife and don't bother to bring binoculars. They need not be an expensive pair, but binoculars are essential to bird viewing. If you become excited about wildlife in the middle of your trip and have no binoculars, many eco-lodges rent them out by the day.

A surprise to many people during their first trip, especially to a habitat like the Amazonian rainforest, is that they do not immediately see or hear hordes of birds upon entering a trail. During large portions of the day, in fact, these habi-tats are mainly quiet, with few birds noticeably active. The birds are there, but many are inconspicuous – small brownish birds near to the ground, and greenish, brownish, or grayish birds in the tops of the vegetation. A frequent, at first dis-combobulating experience, is that you will be walking along a trail, seeing few birds, and then, suddenly, a *mixed-species foraging flock* with many species swooshes into view, filling the bushes and trees around you at all levels – some hopping along the ground, some moving through the brush, some clinging to tree trunks, others in the canopy – more birds than you can easily count or iden-tify – and then, just as suddenly, the flock is gone, moved on in its meandering path through the forest. If the trail system is extensive, sometimes you can move quietly ahead of the flock and let it pass by you again and again. This works espe-cially well for low-moving flocks of antbirds, ovenbirds, woodcreepers, and fly-catchers. High-moving flocks, with birds such as tanagers and cotingas, are much harder to follow and are often best seen from canopy towers built at several jungle lodges throughout the country.

In the Pantanal, the dry season (June to September) causes much of this vast marsh to dry up. The birdlife, especially the water birds, concentrates more and more as the available water becomes restricted. By the end of the dry season spec-tacular numbers of ducks, cormorants, herons, and ibises vie cheek-to-jowl for the little remaining water and the food swimming in it. During the morning, flock after flock leaves the relative safety of isolated nocturnal roosting sites and moves out to the scarce feeding areas. In the late afternoon these flocks again darken the sky as they return to their roosts. During the rainy season, the birds are not rarer, just more spread out.

It would be a shame to leave Brazil without seeing at least some of its spec-tacular birds, such as rheas, macaws, toucans, trogons, and tanagers. If you have trouble locating such birds, be sure and let people around you know of your inter-est – tourguides, resort employees, park personnel. Everyone involved in Brazil's tourist industry wants to share the country's richness of natural beauty, and they can either tell you the best places to go for particular birds or send you to some-one who knows.

Family Profiles

I. Pelicans, Cormorants, and Anhingas

Pelicans (9 species worldwide), *cormorants* (33 species worldwide), and *anhingas* (4 species worldwide) are all families in the order Pelecaniformes. However, only a single species of each of these three families occurs in Brazil. Pelicans are large heavy-bodied seabirds, and, owing to their big, saggy throat pouches, are perhaps among the most recognizable of birds. They have long wings, long necks, large heads, and long bills from which hang the flexible, fish-catching, pouches. The BROWN PELICAN is restricted to coastal ocean waters, mangrove estuaries and the mouth of the Amazon River. Cormorants are medium-sized birds, usually black, with short legs, long tails, and longish bills with hooked tips. The NEOTROPIC CORMORANT (Plate 26) is ubiquitous and easily seen on almost any river, lake or coastal estuary throughout the country. At times, especially in the Pantanal during the dry season, thousands of Neotropic Cormorants concentrate on the receding ponds to feed on the dense fish populations. Most cormorant species breed and roost together in often enormous colonies. Their numbers are directly related to the fish supply in rivers, lakes, marshes, and the ocean.

The ANHINGA (Plate 26) is similar in overall form to cormorants but their bills are long and thin with a sharp point. They have long tails and very long, thin necks, and when they occasionally soar to great heights with tail and wings spread, they resemble soaring hawks or eagles with long necks. Males are all blackish and females and immatures have buffy heads and necks. Anhingas occur both in coastal mangroves and along rivers and lakes in the Amazon and Pantanal.

Natural History
Ecology and Behavior
These pelican relatives all feed mainly on fish, but they catch the fish in quite different ways. The BROWN PELICAN dives into the ocean from heights of 3 to 5 m (10 to 16 ft). NEOTROPIC CORMORANTS and ANHINGAS dive from the surface of lakes, rivers, lagoons, and coastal saltwater areas to pursue fish underwater. Using their large webbed feet for propulsion, cormorants catch fish (and occasionally crustaceans like crabs) in their hooked bills. They often feed in large groups, especially when fish are concentrated in a small area. They roost and nest together in large colonies, usually on island peaks or in the tops of tall trees, and they move between roosting and feeding areas in large "V"-shaped flocks. Anhingas are solitary and spear prey underwater on the tips of their sharp bills. After feeding underwater, cormorants and Anhingas commonly roost for long periods with their wings outstretched to dry.

Breeding
The NEOTROPIC CORMORANT nests in large colonies either on isolated islands or in groves of trees surrounded by water, both of which are relatively predator-free. ANHINGAS nest in trees but usually singly or in loose association with heron and ibis colonies. All of these pelican relatives are monogamous, and both mates share in nest-building, incubation and feeding young. In some groups, such as the pelicans, the male gathers sticks and stones for the nest, but the female actually constructs the nest. Individuals keep the same mate for several seasons and tend to return to the same site to nest. Neotropic Cormorants begin breeding when they are 3 or 4 years old. Two to 4 eggs are incubated for about 4 weeks, and

the young fledge 5 to 8 weeks after hatching. The helpless young of both cormorants and Anhingas push their head and bill deep into the gullet of the returning parent birds to get at the food awaiting them there.

Notes

Anhingas are also known as *darters*, the name derived from the way the birds underwater swiftly thrust their necks forward to spear fish on the points of their bills. Because they often swim with bodies submerged and only long necks and heads above water, they are also often called *snake-birds*. Cormorants have been used for centuries by people in China, Japan and Central Europe as fishing birds. A ring is placed around the cormorant's neck so that it cannot swallow its catch. Then, usually on a long leash, it is permitted to swim underwater to pursue fish. When the bird returns to the surface, it is reeled in, usually with an unswallowable fish clenched in its bill.

Status

None of the species of pelican relatives of Brazil is considered threatened or endangered. However, North American populations of the BROWN PELICAN were severely affected in the 1960s and 1970s by insecticides concentrated in the fish they ate. Control of pollution and protection of nesting sites have restored many of these North American populations.

Profiles

Neotropic Cormorant, *Phalacrocorax brasilianus*, Plate 26a
Anhinga, *Anhinga anhinga*, Plate 26b

2. Terns

On the open ocean, over coastal estuaries, and along Amazonian rivers, *terns* are often present and obvious. They feed on fish and on aquatic and marine invertebrates, and they are often mesmerizing as they dive, swoop and soar in search of their food or in noisy encounters with each other. At rest, terns perch on sandy beaches and mudflats almost always in flocks of single or mixed species.

Terns are members of the Order Charadriiformes, which also includes the shorebirds (Plate 33). The *gulls* and terns are in the family Laridae (88 species worldwide, 22 in Brazil). Terns are smaller, more streamlined forms of gulls. On the coast of Brazil, several species of terns winter or are transient in migration. In the Amazon and Pantanal, however, only two species are regularly present. The LARGE-BILLED TERN (Plate 26) and the smaller YELLOW-BILLED TERN (Plate 26) are restricted to the large rivers and lakes, where they are permanent residents. They are noisy and obvious as they fly along a river or roost on isolated sand islands. The BLACK SKIMMER (Plate 26) is closely related to the gulls and terns but is placed in its own family, the Rynchopidae (3 species worldwide, 1 in Brazil). It is the most bizarre and memorable of all these gull-like species, with its all-black body and huge red bill, the lower part of which extends beyond the tip of the upper part. The skimmer is usually seen roosting on sand bars in the rivers of the Amazonian region. In flight its long, arched wings are distinctive.

Natural History

Ecology and Behavior

Terns feed primarily on fish, which they catch by hovering high over the water and then diving. Terns on rivers of the Amazonian region are sparsely encountered, probably because the fish are generally not concentrated. Skimmers use their peculiar flight and even more peculiar bill to pluck fish and large invertebrates from the water's surface. They fly low over the water with their blade-like bills open and the lower mandible skimming the surface. When they strike a small crustacean or fish, they quickly close the bill and catch it. Frequently they skim a line in the water and then turn to skim back along the same line.

Breeding
As with most seabirds, these terns and the skimmer all breed in noisy colonies, usually on an isolated island or remote sand spit. Generally they are monogamous, male and female sharing brooding and feeding the young. Males often present food to prospective mates in a ritual feeding that apparently provides clues to a female of the male's ability to catch quality prey and to be a provider for their offspring. Because terns nest on the ground, they have little protection from predators, although they will vigorously dive bomb, peck and defecate on intruders into their nesting colony, human or otherwise. They lay up to 4 eggs, which are incubated for about 30 days. Young are fed when they push their bills down into their parents' throats, in effect forcing the parents to regurgitate food stored in their crops – enlargements of the top part of the esophagus. The low river islands on which the skimmer and the two inland tern species nest are frequently flooded, and drowning takes a large proportion of the young.

Notes
Because their nesting colonies are so obvious and concentrated, tern eggs are often collected by humans for food. In some parts of the world, large colonies of these fast-flying birds roost or nest in the vicinity of airports. A single bird sucked into a jet engine can cause severe damage, especially during a take-off or landing.

Status
None of these species is threatened in Amazonian and Pantanal portions of Brazil, but habitat destruction, pollution and human interference on nesting areas make some populations vulnerable. The limited ranges and specialized habitats for the LARGE-BILLED TERN and YELLOW-BILLED TERN make these species more sensitive to increasing water contamination and inroads from growing human populations along Amazonian rivers.

Profiles
Large-billed Tern, *Phaetusa simplex*, Plate 26c
Yellow-billed Tern, *Sterna superciliaris*, Plate 26d
Black Skimmer, *Rynchops niger*, Plate 26e

3. Herons and Egrets

Herons and *egrets* are beautiful medium to large-sized wading birds that enjoy broad distributions throughout temperate and tropical regions around the world. Herons, egrets and the more elusive *bitterns* constitute the heron family, Ardeidae, which includes about 62 species. Twenty-one species occur in Brazil, most of which breed there. Herons frequent all sorts of aquatic habitats: along rivers and streams, in marshes and swamps, and along lake and ocean shorelines. The difference between what is called an egret and what is called a heron is arbitrary and inconsistent. Generally, however, the term egret is reserved for species that are all white. Most herons and egrets are easy to identify. They are the tallish birds standing upright and still in shallow water or along the shore, staring intently into the water. They have slender bodies, long necks (always folded back in a flattened "S" in flight and sometimes when perched or resting, producing a short-necked, hunched appearance), long, pointed bills, and long legs with long toes. Brazilian species range in height from 0.3 to 1.3 m (1 to 4 ft). Most are attired in soft shades of gray, brown, blue, or green, and black or all white. Close up, many are exquisitely marked with small colored patches of facial skin or broad areas of spots or streaks; the *tiger-herons*, in particular, are strongly barred or streaked. During the breeding season both sexes of some species acquire long back and head plumes, and leg and bill color become brighter. The bizarre and poorly known BOAT-BILLED HERON (Plate 27) is sometimes placed as a single species in its own family, Cochleariidae; it occurs from western Mexico south, throughout the Amazon, to northern Argentina.

Natural History
Ecology and Behavior

Until recently, the CATTLE EGRET (Plate 27) was confined to the Old World, where it made its living following herds of large mammals such as elephant and buffalo. How it got to the New World is intriguing. Whereas many of the animals that have recently crossed oceans and spread rapidly into new continents have done so as a result of people's intentional or unintentional machinations, these egrets did it on their own. Apparently the first ones to reach the New World were from Africa. Perhaps blown off-course by a storm, they first landed in northern South America in about 1877. Finding the New World to its liking, during the next decades the species spread far and wide, finding abundant food where tropical forests were cleared for cattle grazing. Cattle Egrets have now colonized much of northern South America, Central America, all the major Caribbean islands, and much of the United States. The Cattle Egret is now common in the Pantanal and cleared areas of the Amazon. Unlike all the other herons and egrets, it rarely enters the water but, instead, in upland areas, eats insects flushed by the feet of large grazing mammals such as cows. The other herons are mainly sit-and-wait hunters along water edges. Some species wait with infinite patience for prey to move and then strike out in a flash with their bill to grab the fish, frog or crab. The SNOWY EGRET (Plate 27), however, often staggers around in the shallows like a drunken sailor trying to scare up prey that are then easy targets for its bill. The North American GREEN HERON, a close relative of the STRIATED HERON (Plate 28), is known to use bait, such as bread stolen from a picnic area, to swish in the water and attract fish to within striking range of its bill. The CAPPED HERON (Plate 28), RUFESCENT TIGER-HERON (Plate 28), BOAT-BILLED HERON, with its grotesquely large bill, and the similar appearing BLACK-CROWNED NIGHT-HERON (Plate 27) are denizens of vegetated edges of forest swamps and small streams. They are often so well camouflaged that you can pass close by them in your canoe without noticing them. At daybreak and again just before sunset they are more likely to be out in the open. The Boat-billed Heron and Black-crowned Night-Heron, however, are nocturnal and your best chance of seeing them is by shining a flashlight in the tangled foliage along waterways at night or finding a small group in a protected roost within dense thickets during the day. The Boat-billed Heron uses its huge bill to grope in the water for frogs, fish, and shrimp.

Breeding

Most herons are social birds, roosting and breeding in colonies, often several species together. Some, however, like the tiger-herons, are predominantly solitary. Herons are known for their often elaborate courtship displays and ceremonies, which continue through pair-formation and nest-building. Generally the female constructs the nest from sticks presented to her by the male. The nests are in trees, reeds or occasionally on the ground. Both sexes incubate the 3 to 7 eggs for 16 to 30 days, and both feed the young for another 35 to 50 days until they fledge.

Herons and egrets often lay more eggs than the number of chicks they can successfully feed. This seems contrary to our usual view of nature, which we regard as finely tuned through natural selection so that behaviors avoid waste. The likely answer to this puzzle is that this behavior allows a pair to raise the maximum number of offspring every year even if food levels are unpredictable from year to year. Females lay eggs one or two days apart, and start incubating with the first egg. Chicks hatch out at the same intervals, and so the young in a single nest are of different ages and quite different sizes. The largest chicks receive the most food, probably because they can more easily attract the adults and get to the food they regurgitate. The larger chicks on occasion will also kill their smaller siblings (*siblicide*), especially if food is scarce. If there is sufficient food, the next biggest chicks will also be able to eat often enough to survive. In years of super-abundant food, even the smallest chicks will be able to eat enough. Thus, laying more eggs than can be reared as chicks most years may be to insure that many chicks are raised in the years of abundance.

Notes

All herons have a distinctive comb on the flattened middle toe of each foot. They use it to groom themselves and spread bits of specialized feathers, called *powder down*, throughout their body surface. Powder down is found in only a very few other birds in the world; its function appears to be to help clean the large body feathers when they become full of fish scales and grime.

Status

Some of Brazil's herons and egrets are fairly rare, but they are not considered threatened species because they are common in other parts of their ranges, outside the country.

Profiles

Boat-billed Heron, *Cochlearius cochlearius*, Plate 27a
Black-crowned Night-Heron, *Nycticorax nycticorax*, Plate 27b
Snowy Egret, *Egretta thula*, Plate 27c
Cattle Egret, *Bubulcus ibis*, Plate 27d
Great Egret, *Ardea alba*, Plate 27e

Cocoi Heron, *Ardea cocoi*, Plate 28a
Whistling Heron, *Syrigma sibilatrix*, Plate 28b
Rufescent Tiger-heron, *Tigrisoma lineatum*, Plate 28c
Capped Heron, *Pilherodius pileatus*, Plate 28d
Striated Heron, *Butorides striatus*, Plate 28e
Little Blue Heron, *Egretta caerulea*, Plate 28f

4. Marsh and Stream Birds

Marsh and *stream birds* are a collection of unrelated species that share a habitat of standing and running water surrounded by grasses, bushes, trees, and other relatively thick vegetation. They do not rely heavily on flight but rather swim in the water or walk on and through vegetation near the water. They tend to be shy and retiring, and they often slink away from danger before a predator (or an approaching canoe with tourists) has a chance to see them.

Storks (family Ciconiidae; 17 species worldwide, 3 of which occur in Brazil) are heron-like birds usually placed together in the same order as herons. They differ by flying with the neck outstretched and often soaring high in the sky on broad wings. Most species of storks are predominantly white with black patches on the wings. The *ibises* are related to storks, and their curved bills, long neck and long legs make them easy to identify. Ibises fly with the head and neck stretched forward and with a slow, flapping flight that is alternated with short glides. Together with the spoonbills, they form the family Threskiornithidae (32 species worldwide, 8 in Brazil). Four ibis species and the ROSEATE SPOONBILL (Plate 30) are relatively easy to see in the Pantanal marshes. The *jacanas* (jha-SAH-nahs) form a worldwide family, Jacanidae, with 8 species. Only one species, the WATTLED JACANA (Plate 31), is found in Brazil, and it is common in marshes of the Amazon and Pantanal. It has incredibly long toes for walking on floating vegetation without sinking. Female jacanas are larger than males, and immatures are lighter and streaked. The *rails*, family Rallidae (140 species worldwide, 28 in Brazil), are often shy and difficult-to-see inhabitants of swampy areas. The large GRAY-NECKED WOOD-RAIL (Plate 31) is common in marshy forested areas throughout tropical Brazil and is the rail you are most likely to encounter. In marshy areas of the Amazon and Pantanal, beautiful duck-like relatives of rails called *gallinules* (Plate 31) can be common. The SUNBITTERN (Plate 31) belongs to the family Eurypigidae, which is represented in the New World by only this one species; it occurs from southern Mexico to southern Bolivia. In Brazil it is found throughout the tropics. When a Sunbittern's wings are spread, the bars and spots on its wings create a striking "sunburst" pattern. The SUNGREBE (Plate 32) is in the family Heliornithidae, and it is not at all related to grebes, such as the LEAST GREBE, but rather is a close cousin to the Sunbittern. It is a small duck-like species that swims under the vegetation hanging low over forested streams. There are two other similar species in the family, one each in tropical Africa and Asia, where they are called *finfoots*. The HOATZIN (Plate 31) is one of the most intriguing and unusual species you will see in the flooded forests and marshes of Amazonian Brazil. There is only one species in its family, Opisthocomidae (closely related to cuckoos). It is restricted to the upper Amazon and its tributaries. This turkey-sized bird looks for all the world like some prehistoric dinosaur with feathers. The HORNED SCREAMER and SOUTHERN SCREAMER (both Plate 30) belong to a uniquely South American family, Anhimidae, which is related to ducks and which has only one additional species in it. These immense birds looks like plump black and white herons on the ground but like an eagle with long legs when they fly. The Horned Screamer has a deep liquid call that carries for miles. It is found throughout the Amazon while the Southern Screamer occurs only in the southern Amazon and Pantanal. The LEAST GREBE (Plate 32), in the Family Podicipedidae (20 species worldwide, 4 in Brazil), is a small duck-like species found in

Brazil only in marshy lakes. Its small size and thin bill immediately separate it from any of the true ducks that also occur on these marshes.

Natural History
Ecology and Behavior
Storks and ibises use their long bills to probe for food in shallow water, grass and mud. They eat small mammals, frogs, and insects. The ROSEATE SPOONBILL uses its special bill to swish back and forth in the water and catch small swimming prey. Rails and gallinules feed on a wide variety of animal and plant material. The GRAY-NECKED WOOD-RAIL is more often heard than seen in flooded forest and thick river-edge vegetation. At dawn and dusk several pairs will sing in a chorus together. Their raucous, almost maniacal laughing call, "to-tooky, to-tooky," gradually tapers off until only one individual is left singing. Occasionally this rail emerges briefly into open areas in the early morning or late afternoon. The WATTLED JACANA is common and easy to see in flooded grasslands and open marshy areas. It uses its immensely long toes to walk on floating vegetation and lily pads. Sharp spurs on the wing are used for fighting other jacanas and against predators. The SUNBITTERN lives along forested streams and flooded forest where it walks along searching for insects, crabs, frogs, crayfish, and small fish. The SUNGREBE swims in among the roots and overhanging leaves of thick vegetation along lakes and streams, where it feeds on frogs, worms, crustaceans, and insects. It runs across the surface of the water and flies low to escape predation, and your best view will probably be as it skitters away from your canoe into the dense vegetation. HOATZINS are usually in loose flocks of 5 to 10 birds in bushes along the edges of slow-moving streams or forested lakes. They announce their displeasure at your presence with hisses and croaks just before they weakly flap their wings to fly to the next branch over the water. They eat only leaves and have a digestive system similar to a cow's that uses fermentation to digest otherwise indigestible plant parts. You will most likely see screamers in grassy marshes as they fly up noisily. Screamers graze on marsh vegetation, and also perch frequently in the tops of trees to make their loud calls. They are strong fliers and can soar to great heights. The LEAST GREBE feeds in marshy ponds and lakes by diving after fish and invertebrates. It can adjust its buoyancy and simply sink out of sight, or it can leap forward out of the water for a more athletic dive.

Breeding
Storks and ibises are monogamous and most nest colonially in trees or in reeds near the water. Nests are made of sticks and contain up to 5 eggs. Chicks take food regurgitated from the adults' mouth and throat. Rails build their nests in moist areas either in reeds or grass. Gallinules and grebes construct large nests on small islands of floating vegetation. Egg numbers per nest are often high and range from 2 to 16 for gallinules and 2 to 8 for grebes. Jacanas are unusual in that they are often *polyandrous* (one female mates with numerous males). Males each defend small territories from other males, but each female has a larger territory that encompasses 2 to 4 male territories. Males build nests of floating, compacted aquatic vegetation, into which the female deposits 3 or 4 eggs. The male incubates the nest for 21 to 24 days and then cares for the chicks by himself. Jacanas also are able to move their young chicks in case of flooding or danger by holding them under their closed wings and running to safety. The SUNBITTERN is well-known for its spectacular courtship and threat display in which the tail and wings are spread to reveal a sunburst pattern of yellows, blacks and rust colors. It makes

a rounded cup-like nest in a tree or bush, and apparently both mates incubate and feed the 2 to 3 young. The SUNGREBE makes a flat nest of sticks and reeds, often on branches of dead trees low over the water. The 2 to 5 eggs are incubated by both parents. The male has a unique adaptation to protect the fledged young. In case of danger, the small chicks climb into pouches in the skin under the wings and the male dives underwater to escape.

The HOATZIN'S 2 to 4 eggs are incubated for 28 days by both parents in a stick nest placed several meters out over the water in a tree branch. Some observations suggest that groups of up to 6 adults may be involved cooperatively in incubating and feeding the young. When in danger, the young jump from the nest into the water and swim underwater to then clamber up another bush. To facilitate their tree-climbing ability they have an extra, opposable, digit on the naked wing that they use like a hand. This extra digit is lost as the chick matures and its feathers and wings develop so it can fly. Grebes are monogamous and build a floating nest of aquatic material. This way a rise or fall in the water level of the marshy lake will not affect the safety of the 2 to 6 eggs or young. When both adults are away from the nest at the same time, they cover the eggs or chicks with vegetation to keep them warm and camouflaged from potential enemies. Both mates are equally involved in incubation and guarding the striped chicks, which soon leave the nest. The young continue to be dependent on the adults for 3 to 4 weeks as they swim around the pond and hide in vegetation at night. Screamers, like their relatives, geese and swans, mate for life. Their nests are in shallow water and made of sticks and vegetation. The 5 eggs are incubated for 40 days and screamers are fully grown in about 4 months.

Notes

The term "skinny as a rail" refers originally not to a railroad track but to the bird. Rails are extremely flattened from side to side so they can fit into narrow spaces – thus the saying. Hoatzins are large birds with few chances to escape hunters, yet virtually no indigenous peoples use hoatzins for food (although their eggs are often eaten). The reason is that among the plants and leaves they eat is one common aroid plant (*Montrichardia*; p. 28) that grows along the edges of Amazonian-region lakes. It has a thick woody stem and heart-shaped leaves. The leaves contain chemicals that when eaten are absorbed by the muscles and convey a smell and taste not unlike a sewer. Even a starving person would likely turn down a serving of Hoatzin.

Status

None of these marsh species is considered threatened in Brazil, but the HORNED SCREAMER populations in Amazonia have fallen dramatically in the last two decades, probably owing to hunting pressure.

Profiles

Jabiru Stork, *Jabiru mycteria*, Plate 29a
Maguari Stork, *Ciconia maguari*, Plate 29b
Green Ibis, *Mesembrinis cayennensis*, Plate 29c
Plumbeous Ibis, *Harpiprion caerulescens*, Plate 29d
Buff-necked Ibis, *Theristicus caudutus hyperorius*, Plate 29e
Bare-faced Ibis, *Phimosus infuscatus*, Plate 29f
Limpkin, *Aramus guarauna*, Plate 30a
Roseate Spoonbill, *Ajaia ajaja*, Plate 30b

Horned Screamer, *Anhima cornuta*, Plate 30c
Southern Screamer, *Chauna torquata*, Plate 30d

Wattled Jacana, *Jacana jacana*, Plate 31a
Sunbittern, *Eurypyga helias*, Plate 31b
Hoatzin, *Opisthocomus hoazin*, Plate 31c
Purple Gallinule, *Porphyrio martinicus*, Plate 31d
Gray-necked Wood-rail, *Aramides cajanea*, Plate 31e
Least Grebe, *Tachybaptus (Podiceps) dominicus*, Plate 32d
Sungrebe, *Heliornis fulica*, Plate 32e

5. Ducks

Members of the Family Anatidae, which includes about 150 species of *ducks, geese,* and *swans,* are all associated with water. They are distributed throughout the world in habitats ranging from open sea to high mountain lakes. Although abundant and diverse in temperate regions, only a relatively few species migrate to or reside in the tropics. Ducks vary quite a bit in size and coloring, but most share the same major traits: duck bills, webbed toes, short-tails, and long, slim necks. Plumage color and patterning vary, but there is a preponderance within the group of grays and browns, and black and white, although many species have at least small patches of brighter colors. In some species male and female look alike, but in others there is a high degree of difference between the sexes. About 24 species occur in Brazil.

Natural History
Ecology and Behavior
Ducks eat aquatic plants, small fish and invertebrates, but some, such as the BLACK-BELLIED WHISTLING DUCK (Plate 32), other whistling ducks, and MUSCOVY DUCK (Plate 32), regularly graze on grasses, moist upland vegetation and terrestrial insects. More typical is the dabbling feeding behavior of the BRAZILIAN DUCK (Plate 32), which dips its bill into the water while swimming. Sometimes it will tip its rear end into the air trying to reach a bit deeper into the water for a morsel, but this species does not dive underwater.

Breeding
Most ducks nest on the ground in protective vegetation near their feeding areas. However, the MUSCOVY DUCK and whistling ducks nest in tree cavities often more than 15 m (50 ft) above the ground. Typically, duck nests are lined with downy feathers that the female plucks from her breast. In most species of ducks the female alone performs the duties of dealing with nesting and caring for the young. In larger species, such as geese and swans, the pair typically mates for life, and both parents are more equally involved in raising the young. The young hatch feathered and able to run within a few minutes (*precocial*); they can swim and feed themselves soon after. The parents' main role is to guard them against predators and teach them how to find food.

Notes
Ducks, geese, and swans have been objects of people's attention since ancient times, chiefly as a food source. These birds typically have tasty flesh, are fairly large and thus economical to hunt, and usually easier and less dangerous to catch than many other animals, particularly large mammals. Owing to their frequent

use as food, several wild ducks and geese have been domesticated for thousands of years; Brazil's native MUSCOVY DUCK, in fact, in its domesticated form is a common farmyard inhabitant in several parts of the world. Wild ducks also adjust well to the proximity of people, to the point of taking food from them – a practice that surviving artworks show has been occurring for at least 2000 years. Hunting ducks and geese for sport is also a long-practiced tradition. As a consequence of these long interactions between ducks and people, and the research on these animals stimulated by their use in agriculture and sport, a large amount of scientific information has been collected on the group; many of the ducks and geese are among the most well-known of birds. The close association between ducks and people has even led to a long contractual agreement between certain individual ducks and the Walt Disney Company.

Status

The populations of all the species profiled here have been affected to some degree by hunting pressures. The MUSCOVY DUCK has suffered a reduction of its populations throughout the Neotropics. When these ducks were more common, local hunters would tether a female to a tree and then kill males that came a-courting; with this method, up to 50 males could be lured to their deaths in a single day. The other species are still relatively common in their appropriate habitats. The only duck in Brazil that is considered endangered, however, is the BRAZILIAN MERGANSER, which occurs now in only a few isolated areas of northeastern Argentina and southern Brazil.

Profiles

Muscovy Duck, *Cairina moschata*, Plate 32a
Brazilian Duck, *Amazonetta brasiliensis*, Plate 32b
Black-bellied Whistling Duck, *Dendrocygna autumnalis*, Plate 32c

6. Shorebirds

Spotting *shorebirds* is usually a priority only for visitors to the Neotropics who are rabid birdwatchers. The reason for the lack of interest is that many shorebirds in Brazil are visitors from their nesting grounds in North America. Of course, being mostly brown and lacking in reasonably distinguishing characteristics may have something to do with it as well. Nevertheless, it can be a treat watching these fellow travellers in their tropical wintering areas as they forage in meadows, along streams, on mudflats and on sandy ocean beaches. When a large flock, often of several species, rises rapidly from a sand bar, it is fun to follow its progress until out of sight. The resident species of shorebirds in Brazil are intriguing for their combination of similarities to and frequently jarring differences from their migratory cousins. Shorebirds are traditionally placed along with the gulls in the avian Order Charadriiformes. They are global in distribution, and we profile species from three families found in Brazil. Most shorebirds, regardless of size, have a characteristic "look." They are usually drably colored birds (especially during the nonbreeding months), darker above, lighter below, with long, thin legs for wading through wet meadows, mud, sand, or surf. Depending on feeding habits, bill length varies from short to very long.

The *sandpipers*, Family Scolopacidae, are a worldwide group of approximately 85 species. About 26 species occur in Brazil, some being quite abundant during much of the year, especially along the coast. All but two of these sandpipers are migrants that nest in the Arctic of North America. However, some nonbreeding individuals of these migrants, such as the SPOTTED SANDPIPER (Plate 33), can be present in Brazil any month of the year. Most of the Brazilian sandpipers range from 15 to 48 cm (6 to 19 in) long. They are generally slender birds with straight or curved bills of various lengths and live on sandy beaches or mudflats along rivers, lakes and the coast.

Plovers, in the Family Charadriidae, are small to medium-sized (15 to 30 cm, 6 to 12 in) shorebirds with short tails and straight, relatively stout, dove-like bills. They are mostly shades of gray and brown but some have bold color patterns such as a broad white or dark band on the head or chest. Worldwide, there are more than 60 species. Ten species occur regularly in Brazil, 3 of which are resident nonmigratory species in the Amazon and Pantanal regions.

The family of the *stilts*, Recurvirostridae, has 10 species worldwide but only one species in Brazil. The BLACK-NECKED STILT (Plate 33) congregates in flocks of 5 to 100 in shallow ponds and muddy areas. The flocks are so noisy you often hear them before you can see them.

Natural History
Ecology and Behavior
Even though shorebirds are all excellent fliers, they spend a lot of time on the ground foraging and resting. When pursued, they often prefer running to flying away. Sandpipers tend to use their bills to probe into the soil or mud for small invertebrates, and different shapes and lengths of bills help the various sandpiper species find different prey even when they are feeding side by side. The plovers use their bills to take prey or even seeds off the soil surface but never probe. Stilts take advantage of their long legs and bill to probe mud in deeper water, sometimes feeding with their heads entirely underwater. Many shorebirds, especially among the sandpipers, establish winter feeding territories along stretches of beach; they use the area for feeding for a few hours or for the day, defending it aggressively from other members of their species. Many of the sandpipers and plovers are gregarious birds, often seen in large groups, especially when they are travelling. Several species make long migrations over large expanses of open ocean.

Breeding
Most shorebird nests are simply small depressions in the ground in which eggs are placed; some of these are in sand, on gravel or on a grass hummock. Seldom do the adults prepare the nest with more than a few pebbles. In almost all these shorebird families monogamy is the rule, and both parents incubate the eggs. Shorebird young are precocial and able to run and feed themselves soon after hatching. Parents usually stay with the young to guard them until they can fly, 3 to 5 weeks after hatching. Adults of many ground-nesting species, such as these shorebirds, protect their nests and young by performing a "broken wing" display. At the approach of a predator, the adult runs in front of the danger, calling, and dragging one of its wings on the ground as if it is severely injured. The predator sees an easy meal and follows after the adult, which is able to keep just out of the striking range of the predator and leads it away from the young hidden in the nest or in the grass. If this fails, species like stilts fly close to the predator and hassle it until it leaves.

Notes

The manner in which flocks of thousands of birds, particularly shorebirds, fly in such closely regimented order, executing abrupt maneuvers with precise coordination, such as when all individuals turn together in a split second in the same direction, has puzzled biologists and engendered some research. The questions include: What is the stimulus for the flock to turn – is it one individual within the flock, a "leader," from which all the others take their "orders" and follow into turns? Or is it some stimulus from outside the flock that all members respond to in the same way? And how are the turns coordinated? Everything from "thought transference" to electromagnetic communication among the flock members has been advanced as an explanation. After studying films of DUNLIN, a North American and Eurasian sandpiper, flying and turning in large flocks, one biologist has suggested that the method birds within these flocks use to coordinate their turns is similar to how the people in a chorus-line know the precise moment to raise their legs in sequence or how "the wave" in a sports stadium is coordinated. That is, one bird, perhaps one that has detected some danger, like a predatory falcon, starts a turn, and the other birds, seeing the start of the flock's turning, can then anticipate when it is their turn to make the turn – the result being a quick wave of turning coursing through the flock.

Status

None of the shorebirds of Brazil is threatened or endangered. However, a major goal for conservation of shorebirds is the need to preserve critical migratory stopover points – pieces of habitat, sometimes fairly small, that hundreds of thousands of shorebirds settle into mid-way during their long migrations to stock up on food. These *staging areas* are vital for shorebird populations, and several such areas likely exist in Brazil. These very sites, however, are also often threatened by development and pollution.

Profiles

Black-necked Stilt, *Himantopus mexicanus*, Plate 33a
Spotted Sandpiper, *Actitis macularia*, Plate 33b
Solitary Sandpiper, *Tringa solitaria*, Plate 33c
Pied Lapwing, *Vanellus cayanus*, Plate 33d
Southern Lapwing, *Vanellus chilensis*, Plate 33e

7. Tinamous and Rhea

The *tinamous* are an interesting group of secretive but very vocal chicken-like birds that are occasionally seen walking on forest trails. However, they represent an ancient group of birds more closely related to ostriches and *rheas* than chickens. The family, Tinamidae, with about 45 species, is confined in its distribution to the Neotropics, from Mexico to southern Chile and Argentina; 24 species occur in Brazil, from coastal dry forest and grasslands to Amazon rainforest, where most of the species live.

Tinamous are medium-sized birds, 23 to 45 cm (9 to 18 in) long, chunky-bodied, with fairly long necks, small heads, and slender bills. They have short legs and very short tails. The back part of a tinamou's body sometimes appears higher than it should be, a consequence of a dense concentration of rump feathers. Tinamous are attired in understated, protective colors – browns, grays, and olives; often the plumage is marked with dark spots or bars. Male and female look alike, with females being a little larger than males. Tinamous are found mainly in primary and secondary forests of the Amazon, and your encounter is most likely to be by ear rather than by eye. The UNDULATED TINAMOU (Plate 34) makes one of the most common sounds of secondary forest in the Amazon and Pantanal regions of Brazil. The call, two low whistles followed by a longer note slurred upwards, is ubiquitous all day long. If you have patience and can stand still for 10 to 20 minutes, you can mimic the whistle and sometimes call in an individual close enough to see it. The slightest movement, however, will send it scurrying away. During the drier seasons, when dry leaves accumulate on the forest floor, you can often detect these birds by the crackling sounds of their feet disturbing the leaves.

Only two species of *rheas* exist (Family Rheidae), and they are both limited to southern South America. These ostrich equivalents are open country species. In Brazil the GREATER RHEA (Plate 30) occurs in the drier grasslands on the margins of the Pantanal region (an excellent place to see them is along the road from Cuiabá to Poconé in the northern Pantanal). Long-legged, long-necked and flightless, they can at times be very shy, and run quickly from danger. At other times, if they do not perceive you as a threat, they will stand still and stare at you for long periods. The Greater Rhea, more than a meter and a half tall (5 ft) and up to 34 kg (75 lb), is the largest bird in Brazil.

Natural History
Ecology and Behavior
Tinamous are among the most terrestrial of birds, foraging, sleeping and breeding on the ground. They are very poor at flying, doing so only when alarmed by a predator, and then merely for a short distance. They are better at running along the ground, the mode of location called *cursorial*. The tinamou diet consists chiefly of fruit and seeds, but they will also eat insects and other invertebrates. Some species use their feet to scratch and dig at the soil to feed on roots and termites. Tinamous often avoid predators by standing still or squatting, easily blending in with the surrounding vegetation. Sometimes they will slowly and quietly, almost ghost-like, walk away from danger. If you get too close to a tinamou, it will fly upwards in a sudden burst of loud wing-beating and fly to a new hiding spot in the undergrowth. In the early evening, one of the most delightful parts of the Neotropical forest is the serenade of melodious whistles that make tinamous such a characteristic part of these forest habitats.

Rheas are usually found in small groups of 5 to 15. They feed mainly on grass, roots, and seeds, but they will also eat lizards and small rodents. They regularly graze among deer or cattle.

Breeding
Tinamous are *polyandrous* (one female mates with several males), like their Ostrich relatives. Each male has a nest on the ground, which he guards and broods. Females wander around choosing a series of males to mate with and dumping a few eggs in each nest. Perhaps this is a way females have of not putting all their eggs in one basket. One nest can have up to 12 eggs, deposited by numerous females. Of course each male also mates with numerous females as they make their rounds, so this mating system is *polygynous* as well as polyandrous. The nest itself is seldom more than an indentation in the forest floor, often hidden in a thicket or at the base of a tree.

Each rhea male defends a large territory, and he tries to attract a harem of females to mate with him. As a nest, he makes a hollow in the ground, and he alone is in charge of incubating the eggs. Each of the females can lay up to 15 eggs, and a male with a harem of 6 to 8 females can have a nest full of 90 or more eggs. Incubation lasts 6 weeks, and the young stay with the father, who guards them for an additional 5 months.

Notes

Outside of protected areas, all tinamous are hunted extensively for food. Tinamou meat is considered tender and tasty, albeit a bit strange-looking; it has been described variously as greenish and transparent. Many species of tinamous have eggs that are large, with an extremely glossy surface. Their colors are also bright, from purple, green and greenish yellow to rusty. Actually seeing them, you have to wonder how these bright eggs can ever escape the attention of the many nest predators that prowl the forest floor. One hypothesis is that in the nest these shiny eggs act like mirrors, reflecting the surrounding vegetation so that they become virtually invisible. Rheas are hunted often and are considered a source of delicious meat.

Status

The tinamous' camouflage coloring and secretive behavior must serve the birds well because, although hunted for food, many species of tinamous apparently maintain healthy populations even in populated countryside. However, in Brazil two species are listed as threatened or endangered. Only one of them, the LESSER NOTHURA, occurs in the southern part of the Pantanal. It is a tiny species (18 cm, 7 in, long) that lives in grasslands and is suffering from loss of its habitat from cattle grazing and grass fires. The GREATER RHEA population in Brazil has been severely reduced through hunting and habitat destruction, but because the species is still common in parts of Bolivia and Argentina, it is not yet considered threatened.

Profiles

Undulated Tinamou, *Crypturellus undulatus*, Plate 34e
Greater Rhea, *Rhea americana*, Plate 30e

8. Guans and Trumpeter

Large, pheasant-like birds strutting about the tropical forest floor or fluttering about in trees and running along high branches, are bound to be members of the guan family, Cracidae. This family, related to pheasants and chickens and distributed from southern Texas to Argentina, contains more than 40 species of *guans*, *chachalacas*, and *curassows*. Twenty-two species are found in Brazil.

Brazilian guans as a group range in length from 56 to 91 cm (20 to 36 in) – as large as small turkeys – and weigh up to 4 kg (9 lb). They have long legs and long, heavy toes. Many have conspicuous crests. The colors of their bodies are generally drab – gray, brown, olive, or black and white; some appear glossy in the right light. They typically have small patches of bright coloring such as yellow, red, or orange on parts of their bills, cheeks, or on a hanging throat sac called a *dewlap*. The SPECKLED CHACHALACA (see p. 328 for description) is by far the most common species of this family in Amazonian Brazil. In the Pantanal it is replaced by the similar CHACO CHACHALACA (Plate 34). At dawn a flock of these pheasant-sized birds will give a chorus of their loud and raucous calls, that, with some imagination, can be rendered as a rapid "chachalaca" repeated over and over.

Then another flock will answer from across the river and the signaling will go back and forth for a half-hour or until it's time to start feeding, usually from the tops of trees in secondary forest or river edges. If you have the great fortune to see a RAZOR-BILLED CURASSOW in the Amazon or a BARE-FACED CURASSOW (Plate 34) in the Pantanal, count yourself among the lucky. It will be an indication that you are in pristine habitat, as these large, and unfortunately delicious, birds are easily hunted and thus rare in many areas. Listen for the series of very low-pitched humming or "booming" noises of the males early in the morning and on moonlit nights.

The GRAY-WINGED TRUMPETER (Plate 34) is similar in appearance to the guans, but it is related instead to the rails and cranes. It is placed in its own small family of three species, Psophiidae (all three are found in Brazil). True to its name, this species has a loud deep call that is not unlike an untuned trumpet. When disturbed, *trumpeters* growl like a dog and thump their body with closed wings. Where they are hunted, trumpeters are very shy, and you will be lucky to see this tall bird slinking away into the undergrowth of primary forest. As it is commonly kept as a pet by local people, you are most likely to see it running around a village bullying the chickens. Trumpeter sexes are similar, both weighing about 1 kg (2.2 lb).

Natural History
Ecology and Behavior
Guans are birds of the forest, and the larger the species, the more it is limited to denser forest. All of the guans roost in trees at night, and some, such as the chachalacas and *piping-guans*, rarely ever descend to the ground. They prefer to eat fruits, seeds, and insects from the tree-tops. The larger guans spend more time on the forest floor, eating fallen fruits and insects, but they often feed in the tree tops as well. The curassows spend all but their roosting time at night on the ground. The smaller species are often in flocks, but the larger species are more solitary. Trumpeters also feed on the forest floor, scratching with their feet to stir up large insects and looking for fallen fruits. They are almost always in flocks of 5 to 20 or more individuals moving elegantly along the forest floor, but they do fly to the tree-tops to escape danger and roost at night.

Breeding
The guans are all monogamous breeders in which the sexes share reproductive duties. The nest is a simple open construction of twigs and leaves placed in a tree or shrub several meters from the ground. Two to 4 eggs are incubated for 22 to 34 days. The young leave the nest soon after hatching to hide in surrounding vegetation, where, unlike most species with precocial young, they are fed by the parents. Within a few days the young can fly short distances. The breeding biology of trumpeters is very poorly known. Nests have been reported from large holes in trees and the top of a palm tree. The female apparently incubates the 6 to 8 eggs alone. The black young are covered with streaks and bars of rusty and cinnamon, and they follow one or both parents away from the nest soon after hatching.

Notes
Curassows are frequently kept as pets in local villages, but they are shy birds in captivity. The trumpeters kept as pets, however, quickly become attached to the owner's home and poultry. They take on the mantle of dominant boss and protector. They readily chase dogs and other wild predators from chickens, and even

unfamiliar humans can expect to be challenged with a growl from these birds, which think they are German Shepherds. They are surprisingly affectionate pets, and if you can get close enough to one to scratch it gently on the back of the head, it will follow you for the rest of the day.

Status

A variety of factors converge to assure that the guans will remain a problem group into the foreseeable future. They are chiefly birds of the forests at a time when Neotropical forests are increasingly being cleared. They are desirable game birds, hunted by local people for food. In fact, as soon as new roads penetrate virgin forests in Central and South America, one of the first chores of settlers is to shoot curassows for their dinners. Unfortunately, curassows reproduce slowly, raising only small broods each year. Exacerbating the problem, their nests are often placed low enough in trees and vegetation to make them vulnerable to a variety of predators, including people. In the face of these unrelenting pressures on their populations, guans are among the birds thought most likely to survive in the future only in protected areas, such as national parks. Three Brazil guan species are listed as threatened or endangered: RED-BILLED CURASSOW, BLACK-FRONTED PIPING-GUAN (both CITES Appendix I listed), and CHESTNUT-BELLIED GUAN.

Profiles

Chaco Chachalaca, *Ortalis canicollis*, Plate 34a
Spix's Guan, *Penelope jacquacu*, Plate 34b
Gray-winged Trumpeter, *Psophia crepitans*, 34c
Blue-throated Piping-Guan, *Pipile cumanensis*, Plate 34d
Bare-faced Curassow, *Crax fasciolata*, Plate 34f

9. Vultures

Birds at the very pinnacle of their profession, eating dead animals, *vultures* are highly conspicuous and among Brazil's most frequently seen birds both in rural areas and in towns and cities. That they feast on rotting flesh does not reduce the majesty of these large, soaring birds as they circle for hours over fields and forest. They are generally black or brown, with hooked bills and curious, unfeathered heads whose bare skin is often richly colored in red, yellow, or orange. Male and female vultures look alike, but males are slightly larger than females.

The family of American vultures, Cathartidae, has only seven species, with representatives from Canada to southern Argentina. Five species occur regularly in Brazil.

Natural History
Ecology and Behavior

Vultures are carrion eaters of the first order. Most soar during the day in groups looking for and, in the case of some species, smelling for food. They can cover many miles daily in their search for dead and rotting bodies and garbage. Apparently their bills and feet are not strong enough to dismember fresh meat. With their super eyesight, fine-tuned sense of smell, and ability to cover so much ground each day searching, vultures are nature's most efficient garbage collectors. The bare skin of their heads and large nostrils on the bill help to avoid problems of rotting gore accumulating on their heads and interfering with seeing, hearing and breathing.

KING (Plate 35), GREATER (Plate 35) and LESSER YELLOW-HEADED VULTURES are usually seen in pairs or solitarily, but the other two species are more social, roosting and foraging in groups of various sizes. BLACK VULTURES (Plate 35), in particular, often congregate in large numbers at feeding places, and it is common to find a flock of them at any village dump. At small to medium-sized carcasses, there is a definite pecking order among the vultures: Black Vultures are dominant to TURKEY VULTURES (Plate 35), and can chase them away; several Black Vultures can even chase away a King Vulture, which is the bigger bird. However, in an area with plenty of food, all three species may feed together in temporary harmony. When threatened, vultures may spit up partially digested carrion, a strong defense against harassment if ever there was one.

Black and Turkey Vultures roost communally, the two species often together. A common observation has been that once an individual finds a food source, other vultures arrive very rapidly to share the carcass. Biologists strongly suspect that the group roosting and feeding behavior of these birds are related, and that the former increases each individual's food-finding efficiency. In other words, a communal roost serves as an information center for finding food.

Breeding
Vultures are monogamous breeders. Both sexes incubate the 1 to 3 eggs, which are placed on the ground in protected places or on the floor of a cave or tree cavity. Eggs are incubated for 32 to 58 days. Both sexes feed the young regurgitated carrion for 2 to 5 months until they can fly. Nest predation is very rare, and given the long length of time the apparently helpless nestlings are exposed to danger, the best explanation is that the stench of the carrion and decaying animal flesh around the nest and chicks keep potential predators away.

Notes
Being such large and conspicuous birds, and being carrion-eaters associated with death, guaranteed that vultures would figure prominently in the art and culture of most civilizations. The vultures of Egypt and Old World mythology, however, are actually feather-challenged eagles and only distantly related to the superficially similar New World vultures. Recent comparative studies of DNA suggest that the New World Vultures are more closely related to storks than to hawks and eagles.

Status
None of the vultures that occur in Brazil is considered rare or threatened.

Profiles
Turkey Vulture, *Cathartes aura*, Plate 35a
Black Vulture, *Coragyps atratus*, Plate 35b
King Vulture, *Sarcoramphus papa*, Plate 35c
Greater Yellow-headed Vulture, *Cathartes melambrotus*, Plate 35d

10. Hawks, Eagles, and Kites

The raptor family, Accipitridae, is an immense group that worldwide includes about 200 species of *hawks*, *eagles*, and *kites* (46 in Brazil). Species in this family vary considerably in size and in patterns of their generally subdued color schemes, but all are similar in overall form – we know them when we see them. They are fierce-looking birds with strong feet, hooked, sharp claws, or *talons*, and strongly hooked bills. The plumages of the two sexes are usually similar, but females are larger than males, in some species extremely so. Juvenile raptors often spend several years in subadult plumages that differ in pattern and brightness from the adults.

Natural History
Ecology and Behavior

Although many raptors are common birds, typically they spread themselves out thinly over large areas, as is the case for all *top predators* (a predator at the pinnacle of the food chain and thus having too few prey available to support large populations of the predator). Some large eagles that feed on monkeys or sloths, such as the HARPY EAGLE (Plate 38), may need a territory of 1000 sq km (385 sq miles) or more to ensure sufficient food for itself and its nestlings. Most species have developed unique hunting techniques to increase efficiency of prey capture. Among the kites, for instance, the AMERICAN SWALLOW-TAILED KITE (Plate 36) soars over forest canopies and open areas searching for reptiles, especially snakes, sunning themselves in the open. The kite swoops down on a reptile and carries it off to a perch to devour. The SNAIL KITE (Plate 36) has a peculiarly long, narrow and curved bill that enables it to specialize on giant snails that inhabit extensive marshy areas, such as the Pantanal. With this bill the kite can easily slip past the otherwise protective door (*operculum*) that the snail closes across the opening of the shell to protect itself. The bill then extracts the juicy body of the snail like some specialized escargot fork. The DOUBLE-TOOTHED KITE (Plate 36) has an unusual association with monkey troops, and you are most likely to see this kite near active primates. As the monkeys jump from branch to branch, they often scare large insects out of hiding. Before these panicked insects can reach refuge, the kite quickly grabs them as they land. Large grasshoppers and katydids are among the most common prey items taken this way by these kites.

Among the hawks, The ROADSIDE HAWK (Plate 38) is a generalist, and eats everything from small birds and mammals to insects and even an occasional lizard or snake. Forest clearings and scrub edges are actually beneficial for this hawk because it has little competition there and these man-made habitats make the type of prey it prefers more common. The CRANE HAWK (Plate 36) is also a generalist in the types of prey it takes, but it uses its long legs to scramble along branches and open vegetation and then reach deep into tree cavities and bromeliads to pluck out sleeping prey, such as bats and frogs.

Breeding

Many raptors are territorial, a solitary individual or a breeding pair defending an area for feeding and, during the breeding season, for reproduction. Displays that advertise a territory and that also may be used in courtship consist of spectacular aerial twists, loops, and other acrobatic maneuvers. Hawk, eagle, and kite nests in general are constructed of sticks that both sexes place in a tree or on a rocky ledge. Some nests are lined with leaves. Usually only the female incubates the 1 to 6 eggs for about a month. The male hunts prey for the female while she sits on the eggs, and after the first chicks hatch out, he continues to give prey to the female, which she then tears up to give in turn to the chicks. When the chicks are a little bigger and the demand for food rises, both mates hunt and feed the chicks directly. The young can fly at 28 to 120 days, bigger species taking longer to fledge than the smaller species.

Notes

Large, predatory raptors have doubtless always attracted people's attention, respect, and awe. Wherever eagles occur, they are chronicled in the history of civilizations. Early Anglo-Saxons were known to hang an eagle on the gate of any city they conquered. Some North American Indian tribes and also Australian Aboriginal peoples deified large hawks or eagles. Several states have used likenesses of eagles as national symbols, among them Turkey, Austria, Germany, Poland, Russia, and Mexico. Eagles are popular symbols on regal coats of arms and one of their kind, a fish-eater, was chosen as the emblem of the USA (although, as most USA schoolchildren know, Benjamin Franklin would have preferred that symbol to be the Wild Turkey.)

Status

Several of Brazil's hawks and eagles are considered threatened or endangered, such as the HARPY EAGLE (CITES Appendix I listed) and CRESTED EAGLE (CITES Appendix II), both of which were formerly much more common in Brazil. However, many of these large raptors enjoy extensive distributions external to the country, ranging from Mexico to northern or central South America, and are more numerous in other regions. The WHITE-NECKED HAWK of Brazil's Atlantic coastal forests is also considered threatened. However, a few hawks adapt well to people's habitat alterations. A case in point is the common ROADSIDE HAWK. It prefers open habitats and, especially, roadsides. It has expanded its range and numbers in Brazil with deforestation and road-building in areas that previously were large tracts of inaccessible closed forest. Conservation measures aimed at raptors are bound to be difficult to formulate and enforce because the birds are often persecuted for a number of reasons (hunting, pet and feather trade, ranchers protecting livestock) and they roam very large areas. Also, some breed and winter on different continents, and thus need to be protected in all parts of their ranges, including along migration routes. Further complicating population assessments and conservation proposals, there are still plenty of Neotropical raptor species about which very little is known. For example, for the approximately 80 species of raptors that breed primarily in Central and South America (excluding the vultures), breeding behavior has not been described for 27 species and nests are unknown for 19 species. The typical prey taken by 6 species is unknown.

Profiles

Crane Hawk, *Geranospiza caerulescens*, Plate 36a
American Swallow-tailed Kite, *Elanoides forficatus*, Plate 36b
Double-toothed Kite, *Harpagus bidentatus*, Plate 36c
Snail Kite, *Rostrhamus sociabilis*, Plate 36d
Plumbeous Kite, *Ictinia plumbea*, Plate 36e
Black-collared Hawk, *Busarellus nigricollis*, Plate 37d
Savanna Hawk, *Heterospizias meridionalis*, Plate 37e
Roadside Hawk, *Buteo magnirostris*, Plate 38a
Great Black Hawk, *Buteogallus urubutinga*, Plate 38b
Harpy Eagle, *Harpia harpyja*, Plate 38c
Ornate Hawk-eagle, *Spizaetus ornatus*, Plate 38d

11. Falcons and Osprey

Closely related to the hawks, eagles and kites, the *falcons* and their allies, the *caracaras*, are placed in their own family, Falconidae. The family has about 60 species worldwide, 16 in Brazil. Externally they look like kites and other hawks. The main differences are found in subtle but consistent divergences in internal structures of the skeleton that indicate separate evolutionary branches.

The OSPREY (Plate 38), or Fishing Eagle, occurs worldwide and is the only species in its family, Pandionidae. Its large size, white and black color pattern, peculiarly bowed wing profile in flight, and its obligatory association with water – coastal estuaries to Amazonian rivers – make it easy to recognize. Its loud whistles are frequent, especially when a neighboring Osprey invades its home space. Although it is common throughout Brazil, it has never been recorded breeding in South America. The population is a migratory and non-breeding one, even though many individuals are present all months of the year.

Natural History
Ecology and Behavior
Typical falcons are best known for their remarkable eyesight and fast, aerial pursuit and capture of moving prey such as flying birds. The PEREGRINE FALCON, which migrates through Brazil, is considered to be the fastest bird in the world, achieving more than 192 kph (120 mph) in a steep stoop on prey. For a prey item to be able to avoid or escape this speed of attack seems impossible, yet many if not most potential prey do escape. The success rate of attack is low, and the falcon must often try numerous times before finally catching something to eat or to feed to its young. The hunting behavior of falcons has, over evolutionary time, shaped the behavior of their prey animals. Falcons hit perched or flying birds with their talons, stunning the prey and sometimes killing it outright. An individual bird caught unawares has little chance of escaping the rapid, acrobatic falcons. But most birds are very wary, and birds in groups have two defenses. First, each individual in a group benefits because the group, with so many eyes and ears, is more likely to spot a falcon at a distance than is a lone individual, thus providing all in the group opportunities to watch the predator as it approaches and so evade it. This sort of anti-predation advantage may be why some animals stay in groups. Second, some flocks of small birds, such as starlings, which usually fly in loose formations, immediately tighten their formation upon detecting a flying falcon. The effect is to decrease the distance between each bird, so much so that a falcon flying into the group at a fast speed and trying to take an individual risks injuring itself – the "block" of starlings is almost a solid wall of bird; the close formation also makes a single victim more difficult to target. Biologists believe that the flock tightens when a falcon is detected because the behavior reduces the likelihood of an attack.

As suggested by its name, one of the most typical of the falcons profiled here, the BAT FALCON (Plate 37), hunts at dusk for early-flying bats. During the day it goes after swallows and other birds, but often it also takes large flying insects. The caracaras are all scavengers and nest robbers. The BLACK CARACARA (Plate 39) is especially fond of raiding dense nesting colonies of Yellow-rumped Caciques for eggs and nestlings. The amount of bare skin on the side of the face of a species is often a reflection of how much scavenging it does. Like the vultures, fewer face feathers on caracaras makes accumulation of gore and blood less likely and the head easier to clean. The LAUGHING FALCON (Plate 39) is a snake specialist and the *forest-falcons* are almost entirely bird predators. One of the easiest ways to see the elusive forest-falcons is to squeak or kiss the back of your hand loudly when you hear one calling nearby. This sound mimics the distress calls of small birds – a call to supper for the forest-falcon.

The OSPREY is the quintessential fisherman. It hovers over the water until a fish rises close enough to the surface. Then the Osprey plunges, sometimes all but the upstretched wings underwater, to grab the fish in its extremely long and sharp talons. The soles of its feet are rough to better hold slippery fish. After emerging from the water and violently shaking itself to rid the feathers of water, it turns the fish head-forward and flies to a nearby dead tree to feast on its bounty.

Breeding

Falcons nest in vegetation, in tree and rock cavities, or on a ledge. Some make stick nests, but others make no obvious nest preparation. Incubation of the eggs takes 25 to 35 days and in most species is performed only by the female. (In caracaras both sexes participate in incubation.) The male feeds the female until the chicks hatch, and then both sexes feed the chicks. The nestlings fledge after 25 to 49 days in the nest, but the parents continue to feed the youngsters for several weeks after they fledge, until they are proficient hunters.

Notes

People have had a close relationship with falcons for thousands of years. Falconry, in which captive falcons are trained to hunt and kill game at a person's command, may be the oldest sport, with evidence of it being practiced in China 4000 years ago and in Iran 3700 years ago. One of the oldest known books on a sport is "The Art of Falconry," written by the King of Sicily in 1248. Although falconry is not as widely practiced today, many countries have aficionados who continue the tradition.

Status

At least two of Brazil's falcons are considered threatened. The ORANGE-BREASTED FALCON (CITES Appendix II listed) was never common in Brazil, but now it can be looked for in only a few sites in the Amazon. The RED-THROATED CARACARA formerly was a fairly common resident and evidently is now declining in the Amazon region. This species feeds mainly on wasp and bee larvae, and insecticide spraying may be affecting both the bird itself as well as the availability of its specialized prey. By contrast, the YELLOW-HEADED CARACARA (Plate 39) has expanded recently into northern parts of the Brazilian Amazon, probably due to forest felling and the creation of vast open areas – its preferred habitat.

Profiles

Bat Falcon, *Falco rufigularis*, Plate 37a
Aplomado Falcon, *Falco femoralis*, Plate 37b
American Kestrel, *Falco sparverius*, Plate 37c
Black Caracara, *Daptrius ater*, Plate 39a
Red-throated Caracara, *Daptrius americanus*, Plate 39b
Yellow-headed Caracara, *Milvago chimachima*, Plate 39c
Crested Caracara, *Polyborus plancus*, Plate 39d
Laughing Falcon, *Herpetotheres cachinnans*, Plate 39e
Osprey, *Pandion haliaetus*, Plate 38e

12. Pigeons and Doves

The *pigeon* family, Columbidae, includes about 255 species worldwide, 23 in Brazil. It is a diverse group with representatives on every continent except Antarctica. In Brazil, members of the group inhabit environments from desert scrub to grasslands and rainforest. In general the smaller species are called doves and the larger species pigeons, but there is considerable inconsistency.

All pigeons are generally recognized as such by almost everyone, a legacy of people's familiarity with domestic and feral pigeons. Pigeons worldwide vary in size from the dimensions of a sparrow to those of a small turkey; Brazil's species range in body length from 15 to 35 cm (6 to 14 in). Doves and pigeons are plump-looking birds with compact bodies, short necks, and small heads. Legs are usually fairly short. Bills are small, straight, and slender. Typically there is a swollen bulge (*cere*) at the base of the bill. Body colors are generally soft and understated grays and browns with an occasional splash of bolder black or white. Some have subtle patches of iridescence, usually on the neck or wings. The female tends to have similar, if somewhat duller, plumage to the male.

Natural History
Ecology and Behavior
Most pigeons and doves are at least partially arboreal, but several spend most of their time on the ground. They eat seeds, ripe and unripe fruits, berries and very rarely an insect. They do not have hard bills for seed cracking and thus swallow their food whole. Their chewing is accomplished in the *gizzard*, a muscular portion of the stomach in which food is smashed against small pebbles and other grit eaten from the soil. As they walk on the ground, all species characteristically bob their heads. Camouflage and rapid flight are the two most important anti-predator tactics used by these birds. Many species of pigeons and doves are gregarious to some degree, and some form large flocks during the nonbreeding season.

Breeding
Doves and pigeons are monogamous breeders. Nests are shallow, open affairs of loose twigs, plant stems and roots placed on the ground, rock ledges or in shrubs and trees. Reproductive duties shared by male and female include nest-building, incubating the 1 or 2 eggs, and feeding the young. All doves and pigeons feed their young regurgitated *pigeon's milk*, a protein-rich fluid produced by sloughing off cells lining the *crop*, an enlarged portion of the esophagus otherwise used for food storage. As the chicks grow older, the proportion of solid food fed them grows greater until no more pigeon's milk is supplied. Incubation time ranges from 11 to 28 days, depending on species size.

Notes
Although many pigeons today are very common, some species met extinction within the recent past. There are two particularly famous cases. The DODO was a large, flightless pigeon, the size of a turkey, with a large head and strong, robust bill and feet. Dodos lived, until the 17th century, on the island of Mauritius, in the Indian Ocean, east of Madagascar. Reported to be clumsy and stupid (hence the expression, "dumb as a dodo"), but probably just unfamiliar with and unafraid of predatory animals, such as people, they were killed by the thousands by sailors who stopped at the island to stock their ships with food. This caused population numbers to plunge; the birds were then finished off by the pigs, monkeys, and cats introduced by people to the previously predator-free island –

animals that ate the Dodos' eggs and young. The only stuffed Dodo in existence was destroyed by fire in Oxford, England, in 1755.

North America's PASSENGER PIGEON, a medium-sized, long-tailed member of the family, suffered extinction because of over hunting and because of its habits of roosting, breeding, and migrating in huge flocks. People were able to kill many thousands of them at a time on the Great Plains in the central part of the USA, shipping the bodies to markets and restaurants in large cities through the mid-1800s. It is estimated that when Europeans first settled in the New World, there were 3 billion Passenger Pigeons, a population size perhaps never equaled by any other bird, and that they may have accounted for up to 25% or more of the birds in what is now the USA. It took only a little more than 100 years to kill them all; the last one died in the Cincinnati Zoo in 1914. The common ROCK DOVE, the urban pigeon with which everyone who has visited a city or town is familiar, is a native of the Old World. Domesticated for thousands of years and transported around the world by people, feral populations have colonized all settled and many unsettled areas of the Earth. In the wild, they breed and roost in cliffs and caves.

Status
In Brazil only two species of the pigeon and dove family are considered threatened: the PURPLE-WINGED GROUND-DOVE, restricted to the coastal Atlantic forest of southeastern Brazil, and the BLUE-EYED GROUND DOVE, endemic to open forests of central Brazil.

Profiles
Pale-vented Pigeon, *Columba cayennensis*, Plate 40a
Ruddy Pigeon, *Columba subvinacea*, Plate 40b
White-tipped Dove, *Leptotila verreauxi*, Plate 40c
Picazuro Pigeon, *Columba picazuro*, Plate 40d
Picui Ground-Dove, *Columbina picui*, Plate 40e
Ruddy Ground-Dove, *Columbina talpacoti*, Plate 40f

13. Parrots

Everyone knows *parrots* as caged pets, so discovering them for the first time in their natural surroundings is often a strange but somehow familiar experience (like a dog-owner's first sighting of a wild coyote). One has knowledge and expectations of the birds' behavior and antics in captivity, but how do they act in the wild? Along with toucans, parrots are probably the birds most commonly symbolic of the tropics. The 300+ parrot species that comprise the Family Psittacidae (the "P" is silent; try referring to parrots as *psittacids* to impress your friends and tour guide!) are globally distributed across the tropics, with a few species spilling over into the temperate zones. In Brazil, 71 different species are found, and they occupy habitats from coastal desert to Amazon forest. Parrot fanciers have their own lexicon of common names that often bear no resemblance to the common names used by ornithologists. In Brazil the common names most widely used divide this family mainly by size: the sparrow-sized *parrotlets* are about 10 cm (4 in) long and the smallest of all; the *parakeets* are long-tailed or short-tailed but small (20 to 30 cm, 8 to 12 in); the *parrots* are larger (30 to 45 cm, 12 to 18 in); and the *macaws* are the largest (60 to 100 cm, 24 to 40 in).

Parrots, regardless of size, share a set of distinctive traits that set them apart from all other birds. They are short-necked with a compact and stocky body. All have a short, hooked bill with a hinge on the upper half that provides great mobility for handling food and for clambering around branches and vegetation. The legs are short, and the feet, with toes that are very dexterous, are highly adapted for grasping. Although most species are green, many depart from this scheme, often in a spectacular fashion, with gaudy blues, reds, and yellows. Their raucous calls in flight, usually in flocks, make them easy to see, but when they land in a tree overhead, they can virtually disappear instantaneously. Only the steady rain of discarded fruit parts gives away their presence. Your best view will probably be when a flock suddenly departs a feeding tree, or when a flock is located loafing and squabbling the afternoon away in an isolated, open tree. To distinguish the various species: listen for differences in their voices; look for the length of the tail; and watch for the way they flap their wings – deep and full strokes or twittering, shallow strokes.

The star attractions of the parrot world in Brazil are the macaws. There are two sizes of macaws; some species, like the CHESTNUT-FRONTED MACAW (Plate 41), are only a bit larger (at 46 cm, 1.5 ft) than the largest parrots, while others, such as the HYACINTH MACAW (Plate 41), are enormous (94 cm, 3 ft). The macaws have the loudest voices of all the parrots here, and you will inevitably hear them long before you see them appear in the sky from behind a line of trees. Their slow but steady wingbeats together with their long tails make them unmistakable.

Natural History
Ecology and Behavior

Parrots are incredibly noisy, highly social seed and fruit eaters. Some species give their assortment of harsh, often screeching vocalizations throughout the day, others only in flight, and others call from communal roosts mainly before leaving and when arriving. Many species roost in groups for the night, sometimes in the thousands in more protected parts of the forest or on islands. Often several species roost together. During early morning, flocks of parrots leave the roost, moving out to cover the forest in search of fruiting trees. They may travel up to 75 km (45 miles) or more in a day. In the afternoon the flocks begin to head back from all directions to the same roosting site. At certain times of the year, parrots of many species concentrate in huge wheeling flocks around high river banks to eat clay from the soil. A possible explanation for this behavior is that the clay, or the chemicals in it, aids in digestion. Another hypothesis is that clay helps counteract some of the potent toxins present in many fruits. If you can find such a parrot "salt lick," be sure to spend some time there; early morning is usually best.

Parrots use their special locomotory talent to clamber methodically through trees in search of fruits and flowers, using their powerful feet to grasp branches and their bills as, essentially, a third foot. Just as caged parrots, they will hang at odd angles and even upside down, the better to reach some delicious morsel. Parrot feet also function as hands, delicately manipulating food and bringing it to the bill. Parrots feed mostly on fruits and nuts, buds of leaves and flowers, and on flower parts and nectar. They are usually considered frugivores, but careful study reveals that when they attack fruit, it is usually to get at the seeds within. The powerful bill slices open fruit and crushes seeds. As one bird book colorfully put it, "adapted for opening hard nuts, biting chunks out of fruit, and grinding small seeds into meal, the short, thick, hooked parrot bill combines the destructive powers of an ice pick (the sharp-pointed upper mandible), a chisel (the sharp-edged lower mandible), a file (ridged inner surface of the upper mandible), and a vise." Thick, muscular parrot tongues are also specialized for feeding, used to scoop out pulp from fruit and nectar from flowers. Parrots, unlike most frugivorous birds, are not ingesting seeds eventually to disperse them when they defecate. They are, more technically, seed predators. However, some studies suggest that because of the large amount of uneaten fruit that they drop to the ground, they make available fruits and their seeds to be dispersed by ground frugivores such as tinamous and rodents. These ground-dwelling species are more properly seed dispersers because they eat the pulp and so do not regularly destroy the seeds contained within.

Breeding

In most Brazilian parrots, the sexes are very similar or identical in appearance; breeding is monogamous and pairing is often for life. Nesting is carried out during the dry season and, for some, into the early wet season. Most species breed in cavities in dead trees, although a few build nests. Macaw nests are almost always placed 30 m (100 ft) or more above the ground. A female parrot lays 2 to 8 eggs, which she incubates alone for 17 to 35 days while being periodically fed regurgitated food by her mate. The helpless young of small parrots are nest-bound for 3 to 4 weeks, those of the huge macaws, 3 to 4 months. Both parents feed nestlings and fledglings.

Notes

Parrots have been captured for people's pleasure as pets for thousands of years; Greek records exist from 400 BC describing parrot pets. The fascination stems from the birds' bright coloring, their ability to imitate human speech and other sounds (strangely enough, they do not appear to mimic sounds in the wild), their individualistic personalities (captive parrots definitely like some people while disliking others), and their long life spans (up to 80 years in captivity). Likewise, parrots have been hunted and killed for food and to protect crops for thousands of years. Some pre-Columbian pottery shows scenes of parrots eating corn and being scared away from crops. Historically, people have killed parrots to protect crops – Charles Darwin noted that in Uruguay in the early 1800s, thousands of parakeets were killed to prevent crop damage. Macaws, the largest parrots, are thought to have been raised in the past for food in the West Indies, and macaw feathers were used as ornaments and had ceremonial functions.

Status

Seventy or more parrot species are threatened or endangered worldwide, and at least 14 species that occur in Brazil are currently among this group. The YELLOW-FACED PARROT, HYACINTH MACAW, and BLUE-WINGED MACAW occur near or in the Pantanal. The GOLDEN PARAKEET (Plate 42) is restricted to small parts of the Amazon forest south of the Río Amazonas. SPIX'S MACAW formerly occurred in a small area of northeastern Brazil; there are now only 40 individuals left, but they are all in captivity – held by private parrot fanciers. These people, however, refuse to cooperate in a captive breeding program to re-introduce Spix's Macaw to the wild – the value of their captive macaws might decline if a wild population was re-established.

Many Brazilian parrot species still enjoy healthy populations and are frequently seen. Unfortunately, however, parrots are subject to three powerful forces that, in combination, take heavy tolls on their numbers: parrots are primarily forest birds, and forests are increasingly under attack by farmers and developers; parrots are considered agricultural pests by farmers and orchardists owing to their seed- and fruit-eating, and are persecuted for this reason; and parrots are among the world's most popular cage birds. Several Brazilian species, especially the larger macaws, are prized as pets, and nests of these parrots are often robbed of young for local sale as pets or to international dealers. To get to the young birds, the nest tree, often a dead palm, is cut down. Few of the chicks survive the tree fall, and one of the few cavity nest sites around has been eliminated for renesting. For every macaw that reaches the market place, perhaps 20 to 50 die in the process. Without fast, additional protection, many more Brazilian parrots soon will be threatened.

Profiles

Scarlet Macaw, *Ara macao*, Plate 41a
Blue-and-yellow Macaw, *Ara ararauna*, Plate 41b
Hyacinth Macaw, *Anodorhynchus hyacinthinus*, Plate 41c
White-eyed Parakeet, *Aratinga leucophthalmus*, Plate 41d
Chestnut-fronted Macaw, *Ara severa*, Plate 41e
Red-bellied Macaw, *Ara manilata*, Plate 41f

Cobalt-winged Parakeet, *Brotogeris cyanoptera*, Plate 42a
Canary-winged Parakeet, *Brotogeris versicolorus*, Plate 42b
Black-headed Parrot, *Pionites melanocephala*, Plate 42c
Black-hooded Parakeet, *Nandayus nenday*, Plate 42d
Golden Parakeet, *Aratinga (Guaruba) guarouba*, Plate 42e

Mealy Parrot, *Amazona farinosa*, Plate 43a
Yellow-headed Parrot, *Amazona ochracephala*, Plate 43b
Orange-winged Parrot, *Amazona amazonica*, Plate 43c
Blue-headed Parrot, *Pionus menstruus*, Plate 43d
Short-tailed Parrot, *Graydidascalus brachyurus*, Plate 43e
Turquoise-fronted Parrot, *Amazona aestiva*, Plate 43f

14. Cuckoos and Anis

Many of the *cuckoos* and *anis* (AH-neez) are physically rather plain but behaviorally rather extraordinary. As a group they employ some of the most bizarre breeding practices known among birds. Cuckoos, *ground-cuckoos*, and anis are considered by some to be in the same family, Cuculidae, which, with a total of 130 species, enjoys a worldwide distribution that includes both temperate and tropical areas; 19 species occur in Brazil. While the cuckoos are shy and solitary birds of woodlands, forests and dense thickets, anis are bold, obvious and gregarious birds of savannahs, brushy scrub and river edges. Anis make you wonder where they perched before the advent of fences. Ground-cuckoos are generally shy inhabitants of dense forest floor and thick grassy areas. They are difficult to see under the best of circumstances but tend to make their presence known by loud and often persistent calls and songs.

Most cuckoos are medium-sized, slender, long-tailed birds. Male and female mostly look alike, attired in plain browns, tans, and grays, often with streaked or spotted patches. Several have alternating white and black bands on their tail undersides. (Many cuckoos of the Old World are more colorful.) They have short legs and bills that curve downwards at the end. The STRIPED CUCKOO (Plate 44) is found commonly in open and cut-over brushlands throughout Brazil. Occasionally it will fly up from the ground or low vegetation and sit motionless on a fence post for many minutes. More often, however, you will be made aware of its presence by what must be the most persistent, and sometimes irritating, song of these open areas – two short whistles, the second note higher, and given over and over every two or three seconds throughout the middle of the day. The SQUIRREL CUCKOO (Plate 44) is a large red-brown species of secondary and primary forest throughout tropical Brazil. Its long tail, with a little imagination resembling a squirrel's tail, is often all you see of it as it runs down a branch.

Anis are conspicuous medium-sized birds, glossy black all over, with iridescent sheens particularly on the head, neck and breast. Their bills are exceptionally large, with humped or crested upper ridges. The SMOOTH-BILLED ANI (Plate 44) is an abundant and obvious bird throughout the cleared areas of Amazonian Brazil and on the marshy margins of lakes and rivers. Its all-black color, loose and floppy flight, and large bill make it easy to recognize. The GREATER ANI (Plate 44) is a much larger edition with a distinct bluish tinge to the all-black body and a white eye. It occurs along forested streams and lakes of the Amazon and Pantanal.

Natural History
Ecology and Behavior
Most of the cuckoos are arboreal. They eat insects, apparently having a special affinity for caterpillars. They even safely consume hairy caterpillars, which are avoided by most other predators because they have painful stinging hairs or even poisons. Cuckoos have been seen snipping off one end of a hairy caterpillar, squeezing its body with the bill and beating it against a branch until the toxic entrails fall out. They then can swallow the remains safely. How they get around the hairs is still a mystery, however. A few cuckoos, such as the GROUND CUCKOO, are ground-dwellers, eating small birds, snakes and lizards as well as insects. They are most often seen around army ant swarms, where they eat large insects and occasionally small antbirds attracted to the swarm.

The highly social anis forage in groups, usually on the ground. Frequently they feed around cattle, grabbing the insects that are flushed out of hiding places by the grazing mammals. They eat mostly bugs, but also a bit of fruit. Anis live in groups of 8 to 25 individuals, each group containing 2 to 8 adults and several juveniles. Each group defends a territory from other groups throughout the year. The flock both feeds and breeds within its territory. Ani vocalizations are usually loud and discordant – when the members of a GREATER ANI flock start calling, it sounds like a boiler factory.

Breeding
Cuckoos in the Old World are highly evolved brood parasites. They build no nests of their own, and the females lay their eggs in the nests of other species (the hosts). Immediately after hatching, the young cuckoo nestlings push the rightful heirs out of the nest, and the host adults then raise the young cuckoos as their own offspring. In the New World only a few cuckoo species, such as the STRIPED CUCKOO and the PHEASANT CUCKOO, are brood parasites. The rest are typical monogamous breeders. The male feeds the female in courtship, especially during her egg-laying period. Both sexes build the plain platform nest that is made of twigs and leaves and placed in a tree or shrub. Both sexes incubate the 2 to 6 eggs for about 10 days, and both parents feed the young.

Anis, consistent with their highly social ways, are communal breeders. In the most extreme form, all individuals within the group contribute to a single nest, several females laying eggs in it – up to 29 eggs have been found in one nest. Many individuals help build the stick nest and feed the young. Although this behavior would seem to benefit all the individuals involved, actually it is the dominant male and female that gain the most. Their eggs go in the communal nest last, on top of all the others, which often get buried. Also some females roll eggs out of the nest before depositing their own; thus it pays to be last.

Notes

The name cuckoo comes from the calls made by a common species in Europe, which is also the source of the sounds for cuckoo clocks. Recent research on cuckoos suggests that they may actually be three families – the typical cuckoos, the ground-cuckoos, including the STRIPED CUCKOO, and the anis. Some ornithologists even want to include the Hoatzin as a fourth family in this group.

Status

The STRIPED CUCKOO has been expanding its range within Brazil, it being a species that does well in the forest edge, thicket, and open areas that increasingly are created through deforestation. None of Brazil's cuckoos is considered threatened or endangered.

Profiles

Striped Cuckoo, *Tapera naevia*, Plate 44a
Squirrel Cuckoo, *Piaya cayana*, Plate 44b
Greater Ani, *Crotophaga major*, Plate 44c
Smooth-billed Ani, *Crotophaga ani*, Plate 44d
Guira Cuckoo, *Guira guira*, Plate 44e

15. Owls

Most *owls* are members of the Family Strigidae, which has about 120 species worldwide, 17 in Brazil. Almost all species are nocturnal, and they share distinctive features such as large heads with forward-facing eyes, hooked bills, plumpish bodies and sharp claws (talons). They tend to be camouflaged in colors of gray, brown and black. The group includes species that range in size from 15 to 75 cm (6 to 30 in). The sexes are similar, but females tend to be considerably larger. Because it is frequently active during the day, the FERRUGINOUS PYGMY-OWL (Plate 45) is one owl species that you are likely to see. It is the size of a large sparrow, and its high-pitched, staccato whistles are common in scrub areas and forest edges. Recent studies of this broadly distributed, tiny owl species show that it may actually be made up of a "swarm" of different species across South America. In extensive grassy areas, an unusual owl, the BURROWING OWL (Plate 45), often stands on a fence post or on the ground bobbing up and down on its long legs. It is regularly active during the day and one of the most obvious owls in open habitats of Brazil. It also has a tremendous distribution from southern Canada to southern Argentina.

Natural History
Ecology and Behavior

In general, owls occupy a variety of habitats: forests, clearings, fields, grasslands, mountains, and marshes. They are considered the nocturnal "ecological replacements" of the day-active hawks, eagles, and falcons. Although most owls hunt at night, some hunt at twilight (*crepuscular* activity) and a few during the day. Owls eat a broad range of animals, from small mammals, birds and reptiles to insects and earthworms. Larger owls often develop a taste for smaller owls. Owl vision is good in low light (mainly in black and white, as they are considered to be largely color-blind). In the absence of moonlight and under the cloak of a forest canopy, however, owls hunt using their ears to locate prey. Not only are the ears themselves extremely sensitive but the two ears have different-sized openings. The effect of this asymmetry is comparable to the way you turn your head back and forth to better locate a sound. With its ear structure, an owl can locate sounds without turning its head, especially important in flight. In addition, owls have soft flight feathers and a sound baffle of fringed feathers on the leading edge of the wing that provide a cloak of silence during flight; few prey can hear them coming. They swallow small prey whole, but instead of digesting or defecating the hard bones, fur and feathers, they regurgitate these parts in compact *owl pellets*. These gray oblong pellets often accumulate beneath an owl's perch. If you come across some of these pellets, pull them apart to see what the owl has been dining on.

Breeding

Most owls are monogamous breeders. They do not build nests themselves, but either take over nests abandoned by other birds or nest in cavities such as a tree or rock hole. Incubation of the 1 to 10 eggs is usually conducted by the female alone for 4 to 5 weeks, but she is fed regularly by her mate. Upon hatching, the female broods the young while the male continues to hunt for her and the young. The chicks fledge after 4 to 6 weeks in the nest.

Notes

For owls active at night, try locating them by their call notes and songs. When you locate an owl this way, shine a flashlight on it to see it well. Often owls will sit for a long time on the same perch calling and looking around, even in the bright beam of your flashlight. Note the body size and facial patterns to identify them. Also, watch for the "ear" tufts, which are usually evident on species that have them; but they can also be flattened and difficult to see.

The forward-facing eyes of owls are a trait shared with only a few other animals: humans, most other primates, and to a degree, the cats. Eyes arranged in this way allow for almost complete binocular vision (both eyes can see the same object but from a slightly different angle), a prerequisite for good depth perception, which, in turn, is important for quickly judging distances when catching prey. However, owl eyes cannot move much, so owls swivel their heads to look left or right.

Owls in many parts of the world, including Brazil, are considered an omen of bad luck, or even worse, death. Many indigenous people kill owls when they encounter them to avoid any future visits and bad news brought by the owl.

Status

Owls in Brazil are threatened primarily by forest clearing, but no species is considered endangered.

Profiles

Tropical Screech-owl, *Otus choliba*, Plate 45a
Spectacled Owl, *Pulsatrix perspicillata*, Plate 45b

Ferruginous Pygmy-owl, *Glaucidium brasilianum*, Plate 45c
Black-banded Owl, *Strix huhula*, Plate 45d
Burrowing Owl, *Speotyto cunicularia*, Plate 45e

16. Nightjars and Potoos

Species of birds known as *nightjars* are in the Family Caprimulgidae, which has about 70 species worldwide, 23 species in Brazil. Like their closest relatives, the owls, nightjars are primarily nocturnal. They have a very characteristic appearance. In the New World, most range in size from 16 to 32 cm (6 to 12 in) long. They have long wings, medium or long tails, and big eyes. Their small, stubby bills enclose big, wide mouths that they open in flight to scoop up flying insects. Many species have bristles around the mouth area, which act as a food funnel. With their short legs and weak feet, they are poor walkers – flying is their usual mode of locomotion. The plumage of these birds is uniformly cryptic: mottled, spotted, and barred mixtures of browns, grays, tans, and black. They often have white patches on their wings or tails that can be seen only in flight. The PAURAQUE (Plate 46) is the most easily seen nightjar in Brazil.

The closely related *potoos* are placed in their own family, the Nyctibiidae, with a total of 7 species that occur from Mexico south into Argentina. In Brazil there are 5 species, but you are likely to find only one or two of them, the COMMON POTOO (Plate 46) and the GREAT POTOO (Plate 46). At night, when it is active, the Common Potoo gives a mournful series of long, slow and low descending whistles. During the day, potoos sit on branches, usually out in the open, and with their camouflaged coloring and their bills pointed into the air, they look like dead branches.

Natural History
Ecology and Behavior

Most nightjars are night-active birds, with some becoming active at twilight (*crepuscular* activity). They feed on flying insects, which they catch on the wing, either by forays out from a perched location on the ground or from tree branches, or with continuous circling flight. You can see some species feeding on insects drawn to lights at night. Others you will see only as you flush them from their daytime roost on the ground or in low vegetation. Their camouflage coloring makes them difficult to see, even when you are close to them. The potoos are solitary species that hunt at night for large insects and small birds, lizards and occasionally mammals. A potoo's immense mouth opens like a cavern to catch prey in flight.

Breeding

Nightjars breed monogamously. No nest is built, but instead the female lays her 1 or 2 eggs on the ground in a small depression, usually under a bush or a rock. Either the female alone or both sexes incubate the eggs for 18 to 20 days, and both parents feed the young once they hatch. As is typical of many ground-nesting species, regardless of family, nightjars engage in *broken-wing displays* to distract predators from the nest and young. They flop around on the ground, often with one or both wings held down as if injured, making gargling or hissing sounds, all the while moving away from the nest. Potoos build no nest but lay a single egg in a crevice of a large branch or stump, usually high up in a tree. Potoo breeding biology is poorly known, but apparently both sexes are involved with incubation.

Notes

Other names for nightjars are *goatsuckers* and *nighthawks*, both of which are misleading nicknames. At twilight some species fly low over the ground near grazing animals, such as goats. The birds often fly right next to the mammals to catch insects being scared up as they walk through the grass. Evidently the assumption was that these birds were after the goats' milk, and a legend was born. These often pointed-winged species of birds were also mistaken for hawks flying around at dusk and at night, when accurate identification was difficult, and the name "nighthawk" has stuck ever since. One of the nightjars, North America's COMMON POORWILL, may be the only bird known actually to hibernate, as some mammals do, during very cold weather. During their dormant state, poorwills save energy by reducing their metabolic rate and their body temperature, the latter by about 22 °C (40 °F).

Status

Only one of the Brazilian nightjars is listed as threatened, the WHITE-WINGED NIGHTJAR of southern Brazil. It occurs in a very limited area, and habitat destruction is reducing its population.

Profiles

Sand-colored Nighthawk, *Chordeiles rupestris*, Plate 46a
Pauraque, *Nyctidromus albicollis*, Plate 46b
Nacunda Nighthawk, *Podager nacunda*, Plate 46c
Common Potoo, *Nyctibius griseus*, Plate 46d
Great Potoo, *Nyctibius grandis*, Plate 46e

17. Swifts and Swallows

Swifts and *swallows* are remarkably similar in appearance and behavior, but they are not closely related. They both rely on the same feeding technique, catching insects on the wing during long periods of sustained flight. Swifts, although superficially resembling swallows, are instead closely related to hummingbirds. There are 80 or so species of swifts (Family Apodidae) worldwide in temperate and tropical areas; 15 species are found in Brazil, some albeit rarely. Swifts, like swallows, are slender, streamlined birds, with long, pointed wings. They are 9 to 25 cm (3.5 to 10 in) long and have very short legs, short tails or long, forked tails, and very short but broad bills. Swifts' tails are stiffened to support the birds as they cling to vertical surfaces. The sexes look alike: sooty-gray or brown, with white or grayish rumps or flanks. Many are glossily iridescent. The most widespread and among the largest species in Brazil is the WHITE-COLLARED SWIFT (Plate 47). Although they nest on cliff faces behind waterfalls high in the mountains, they can be expected anywhere in the lowlands, often in immense and noisy flocks high in the air as they seek insect concentrations. The SHORT-TAILED SWIFT (Plate 47) is a species of the Amazon region; its tailless appearance and light gray rump are the best characters to use to distinguish it from several similar species found in the same area.

The swallow family, Hirundinidae, is related to perching birds such as flycatchers, warblers and sparrows. There are 80 species of swallows worldwide, and 16 species in Brazil, 4 of which winter here or pass through on their way to or from North American breeding grounds. Swallows are small, streamlined birds, 11.5 to 21.5 cm (4.5 to 8.5 in) long, with short necks, bills and legs. They are wonderfully adapted for fast and sustained flight, having long, pointed wings and, often, forked tails. They have amazing ability to maneuver in the air as they pursue flying insects or chase each other for competitive or amorous intentions. Some swallows are colored in shades of blue, green or black, but many are gray or brown. The sexes generally look alike, at least to us.

Natural History
Ecology and Behavior
Among the birds, swifts and swallows represent the pinnacle of flying prowess and aerial pursuit of insects. It seems as if they fly effortlessly all day, circling low over water and land, or flying in seemingly erratic patterns high overhead. Swifts especially are perpetual fliers, rarely roosting except at night, when they come together in large groups to spend the non-flying hours gathered on a vertical cliff face behind a waterfall, inside a hollow tree or among the fronds of a palm tree. They roost on these vertical surfaces clinging with their tiny but sharply-clawed feet and bracing themselves against the sides of the roost with their stiff tail feathers. A swift spends more time airborne than any other type of bird, even copulating in the air in a death-defying tail-spin that gives meaning to the concept of sexual thrills. The name swift is apt, as these are the fastest flying birds in level flight, moving along at up to 160 kph (100 mph). Swifts can be told from swallows by their faster, more twittering wingbeats, made possible by an exceptionally short arm bone (the humerus). Some species of swifts hunt every day for insects hundreds of miles from their nesting area. The chicks of swifts have the ability to go into short-term physiological inactivity (*torpor*) during extended periods of inclement weather, when no insects are flying. They can endure the lack of food for up to a week by lowering their body temperatures and energetic requirements (and thus their need for food).

Swallows also take insects on the wing as they fly back and forth over water and open areas. Some also eat berries. Swallows perch more frequently than swifts, often resting during the hottest parts of the day on tree branches over water or open areas. Directly after dawn, however, and at dusk, swallows are always airborne. Because swallows depend each day on capturing enough insects, their daily habits are largely tied to the prevailing weather. Flying insects are thick in the atmosphere on warm, sunny days, but relatively scarce on cold, wet ones. Therefore, on good days, swallows can catch their fill of bugs in only a few hours of flying, virtually anywhere. But on cool, wet days, they may need to forage all day to find enough food, and they tend to do so over water or low to the ground, where under such conditions bugs are more available.

Breeding
Swifts are monogamous, and most are colonial breeders, but some nest solitarily. The sexes share nesting chores. Nests are usually attached to vertical surfaces of rocks, tree cavities or palm fronds, depending on the species of swift. The nests consist of plant pieces, twigs and feathers glued together with the birds' saliva. One to 6 eggs are incubated for 16 to 28 days, with young fledging at 25 to 65 days of age. Swallows are also monogamous; many species breed in dense colonies of hundreds to thousands of pairs. They make nests of mud and some plant material which they attach to vertical surfaces, or they nest in cavities of trees, or tunnel into vertical banks. Both sexes or the female alone incubates the 3 to 7 eggs for 13 to 16 days. Both parents help feed the young for 18 to 28 days, until the young fledge.

Notes

Nests of swifts in some parts of the Old World are almost totally made of saliva, and these nests are harvested to make birds' nest soup. Swallows have a long history of beneficial association with people. In the New World, owing to their insect-eating habits, they have been popular with people going back to the time of the ancient Mayan civilization. Mayans, it is believed, respected and welcomed swallows because they reduced insect damage to crops. In fact, Cozumel (the word refers to swallows), off Mexico's Yucatán Peninsula, is the Island of Swallows. People's alterations of natural habitats, harmful to so many species, are often helpful to swallows, which adopt buildings, bridges, road culverts, road banks, and quarry walls as nesting areas. BARN SWALLOWS (Plate 48) in some areas of North America have for the most part given up nesting in anything other than human-crafted structures. The result of this close association is that, going back as far as ancient Rome, swallows have been considered good luck. Superstitions attached to the relationship abound; for example, it is said that the cows of a farmer who destroys a swallow's nest will give bloody milk. Arrival of the first migratory Barn Swallows in Europe is considered a welcoming sign of approaching spring, as is the arrival of CLIFF SWALLOWS at some of California's old Spanish missions.

Status

So little is known of many species of swifts that we are uncertain of their populations' sizes or vulnerabilities. None of the swallows that breeds or winters in Brazil is threatened.

Profiles

White-collared Swift, *Streptoprocne zonaris*, Plate 47a
Short-tailed Swift, *Chaetura brachyura*, Plate 47b
Fork-tailed Palm-swift, *Tachornis squamata*, Plate 47c
White-banded Swallow, *Atticora fasciata*, Plate 47d
Southern Rough-winged Swallow, *Stelgidopteryx ruficollis*, Plate 47e
Barn Swallow, *Hirundo rustica*, Plate 48a
White-winged Swallow, *Tachycineta albiventer*, Plate 48b
Brown-chested Martin, *Phaeoprogne tapera*, Plate 48c

18. Hummingbirds

Hummingbirds are birds of extremes. They are among the most recognized kinds of birds, the smallest of birds, and arguably the most beautiful, albeit on a small scale. Fittingly, much of their biology is nothing short of amazing. Found only in the New World, the hummingbird family, Trochilidae, contains about 330 species, 83 of which call Brazil home. The variety of forms encompassed by the family, not to mention the brilliant iridescence of most of its members, is indicated by the diversity and inventiveness needed by biologists to give descriptive names to these species: emeralds, barbthroats, plovercrests, coquettes, sapphires, fairies, woodstars, woodnymphs, brilliants, sabrewings, sungems, woodstars, sicklebills and visorbearers. Hummingbirds live in a broad spectrum of habitats from Alaska to southern Argentina. All they seem to require to live in a region is a reliable supply of flower nectar and a few insects for protein.

Almost everyone can identify hummingbirds (call them hummers to sound like an expert). They are mostly tiny birds, usually clad in iridescent metallic greens, reds, violets and blues, that whiz by us at high speeds, the smallest of them more resembling big insects than respectable birds. Most hummers are in the range of only 6 to 13 cm (2.5 to 5 in) long, although a few of the larger kinds reach 20 cm (8 in), and they tip the scales at an almost imperceptibly low 2 to 9 g (most being 3 to 6 g, 0.1 to 0.2 oz) – the weight of a large paper-clip! Bill length and shape vary extensively among species. Many of them have distinctively formed bills to fit precisely into a species or genus of flowers from which that hummingbird species delicately draws its liquid food. Males are usually more colorful than females, and many males have *gorgets*, bright, glittering throat patches that in the right light are red, violet, green or blue. A little turn of the head, however, will change the reflection to black. Not all hummers are so vividly outfitted, however. One group, called the *hermits* (supposedly because of their solitary ways), has dull greenish-brown and gray plumages. Hummers have tiny legs and feet; in fact, they are included by most ornithologists with the swifts (p. 157) in the avian Order Apodiformes, which means "without feet." With so many species to be seen in Brazil, we can only begin to introduce you to some of its hummingbirds. The 12 species we have chosen to profile include a cross section of the ranges of sizes, colors and adaptations you can see in various habitats throughout the Amazon and Pantanal regions of the country. These species are also the ones you are most likely to see and be able to identify by their habitats and distinctive traits.

Natural History
Ecology and Behavior
Because of their many anatomical, behavioral and ecological specializations, hummingbirds have long attracted the research attention of biologists. The outcome is that we know quite a lot about these tiny birds:

1   Hummers are capable of very rapid, finely controlled, acrobatic flight, more so than any other type of bird. The bones of their wings have been modified to allow for stationary hovering flight as well as the unique ability to fly backwards. Their wings beat in a figure-8-shaped wingstroke and at a speed beyond our ability to distinguish the individual beats – up to 80 times per second. Because most people see hummers only during the birds' foraging trips, they often appear to be flying continuously, as they zip from flower to flower. They do, however, perch every now and again, providing the best chance to see them well.

2   Hummingbirds have very fast metabolisms, a necessary condition for small, warm-blooded animals. To pump enough oxygen and nutrient-delivering blood around their little bodies, their hearts beat up to 10 times faster than human hearts – 600 to 1000 times per minute. To obtain sufficient energy to fuel their high metabolism, hummingbirds must eat many times each day. They can starve quickly without almost constant feeding. At night, when they are inactive, they burn much of their available energy reserves and on cold nights, if not for special mechanisms, they would surely starve to death. The chief method to avoid energy depletion on cold nights is to enter into a sleep-like state of *torpor*, during which the body's temperature is lowered to just above that of the outside world, from 17 to 28 °C (30 to 50 °F) below their normal daytime operating body temperature. This torpor means they virtually stop using and needing energy; in effect, they hibernate each night. If you ever find a hummingbird perched as if in a daze early on a cool morning,

it is not sick – just not yet warmed up and ready for its active daytime life.

3   All hummingbirds are *nectarivores* – they get most of their nourishment from consuming nectar from flowers (thus the name for hummingbird in Portuguese is "bezaflor," which means *flower-kisser*). They have long, thin bills and specialized tongues, which they can extend incredible distances into the long thin flowers for the nectar reward that awaits them at the bottom. This is done while the hummingbird hovers, but a few species must land on the flower and even turn their heads upside down to get access to the nectar. The advantage for the flower to provide this nectar reward is that the hummingbird's head must pass by the male parts of the flower, which have pollen on their surfaces. This pollen sticks to the feathers of the hummingbird, and then some of it is jostled to drop off on the female parts of the next flower – thus achieving *pollination*, or sex via an intermediary. Because nectar is primarily a sugar and water solution, hummingbirds need to obtain additional nutrients, such as proteins, from other sources, especially when feeding growing chicks. Thus, they also eat insects and spiders, which they catch in the air or pluck from leaf surfaces or even from spider webs. Some recent studies suggest that these arthropods make up a much larger proportion of a hummingbird's diet than is generally believed, some going so far as to suggest that some hummingbird species visit flowers more often to catch bugs there than to gather nectar.

4   Hummingbird-pollinated flowers are often shaped to permit only a single or a few species of hummingbirds with the matching shape and length of bill to be able to reach the nectar source. The advantage to the hummingbirds is that insects and other species of hummingbirds cannot compete for the nectar in that species of flower. The advantage to the flower is that these specialized hummingbirds won't be wandering around visiting lots of other species of flowers and dropping pollen in all the wrong places. The specialization ensures that the next flower visited is highly likely to be of the same species, and thus these plant species don't have to produce much extra pollen. They can use that energy instead to make better roots, more leaves and other useful parts that otherwise might have been sacrificed. Interlopers in this *mutualistic* interaction are a group of pollen-eating mite species. Mites are minuscule arthropods, allied with the spiders and ticks. Some mites may spend their lives on a single plant, feeding and reproducing, but others, perhaps searching for mates or new sites to colonize, try to reach other plants. Walking to another plant for such a small animal is almost out of the question. What to do? The mites jump onto the bills of hummingbirds when the birds visit flowers and become hitchhikers on the bird, usually hiding in their nostrils. The passengers leap off the bird's bill during a subsequent visit to a plant of the same species that they left, necessary because the mites are specialized for certain plants. Recent research suggests that the passenger mites monitor the scents of flowers to identify the correct type, to know when to get off the bus.

5   Many hummers are highly aggressive birds, energetically defending individual flowers or feeding territories from all other hummingbirds, regardless of species, as well as from large insects. Not all are territorial, however. Some are *trapline feeders*, repeatedly following a regular route around a large undefended section of the habitat and checking the same series of widely spaced flowering plants for their nectar. Unlike many plants that put out all their flowers at the same time, and then only for a short period, these trapline types

of plants put out only one or a few flowers each day, but they continue doing so for several weeks, so the hummingbirds can learn about and depend on this nectar source. Some traplines can be more than a kilometer (0.6 mile) long. Whether a bird defends a territory or not depends on the balance of the costs of energy used and the benefits of energy (in terms of resources) gained. If the flowers in an area are superabundant, providing sufficient food for all, or if the flowers are so spread out that no one hummingbird could possibly defend them all (as in trapline flowers), then owning and defending a territory is not cost-effective. If the opposite is the case, and by keeping away interlopers from a defendable area with limited nectar, a hummingbird can keep more of the nectar for itself, then a defended territory is worthwhile.

Predators on hummingbirds include small agile hawks and falcons, large frogs, and insects such as preying mantises, which ambush the small birds as they feed at flowers. Another hazard is large spider webs, from which sometimes a poor hummingbird cannot extricate itself.

Breeding

Hummingbirds are polygamous breeders in which females do almost all the work. In some species a male in his territory advertises for females by singing squeaky songs. A female enters the territory and, following often spectacular aerial courtship displays, mates. She then leaves the male's territory to nest on her own. Other species are lec breeders, especially some of the hermits. Three to 25 males gather in a cleared area of the forest undergrowth, each with a tiny mating territory in that area in which he sings his squeaky little song in the hope of impressing and attracting a passing female to mate with him. The males spend hours there each day during the breeding season, singing their little hearts out. When a female enters a lec area, she chooses a lucky stud from among the males there and mates with him. A male might spend months at a lec but have only one 15-minute mating interaction with a female, or, if his song is pitiful and unimpressive, mate with no females. Other males, presumably the Placido Domingos and Garth Brooks of the hummingbird-world, attract more females with their songs and mate with many of them in a season. (This is not to imply that Placido and Garth are promiscuous.) The females construct their tiny nests from plant parts, mosses, lichens, feathers, animal hairs and spider webbing. The nests are placed perched on the top of small branches, often attached with spider webbing. Hermits use this spider webbing to weave together the sides of the tip of a large-leafed plant. They then add plant material to construct a nest that hangs on the underside of the leaf, protected from rain and predators. The female lays 2 eggs, incubates them for 15 to 19 days, and feeds the chicks regurgitated nectar and insects for 20 to 26 days until they fledge.

Notes

Intriguingly, some hummingbirds are as curious about us as we are of them. A common occurrence while following a trail is to be closely approached by a passing hummingbird, which stops in midair to size up the large primate, darts this way and that to view the intruder from all angles, then, its curiosity apparently satisfied, zips off into the forest. You can increase your chances of this type of encounter by wearing a bright red bandanna, or tying it to your pack as you hike. Hummers always seem eager to investigate a new source of nectar, and the red color is usually their cue to a freshly opened flower. Eco-lodges often have hummingbird feeders on their porches. Dozens of flashy large hummingbirds chase each other to gain access to the sugar water while you sit only a meter or two away.

Several groups of Indians used colorful, iridescent hummingbird feathers in their wedding ornaments. Hummingbird bodies have a long mythical history in Latin America of being imbued with potent powers as love charms. Having a dead hummer in the hand or pocket is thought by some even today to be a sure way to appear irresistible to a member of the opposite sex. Even powdered hummingbird is sold for this purpose. The Arakmbut forest people of Amazonian Brazil believe that a hummingbird seen in the forest is a sure sign of a Jaguar being nearby; when spotting such a bird while in the forest, they become more cautious and often return home quickly.

Status
At least 30 species of hummers are currently threatened or considered vulnerable to threat, but none of them occurs in Brazil. Several Brazilian species are very uncommon in the country, but are more abundant in other parts of their ranges.

Profiles
Long-billed Starthroat, *Heliomaster longirostris*, Plate 48d
White-necked Jacobin, *Florisuga mellivora*, Plate 48e
Crimson Topaz, *Topaza pella*, Plate 49a
Swallow-tailed Hummingbird, *Eupetomena macroura*, Plate 49b
Rufous-breasted Hermit, *Glaucis hirsuta*, Plate 49c
Long-tailed Hermit, *Phaethornis superciliosus*, Plate 49d
Black-eared Fairy, *Heliothryx aurita*, Plate 49e
Glittering-throated Emerald, *Amazilia fimbriata*, Plate 50a
Black-throated Mango, *Anthracothorax nigricollis*, Plate 50b
Versicolored Emerald, *Amazilia versicolor*, Plate 50c
Racket-tailed Coquette, *Discosura longicauda*, Plate 50d
Fork-tailed Woodnymph, *Thalurania furcata*, Plate 50e

19. Trogons

Although not as familiar to most people as other gaudy tropical birds such as toucans and parrots, *trogons* are generally regarded by wildlife enthusiasts as among the globe's most visually impressive and glamorous birds. The family Trogonidae inhabits tropical and semi-tropical regions throughout the Neotropics, Africa and southern Asia. It consists of about 40 species (9 in Brazil), all of them colorful, medium-sized birds with compact bodies, short necks and short, almost parrot-like bills. The largest of these species, the *quetzals*, are the most dazzling. Considering the broad and widely separated geographical areas over which the species of this family are spread, the uniformity of the family's body plan and plumage pattern is striking. Males are consistently more colorful than the females and have metallic or glittering green, blue or violet heads, backs and chests. Their breasts and undersides are contrasting bright red, yellow or orange. The duller females usually have the bright back and head colors replaced with brown or gray, but they share the males' brightly colored breasts and bellies. The characteristic tail is long and squared off, with horizontal black and white stripes on the underside. Trogons usually sit erect with their distinctive tails pointing straight down to the ground.

Natural History
Ecology and Behavior
You usually see trogons by themselves or occasionally in pairs. In spite of their persistent calls, they are often difficult to locate and see. Their bright colors meld into the colors of the foliage, and except during their fast and darting flight, they tend to sit still for long periods. At a fruiting tree they will fly up to a fruit and grab it in the bill without landing. They take big insects and occasionally small lizards in much the same way. They are probably most easily seen as part of a *mixed species feeding flock* in the canopy. At these times they move around more and tend to sit out in the open for short periods.

Breeding
Trogons are monogamous, nesting in tree cavities and occasionally in excavations in arboreal ant or termite nests. Generally the female incubates the 2 or 3 eggs overnight, and the male takes over during the day. Incubation is 17 to 19 days. Young are tended by both parents, and fledging is at 14 to 30 days.

Notes
The RESPLENDENT QUETZAL of Central America, a large trogon with extremely long tail feathers, is revered and held sacred by several indigenous groups. The skin of trogons and quetzals is so thin that it has been described as being like wet toilet paper. Why this is so is a question no one yet has been able to answer satisfactorily, but it does mean that you are unlikely to ever see trogons fighting with each other; the slightest cut would be severe.

Status
The trogons and quetzals of Brazil are fairly common, and apparently none is threatened. However, the RESPLENDENT QUETZAL of Central America is considered endangered (CITES Appendix I listed) because of hunting and continuing destruction of its cloud forest habitat.

Profiles
Pavonine Quetzal, *Pharomachrus pavoninus*, Plate 51a
White-tailed Trogon, *Trogon viridis*, Plate 51b
Blue-crowned Trogon, *Trogon curucui*, Plate 51c
Violaceous Trogon, *Trogon violaceus*, Plate 51d
Collared Trogon, *Trogon collaris*, Plate 51e

20. Kingfishers

Kingfishers are handsome, bright birds, and most of Brazil's are easy to see. Generally found along forest streams, large rivers and lakes, they are included in the worldwide Family Alcedinidae (but the New World species are sometimes split into their own family, Cerylidae). Nearly 100 species occur throughout the world in temperate and tropical areas, and 5 of the 6 New World species are found in Brazil. They range in size from 12 to 46 cm (5 to 16 in), but all are similar in form: large heads with very long, robust, straight bills, short necks, and short legs. Their colors are blue-gray or oily green above with white and chestnut breasts. The largest species in Brazil, the RINGED KINGFISHER (Plate 52), is loud and obvious on large rivers and lakes. Its blue-gray back and head, along with its large size, separate it from the other local kingfishers. It often flies high overhead as it moves from one water area to another, giving its far-carrying "check" call. An oily green back and head is characteristic of the other four species in Brazil.

Natural History
Ecology and Behavior
New World kingfishers, as their name suggests, are all mainly *piscivores*, or fish-eaters. Usually seen hunting alone, a kingfisher sits quietly on a low branch over water attentively scanning the water below. When it sees a fish, it swoops down and dives head first into the water, sometimes as deep as 60 cm (24 in) to catch the unwary fish in its bill. If successful, the kingfisher returns to its perch, beats the hapless fish several times on the branch and then swallows it head first. The RINGED KINGFISHER will also hover over the water several seconds before making the plunge. Occasionally they will go after tadpoles and large aquatic insects. Kingfishers have a buzzy and fast flight when moving low over the water's surface.

Kingfishers are highly territorial, noisily defending their territory from other members of the same species (see Close-up, p. 237) with noisy chattering, chasing, and fighting. They inhabit forests and waterways.

Breeding
Kingfishers are monogamous breeders that nest in tunnels excavated from vertical or near vertical banks over water. Both mates help defend their territory, and both also help dig the nest tunnel, which can be 0.75 to 1.5 m (2 to 5 ft) deep. Both parents incubate the 3 to 8 eggs for a total of 19 to 26 days. They feed their young increasingly large fish until they fledge at 25 to 38 days old. Fledglings continue to be fed outside the nest by the parents for up to 10 weeks. Eventually the parents expel the young from the territory, and the young must then establish their own. Kingfishers are notoriously bad housekeepers, and the stench of decaying fish and droppings is often your first clue that a nest tunnel is nearby. This very stench, however, may be so overpowering that it overwhelms the delicate olfactory senses of predators and discourages them from entering to eat what would otherwise be easy prey.

Notes
Kingfishers are the subject of a particularly rich mythology, a sign of the bird's conspicuousness and its association throughout history with oceans, lakes, and rivers. The power over wind and waves that was attributed by sailors to the god Halcyon was passed on to the Halcyon bird, or kingfisher, which became credited with protecting sailors and calming storms. The seven days before and after the winter solstice were thought to be the days when this kingfisher nested and were thus days of peace and calm, the "halcyon" days.

Status
All the New World kingfisher species are moderately common to abundant and none is considered threatened.

Profiles
Ringed Kingfisher, *Ceryle torquata*, Plate 52a
Green Kingfisher, *Chloroceryle americana*, Plate 52b
Green-and-rufous Kingfisher, *Chloroceryle inda*, Plate 52c
Amazon Kingfisher, *Chloroceryle amazona*, Plate 52d
American Pygmy Kingfisher, *Chloroceryle aenea*, Plate 52e

21. Jacamars and Puffbirds

Two interesting and closely related Neotropical families distantly related to king-fishers are the *jacamars* and *puffbirds*. The jacamar family (Galbulidae) includes 18 species, with 15 in Brazil, and the puffbird family (Bucconidae) includes about 30 species, with 23 in Brazil. Species of both families are generally forest dwellers, mostly in warm lowlands. Jacamars are by far the flashier members of the two families, with most having glittering green and blue backs and heads, and noisy vocalizations. Some ornithologists have described them as over-sized humming-birds because of their colors and long, sharp bills. They are, however, much larger than hummingbirds (15 to 31 cm, 6 to 12 in, long) and have distinctly different behavior. Puffbirds are, in contrast, much duller in color – mainly subdued browns and grays or black and white. Their size range is somewhat smaller than that for jacamars, 15 to 28 cm (6 to 11 in), and their bills, although moderately long, are usually very thick and often end in a small hook.

Natural History
Ecology and Behavior

You are most likely to see jacamars along small forest streams and at forest clear-ings. Here they sit, usually in pairs or family groups, chattering away, moving their heads back and forth and waiting for a large butterfly, dragonfly, or other tasty insect to fly by. One of them then darts out and deftly snatches the insect out of the air with the tip of its long bill and then returns to a perch, often the same one from which it launched the aerial attack. After slamming the insect against the perch a couple of times, it removes the wings and swallows the body. If you find a pile of discarded butterfly and other insect wings on a path, this is a good sign for you to look up and search for a jacamar roosting overhead. They often have a series of favorite perches they use through the day, so if it's not there when you first look, check again later.

Most puffbirds are less gaudy and noticeable than jacamars. However, a few species are show-offs, and you have a better chance of seeing them. The WHITE-NECKED PUFFBIRD (Plate 53) is striking with its black and white colors, but you will see it only if you look for it in the canopy, where it often sits on an open branch by itself for an hour or more without moving. If you are visiting one of the canopy towers built in Amazonian Brazil, you will have a better possibility of seeing one without straining your neck staring at the tops of trees from the ground. It and most other puffbirds hunt by waiting patiently for a lizard, small snake or large insect to walk or run on a nearby trunk or on the ground. Then the puffbird swoops from its perch and snatches the luckless prey in its bill. The BLACK-FRONTED NUNBIRD (Plate 53) makes itself so obvious, vocally and visu-ally, that you will have a hard time not noticing it. Usually 2 to 6 individuals will sit on a branch together high up in a tree and sing their rollicking and raucous song for several minutes, each one trying to sing louder than its neighbor. Appar-ently the name "nunbird" was applied by some scientist unappreciative of the local chorus of nuns in black and white habit he had to endure in his childhood church. This species hunts for large insects and lizards running on tree trunks and branches in the mid-levels of primary forests of the Amazon region and is usually associated with *mixed-species foraging flocks* in the canopy. Occasionally a family group of nunbirds will follow a troop of monkeys and catch the large insects scared into flight by movements of the monkeys. The most commonly seen puff-bird in Amazonian Brazil, and the most bizarre in appearance, is the SWALLOW-

WINGED PUFFBIRD (Plate 53). This black, white, and reddish brown species appears to have no tail. It sits, usually in pairs or small groups, in isolated tree tops in the middle of cleared fields or along large rivers of the Amazon. All of a sudden one or all of the group will fly out a long distance, swoop to catch a small insect in the air and then return to the same perch. Their wings are long and tapered, and misidentifications as swallows are common. Even at rest they resemble husky swallows, or as one wag put it, "like swallows on steroids."

Breeding

Jacamars nest in short, horizontal burrows they dig in steep hillsides or in river banks. Both parents incubate the 2 to 4 eggs for a total of 20 to 22 days. They feed insects to the young for 19 to 26 days until fledging. Little is known about breeding in puffbirds, but some nest in burrows on the forest floor and some in burrows excavated from arboreal termite nests. The WHITE-FRONTED NUNBIRD surrounds its tunnel entrance with sticks to hide the hole. Numerous adults appear to feed the young in a helpers-at-the-nest behavior also known from several other families such as jays. Both mates share in tunnel excavation, incubation and feeding the young. The SWALLOW-WINGED PUFFBIRD digs vertical nesting tunnels in sandy soil that are up to 2 m (6.5 ft) deep.

Notes

Puffbirds of several species have been called stupid because they often sit still, depending on camouflage, and permit close approach. But these birds actually can be quite stealthy in their behavior and movements; you will likely pass by many of these birds near forest trails without noticing them.

Status

Among the puffbirds, LANCEOLATED MONKLET populations appear to be declining, and this species may be near-threatened.

Profiles

Rufous-tailed Jacamar, *Galbula ruficauda*, Plate 53a
Paradise Jacamar, *Galbula dea*, Plate 53b
White-necked Puffbird, *Notharchus macrorhynchos*, Plate 53c
Black-fronted Nunbird, *Monasa nigrifrons*, Plate 53d
Swallow-winged Puffbird, *Chelidoptera tenebrosa*, Plate 53e

22. Motmots

With beautiful coloring but a ridiculous name, *motmots*, related to the kingfishers, have several distinctive features. The 9 species in the Family Momotidae are all Neotropical; 4 occur in Brazil. They occur in all types of forest, from primary to flooded, secondary to open orchards, suburban parks and even tropical dry forest areas. Motmots are colorful, long, slender, medium-sized birds (32 to 48 cm, 16 to 19 in, long). They all have long, broad bills somewhat curved down at the ends and with serrate edges, adapted to grab and hold their animal prey. The most peculiar feature, however, is their tail. In some species, two central feather shafts grow much longer than the others. With preening, feather barbs just above the ends of the shafts drop off, producing a short length of naked shaft and an isolated feather patch on the end called a *racket*. General motmot colors are soft hues of cinnamon, and the BLUE-CROWNED MOTMOT (Plate 54) adds a black face and blue-green to turquoise head. Its deep, hollow call of

"BOO-boop," probably the source of the common name of motmots, is given at 3- to 5-second intervals for long periods. The Blue-crowned is the motmot you will most likely encounter either in primary forests or in cut-over areas almost anywhere in eastern and northwestern Brazil. Male and female motmots are similar in size and color.

Natural History
Ecology and Behavior
Motmots are predators on large insects, spiders, and small frogs, lizards and snakes, which they snatch off leaves or from the ground while they are in flight. Typically they perch quietly on tree branches, regularly swinging their long tails from side to side, until they spot a suitable meal moving. They then dart out quickly and seize the prey in their bill, carry it back to their perch and eat it. If the prey is large and struggling, the motmot will thwack it against the branch several times to dispatch it before swallowing it. Motmots are also frugivores, eating small fruits up to the size of plums, which they collect from trees while hovering. You will find motmots almost always by themselves, even though they may pair for the entire year. Pairs tend to separate during the day to feed. They start their daily activities before dawn and continue to well past twilight, after most diurnal birds have gone to bed.

Breeding
Some of their low-key courtship activities include calling back and forth high up in the trees, and holding bits of green leaves in their bills. Motmots are burrow nesters, like their kingfisher cousins. Both male and female help dig the burrow, often placed in the vertical bank of a riverside or road cut. Tunnels can be up to 4 m (13 ft) long, but most are on the order of 1.5 m (4 ft). Both parents incubate the 2 to 4 eggs. Young are fed and brooded by male and female for 24 to 30 days, at the end of which the juvenile motmots are able to fly from the burrow entrance.

Notes
Because of the characteristic swinging of the tail from side to side, one common name for motmots in South America is "clock-maker," evidently referring to the pendulum-like ticking of the tail. This group is one of the few in which there are more species in Central America than in South America, and this is likely the result of a different and probably unique historical origin and subsequent historical movements of this group.

Status
None of Brazil's motmot species is considered endangered or threatened.

Profiles
Blue-crowned Motmot, *Momotus momota*, Plate 54d
Broad-billed Motmot, *Electron platyrhynchum*, Plate 54e

23. Barbets and Toucans

The *barbets* and *toucans* are two closely related groups considered as separate families by some experts and as part of the same family by others; both groups are cousins to the woodpeckers. The barbets have a broad distribution in the tropics of Africa, southern Asia and the Neotropics (family Capitonidae), with a total of 75 species, 5 of which are found in Brazil. Barbets are colorful, with patches of red, orange, yellow, black, and white. Males are generally brighter than females. Several species are known for duet singing between mates. Often one mate sings every other note (an *antiphonal* duet) and the other mate fills in the missing notes in such a perfect, coordinated manner that it sounds like one seamless composition. Ranging in size from 15 to 20 cm (6 to 8 in), barbets are stocky birds with stout but not long bills; they are considerably smaller than toucans. The BLACK-SPOTTED BARBET (Plate 54) is common in primary and secondary forests of the western Amazonian forests. It is frequently in mixed species feeding flocks in the canopy.

Toucans are stunning, and no other word suits them better. Their shape, brilliant color patterns and tropical quintessence make them one of the most popular "poster animals" for the tropical forests of the Americas. Most ecotravellers want to see toucans, and with a little luck, they will. The toucan family, Ramphastidae, has about 40 species, all restricted to the Neotropics. Brazil has 23 species, including some of the smaller types called *aracaris* (AH-rah-SAH-rees) and *toucanets*. Your first sighting of a toucan in the wild will be exciting – the large size of the bird, the bright colors, the enormous almost cartoonish bill all combine to surpass the toucan of your imagination. If you see it in flight, it will somewhat resemble a flying banana, as it alternately flaps and sails in its undulating flight (smaller species fly more directly with a buzzy flight). The toucans' most distinctive mark, their bill, looks so ungainly and heavy you might wonder how they can maintain their balance perched on a branch or in flight. Actually, the bill is mostly hollow and light-weight.

The large toucans (Plate 54) in Brazil are most common in primary forest, but a fruiting tree in secondary (recently cut) forest nearby can easily tempt them. The greatest variety of toucans is among the aracaris (Plate 55), with their numerous variations on the theme of yellow breast, dark back and squealing vocalizations. You will usually see aracaris as a flock flying by one at a time in a long procession (moving from tree to tree in "strings").

Natural History
Ecology and Behavior
Barbets and toucans live in moist forests. You often see barbets in mated pairs among large mixed species foraging flocks in the subcanopy. They commonly eat fruits and seeds, but they also take insects and even small lizards. Almost all toucans are social and gregarious. When they forage at a fruiting tree they reach with their long bills to the outermost fruits, grasp one with the tip of the bill, toss it in the air and swallow it. Toucans also raid other birds' nests to eat eggs and nestlings. Toucans have a mean reputation among smaller birds, and not just because of their nest-robbing proclivities. Apparently toucans take umbrage at other bird species feeding in the same fruiting tree and may at times eat adult birds of small sizes. When a flock of toucans lands in a tree, most of the other birds, even large parrots such as macaws, will quickly abandon the site.

Breeding
Both barbets and toucans nest in tree cavities, either natural cavities or those built originally by woodpeckers. Barbets occasionally use their bills to enlarge holes in softer or dead wood. Nests can be any height above ground up to 30 m (100 ft) or more. Both sexes incubate and feed the 2 to 4 young. Toucans and barbets are apparently monogamous. Some species of toucans like the Central American COLLARED ARACARI seem to breed cooperatively, with numerous helpers at the

nest (usually relatives) in addition to the mother and the father bringing food to the young. Frugivorous birds such as toucans are critical for dispersing seeds away from the parent trees and so helping maintain the healthy plant diversity of these forests (see Close-up, p. 196).

Notes

The colorful rump and tail feathers of toucans are commonly used to construct the feathered crowns of the native people in the Amazonian region of Brazil. If someone tries to sell or even give you one of these crowns, however, you must decline; it is against both Brazilian and international law to export or even possess them.

Status

Habitat clearing and hunting are the main factors explaining declines of toucan populations in some parts of Brazil, but none of the species is considered threatened at this time.

Profiles

Toco Toucan, *Ramphastos toco*, Plate 54a
Cuvier's Toucan, *Ramphastos cuvieri*, Plate 54b
Black-spotted Barbet, *Capito niger*, Plate 54c
Spot-billed Toucanet, *Selenidera maculirostris*, Plate 55a
Curl-crested Aracari, *Pteroglossus beauharnaesii*, Plate 55b
Lettered Aracari, *Pteroglossus inscriptus*, Plate 55c
Red-necked Aracari, *Pteroglossus bitorquatus*, Plate 55d
Chestnut-eared Aracari, *Pteroglossus castanotis*, Plate 55e

24. Woodpeckers

Everyone knows what a *woodpecker* is, at least by name and perhaps by their cartoon incarnations. They are highly specialized forest birds that occur almost everywhere in the world (even in some places without trees) except Australia, New Zealand and Antarctica. The family, Picidae, includes more than 200 species that range in size from the tiny *piculets* (9 cm, 3.5 in, long) to the largest woodpeckers (50 cm, 1.7 ft). Forty-six species of various sizes occur throughout Brazil's diverse habitats. They all share strong, straight and chisel-like bills, very long and barbed tongues, and sharp toes that spread widely for clinging to tree trunks. All but the small piculets also have stiffly reinforced tail feathers that support them as they climb on vertical surfaces. To accommodate their constant banging and drumming with their bills on wood surfaces, they have extra-spongy bone at the base of the bill to absorb shock waves. They come in mostly subdued shades of gray, green, black, and white, frequently with bars and streaks. Most, however, have bright patches of crimson, especially males.

Natural History
Ecology and Behavior

Woodpeckers are adapted to cling to a tree's bark and move lightly over its surface, listening and looking for insects. They drill holes into bark where they hear insects chewing on the wood and then use their long, often sticky tongues to extract the juicy morsels, which include both adult insects and grubs. Some species, such as YELLOW-TUFTED WOODPECKERS (Plate 57), commonly act like flycatchers as they sally out from perches high in trees to catch flying insects in the air. Many species also eat fruit, nuts and nectar from flowers. The piculets use the smallest branches of trees and bushes, usually low in the forest, and, lacking a long stiff tail like the other woodpeckers, clamber about pecking on horizontal branches. In flight, woodpeckers typically undulate up and down with an alternating short burst of rapid wing beating; this causes a rise in altitude that is followed by a short period of folded-wing gliding in which altitude is lost. They sleep and rest in cavities they excavate from trees. Woodpeckers use their bills and their pecking ability in three ways: for drilling holes to get insect food; for excavating holes for roosting and nesting; and for *drumming*, that is, extra rapid beats usually on a hollow surface that amplifies the sound for communication to other woodpeckers.

The holes that woodpeckers excavate for their own nests are used over and over again by a plethora of birds and mammals that cannot excavate their own cavities. Some of these interlopers use abandoned woodpecker holes, but others, such as some aracaris, will at times evict woodpeckers from their active cavity. These cavities are vital for protection from nest predators and are thus at a premium. Their availability may affect the population sizes of many species dependent on them. A species or group of species whose presence or absence directly affects the ability of many other species to persist in a habitat is called a *keystone species*. In this case, the protection of woodpeckers, which can be considered keystone species, is important because their absence would harm a large number of other bird species.

Breeding
Woodpeckers are monogamous, and some live in large social or family groups. Tropical woodpeckers usually remain paired throughout the year. Both mates are involved with the nest excavation, the interior of which they line with wood chips. Both sexes incubate the 2 to 4 eggs for 11 to 18 days, males typically taking the night shift. They feed the young for 20 to 35 days until fledging. Juveniles remain with the parents outside the nest for several months.

Notes
Woodpeckers often damage trees and buildings in their quest for food and nest sites. They also eat fruits from orchards and gardens and so are considered to be pests in some parts of the tropics.

Status
Three of Brazil's woodpecker species are considered threatened or endangered, the HELMETED WOODPECKER, the TAWNY PICULET, and the OCHRACEOUS PICULET. However, these three species are all found in the rapidly disappearing forests of eastern Brazil, and none of the woodpecker species in the Amazon or Pantanal regions of Brazil is considered threatened.

Profiles
White Woodpecker, *Melanerpes candidus*, Plate 56a
Campo Flicker, *Colaptes campestris*, Plate 56b
Lineated Woodpecker, *Dryocopus lineatus*, Plate 56c
Red-necked Woodpecker, *Campephilus rubricollis*, Plate 56d
Crimson-crested Woodpecker, *Campephilus melanoleucos*, Plate 56e
White-wedged Piculet, *Picumnus albosquamatus*, Plate 57a
Spot-breasted Woodpecker, *Colaptes punctigula*, Plate 57b
Pale-crested Woodpecker, *Celeus lugubris*, Plate 57c

Yellow-tufted Woodpecker, *Melanerpes cruentatus*, Plate 57d
Cream-colored Woodpecker, *Celeus flavus*, Plate 57e

All of the bird families considered below are *passerine*, or *perching birds*, members of the Order Passeriformes (see p. 124).

---

25. Woodcreepers

Woodcreepers, Family Dendrocolaptidae, are small to medium-sized brown birds that pursue a mostly arboreal existence. About 50 species are distributed from Mexico to Argentina, 35 in Brazil. They occur in moist forest, tropical dry and thorn forest. Although their long stout bills, stiff tail feathers and tree-trunk climbing recall woodpeckers, these birds are more closely related to flycatchers; the similarities to woodpeckers are superficial and coincidental – what biologists term *evolutionary convergence*. Most are slender birds that range in size from 20 to 36 cm (8 to 14 cm). The sexes look alike, with plumages of various shades of brown, chestnut, and tan. Most have spotting, streaking or banding, but different species are confusingly similar and their identification to species is frustrating at best.

Natural History
Ecology and Behavior
Woodcreepers feed by hitching upwards on tree trunks and also horizontally along branches, peering under bark and into moss clumps and epiphytes, using their stout bills to probe and catch prey in tight nooks and crannies. Unlike woodpeckers, they do not drill holes in search of prey or drum with their bills. The foraging procedure among the various species follows a standard theme but with many variations. An individual flies to the base of a tree and then spirals up the trunk, using its stiff tail for support and sharp toenails for purchase on the bark's surface. Near the top of the tree the bird flies down to the base of the next tree and repeats the process. Some species, however, use smaller trees or even bamboo, others tend to stay higher in the canopy, and some frequently follow army ant swarms to catch large insects flying up to escape the horde. In these cases the woodcreepers will hunt from the base of a tree near the ground or sometimes right on the ground. They will also fly out to catch insects on the wing. Usually woodcreepers are solitary but occasionally a pair will forage together. Some species, however, commonly forage in mixed species foraging flocks of the forest undergrowth or the canopy.

Breeding
Most woodcreeper species practice standard monogamy, with the sexes equally sharing nesting chores and care of the young. In some, however, they form no real pair bonds, and after mating females nest alone. Nests are usually in tree crevices or holes and occasionally in arboreal termite nests. Parents line nests with wood chips. The 2 or 3 eggs are incubated for 17 to 21 days and young fledge 18 to 24 days after hatching.

Notes
Some woodcreepers have reputations for being extremely aggressive toward other species, for example, harassing and evicting roosting or nesting woodpeckers from tree cavities.

Status

Most woodcreepers are common in Brazil. Only the MOUSTACHED WOOD-
CREEPER of dry forests in eastern Brazil is threatened.

Profiles

Red-billed Scythebill, *Campyloramphus trochilirostris*, Plate 58a
Wedge-billed Woodcreeper, *Glyphorynchus spirurus*, Plate 58b
Long-billed Woodcreeper, *Nasica longirostris*, Plate 58c
Buff-throated Woodcreeper, *Xiphorhynchus guttatus*, Plate 58d
Narrow-billed Woodcreeper, *Lepidocolaptes angustirostris*, Plate 58e

26. Ovenbirds

More diverse than the woodcreepers (discussed above), the *ovenbirds* are even
more difficult to tell apart. There are a mind-numbing 240+ species of this family (Furnariidae), which occurs from Mexico to Argentina. Brazil has 100 species,
many of which are differentiated by no more than subtle differences in shades of
brown. We profile four species which you can easily identify and which you are
most likely to see in various Brazilian habitats, from open scrub forests to the
moist forests of the Amazon.

Natural History
Ecology and Behavior

Ovenbirds are all insectivores that mainly glean their resting prey from undersides of leaves and branches. Most ovenbirds live low in their habitats or even on
the ground, but a few are regular in the canopy of tall forests. Although dully colored and unobtrusive in behavior, they are interesting because of the diversity of
ecological niches they occupy. They have invaded almost every habitat in South
America. In this remarkable "radiation," the various species have developed such
a breadth of adaptations that they have become similar to and behave like unrelated families that occupy those respective niches in other parts of the world.
Thus, there are ovenbird "replacements" of thrushes, wheatears, pipits, dippers,
larks, wagtails, nuthatches and chickadees (tits).

Breeding

Many ovenbirds appear to mate for life. Virtually all species of ovenbirds use closed
nests. Some such as *xenops* make tunnels in vertical banks, others use tree cavities
or construct elaborate structures of twigs or mud. The nests of the family's name-
sake, the several species called *horneros* (genus *Furnarius*), are mind-boggling. The
PALE-LEGGED HORNERO (Plate 59) builds large domed nests (Plate 59) out of clay,
sometimes 30 cm (1 ft) in diameter. The shape is much like a small-scale replica of
the old bread ovens also made of clay that were used by early European colonists
in the New World. Usually these nests are placed in exposed areas 1 or 2 m (3 to
6 ft) off the ground. The sun bakes the clay brick hard and few predators can break
down its walls. More clever predators, however, try to use the entrance of the nest
to gain access to eggs or chicks, but are usually foiled by the large but false tunnel
that leads down into the clay mass and then ends abruptly. The actual nest
entrance leads up unobtrusively from the fake tunnel. The oven-shaped nests are
a common part of the scenery in much of Brazil. They are so durable that each one
lasts for years. Often, other species of birds use these cavities for their own nests
after the ovenbirds have abandoned them.

Notes

The hanging nests of the RUFOUS-FRONTED THORNBIRD (Plate 59) are obvious in open forests of central Brazil. Made of interlaced dry twigs, the bulky construction is placed in a large bush or tree usually near a waterway. Shaped like a boot or an American football and often hanging suspended from a small branch, the single entrance is in the "toe" and usually has at least two chambers inside. A nest is used for several years, and additional chambers are often added each year. One chamber serves as the incubating area for eggs and nestlings and the other chambers serve as dormitories or perhaps baffles for intruding predators.

Status

Most ovenbirds in Brazil are common and have extensive ranges, but 7 Brazilian species are threatened or endangered. All but 1 of these are from the Atlantic coastal forests. The HOARY-TAILED SPINETAIL is the only ovenbird in the Brazilian Amazon that is threatened. These 7 species are considered vulnerable because of their extremely small ranges and specialized habitats. Habitat destruction and brush fires easily push such species to very low populations and even extinction.

Profiles

Plain Xenops, *Xenops minutus*, Plate 59a
Rufous Cacholote, *Pseudoseisura cristata*, Plate 59b
Pale-legged Hornero, *Furnarius leucopus*, Plate 59d
Rufous-fronted Thornbird, *Phacellodomus rufifrons*, Plate 59e

27. Antbirds

Antbirds are small and medium-sized, often drab inhabitants of the lower parts of forest vegetation. Many are difficult to see, but often they are loud and vocal. The family of antbirds, Formicariidae, has about 200 species, all restricted to the Neotropics, with 164 in Brazil. The name comes not from their eating ants but from the behavior of some of these species to use army ants to scare up insect prey for them. Antbirds range in size from 8 to 36 cm (3 to 14 in). The smaller ones are called *antwrens* and *antvireos*. The mid-sized ones are the *antbirds*, and larger species are called *antshrikes, antthrushes,* and *antpittas*. In detail these species are quite varied in appearance and body shape. Males are generally colored with understated shades of brown, gray, black, and white. Females are generally duller than the males, with olive brown or chestnut predominating. Some species have bright red eyes or patches of bright bare skin around the eye. Some, like the GREAT ANTSHRIKE (Plate 59), are bold and often emerge from the scrubby bushes to sing and scold. Others, like the THRUSH-LIKE ANTPITTA (Plate 60), are shy and incredibly difficult to see as they run through undergrowth.

Natural History
Ecology and Behavior

Antbirds generally occur in thick vegetation in secondary and primary forests. A few species run on the forest floor, but most are in low to middle parts of the forest. A very few are up in the canopy. Most species are insectivorous, but some of the larger species also eat fruit, lizards, snakes, and frogs. Most species glean for their prey by searching the undersides of leaves and branches. A few hawk for flying insects, and a number always follow army ant swarms (that is, they are *obligate* ant followers). These species wait at the advancing line of army ants as they raid the forest floor (see p. 75). Panicked insects run or fly up from the ant onslaught into the waiting bills of the antbirds. Often several species of antbirds, along with woodcreepers and many other bird species, jostle each other for the best positions to catch the escaping insects.

Breeding
Many antbirds appear to mate for life. Courtship feeding occurs in some of these birds, males passing food to females prior to mating. Many antbirds build cup nests out of pieces of plants that they weave together. Nests are usually placed in a fork of branches low in a tree or shrub, but some species nest in tree cavities. Male and female share nest-building duty, as well as incubation of the 2 or 3 eggs and eventually feeding insects to the young. Incubation is 14 to 20 days, and young remain in the nest for 9 to 18 days. Some of the obligate ant following species have abbreviated courtship and nesting behavior, apparently to facilitate their following the army ants when these mobile insect colonies move on from their temporary bivouacs in the forest. In some species, family groups remain together, male offspring staying with the parents, even after acquiring mates themselves.

Notes
The strange compound names of these birds, such as antwrens and antshrikes, arose partially because, to the naturalists who first named them, there were obvious parallels in size and, at least superficially, appearance, of these various species to North American, European, and Asian wrens and shrikes. These common names are only confusing because some birds similarly named, such as the ant-tanagers, really are tanagers (p. 189) that follow army ants and are not members of the antbird family. Some ornithologists prefer to consider the ground-dwelling antpittas and antthrushes as their own separate family, Formicariidae, and the "typical" antbirds as the Family Thamnophilidae.

Status
Sixteen Brazilian antbirds are presently considered threatened or endangered. Of these, all are from the eastern Atlantic forests except the RÍO BRANCO ANTBIRD, which is restricted to the Amazon region north of Manaus, on the Venezuelan border.

Profiles
Great Antshrike, *Taraba major*, Plate 59c
Black-spotted Bare-eye, *Phlegopsis nigromaculata*, Plate 60a
Barred Antshrike, *Thamnophilus doliatus*, Plate 60b
Mato Grosso Antbird, *Cercomacra melanaria*, Plate 60c
White-plumed Antbird, *Pithys albifrons*, Plate 60d
Thrush-like Antpitta, *Myrmothera campanisona*, Plate 60e

28. Manakins

The *manakins*, family Pipridae, are a Neotropical group of about 60 species, with 36 in Brazil. They are small, compact, stocky passerine birds, 9 to 19 cm (3.5 to 7.5 in) long, with short tails and bills, and two attention-grabbing features: brightly colored plumages and some of the most elaborate courtship displays among birds. Some male manakins are outstandingly beautiful, predominantly glossy black but with brilliant patches of bright orange-red, yellow, or blue on their heads and/or throats. Some have deep blue on their undersides and/or backs. The exotic appearance of male manakins is sometimes enhanced by long, streamer-like tails, up to twice the length of the body, produced by the elongation of two of the central tail feathers. Females, in contrast, are duller and less ornate, usually shades of yellowish olive-green or gray. To accompany the bird's courtship displays, the wing feathers of some species, when moved in certain ways, make whirring or snapping sounds.

The BLUE-CROWNED MANAKIN (Plate 61) is one of the most common species of manakins in the western Amazon region. The males of this species, however, are relatively solitary and rarely form organized mating lecs (see below) in primary forest. The males of the WHITE-BEARDED MANAKIN (Plate 61), in contrast, form noisy and active lecs in secondary forests. Listen for their explosive wing-snapping and nasal calls from the understory.

Natural History
Ecology and Behavior
Manakins are highly active forest birds. Primarily residents of the forest understory, they eat mostly small fruits, which they pluck from bushes and trees while in flight, and they also take insects from the foliage. Largely *frugivorous*, manakins are important seed dispersers of the fruit tree species from which they feed. The cozy relationships between fruit trees and the birds that feed on them are explored in the Close-up on p. 196. Manakins are fairly social animals when it comes to feeding and other daily activities, but males and females do not pair. They employ a non-monogamous mating system and, in fact, most of our knowledge about manakin behavior concerns their breeding behavior – how females choose males with which to mate and, in particular, male courting techniques. To use the ornithological jargon, manakins are *promiscuous* breeders. No pair-bonds are formed between males and females. Males mate with more than one female and females probably do the same. After mating, females build nests and rear young by themselves. Males, singly, or in pairs or small groups, during the breeding season stake out display sites on tree branches, in bushes, or on cleared patches of the forest floor, and then spend considerable amounts of time giving lively vocal and visual displays, trying to attract females. An area that contains several of these performance sites is called a *lec*, and thus manakins, along with other birds such as some grouse, some cotingas, and some hummingbirds, are *lecking* breeders.

At the lec, male manakins *dance*, performing elaborate, repetitive, amazingly rapid and acrobatic movements, sometimes making short up and down flights, sometimes rapid slides, twists, and turn-arounds, sometimes hanging upside down on a tree branch while turning rapidly from side to side and making snapping sounds with their wings. The details of a male's dance are *species specific*, that is, different species dance in different ways. Females, attracted to lecs by the sounds of male displays and by their memories of lec locations – the same traditional forest sites are used from one year to the next – examine the energetically performing males with a critical eye and then choose the ones they want to mate with, sometimes making the rounds several times before deciding. In a few species, two and sometimes three males (*duos and trios*) join together in a coordinated dance on the same perch. In their dance the males alternate *leapfrog hops* with bouts of slow, *butterfly flight*. In these curious cases, one male is dominant, one subordinate, and only the dominant of the pair eventually gets to mate with interested females. Why the subordinate male appears to help the dominant one obtain matings (are they closely related? Do subordinate males stand to inherit display sites when the dominants die? Do subordinates achieve "stolen" matings with females when the dominants are temporarily distracted?), why the manakins dance at all, and on what basis females choose particular males to become the fathers of their young, are all areas of continuing scientific inquiry.

Breeding

Males take no part in nesting. The female builds a shallow cup nest that she weaves into a fork of tree branches, 1 to 15 m (3 to 50 ft) from the ground. She incubates the 1 or 2 eggs for 17 to 20 days, and rears the nestlings herself, bringing them fruit and insects, for 13 to 20 days. Manakins, like most birds that use open, cup-like, nests, often suffer very high rates of nest destruction. In one small study, only about 7% of eggs survived the incubation stage and hatched. Most nests were lost to predators, for which the suspect list is quite lengthy: ground-dwelling as well as arboreal snakes, birds such as motmots, puffbirds, toucans, and jays, large arboreal lizards, and mammals such as opossums, capuchin monkeys, kinkajous, and coatis.

Notes

Colorful manakin feathers were often used by the indigenous peoples of Central and South America for ornamental purposes, especially for clothing and masks used during dances and solemn festivals.

Status

Two Brazilian species of manakins are considered threatened – the BLACK-CAPPED MANAKIN of extreme southeastern coastal Brazil and the GOLDEN-CROWNED MANAKIN, which is known only from a tiny area of primary forest south of the Río Amazonas in central Brazil.

Profiles

Blue-crowned Manakin, *Pipra coronata*, Plate 61a
White-bearded Manakin, *Manacus manacus*, Plate 61b
White-crowned Manakin, *Pipra pipra*, Plate 61c
Golden-headed Manakin, *Pipra erythrocephala*, Plate 61d
Helmeted Manakin, *Antilophia galeata*, Plate 61e

29. Cotingas

Owing to their variety of shapes, sizes, ecologies, and breeding systems, as well as to their flashy coloring, *cotingas* are usually considered to be among the Neotropic's glamour birds. The Family Cotingidae is closely allied with the manakins and flycatchers and contains about 70 species, with 48 in Brazil. The cotingas include species from tiny, warbler-sized birds to large, crow-sized birds. Primarily fruit- and insect-eaters, some eat only fruit (which among birds is uncommon). In some species the sexes look alike, but in many the males are stunningly attired in bright spectral colors while the females are plain. There are territorial species that breed *monogamously* and *lecking* species that breed *promiscuously* (see below); all in all a very eclectic family.

Among the Brazilian cotingas are *pihas*, *"typical" cotingas*, *cocks-of-the-rock*, *umbrellabirds*, and *fruitcrows*, the last two being quite large. Perhaps the only generalizations that apply to these birds are that all have short legs and relatively short, rather wide bills, the better to swallow fruits. Males of some of the group are quite ornate, with patches of gaudy plumage in unusual colors. For instance, some of the typical cotingas are lustrous blue and deep purple, and some are all white; others are wholly black, or green and yellow, or largely red or orange or gray. The GUIANAN COCK-OF-THE-ROCK (Plate 63) is one of the most dramatic species of cotingas in Brazil, and it is also a lecking species. Three to 80 large, bright red and crested males gather to attract rather dull-colored females at historical sites often used for decades. Males of the almost equally handsome BLACK-NECKED RED-COTINGA (Plate 62) also lec in forests of northwestern Brazil. They are noisy and sometimes easy to see at historical courting sites. PURPLE-THROATED FRUITCROWS (Plate 63) live in highly social flocks of 5 to 10 individuals. They seldom leave the canopy of primary forest in the Amazon. Listen for their distinctive calls, which are loud and slurred whistles interspersed by rude hacking noises, like someone getting ready to spit. If you try mimicking their whistles, you can often attract them in close to you as they investigate an intruder into their territory. One Brazilian cotinga that you will hear over and over in the forests of the Amazon, but probably never see, is the SCREAMING PIHA (Plate 62). Its ear-splitting shrill whistles are given by numerous males from the tops of widely separated, tall trees in primary forest. Their plain gray plumage makes them almost impossible to see, but females are more interested in how individual males sing in their lecs than in how colorful they are.

Natural History
Ecology and Behavior
Cotingas primarily inhabit the high canopy of the forest. They are fruit specialists, a feature of their natural history that has engendered much study. They eat small and medium-sized fruits that they take off trees, often while hovering. Some cotingas, such as fruitcrows and pihas, supplement the heavily frugivorous diet with insects taken from the treetop foliage, but others, particularly the species called *fruiteaters*, feed exclusively on fruit. This dependence creates both problems and benefits (for details, see Close-up, p. 196); one consequence is that when young are fed only fruit, the nestling period can be unusually long because rapidly growing nestlings require protein that an all-fruit diet provides only at a low rate. Because of the cotingas' feeding specialization on fruit, they are vital as dispersers of tree seeds. Owing to their high-canopy habits, the precise fruits cotingas go after often are difficult to determine. They feed heavily at palms, laurels, and incense trees, and also at, among others, members of the blackberry/raspberry family.

Breeding
Some cotingas pair up, defend territories from *conspecifics* (individuals of the same species), and breed conventionally in apparent monogamy. But others, such as umbrellabirds, cocks-of-the-rock, and pihas, are lecking species, in which males individually stake out display trees and repeatedly perform vocal and visual displays to attract females. Females enter display areas, called *lecs*, assess the jumping and calling males, and choose the ones they wish to mate with. With this type of breeding, females leave after mating and then nest and rear young alone. Nests, usually placed in trees or bushes, are generally small, open, and inconspicuous, some nest cups being made of loosely arranged twigs, some of mud, and some of pieces of plants. Many species lay only a single egg, some 1 or 2 eggs. Incubation

is 17 to 28 days and the nestling period is 21 to 44 days, both stages quite long for passerine birds.

Notes

Because they are often dubbed onto the soundtrack of most movies and TV programs with a "jungle" setting, calls of the SCREAMING PIHA likely will be a strangely familiar part of your first hike into the Amazon forest. The sound is now so widely used by the entertainment industry that it could be considered trite – until you stand in the midst of a small group of these males each calling from the top of a different tree. Even from a kilometer (half-mile) away, the sound penetrates the vegetation; if you are directly beneath a calling male, you may well have to hold your hands over your ears to stop the ringing.

Status

Of the 48 Brazilian cotingas, 8 are considered threatened, and they are all found in the eastern Atlantic forests of the coast. The tiny geographical ranges of these cotingas together with rapid deforestation make them vulnerable.

Profiles

Black-necked Red-Cotinga, *Phoenicircus nigricollis*, Plate 62a
Plum-throated Cotinga, *Cotinga maynana*, Plate 62b
Screaming Piha, *Lipaugus vociferans*, Plate 62c
Pompadour Cotinga, *Xipholena punicea*, Plate 62d
Masked Tityra, *Tityra semifasciata*, Plate 62e
Amazonian Umbrellabird, *Cephalopterus ornatus*, Plate 63a
Purple-throated Fruitcrow, *Querula purpurata*, Plate 63b
Guianan Cock-of-the-Rock, *Rupicola rupicola*, Plate 63c
Bare-necked Fruitcrow, *Gymnoderus foetidus*, Plate 63d

30. American Flycatchers

The *American flycatchers* comprise a huge group of passerine birds that is broadly distributed over most habitats from Alaska and northern Canada to the southern tip of South America. The flycatcher family, Tyrannidae, is considered among the most diverse of avian groups. Some experts even combine American flycatchers, manakins (Pipridae) and cotingas (Cotingidae) into one megafamily, but we will follow the narrower definition of what constitutes the flycatcher family. With more than 380 species, the flycatchers usually contribute a hefty percentage of the avian biodiversity in every locale. For instance, it has been calculated that flycatchers make up fully one tenth of the land bird species in South America, and perhaps one-quarter of Argentinean species. In Brazil the group is represented by a healthy contingent of about 220 species.

Flycatchers range in length from 6.5 to 30 cm (2.5 to 12 in). At the smallest extreme are some of the world's tiniest birds, weighing, it is difficult to believe, only some 7 g (¼ oz). Their bills are usually broad and flat, the better to snatch flying bugs from the air. Tail length is variable, and some species even have long, forked tails, which probably aid the birds in their rapid, acrobatic, insect-catching maneuvers. Most flycatchers are dully turned out in shades of gray, brown, and olive-green, and the sexes are generally similar in appearance. Many species have some yellow in their plumage, and a relatively few are quite flashily-attired in, for example, bright expanses of red or vermilion. A great many of the smaller, drabber flycatchers, clad in olives and browns, are extremely difficult to tell apart in the field, even for experienced birdwatchers. One set of frequently seen flycatchers that are easy to see and identify all share bright yellow breasts and some variation on a theme of white eyelines and dark heads. The most likely species of this group of flycatchers you will see in Brazil include the GREAT KISKADEE (Plate 66), the LESSER KISKADEE (Plate 66), the BOAT-BILLED FLYCATCHER (Plate 66), the SOCIAL FLYCATCHER (Plate 66), and the TROPICAL KINGBIRD (Plate 66). These are all widespread species found in open areas and can be distinguished by presence or absence of rufous (reddish brown) coloring in the wings and tail, size of the bill, and habitat.

Natural history
Ecology and Behavior
Flycatchers are common over a large array of different habitat types, from moist forests, treeless plains and grasslands to marshes and mangrove swamps. As their name implies, flycatchers are primarily insectivores, obtaining most of their food by employing the classic flycatching technique. They perch motionless on tree or shrub branches or on fences or telephone wires, then dart out in short, swift flights to snatch from the air insects foolhardy enough to enter their field of vision; the bird then returns time and again to the same perch to repeat the process. Many flycatchers also snatch insects from foliage as they glean the vegetation, and many also supplement their diets with berries and seeds. Some of the larger flycatchers will also take small frogs and lizards, and some, such as the GREAT KISKADEE, consider small fish and tadpoles delicacies to be plucked from shallow water at the edges of lakes and rivers. A few species, like the PIRATIC FLYCATCHER (Plate 66), have ceded flycatching to their relatives and are now, as adults, almost completely *frugivorous*.

Many flycatchers show marked alterations in their lifestyles as seasons, locations, and feeding opportunities change. Such ongoing capacity for versatile behavior in response to changing environments is considered a chief underlying cause of the group's great ecological success. An excellent example is the EASTERN KINGBIRD'S (Plate 65) drastic changes in behavior between summer and winter. Breeding during summer in North America, these black and white flycatchers are extremely aggressive in defending their territories from birds and other animals, and they feed exclusively at that time on insects. But a change comes over the birds during the winter, as they idle away the months in South America's Amazon Basin. There, Eastern Kingbirds congregate in large, nonterritorial flocks with apparently nomadic existences, and they eat mostly fruit.

Breeding
Almost all of the relatively few flycatchers that have been studied inhabit exclusive territories that mated, monogamous pairs defend for all or part of the year. Some forest-dwelling species, however, breed *promiscuously*: groups of males call and display repeatedly at traditional courting sites called *lecs*, attracting females that approach for mating but then depart to nest and raise young by themselves. Many flycatchers are known for amazing courtship displays, males showing off to females by engaging in aerial acrobatics, including flips and somersaults. In monogamous species, males may help females build nests. Some build cup nests, roofed nests, or globular hanging nests placed in trees or shrubs, others construct mud nests that they attach to vertical surfaces such as rock walls, and some nest in holes in trees or rocks. Tropical flycatchers generally lay 2 eggs that are incubated only by the female for 12 to 23 days; nestlings fledge when 14 to 28 days old.

The *tody flycatchers* construct large, hanging, woven, or "felted," nests that take up to a month or more to build. These nests tend to hang from slender vines or weak tree branches, which provides a degree of safety from climbing nest predators such as snakes and small mammals. Often, however, such efforts are ineffective – nest predation rates are quite high. In response, some of the tody flycatchers purposefully build their nests near to colonies of stinging bees, apparently seeking additional protection from predators. The PIRATIC FLYCATCHER lives up to its name. This scoundrel species drives hard-working caciques, oropendolas and even other flycatchers from their nests and usurps them for its own.

Notes
Flycatchers in Brazil are notorious because of the difficulty of distinguishing the many similar species in the field. Some can only be readily distinguished by their voices, so if you have feelings of frustration trying to figure this group out, you are not alone.

Status
Nine species of flycatchers in Brazil are listed as threatened or endangered, but only one of them, the RUFOUS-SIDED PYGMY TYRANT, enters the northeastern part of the Pantanal region. The rest are restricted to the eastern coastal habitats of Atlantic Brazil.

Profiles
White-headed Marsh-Tyrant, *Arundinicola leucocephala*, Plate 64a
Spotted Tody-Flycatcher, *Todirostrum maculatum*, Plate 64b
Cattle Tyrant, *Machetornis rixosus*, Plate 64c
Vermilion Flycatcher, *Pyrocephalus rubinus*, Plate 64d
Drab Water-Tyrant, *Ochthornis littoralis*, Plate 64e
Eastern Kingbird, *Tyrannus tyrannus*, Plate 65a
Fork-tailed Flycatcher, *Tyrannus savana*, Plate 65b
White-rumped Monjita, *Xolmis velata*, Plate 65c

Sirystes, *Sirystes sibilator*, Plate 65d
Black-backed Water-Tyrant, *Fluvicola albiventer*, Plate 65e
Tropical Kingbird, *Tyrannus melancholicus*, Plate 66a
Boat-billed Flycatcher, *Megarhynchus pitangua*, Plate 66b
Great Kiskadee, *Pitangus sulphuratus*, Plate 66c
Lesser Kiskadee, *Pitangus lictor*, Plate 66d
Social Flycatcher, *Myiozetetes similis*, Plate 66e
Piratic Flycatcher, *Legatus leucophaius*, Plate 66f

31. Jays

Jays are members of the Corvidae, a passerine family of 115 species that occurs just about everywhere in the world – or, as ecologists would say, corvid distribution is *cosmopolitan*. The group also includes the *crows, ravens,* and *magpies.* Although on many continents birds of open habitats, jays of the Neotropics are primarily woodland or forest birds. Jays, aside from being strikingly handsome birds, are known for their versatility, adaptability, and for their seeming intelligence. In several ways, the group is considered by ornithologists to be one of the most highly-developed of birds. They are also usually quite noisy.

Members of the family range in length from 18 to 77 cm (7 in to 2.5 ft), many near the higher end – large for passerine birds. *Corvids* have robust, fairly long bills and strong legs and feet. Many of them (crows, ravens, rooks, jackdaws) are all or mostly black, but the jays are different, being attired in bright blues, purples, greens, yellows, and white. In corvids, the sexes generally look alike. The COMMON RAVEN is the largest passerine bird in the world, but although its range encompasses several continents, it does not extend to Brazil. The only representatives of this family in Brazil are 8 species of jays, most of which you will see in small family groups (theirs, not yours).

Natural History
Ecology and Behavior
Jays eat a large variety of foods (and try to eat many others) and so are considered *omnivores*. They feed on the ground, but also in trees, eating carrion, insects (including some flying ones), fruits and nuts, and also robbing bird eggs and nestlings. They are considered to be responsible for a significant percentage of the nest predation on many songbird species, particularly those with open-cup nests. Bright and versatile, they are quick to take advantage of new food sources and to find food in agricultural and other human-altered environments. Jays use their feet to hold food down while tearing it with their bills. Hiding food for later consumption, *caching*, is practiced widely by the group.

Most corvids are quite social, Brazilian jays being no exception. Many of these species remain all year in small groups of relatives, 5 to 10 individuals strong. They forage together within a restricted area, or *home range*, and at the appropriate time, breed together on a group-defended territory. Jays are usually raucous and noisy, giving varieties of harsh, grating, loud calls as the foraging flock straggles from tree to tree, but at times they can be amazingly quiet and unobtrusive, especially during the breeding season.

Breeding
Several species of jays raise young cooperatively. Generally the oldest pair in the group breeds and the other members serve only as *helpers*, assisting in nest construction and feeding the young. Courtship feeding is common, the male feeding the female before and during incubation, which she performs alone. Bulky, open nests, constructed primarily of twigs, are placed in trees or rock crevices. Two to 7 eggs are incubated for 16 to 21 days, the young then being fed in the nest by parents and helpers for 20 to 24 days.

Notes
Although members of the crow family are considered by many to be among the most intelligent of birds, and by ornithologists as among the most highly evolved, corvid folklore is rife with tales of crows, ravens, and magpies as symbols of ill-omen. This undoubtedly traces to the group's frequently all-black plumage and habit of eating carrion, both sinister traits. COMMON RAVENS, in particular, have long been associated in many Northern cultures with evil or death, although these large, powerful birds also figure more benignly in Nordic and Middle Eastern mythology. Several groups of indigenous peoples of northwestern North America consider the Raven sacred and sometimes, indeed, as a god.

Status
Some of the 8 species of jay that occur in Brazil are fairly rare, but none is considered threatened. Many corvids adjust well to people's activities, often expanding their ranges when they can feed on agricultural crops.

Profiles

Violaceous Jay, *Cyanocorax violaceus*, Plate 67d
Purplish Jay, *Cyanocorax cyanomelas*, Plate 67e

32. Wrens and Gnatcatchers

Wrens are small, brownish species with an active, snappish manner and, characteristically, erect, upraised tails. Most skulk in thick undergrowth, but a few are *arboreal*, staying in trees in more open areas. Approximately 75 wren species comprise the family Troglodytidae, a group that except for one Eurasian species is confined to the Western Hemisphere; 18 species occur in Brazil. Among other traits, wrens are renowned for their singing ability, vocal duets, and nesting behavior. They range in length from 10 to 22 cm (4 to 9 in) and usually appear in shades of brown or reddish brown, with smaller bits of tan, gray, black, and white. Some of these birds are tiny, weighing in at less than 15 g (half an ounce). Wings and tails are frequently embellished with finely barred patterns. Wrens have rather broad, short wings and owing to this, are considered poor flyers. The sexes look alike. The marsh-inhabiting DONACOBIUS (Plate 67) occurs in small colonies. It is so large and unusually colored that for years ornithologists considered it a mockingbird. Only with recent DNA studies has it found a more comfortable home in the wren family.

Gnatcatchers and *gnatwrens* are variously placed in the huge and worldwide family of Old World warblers, Sylviidae (361 species) or split by some experts into their own New World family called Polioptilidae. Unlike the New World Warblers, which have nine long flight (primary) feathers in each wing, gnatwrens and gnatcatchers have 10 – only an ornithologist would consider counting obscure feathers, but it is a distinctive if not readily seen trait. The gnatcatchers and gnatwrens are all small birds that are clad in understated colors of gray, black, white, and tawny, and they display a long, slender tail that is often carried cocked up over the back.

Natural History
Ecology and Behavior

Most wrens are *cryptically colored* and fairly secretive in their habits as they sneak, hop and poke around the low levels of the forest, and through thickets, grasslands, and marshes, searching for insects. They are completely *insectivorous* or nearly so. Often spending the year living in pairs, they defend territories in which during the breeding season they will nest. The HOUSE WREN (Plate 68) is the same species as in North America and familiar to many. It is ubiquitous throughout Brazil, except for in undisturbed forested areas. Some of the larger wrens, such as the THRUSH-LIKE WREN (Plate 67), spend their days higher in the trees in small family flocks, and, owing to their size, are a bit bolder in their movements. Their loud songs also make them obvious. After breeding, wrens will use their nests as roosting places – or "dormitories," as one researcher puts it. Some species actually build specific nests for roosting that are of a different structure than nests for raising young. The vocalizations of wrens have been studied extensively. Especially talented, a pair of the DONACOBIUS will call back and forth as they lose sight of each other while foraging in dense marsh grasses, keeping in contact. Mated pairs of some wren species sing some of the bird world's most complex duets, male and female rapidly alternating in giving parts of one song (as we think of it), so rapidly and expertly that it actually sounds as if one individual utters the entire sequence. Such duets probably function as "keep-out" signals, warning away from the pair's territory other members of the species, and in maintaining the pair-bond between mated birds. The MUSICIAN WREN has to be heard to be believed. If you hear what sounds like a child learning to whistle in the undergrowth of the Amazonian forest, it is probably this species. It is most easily seen as it participates in undergrowth mixed-species foraging flocks that move low through denser parts of the forest.

The gnatcatchers and gnatwrens are also insectivorous. They often associate with large mixed-species foraging flocks in the low to mid-story of primary and secondary forests. They are visually inconspicuous, but their noisy calls often make them obvious.

Breeding

The wrens of Brazil are mainly monogamous, but some like the DONACOBIUS breed *cooperatively*, with members of the small family group helping out at the single nest of the parents. Nests, generally of woven grass, are placed in vegetation or in tree cavities. They are small but elaborate nests, roofed, with inconspicuous side entrances. Intriguingly, in some species the male builds many more nests on his territory than his mate (or mates, in *polygynous* species) can use, apparently as a courtship signal, perhaps as an inducement for a female to stay and mate. Only the female incubates the 2 to 5 eggs, for 13 to 19 days. Sometimes she is fed by the male during this period. Nestlings are fed by both parents for 14 to 19 days, until fledging.

The gnatcatchers and gnatwrens are monogamous and form territories with a single pair breeding in each. The gnatcatchers make elaborate but tiny nests of fine grasses, hairs, spider webbing, and moss that are affixed to the top of a small horizontal branch.

Notes

The HOUSE WREN has one of the most extensive ranges of any bird species in the Western hemisphere. It nests from North America to throughout South America. One of the reasons for its extensive range is that it often nests in association with people and their structures. These birds root about near and in human settlements, looking for insects. Nests are often placed in crannies and crevices within buildings or other structures. (Many wrens nest in naturally occurring cavities, hence the family name, Troglodytidae, or "cave dweller.")

Status

Most of the wren, gnatcatcher, and gnatwren species that occur in Brazil are fairly common, and none is threatened.

Profiles

Thrush-like Wren, *Campylorhynchus turdinus*, Plate 67a
Donacobius, *Donacobius atricapillus*, Plate 67c

Southern Nightingale Wren, *Microcerculus marginatus*, Plate 68a
House Wren, *Troglodytes aedon*, Plate 68b
Buff-breasted Wren, *Thryothorus leucotis*, Plate 68c
Long-billed Gnatwren, *Ramphocaenus melanurus*, Plate 68d
Masked Gnatcatcher, *Polioptila dumicola*, Plate 68e

33. Thrushes and Mockingbirds

The more than 300 species of *thrushes* inhabit most terrestrial regions of the world and include some of the most familiar park and garden birds. The family, Turdidae, has few defining, common features that set its members apart from other groups, as perhaps could be expected; so large an assemblage of species is sure to include a significant amount of variation in appearance, ecology, and behavior. *Thrushes, robins, nightingale thrushes,* and *solitaires* of the Western Hemisphere are slender-billed birds that range from 12.5 to 31 cm (5 to 12 in) in length. In Brazil there are 17 species of this family, some of which are migrants from nesting grounds in North America. Generally they are not brightly colored; instead, they come in drab browns, grays, brown-reds, olive, and black and white. The sexes are very similar in appearance. During their first months of life, young thrushes are clad in distinctively spotted plumages.

Many species of thrushes have adapted to living near humans and benefitting from their environmental modifications. On five continents, a thrush is among the most common and recognizable of garden birds, including North America's AMERICAN ROBIN, Europe's REDWING and BLACKBIRD, and southern Brazil's RUFOUS-BELLIED THRUSH (Plate 69). Thrushes in general are famous for their rich and musical sounds, and one of the champion songsters of the world is the LAWRENCE'S THRUSH (Plate 69). It is easily overlooked in the primary forests of the Amazon, but it is one of the most remarkable mimics in South America. It sings high in the forest all day long, and the song of a single individual may include song phrases of up to 35 other species; with some patience, this songster supreme can usually be found on its favorite perch day after day.

Although superficially similar to the thrushes, the family of *mockingbirds*, Mimidae, is now thought to be most closely related to the starlings. The *mimids*, which also include *thrashers* and *catbirds*, are found only in the New World. These medium-sized birds (20 to 30 cm, 8 to 12 in) have long tails and rather short and rounded wings. Most species have strong, moderately long bills, often down-curved. The species tend toward gray, brown or rufous, often with flashes of white in the tail and wings. There is no distinct difference in the plumages of the sexes. Only a few species actually mimic calls and songs of other species. Of the 30+ species in the family, only 3 are found in Brazil, 2 of them in the Pantanal area: the CHALK-BROWED MOCKINGBIRD (Plate 67) and the WHITE-BANDED MOCKINGBIRD.

Natural History
Ecology and Behavior
Many thrushes eat fruits, some are primarily *insectivorous*, and most are at least moderately *omnivorous*. Although generally arboreal birds, many thrushes frequently forage on the ground for insects, other arthropods, and, a particular favorite, delicious earthworms. Some of the thrushes in Brazil associated with gardens forage like the familiar thrushes from North America or Europe – they hop and walk along the ground, stopping at intervals, cocking their heads to peer downwards. These birds are residents of many kinds of habitats – deep forest, forest edge, clearings, and other open areas such as shrub areas and grasslands, gardens, parks, suburban lawns, and agricultural areas. Many thrushes are quite social, spending their time during the nonbreeding season in flocks of the same species, feeding and roosting together. Some of the tropical thrushes, like the BLACK-BILLED THRUSH (Plate 69), evidently make seasonal migrations within the Amazon, following changing food supplies.

The mockingbirds feed on fruits, seeds, and insects. Many feed on the ground using their curved bills to dig and probe for prey in soft soils and leaf litter. With their long tails and the open habitat they prefer, they are often one of the most conspicuous bird species present. They tend to be highly territorial and often solitary throughout the year.

Breeding

Thrushes breed monogamously, male and female together defending exclusive territories during the breeding season; pairs may associate year round. Nests, usually built by the female and placed in tree branches, shrubs, or crevices, are open and cup-shaped, made of grass, moss, and like materials, and often lined with mud. Two to 6 eggs (usually 2 or 3) are incubated by the female only for 12 to 14 days. Young are fed by both parents for 12 to 16 days prior to their fledging. The mockingbirds are monogamous, and both sexes participate in building the bulky, open cup-shaped nest of twigs and lining it with hair or grass. It is placed low in a bush or occasionally on the ground. The 2 to 4 eggs are generally incubated by the female alone for about 2 weeks. The chicks are then fed by both parents for another 13 to 19 days until they fledge.

Notes

English colonists in the New World gave the AMERICAN ROBIN, a thrush, its name because it resembled England's common ROBIN, an Old World flycatcher – both birds have reddish breasts. The New World bird, however, is more closely related to Europe's BLACKBIRD, also a common garden bird and a true thrush; and you wonder why common names of birds can be so confusing.

Status

Although several thrushes and mockingbirds in many different parts of the world are vulnerable to threats or are now considered threatened, none of the species that breeds in Brazil is in imminent danger.

Profiles

Chalk-browed Mockingbird, *Mimus saturninus*, Plate 67b
Rufous-bellied Thrush, *Turdus rufiventris*, Plate 69a
Pale-breasted Thrush, *Turdus leucomelas*, Plate 69b
Black-billed Thrush, *Turdus ignobilis*, Plate 69c
Lawrence's Thrush, *Turdus lawrencii*, Plate 69d

34. Wood Warblers and Vireos

More than 110 species of the spritely and often beautiful family of New World *wood warblers* (Parulidae) are found from Alaska to Argentina. In Brazil, 21 species occur: 7 species that are migrants from nesting grounds in North America, and 14 species that are non-migratory. Most of the migratory species are easy to see as they forage high in trees of secondary and primary forests, but they do little singing on their wintering grounds and for most of their stay in Brazil are clad in subdued colors that make them difficult to identify. The non-migratory species, in contrast, sing loudly and wear the same plumage all year round. Unfortunately, they tend to skulk in the dense undergrowth, and many of them at their brightest plumage are as dull as the winter plumages of the migratory species. The plumages of both sexes of non-migratory species tend to be similar, but in migratory species, only the males acquire a brilliant summer plumage. Warblers all have thin, narrow bills and both migratory and non-migratory species regularly participate in *mixed species foraging flocks*.

The family of *vireos*, Vireonidae, has about 44 species throughout the New World (14 species in Brazil). They are small to medium-sized birds varying from 10 to 18 cm (4 to 7 in) in length. They have stout legs and a short neck. Most experts divide the family into three subgroups: the *typical vireos*, with a medium bill slightly hooked at the tip; the *shrike-vireos*, with a stout bill with a hooked tip; and the *pepper-shrikes*, with a heavy bill flattened sideways with a large hook at the tip. Most species of vireos are plainly colored in greens, olives, and grays above, with grays, yellows or buff below. The shrike vireos and pepper-shrikes, however, are more brightly colored, with greens, reds, and blues.

After the House Wren (Plate 68), the RED-EYED VIREO (Plate 70) has the widest nesting range of any bird species in the Western hemisphere. Migrant populations nest throughout most of eastern North America and winter in the Amazon. Other populations are resident nesters throughout the northern two-thirds of South America.

Natural History
Ecology and Behavior
Wood warblers are largely insect eaters. Some species, such as the *redstarts*, sally out like flycatchers to snatch flying insects in the air. Some species probe flowers and buds with their thin bills for insects hiding there. Most species, however, glean insects from undersides of leaves and twigs. The quality of songs among these warblers ranges from loud and clear notes to insect-like trills and buzzes. Found only along forested streams, the FLAVESCENT WARBLER (Plate 70) is resident year-round and is largely terrestrial. Its loud ringing song and large fanned tail make it easy to find and identify.

Vireos eat mainly insects gleaned from leaves and branches; however, small fruits are eaten at times. The tropical species are typically found in mixed-species foraging flocks from the canopy down to mid-levels of the forest.

The migratory distances for warbler and vireo species nesting in North America involve thousands of kilometers. The BLACKPOLL WARBLER, for instance, winters as far south as Bolivia and nests as far north as northern Canada. For many years, North American scientists interested in warblers and many other songbirds concentrated their research on the birds' ecology and behavior during breeding, essentially ignoring the fact that the birds spent more than half of each year wintering in the tropics, many of them in South America. Now, with the realization that the birds' biology during the nonbreeding season is also important for understanding their lives, their ecology and behavior during the winter have become areas of intense interest. Being addressed in research studies are such questions as: Are species that are territorial during breeding also territorial on their wintering grounds, and if so, in what way? Do individual birds return to the same spot in the tropics each year in winter as they do for nesting during the North American spring? Do migratory birds compete for food on their wintering grounds with those species that remain all year in the tropics? Why do the migratory species of warblers have dull plumages on the wintering grounds, and why do the non-migratory species have the same plumage all year around?

Breeding
Most warbler species place their nests in trees or shrubs, but some nest on the ground or in tree cavities. The nest shape is usually an open cup-like structure,

but in the tropics many species build a domed nest with an entrance at the side. Warblers are primarily monogamous, but the females do most if not all the nest construction. The 2 to 4 eggs are incubated by the female for about 12 days. After hatching, the chicks are fed by both parents for 8 to 12 days in the nest, and continue to be fed by the parents for a few weeks after leaving the nest.

Vireos build small cup-shaped nests in the horizontal fork of a tall bush or tree, usually attached by the rim of the nest so it is a semi-hanging construction. The 2 to 5 white eggs are incubated by both parents, and hatched young are fed by both parents, which carry insects to the nest in their bills. The typical vireos defend breeding territories with songs that are usually short and simple. The shrike-vireos and pepper-shrikes have loud but more melodious songs.

Status

No warblers that occur in Brazil are known to be threatened. Two other warblers, however, are now endangered – KIRTLAND'S WARBLER, which breeds in the USA (Michigan) and winters in the Bahamas, and SEMPER'S WARBLER, which occurs only on the Caribbean island of St. Lucia. Kirtland's Warbler, which nests only in stands of young Jack-pine trees, has been victimized by its own specialization on one type of breeding habitat combined with a shrinking availability of that habitat, by destruction of its wintering habitat, and by BROWN-HEADED COWBIRDS, which lay their eggs in the nests of warblers and other species, reducing their reproductive success (see p. 193). It is suspected that mongooses, which were introduced to St. Lucia by people and which are predators on bird nests, play a major role in endangering Semper's Warbler, which nests on or near the ground. Ten to 12 additional American warbler species are probably now at risk, but there is at present insufficient information about their populations to judge their statuses with any certainty. The BACHMAN'S WARBLER, which nested throughout the southeastern US and wintered in Cuba, apparently became extinct in the 1960s. The population of RED-EYED VIREO on the island of Fernando de Noronha, off the coast of northeastern Brazil, is considered by some to be a separate species, the NORONHA VIREO. Its restricted distribution and its unwary behavior on this island have led conservation biologists to consider it threatened.

Profiles

Rufous-browed Peppershrike, *Cyclarhis gujanensis*, Plate 69e
Slaty-capped Shrike-Vireo, *Vireolanius leucotis*, Plate 70a
Red-eyed Vireo, *Vireo olivaceus*, Plate 70b
Flavescent Warbler, *Basileuterus (Phaeothlypis) flaveolus*, Plate 70d
Tropical Parula, *Parula pitiayuma*, Plate 70e

35. Conebills and Honeycreepers

This group of species does not fit obviously into any single family, and no two ornithologists seem to agree on who their closest relatives are. Some experts place the *conebills* and *honeycreepers* in the tanager family, Thraupidae. Others have them related to the finches and placed as a subfamily within the Emberizidae. Yet others place some of them with the wood warblers, Parulidae. All these species are associated with flowers, and many of them are very colorful. Although the conebills are primarily in the higher altitudes, a few occur in the lowlands. Honeycreepers and *dacnis* are most common in the lowlands. You will most likely see the dacnis and honeycreepers in high canopy flocks of the lowland forests. An easy way to see them well is from one of the canopy towers constructed by lodges in primary forest. The BANANAQUIT (Plate 70), which is either lumped into the warbler group or is the only member of its own family, Coerebidae (its classification is controversial), is a tiny yellow and olive/grayish bird with a broad Neotropical distribution: from southern Mexico and the Caribbean to northern Argentina. It is a common species in urban areas and disturbed habitats – so people have been a boon to its spread. In Amazonia its presence indicates that the primary forest has been largely disturbed in the area. In all, 12 species of this group occur in Brazil.

Natural History
Ecology and Behavior
Conebills, bananaquits, dacnis, and honeycreepers probe flowers, but only occasionally for nectar. More frequently they are searching for insects. They also commonly eat fruits, and are most easily seen in *mixed species foraging flocks* moving through the upper parts of the forest.

Breeding
Most species in this group build open, cup-shaped nests of moss and grass. They are presumably monogamous, but little is known about their breeding biology. Unusual among birds, BANANAQUITS build not only breeding nests, but also lighter, domed dormitory nests, where they sleep individually. Both Bananaquit sexes build the round, domed, breeding nest. Only the female incubates the 2 or 3 eggs, for 12 to 13 days. Both parents feed the chicks in the nest for 17 to 19 days by regurgitating food to them.

Status
Some of the species in this group have extremely small geographical ranges, which makes them vulnerable; extensive habitat destruction in these areas could easily threaten these birds. At the present time, however, in Brazil only the BLACK-LEGGED DACNIS, an endemic of the coastal Atlantic forest, is considered threatened.

Profiles
Chestnut-vented Conebill, *Conirostrum speciosum*, Plate 70c
Bananaquit, *Coereba flaveola*, Plate 70f
Green Honeycreeper, *Chlorophanes spiza*, Plate 71a
Blue Dacnis, *Dacnis cayana*, Plate 71b
Black-faced Dacnis, *Dacnis lineata*, Plate 71c
Yellow-bellied Dacnis, *Dacnis flaviventer*, Plate 71d
Purple Honeycreeper, *Cyanerpes caeruleus*, Plate 71e

36. Tanagers

Tanagers comprise a large New World group of beautifully colored, small passerine birds, most of which are limited to tropical areas. They are among the tropics' most common and visible birds, primarily due to their habit of associating in *mixed-species foraging flocks* that gather in the open, often near human habitation, to feed in fruit trees, and they are a treat to watch. All told, there are some 230 species of tanagers (family Thraupidae), the group including the *typical tanagers* and the *euphonias*. Some of the tanagers, such as the SUMMER TANAGER (male all red, female yellow-olive), breed in North America and migrate to winter in

Brazil and other parts of South America. Tanagers inhabit all forested and shrubby areas of the American tropics, over a wide range of elevations, and are particularly numerous in wet forests and forest edge areas. Not devotees of the dark forest interior, most prefer the lighter, upper levels of the forest canopy and more open areas; some prefer low, brushy habitat. More than 80 species of tanagers call Brazil home.

Tanagers vary from 9 to 28 cm (3.5 to 11 in) in length, with most concentrated near the smaller end of the range. They are compact birds with fairly short, thick bills and short to medium-long tails. Tanagers' outstanding physical attribute is their bright coloring – they are strikingly marked with patches of color that traverse the entire spectrum, rendering the group among the most fabulously attired of birds. It has been said of the typical tanagers (genus *Tangara*) that they must "exhaust the color patterns possible on sparrow-sized birds." Yellows, reds, blues, and greens predominate, although a relatively few species buck the trend and appear in plain blacks, browns, or grays. The sexes usually look alike. Euphonias are small, stout tanagers, whose appearances revolve around a common theme: males blue-black above, with yellow foreheads, breasts, and bellies; and females all dull olive. We profile typical species found commonly in the Amazon and Pantanal of Brazil. They all tend to be relatively easy to distinguish by their color patterns and habitat preference.

Natural History
Ecology and Behavior
Most tanager species associate in mixed-species tanager flocks, usually together with other types of birds. Finding five or more tanager species in a single group is not uncommon. A mixed flock will settle in a tree full of ripe fruit such as berries and enjoy a meal. These flocks move through forests or more open areas, searching for fruit-laden trees and also gleaning for insects. Although most species are arboreal, a few are specialized ground foragers, taking seeds and bugs. Tanagers usually go after small fruits that can be swallowed whole, such as berries, plucking the fruit while perched. After plucking it, a tanager rotates the fruit a bit in its bill, then mashes it and swallows. (Ecologists divide frugivorous birds into *mashers*, such as tanagers, and *gulpers*, such as trogons and toucans, which swallow fruit whole and intact.) One explanation is that mashing permits the bird to enjoy the sweet juice prior to swallowing the rest of the fruit. This fits with the idea that mashers select fruit based partially on taste, whereas gulpers, which swallow intact fruit, do not. Tanagers, as mashing frugivores, sometimes drop the largest seeds from the fruits they consume before swallowing but, nonetheless, many seeds are ingested; consequently, these birds are active seed dispersers (see Close-up, p. 196). Some ecologists believe tanagers to be among the most common dispersers of tropical trees and shrubs, that is, they are responsible for dropping the seeds that grow into the trees and shrubs that populate the areas they inhabit. Euphonias, for example, are crucial for the mistletoe life cycle because, after eating the berries, they deposit their seed-bearing droppings on tree branches, where the seeds germinate, the mistletoe plants starting out there as parasites on the host tree.

Some tanagers, such as the *ant-tanagers*, are frequent members of mixed-species flocks of the undergrowth (along with antbirds, woodcreepers, and others) that spend their days following army ant swarms, feeding on insects that rush from cover at the approach of the devastating ants. Euphonias specialize on mistletoe berries, but eat other fruits and some insects as well. Some tanagers are *altitudinal migrants*, seasonally moving to higher or lower elevation habitats.

Breeding

Most tanagers appear to breed monogamously, although a number of bigamists have been noted (BLUE-GRAY TANAGER, Plate 75, among them). Breeding is concentrated during the transition from dry to wet season, when fruit and insects are most plentiful. In many species, male and female stay paired throughout the year. Males of many species give food to females in nuptial feeding, and during courtship displays make sure that potential mates see their brightly colored patches. Either the female alone or the pair builds a cup nest in a tree or shrub. Two eggs are incubated by the female only for 12 to 18 days and young are fed by both parents for 12 to 18 days prior to their fledging. A pair of tiny euphonias build a nest with a roof and a side entrance, often within a bromeliad plant.

Notes

The word tanager comes from the Brazilian Tupi Indian word "tangara," which is also used as the genus name for a group of tanagers.

Status

Four Brazilian tanagers are currently considered threatened or endangered. One species, the CONE-BILLED TANAGER, occurs near the northern Pantanal but is known from only a single specimen collected early in the century. In addition, several of the euphonias are increasingly scarce and the reason may be that, although they are not hunted for the international pet trade, they are prized as cage birds within South American countries.

Profiles

Yellow-backed Tanager, *Hemithraupis flavicollis*, Plate 72a
Guira Tanager, *Hemithraupis guira*, Plate 72b
Hooded Tanager, *Nemosia pileata*, Plate 72c
Yellow-bellied Tanager, *Tangara xanthogastra*, Plate 72d
Burnished-buff Tanager, *Tangara cayana*, Plate 72e
Turquoise Tanager, *Tangara mexicana*, Plate 73a
Bay-headed Tanager, *Tangara gyrola*, Plate 73b
Green-and-gold Tanager, *Tangara schrankii*, Plate 73c
Paradise Tanager, *Tangara chilensis*, Plate 73d
Opal-rumped Tanager, *Tangara velia*, Plate 73e

Thick-billed Euphonia, *Euphonia laniirostris*, Plate 74a
White-vented Euphonia, *Euphonia minuta*, Plate 74b
Chestnut-bellied Euphonia, *Euphonia rufiventris*, Plate 74c
White-lored Euphonia, *Euphonia chrysopasta*, Plate 74d
Swallow Tanager, *Tersina viridis,* Plate 74e

Gray-headed Tanager, *Eucometis penicillata*, Plate 75a
Palm Tanager, *Thraupis palmarum*, Plate 75b
Masked Crimson Tanager, *Ramphocelus nigrogularis*, Plate 75c
Silver-beaked Tanager, *Ramphocelus carbo*, Plate 75d
Blue-gray Tanager, *Thraupis episcopus,* Plate 75e
Flame-crested Tanager, *Tachyphonus cristatus*, Plate 76a
White-shouldered Tanager, *Tachyphonus luctuosus,* Plate 76b
Red-billed Pied Tanager, *Lamprospiza melanoleuca*, Plate 76c

Fulvous Shrike-Tanager, *Lanio fulvus*, Plate 76d
Magpie Tanager, *Cissopis leveriana*, Plate 76e

37. American Orioles and Blackbirds

Diversity is the key to comprehending the *American orioles* and *blackbirds*. The passerine family Icteridae includes about 95 species, 36 of which occur in Brazil. They vary extensively in size, coloring, ecology, and behavior, but they also partition neatly into very different groups called *blackbirds, caciques (kah-SEE-kays), cowbirds, grackles, meadowlarks, orioles* (distinct from the unrelated family of birds called orioles in Eurasia and Africa), and *oropendolas*. These *icterids* range over most of North, Central, and South America. Distinguishing this varied assemblage from most other birds is a method for feeding known as *gaping* – a bird places its closed bill into crevices or under leaves, rocks or other objects, then forces the bill open, exposing the previously hidden space to its prying eyes and hunger. The icterid group inhabits marshes and almost all types of terrestrial habitats. Many of these birds have adapted well to human settlements and are common denizens of gardens, parks, and urban and agricultural areas.

Icterids range in length from 15 to 56 cm (6 in to 1.8 ft) – medium to fairly large-sized birds. Bills are usually sharply pointed and conical. Black is the predominant plumage color in the group, but many combine black with bright reds, yellows, or oranges. In some species, the sexes are alike (particularly in the tropical species), but in others, females look very different from males, often more cryptically outfitted in browns, grays, or streaked plumage. Pronounced size differences between the sexes, females being smaller, are common; male oropendolas, for instance, may weigh twice as much as females. Bills and eyes are sometimes brightly colored. The wide ranges of sizes, shapes, colors, mating systems, and breeding behaviors of these birds have attracted considerable interest from avian researchers.

Natural History
Ecology and Behavior
Icterids occur in all sorts of habitat types – woodlands, thickets, grassland, marshes, forest edges, and the higher levels of closed forests – but they are especially prevalent in more open areas. Their regular occupation of marshes has always been viewed as interesting, as they are not otherwise obviously adapted for living in aquatic environments – they do not have webbed feet, for example, nor are they able to float or dive. They are *omnivorous* and eat a wide variety of foods including insects and other small animals, fruit, and seeds. A common feature of the group is that although they are primarily seed-eaters (*granivores*) during the nonbreeding periods, they become *insectivorous* during breeding, and feed insects to the young. Gaping for food is frequent and will be seen repeatedly if you observe these birds for any length of time. Oropendolas and caciques join in mixed-species foraging flocks in the canopy; in a single fruit tree you may see two or more species feeding with several species of tanagers, honeycreepers, and others. Outside of the breeding season, icterids, particularly the blackbirds and grackles, typically gather in large, sometimes enormous, flocks that can cause damage to roosting areas and agricultural crops.

Breeding

Icterid species pursue a variety of breeding strategies. Some, such as the orioles, breed in classically monogamous pairs, male and female defending a large territory in which the hanging pouch nest is situated. The caciques and the oropendolas nest in colonies. The members of an oropendola colony weave large, bag-like or pouch-like nests that hang from the ends of tree branches, many on the same tree. In Costa Rica, researchers documented a rare form of non-monogamous breeding. Three to 10 male MONTEZUMA'S OROPENDOLAS establish a colony in a tree (often an isolated one) and defend a group of 10 to 30 females that will mate and nest in the colony. The males engage in fighting and aggressive displays, competing among themselves to mate with the females. The most dominant males (the *alpha* birds) in each colony, usually heavier males, obtain up to 90% of all matings, and therefore, are the fathers of most of the colony's young. Caciques, also with pouch-like nests, breed either solitarily in the forest or in colonies. In one study it was noted that each cacique in a colony tries to locate its nest toward the center of the colony, presumably because there is less of a chance of suffering nest predation at the colony's center. The TROUPIAL (Plate 77) has the peculiar habit of using recently abandoned colonies of cacique nests and laying its eggs in one of them instead of building its own nest.

Breeding colonies of caciques and oropendolas are often located in trees that contain or are near large bee or wasp nests. The wasps or bees swarm in large numbers around the birds' nests. Apparently the birds benefit from this close association because the aggressiveness the stinging insects show toward animals that try to raid the birds' hanging nests offers a measure of protection. Icterid nests range from hanging pouches woven from grasses and other plant materials to open cups lined with mud to roofed nests built on the ground, hidden in meadow grass. Nests are almost always built by females. The female also incubates the 2 or 3 eggs, for 11 to 14 days, while the male guards the nest. Nestlings are fed for 10 to 30 days either by both parents (monogamous species) or primarily by the female (polygamous species).

Most of the cowbirds, like some cuckoo species, are *brood parasites*, building no nests themselves. Rather, females, after mating with one or more males, lay their eggs, one in each nest and up to 14 or more per season, in the nests of other species – other icterids as well as species in other families. The *host* species then incubate and raise these foster young. Some of the cowbirds specialize on icterid hosts – the GIANT COWBIRD (Plate 77) parasitizes only caciques and oropendolas. Its occurrence is apparently restricted only by the presence of colonies of its hosts, various cacique and oropendola species. Some host species have evolved the abilities to recognize cowbird eggs and eject them from their nests, but others have not. The cowbirds benefit from this selfish behavior by being freed from nest-building and tending chores – what must amount to significant savings of energy and also decreased exposure to predators. The host species suffer reproductive harm because a female cowbird often ejects a host egg when she lays her own (when the nest is left unguarded). Also, more often than not, the cowbird's young are larger than the host's own, and are thus able to out-compete them for food brought to the nest by the adult birds. The host's own young often starve or are significantly weakened.

How can brood parasitic behavior arise? Evolutionary biologists posit that one way would be if, long ago, some female cowbirds that built nests had their nests destroyed mid-way through their laying period. With an egg to lay but no nest in which to place it, females in this situation may have deposited the eggs in the nests of other species, which subsequently raised the cowbird young. Alternatively, the nesting behavior of the Troupial, which uses old cacique nests, suggests another possible evolutionary road to brood parasitism: if a female Troupial didn't bother to wait for the caciques to finish using their nests before she laid her egg, she could quickly develop a brood parasitic lifestyle.

Notes

"Cacique" is an interesting name for a bird: in Spanish it means "chief" or "boss;" in Mexico, it also has the suggestion of "tyrant;" in Chile and some other parts of South America, it means "one who leads an easy life."

Status

In North America, the BROWN-HEADED COWBIRD, an open country species like all other cowbirds, has been able to expand its range with deforestation. Because it does not regularly penetrate into extensive forests, many forest-dwelling songbird species, especially migrants from South America, were long-protected from this brood parasite. Now, with only small forest remnants (which are readily entered by cowbirds) left throughout much of eastern North America, these other small songbirds have been overwhelmed not only by loss of habitat but also by increased rates of cowbird parasitism. This combination of factors together with habitat destruction in Brazil may help explain the precipitous decline of some North American species that winter in Brazil. In Brazil, two species of icterids are endangered, the SAFFRON-COWLED BLACKBIRD and FORBES BLACKBIRD, both found in eastern parts of the country.

Profiles

Red-breasted Blackbird, *Sturnella militaris*, Plate 77a
Giant Cowbird, *Schaphidura oryzivora*, Plate 77b
Scarlet-headed Blackbird, *Amblyramphus holosericeus*, Plate 77c
Troupial, *Icterus icterus*, Plate 77d
Oriole Blackbird, *Gymnomystax mexicanus*, Plate 77e
Crested Oropendola, *Psarocolius decumanus*, Plate 78a
Olive Oropendola, *Psaracolius bifasciatus*, Plate 78b
Yellow-rumped Cacique, *Cacicus cela*, Plate 78c
Red-rumped Cacique, *Cacicus haemorrhous*, Plate 78d
Epaulet Oriole, *Icterus cayanensis*, Plate 78e

38. Sparrows and Finches

The New World *sparrows* and *finches* are a large, diverse group, totaling about 320 species, that includes some of South America's most common and visible passerine birds. The group's classification is continually being revised, but here we can consider them to be separate families: the sparrows, *seedeaters*, and *grassquits* in Family Emberizidae, and the *grosbeaks* and *saltators* in Family Cardinalidae. The *siskins* are in the closely related family Fringillidae. These groups are almost *cosmopolitan* in distribution, meaning representatives occur just about everywhere, in all kinds of habitats and climates, from Alaska and northern Canada south to Tierra del Fuego.

Sparrows and finches are generally small birds, 9 to 22 cm (3.5 to 9 in) in length, with relatively short, thick, conical bills, that are specialized to crush and open seeds. In some species, the upper and lower halves of the bill can be moved from side-to-side, the better to manipulate small seeds. Sparrows have relatively large feet that they use in scratching the ground to find seeds. Coloring varies greatly within the group but the plumage of most is dull brown or grayish, with many sporting streaked backs. The sexes generally look alike. We profile 15 species of these birds that are common and easily seen in various habitats throughout Brazil.

Natural History
Ecology and Behavior
Sparrows and finches are mostly seed-eaters (*granivores*), although many are considered almost *omnivorous*, and even those that specialize on seeds for much of the year often feed insects to their young. Some species also eat fruit. Sparrows in Brazil mainly inhabit open areas such as grassland, parkland, brushy areas, and forest edge. They are birds of thickets, bushes, and grasses, foraging mostly on the ground or at low levels in bushes or trees. Because many species spend large amounts of time in thickets and brushy areas, they can be quite inconspicuous. Whereas in North America sparrows constitute perhaps the most important group of seed-eating birds, they are less dominant in the Neotropics. Other groups of birds, such as pigeons (p. 148), occupy more of the seed-eating niche in South American countries than do sparrows and, as a consequence, one encounters sparrows much more often in North than in South America.

Most species are strongly territorial, a mated pair aggressively excluding other members of the species from sharply defined areas. In the *typical sparrows*, pairs often stay together all year; other species within the group often travel in small family groups. Sometimes territories are defended year round and almost all available habitat in a region is divided into territories. The result is that those individuals that do not own territories must live furtively on defended territories, always trying to avoid the dominant territory owner, retreating when chased, and waiting for the day when the owner is injured or dies and the territory can be taken over. Only when one of these *floaters* ascends to territorial ownership status can he begin to breed. In species that have this kind of territorial system, such as the RUFOUS-COLLARED SPARROW (Plate 81), the "floater" individuals that live secretly on other individual's territories, waiting and watching, were termed by their discoverer an *avian underworld*, and the name has stuck.

Breeding
Most sparrows and finches are monogamous breeders. The female of the pair usually builds a cup-shaped or, more often in the tropics, a domed nest, from grasses, fine roots, and perhaps mosses and lichens. Nests are concealed on the ground or low in a shrub or tree. The female alone incubates 2 or 3 eggs, for 12 to 14 days. Both male and female feed nestlings, which fledge after 10 to 15 days. Most breeding is accomplished during the beginning of the warm rainy season. Some species, such as the abundant and conspicuous RUFOUS-COLLARED SPARROW, breed almost continually through the year.

Notes
The New World sparrows and finches have been especially well-studied by scientists, and thus they have contributed substantially to our general knowledge of birds. For instance, studies of North America's SONG SPARROW and the Neotropic's RUFOUS-COLLARED SPARROW provided the basis for much of the information we have about avian territoriality and many other kinds of behavior.

Status

Seven species of finches and seedeaters are threatened or endangered in Brazil. Two of them, the BLACK-MASKED FINCH and the BLACK-AND-TAWNY SEEDEATER, include the grasslands of the Pantanal in their restricted range. Cattle grazing and grass burning have severely affected their populations.

Profiles

Buff-throated Saltator, *Saltator maximus*, Plate 79a
Slate-colored Grosbeak, *Pitylus grossus*, Plate 79b
Red-crested Cardinal, *Paroaria coronata*, Plate 79c
Red-capped Cardinal, *Paroaria gularis*, Plate 79d
Grayish Saltator, *Saltator coerulescens*, Plate 79e
Lesser Seed-finch, *Oryzoborus angolensis*, Plate 80a
Blue-black Grassquit, *Volatinia jacarina*, Plate 80b
Rusty-collared Seedeater, *Sporophila collaris*, Plate 80c

Yellow-bellied Seedeater, *Sporophila nigricollis*, Plate 80d
White-bellied Seedeater, *Sporophila leucoptera*, Plate 80e
Blue-black Grosbeak, *Cyanocompsa cyanoides*, Plate 81a
Rufous-collared Sparrow, *Zonotrichia capensis*, Plate 81b
Yellow-browed Sparrow, *Ammodramus aurifrons*, Plate 81c
Saffron Yellow-Finch, *Sicalis flaveola*, Plate 81d
Chestnut-bellied Seedeater, *Sporophila castaneiventris*, Plate 81e

Environmental Close-up 5
Frugivory: Animals That Eat Fruit and the Trees That Want Them To

Frugivory from the Animal's Point of View

A key feature of tropical forests, and of the animal communities that inhabit them, is the large number of birds (cotingas, finches, manakins, parrots, orioles, tanagers, toucans, and trogons make up a partial list), mammals, and even some fish that rely on fruit as a diet staple. Frugivory represents a trade-off, each participant – the fruit-bearing tree and the fruit-eating animal – offering the other something of great value (and therefore it is a kind of mutualism – see p. 52). The complex web of relationships between fruit-eaters and fruit-producing trees is particularly interesting because it nicely demonstrates ecological interactions between plant and animal, between food producer and food consumer, between predator and prey, and the mutual dependence sometimes engendered by such relationships.

Benefits of Frugivory for Animals

Most small and medium-sized tropical forest birds, many mammals, and some fish eat either fruits or animals such as insects, or they eat both. But it is the fruit-eating habit that accounts for much of the incredible ecological success of animals in the tropics. For birds, many more species occupy the Earth's tropical areas than temperate zones and, ecologists believe, about 20% of the difference is directly attributable to the tropical birds' superior abilities to exploit fruit resources. In fact, probably 50% of tropical bird biomass (the summed weight of all tropical birds alive at one time) is supported by fruit-eating. You would think, therefore, that fruit must be tremendously profitable "prey" for birds, and in several ways it is:

1 Fruit is conspicuous. First consider insects as food. Palatable insects are often small and/or inconspicuous; they hide or blend in extremely well with their surroundings. Finding such insects is a chore that takes a lot of time. Ripe fruit, on the other hand, usually attracts attention to itself, being sweet-smelling, brightly colored, and displayed out in the open.

2 Fruit is easy to stalk, run down, catch, kill, and devour. Insects, as far as we can tell, are absolutely loath to be eaten – they run, hide, and resist to the end; some even spray noxious chemicals at their attackers. Fruit, however, never attempts escape and, in fact, when it is ripe and so most attractive to frugivores, it is most easily separated from the tree that bears it.

    The underlying reason for points (1) and (2), which becomes more clear when considering frugivory from the trees' point of view (see below), is that fruits are made to be consumed by animals. It is their raison d'être. Owing to this, trees could hardly be expected to make their fruit difficult to locate or pluck. Thus we have a major ecological insight: insects benefit by not being eaten, but unless a fruit is eaten, the plant gains nothing from the effort to produce it.

3 Fruit is abundant. When a bird locates a tree with fruit, there is often a large amount available for consumption. Thus, meeting a day's nutritional requirements means finding one or, at most, a few, fruit-bearing trees.

4 Fruit in the tropics is usually available year-round. There are wide-ranging consequences of points (3) and (4) for avian frugivores. That fruit is always available and abundant means that birds can safely specialize on it – evolve special ways to pluck, eat, and digest it – without encountering times of the year when no fruit is available, forcing the birds to search for food that they are ill-equipped to handle. Owing to fruit's abundance, species that concentrate on fruit often are quite successful, meaning that within a given area the numbers of individuals of these species can be quite large. But the greatest influence of frugivory on the lives of birds is that, because fruit is abundant and easy to locate and eat, birds can fulfill nutritional needs in only a few hours, leaving many hours each day available to pursue other activities. In contrast, an avian insectivore or piscivore (specializing on insects or fish, respectively), to survive may have to hunt most of each day.

The abundance of fruit, in fact, probably permitted the evolution of polygamous and promiscuous breeding in tropical birds. Take the manakins and cotingas that breed promiscuously. Males establish display sites on tree branches or on ground courts. Several of these display sites near each other constitute a lec. Females visit lecs, attracted by the males' vocalizations and dancing display antics, compare the males displaying, and choose one or more to mate with. Afterwards, the females go off by themselves to nest and raise their young. At their lecs, male manakins, for instance, spend up to 80% to 90% of daylight hours during the breeding season displaying and trying to attract females (the more they are able to convince to mate with them, the more offspring the males will have in the next generation). The free time frugivory affords permits both the prolonged display time in these breeding systems as well as the requisite ability of females to raise young themselves.

Also, when food is fairly scarce or difficult to locate or catch, to insure adequate supplies for themselves and their young, birds may need to defend individual territories and struggle to keep out other members of their species. Furthermore, male and female may need to continue their pairing past actual mating because one parent foraging alone cannot provide sufficient food for the young. But establishing a territory to defend the fruit it holds is unnecessary because there is usually fruit enough for all that want it. (In fact, usually birds cannot eat all the fruit that ripens on a tree.) It is far more efficient to forage in groups, to be social feeders, as are toucans and parrots, and so to each day have help in finding trees bearing ripe fruit (sometimes easier said than done because trees within a small area usually do not ripen simultaneously).

Problems of Frugivory

Have birds encountered difficulties in the process of specializing on fruit? Yes, there are some associated problems:

1   Fruits, although providing plentiful carbohydrates and fats, are relatively low in protein, so these birds, although easily meeting their daily calorie needs, sometimes have "protein deficits" that they must ease by feeding occasionally on insects or other animals (the occasional snail or frog, the odd lizard). Few bird species eat fruit exclusively. The ones that do, such as many cotingas, need to make special provision for their all-fruit diet. For instance, because rapidly growing young need good amounts of protein, cotinga nestlings, fed only fruit by their parents, grow relatively slowly, and so spend perhaps 50% more time in the nest than non-frugivorous birds of the same size. Many of these birds nest in tree cavities where their slow-developing young are better-protected from the many nest predators roaming tropical habitats. Also, some of these birds seek out unusual fruits that are high in proteins and fats, such as avocados.
2   Eating liquidy fruit pulp means that frugivores consume a lot of water, which is both bulky and heavy, and which must be transported for a time (which uses up energy) and disposed of regularly.
3   The birds' nutrition comes from the fleshy fruit pulp. The seeds that are eaten incidentally are usually indigestible or even poisonous and must be, like water, carried for a while and then disposed of – either by regurgitation or after being passed through the digestive tract.
4   When a species specializes on a particular type of fruit, it becomes vulnerable to any temporary or permanent decline in the fruit's availability. (It appears that most avian frugivores avoid such vulnerability by not being overly specialized: in an observational study that followed the feeding habits of 70 fruit-eating species in the tropics, researchers discovered that each bird species consumed, on average, 10 species of fruits.)

Frugivory from the Tree's Point of View

It is clear what birds get from frugivory, but what of the trees, which are picked clean of the fruit that they spend so much time and energy producing? The answer is that the trees, by having birds eat, transport, and then drop their seeds, achieve efficient reproduction – something well worth their investment in fruit. The trees make use of birds as winged, animate, seed dispersal agents.

Why don't trees just let their seeds drop to the ground? It turns out that seeds dropped near the parent most often do not survive. They die because they must compete with the much larger parent for sun and other nutrients. Also, specialized insects that eat seeds can more easily find and destroy seeds that are in large accumulations, like under the mother tree. Seeds carried some distance from the parent tree have a better chance of germination and survival, and they will not compete with the parent tree (also, because in the tropics trees of the same species usually do not grow near each other, seeds dropped by birds are unlikely to be regularly competing with any trees of the same species). Furthermore, because they are more spread out, seed predators are less likely to find them. Thus, seed dispersal by birds enhances a parent tree's prospects for successful reproduction, and also allows the tree to colonize new sites.

The tree's use of animal power for seed dispersal is exquisitely fine-tuned. As seeds are being readied, fruit is green, hard, and bitter-tasting – unappealing fare to birds (and to people!). When the seeds mature and are ready for dispersal and germination, the surrounding fruit brightens in color, becomes softer and easier to pluck from the tree, and in a coup de grâce, trees inject sugars into fruits, making them sweet and very attractive.

Not all animals attracted to fruits are good seed dispersers. Some, notably the parrots, eat and digest seeds, acting as predators rather than dispersers. These seed destroyers, however, in the course of their movements from branch to branch often knock out of the canopy many fruits that fall to the forest floor. Here, frugivorous animals that can't climb trees well, such as tinamous and agoutis, await this largesse. They eat the fruit, dispersing seeds later when they defecate, or cache it in the ground for later consumption, where seeds may later germinate.

Ecological Consequences of Frugivory for Birds, Trees, and Ecosystems

As tropical birds have benefitted in several ways by specialization on fruit, so too have trees. In fact, ecologists now suspect that together with pollination by insects, bats, and birds, seed dispersal by birds and other vertebrate animals was and is responsible for the initial spread and current domination of the Earth by flowering plants. They estimate that upwards of 80% of trees and shrubs in tropical wet forests have their seeds dispersed by animals. These plants provide the nutrients to support large, healthy populations of frugivorous birds and bats. Moreover, the great species diversity of plants in the tropics may be largely linked to frugivorous animals continually eating fruits and spreading seeds into new areas. Such constant dispersal, which also allows continual, healthy genetic mixing, is beneficial for plant populations, always working to decrease the chances that individual species will go extinct. In fact, the more successful a tree species is at being "preyed upon" by birds, the more its seeds will be dropped over a wide area, and the more abundant it will become.

One potential problem for trees, though, is that if their fruit is eaten by only one or two bird species, that strict dependence for seed dispersal brings vulnerability. If the bird that disperses such a specialist tree for some reason declines in abundance and becomes extinct, so too, in short order, will the tree species. Most tree species, however, enjoy the seed dispersal services of at least several bird species.

The trade-offs that the birds and trees make, the conflicting strategies to survive and complete their life cycles, are fascinating. Think about it from one evolutionary perspective: the beneficial aspect of the interaction for the tree – having a bird transport its seeds – is the negative aspect for the animal, which has no "desire" to carry seeds from which it gets no benefit. The beneficial aspect for the bird – the fruit pulp that the plant manufactures to attract animals – is the negative part of the interaction for the plant, which loses the energy and nutrients required to make the fruit. Frugivory is one of the tropic's most important and compelling ecological interactions, and one that currently attracts strong interest from ecological researchers. Frugivory may even have been a causative factor in the early evolution of color vision, as the first fruit-eaters that could easily distinguish ripe and unripe fruit plainly would have had advantages over those that could not.

A Fruitful Connection between Land and Water

The PIRANHA, thanks to cartoons and horror movies, is etched into our minds as a bloodthirsty fish of the Amazon. Here it supposedly reduces large animals, unlucky enough to fall into the water, to nothing but bones within minutes. Although some do eat flesh, their reputations are greatly exaggerated. They do occasionally bite swimmers, but this behavior is very rare in Brazil. We regularly swim near these intriguing fish, and in 30 years have never had so much as a nibble – except on a fishing line. The biggest threat these fish pose to people may be when freshly caught piranha are flopping around on the bottom of a fisherman's canoe, with bare toes exposed to their sharp teeth.

There are about 25 piranha species in the Amazon Basin – some black and others white; a few are red-bellied. Regardless of their reputation, piranhas also eat a lot of fruits floating in the water. All species are primarily frugivores when young, and, even as adults, fruits are an occasional to major part of their diets, depending on the species. Only six species of piranhas (red-bellied species in the genus *Pygocentrus*), however, are primarily flesheaters as adults. Even then the flesh they eat is usually in the form of fins and scales of other fish. In Brazil, apparently two or three extremely similar species of this red-bellied genus (*Pygocentrus*) occur (Plate 99).

During the rainier season in Brazil, rivers flood and low forest, dry for most of the year, has up to 1 m (3.3 ft) or more of water standing at the bases of the trees. Many of these trees time their flowering and fruiting to coincide with this flooding, their fruits dropping to float in the water below. Fish, including piranhas, swim in among the bases of the trees to devour the fruits or chew at their outer coverings. Many seeds are dropped or pass through the fish digestive system to be defecated somewhere else in the flooded forest. The seeds fall to the forest floor, and if lucky, germinate when the floods recede. Not only does this story dispel the undeserved super-carnivore reputation of piranhas, it also dispels the idea that aquatic and terrestrial systems are very separate. That an aquatic fish serves as a major seed disperser for a terrestrial tree is just one of many examples of how differently we must look at and study this diverse area.

Chapter 10

Mammals

Introduction

Leafing through this book, you may have noticed that there are many more profiles of birds than mammals. At first glance you might think this odd, especially because people themselves are mammals and, because of that direct kinship, might often be keenly interested and motivated to see and learn about mammals. What's going on? Aren't mammals as good as birds? Why not include more of them? There are several reasons for the discrepancy – good biological reasons. One is that, even though the tropics generally have more species of mammals than temperate or Arctic regions, the total number of mammal species worldwide, and the number in any region, is almost always much less than the number of birds. In fact, there are only 4629 mammal species in the world, as compared with

9040 birds, and that relative difference is reflected in Brazil's fauna. Another compelling reason not to include more mammals in a book on commonly sighted wildlife, is that throughout the Brazilian Amazon you will rarely see mammals – especially if you are a short-term visitor. Mammals are delicious fare for any number of predatory beasts (eaten in good numbers by reptiles, birds, other mammals, and even the odd amphibian), but most mammals lack a basic protection from predators that birds possess, the power of flight. Consequently, most have been forced into being active nocturnally, or, if active during daylight hours, they are highly secretive. Birds often show themselves with abandon, mammals do not. An exception is monkeys. They are fairly large and primarily arboreal, which keeps them safe from a number of kinds of predators, and thus permits them to be noisy and relatively conspicuous. Only in the Pantanal do you have a good chance of seeing lots of large mammals besides monkeys, but even then these obvious mammals will represent only a small proportion of all the mammal species in the area. A final reason for not including more mammals in the book is that about 141 (27%) of the 524 mammal species occurring in Brazil are bats. They are for the most part nocturnal animals that, even if you are lucky enough to get good looks at them, are very difficult for anyone other than an expert to identify to species.

General Characteristics and Classification of Mammals

Mammals as a group first arose, so fossils tell us, approximately 245 million years ago, splitting off from the primitive reptiles during the late Triassic Period of the Mesozoic Era, somewhat before the birds did the same thing. Four main traits distinguish mammals from other vertebrates, and each of these traits helped mammals spread into most of the habitats around the world. Hair on their bodies insulates and helps maintain constant internal temperatures as well as protecting the skin from injuries; milk production for the young frees mothers from having to search for specific foods for their offspring; the bearing of live young instead of eggs allows breeding females to be mobile and hence safer than if they had to guard eggs for several weeks; and advanced brains together with highly integrated sensory systems contribute to mammals' breadth of survival mechanisms.

Mammals are quite variable in size and form, many being highly adapted – changed through evolution – to specialized habitats and lifestyles: bats specialized to fly, marine mammals specialized for their aquatic world, deer to run swiftly, etc. The smallest mammals are the *shrews*, tiny insect eaters that weigh as little as 2.5 g (a tenth of an ounce). The largest are the whales, weighing in at up to 160,000 kg (350,000 lb, half the weight of a loaded Boeing 747) – as far as anyone knows, the largest animals that have ever lived.

Mammals are divided into three major groups, primarily according to reproductive methods. The *monotremes* are an ancient group that actually lays eggs and still retains some other reptile-like characteristics. Only three species of them survive, one platypus and two spiny anteaters, and they are found only in Australia and New Guinea. The *marsupials* give birth to live young that are relatively undeveloped. When born, the young crawl along mom's fur to attach themselves to her nipples, usually inside her pouch, where they find milk supplies and finish their development. There are about 240 marsupial species, including kangaroos, koalas, wombats, and opossum, and they are limited in distribution to Australia and the Neotropics (the industrious but road-accident-prone VIRGINIA OPOSSUM also inhabits much of Mexico and the USA). The majority of mammal species are *eutherians*. These animals are distinguished from the other groups by having a well-developed placenta, which efficiently connects a mother to her developing babies, allowing for long internal development. This trait, which allows embryos to develop to a fairly mature form in safety, and for the female to be mobile until birth, has allowed these mammals to colonize successfully and prosper in many habitats. These typical mammals include those with which most people are intimately familiar: rodents, rabbits, cats, dogs, bats, primates, elephants, horses, whales – everything from house mice to ecotravellers. The 4600 species of living mammals are grouped into about 115 families, which are in turn categorized into about 20 orders.

Features of Tropical Mammals

There are several important features of tropical mammals and their habitats that differentiate them from temperate zone mammals. First, tropical mammals face different environmental stresses than do temperate zone mammals, and they respond to stresses in different ways. Many temperate zone mammals, of course, must endure extreme variation within a year; from cold winters with snow and low food supplies to hot summers with dry weather and abundant food. Many mammals respond with hibernation, staying more or less dormant for several months until conditions improve. Tropical mammals, except in the high altitude mountains, do not encounter such extreme annual changes, but they do face dry seasons, up to 5 months long, that sometimes severely reduce food supplies. For some surprising reasons, they cannot alleviate this stress by hibernating, waiting for the rainy season to arrive with its increased food supplies. When a mammal in Canada or Alaska hibernates, many of its predators leave the area. This is not the case in the tropics. A mammal sleeping away the dry season in a burrow would be easy prey to snakes and other predators. Moreover, a big danger to sleeping mammals would be … army ants (p. 75)! These voracious insects are very common in the tropics and would quickly eat a sleeping mouse or squirrel. Also, external parasites, such as ticks and mites, which are inactive in extreme cold, would continue to be very active on sleeping tropical mammals, sucking blood and doing considerable damage. Last, the great energy reserves needed to be able to sleep for an extended period through warm weather may be more than any mammal can physically accumulate. Therefore, tropical mammals need to stay active throughout the year. One way they counter the dry season's reduction in their normal foods is to switch food types seasonally. For instance, some rodents that eat mostly insects during the rainy season switch to seeds during the dry; some bats that feed on insects switch to dry-season fruits.

    The abundance of tropical fruit brings up another interesting difference between temperate and tropical mammals: a surprising number of tropical mammals eat a lot of fruit, even among the carnivore group, which, as its name implies, should be eating meat. All the carnivores in Brazil, save the PUMA,

JAGUAR and otters, are known to eat fruit on occasion. Upon reflection, that these mammals consume fruit makes sense. Fruit is very abundant in the tropics, available throughout much of the year, and, at least when it is ripe, easily digested by mammalian digestive systems. A consequence of such *frugivory* (fruit-eating) is that many mammals have become, together with frugivorous birds, major dispersal agents of fruit seeds, which they spit out or which travel unharmed through their digestive tracts to be deposited in feces far from the mother tree (see Close-up, p. 196). Some biologists believe that, even though the carnivores plainly are specialized for hunting down, killing, and eating animal prey, it is likely that fruit has always been a major part of their diet.

Finally, there are some differences in the kinds of mammals inhabiting tropical and temperate regions. For instance there are few social rodents like beavers and prairie dogs and very few rabbit species. On the other hand, some groups occur solely in the tropics and do extremely well there. There are about 75 to 100 species of New World monkeys (depending on which primate specialist you consult), all of which occur in tropical areas. Arboreal mammals such as monkeys and sloths are plentiful in tropical forests, probably because there is a rich, resource-filled, dense canopy to occupy and feed in. Also, the closed canopy blocks light to the ground, which allows only an undergrowth that is sparse and poor in resources, and consequently permits few opportunities for mammals to live and feed there. Bats thrive in the tropics, being very successful both in terms of number of species and in their abundances. Nine families of bats occur in Brazil, including more than 140 species; only 4 families and 40 species occur in the entire USA, an area similar in size to that of Brazil. While most of the North American bats are insect-eaters, the Brazilian bats are quite varied in lifestyle, among them being fruit-eaters, nectar-eaters, fish-eaters and even a few that consume other animals or their blood.

The social and breeding behaviors of various mammals are quite diverse. Some are predominantly solitary animals, males and females coming together occasionally only to mate. Others live in family groups. Like birds, female mammals have most of the say in choosing a mate. Unlike most bird species, in which both mates are necessary to raise the young, and monogamy (one male mates with one female) is thus common, milk production among female mammals usually frees the male from caring for the young. He is better off and more likely to get more of his genes into the next generation by convincing additional females to mate with him. This leads to polygyny (one male mates with a harem of several females) or promiscuity (a sexual free-for-all where dominant males tend to mate with a mind-blurring array of females) as the most common mating systems among mammals. Monogamy is uncommon but polyandry (one female mates with several males) is even rarer among mammals than birds. Depending on resources like food availability and access to mates, some mammal species are rigorously territorial, others are not.

Seeing Mammals in Brazil

No doubt about it, except in the Pantanal, mammals are tough to see. You could go for two weeks and, if in the wrong places at the wrong times, see very few of them. A lot of luck is involved – a tapir, a small herd of peccaries, or a porcupine happens to cross the trail just ahead of you, or by chance someone in your group spots a sloth in a tree. We can offer three pieces of mammal-spotting advice: first, if you have time and are a patient sort, stake out a likely looking spot near a stream or watering hole, be quiet, and wait to see what approaches. Second, try taking quiet strolls along paths and trails very early in the morning. At this time, many nocturnal mammals are quickly scurrying to their day shelters. Third, although only for the stout-hearted, try searching with a flashlight at night around field stations or campgrounds. After scanning the ground (for safety's sake as well as for mammals), shine the light toward the middle regions of trees and look for bright, shiny eyes reflecting the light. You will certainly stumble across some kind of mammal or another; then it is simply a matter of whether you scare them more than they scare you. Doing the same thing at night from a canoe can also be a good way to spot eye-shine of mammals in the vegetation along the edge of a stream or forested lake.

Some mammals, of course, you can see more reliably. Monkeys, for instance, are often easy to see in many of Brazil's national parks, and squirrels and peccaries are frequently sighted in forests of the Amazon. Banish all thoughts right now of ever encountering the Jaguar, which is found regularly now only in isolated regions. Even there, however, your chances of encountering one are slim, although their tracks (Plate 92) on river beaches and muddy roads are a regular sight in some areas.

Family Profiles

1. Opossums

Marsupials are an ancient group, preceding in evolution the development of the *true*, or *placental*, mammals, which eventually replaced the marsupials over most parts of the terrestrial world. Marsupials alive today in the Australian and Neotropical regions therefore are remnants of an earlier time when the group's distribution spanned the Earth. Of the eight living families of marsupials, only three occur in the New World, and only one, the *opossums*, occurs in Brazil. This family, Didelphidae, is distributed widely over the northern Neotropics (with one member, the VIRGINIA OPOSSUM, reaching far northwards into the USA). Forty-three species represent the family in Brazil. They are a diverse group, occupying essentially all of the country's habitats. Some, such as the COMMON OPOSSUM (also called SOUTHERN OPOSSUM; Plate 82), are abundant and frequently sighted, while others are rarer or shier.

All opossums are essentially alike in body plan, although species vary considerably in size. Their general appearance probably has not changed much during the past 40 to 65 million years. Basically, these mammals look like rats, albeit in the case of some, such as the Common Opossum, like large rats. Their distinguishing features are pointed snouts, short legs, a long, often hairless tail, which is usually *prehensile* (that is, opossums can wrap it around a tree branch and hang from it), and large, hairless ears. Opossums come in a narrow range of colors – shades of gray, brown, and black. Male and female opossums generally look alike, but males are usually larger than females of the same age. Females in about half of the species have pouches for their young on their abdomens.

Opossum hind feet have five digits each, one digit acting as an opposable thumb.

Natural History
Ecology and Behavior

Most opossums are night-active omnivores, although some also can be seen during the day. Their reputation is that they will eat, or at least try to eat, almost anything they stumble across or can catch; mostly they take fruit, eggs, invertebrates, and small vertebrate animals. The COMMON OPOSSUM forages mainly at night, often along ponds and streams, sometimes covering more than a kilometer (half-mile) per night within its home range, the area within which it lives and seeks food. Opossums that have been studied are not territorial – they do not defend part or all of their home ranges from others of their species. Some opossums forage mainly on the ground, but most are good climbers and are able to forage also in trees and shrubs. Some species are chiefly arboreal. The terrestrial BROWN FOUR-EYED OPOSSUM (Plate 82) and the arboreal LONG-FURRED WOOLLY MOUSE OPOSSUM (Plate 82) are both quite shy and wary. They concentrate on insects for food, but during times of the year when there are lots of fruit, your best chance to see them is at a fruiting tree. After a night's foraging, an opossum spends the daylight hours in a cave, a rock crevice, or a cavity in a tree or log.

Predators on opossums include owls, snakes, and carnivorous mammals. Some opossums apparently are somewhat immune to the venom of many poisonous snakes. The response of the Common Opossum to threat by a predator is to hiss, growl, snap its mouth, move its body from side to side, and finally, to lunge and bite. They often try to climb to escape. The VIRGINIA OPOSSUM, a common North and Central American species, is famous for faking death ("playing possum") when threatened, but that behavior is rare or absent in the Common Opossum.

The Common Opossum has what can be considered a commensal relationship with people. Throughout its range in northern South America, populations of these opossums are concentrated around human settlements, particularly near garbage dumps, where they feed. They also partake of fruit crops and attack farmyard birds. Consequently, this species of opossum is more likely to be seen near towns or villages than in uninhabited areas. Of course, these opossums pay a price for the easy food – their picture commonly is found in the dictionary under "road kill."

Breeding

Opossums are unsociable animals and usually observed singly. The exception is during the breeding season, when males seek and court females, and two or more may be seen together. Female opossums give birth only 12 to 14 days after mating. The young that leave the reproductive tract are only about 1 cm (a half inch) long and weigh less than half a gram (one-hundredth ounce). These tiny opossums, barely embryos, climb unassisted along the mother's fur toward her nipples. They then grasp a nipple in their mouth, either within the pouch, or, if a species without a pouch like the BROWN FOUR-EYED OPOSSUM or the mouse opossums, directly on her chest. The nipple swells to completely fill the young's mouth, essentially attaching it to the mother for about 2 months. Usually more young are born (up to 20) than make it to the nipples to attach correctly. In studies, 6 young, on average, are found on the females' nipples (they have up to 13 nipples). Following this attached phase, the female continues to nurse her young for another month or more, often in a nest she constructs of leaves and grass in a tree cavity or burrow.

Notes

COMMON OPOSSUMS are known as foul-smelling beasts. Their reputation probably stems from the fact that they apparently enjoy rolling about in fresh animal droppings. Also, when handled, they employ some unattractive defense mechanisms – tending to squirt urine and defecate.

Status

Eleven of Brazil's opossum species are considered threatened, primarily by habitat destruction, and, of these, four occur in the Amazon–Pantanal area: BLACK-SHOULDERED OPOSSUM, BUSHY-TAILED OPOSSUM, EMILIA'S GRACILE MOUSE OPOSSUM and EMILIA'S SHORT-TAILED OPOSSUM. Opossum meat is not regarded as tasty, so these mammals are rarely hunted for food. Opossums, chiefly COMMON OPOSSUMS, are killed intentionally near human settlements to protect fruit crops and poultry, and unintentionally but frequently by cars.

Profiles

Brown Four-eyed Opossum, *Metachirus nudicaudatus*, Plate 82a
Common Opossum, *Didelphis marsupialis*, Plate 82b
Long-furred Woolly Mouse Opossum, *Micoureus demerarae*, Plate 82c

2. Anteaters, Sloths, and Armadillos

Anteaters, sloths, and *armadillos* are three types of very different-looking mammals that, somewhat surprisingly, are closely related. The group they belong to is order Edentata, meaning, literally, without teeth. However, because all but the anteaters have some teeth, the name is a misnomer. The *edentates* are New World mammals specialized to eat ants and termites, or to eat leaves high in the forest canopy. Although the edentates might look and behave differently, they are grouped together because they share certain skeletal features and aspects of their circulatory and reproductive systems that indicate close relationships. Because anteaters and sloths are so unique and found only in the tropical and semi-tropical forests of Central and South America, they are perhaps the quintessential mammals of the region, the way that toucans and parrots are the quintessential Neotropical birds. If given a choice of mammals, most visitors to Brazil would probably prefer to see a Jaguar, but it is far more likely that the characteristic Neotropical mammal they spot will be a sloth.

The anteater family, Myrmecophagidae, has 4 species, all restricted to Neotropical forests, and three of which are found in Amazonian Brazil: the very rare, 2-meter-long (6.5 ft) GIANT ANTEATER (Plate 83), the SOUTHERN TAMANDUA (Plate 83), and the small PYGMY or SILKY ANTEATER (Plate 82). Because the last species is a nocturnal tree-dweller, the anteater you are most likely to see during your trip is a tamandua.

There is nothing else like a sloth. Sloths vaguely resemble monkeys ("deformed monkeys," according to one chronicler), but their slow-motion lifestyle is the very antithesis of most primates' hyperkinetic lives. There are two families of sloths, the two-toed and three-toed varieties, distinguished by the number of claws per foot. There are five sloth species, all of which occur in Brazil. The two-toed sloths (family Megalonychidae) weigh about 5 to 8 kg (11 to 17.5 lb) and are active only at night. The much smaller three-toed sloths (family Brady-podidae, meaning slow-footed) weigh, on average, about 4 kg (9 lb), are pale yellowish or brown with a round, white face with dark side stripes, and are active both during day and night. Their hair is long and stiff, producing a shaggy look. Long limbs end in feet with three curved claws that they use as hooks to hang from tree branches.

Armadillos are strange ground-dwelling mammals that, probably because of the armor plating on their backs, are protected from many predators. The family, Dasypodidae, contains about 20 species that are distributed from the southern tip of South America to the central USA, with 11 species in Brazil. The endangered GIANT ARMADILLO (Plate 83) (up to 1.5 m, 5 ft, in length, including the tail, and weighing about 30 kg, 65 lb) is rare in the forests of the Amazon and open grasslands of southeastern Brazil, but where present, huge holes it makes in the forest floor advertise the fact. Because all the other species of Brazilian armadillos are entirely nocturnal, you are most likely to see only the Nine-banded Armadillo, which is often also active during the day. It is also the species that extends into the USA. All these armadillos are grayish or yellowish, with many crosswise plates of hard, horn-like material on their backs (bony plates underlie the outer horny covering).

Natural History
Ecology and Behavior

Anteaters are mammals highly specialized to feed on ants and termites; some also dabble in bees. From an anteater's point of view, the main thing about these social insects is that they live in large colonies, so that finding one often means finding thousands. The anteaters' strong, sharp, front claws are put to use digging into ant colonies in or on the ground, and into termite nests in trees (the very abundant, dark, globular, often basket-ball sized *termitarium* attached to the trunks and branches of tropical trees). Their long, thin snouts are used to get down into the excavation, and their extremely long tongues, coated with a special sticky saliva, are used to extract the juicy insects. The SOUTHERN TAMANDUA and SILKY ANTEATER are largely arboreal. They have prehensile tails for hanging about and moving in trees, allowing them to get to hard-to-reach termite nests. Particular about their food, anteaters don't generally go after army ants or large, stinging ants that might do them harm. Tamanduas rest in hollow trees or other holes during midday, but are otherwise active, including nocturnally. They forage both on the ground and in trees, usually solitarily. Each individual's home range, the area in which it lives and seeks food, averages about 70 hectares (170 acres). Anteaters are fairly slow-moving animals and their metabolic rates low because, although ants and termites are plentiful and easy to find, they don't provide a high nutrition, high energy diet. Deceptively placid and shy, anteaters, especially the GIANT ANTEATER, if attacked, can rear back and slash with deadly accuracy and force, using their powerful front legs and sharp claws to disembowel or severely injure enemies.

Sloths are active almost exclusively in trees, feeding on leaves as they hang upside down. "Active" is probably the wrong word to describe their behavior. Sloths, particularly the three-toed ones, move incredibly slowly – so much so that at one time it was mistakenly thought that a sloth spent its entire life moving about slowly in a single tree. Detailed observations have shown that sloths do indeed switch trees, but, on average, only once every two days. When switching, they do not cross open ground, but move between the trees' overlapping branches. This is smart, both because slowly descending to the ground and then climbing another tree would be a waste of time and energy, and because a slow-

moving sloth on the ground would be easy, defenseless prey for a variety of predators – snakes, large cats, and eagles. (One person clocked a female sloth on the
ground as moving only 4.5 m, 14 ft, in a minute – and that was in rapid response
to the call of her offspring!) Sloths can swim, however, and you should look for
them crossing small rivers.

Besides their slow movements that probably help sloths escape notice from
predators searching the canopy, the surface of their hair has many grooves and
pits in which algae and fungi readily grow to turn the animal greenish and camouflaged. Not only do sloths support plants on their bodies, they support insects
as well. A number of different beetle and moth species spend at least parts of their
life cycles living on sloths. One moth species, a "sloth moth," lives as an adult in
the hair of a sloth, reproducing by laying its eggs in sloth droppings. While the
three-toed sloths are docile and non-aggressive, the two-toed sloths are dangerous
and can do considerable damage, even in slow motion, with their front claws. All
species of sloths apparently come down from their elevated perches only about
once per week, to urinate and defecate at the base of a tree. Why they do so,
instead of just defecating from the heights, remains a mystery. The three-toed
sloths, but not the two-toed sloths, take extra time to dig a small hole, void themselves, and cover the droppings. During this 30-minute period, the animals are
dangerously vulnerable to predators.

Leaves are notoriously difficult to digest, so a diet purely of leaves provides
little nutrition. That means the sloths must eat a lot of them to survive. Sloths
have very low metabolic rates and relatively low body temperatures; in fact, at
night, sloths save energy by lowering their body temperatures to almost match
that of the environment. Sloths are solitary and apparently territorial – only one
per tree is permitted (or a female together with her young). Look for sloths in
large, leafy trees (particularly *Cecropias*), as they hang upside down, their hook-
like claws grasping the branches. Two-toed sloths will often eat fruits in addition
to leaves, so also look for them at night in fruiting trees.

Some armadillos, such as the GIANT ARMADILLO, specialize on ants and termites. This species uses its immense bulk and large claws on its front feet to
quickly dig out these insects from their nests in the ground. The NINE-BANDED
ARMADILLO (Plate 82), however, is more omnivorous, eating many kinds of
insects, small vertebrates, and also some plant parts. Usually they spend the day
foraging alone, but several family members may share the same sleeping burrow
they have dug out with their sharp claws. They are generally slow-moving creatures that, save for their armor plating, would be easy prey for predators. When
attacked, they curl up into a ball so that their armor faces the attacker, their soft
abdomens protected at the center of the ball. Few natural predators can harm
them. However, like opossums, they are frequently hit on roads by automobiles.

Breeding

Female anteaters bear one offspring at a time, and lavish attention on it. At first
the newborn is placed in a secure location, such as in a tree cavity, and the
mother returns to it at intervals to nurse. Later, when it is old enough, the young-
ster rides on the mother's back. After several months, when the young are about
half the mother's size, the two part ways. Breeding may be at any time of year.
Sloths also produce one young at a time. Following 6 months of pregnancy, the
offspring is born. It is then carried about and fed by the mother for about 4
months, at which point it is put down and must forage for itself. Until it is a year

old or so, the juvenile forages within its mother's home range; then it moves out on its own. Sloths not only move slowly, they grow slowly. Apparently they do not reach sexual maturity until they are 3 years old, and they may live for 20 to 30 years. Female armadillos, after 70-day pregnancies, produce several young at a time, usually four. For some unknown reason, each litter of armadillo young arises from a single fertilized egg, so that if a female has four young, they are always identical quadruplets.

Notes

GIANT ANTEATERS are also known as Ant Bears, for obvious reasons. Frequently, three-toed sloths are captured and released into city parks and plazas, where they survive amazingly well.

Status

Overall, the edentate mammals are not doing badly, but all suffer population declines from habitat destruction. One problem in trying to determine the status of their populations is that many are nocturnal, and some of the armadillos spend most of their time in burrows. The result is that nobody really knows the real health of some populations. However, in Brazil one species of armadillo (BRAZILIAN THREE-BANDED ARMADILLO) is considered threatened. The GIANT ARMADILLO, because of over-hunting, is considered endangered (CITES Appendix I listed). The GIANT ANTEATER has been exterminated from much of its range in South and Central America, and is considered threatened. Tamanduas are found throughout Brazil but, outside of protected areas, they are sometimes killed as pests by locals. The SILKY ANTEATER is thought to be fairly common, but because their populations naturally are sparse and also because they are so difficult to spot, good information on them is lacking. Three of Brazil's sloth species apparently are fairly common, although, again, there is no good information on their populations. Some biologists suspect that three-toed sloths are one of the most abundant larger mammals of Neotropical forests. One sloth, the MANED THREE-TOED SLOTH, from Brazil's shrinking Atlantic Forest, is endangered (CITES Appendix I and USA ESA listed).

Profiles

Nine-banded Armadillo, *Dasypus novemcinctus*, Plate 82e
Giant Armadillo, *Priodontes maximus*, Plate 83c
Southern Two-toed Sloth, *Choloepus didactylus*, Plate 83a
Brown-throated Three-toed Sloth, *Bradypus variegatus*, Plate 83b
Giant Anteater, *Myrmecophaga tridactlyla*, Plate 83d
Southern Tamandua, *Tamandua tetradactyla*, Plate 83e
Silky Anteater, *Cyclopes didactylus*, Plate 82d

3. Bats

Because they are so hard to see or hear, *bats* have always been considered foreign, exotic, and mysterious, even in our own backyards. Unlike any other mammals, they engage in sustained, powered flight ("rats with wings," in the memorable phrasing of an unappreciative acquaintance). Bats are active at night and navigate the dark skies chiefly using "sonar," or *echolocation*: by broadcasting ultrasonic sounds – extremely high-pitched chirps and clicks – and then gaining information about their environment by "reading" the echoes. They also use this sonar to locate prey such as flying insects and surfacing fish. Although foreign to people's primate sensibilities, bats, precisely because their lives are so very different from our own, are increasingly of interest to us. In the past, of course, bats' exotic behavior, particularly their nocturnal habits, engendered in most societies not ecological curiosity but fear and superstition.

Bats are widely distributed, inhabiting most of the world's tropical and temperate regions, except for some oceanic islands. With a worldwide total of about 980 species, the bats are second in diversity among mammals only to the rodents. Ecologically, they can be thought of as night-time replacements for birds, which dominate the daytime skies. Bats of the Neotropics, although often hard to see and, in most cases, difficult for anyone other than experts to identify (because of their great diversity), are tremendously important mammals. Their numbers tell the story: 39% of all Neotropical mammal species are bats, and there are often more species of bats in some Neotropical forests than of all other mammal species combined. Researchers estimate that bats make up most of the mammalian biomass (the total amount of living tissue, by weight) in any given Neotropical region. Of the 524 species of mammals that occur in Brazil, more than 140 are bats. We profile 10 species that represent a spectrum of the types of bats you are most likely to encounter.

Bats have true wings that are made of thin, strong, highly elastic membranes that extend from the sides of the body and legs to cover and be supported by the elongated fingers of the arms. (The name of the order of bats, Chiroptera, refers to the wings: *chiro*, meaning hand, and *ptera*, wing.) Other distinctive anatomical features include bodies covered with silky, longish hair; toes with sharp, curved claws that allow the bats to hang upside down and are used by some to catch food; scent glands that produce strong, musky odors; and, in many, very odd-shaped folds of skin on their noses (*noseleaves*) and prominent ears that aid in echolocation. Like birds, bats' bodies have been modified through evolution to conform to the needs of energy-demanding flight: they have relatively large hearts, low body weights, and high metabolisms.

Bats come in a variety of sizes but are fairly standardized in form. Females in most species are larger than males, presumably so they can fly when pregnant. Bat species in Brazil weigh 5 to 200 g (0.2 to 7 oz) and have wingspans of 5 to 80 cm (2 to 31 in). At night in almost any habitat this group of mammals takes over. At dusk, when it is not yet too dark to see them, some species are already flying over streams and forests. During the night as you walk along a closed forested path, bats frequently will fly past the light beam of your flashlight. They may even brush your body with their wings as they swiftly fly by in hot pursuit of a scrumptious insect. Don't panic – they are harmless, unless you act like an insect. Contrary to folk-stories, bats absolutely do NOT make nests in your hair.

Natural History
Ecology and Behavior
Most Neotropical bat species specialize in eating insects (a single individual has been estimated to eat up to 1200 insects per hour!). They use their sonar to detect insects, which they catch on the wing, pick off leaves, or scoop off the ground. Bats use several methods to catch flying insects. Small insects may be captured directly in the mouth; some bats use their wings as nets and spoons to trap insects and pull them to their mouth; and others scoop bugs into the fold of skin membrane that connects their tail and legs, then somersault in midair to move the catch to their mouth. Small bugs are eaten immediately on the wing, while larger

ones, such as big beetles, are taken to a perch and dismembered. However, not all species are insectivores. Neotropical bats have also expanded ecologically into a variety of other feeding niches: some specialize in eating fruit, feeding on nectar and pollen at flowers, preying on vertebrates such as frogs or birds, eating fish, or drinking blood.

Bats are highly gregarious animals, roosting and often foraging in groups. They spend the daylight hours in *day roosts*, usually tree cavities, shady sides of trees, caves, rock crevices, or, these days, in buildings or under bridges. Some bats make their own individual roosting sites in trees by biting leaves so that they fold over, making small tents that shelter them from predators as well as from the elements. More than one species of bat may inhabit the same roost, although some species will associate only with their own kind. For most species, the normal resting position in a roost is hanging by their feet, heads down, which makes taking flight as easy as letting go and spreading their wings. Many bats leave roosts around dusk and then move to foraging sites at various distances from the roost. Night activity patterns vary, perhaps serving to reduce food competition among species. Some tend to fly and forage intensely in the early evening, become less active in the middle of the night, then resume intense foraging near dawn; others are relatively inactive early in the evening, but more active later on. Bats do not fly continuously after leaving their day roosts, but group together at a *night roost*, a tree for instance, where they rest and bring food. Fruit-eaters do not rest in the tree at which they have discovered ripe fruit, where predators might find them, but they make several trips per night from the fruit tree to their night roost.

If you see any bats well on your trip to Amazonian Brazil, they likely will be LONG-NOSED BATS (Plate 85). They roost in groups up to 30 or more on the underside of logs and along banks of rivers and lakes. They hang in a line, evenly spaced but so well camouflaged that you will have to look carefully to see them. They readily take flight in the daytime if you come too close, and fly ahead of your canoe like a flock of large, whitish butterflies. At dusk they begin to feed on tiny insects low over the water. The WHITE-LINED SAC-WINGED BAT (Plate 84) is one of the most frequently encountered bats of Brazil's forests. By day they roost in groups of 5 to 50 in hollow trees or caves, rocks, or buildings; they are often seen under overhangs at ecotourist facilities. They leave roosts just before dark to commence their insect foraging, which they do under the forest canopy, usually within 300 m (1000 ft) of their roosts. Individual males defend territories in the day roosts, and they have harems of up to 9 females each. After birth, a mother carries her pup each night from the day roost and leaves it in a hiding place while she forages. Pups can fly at about 2 weeks old, but continue to nurse for several months. The GREATER FISHING BAT (Plate 84) is relatively large and orange-colored. Fishing bats (sometimes called *bulldog bats*) roost in hollow trees and buildings near fresh or salt water. They have very large hind feet and claws that they use to pull fish, crustaceans, and insects from the water's surface. These bats fly low over still water, using their sonar to detect the ripples of a fish just beneath or breaking the water's surface. Grabbing the fish with their claws, they then move it to their mouth, land, hang upside down, and feast.

The COMMON LONG-TONGUED BAT or NECTAR BAT (Plate 85) is a small bat with a misleading name. Although it can hover for a few seconds at flowers to take pollen or nectar, most of its omnivorous diet consists of fruit and insects. It roosts in large groups in both dry and wet forest habitats. Young use their teeth to cling to their mothers' fur after birth, being carried along during foraging trips;

pups can fly on their own at about a month old. The SHORT-TAILED FRUIT BAT (Plate 85) is another small and very common species that lives in large groups, up to several hundred, usually in caves or tree cavities. They are primarily fruit-eaters, but also seasonally visit flowers for nectar. Usually they pick fruit from a tree, then return to a night roost to consume it. After giving birth, females carry their young for a week or two during their nightly foraging; older young are left in the day roost. Because of their abundance and frugivory, these bats are critical dispersers of tree seeds in Neotropical forests. A medium-sized fruit-eater in wet and dry forests, the JAMAICAN FRUIT-EATING BAT (Plate 84) also takes insects and pollen from flowers. It plucks fruit and carries it to a night roost 25 to 200 m (80 to 650 ft) away to eat it. Observers estimate that nightly each bat carries away from trees more than its own weight in fruit. These fruit bats roost in caves, hollow trees, or in foliage. Breeding is apparently polygynous (a single male mates with more than one female), because small roosts are always found to contain one male plus several females (up to 11) and their dependent young.

Vampire bats are the only mammals that feed exclusively on blood; the only true mammalian parasites. Only three living species of these notorious blood-eating vampires are known, and they range from northern Mexico south to Argentina. All three are found in Brazil, and two of them eat blood only from birds (including poultry if available). The COMMON VAMPIRE BAT (Plate 84), however, concentrates on mammalian blood. Day roosts are in hollow trees and caves, and they can be instantly recognized by the accumulation of their tar-like droppings. At night, vampires fly out, using both vision (they have larger eyes and better vision than most bats) and sonar to find victims. They not only fly well and quietly, they use the extra long thumb on their wing like a front foot to allow agile walking, running, and hopping – of great assistance in perching on, feeding on, and avoiding swats by their prey. They use their sharp incisor teeth to bite the awake or sleeping animal, often on the neck, and remove a tiny piece of flesh. An anti-clotting agent in the bat's saliva keeps the small wound oozing blood. The vampire laps up the oozing blood – it does not suck it out. The feeding is reported to be painless (we won't ask how researchers know this, but, with a shudder, we can guess). Because blood is mostly water and proteins, which, unlike fats and carbohydrates, cannot be stored easily, each bat must consume a blood meal (of about half its body weight) at least every 60 hours or starve to death. Vampires breed at any time of the year; older young are fed blood from the mother's mouth for several months until they can get their own. Although they rarely feed on humans, when they do, they prefer biting people at sleep on the nose or toes. If you see the local people sleeping with a basket over their heads and their feet, or if your host insists you sleep under mosquito netting even when there are no mosquitos around, consider taking appropriate protection. If you don't, those scabs on the end of your nose or fingers in the morning will give you great bragging rights back home.

The SUCKER-FOOTED BAT (Plate 85) is a tiny bat with peculiar, circular adhesive cups on its thumbs and feet. It roosts most commonly in small family groups (2 to 9) in rolled up banana or *Heliconia* leaves or fronds. The "sucker" cups adhere to the leaves. When in a few days the leaf matures and unfurls, the family must seek a new home. Interestingly, unlike most bats, the Sucker-foots in their roosts are head upwards. They are common in rainforests and gardens and can be a startling surprise as they fly suddenly out of the young rolled leaf you have just disturbed along the trail. During the night they feed on insects in openings of the forest and along rivers. The BLACK MYOTIS (Plate 85) is a common representative of a group of tiny bats that are distributed widely over the Neotropics. They roost in large groups in hollow trees and buildings; males usually roost separately from females and their young. At sunset they leave the roost in search of flying insects, and return just before dawn. Young are carried by the mother for a few days after birth, but are then left behind with other young in the roost when the female leaves to forage. Pups can fly at about 3 weeks of age, are weaned at 5 to 6 weeks, and are reproductively mature at only 4 months.

Bats are beneficial to forests and to people in a number of ways. Many Neotropical plants have bats, instead of bees or birds, as their main pollinators. These species generally have flowers that open at night and are white, making them easy for bats to find. They also give off a pungent aroma that bats can home in on. Nectar-feeding bats use long tongues to poke into flowers to feed on nectar – a sugary solution – and pollen. As a bat brushes against a flower, pollen adheres to its body, and is then carried to other plants, where it falls and leads to cross-pollination. Fruit-eating bats, owing to their high numbers, are important seed dispersers (see Close-up, p. 196), helping to regenerate forests by transporting and dropping fruit seeds onto the forest floor. Also, particularly helpful to humans, bats each night consume enormous numbers of annoying insects.

Bats eat a variety of vertebrate animals; unfortunately for some of them, they play right into the bat's hands . . . uh, feet. One bat that specializes on eating frogs, it has been discovered, can home in on the calls that male frogs give to attract mates. These frogs are truly in a bind: if they call, they may attract a deadly predator; if they do not, they will lack for female company. Some types of bat prey, on the other hand, have developed anti-bat tactics. Several groups of moth species, for instance, can sense the ultrasonic chirps of some echolocating insectivorous bats; when they do, they react immediately by flying erratically or diving down into vegetation, decreasing the success of the foraging bats. Some moths even make their own clicking sounds, which apparently confuse the bats, causing them to break off approaches.

Relatively little is known about which predators prey on bats. The list, however, includes birds-of-prey (owls, hawks), snakes, other mammals such as opossums, cats, and (yes) people, and even other bats, such as the carnivorous FALSE VAMPIRE BAT. Crane Hawks (Plate 36) use their long legs to reach deep into tree cavities and capture sleeping bats. Tiny bats, such as the 3 to 5 g (0.1 to 0.2 oz) Black Myotis, are even captured and eaten by large spiders and cockroaches. Bats, logically, are usually captured in or near their roosts, where predators can reliably find and corner them. One strong indication that predation is a real problem for bats is that many species reduce their flying in bright moonlight. Bats showing this "lunar phobia" include the Jamaican Fruit-eating Bat, Vampire Bats and Short-tailed Fruit Bat. On the other hand, others, like the very small White-lined Sac-winged Bat, do not decrease their activity levels under a full moon, perhaps because they hunt mostly in the darker understory of forests.

Breeding

Bat mating systems are diverse. The males of some species have harems of 2 to 5 females, but various species employ monogamy, polygyny, and/or promiscuity; the breeding behavior of many species has yet to be studied in detail. Some Brazilian species breed at particular times of the year, but others have no regular breeding seasons. Most bats produce a single pup at a time. Females of many species of bats, both in temperate areas and the tropics, store sperm and can delay fertilization or the beginning of the development of the embryo. This ability is apparently so that the time of birth for the young bats can be more finely coordinated with periods of abundant insects and fruit.

Notes

Bats have frightened people for a long time. The result, of course, is that there is a large body of folklore that portrays bats as evil, associated with or incarnations of death, devils, witches, or vampires. Undeniably, it was the bats' alien lives – their activity in the darkness, flying ability, and strange form – and people's ignorance of bats, that were the sources of these myriad superstitions. Many cultures, worldwide, have evil bat legends, from Japan and the Philippines, to Europe, the Middle East, Australia and Central and South America. Many ancient legends tell of how bats came to be creatures of the night. But the association of bats with vampires – blood-sucking monsters – may have originated in recent times with Bram Stoker, the English author who in 1897 published *Dracula* (the title character, a vampire, could metamorphose into a bat). Vampire bats are native only to the Neotropics. Stoker may have heard stories of their blood-lapping ways from travellers, and for his book, melded the behavior of these bats with legends of vampires from India and from Slavic Gypsy culture. Although not all New World cultures imparted evil reputations to bats, it is not surprising, given the presence of vampire bats, that some did. The Mayans, for instance, associated bats with darkness and death; there was a "bat world," a part of the underworld ruled by a bat god, through which dead people had to pass.

Speaking of vampire bats, they presumably are much more numerous today than in the distant past because they now have domesticated animals as prey. Before the introduction of domesticated animals to the Neotropics, vampires would have had to seek blood meals exclusively from wild animals such as deer and peccaries (two species, however, are specialists on bird blood); now they have, over large parts of their range, herds or flocks of large domesticated animals to feed on. In fact, examinations of blood meals reveal that vampire bats in settled areas feed almost exclusively on ranch and farm animals – cattle, horses, poultry, etc. Vampire bats rarely attack people, although it is not unheard of. Out of fear and ignorance, there is a tendency for local people to kill any large bat. Most of these large bats, however, are fruit and insect-eating bats that are critical for pollination, seed dispersal and insect control. Vampire bat eradication can only be justified in agricultural areas, but it must discriminate and leave unharmed all the other bats species in the area as well as vampire bats living away from settled areas. In some regions, bats, especially vampire bats, may transmit rabies. As most of them will bite in self-defense, it's best to avoid handling any bat bare-handed. If you must handle bats, make sure you have your rabies prophylactic shots and wear gloves.

Status

Determining the statuses of bat populations is difficult because of their nocturnal behavior and habit of roosting in places that are hard to census. With some exceptions, all that is known for most Neotropical species is that they are common or not common, widely or narrowly distributed. Some species are known from only a few museum specimens, or from their discovery in a single cave, but that does not mean that there are not healthy but largely hidden wild populations. Because many forest bats roost in hollow trees, deforestation is obviously a primary threat.

Ten species of Brazilian bats are included in the IUCN Red List of Threatened Animals. Of these, five occur in the Amazon–Pantanal area: LITTLE BIG-EARED BAT, RECIFE WHITE-LINED FRUIT BAT, EGA LONG-TONGUED BAT, ALLEN'S ROUND-EARED BAT, and NEGLECTED DOG-FACED BAT. All the bats we chose to profile here are common. Many bat populations in temperate regions in Europe and the USA are known to be declining and under continued threat by a number of agricultural, forestry, and architectural practices. Traditional roost sites have been lost on large scales by mining and quarrying, by the destruction of old buildings, and by changing architectural styles that eliminate many building overhangs, church belfries, etc. Many forestry practices advocate the removal of hollow, dead trees, which frequently provide bats with roosting space. Additionally, farm pesticides are ingested by insects, which are then eaten by bats, leading to death or reduced reproductive success.

Profiles

Greater Fishing Bat, *Noctilio leporinus*, Plate 84a
Jamaican Fruit-eating Bat, *Artibeus jamaicensis*, Plate 84b
Common Vampire Bat, *Desmodus rotundus*, Plate 84c
White-lined Sac-winged Bat, *Saccopteryx bilineata*, Plate 84d
Hairy-legged Fruit Bat, *Sturnira lilium*, Plate 84e
Short-tailed Fruit Bat, *Carollia perspicillata*, Plate 85a
Sucker-footed Bat, *Thyroptera tricolor*, Plate 85b
Common Long-tongued Bat, *Glossophaga soricina*, Plate 85c
Long-nosed Bat, *Rhynchonycteris naso*, Plate 85d
Black Myotis, *Myotis nigricans*, Plate 85e

4. Primates

Most people, it seems, find *monkeys* (*macaco* in Portuguese) striking, even transfixing, when first encountered, but then responses diverge. Some people adore the little primates and can watch them for hours, whether it be in the wild or at zoos. Others, however, find them a bit, for want of a better word, unalluring – even to the point of making people slightly uncomfortable. It is probably the same characteristic of monkeys that both so attracts people and turns them off, and that is their quasi-humanness. Whether or not we acknowledge it consciously, it is this trait that is the source of all the attention and importance attached to monkeys and apes. They look like us, and, truth be told, they act like us, in a startlingly large number of ways. Aristotle, 2300 years ago, noted similarities between human and nonhuman primates, and Linnaeus, the Swedish originator of our current system for classifying plants and animals, working more than 100 years pre-Darwin, classed people together in the same group with monkeys. Therefore, even before Darwin's ideas provided a possible mechanism for people and monkeys to be distantly related, we strongly suspected there was a link; the resemblance was too close to be accidental. Given this bond between people and other primates, it is not surprising that visitors to parts of the world that support nonhuman primates are eager to see them and are very curious about their lives. Fortunately, Brazil provides homes for many monkey species, some of them still sufficiently abundant in protected areas to be readily located and observed.

Primates are distinguished by several anatomical and ecological traits. They are primarily arboreal animals. Most are fairly large, very smart, and highly social – they live in permanent social groups. Most have five very flexible fingers and toes per limb. Primates' eyes are in the front of the skull, facing forward (eyes in the front instead of on the sides of the head are required for binocular vision and good depth perception, without which swinging about in trees would be an extremely hazardous and problematic affair), and primates have, for their sizes, relatively large brains. Unlike most other mammals, primates have color vision. Female primates give birth usually to a single, very helpless, infant.

Monkeys are distributed mainly throughout the globe's tropical areas and many subtropical ones, save for the Australian region. They are divided into four groups:

1 *Prosimians* include several families of primitive primates from the Old World. They look the least like people, are mainly small and nocturnal, and include lemurs, lorises, galago (bushbaby), and tarsiers.
2 *Old World Monkeys* (family Cercopithecidae) include baboons, mandrills, and various monkeys such as rhesus and proboscis monkeys.
3 *New World Monkeys* (families Callitrichidae and Cebidae) include many kinds of monkeys, marmosets, and tamarins.
4 The *Hominoidea* order contains the gibbons, orangutans, chimpanzees, gorillas, and ecotravellers.

New World monkeys, in general, have short muzzles and flat, unfurred faces, short necks, long limbs, and long tails that are prehensile in some of the larger species – used as fifth limbs for climbing about in trees. They are day-active animals that spend most of their time in trees, usually coming to the ground only to cross treeless space that they cannot traverse within the forest canopy. About 75 to 100 species of New World Monkeys are distributed from southern Mexico to northern Argentina, and 75 occur in Brazil (if you agree with authorities who consider every isolated population to be a separate species). The New World monkeys are conveniently divided into two major families: the marmosets and tamarins (family Callitrichidae) and the "typical" monkeys (family Cebidae).

The *marmosets* and *tamarins* (*mico* in Portuguese) are tiny to small in size (70 to 600 g, 2.5 to 21 oz) with long tails that are NOT prehensile. Their feet have claws instead of flattened nails, and they typically give birth to twins. Because they are so small, local hunters seldom waste expensive shells on them, and so they can be common even in secondary forests near inhabited areas. Fourteen species of marmosets and 17 species of tamarins occur in Brazil, including the enigmatic and very rare GOELDI'S MONKEY (which is sometimes placed by itself in its own family, Callimiconidae). The *typical monkeys* are larger (800 to 1500 g, 1.8 to 3.3 lb) and have long tails that in the largest species are prehensile. Their feet have flattened nails, and they give birth to a single young. They are actively hunted and so are among the first native species to disappear from an area after people settle there.

Natural History
Ecology and Behavior
The tamarins and marmosets of Brazil travel in noisy troops giving chirps and twitters that sound more bird-like than primate-like. They feed in mid levels of the forest and dense vine tangles on fruits, insects, flower nectar and occasionally lizards and birds.

Titis are small monkeys (1.2 kg, 2.6 lb) with thickly furred, nonprehensile tails that hang straight down. They travel in small family groups and feed on fruits and frequently on leaves, especially bamboo. They have very small home ranges that often center on a dense tree fall or vine tangle, where they spend their nights. Although the DUSKY TITI MONKEY (Plate 87) of Amazonian Brazil is rarely seen, you will almost certainly hear it. The male and female duet early in the morning and at dusk with loud chimpanzee-like whoops that no one can miss. Because of its small home range, small size and retiring behavior, this is often the only monkey species remaining in extensively cleared parts of the forest. Apparently all it needs to prosper is a small patch of trees and some dense tangle to hide in.

The COMMON SQUIRREL MONKEY (Plate 87) lacks a prehensile tail and, with its white eye mask, black snout and large noisy troop behavior, is unmistakable throughout the Amazon. Squirrel moneys feed on fruits, insects and some leaves and are often found associating with a troop of capuchin monkeys. A troop (5 to 40 individuals) usually consists of several adult males and many females and their dependent young, although during nonbreeding portions of the year the sexes may separate into uni-sex groups. Squirrel monkeys apparently do not defend exclusive territories: observers have noticed that the home ranges of troops frequently overlap, and they will often tolerate a coalescing of troops into a monstrous supertroop. During a one-month period, a troop may range back and forth over an area (home range) of about 2 sq km (0.8 sq miles). These monkeys are commonly spotted in trees near water – along lake shores, rivers, and swamps.

The WHITE-FRONTED CAPUCHIN (Plate 87) and BROWN CAPUCHIN (Plate 87) are larger monkeys (2.3 kg, 5 lb) that often travel together in large and noisy troops with squirrel monkeys. Capuchins are highly arboreal, but also versatile – they forage over all levels of the forest, from canopy to lower tree trunks, and they also occasionally come to the ground to feed. Their diet is broad, consisting mainly of ripe fruit and insects, but also bird eggs, young birds, baby squirrels, and small lizards. (Although they rarely attack larger animals, one male capuchin was observed to attack a 1.7 m (6 ft) long Green Iguana (Plate 23) and break off and eat the end of its tail.) In one study, a troop was found to consume 20% animal prey (mostly insects), 65% fruit, and 15% green plant material; but insects make up 50% of the diet during some periods of the year. Capuchins are very active monkeys, spending 80% or more of daylight hours moving through the forest, foraging in any number of ways, such as looking through leaves and leaf litter, pulling bark off trees, and rolling over sticks and logs. A troop, 2 to 30 strong (often 6 to 10), consisting usually of a single adult male plus females and their young, travels an average of about 2 km (1.2 miles) per day, while remaining within a fairly small home range of a few square km (about a square mile). Troops maintain exclusive territories, aggressively defending their turf whenever they meet other troops of the same species at territorial boundaries.

The COMMON WOOLLY MONKEY (Plate 88) is a large species (males regularly weigh more than 10 kg, 22 lb) with a truly prehensile tail. The body color can vary from gray to brown, but the face is almost always darker. Woolly monkeys feed mostly on fruit and seeds and occasionally on insects and leaves from the canopy of tall forests of the Amazon. They move in large, noisy troops giving musical trills, barks and whoops, and each troop needs a minimum of 500 hectares (1200 acres) for a home range. This species is considered in Brazil the most desirable monkey for eating, and this hunting pressure, combined with a female being able to give birth only every other year, makes it especially vulnerable to human pressures. Even when protection is provided, populations take a long time to recover.

The WHITE-BELLIED SPIDER MONKEY (Plate 88) is the longest monkey species in Amazonian Brazil, with males reaching up to 1.5 m (5 ft), including the tail. These monkeys stay mostly within a forest's upper canopy, rarely descending to the ground, and move quickly through trees using their fully prehensile tail as a fifth limb to climb, swing, and hang. They are known to feed occasionally at night, but they typically feed in the early morning and late afternoon. Spider monkeys eat young leaves and flowers but are especially fond of hard palm fruits. During the day, troops, varying in size from 2 to 25 or more (groups of 100 or more have been reported), range over wide swaths of forest, but stay within a home range of 2.5 to 4.0 sq km (1 or 2 sq miles). Troops usually consist of an adult male and several females and their dependent offspring. Spider monkeys are commonly observed in small groups, often two animals, but frequently they are members of a larger troop; the troop breaks up daily into small foraging parties, then coalesces each evening at a mutual sleeping tree.

Howlers inhabit a variety of forest habitats. The RED HOWLER MONKEY (Plate 88) is relatively common in the Amazon and the BLACK HOWLER MONKEY (Plate 88) is fairly easy to find in gallery forests of the Pantanal. Howlers are highly arboreal and rarely come to the ground; typically they spend most of their time in the upper reaches of the forest. In contrast to many other monkey species, howlers are relatively slow-moving and more deliberate in their canopy travels. They eat fruit and a lot of leafy material; in fact, in one study, leaves comprised 64% of their diet, fruit and flowers, 31%. Because of their specialization on a super-abundant food resource – leaves – their home ranges need not be, and are not, very large. Most troops have 10 to 20 individuals, which are made up of females, associated young, and usually one male in Red Howler (and perhaps Black Howler) troops. Howlers are frequently inconspicuous because they are slow-moving and often quiet, and many people on trails pass directly below howlers without noticing them. They are most assuredly not inconspicuous, however, when the males let loose with their amazing lion-like roaring, which is amplified and modulated by a special bony plate over the throat. Their very loud, deep choruses of roars, at dawn, during late afternoon, and, frequently, during heavy rain, are a characteristic and wonderful part of the rainforest environment. (The initial response of a newcomer to the Neotropics, upon being awakened in the morning by howling howlers, is sure to be "Now what the heck is THAT?"). These vocalizations are probably used by the howlers to communicate with other troops, to advertise their locations and to defend them; although troops of these monkeys do not maintain exclusive territories, they do appear to defend current feeding sites. The males' howling can be heard easily at 3 km (1.8 miles) away in a forest or 5 km (3 miles) away across water.

Saki monkeys (Plate 89) are medium-sized (up to 2.25 kg, 5 lb) species with long thick hair and nonprehensile tails that are thickly furred. They forage primarily on fruits, seeds and a few leaves, and usually are seen in small family groups of 2 to 4. They wander and feed from the lower canopy down to mid levels of forests in the Amazonian region and are often hard to see because of their shy and retiring behavior. You are most likely to see sakis along streams and lakes as they sit without moving in a low tree, only their long bushy tails hanging straight down telling you they're not just another tangle of dead leaves.

The *night*, or *owl*, *monkeys* are, as their name suggests, active primarily at night. They are relatively small (1 kg, 2.2 lb) with a two-colored tail tipped in black that is non-prehensile. At night, their large eyes reflect light, and they can only be mistaken for an opossum or Kinkajou, neither of which has the striking black and white facial pattern. They feed mostly on fruits in small family groups. The taxonomy of the night monkeys is controversial, with some scientists identifying up to 8 species in Central and South America. In the southeastern part of Amazonian Brazil, the BLACK-HEADED NIGHT MONKEY (Plate 89) occurs. Your best chance of seeing it is from a canoe at night as you drift along the edge of a forested lake or stream. Look for eye-shine and listen for its low, distinctive three-note hoots that sound like an owl. Occasionally you can see them in the light late in the afternoon as they begin to forage, usually at forest edges.

A variety of animals prey on Brazil's monkeys, including boa snakes (Plate 20), birds-of-prey such as eagles (Plate 38), arboreal cats such as Jaguarundi and Margay (Plate 92), and people. Other causes of death are disease, such as yellow fever, and parasite infestations, such as that by *botflies*. Botflies lay their eggs on mosquitos, monkeys being exposed when infected mosquitos land on them to feed. Botfly larvae burrow into a monkey's skin and develop there for 10 weeks before emerging as adults. Many howlers, for instance, are observed to have severe botfly infestations of their necks, seen as swollen lumps and the holes created when adult botflies emerge from the monkey's body. In one Panamanian study, each member of a howler population had an average of 2 to 5 botfly parasites; several monkeys in the study died, apparently of high levels of botfly infestation.

Monkeys are especially crucial elements of rainforest ecosystems because they are seed dispersers for many hundreds of plant species, particularly of the larger canopy trees. Mammals transport seeds that stick to their fur from the producing tree to the places where the seeds eventually fall off. Mammals that are *frugivores* (fruit-eaters) also carry fruit away from a tree, then eat the soft parts and drop the seeds, which may later germinate; or they eat the fruit whole and transport the seeds in their digestive tracts. The seeds eventually fall, unharmed, to the ground and germinate (see Close-up, p. 196). Monkeys, it turns out, are major seed dispersers. For example, in Panamá, a troop of capuchins was estimated to disperse each day more than 300,000 tiny seeds of a single tree species; up to two-thirds of the seeds that passed through the monkeys' digestive systems later germinated (a proportion that was actually higher than seeds that made it to the ground without passing through an animal gut). Monkeys also assist plants in another way: Capuchins eat so many insects that they probably have a significant effect in reducing insect damage to trees. Because some monkeys eat leaves, they also harm trees, but reports are very rare of primates stripping all the leaves from trees, killing them. Also, monkeys at times are seed predators. They extract seeds from fruit and chew them, destroying them, and also eat young fruits and nuts that contain seeds too undeveloped ever to germinate.

Most monkey troops are quite noisy as they forage, moving quickly about in trees and also vocalizing. A variety of other animals take advantage of monkey foraging, apparently attracted by the noise-making: squirrel monkeys and the Double-toothed Kite (Plate 36) regularly follow capuchins, catching large insects that the capuchins scare up as they move. Various ground-dwellers such as agouti (Plate 95) and peccaries (Plate 93) often congregate under foraging troops, feeding on dropped fruit.

Breeding

Female monkeys in Brazil usually produce a single young (tamarins and marmosets two) that is born furred and with its eyes open. The tamarins, marmosets, and most of the small "typical" monkeys, such as titis, night monkeys and sakis, are monogamous, but the SADDLE-BACKED TAMARIN (Plate 86) appears to be occasionally polyandrous – one female mates with two males (such a rare behavior among mammals that scientists are still amazed). The male of these species carries the young until they are large enough to forage on their own. The other monkeys are polygynous, with a male having a harem of 2 to 5 females. The squirrel monkeys, however, are promiscuous, and a male mates with several females in the troop in a sexual scramble. In polygynous and promiscuous species the female carries the young. Squirrel monkeys, which live up to 21 years in captivity, begin reproducing at 3 (females) to 5 (males) years old. The young cling to their mother after birth and are not truly independent until about a year old. Pregnancy is between 160 and 172 days. Mating is during the dry season, with births occurring during the wet season. Female capuchins reach sexual maturity at 3 to 4 years of age, then give birth at 1 to 2 year intervals. Most births occur during the dry season. Young cling to the mother's fur immediately following birth, and are carried by the mothers for 5 to 6 months, until they can travel on their own. Pregnancy is about 180 days. Capuchins live up to 46 years in captivity. Spider monkeys appear to have no regular breeding seasons. Females reach sexual maturity at about 4 years old (males at about 5), then give birth every 2 to 4 years after pregnancies of about 230 days. Young, which weigh about 500 g (1 lb) at birth, are carried by the mother for up to 10 months and are nursed for up to a year. Upon reaching sexual maturity, young females leave their troops to find mates in other troops; males remain with their birth troop. Spider monkeys have lived for 33 years in captivity. Female howlers reach sexual maturity at 3 to 4 years of age. They give birth following pregnancies of about 180 days. At 3 months, youngsters begin making brief trips away from their mothers, but until a year old, they continue to spend most of their time on their mother's back; they are nursed until they are 10 to 12 months old. Howlers have survived in the wild for up to 20 years.

Notes

The current range of the RED-BACKED SQUIRREL MONKEY, restricted to fragmented regions on the Pacific coasts of Panamá and Costa Rica, is at least 500 km (300 miles) distant from the nearest South American squirrel monkey populations. The discontinuous nature of the distributions is puzzling, and it has led biogeographers to suggest that squirrel monkeys may have arrived in Central America only with the help of people; that is, they may have been introduced there by travellers from South to Central America in Pre-Columbian times.

Owing to their active lifestyles, intelligence, and mischievousness, capuchins are sought after as pets and as "organ-grinder" monkeys; consequently, they are probably the most numerous captive monkeys in North America and Europe. Trade in wild-caught capuchins for pets, however, is now illegal.

Status

All New World monkeys are listed in CITES Appendix II as species that, although they may not be currently threatened, need to be highly regulated in trade, or they could soon become threatened. The IUCN Red List includes 20 species of Brazilian primates, only seven of which occur in the Amazonian or

Pantanal sections of the country – GOELDI'S MONKEY, SILVERY TUFTED-EAR MARMOSET, BLACK-HEADED MARMOSET, BALD UKARI, WHITE-BELLIED SPIDER MONKEY, LONG-HAIRED SPIDER MONKEY, and KA'APORI CAPUCHIN MONKEY. Main menaces to monkeys are deforestation – elimination of their natural habitats – and poaching. The larger monkeys – especially woolly, spiders, and howlers – are often hunted for their meat, and therefore are usually rare near human settlements.

Profiles

Black-chested Moustached Tamarin, *Saguinus mystax*, Plate 86a
Golden-handed Tamarin, *Saguinus midas*, Plate 86b
Saddle-backed Tamarin, *Saguinus fuscicollis*, Plate 86c
Silvery Marmoset, *Callithrix argentata*, Plate 86d
Dusky Titi Monkey, *Callicebus moloch*, Plate 87a
Common Squirrel Monkey, *Saimiri sciureus*, Plate 87b
Brown Capuchin Monkey, *Cebus apella*, Plate 87c
White-fronted Capuchin Monkey, *Cebus albifrons*, Plate 87d

Black Howler Monkey, *Alouatta caraya*, Plate 88a
Red Howler Monkey, *Alouatta seniculus*, Plate 88b
Common Woolly Monkey, *Lagothrix lagothricha*, Plate 88c
White-bellied Spider Monkey, *Ateles belzebuth*, Plate 88d
Monk Saki Monkey, *Pithecia monachus*, Plate 89a
Brown-bearded Saki Monkey, *Chiroptes satanas*, Plate 89b
Guianan Saki Monkey, *Pithecia pithecia*, Plate 89c
Black-headed Night Monkey, *Aotus nigriceps*, Plate 89d

5. Carnivores

Carnivores are ferocious mammals – including the cat that sleeps on your pillow and the dog that takes table scraps from your hand – that are specialized to kill and eat other vertebrate animals. They all share clawed toes and teeth customized to grasp, rip, and tear flesh – witness their large, cone-shaped canines. Most are meat-eaters, but many are at least somewhat omnivorous, taking fruits and other plant materials. Carnivore populations tend to be sparse and individuals notoriously difficult to see at any time. They range in size from weasels 9 cm (3.5 in) long to bears 3 m (10 ft) long. Four families within the Order Carnivora have Brazilian representatives: *dogs, raccoons, weasels,* and *cats.* Of these, only the raccoon family is unique to the New World; the others are widely represented throughout the Old World as well.

The 36 species in the worldwide dog family (Canidae) include wolves, coyotes, foxes, and hunting dogs. They are all highly adapted for running; their feet are arranged so that they bear weight on the toes; and they tend to be highly vocal. The raccoon family (Procyonidae) includes medium-sized species that carry their full weight on the soles of the feet and have long tails, both of which help with maneuverability and balance in their largely arboreal habitats. They are omnivorous and largely nocturnal. The weasel family (Mustelidae) includes weasels, stoats, skunks, minks, wolverines, and badgers and is characterized by relatively long bodies, short legs, and walking on the soles of the feet. Most have dense, soft fur and a gland that produces chemicals with powerful odors. Their extremely powerful jaws and sharp teeth can kill large prey quickly. Members of the cat family (Felidae) bear weight on their toes and have retractable claws. They are completely carnivorous and use their extremely sharp and long teeth to dispatch prey with a bite to the back of the head or neck. They tend to have excellent vision, including color vision. They have a short nose and their eyes are set at the front of the head to maximize depth perception.

Natural History
Ecology and Behavior

Dogs. The dogs have 6 representatives in Brazil. If you encounter any of them, it will probably be in the form of tracks or *scats* (droppings). The CRAB-EATING FOX (Plate 90) is nocturnal and feeds on mice, frogs, crabs, insects, and fruit. It avoids the extensive forest of the Amazon and is most common in open grassy areas and savannah of the Pantanal area. Its long, thin droppings and footprints are common in some areas. It preys on small mammals and birds, but occasionally scavenges dead animals. Also, in open grassy areas of the Pantanal, the MANED WOLF (Plate 90) is a prize observation. Solitary and active during the day or night, these long-legged wolves eat small vertebrates, invertebrates, grass, and lots of fruit (up to 60% of their diet at some times of the year). Two diurnal canids, BUSH DOG and SHORT-EARED DOG, both occur throughout the Amazon forest, but they are rarely seen and relatively little is known about them.

Raccoons. The raccoons make up a New World group of about 15 species (until recently, the Asian Red Panda was thought also to be in this group). Five species occur in Brazil, but you are only likely to see a few of them. The most visible ones are *coatis*. Although adult males are usually solitary, female SOUTH AMERICAN COATIS (Plate 90) and juveniles often occur in large groups of up to 30 that move through the undergrowth and mid-levels of trees making barks, whines, and other noises. Coatis are immediately recognized by their long tails held vertically as they walk on the ground or along branches. They use their long noses and hand-like fore-paws to investigate every nook and cranny for insects, fruits, and small vertebrates. The other frequently seen *procyonid* in Brazil is the KINKAJOU (Plate 90), which is limited to moist forests of the Amazon. Kinkajous are nocturnal, solitary, and spend most of their time in trees, foraging for fruits and arboreal vertebrates. Alone among the procyonids, their long, thin tail is fully prehensile, permitting them to grasp branches with it and hang upside down. Your best chance for seeing one is by walking out into the forest at night and looking for their eye-shine reflected in the light of your flashlight. They can often be spotted moving about tree branches at night, making squeaking sounds; several often feed together in a single tree. If you are really lucky, you may catch a glimpse of a CRAB-EATING RACCOON (Plate 90) as you quietly float in a canoe at night along a forested stream or lake. This species occurs from Costa Rica to Argentina, but nowhere is it common, and its natural history is poorly known. They are associated with open areas along water and, although omnivores, seem to prefer to eat clams, fish, and crabs. They spend the day sleeping in dens, and the best evidence of their presence, short of seeing one, is looking for their small, human-like foot- and hand-prints in wet mud along water.

Weasels. The weasel family comprises about 70 species of small and medium-sized, slender-bodied carnivores that are distributed globally except for Australia and Antarctica. In Brazil the family is represented by 9 species of weasels, skunks, and otters, but only 3 are commonly sighted. TAYRA (TIE-rah, Plate 91) are large tree climbers that will often descend to search the ground for a variety of foods –

fruit, bird eggs or nestlings, lizards, rodents, rabbits, and insects. Although they are often wary animals, they can be quite bold at times and are among the most frequently sighted of the *mustelids*, especially when attracted to fruits in gardens and orchards. The GIANT OTTER (Plate 91) once occurred throughout Amazonian South America from Venezuela to northern Argentina, but it is now absent from most of this range. Its huge size (up to 2 m, 6.5 ft, and 34 kg, 75 lb) and noisy vocalizations in family groups of 5 to 8 make it easy to find. Its luxurious pelt makes it a target of intense persecution by people. It remains now only in isolated and highly protected patches of its former range. Otters are active both during the day and at night, hunting in streams, rivers, and ponds for fish and crustaceans such as crayfish. Although otters always remain in or near the water, they spend their inactive time in burrows on land. Adapted with webbed feet, flattened tail and a sleek form for moving swiftly and smoothly through water, they move on land awkwardly, with a duck-like waddle. There are only a few places left in Amazonian Brazil where you can still hear the haunting whistles, screams, and hums of a group of these wondrous animals as they frolic in the water of an isolated stream or lake. If you do experience the sight and sounds of this otter, it will be a memory you will never forget. The smaller NEOTROPICAL OTTER (Plate 91), with its rounded, tapered tail and white chest, is fairly easy to distinguish from its giant relative.

Cats. Because all 8 species of cats that occur in Brazil are fairly rare, some to the point of being endangered, and because of their mainly nocturnal habits, your chances are slim of seeing even a single wild cat on any brief trip. More than likely, all that you will see of cats are traces; some tracks in the mud near a stream or scratch marks on a tree trunk or log. (Although some communication is vocal, cats also signal each other by making scratch marks on vegetation and by leaving urine and feces to scent-mark areas.)

In Brazil, the cat species can be placed into two groups – spotted or unspotted. The spotted species generally are yellowish, tan, or cinnamon on top and white below, with black spots and stripes on their heads, bodies, and legs. The smallest is the ONCILLA, or LITTLE SPOTTED CAT, the size of a small house cat. The largest is the JAGUAR (Plate 92), which is the largest New World cat and the region's largest carnivore, weighing between 60 and 120 kg (130 to 260 lb). The unspotted cats are the mid-sized JAGUARUNDI (Plate 92), which is blackish, brown, gray, or reddish, and the PUMA (Plate 92), or MOUNTAIN LION, which is tan or grayish and almost as large as the Jaguar. The Puma, which occurs from the Arctic Circle of North America to Tierra del Fuego in extreme southern South America, has one of the largest geographical ranges of any mammal. Female cats of most species are smaller than males, up to a third smaller in the Jaguar. The cats are finely adapted to prey on vertebrate animals, and hunting methods are extremely similar among the various species. They do not run to chase prey for long distances. Rather, cats slowly stalk their prey or wait in ambush, then capture the prey after pouncing on it or after a very brief, fast chase. Biologists are often impressed by the consistency in the manner that cats kill their prey. Almost always it is with a sharp bite to the neck or head, breaking the neck or crushing the skull. Retractile claws, in addition to their use in grabbing and holding prey, give cats good abilities to climb trees, and some of them are partially arboreal animals, foraging and even sleeping in trees.

Aside from some highly social large cats of Africa, most cats are solitary animals, foraging alone, individuals coming together only to mate. Some species are territorial but in others individuals overlap in the areas in which they hunt. Cats, with their big eyes to gather light, are often nocturnal, especially those of rainforests, but some are also active by day. When inactive, they shelter in rock crevices or burrows dug by other animals. Cats are the most carnivorous of the carnivores, that is their diets are more centered on meat than any of the other families. Little is known of the natural history of forest-dwelling Oncillas beyond that they eat birds and small rodents. MARGAYS (Plate 92) are mostly arboreal forest cats that forage in trees for rodents and birds. OCELOTS (Plate 92) eat rodents, snakes, lizards, and birds. They are probably more common than Oncillas and Margays and, although they are quite secretive, they are the most frequently seen of the spotted cats. Active mainly at night, they often spend daylight hours asleep in trees. They also tend to be the most adaptable to human presence, especially if a chicken coop is involved. The Jaguar can be active day or night. These cats inhabit low and middle elevation forests, savannahs and grasslands, hunting for large prey such as peccary and deer, but also monkeys, birds, lizards, even caiman. Jaguarundi are both day and night active, and are usually seen in forests. They eat small rodents, rabbits, and birds. Puma occupy various habitat types from subalpine areas to evergreen forest to desert scrub, and they prey on deer and other large mammals.

Breeding

Most dogs are monogamous and although they often dig their own dens for the young, they are not above taking over a hole made by an armadillo or some other burrowing animal, enlarging and modifying it for their own use. The large litter of young is born naked and blind and is fed by both parents even after they emerge from the den. Among all the Brazilian procyonids, females raise young without help from males. Young are born in nests made in trees. Duration of pregnancy varies from about 65 days in raccoons, to about 75 days in coatis, to about 115 days in KINKAJOUS. Raccoons have 3 to 7 young per litter, coatis, 1 to 5 young, and Kinkajous, always only 1. Female mustelids give birth in dens under rocks or in crevices, or in burrows under trees. Pregnancy for TAYRA, skunks, and otters usually lasts about 60 to 70 days. Tayra produce an average of 2 young per litter, skunk, 4 or 5, and otter, 2 or 3. As is true for many of the carnivores, mustelid young are born blind and helpless. Male and female cats of the Neotropics come together only to mate; the female bears and raises her young alone. She gives birth in a den that is a burrow, rock cave, or tree cavity. The young are sheltered in the den while the female forages; she returns periodically to nurse and bring the kittens prey to eat. Most of the cats have 1 or 2 young at a time, although PUMA and JAGUAR may have up to 4. Pregnancy is about 75 days in the smaller cats, about 100 in the large ones. Juvenile Jaguars remain with their mother for up to 18 months, learning to be efficient hunters, before they go off on their own.

Notes

JAGUAR rarely attack people, who normally are given a wide berth; these cats tend to run away quickly when spotted. Cats in Brazil are sometimes seen walking at night along forest trails or roads. General advice if you happen to stumble across a large cat: do not run because that often stimulates a cat to chase. Face the cat, make yourself large by raising your arms, and make as much loud noise as you can.

The Arakmbut people of Amazonian Brazil place chosen small children on a balsa wood platform, wash them carefully, then paint spots on them to enable them to become jaguar spirits. These children are thought to grow to become powerful warriors who, when the need arises, can transform themselves into real jaguars to kill the community's enemies.

Mustelids have scent glands on their backsides that produce a secretion called *musk*, which has a strong, characteristic odor. These secretions are used to communicate with other members of the species by marking territories as well as signal availability for breeding and courtship. In skunks, these glands produce particularly strong, foul-smelling fluids that with startlingly good aim can be violently squirted in a jet at potential predators. The fluids are not toxic and cannot cause blindness as is sometimes commonly believed, but they can cause temporary, severe irritation of eyes and nose. Most predators that approach a skunk once rarely repeat the exercise.

One facet of mustelid natural history that is particularly helpful to people, though not universally appreciated, is that these carnivores eat a staggering number of rodents. For instance, it has been calculated that weasels each year in New York State eat some 60 million mice and millions of rats. In fact, in the past, TAYRA were kept as pets in parts of South America to protect homes and belongings from rodents.

Status

All of the Neotropical cats are now threatened or actually endangered (MARGAY, ONCILLA, MARSH CAT, and JAGUAR are listed by CITES Appendix I and USA ESA, as are Central American populations of PUMA, JAGUARUNDI, and OCELOT). Their habitats are increasingly cleared for agricultural purposes, they were, and still are to a limited extent, hunted for their skins, and large cats are killed as potential predators on livestock and pets. Jaguar have been eliminated from much of Brazil and are present only in small numbers in protected areas.

Many mustelids in the past were trapped intensively for their fur, which is often soft, dense, and glossy, just the ticket, in fact, to create coats of otter or weasel, mink or marten, sable or fisher. The GIANT OTTER is sufficiently rare to be considered endangered (CITES APPENDIX I, USA ESA, and IUCN Red List). The COLOMBIAN WEASEL and BUSH DOG are also considered threatened species in Brazil, on the IUCN Red List. TAYRA are common animals that usually do well even where people disturb their natural habitats. Another Brazilian mustelid, the GRISON (Plate 91), a grayish and black weasel-like animal, is fairly rare and may be threatened.

Profiles

Kinkajou, *Potus flavus*, Plate 90a
Crab-eating Raccoon, *Procyon cancrivorous*, Plate 90b
Crab-eating Fox, *Cerdocyon thous*, Plate 90c
South American Coati, *Nasua nasua*, Plate 90d
Maned Wolf, *Chrysocyon brachyurus*, Plate 90e

Giant Otter, *Pteronura brasiliensis*, Plate 91a
Neotropical Otter, *Lontra longicaudis*, Plate 91b
Tayra, *Eira barbara*, Plate 91c
Grison, *Galictis vittata*, Plate 91d

Jaguarundi, *Herpailurus yaguarondi*, Plate 92a
Ocelot, *Felis (Leopardus) pardalis*, Plate 92b

Margay, *Felis (Leopardus) wiedii*, Plate 92c
Jaguar, *Panthera onca*, Plate 92d
Puma, *Puma concolor*, Plate 92e

6. Peccaries and Deer

Peccaries and *deer* are two Neotropical representatives of the Order Artiodactyla, the globally distributed hoofed mammals (*ungulates*) with even numbers of toes on each foot. Other *artiodactyls* are pigs, hippos, giraffes, antelope, bison, buffalo, cattle, gazelles, goats, and sheep. In general, the group is specialized to feed on leaves, grass, and fallen fruit.

Three peccary species comprise the family Tayassuidae. They are confined in their distributions to the Neotropics, although one species pushes northwards into the southwestern USA, where it is often called JAVELINA; two species, the COLLARED PECCARY (Plate 93) and the WHITE-LIPPED PECCARY (Plate 93), occur in Brazil. Peccaries are small to medium-sized hog-like animals covered with coarse, bristly, longish hair, with slender legs, large heads, small ears, and short tails. They have enlarged, sharp and pointed, tusk-like canine teeth. The Collared Peccary is the smaller of the two Brazilian species, adults typically weighing 17 to 30 kg (35 to 75 lb). They come in black or gray as adults, with a band of lighter-colored hair at the neck that furnishes their name; youngsters are reddish brown or buff-colored. The White-lipped Peccary, named for the white patch of hair on its chin, weighs 25 to 40 kg (55 to 85 lb). Collared Peccaries are more abundant than the White-lipped Peccary, occur in more habitats, and are seen more frequently.

The deer family, Cervidae, has 43 species worldwide, six in Brazil. Only three, however, are common enough that you are likely to see them. The RED BROCKET DEER (Plate 93) is a denizen of dense forest throughout Brazil, and the MARSH DEER (Plate 93) and PAMPAS DEER (Plate 93) occur in the Pantanal. Deer are large mammals with long, thin legs, short tails, and big ears. Males have antlers that they shed each year and regrow. The Marsh Deer is the largest deer species in South America (1.1 m, 3.6 ft, at the shoulder) and occurs in extensive marshy areas. The smaller Pampas Deer (0.75 cm, 2.5 ft, at the shoulder) at one time occurred in natural grassy areas throughout eastern South America south of the equator. It now occurs in only a few areas of its former range.

Natural History
Ecology and Behavior

Peccaries are day-active, highly social animals, rarely encountered singly. COLLARED PECCARIES travel in small groups of 3 to 25 or so, most frequently 6 to 9; WHITE-LIPPED PECCARY herds generally are larger, often with 50 to 100 or more individuals (smaller herds occur where they are heavily hunted). They travel single file along narrow forest paths, spreading out when good foraging sites are found. These animals are omnivores, but mainly they dig into the ground with their snouts, *rooting* for vegetation. Peccaries feed on roots, underground stems, and bulbs, but also leaves, fruit (the White-lipped Peccary, with extra-strong jaw muscles, is better adapted for eating hard palm fruits), insects, and even small vertebrates that they stumble across. Because White-lipped Peccaries are larger than Collared Peccaries and travel in larger groups, they need to wander long distances each day to locate enough food. Like pigs, peccaries often wallow in mud and shallow water, and there is usually a customary wallowing spot inside their home range, the area within which a group lives and forages. During dry seasons, peccaries may gather in large numbers near lakes or streams. Because peccaries are hunted by people, they are usually quiet, wary, and therefore, sometimes hard to notice or approach. Besides their tracks, you can detect that a group has just passed by a cloyingly sweaty smell that lingers after them for a half hour or more in the undergrowth of a forest. Peccaries are preyed upon by large snakes such as boas, and by Puma and Jaguar.

Deer eat leaves and twigs from trees and shrubs that they can reach from the ground (*browsing*), and grass (*grazing*). The RED BROCKET DEER, in particular, also eats fruit and flowers, chiefly those that have already fallen to the ground. Red Brocket Deer are almost always solitary. They are active during daylight hours but also often at night, although they are most commonly seen during early mornings and at dusk. The huge MARSH DEER is limited to extensive marshy grasslands, and in Brazil is most easily seen in the northern parts of the Pantanal, where it feeds almost always in or near water on a wide range of plants, from water lilies to grass and legumes. Its large hooves can each spread more than 10 cm (4 in) apart so the deer can walk and run more easily across mud and aquatic vegetation. The smaller PAMPAS DEER you will likely see in drier parts of the Pantanal, where it feeds on upland grasses and herbs. Deer are *cud-chewers*. After foraging and filling a special chamber of their stomach, they find a sheltered area, rest, regurgitate the meal into their mouths and chew it well so that it can be digested. Predators on deer include the big cats – Puma and Jaguar; eagles may take young fawns.

Breeding

Female peccaries have either 1 or 2 young at a time, born 4 to 5 months after mating. The young are *precocial*, meaning that they can walk and follow their mother within a few days of birth. Deer, likewise, give birth to 1 or 2 young that, within a week or two, can follow the mother. Until that time, they stay in a sheltered spot while their mother forages, returning at intervals to nurse them. The fawns of most species have small white spots on their flanks and back. The breeding season for MARSH DEER is quite long in the Pantanal. Fawns are generally born between May and September. The RED BROCKET DEER is less distinctly seasonal in breeding.

Notes

Both species of peccaries enjoy reputations for aggressiveness toward humans, but experts agree that the reputation is exaggerated. There are stories of herds panicking at the approach of people, stampeding, even chasing people. These are large enough beasts, with sufficiently large and sharp canine teeth, to do damage. If you spot peccaries, err on the side of caution; watch them from afar and leave them alone. Be quiet and they might take no notice of you; their vision apparently is poor. If you are charged, a rapid retreat into a tree could be a wise move.

To the Arakmbut forest people of Amazonian Brazil, disease symptoms originate with the spirits of the various game animals they take. For instance, armadillos are thought to be responsible for coughs and bronchial disorders. Peccaries are responsible for a broad array of symptoms. COLLARED PECCARY spirits cause severe stomach pain (the spirit jumping on one's abdomen) and WHITE-LIPPED PECCARY spirits cause loose jaw, teeth chattering, headache, and fever. Many indigenous people throughout South America, including in Brazil, believe that the spirits of their dead relatives reside in deer; many people, therefore, will not hunt or kill deer.

Status

Peccaries were hunted for food and hides long before the arrival of Europeans to the New World, and such hunting continues. COLLARED PECCARIES, CITES Appendix II listed, are still locally common in protected wilderness and more rural areas. WHITE-LIPPED PECCARIES, also CITES Appendix II listed, are less common, and less is known about their populations; they soon may be threatened. Deer are likewise hunted for meat, skins, and sport. Deer range widely in Brazil but, owing to hunting pressures, are numerous only in remote areas. RED BROCKET DEER employ excellent anti-hunting tactics, being solitary animals that keep to dense forests. The huge MARSH DEER is so limited to its peculiar habitat that susceptibility to cattle diseases, over hunting and habitat destruction have caused it to be considered threatened (IUCN Red List).

Profiles

Collared Peccary, *Tayassu tajacu*, Plate 93a
White-lipped Peccary, *Tayassu pecari*, Plate 93b
Pampas Deer, *Ozotoceros bezoarticus*, Plate 93c
Red Brocket Deer, *Mazama americana*, Plate 93d
Marsh Deer, *Blastocerus dichotomous*, Plate 93e

7. Rodents and Rabbit

Rodents and *rabbits* superficially resemble each other with their large, front incisor teeth. They are, however, only distantly related. Rodents (order Rodentia) are distributed worldwide from the Arctic to the tropics, and they include *mice, rats, squirrels, chipmunks, marmots, gophers, beavers*, and *porcupines*. Worldwide there are more than 2000 species, representing 44% of the approximately 4629 known mammalian species. More individual rodents are estimated to be alive at any one time than individuals of all other types of mammals combined. Nevertheless, many ecotravellers will discover among rodents a paradox: although by far the most diverse and abundant of the mammals, rodents are, with a few obvious exceptions in any region, relatively inconspicuous and rarely encountered. Rodents' near-invisibility to people, particularly in the Neotropics, can be explained best by the facts that most rodents are very small, secretive or nocturnal, and many of them live in subterranean burrows. Of course, many people do not consider it a hardship that rodents are so rarely encountered.

High rodent abundance and diversity are likely related to their efficient, specialized teeth and associated jaw muscles, as well as to their broad, nearly omnivorous, diets. Rodents are characterized by having four large incisor teeth, one pair front-and-center in the upper jaw, one pair in the lower (other teeth, separated from the incisors, are located farther back in the mouth). With these strong, sharp, chisel-like front teeth, rodents "make their living": gnawing (*rodent* is from the Latin *rodere*, to gnaw), cutting, and slicing vegetation, fruit, and nuts, killing and eating small animals, digging burrows, and even, in the case of beavers, imitating lumberjacks.

The Neotropics contain some of the largest and most interesting of the world's rodents, and more than 165 species occur in Brazil. However, only a few representatives of 6 families are commonly spotted by visitors, and we profile 11 species from these families. Squirrels are members of the Family Sciuridae, a worldwide group of 273 species that occurs on all continents except Australia and Antarctica. The family includes *ground, tree*, and *flying squirrels*; only 7 species occur in Brazil. Family Erethizontidae contains the 12 species of New World porcupines, which are distributed throughout the Americas save for the southern third of South America. Six species of these sharp-spined mammals are native to Brazil. The 78 species of *spiny* or *tree rats* are placed in the Family Echimyidae and are almost all restricted to rainforests. About 45 species occur in Brazil, but their classification is very poorly known. Three other families that are restricted to tropical America contain a few large rodents that all share an ungulate-type body form with long legs: Family Agoutidae contains the PACA (Plate 95), Family Dasyproctidae includes the *agoutis*, and Family Hydrochaeridae contains a single species, the CAPYBARA (Plate 96), which is the world's largest rodent.

Porcupines generally are fairly large, heavyset rodents (although Brazil has some small species that weigh only 0.95 kg, 2 lb) with many sharp spines covering their bodies and often the tail. The spines easily break off to embed themselves in the skin of a predator unfortunate or naive enough to try to bite a porcupine. The most common Brazilian species, the BRAZILIAN PORCUPINE (Plate 95), weighs 3.2 to 5.3 kg (7.3 to 11.7 lb) and occurs in forests throughout the Amazonian region. A long prehensile tail, with bare top, is always curled under rather than over a branch for climbing. It has short limbs and small feet with long, curved claws that aid in gripping and climbing trees.

The spiny and tree rats are touted by some experts as the most common terrestrial mammals in the rainforests of Brazil. Many of them have long bristles or flat spines on the back, such as the SPINY TREE RAT (Plate 94). Unlike porcupine spines, these rat spines are not barbed and do not readily detach. Another large forest rat you are likely to encounter in the Amazon is the AMAZON BAMBOO RAT (Plate 94), which has no spines on the back. Instead of seeing this large rat, however, you are much more likely to hear its incessant series of loud quacks given in the middle of the night. You can be forgiven for mistaking these sounds for some loud frog, but they are quite unlike any amphibian in the Amazon: these hollow and ventriloquial sounds are given at increasingly softer levels and more widely spaced intervals until they stop. If you follow the sound, the final approach to the rat itself will be facilitated by its commanding aroma, which has a strong musky component.

Agoutis, PACA and CAPYBARA are large, almost pig-like rodents, usually brownish, with long legs, short hair, and squirrel-like heads. The BLACK AGOUTI (Plate 95) weighs only 5 kg (11 lb), but is common in secondary and primary forest throughout the western Amazon of Brazil. Paca weigh up to 12 kg (26 lb) and are distinguished by the four rows of white spots along their flanks. The huge Capybara (to 65 kg, 140 lb) is regularly found throughout the Amazon and Pantanal, usually near rivers or marshes. The closely related Acouchys ("Ah-coo-CHEEZ;" Plate 95) of the Amazon forest floor are smaller (1 kg, 2.2 lb) and look more like a respectable rodent, albeit short-tailed.

Rabbits, even though they look like rodents, are in a separate order, the Lagamorpha. The group is differentiated from rodents by four instead of two front incisor teeth on the upper jaw, large hind legs, and long ears. Only one species occurs in Brazil, the BRAZILIAN RABBIT, and it looks for all the world like the cottontail so common throughout North America; it is even in the same genus, *Sylvilagus*. Most ecotravellers to Brazil will see this species in clearings and grassy areas in the Pantanal area.

Natural History
Ecology and Behavior
Rodents are important ecologically primarily because of their great abundance. They are so common that they make up a large proportion of the diets of many carnivores. For instance, in a recent study of Jaguar, it was discovered that rodents were the third most frequent prey of the large cats, after sloths and iguanas. In addition, rodents, owing to their ubiquitousness and numbers, are themselves important predators on seeds and fruit. That is, they eat seeds and seed-containing fruit, digesting or damaging the seeds, rendering them useless to the plants that produced them for reproduction. Of course, not every seed is damaged (some fall to the ground as rodents eat, others pass unscathed through their digestive tracts), and so rodents, at least occasionally, also act as seed dispersers (see Close-up, p. 196). Pacas, acouchys and agoutis are scatter hoarders, that is they move excess seeds to caches away from the fruiting tree, where they bury the seeds. Often the location of some of these caches is forgotten and the seeds germinate to produce new plants. Burrowing is another aspect of rodent behavior that has significant ecological implications because of the sheer numbers of individuals that participate. When so many animals move soil around (rats and mice, especially), the effect is that over several years the entire topsoil of an area is turned, keeping soil loose and aerated, and therefore more suitable for plant growth.

The NORTHERN AMAZON RED SQUIRREL (Plate 94), GUIANAN SQUIRREL (Plate 94), and the AMAZON DWARF SQUIRREL (Plate 94) are all solitary, day-active species, generally seen in trees and, occasionally, foraging on the ground. The large red squirrel typically feeds on fruits and large palm nuts. It is usually found low in the forest and often on the ground or in the understory, where it frequently hides (caches) food for later meals by burying it in the ground or placing it in tree cavities. In contrast, the dwarf squirrel's diet is largely made up of insects, spiders, and other arthropods it searches out on branches, tangles, and other vegetation, from high in the canopy to the forest floor. It also apparently eats bark and fungi. This species is quickly and reliably attracted to squeaking noises that mimic a bird or small mammal in distress. This behavior may indicate that dwarf squirrels, like other insectivorous squirrel species, are also partially carnivorous. Although the natural history of these Brazilian species is poorly known, Central American species closely related to the Northern Amazon Red Squirrel are known to have females that defend exclusive living and feeding areas from other females. Males are not territorial; their home ranges, the areas over which they range daily in search of food, overlap those of other males and those of females.

BRAZILIAN PORCUPINES are solitary, nocturnal animals, almost always found in trees. They move slowly along branches, using their prehensile tail as a fifth limb. They feed on leaves, green tree shoots, and fruit. During the day they sleep in tree cavities or on branches hidden amid dense vegetation. The AMAZON BAMBOO RAT is active only at night and spends the daytime resting in thick tangles of vegetation, usually in or near bamboo thickets. They are almost entirely arboreal and feed in family groups mainly on leaves, shoots and stems. Their calls at night are often in duets. The much quieter SPINY TREE RAT is also nocturnal but more likely to be seen as it forages in vine tangles and the edge of tree falls, from the forest floor to the canopy.

PACA are usually only active at night, foraging individually for fruit, nuts, seeds, and vegetation. They sleep away daylight hours in burrows. Along with the agouti, they can sit up on their hind legs and eat, holding their food with their front paws, much like a squirrel or rat. Several observers have noted that Paca, although usually terrestrial, will, if startled or threatened, dive into nearby water if available. The smaller agoutis are completely terrestrial and naturally day-active, but many populations have become increasingly nocturnal in their habits in areas where they are intensively hunted. They mainly eat seeds and fruit, but also flowers, vegetation, and insects. When threatened or startled, agoutis usually run, giving warning calls or barks as they go, presumably to warn nearby relatives of danger. They make so much noise running through the undergrowth vegetation that it is easy to mistake them for much larger peccaries. The even smaller acouchys make enough noise to sound like elephants. In addition to running noisily through the undergrowth to escape danger, they squeal loudly as they run away. In Brazil, the immense CAPYBARA is always closely associated with river banks, lake edges and forested swamps, and in the dry season it can be found in groups of up to 20, depending on the availability of water. It is normally diurnal, but under human hunting pressure often becomes more active at night. At the slightest hint of danger, it leaps into the water and disappears under the surface, later emerging far away. If it is present, its huge and distinctive foot prints are common on sandy river beaches and in the mud along lake shores. It feeds largely on aquatic vegetation but also on fruits. These species, all relatively large and tasty, are preyed on by a variety of mammals and reptiles, including large snakes and such carnivores as Jaguarundi.

Breeding

Relatively little is known of the breeding behavior of most Neotropical tree squirrels and of many other rodents. Tree squirrel nests consist of a bed of leaves placed in a tree cavity or a ball of leaves on a branch or in a tangle of vegetation. One to 3 young are born per litter, although 2 is the norm. Females of species closely related to red squirrels have 2 or 3 litters per year. Actual mating in this species takes place following sex chases, in which 4 or more males chase a female for several hours, the female apparently choosing the male that runs the fastest or lasts the longest to mate with. Pregnancy is about 45 days; young nurse for 8 to 10 weeks. Breeding tends to be during the dry season.

Porcupines have 1 to 3 young per litter. Pregnancy periods are relatively long, and, as a result, the young are *precocial* – born eyes open and in an advanced state. They are therefore mobile and quickly able to follow the mother.

Paca, agouti and acouchy appear to live in monogamous pairs on territories, although male and female often tend to forage separately. Capybaras are polygynous with a fluid social system depending on how much water there is to spread out into. All these species have precocial young, usually in litters of 1 or 2 for the Paca, agouti, and acouchy but up to 7 for the Capybara. A day after their birth, a mother agouti leads her young to a burrow where they hide, and to which she returns each day to feed them. Pregnancies for acouchy last 99 days, for agouti and Paca 115 to 120 days, and for Capybara 150 days.

Notes

Through the animals' constant gnawing, rodents' chisel-like incisors wear down rapidly. Fortunately for the rodents, their incisors, owing to some ingenious anatomy and physiology, continue to grow throughout their lives, unlike those of most other mammals.

Contrary to folk wisdom, porcupines cannot "throw" their quills, or spines, at people or predators. Rather, the spines detach quite easily when touched, such that a predator snatching a porcupine in its mouth will be impaled with spines and hence, rendered very unhappy. The spines have barbed ends, like fishhooks, which anchor them securely into the offending predator.

PACA, AGOUTI, and CAPYBARA meat is considered to be among the most superior of wild meats, because it is tasty, tender, and lacks much of an odor; as such, when it can be purchased in Brazil, it is very expensive. All three mammals are favorite game animals throughout their ranges. In Venezuela, Capybara meat is considered to be the holiday meal for Easter dinner, and Capybaras are widely raised in captivity to meet the demand for this market. In some parts of Brazil, the local people depend heavily on large tree rats as a meat source, which they trap at night in the forest. Some attempts are being made to raise these rats in captivity and farm them as a more dependable resource.

Status

Twelve of Brazil's rodents are listed as threatened by the IUCN Red List. Of these, three rats and the AZARA'S AGOUTI occur in the Amazon or Pantanal area. Habitat destruction and hunting them for food have been the main causes for their decline. One species of porcupine, southeastern Brazil's BRISTLE-SPINED PORCUPINE, is now highly endangered (listed as such by USA ESA).

Profiles

Amazon Bamboo Rat, *Dactylomys dactylinus*, Plate 94a
Spiny Tree Rat, *Mesomys hispidus*, Plate 94b
Northern Amazon Red Squirrel, *Sciurus igniventris*, Plate 94c
Amazon Dwarf Squirrel, *Microsciurus flaviventer*, Plate 94d
Guianan Squirrel, *Sciurus aestuans*, Plate 94e
Brazilian Porcupine, *Coendou prehensilis*, Plate 95a
Green Acouchy, *Myoprocta pratti*, Plate 95b
Red-rumped Agouti, *Dasyprocta agouti*, Plate 95c
Black Agouti, *Dasyprocta fuliginosa*, Plate 95d
Paca, *Agouti paca*, Plate 95e
Capybara, *Hydrochaeris hydrochaeris*, Plate 96a

8. Manatee and Tapirs

Along with the *dugongs* of the Indian Ocean, the *manatees*, or *sea cows*, form the tropical order Sirenia. Despite their similarities to seals and cetaceans (whales and dolphins), they are unrelated to either group and are the only completely aquatic herbivorous mammals in the world. Except for bristles on the snout, they are basically hairless and look like walruses without tusks. They have tiny eyes and back molar teeth that resemble those of elephants. As adaptations for their aquatic life, they have evolved streamlined bodies; their hind feet have developed into a horizontal fluke and their fore-legs into flippers. Only two species of manatees are in the New World tropics. The AMAZONIAN MANATEE (Plate 96), a freshwater species, occurs along the Amazon River and its major tributaries as far west as northeastern Brazil, and is only 2.8 m (9 ft) long. Because of its shy and often nocturnal behavior, it is extremely difficult to see as it feeds on aquatic vegetation in a quiet lake, only infrequently rising with its body in a vertical position to put its snout just above the water's surface to breathe. The larger WEST INDIAN MANATEE (up to 4.5 m, 13 ft, long) is found in brackish and salt water from Florida to northern Venezuela and coastal Brazil.

Although *tapirs* are related only distantly to manatees, we include them here because they are almost always associated with swamps, lakes, and river edges. They swim well, often with little more than their long snout extending above the water's surface. In fact, if you are going to see one, it will most likely be from a canoe as you come upon a swimming tapir just emerging from the water. There are only four species of tapirs (family Tapiridae) in the world, three in the New World tropics and one in southeast Asia. Only one of the New World species is found in Brazil. Although they look like they should be related to pigs or hippopotamus, they are actually related to rhinoceros and horses (in the Order Perissodactyla, made up of hoofed animals (*ungulates*) with odd numbers of toes on some of the feet). Tapirs have three toes on the hind feet and four on the front feet. Their peculiarly elongated snout functions somewhat like an elephant's trunk in grasping vegetation to eat. They have excellent hearing and smelling abilities but relatively poor eyesight. They are the largest terrestrial animals in Brazil, some males weighing up to 300 kg (660 lb). The BRAZILIAN TAPIR (Plate 96) has the widest range of any tapir species in the world and is found throughout South America west of the Andes and north of Argentina. In Brazil it occurs in isolated areas of forest throughout the Amazon and Pantanal. Your encounter is most likely to consist solely of seeing its distinctive footprints on muddy paths and along sandy river beaches.

Natural History
Ecology and Behavior
The AMAZONIAN MANATEE in Brazil feeds mainly at night on aquatic vegetation such as floating grasses and water hyacinths. During the dry season, when many lakes and small rivers dry up, manatees may retreat to deeper channels in the main rivers, where they fast for several weeks or more. Generally this species is extremely difficult to see, but its impressive production of floating dung (like horse apples) is the best sign of its presence. Manatees usually occur alone except during courtship, but they do communicate with each other by sounds they produce underwater. Individuals take about 5 to 6 years to reach sexual maturity.

Tapirs are active primarily at night and hide in dense thickets of undergrowth during the day. They browse on leaves and vegetation as well as fruits fallen to the ground. Tapirs follow habitual trails through vegetation, and routinely cross rivers at the same place, thus forming obvious tunnels through the undergrowth and gulleys at river banks where they are most likely to be seen (and shot if being hunted). Individuals use established wallowing areas in which they apply a layer of mud to their skin to help protect them from horseflies and other biting insects that plague them throughout the year. Although generally solitary, tapirs, by using these habitual trails and wallowing areas together with communal defecation sites, at least loosely associate and communicate with each other. They are shy and retiring, and except for grunts of alarm and high whistles during the mating season, are quiet.

Breeding
Manatees give birth to a single calf after a gestation period of 13 months. The calf is dependent on the mother and accompanies her closely for 2 or more years. Thus, a female gives birth only every 3½ years or more. Tapirs remain together as mated pairs for only a few weeks of courtship and then separate. Occasionally males will fight to the death over a sexually receptive female. Females are entirely responsible for rearing and caring for the young, which have peculiar horizontal

stripes and spots. Usually a single but rarely two calves are born after a gestation period of 13 months. The calf remains with the mother for up to a year. This long gestation period and extended care of the young mean a female can reproduce only every 17 months.

Notes

At least two researchers have noted that tapirs, which can become infested with blood-sucking, disease-carrying ticks, have let other mammals – a coati in one case, a tame peccary in the other – approach them and pick and eat the ticks on their bodies. If this occurs regularly, it is a mutualistic association: tapirs obviously benefit because they are freed temporarily from the harmful ticks, and the tick-eaters receive the nutritional value of the bloodsuckers (yech!). Manatees, as they floated vertically in the water, were apparently the source of the myth of mermaids. Evidently lonely sailors who had been on board ship way too long imagined these forms to be female humans with fins.

Status

Because they are so heavily hunted, tapirs are very shy and cautious animals. This hunting pressure may be forcing them more and more into nocturnal activity, and, together with low population sizes, may explain why they are so rarely seen. Because they are hunted for meat, and also due to deforestation, all three Neotropical tapirs are now rare and considered endangered, listed by both CITES Appendix I and USA ESA. Both species of New World manatees have been hunted and killed extensively. Their populations have been severely reduced, and they are considered endangered (CITES Appendix 1, USA ESA, and IUCN Red List).

Profiles

Brazilian Tapir, *Tapirus terrestris*, Plate 96b
Amazonian Manatee, *Trichechus inunguis*, Plate 96e

9. Dolphins

All *dolphins*, *porpoises*, and *whales* belong to order Cetacea, and all but a few freshwater forms are restricted to the *marine* environment (sea water). They never leave the water and generally come to the surface only to breathe. Their hind legs have been lost through evolution and their forelegs modified into paddle-like flippers. Their tails have become broad and flattened into what are called *flukes*. A single or double nostril, called a *blowhole*, is on top of the head. Although cetacean eyes are relatively small, hearing is well developed. Cetaceans are often divided into two broad categories, *baleen* and *toothed whales*. The baleen group consists of large whale species that have mouths that look like immense radiator grills, filled with long, vertical, brownish strands of baleen, or whalebone. The largest mammal, and probably the largest animal ever, the BLUE WHALE, is a member of this group. It reaches 30+ m (100 ft) in length and 150 tons in weight. Members of the other group have mouths with short, sharp teeth instead of baleen.

In the same group as the toothed whales are the smaller dolphins and porpoises. In the Amazon, the last thing many ecotravellers expect is a dolphin, but wonder of wonders, here they are. Two species of freshwater dolphins occur in the main channels and tributaries of the Río Amazonas and Río Madeira. Look for the PINK RIVER DOLPHIN (Plate 96) in the Amazon and Orinoco River basins. It rises from under the water to exhale noisily at the surface, especially along the edge of a river or in a quiet, isolated lake. It is large (males reach nearly 3 m, 10 ft, in length) and is light gray in color (despite their name they actually show little pink coloring). The GRAY, or ESTUARINE, DOLPHIN (Plate 96) is the second smallest cetacean in the world (1.4 m, 4.5 ft), and in Brazil is often seen in the large rivers of the Amazon region, but also out the mouth of the Amazon, and along the coast of northern South America to Panamá.

Natural History
Ecology and Behavior
In Asia and South America, five similar species of dolphins have evolved unique adaptations to live in freshwater. The most widespread of these species in South America, the PINK RIVER DOLPHIN, feeds chiefly on fish as well as other aquatic organisms such as crabs, which they generally catch in deep shady water near the banks of rivers or at points where smaller tributaries enter larger rivers. They use their excellent eyesight to locate prey in clear water, but in turbid water they emit a series of clicking noises, 30 to 80 per second, which they then use as sonar by listening for them to bounce off potential prey items. They use their ability to flex their necks back and forth to broadcast and scan these clicking sounds over a large area. They also give numerous other sounds including a screeching alarm call. During the dry season these dolphins are often confined to the main channels of deep rivers, but during the rainy season, they will pursue fish well into flooded forest areas and swamps. This species tends to occur alone or in pairs, and it rarely jumps out of the water. The second species of dolphin found in Amazonian Brazil, the GRAY DOLPHIN, is more like typical marine dolphins. They tend to be highly social, sometimes seen in pods of up to 20, but they are shier than the Pink River Dolphin, and often harder to see. The sound of their blow when reaching the surface to breathe after a dive can barely be heard more than 15 m (50 ft) away. It is much softer than the explosive sounds made by surfacing Pink River Dolphins. The smaller Gray Dolphin, however, is more likely to leap out of the water and make its presence known. It feeds primarily on crabs, prawns, and catfish, which it locates underwater at close distances with sonar clicks.

Breeding
Dolphins in the Amazon reproduce seasonally, usually giving birth during the flood season. The gestation period is 10.5 months and a single young is produced every 2 years. The calf is cared for by the mother for almost a year.

Notes
The PINK RIVER DOLPHIN has received considerable attention in the sexual fantasies of local people. In most parts of the Amazon, dolphins are treated with respect and even fear. These people believe that dolphins turn themselves into beautiful women who seduce innocent men and drown them. Alternatively, the dolphins are often blamed for impregnating unwed mothers. Whatever the source of these folk tales, they can serve the useful function of protecting the dolphins from being hunted.

Status
All cetaceans are CITES Appendix I or Appendix II listed. The freshwater dolphins of the Amazon are common and widespread, but water contaminants and fishing with explosive charges have evidently reduced populations in some parts of their range. The IUCN Red List includes the PINK RIVER DOLPHIN as threatened in Brazil.

Profiles
Gray Dolphin, *Sotalia fluviatilis*, Plate 96c
Pink River Dolphin, *Inia geoffrensis*, Plate 96d

Environmental Close-up 6
Of Kingfishers and Competition: Big Bills and Little Bills and How They Got That Way

Take a long look at the beautiful birds shown in Plate 52 – Brazil's five kingfisher species. The step-wise size differences you see there may not be just a coincidence. Some researchers interpret this pattern of closely related species having such distinctly different sizes as an adaptation against competition. Competition in nature is defined as an interaction in which two or more individuals, populations, or species use the same resource (see also p. 52). As they use this resource, they make it rarer and harder to find, and there is a contest between rivals to get to the remaining resource first. The resource over which the rivalry takes place can be food, nesting sites, water, sunlight or even females to mate with. Whatever this important resource, it is called a *limiting resource* because even though there may be an abundance in the environment of everything else needed successfully to live and have young, the paucity of this one resource serves to limit or restrict the likelihood of having young and surviving. Among kingfishers, studies show that bill size is important for efficiently catching a certain size of fish. The larger the bill, the larger the size of fish that can be taken efficiently. If fish is a limiting resource, then different species of kingfishers can live together on the same stream or lake only because their different bill sizes force them to take different sizes of fish, and competition rivalry is reduced or eliminated. That one kingfisher species seldom, if ever, chases an individual of another species from its territory reinforces this hypothesis of reduced competition by having different body and prey sizes. In other words, Brazil's various kingfisher species need not be aggressive toward one another because they do not seek the same food.

Kingfishers are not the only animals to show this pattern of different sizes as a response to competition. Tiger beetles (see Plate 2b) eat small insects and spiders on the ground. They use their large, sickle-shaped mandibles to capture, subdue and puree their prey. Generally, the tiger beetle species in any one habitat, such as a sandy river beach, primary forest floor or muddy pond edge, are of different sizes. In some cases, however, even if their bodies are about the same length, their mandibles are very different in size. Studies of these marauding beetles show that the size of food they can most successfully capture and eat is directly related to the length of their mandibles. Thus, just as with the kingfishers, a *community* of tiger beetle species can occupy the same habitat by eating different parts of the available menu, in this case tiny to small insects, because competition for the limiting resource is reduced or eliminated.

Finally, the effects of competition may be complicated by the result of competitive events in the distant past. In some cases there is no time to evolve different bills, legs, tails or behavior to divide the limiting resource, and direct competition occurs. When such strong competition does occur, one species wins out quickly and drives the losers out of the area or into local extinction (called *competitive exclusion*). Often, the species we see in nature now, and the ways we see species interacting, are the results of competition hundreds or thousands of years ago. With no "time machine" to see which species were winners and which were losers, we might only guess at what happened or see no reason to even consider competition as a significant factor in understanding surviving species and their communities. Although competition among species may be largely invisible to us, and much of it that is significant to understanding the form and behavior of current species occurred in the distant past, it is among the most important ecological concepts to comprehend; it is, in fact, considered one of the basic ordering forces of nature.

Chapter 11

Freshwater Fish of the Amazon

by Richard Francis

- Introduction
- Catfish and Characins
- Knifefish
- Cichlids
- Habitats and Niches
- Conservation

Introduction

We are terrestrial creatures. So it is not surprising that most visitors view the Amazon River primarily as a highway into the rainforest and/or a platform from which to view the forest inhabitants. But for the indigenous people of this region, the river is much more than a highway; it is the focus of almost every aspect of their lives. The river also is the focus for many other, non-human, forest inhabitants; indeed, it is no exaggeration to say that the river is the lifeblood of the rainforest itself, without which Amazonia as we know it would not exist.

The tremendous biodiversity of the Amazonian rainforest is now well publicized and fairly well known. What is much less known is the biodiversity of the Amazon River itself, which exceeds that of all other rivers, indeed all other freshwater systems of any kind. Biologists have not yet plumbed the depths of this biodiversity; dozens of new species of fish are discovered each year, many of them bizarre and unlike any found elsewhere. But we already know this much: there are between 2500 and 3000 species of fish in the Amazon itself (about 10 times that of all of Europe), making it the richest ichthyological region on Earth. There are more species of catfish in the Amazon – about 500 – than the total number of freshwater fish species in North America. What accounts for this great biodiversity?

One factor in the Amazon's biodiversity is its size. The Amazon River is vast, the largest river system on Earth. It flows for 6200 km (3900 miles) between its headwaters in the Andes and its delta in the Atlantic Ocean. And the river is so wide in some places that it looks more like a large lake; standing on one side of the river, you cannot see the opposite shore. But the true measure of a river is the volume of water it contains and in this respect the Amazon River far exceeds any other. About one-fifth of the world's freshwater that is discharged into the ocean each year can be traced to the Amazon. By way of comparison, the Amazon's discharge is 10 times greater than that of the Mississippi River, and 3500 times that of the Thames. Perhaps most astonishing is the fact that the river flows far into the Atlantic Ocean, especially during the flood season. The freshwater plume is still visible by air 240 km (150 miles) out from the Brazilian coastline.

But if size alone mattered, the Nile and Mississippi rivers would contain more species than they do, which is about one-tenth of the fish species found in the Amazon. The second factor in the Amazon's favor is the fact that it is a tropical river system, and tropical ecosystems, whether terrestrial, marine or freshwater, are richer than any other. But there must be another factor as well, as the Amazon contains about two to three times as many species as the Congo, which is both large and tropical.

The third factor favoring species diversity in the Amazon is its age. In general, the older an ecosystem, the more species it sustains. The Amazon may be the oldest river system on Earth. Indeed it originated before the break-up of the southern super-continent, Gondwanaland (India, Africa, Australia, Antarctica and South America combined), about 80 to 90 million years ago. Hence, the Amazon River has been around long before the Atlantic Ocean, which is its current outlet. This explains a seeming anomaly in the Amazon fish fauna. The Amazon's famous freshwater stingrays (Plate 102) are more closely related to Pacific Ocean stingrays than to Atlantic Ocean stingrays. That's because, in the past, starting in the Gondwana days, the Amazon flowed to the Pacific Ocean, not the Atlantic. The eastward flow only commenced after the rise of the Andes, about 15 million years ago, which deprived the river of its Pacific outlet. There was an extended period, while the eastern Guinea and Brazilian highlands were still joined, during which the Amazon had no outlet at all, forming instead a vast lake and swamp ecosystem, the largest ever on Earth. It was only 10 million years ago that the Amazon penetrated the eastern highlands and reached the Atlantic ocean.

Catfish and Characins

More than 80% of the fish species found in the Amazon belong to a large subgroup of bony fishes in which the front vertebrae of the backbone are modified to conduct sound from the swim bladder to the inner ear. This acoustic specialization is especially valuable in the low-visibility environments found throughout much of the Amazon. Three groups of these acoustic specialists, in particular, dominate the fish fauna.

Characins. The most speciose group of Amazonian fishes are the characins ("KAHR-ah-sinz") and their relatives. The *true characins* (family Characidae) include all of the *tetra* species (Plate 99) favored by aquarists, as well as the *piranhas* and their vegetarian counterparts, the PACU and TAMBAQUI (Plate 99). Characins exhibit a wide variety of adaptations for diverse modes of food consumption and predominate in virtually every Amazonian habitat. Several families of closely related fishes are grouped with the true characins as *characoid fishes*. The JARAQUI (Plate 100) belongs to a family (Curimatidae) of carp-like detritus feeders; the ARACU (Plate 100) is a member of a family (Anostomidae) of fruit-eating fishes commonly referred to as *headstanders*, because of the characteristic way in which they orient themselves in the water. Other families of characoid fishes are primarily fish-eaters. The *pike-characins* (Ctenolucidae) are so called because of their pike-shaped bodies; they are lunge or ambush fish predators that feed near the surface. The TRAIRA (Erythrinidae; Plate 100), another important fish predator, belongs to a small group of primitive tube-shaped characins that may represent the baseline condition for characoid fishes as a whole.

Catfish. The Amazon is justly famous for its catfishes; no other ecosystem on Earth comes close with respect to the number and diversity of catfish species. Many Amazonian catfishes are not the typical bottom-hugging scavengers that the term "catfish" typically conjures. The DOURADA (Gilded Catfish; Plate 101), for example, renowned for its flesh by indigenous groups and for its epic migrations by biologists, is an active predator in the upper portions of the water column. Its large dorsal fin is often seen protruding above the water surface like that of a shark. The Dourada belongs to a family (Pimelodelidae, the *long-whiskered catfish*) of large predatory catfish that includes the PIRAIBA (Giant Catfish; Plate 101), the SURUBIM (Tiger Flathead; Plate 101), and the PIARARA (Redtail Catfish), a favorite of sport-fishing enthusiasts.

Long-whiskered (pimelodelid) catfish have smooth skins, but many Amazonian catfish are heavily armored. The largest armored catfish (family Doradidae) are commonly referred to as *bacu* in Brazil; they are also called "thorny catfish" because each of their lateral plates bears a hook or spine, and "talking catfish" because they are prone to make noises with their swim-bladder. Many bacu catfish, such as the BACU-PEDRA (Rock Bacu; Plate 101) are fruit-eaters and important dispersal agents for lowland forest trees; others, such as the CUIU-CUIU (Ripsaw Catfish; Plate 101) vacuum up detritus with huge suction mouths.

The *suckermouth catfish* (family Loricaridae), such as the acari (plecostomus), derive their common name from their capacity to attach themselves by their mouths to hard surfaces such as rocks, from which they remove algae. In nature, they prefer clear flowing water, but these intermediate-sized catfish have also become popular aquarium species; in captivity they attach themselves to aquarium glass and rasp their way around the tank while removing algae. The third group of armored catfish (family Callichthyidae), often referred to as *smooth-armored catfish* because their plates lack hooks or spines, are even more popular in home aquariums. This group includes the TABATINGA (Skunk Corydoras; Plate 102) and hundreds of closely related species. These diminutive and extremely peaceful creatures play the more traditional catfish role of bottom scavengers. There are several other groups of Amazonian catfish as well, such as the so-called *banjo catfish* (Aspredinidae) which includes the GUITARITA (Plate 102), and the group of parasitic species known as *candiru* (family Trichomycteridae; Plate 102), infamous for their capacity to invade human orifices.

Knifefish

The *knifefishes* are the third major component of that super-group of acoustic specialists. Knifefish, however, do not rely much on acoustics to navigate their home waters; they rely instead on a highly evolved electrical sense, which is also useful in low-visibility conditions. Knifefish also generate weak electrical fields that they use to detect their prey and to communicate with each other. Several distinct groups of electric fishes are collectively referred to as knifefish; the CARAPO (Plate 98) belongs to one of the largest families (Gymnotidae) of weakly electrical fish. The PORAQUE (Elecric Eel; family Electrophoridae; Plate 98), however, generates powerful high-voltage pulses by means of which it stuns its prey and predators alike.

Cichlids

In contrast to the characins, catfish and knifefish, *cichlids* ("sick-lids") lack the modified front vertebrae; they are not acoustic specialists. They are, however, considered among the most advanced fish groups, and they are an important component of the Amazonian fish fauna. Cichlids are renowned for their care of their young. All cichlids guard their young for extended periods and this is thought to be an important factor in their success in the Neotropics and elsewhere. Most cichlids are carnivorous to some extent, none more so than the celebrated TUCUNARE (Plate 97), a formidable bass-like predator that pursues its prey – other fishes – relentlessly. The JACUNDA (Pike-cichlid; Plate 98) is another formidable fish predator, but this pike-shaped cichlid captures its prey by ambush rather than pursuit. Several other Amazonian cichlids are famous aquarium species, especially the SCALARE (Scalare Angel, or Cara Bandeira; Plate 97) and the DISCUS (Acara-morere; Plate 97), the latter being one of the most beautiful creatures on Earth.

Habitats and Niches

So far, I have spoken of the Amazon as if it is a homogeneous ecosystem but it is far from that. Let us now look at the different sorts of environments this river system provides. Most visitors are soon struck by the muddy brown color of the main river. It is loaded with sediments eroded from the Andes and the underwater visibility is close to nil. But much of the river system is not muddy, or *whitewater*, as the locals refer to it. There are large sections of *clearwater* as well, in which visibility is good and there is little sediment. These clearwater sections have their headwaters in the ancient Guinea and Brazilian highlands in which there is little erosion. The Xingu and Tapajos Rivers are two of the Amazon's main clearwater tributaries, the upper reaches of which have many cataracts and waterfalls. A third water type, found west of the clearwater tributaries, is perhaps the most distinctive; it is called *blackwater* and the Río Negro is an example. Blackwaters develop over the nutrient-poor sandy soils deposited over much of the

Amazon lowlands (see Close-up, p. 37). The chemistry of these rivers approximates that of distilled water; they are almost chemically pure, so they are extremely soft. This water is also quite acidic, more so than a carbonated soft drink. The distinct tea-black color results from the heavy load of organic material (including plant defense compounds; see Close-up, p. 37) that will not decompose because of the lack of sufficient nutrients to support the micro-organisms required for that process.

The whitewater–clearwater–blackwater distinction does not begin to cover the diversity of Amazon habitats; each of the three water types supports distinct, diverse habitats, each of which hosts a characteristic suite of fish species. Many of these habitats undergo dramatic changes through the course of the year as a result of the Amazon's dramatic seasonal fluctuations. Virtually all rivers experience seasonal fluctuations in volume, but none as dramatic as the Amazon's. The seasonal changes promote species diversity in the lowland forest/river ecosystem by creating two completely different habitats in the same space.

The low-water season extends roughly from July to October; the rainy season, during which the main river channel extends from 5 km (3 miles) wide to as much as 65 km (40 miles) wide and water levels rise up to 9 m (30 ft), commences in November and extends through February. The flood stage reaches its peak during the high-water season (February to May) and the waters begin to recede again in June, a process that continues until the next rainy season commences in November. During the rainy and high-water seasons, large areas of the lowland forest are inundated with up to 9 m (30 ft) of water. These flooded forests, or *igapó*, constitute one of the most distinctive aquatic environments on Earth. Countless individuals of hundreds of fish species migrate into the igapó from the main river channels, to feed in these nutrient-rich waters (see also Close-up, p. 200). Many of them, such as the famous TAMBAQUI (Plate 99), are fruit and seed-eaters. Frugivory is not at all common among the world's fishes but the igapó supports many such species, including fruit-eating catfish. Among the predatory fishes that penetrate far into the forest at this time of year are the insect-eating ARAWANA (Plate 98) and the voracious fish-eating TRAIRA (Plate 100). Many other fishes, such as the JARAQUI (Plate 100), suction up the abundant detritus on the submerged tree trunks and forest floor.

Lakes and Meadows. When the waters recede, the fish migrate back to the main river channels. The annual return migration of fattened Tambaqui is the target of an important Amazonian fishery. Many fish, however, become trapped and die on the forest floor. Others, for whom the way to the river is blocked, seek refuge in the numerous floodplain lakes, the largest of which endure throughout the entire dry season. The PIRARUCU (Plate 98) retreats to these lakes, as do piranha (Plate 99), which makes them less than ideal for swimming. Most piranha attacks occur in these floodplain lakes during the dry season. Both Pirarucu and piranha make out like bandits during the dry season, as their prey species become increasingly concentrated. In addition to avoiding predators, the prey fish have another huge problem to deal with in these lakes: low oxygen levels. This problem becomes increasingly acute as the lakes shrink in size during the dry season. Many fishes reduce their activity levels, rendering them even easier targets for predators like the Pirarucu, which, like several other Amazonian species, has evolved the capacity to breathe air. Adult Pirarucu, in fact, lack gills altogether, and must come regularly to the surface to gulp air.

Pirarucu use their swim-bladders as a lung; other air-breathers manage to extract oxygen from the air by other means. The so-called *lungfish* belongs to an ancient lineage dating back to the Devonian Period; it has evolved true lungs and can survive extended periods without any water at all. The PORAQUE (Plate 98), or Electric Eel, by contrast actually uses its mouth as a lung. It is lined with highly vascularized protuberances in which oxygen is taken into the bloodstream. It is thought that the eel's powerful electric discharges evolved primarily to protect this fragile mouth-lung from the spines of its prey; stunned fish put up no resistance and can be quickly swallowed.

Along the edge of the main river channels and in the larger floodplain lakes can be found large tangled mats of vegetation, sometimes exceeding a hectare (2.5 acres) in size. These "floating meadows" consist primarily of grasses and herbaceous plants, and their dense root mats host a very rich assemblage of fishes (over 100 species per hectare, 2.5 acres). Few of these fishes feed directly on the vegetation, however; most sustain themselves on the nutrient-rich organic material that accumulates in the root mats. Large, heavily armored CUIU-CUIU CATFISH (Plate 101) vacuum up huge quantities of detritus, rich in bloodworms and shrimp, while carp-like characins called *curimata* (Plate 100c) suction up the fine detritus to extract the bacteria and algae it contains. Many Amazonian fishes spend their larval stages beneath floating meadows, as do adult tetras and other small characins. Predators abound here too, none more formidable than the TUCUNARE (Plate 97), a voracious bass-like cichlid.

Sandy Banks. Deposits of sand and mud along the river banks, especially prominent during the low-water period, support a diverse fish community. Here, where the turtles bask and the stingrays bury themselves, is a particularly rich assemblage of predators, including the PIRAPOUCOU (Golden Pike-characin; Plate 100). Pirapoucou typically hang motionless in the water, awaiting the approach of unwary prey. The MADALENA (Plate 100), on the other hand, is a notorious scale-eater, a habit thought to be the ancestral condition for piranhas as well. They ram their victims, dislodging the scales with the aid of tooth-like projections from the outer jaw. Groups of Madalena are understandably avoided by most other fish species.

Deep water. In the main river channels the water depth often exceeds 30 m (100 ft). Formerly it was thought that these deepwater reaches were largely devoid of life. We now know otherwise. Most of the new species of Amazonian fishes discovered over the last 10 years come from these deep waters, as a result of the efforts of several research expeditions. These new species include a host of knifefishes, one of which eats only the tails of other knifefishes. The PIRAIBA (Giant Catfish; Plate 101) also hunts these deep channels, as do several other large predatory catfishes.

Toward the Sea. The igapó is not the only type of flooded forest. For up to 300 km (185 miles) from the river's mouth, there are pronounced tidal fluctuations in the river and twice daily flooding of adjacent forest areas. Many of the trees of the igapó are also found in these tidal flooded forests but the fish community is quite different and much less diverse. Among the notable denizens of this habitat is a fruit-eating catfish known as the BACU-PEDRA (Plate 101). During the fruiting season (April to July) this large and heavily armored catfish follows the high tide into the forest and waits beneath the trees for falling fruit. It has a very large stomach into which it packs a massive amount of fruit during the few hours before the tide goes out.

The third type of flooded forest is known as *swamp forest* and it also occurs in the lower Amazon. In contrast to the other two flooded forest types, swamp forests are almost permanently inundated. The tree diversity here is low, dominated by several species of palm, including the famous Buriti, the fruit of which is fed on by a diverse assemblage of terrestrial animals, including several species of macaw. Most of the fruit falls into the water, however, where it is eagerly consumed by several types of bacu catfish (thorny catfish, family Doradidae), cousins of the Bacu-pedra. The Poraque, or Electric Eel, also frequents these waters. It particularly favors the fruits of the beautiful Assai Palm; according to folklore, it wraps itself around the trunk, sending shocks up the tree to dislodge the fruits.

Near the coast, the water becomes brackish, an environment unsuitable to most characins and catfish but ideal for the TRAHOLTO, or Four-eyed Fish (Plate 99). This denizen of tidal mudflats preys on insects floating on the water surface, which it detects with its huge periscopic eyes. Marine fishes, not Amazonian fishes, predominate in the brackish waters. Few marine species penetrate far up the Amazon, however; among those that do are the Sawfish and BULL SHARK (Plate 102). The Bull Shark, in fact, travels up the entire course of the main channel, all the way to the base of the Andes, some 5000 km (3100 miles) upstream. Though this shark is notorious for its attacks on humans in other large river systems throughout the world, there is little evidence of such attacks in the Amazon.

Conservation

The Amazon River, like the Amazon forests, is threatened on a number of fronts. It has undergone more changes in the last four decades than in the last four centuries, and more changes in the last four centuries than the last four millennia. Not surprisingly, the threats are caused by people. The clearwater rivers of the Brazilian and Guinea highlands are being inundated with toxic wastes from mining operations. The lowland forests are being removed at a rapid rate for cattle ranching, with devastating consequences for the floodplain habitats. And virtually all of the large fishes are under siege from commercial fishing operations, which are now able to transport their meat to quite distant locations. No longer is fishing primarily a subsistence activity; it is big business. The next decade will be crucial in determining whether much of the Amazon River is severely, and perhaps irreversibly, damaged for short-term gain, or rather remains the biological paradise that it has long been.

References and Additional Reading

If, in the course of your travels through the Amazon and Pantanal of Brazil, you find yourself becoming more and more interested in the wildlife and plants around you, one of our major goals in writing this book will have been achieved. If you would like to satisfy your heightened natural history interest with additional reading, perhaps to find out about Brazil's *other* wildlife (the 80% of it that we had not the space to cover in this book), we list below some of the best and most detailed reference books and articles that would assist you in these goals. We used these references ourselves as we wrote this book.

Bates H. W. (1988) *The Naturalist on the River Amazonas*. Penguin Books, Baltimore, MD.

Campbell J. A. and W. W. Lamar (1989) *The Venomous Reptiles of Latin America*. Cornell University Press/Comstock, Ithaca, NY.

Carwardine M. (1995) *Whales, Dolphins and Porpoises: Eyewitness Handbooks*. DK Publishing, New York.

Collins M. (editor) (1990) *The Last Rain Forests*. Oxford University Press, Oxford, UK.

D'Abrera B. (1984) *Butterflies of South America*. Hill House, Victoria, Australia.

Duellman W. E. (editor) (1999) *Patterns of Distribution of Amphibians: A Global Perspective*. Johns Hopkins University Press, Baltimore, MD.

Duellman W. E. and L. Treub (1994) *Biology of Amphibians*. Johns Hopkins University Press, Baltimore, MD.

Eisenberg J. F. and K. H. Redford (1999) *Mammals of the Neotropics: The Central Neotropics, vol. 3*. University of Chicago Press, Chicago, IL.

Emmons L. H. (1997) *Neotropical Rainforest Mammals, 2nd ed.* University of Chicago Press, Chicago, IL.

Ernst C. H. and R. W. Barbour (1989) *Turtles of the World*. Smithsonian Institution Press, Washington, D.C.

Forsyth A. and K. Miyata (1987) *Tropical Nature*. Charles Scribner's Sons, New York, NY.

Gentry A. H. (1993) *A Field Guide to the Families and Genera of Woody Plants of Northwest South America (Colombia, Ecuador, Perú)*. University of Chicago Press, Chicago, IL.

Gill F. B. (1994) *Ornithology, 2nd ed.* W. H. Freeman, San Francisco, CA.

Hairston N. G. (1994) *Vertebrate Zoology: An Experimental Field Approach*. Cambridge University Press, Cambridge.

Henderson A. (1995) *The Palms of the Amazon*. Oxford University Press, New York.

Hilty S. L. and W. L. Brown (1986) *A Guide to the Birds of Colombia*. Princeton University Press, Princeton, NJ.

Hogue C. L. (1993) *Latin American Insects and Entomology*. University of California Press, Los Angeles, CA.

IUCN 2000 (2000) *IUCN Red List of Threatened Animals*. The World Conservation Union (IUCN), Gland, Switzerland.

Janzen D. H. (1983) *Costa Rican Natural History*. University of Chicago Press, Chicago, IL.

Kricher J. (1997) *A Neotropical Companion: An Introduction to the Animals, Plants, and Ecosystems of the New World Tropics, 2nd ed*. Princeton University Press, Princeton, NJ.

Ladle J. (editor) (1999) *Insight Guide: Brazil, 5th ed*. Insight Guides, London, UK.

Lamar W. W. (1997) Checklist and common names of the reptiles of the Peruvian Lower Amazon. *Herpetological Natural History* 5:73–76.

de la Peña M. and M. Rumboll (1998) *Collins Illustrated Checklist: Birds of Southern South America and Antarctica*. Harper Collins Publishers, London.

Perrins C. M. and A. L. A. Middleton (1985) *The Encyclopedia of Birds*. Facts on File Publications, New York, NY.

Pough F. H., R. M. Andrews, J. E. Cadle, M. L. Crump, A. H. Savitzky and K. D. Wells (1998) *Herpetology*. Prentice Hall, Upper Saddle River, NJ.

Rodriguez L. and W. Duellman (1994) *Guide to the Frogs of the Iquitos Region, Amazonian Perú*. Natural History Museum, University of Kansas, Lawrence, KS.

Selby N., A. Draffen, R. Jones, C. McAsey and L. Pinheiro (1999) *Brazil* (4th ed.) Lonely Planet Publications, Victoria, Australia.

Terborgh J. (1992) *Diversity and the Tropical Rain Forest*. Scientific American Library, W. H. Freeman, San Francisco, CA.

Vaughn T. A. (1997) *Mammalogy, 3rd ed*. Saunders, Philadelphia, PA.

Habitat Photos

1 Meeting of the clear dark water of the Río Negro and the white, silt-laden water of the Río Solimões to form the Brazilian Río Amazonas near the city of Manaus. © G. Prance

2 Typical seasonally flooded varzea forest on the edge of Lake Janau Aca in Amazonian Brazil. © G. Prance

3 Aerial view of seasonally flooded varzea forest at the junction of a small blackwater river and larger whitewater river in Amazonian Brazil. © G. Prance/Visuals Unlimited

4 Trunk of giant fig tree (*Ficus* sp.) on the edge of Lake Janau Aca in Amazonian Brazil. © G. Prance

5 Giant water lilies (*Victoria amazonica*) on an Amazonian pond. © M. & B. Hunn/Visuals Unlimited

6 Typical flooded igapo forest along the Río Negro of northwestern Brazil. © G. Prance/Visuals Unlimited

7 View from the canopy of terra firme forest along the Río Ariau northwest of Manaus.
© J. Dermid/Visuals Unlimited

8 Undergrowth and floor of terra firme forest near the Río Anajas in Amazonian Brazil. © G. Prance/Visuals Unlimited

9 Flowering bromeliad in the canopy of terra firme forest of the Brazilian Amazon. © D. Matherly/Visuals Unlimited

10 Aerial view of marshy areas in the northern Pantanal during flood season. © G. Prance

11 Aerial view of flooded savannah at the end of the rainy season in the southern Pantanal. © G.Prance

12 Aerial view of flooded scrub forest (*Vochysia* sp.) at height of flood season in the northern Pantanal. © G. Prance

13 Carunda Palm (*Copernicia alba*) savannah of the central Pantanal in the dry season. © G.Prance

14 Savannah fire in the Pantanal during the dry season. © G. Prance

15 Hills surrounding the northern edge of the Pantanal near the town of Acorizal. © G. Prance

16 Spectacular dry season blossoming of a Tabebuia tree (*Tabebuia impetiginosa*) near Corumbá in the southern Pantanal. © G. Prance

17 Palm swamp (*buritales*) in the northern Pantanal near the town of Acorizal. © G. Prance

18 Flooded Carunda Palm (*Copernicia alba*) in the northern Pantanal. © G. Prance

19 Strangler Fig (*Ficus aurea*) wrapping its roots around a host tree in a Pantanal gallery forest. © F. Pölking/Visuals Unlimited

20 Forest islands on raised soil mounds isolated by flood waters in the northern Pantanal, near the town of Poconé. © J. Adis

Explanation of habitat symbols used in the plate section:

= Terra firme lowland forest (p. 15).

= Varzea forest (also called flooded or riverine forest; p. 27).

= Igapó forest (also called white sand forest; p. 15).

= Forest edge and streamside. Some species typically are found along forest edges or near or along streams; these species prefer semi-open areas rather than dense, closed, interior parts of forests. Also included here: open woodlands, tree plantations, and shady gardens.

= Pastureland, non-tree plantations, savannah (grassland with scattered trees and shrubs), gardens without shade trees, roadside. Species found in these habitats prefer very open areas.

= Freshwater. For species typically found in or near lakes, streams, rivers, marshes, swamps.

= Saltwater/marine. For species found in or near the ocean, ocean beaches, or mangroves.

REGIONS (see Map 3, p. 34):

NEA   Northeastern Amazon
CMF   Coastal Mangrove Forest
NWA   Northwestern Amazon
SAM   Southern Amazon
PAN   Pantanal

Identification Plates

Plates 1–102

Abbreviations on the Identification Plates are as follows:

M;   male
F;   female
IM; immature
LF; left front footprint
LH; left hind footprint

The species pictured on any one plate are not necessarily to scale. In a few cases, a horizontal line on a plate separates animals at different scales.

Plate 1a
Helicopter Damselfly
Mecistogaster ornata
ID: Long (15 cm, 6 in), thin body; large wings flap slowly as flies through the middle and upper levels of moist primary lowland forests on sunny days. Look for large white or yellow wing-tips.

REGION: NEA, NWA, SAM

Plate 1b
Leaf-mimicking Katydid
Cycloptera speculata
ID: Green or brown body and wings (6 cm, 2.4 in long) look like a live or dead leaf; during the day sits on vegetation that matches its coloration; active at night, when it is often attracted to lights.

REGION: NEA, NWA, SAM, PAN

Plate 1c
Nasute Termite
Nasutitermes sp.
ID: Body mainly white; worker with mandibles and soldier with "nozzle head" for spraying enemies; forest undergrowth; active during the day.

REGION: NEA, NWA, SAM, PAN

Plate 1d
Evening Cicada
Fidicina mannifera
ID: Delicate colors; wings held over back tent-like; large (5 cm, 2 in), often making it easy to see resting on vertical trunks of moist forest usually during the day; active at night feeding; begins calling at sundown, although other similar sounding species call during the day.

REGION: NEA, NWA, SAM, PAN

Plate 1e
Peanut Bug
(also called Lantern Bug)
Fulgora laternaria
ID: Large (10 cm, 4 in), well-camouflaged; often spends the day in small groups roosting on vertical tree trunks in moist primary and tall secondary forest; active at night. Large "eye" spots on wings revealed in flight.

REGION: NEA, NWA, SAM

Plate 1f
Antlion
Myrmeleon sp.
ID: Small (5 to 10 mm, 0.2 to 0.4 in) larvae at the bottom of inverted cones (1 to 2.5 cm, 0.4 to 1 in, across at their tops) in dry sand in open lowland areas; also in shade of vegetation or buildings; dragonfly-like adult (3 to 4 cm, 1.6 to 1.7 in length) with long antennae with clubbed ends, attracted to lights at night.

REGION: NEA, NWA, SAM, PAN

Plate I 263

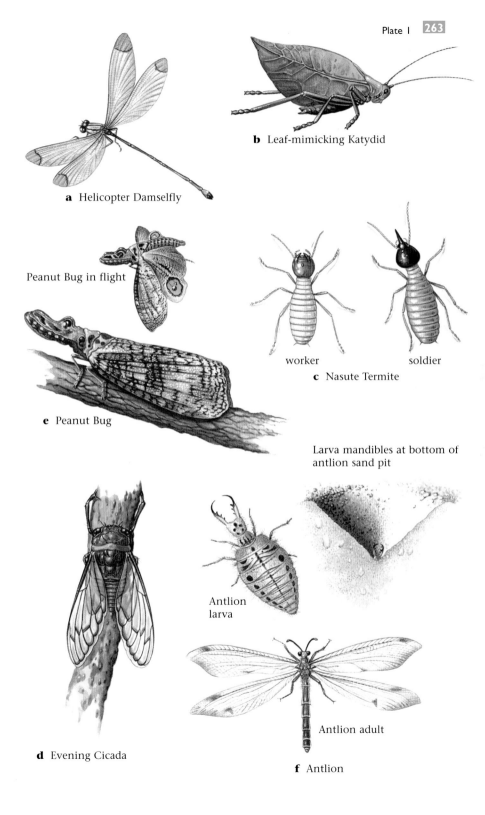

a Helicopter Damselfly

b Leaf-mimicking Katydid

Peanut Bug in flight

e Peanut Bug

worker   soldier

c Nasute Termite

Larva mandibles at bottom of antlion sand pit

Antlion larva

Antlion adult

d Evening Cicada

f Antlion

Plate 2a
Headlight Click Beetle
Pyrophorus sp.

ID: Large (4 cm, 1.5 in), slender beetles with rounded heads and pointed rear ends; overall brown-olive color; active at night they fly slowly, with two round phosphorescent light patches on top of the body just in back of the head and one broad lighted area on the underside glowing eerily; adults are easily attracted to artificial lights at night; placed on their backs, they will bend the head and wings backward and then suddenly straighten out with a clicking sound to jump up in the air several centimeters (an inch or two); the larvae, which live in the soil, also glow and are predators on other beetle larvae.

REGION: NEA, NWA, SAM, PAN

Plate 2b
Nocturnal Riverine Tiger Beetle
Tetracha (Megacephala) sobrina

ID: Active only at night along moist mud and sand rivers, lakes, and grassy areas; bright metallic red, green and blue (1.7 cm, 0.7 in); it seldom flies but runs quickly in search of prey or to hide in crevices or under vegetation; most easily seen by flashlight along open sandy beaches at the water's edge or attracted to lights at night; larvae make vertical tunnels in the sand in which they await their insect prey.

REGION: NEA, CMF, NWA, SAM, PAN

Plate 2c
Harlequin Long-horned Beetle
Acrocinus longimanus

ID: Large (6 cm, 2.4 in) and colorful, most often seen when attracted to lights at night in moist primary lowland forest; male's front legs (7 cm, 2.8 in) are half again as long as those of the female.

REGION: NEA, NWA, SAM

Plate 2d
Giant Metallic Wood-boring Beetle
Euchroma gigantea

ID: Large (7 cm, 2.8 in long) and brilliantly colored, shining green and red; active during the day and obvious as it flies slowly and noisily at mid levels through moist forest; often seen on the trunks of trees it attacks, such as Ceiba (p. 15) and other soft wood, or on dead individuals of the plant family Bombacaceae.

REGION: NEA, NWA, SAM

Plate 2e
Green Dung Beetle
Oxysternon conspicillatum

ID: Dark metallic green (2.7 cm, 1 in); male with a prominent horn; commonly attracted to fresh dung in moist lowland primary and tall secondary forest; active during the day; most other species in this group are similar in shape but black.

REGION: NEA, NWA, SAM

Plate 2f
Palm Weevil
Rhynchophorous palmarum

ID: Large (5 cm, 2 in), entirely black with a snout almost as long as its body; parallel grooves on wing coverings that do not completely cover the body; found on palm trunks.

REGION: NEA, NWA, SAM, PAN

Plate 2   265

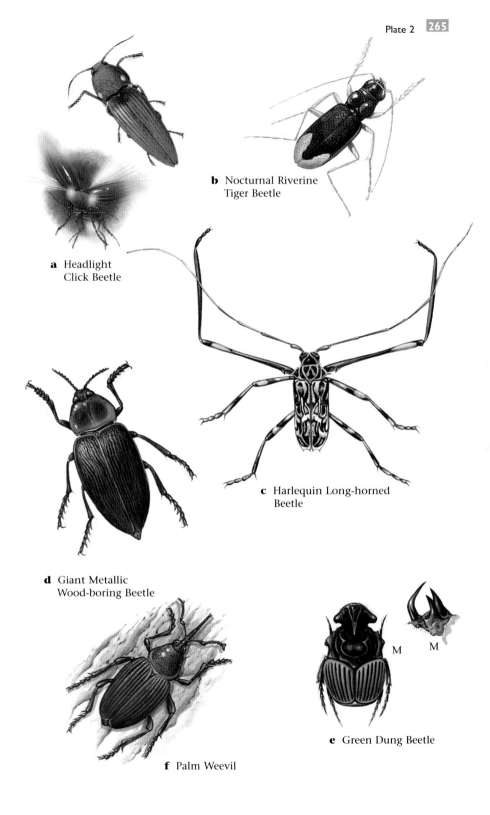

b Nocturnal Riverine Tiger Beetle

a Headlight Click Beetle

c Harlequin Long-horned Beetle

d Giant Metallic Wood-boring Beetle

M   M

e Green Dung Beetle

f Palm Weevil

Plate 3a
Brazilian Morpho Butterfly
Morpho deidamia
ID: Very large (wingspan 10 cm, 4 in) bright blue male with black wing tips is unmistakable; female is larger with narrower blue band on wings; flaps lazily along open corridors through forest or along river edges of lowland forest during sunny days. At rest on vertical surfaces the camouflaged underwings hide the butterfly.

REGION: NEA, NWA, SAM

Plate 3b
Mazaeus Mechanitis Butterfly
Mechanitis mazaeus
ID: Bright orange, black, and yellow "tiger" pattern (wingspan 6.5 cm, 2.5 in); poisonous and distasteful, it serves as a "model" to be mimicked by other, less dangerous, butterfly species; mid-levels of moist primary and tall secondary forest; active on sunny days.

REGION: NEA, NWA, SAM

Plate 3c
Amphione Dismorpha Butterfly
Dismorphia amphione
ID: Bright orange, black, and yellow "tiger" pattern (wingspan 6 cm, 2.4 in); lacks toxins and is cheating by mimicking the distasteful and similar appearing model species, such as Mazaeus Mechanitis Butterfly; mid-levels of moist primary and tall secondary forest; active on sunny days.

REGION: NEA, NWA, SAM

Plate 3d
Sulphur Butterfly
Phoebis sp.
ID: Males yellowish orange above and below (wingspan 3.5 cm, 1.43 in); females with black edges on yellowish wings, but some individuals are whitish. Males commonly "puddle" in large concentrations along watercourses.

REGION: NEA, NWA, SAM, PAN

Plate 3e
Lelius' Urania Moth
Urania lelius
ID: Brilliant green and black color (wingspan 7 cm, 6.5 in); common on moist river beaches where males "puddle" to suck sodium and other essential chemicals from the sand; also often in large numbers migrating over the canopy of moist lowland forest; active on sunny days.

REGION: NEA, NWA, SAM

Plate 3f
Glaucous Kite Swallowtail
Eurytides glaucolaus
ID: Large (wingspan 8 cm, 3 in) and showy, this whitish swallowtail is common along river beaches and sand bars, where males often gather in large concentrations to "puddle."

REGION: NEA, NWA, SAM

Plate 3 267

a Brazilian Morpho Butterfly

b Mazaeus Mechanitis Butterfly

c Amphione Dismorpha Butterfly

d Sulphur Butterfly

e Lelius' Urania Moth

f Glaucous Kite Swallowtail

Plate 4a
Window-winged Atlas Moth
Rothschildi sp.
ID: Large (wingspan 12 cm, 4.7 in) and mainly brown to reddish brown with white lines on ends of wings and a prominent translucent triangle in the center of each wing.
REGION: NEA, NWA, SAM, PAN

Plate 4b
Snake-mimicking Sphinx Moth
Hemeroplanes tritolemus
ID: Medium-sized (wingspan 8 cm, 3 in); brown with silver streaks; wings extended are long, thin, and pointed; at rest form a distinct triangle over the back; larvae are called "viper" worms because their coloring, shape, and behavior closely resemble a small and aggressive *Bothrops* snake (Plate 21).
REGION: NEA, NWA, SAM

Plate 4c
Claudina's Red-winged Agrias
Agrias claudina
ID: Fast-flying with bright red fore wings and blue hind wings (wingspan 7 cm, 2.7 in); camouflaged under wings make it difficult to see perched on the ground or on low bushes of lowland forest. Often attracted to feces, rotting fruits or dead animals on forest floor.
REGION: NEA, NWA, SAM

Plate 4d
Green Long-winged Butterfly
Philaethria dido
ID: Large (wingspan 8 cm, 3 in); pale green wings with dark brown margins diagnostic; active in and above the canopy of lowland forests but descends at midday to fly low along the edge of light gaps.
REGION: NEA, NWA, SAM

Plate 4e
Owl Butterfly
Caligo sp.
ID: Very large (wingspan 13 cm, 5 in) and blue-gray above. Underside of hind wings with two large "owl eyes." Perches on tree trunks in dense shade throughout most of the day, flying late in the afternoon and early morning.
REGION: NEA, NWA, SAM, PAN

Plate 4f
Aurorina Clear-winged Satyr
Cithaerias aurorina
ID: Brownish (wingspan 5 cm, 2 in) with clear fore wings and reddish patches on hind wings; common during the day on forest floor and along shaded trails of moist forest.
REGION: NEA, NWA, SAM

Plate 4 269

a Window-winged Atlas Moth

b Snake-mimicking Sphinx Moth

larva

c Claudina's Red-winged Agrias

d Green Long-winged Butterfly

e Owl Butterfly

f Aurorina Clear-winged Satyr

Plate 5a

Chestnut-colored Robber Fly

Diomites castaneus

ID: Brownish-yellow color; sits on ground or low vegetation in moist lowland forest waiting to pounce on small insects flying by on sunny days; wings produce loud buzzing in flight.

REGION: NEA, NWA, SAM

Plate 5b

Leaf-cutter Ant

Atta sp.

ID: Tan and brown; travel in long narrow columns carrying leaf or flower bits like open umbrellas; often create obvious well-worn paths through leaf litter on the ground of lowland moist forest; several size castes in a colony.

REGION: NEA, NWA, SAM, PAN

Plate 5c

Burchell's Army Ant

Eciton burchelli

ID: Tan and brown; travel in massive attack columns through moist lowland forest floor and lower vegetation searching for insect prey; several castes in a colony; soldiers have very impressive mandibles.

REGION: NEA, NWA, SAM, PAN

Plate 5d

Giant Hunting Ant

(also called Paraponera Ant)

Paraponera clavata

ID: Medium-sized (2 cm, 0.75 in), all brownish black; usually alone or in small groups; listen for their warning sounds and avoid at all costs being stung – an experience in pain you will not soon forget; lowland moist forests, canopy to forest floor.

REGION: NEA, NWA, SAM, PAN

Plate 5e

Merian's Orchid Bee

Eulaema meriana

ID: Bumblebee-like; black body with bright yellow and orange rings on the rear; listen for its deep humming during the day; a non-aggressive resident of moist lowland forest.

REGION: NEA, NWA, SAM

Plate 5f

Neotropical Colonial Spider

Anelosimus eximus

ID: Most easily recognized by the huge gossamer webs that stretch for meters (yards) high along riverside vegetation and forest borders. Hundreds of spiders can live together, each with its own small web united with those of its neighbors.

REGION: NEA, NWA, SAM

Plate 5g

Forest Crab

Fredius sp.

ID: A flat, brownish land crab (shell up to 6 cm, 2.4 in, across) with huge pincher claws (*chelipeds*). Usually found in moist areas of the forest floor and along forest streams. During the day often hidden under leaves or at the base of trees. Most active at night, but if disturbed at any time of the day, it will raise its open pinchers in a very intimidating threat posture.

REGION: NEA, NWA, SAM, PAN

Plate 5 271

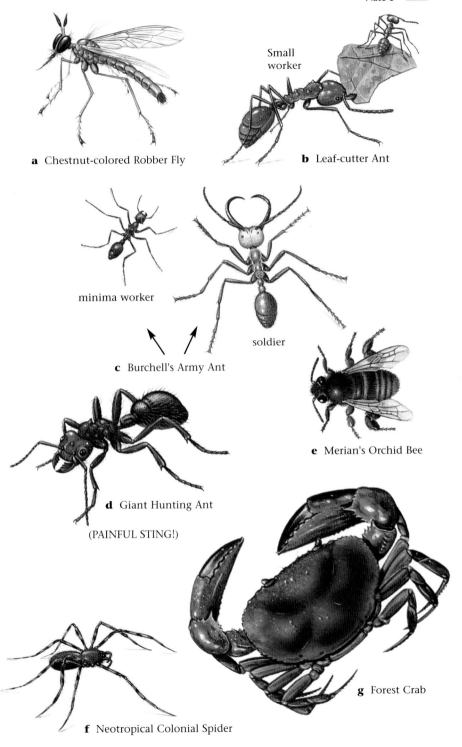

a Chestnut-colored Robber Fly

Small worker

b Leaf-cutter Ant

minima worker

soldier

c Burchell's Army Ant

e Merian's Orchid Bee

d Giant Hunting Ant

(PAINFUL STING!)

g Forest Crab

f Neotropical Colonial Spider

Plate 6a

South American Caecilian
(also called Ringed Blue Caecilian)
Siphonops annulatus

ID: Medium-sized (to 50 cm, 20 in, long and 1.5 cm, 0.6 in, wide; but most are smaller); resembles large blue worm; smooth skin with closely spaced lighter blue rings; eye evident as slightly raised, dark spot below surface of skin.

HABITAT: Found in primary and secondary forest; normally found only underground, but sometimes seen on surface after heavy rain.

REGION: NEA, NWA, SAM, PAN

Plate 6b

Amazonian Salamander
Bolitoglossa altamazonica

ID: Small (to 4.9 cm, 2 in, excluding tail); slim; dark gray to reddish brown; with or without dark blotches or stripe running down length of body; with or without cream bar across snout; underside dark gray, sometimes with white flecks; hands and feet extensively webbed.

HABITAT: Nocturnal; by day often found in leaf litter on ground; at night on leaves of shrubs; in primary and secondary forest.

REGION: SAM

Plate 6c

Common Lesser Toad
Bufo granulosus

ID: Medium-sized (to 5.5 cm, 2.2 in); rough, granular skin; large eyes; light brown to yellowish gray, with irregular dark gray or brown markings; belly gray, often marbled darker gray; dark bony ridges on head, encircling eye.

HABITAT: Terrestrial, nocturnal; found in open, disturbed areas such as clearings.

REGION: NEA, NWA, SAM, PAN

Plate 6d

South American Common Toad
Bufo typhonius

ID: Medium-sized (to 8 cm, 3.2 in); rough skin; pointed snout; medium to dark brown or gray, with or without irregular darker blotches or spots, and frequently with white or yellow stripe running down center; distinct, high bony crests between eyes and continuing onto shoulders; line of small pointed tubercles (bumps) along each side of upper body.

HABITAT: Terrestrial, active by day; most often found in primary forest, sometimes in secondary forest.

REGION: NEA, NWA, SAM

Plate 6   **273**

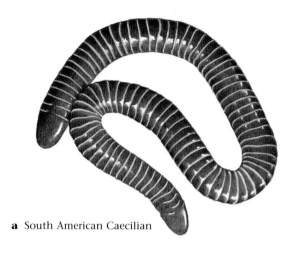

a South American Caecilian

b Amazonian Salamander

c Common Lesser Toad

d South American Common Toad

Plate 7a

Marine Toad
(also called Giant Toad or Cane Toad)
Bufo marinus

ID: Large (to 20 cm, 8 in); robust; grayish tan to reddish brown with rough skin covered with "warts;" with or without darker spots; large, triangular parotoid glands on shoulders behind eyes; extensive webbing between toes; underside cream with grayish brown spots; eyes pale green with fine black lines.

HABITAT: Terrestrial, active by day and night; most commonly found in clearings, along forest edges, near edges of temporary ponds, and around human habitation; rarely observed in forest.

REGION: NEA, NWA, SAM

Plate 7b

Cururu Toad
Bufo paracnemis

ID: Large (to 21 cm, 8.4 in); brown to yellow-brown with large bony crests on head; large bean-shaped parotoid glands behind the eyes; skin rough, covered with blunt, spiny "warts;" often with darker brown spots on upper surface of body; belly and throat white with dark flecks.

HABITAT: Terrestrial, nocturnal; most commonly found in open areas breeding in both temporary and permanent bodies of water.

REGION: PAN

Plate 7c

Amazon Horned Frog
Ceratophrys cornuta

ID: Large (to 12 cm, 4.8 in); green or tan with robust body and large mouth; dark green or brown markings; upper eyelids with spike-like projections of skin, resembling horns; fingers not webbed, toes half webbed; underside white.

HABITAT: Terrestrial, nocturnal; juveniles active by day; often hidden in leaf litter; breed in forest ponds and swamps.

REGION: NEA, NWA, SAM

Plate 7d

Knudsen's Frog
Leptodactylus knudseni

ID: Large (to 17 cm, 6.8 in); robust body and limbs; brown, usually with dark bars, but occasionally uniform or with spots; prominent fold of skin on each side of upper body; light orange markings on posterior surface of darkly colored thigh; belly sometimes with yellow spots; lips without light vertical bars.

HABITAT: Terrestrial, nocturnal; found in primary forest.

REGION: NEA, NWA, SAM

Plate 7e

Smoky Jungle Frog
Leptodactylus pentadactylus

ID: Large (to 17 cm, 6.8 in); robust body and limbs; reddish brown with transverse blotches of dark gray, dark brown, or reddish brown; upper lip tan with 4 or 5 black vertical bars; snout wide and rounded; underside cream to gray with bold black markings on belly; no webbing on hands, slight webbing on feet; prominent fold of skin on each side of upper body.

HABITAT: Terrestrial, nocturnal; in primary forest.

REGION: NEA, NWA, SAM

Plate 7 275

a Marine Toad

b Cururu Toad

c Amazon Horned Frog

d Knudsen's Frog

e Smoky Jungle Frog

Plate 8a
Rufous Frog
Leptodactylus fuscus
ID: Medium-sized (to 5.5 cm, 2.2 in); brown, spotted or blotched; with or without light lip stripe; often with light stripe on back surface of thigh; six distinct prominent folds of skin running down length of body.

HABITAT: Terrestrial, nocturnal; primarily found in open areas, sometimes in secondary forest.

REGION: NEA, NWA, SAM, PAN

Plate 8b
Basin White-lipped Frog
Leptodactylus mystaceus
ID: Medium-sized (to 6 cm, 2.4 in); robust body and pointed snout; gray or tan with darker gray or brown markings; smooth skin; no webbing between fingers or toes; distinctive dark brown or black face mask, bordered below by wide white stripe; underside white.

HABITAT: Terrestrial, nocturnal; juveniles active by day; found in clearings, secondary forest, and primary forest; males call from around small pools or from cavities in ground.

REGION: NEA, NWA, SAM

Plate 8c
Pointed-belly Frog
Leptodactylus podicipinus
ID: Medium-sized (5.4 cm, 2.2 in); grayish brown with scattered darker irregular spots; dark triangular mark between eyes; yellowish glandular patches on flanks and in groin; body fairly stout, slightly warty; broad head; eyes large; fingers and toes webbed at base; toes long, fringed.

HABITAT: Terrestrial, nocturnal; most commonly found by the edges of rivers and along banks of quiet pools in open areas and in swamps and other flooded areas.

REGION: NEA, SAM, PAN

Plate 8d
Cei's White-lipped Frog
Leptodactylus chaquensis
ID: Medium-sized (to 8.5 cm, 3.4 in); gray to green-brown with light stripes and light and dark spots; thickened folds of skin running down length of body; belly white, not spotted; posterior surface of thighs green; fingers not webbed, toes webbed at base and fringed.

HABITAT: Terrestrial, nocturnal; often found in large numbers breeding in flooded roadside ditches and puddles and in swamps.

REGION: PAN

Plate 8e
Napo Tropical Bullfrog
Adenomera hylaedactyla
ID: Small (to 2.8 cm, 1.1 in); pale tan with brown spots to dull gray, with or without cream to dull red stripe running down center of body; underside creamy white; dark brown triangular mark on back of head; snout fairly long and pointed; no webbing or fringes on toes.

HABITAT: Terrestrial, nocturnal; most commonly found in open areas, such as in clearings, along forest and river edges, and in secondary forest.

REGION: NEA, NWA, SAM, PAN

Plate 8 277

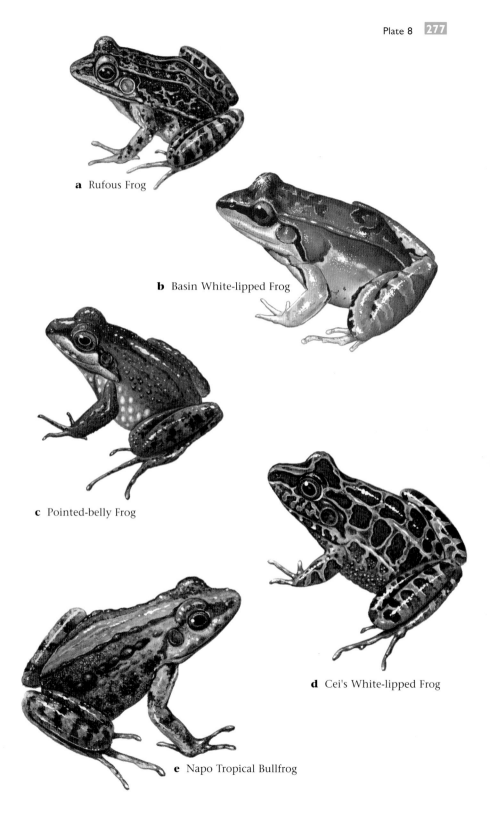

a Rufous Frog

b Basin White-lipped Frog

c Pointed-belly Frog

d Cei's White-lipped Frog

e Napo Tropical Bullfrog

Plate 9 (*See also*: Rainfrogs, p. 84; Treefrogs, p. 87)

Plate 9a
Cuyaba Dwarf Frog
Physalaemus nattereri

ID: Medium-sized (to 5.0 cm, 2.0 in); gray or light brown with irregular bright white-edged or yellow-edged transverse bands; two large black eye-shaped spots in groin; head short, snout very short.

HABITAT: Terrestrial and fossorial (burrowing), nocturnal; common in temporary ponds and swamps in open areas.

REGION: SAM, PAN

Plate 9b
Peter's Dwarf Frog
Physalaemus petersi

ID: Small (to 4 cm, 1.6 in); toad-like, with pointed snout; brown, covered with small red or orange tubercles (bumps); sides of body often cream towards the front, becoming orange toward the rear, with large black spots; hands and feet without webbing.

HABITAT: Terrestrial, nocturnal; found both in primary and secondary forest.

REGION: NWA, SAM

Plate 9c
Río Mamore Robber Frog
Eleutherodactylus fenestratus

ID: Small (to 4.5 cm, 1.8 in); brown with darker markings; posterior surfaces of thighs brown without prominent markings; scattered, enlarged tubercles (bumps) on body; long legs; no toe webbing.

HABITAT: Found both on low bushes and on the ground; nocturnal; found along streams, in clearings and other open areas, and around human habitation.

REGION: NEA, NWA, SAM

Plate 9d
Carabaya Robber Frog
Eleutherodactylus ockendeni

ID: Small (to 3 cm, 1.2 in); tan to reddish brown with dark brown markings in the shape of an H or W in the shoulder region; with or without dark brown bar between eyes; fingers and toes long, with expanded discs on tips; top part of iris usually metallic green, lower red.

HABITAT: Active by day on the ground, and at night on low vegetation; in both primary and secondary forest.

REGION: NEA, NWA, SAM

Plate 9e
Common Laughing Frog
Osteocephalus taurinus

ID: Medium-sized (to 10.3 cm, 4.1 in); tan to reddish brown with dark markings; side of body tan to creamy white with dark brown spots; dark crossbars on limbs; skin of females smooth, skin of males covered with spiny tubercles (bumps).

HABITAT: Arboreal, nocturnal; found in both primary and secondary forest; in some areas, common in roofs and houses and in palms near human habitation; breeding occurs at temporary ponds in forest.

REGION: NEA, NWA, SAM

Plate 9 279

a Cuyaba Dwarf Frog

b Peter's Dwarf Frog

c Río Mamore Robber Frog

d Carabaya Robber Frog

e Common Laughing Frog

Plate 10a
Tiger-striped Leaf Frog
Phyllomedusa tomopterna
ID: Medium-sized (to 5.7 cm, 2.3 in); bright green; flanks and hidden surfaces of thighs orange with purple-brown vertical bars; no webbing between fingers and toes; distinct extensions of skin (calcars) present on heels.

HABITAT: Arboreal, nocturnal; most commonly found on branches of dense vegetation overhanging ponds in forest.

REGION: NEA, NWA, SAM

Plate 10b
White-lined Leaf Frog
Phyllomedusa vaillanti
ID: Medium-sized (to 8.4 cm, 3.4 in); green with rough skin; elongated, slightly elevated parotoid glands with distinctive row of white granules running along length of gland; underside grayish brown with two cream spots on throat and one large green spot on chest.

HABITAT: Arboreal, nocturnal; most commonly seen while breeding at forest ponds.

REGION: NEA, NWA, SAM

Plate 10c
Veined Treefrog
Phrynohyas venulosa
ID: Medium-sized (to 11 cm, 4.4 in); brown or tan with or without darker markings; underside uniform gray or pale tan; skin thick and glandular, usually with scattered pustules; males with paired lateral vocal sacs.

HABITAT: Arboreal, nocturnal; most commonly found in open, disturbed areas such as clearings.

REGION: NEA, NWA, SAM, PAN

Plate 10d
Common Flat Treefrog
Scinax rubra
ID: Small (to 4.4 cm, 1.8 in); tan or dull green with yellow spots rimmed with black on hidden surfaces of thigh and groin; skin smooth; usually with wide cream or tan stripe running down each side of back.

HABITAT: Arboreal, nocturnal; most commonly found in open, disturbed areas such as in clearings and around human habitation; less commonly found in secondary forest.

REGION: NEA, NWA, SAM

Plate 10e
Mato Grosso Snouted Treefrog
Scinax acuminatus
ID: Small (to 4.5 cm, 1.8 in); robust, with rough skin; dark gray with dark brown triangular marking between eyes; often with dark brown saddle-shaped spot near rump and curved stripe running down each side of upper body; tips of fingers and toes expanded into wide discs.

HABITAT: Arboreal, nocturnal; found in open areas around lakes and ponds, and often associated with human residences.

REGION: SAM, PAN

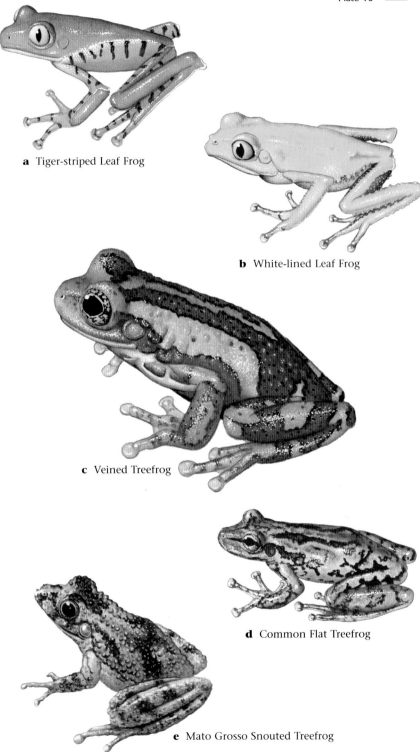

Plate 10 281

a Tiger-striped Leaf Frog

b White-lined Leaf Frog

c Veined Treefrog

d Common Flat Treefrog

e Mato Grosso Snouted Treefrog

Plate 11a
Short-legged Treefrog
Hyla leali
ID: Small (to 2.6 cm, 1 in); pinkish tan with long body and short legs; most with brown X-shaped mark across shoulders; fingers short; underside cream; white spot on upper lip below eye.

HABITAT: Arboreal, nocturnal; most commonly found in disturbed, open areas; breed in temporary or semi-permanent ponds at edge of forest.

REGION: NWA, SAM

Plate 11b
Lesser Treefrog
Hyla minuta
ID: Small (to 2.4 cm, 1 in); tan, reddish, or golden brown with irregular dark brown markings; skin smooth; snout broadly rounded; thighs orange tan; when frog is sitting, a narrow cream stripe on rump touches cream stripes on heels; underside creamy white.

HABITAT: Arboreal, nocturnal; most commonly found in primary forest, especially around ponds, where it breeds.

REGION: NEA, NWA, SAM, PAN

Plate 11c
Dwarf Treefrog
Hyla nana
ID: Tiny (to 2.2 cm, 0.9 in); dull golden-yellow to tan with fairly distinct brown stripe running down along each side of body, from nose to groin; large eyes; fingers not webbed, toes almost fully webbed.

HABITAT: Arboreal, nocturnal; found in high densities around swamps when breeding.

REGION: NEA, SAM, PAN

Plate 11d
Sarayacu Treefrog
Hyla parviceps
ID: Small (to 2.6 cm, 1 in); tan to reddish brown with dark brown markings; single cream bar extending from beneath eye to upper jaw; thighs black with one or two cream spots on forward-facing surfaces; underside grayish white with black mottling on belly; bright orange spot on underneath surface of hind limb; skin smooth with scattered small tubercles (bumps).

HABITAT: Arboreal, nocturnal; common in primary and secondary forest; breeds in swamps.

REGION: NEA, NWA, SAM

Plate 11e
Red-skirted Treefrog
Hyla rhodopepla
ID: Small (to 3 cm, 1.2 in); yellow (often white at night) with red flecks; wide red or reddish brown stripe from tip of snout to eyes and continuing behind eyes on each side of body; underside yellow or white; skin smooth.

HABITAT: Arboreal, nocturnal; found in both primary and secondary forest and along forest edges; congregate at small ponds, pools, and swamps for breeding.

REGION: NEA, NWA, SAM

Plate 11   283

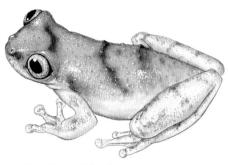

a Short-legged Treefrog

b Lesser Treefrog

c Dwarf Treefrog

d Sarayacu Treefrog

e Red-skirted Treefrog

Plate 12a
Upper Amazon Treefrog
Hyla bifurca
ID: Small (to 3.5 cm, 1.4 in); brown with cream bar on head between eyes, extending along each side of body; cream spot on rump and on each heel; webbing between toes and concealed surfaces of limbs and body orange-brown.

HABITAT: Arboreal, nocturnal; usually found on low vegetation near temporary ponds at the edge of secondary forest or in open, disturbed areas.

REGION: SAM

Plate 12b
Common Clown Treefrog
Hyla leucophyllata
ID: Small (to 4.4 cm, 1.8 in); creamy yellow with dark brown hourglass-shaped mark in center of back; extensive membrane of skin from side of body to posterior edge of upper arm; side of head and flanks brown; hidden surfaces of limbs and webbing between toes orange; some with zebra-like pattern of cream and dark brown; skin smooth.

HABITAT: Arboreal, nocturnal; most commonly found when breeding at night in ponds in forest or disturbed areas, such as water-filled ditches along road and forest edges.

REGION: NEA, NWA, SAM

Plate 12c
Triangle Treefrog
Hyla triangulum
ID: Small (to 4.5 cm, 1.8 in); creamy tan with or without one or more round brown spots; at night the hand and foot webbing and hidden surfaces of limbs are pink; by day these areas are red.

HABITAT: Arboreal, nocturnal; usually found on low vegetation near temporary ponds at the edge of secondary forest or in open, disturbed areas.

REGION: NEA, NWA, SAM

Plate 12d
Jade Treefrog
Hyla granosa
ID: Medium-sized (to 5.4 cm, 2.2 in); green with finely granular skin; sometimes with tiny red or gold flecks; reddish at night; underside pale green; iris cream, with gold ring around pupil and blue border around rim.

HABITAT: Arboreal, nocturnal; most commonly found near ponds in primary and secondary forest.

REGION: NEA, NWA, SAM

Plate 12e
Polkadot Treefrog
Hyla punctata
ID: Small (to 4.5 cm, 1.8 in); tan or pale green with red flecks and spots giving overall reddish appearance at night; stripe (yellow above, red below) running along each side of body; by day red flecks and spots are less distinct; individuals of some populations have brilliant yellow splotches by day; skin smooth; green throat, white belly; iris white with fine black reticulations.

HABITAT: Arboreal, nocturnal; commonly found around permanent, semi-permanent, and temporary ponds in forests and clearings.

REGION: NEA, NWA, SAM, PAN

Plate 12 285

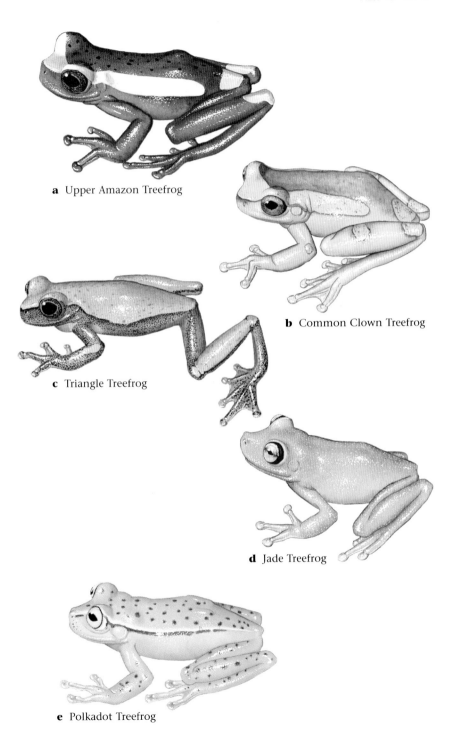

a Upper Amazon Treefrog

b Common Clown Treefrog

c Triangle Treefrog

d Jade Treefrog

e Polkadot Treefrog

Plate 13a

Marbled Treefrog
Hyla marmorata

ID: Medium-sized (to 5.5 cm, 2.2 in); grayish tan to greenish tan with dark brown or black mottling; armpits, groin, and posterior surfaces of thighs orange-yellow with black spots or mottling on thighs; distinctive white or yellow belly with bold black spots or mottling; scalloped fringes of skin along outer edges of hands and feet.

HABITAT: Arboreal, nocturnal; found in primary and secondary forest, but migrate to temporary ponds in clearings and forest edges to breed following heavy rains.

REGION: NEA, NWA, SAM

Plate 13b

Quacking Treefrog
Hyla lanciformis

ID: Medium-sized (to 9.4 cm, 3.8 in); tan with long, pointed snout; brown cross-bars on back; some with narrow dark stripe running down center of body; distinctive brown face mask and white stripe on upper lip; long limbs; chest brown with cream spots.

HABITAT: Arboreal, nocturnal; found in open disturbed areas such as clearings and around human habitation.

REGION: NEA, NWA, SAM

Plate 13c

Giant Gladiator Frog
Hyla boans

ID: Large (to 11.8 cm, 4.7 in); tan or brown with long limbs; brown blotches on back; often with irregular white or silver patches on upper part of body; broad head and large eyes; toes and all fingers except first fully webbed.

HABITAT: Arboreal, nocturnal; when not breeding, usually found in trees in forest; during dry season, frogs breed along edges of slow-moving streams; call from trees and the ground by edge of river.

REGION: NEA, NWA, SAM

Plate 13d

Troschel's Treefrog
Hyla calcarata

ID: Medium-sized (to 6.1 cm, 2.4 in); light brown with large triangular extension of skin (calcar) on each heel; bold black bars on flanks and hidden surfaces of thighs; no webbing between fingers, toes one-half to two-thirds webbed.

HABITAT: Arboreal, nocturnal; found on branches in primary and secondary forest, often near swamps.

REGION: NEA, NWA, SAM

Plate 13e

Map Treefrog
Hyla geographica

ID: Medium-sized (to 8.3 cm, 3.3 in); brown with irregular darker markings, often with narrow dark brown stripe down center of back; flanks and thighs with narrow, dark, vertical bars; broad head; small triangular projection of skin (calcar) on heel; fingers half webbed, toes three-fourths webbed; dark reticulations on lower eyelid.

HABITAT: Arboreal, nocturnal; usually found in secondary forest near lakes, ponds, or swamps.

REGION: NEA, NWA, SAM, PAN

Plate 13   287

a Marbled Treefrog

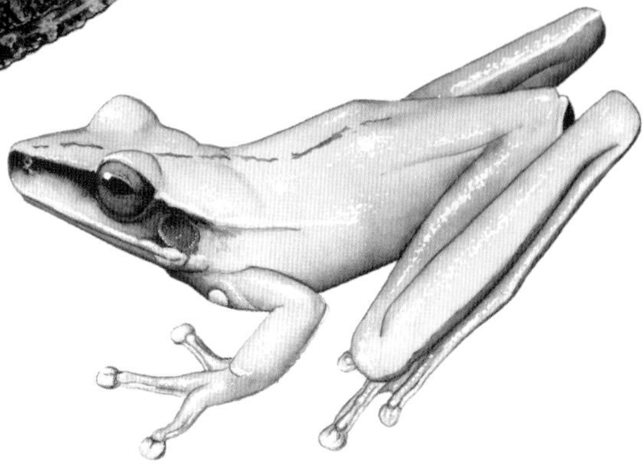

b Quacking Treefrog

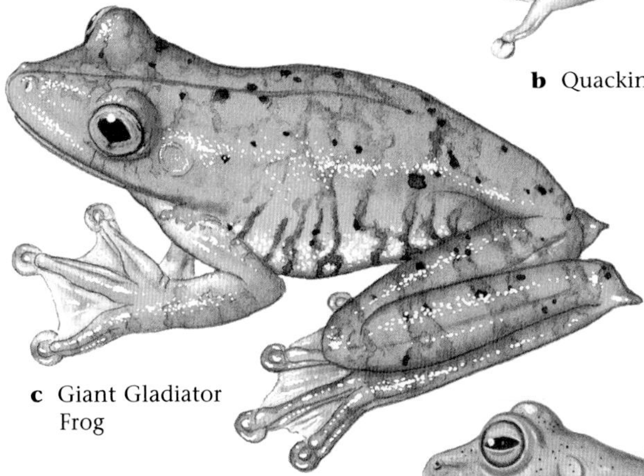

c Giant Gladiator Frog

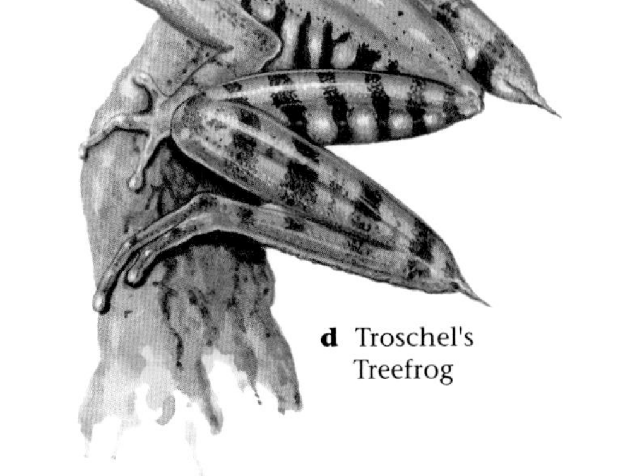

d Troschel's Treefrog

e Map Treefrog

Plate 14a
Amazon Rocket Frog
Colostethus marchesianus

ID: Tiny (to 1.8 cm, 0.7 in); tan to reddish brown with small black spots; conspicuous brown stripe, bordered below by white stripe, running down each side of body; belly white, throat light yellow; no webbing on fingers or toes; eyes gold with black flecks.

HABITAT: Terrestrial, active by day; found in primary and secondary forest, in moist areas; male carries tadpoles to small pools of water or slow-moving streams in forest.

REGION: NEA, NWA, SAM

Plate 14b
Río Madeira Poison-dart Frog
Dendrobates quinquevittatus

ID: Tiny (to 2.0 cm, 0.8 in); very distinctive pattern of black with five conspicuous yellow, pale green, or light blue stripes running down length of body; throat, belly and undersides of limbs pale blue with irregular black spots; small gold or metallic orange spots at limb insertions.

HABITAT: Terrestrial, active by day; primary forest; males carry tadpoles to water, often in fallen Brazil nut fruit capsules.

REGION: SAM

Plate 14c
Brilliant-thighed Poison-dart Frog
Epipedobates femoralis

ID: Small (to 2.9 cm, 1.2 in); brown with cream or tan stripe running along each side of body; white stripe on flank; pale yellow spot on front surface of arm and on front surface of thigh; throat and chest black; belly and underparts of limbs blue with black mottling.

HABITAT: Terrestrial, active by day; most commonly found in primary forest, but also in secondary forest; both males and females have been reported carrying tadpoles to water.

REGION: NEA, NWA, SAM

Plate 14d
Spot-legged Poison-dart Frog
Epipedobates pictus

ID: Small (to 2.5 cm, 1 in); dull greenish gray to dark brown or, more commonly, black with distinctive narrow yellow or metallic green stripe across tip of snout, continuing to groin; shorter yellow or metallic green stripe runs along lower jaw from under eye to upper arm; small yellow spot in armpit, a second in groin; underside blue and black.

HABITAT: Terrestrial, active by day; common in second-growth forests and forest edges; individuals frequently sleep on leaves of low herbs at night; males carry tadpoles to isolated pools or streams.

REGION: NEA, NWA, SAM, PAN

Plate 14 289

a Amazon Rocket Frog

b Río Madeira Poison-dart Frog

c Brilliant-thighed Poison-dart Frog

d Spot-legged Poison-dart Frog

Plate 15a

Amazon River Frog
(also called Amazon Bullfrog)
Rana palmipes

ID: Large (to 12.6 cm, 5 in); olive-tan to green with smooth skin; robust hind limbs; usually with small brown or black spots; rear surfaces of legs mottled pale yellow and black; underneath cream to pale yellow with small black spots; pointed snout; distinct tympanum (external ear disc) almost as large as eye; fingers lack webbing, but toes nearly fully webbed; distinct skin folds along upper sides of body.

HABITAT: Terrestrial, active both day and night; commonly found in forest and open areas near ponds, lakes, swamps, and slow-moving streams.

REGION: NEA, NWA, SAM

Plate 15b

Bolivian Bleating Frog
Hamptophryne boliviana

ID: Small (to 4.4 cm, 1.8 in); tan to reddish brown with moderately robust body and pointed snout; large brown blotch in center of back, with or without faint narrow, white stripe running down middle of back; sides of body dark brown; throat dark brown with white flecks, belly white with brown spots; fingers and toes not webbed.

HABITAT: Terrestrial, nocturnal; found in primary and secondary forest; breeds at shallow, temporary ponds in forest.

REGION: NEA, NWA, SAM

Plate 15c

Swimming Frog
(also called Paradoxical Frog)
Pseudis paradoxa

ID: Medium-sized (to 5.8 cm, 2.3 in); green with brown markings; dark line on head running from nostril through eye to tympanum (external ear); pale yellow and black reticulations on lower surfaces of thighs; fingers not webbed, toes fully webbed; body stout; long hind legs.

HABITAT: Fully aquatic; lives and breeds in permanent marshes and ponds.

REGION: NEA, NWA, SAM, PAN

Plate 15d

Surinam Toad
Pipa pipa

ID: Large (to 17.1 cm, 6.8 in); bizarre-looking; tan to brown with flattened body and broad, triangular head; usually with darker brown blotches; skin bumpy; snout pointed; eyes tiny; fingers not webbed, toes fully webbed; tips of fingers split into two; dark T-shaped mark on chest.

HABITAT: Fully aquatic; most often found in ponds and swamps in forest.

REGION: NEA, NWA, SAM

Plate 15   291

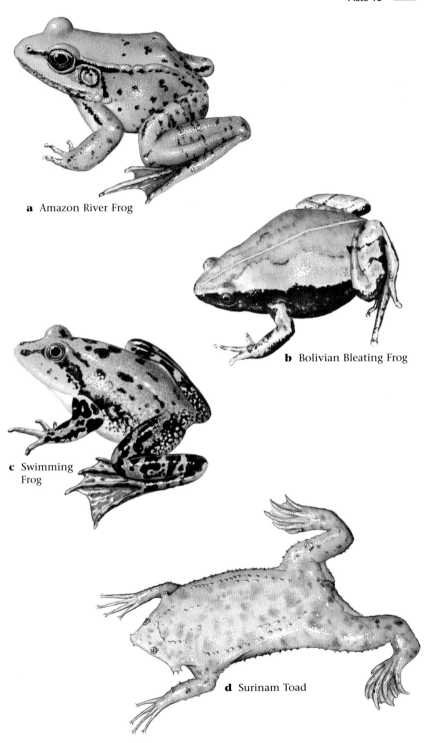

a Amazon River Frog

b Bolivian Bleating Frog

c Swimming Frog

d Surinam Toad

Plate 16a
Spectacled Caiman
Caiman crocodilus

ID: Medium-sized (to 2 m, 6.5 ft, although most are smaller); brown or olive-brown, often with wide black bars on body and tail; *spectacled* refers to the bony ridges between the eyes.

HABITAT: Forests, in or near streams, swamps, ponds, lakes, and rivers; nocturnal.

REGION: NEA, NWA, SAM, PAN

Note: Regulated for conservation purposes; CITES Appendix II listed.

Plate 16b
Black Caiman
Caiman niger

ID: Large (to 6 m, 19.5 ft, but most less than 4 m, 13 ft); very dark olive, brown, or, most often, blackish, with white markings or partial bands; snout broad and rounded; juveniles have yellow bands on body and tail.

HABITAT: Large bodies of water, mostly large lakes, in forest; also large rivers and swampy areas near lakes, rivers; nocturnal.

REGION: NEA, NWA, SAM

Note: This species is endangered, CITES Appendix I listed.

Plate 16c
Smooth-fronted Caiman
Paleosuchus trigonatus

ID: Small (to 1.5 m, 4.9 ft); moderately rounded snout; dark olive with darker bands on body and tail; often with lighter blotches on sides of jaws.

HABITAT: Larger streams, small rivers, small ponds, and swamps in forest; nocturnal; also on forest floor, where it forages.

REGION: NEA, NWA, SAM

Note: Regulated for conservation purposes; CITES Appendix II listed.

Plate 16d
Yellowfoot Tortoise
Geochelone denticulata

ID: Large (to 57 cm, 23 in, but most smaller); moderately domed shell; distinctly textured, raised concentric "growth rings" on each upper shell plate; upper shell dull brown to black, usually with pale tan to yellow area at center of each plate; scales on front limbs yellow to orange; rear limbs with stubby, elephant-like feet.

HABITAT: Terrestrial in forest; day- and perhaps night-active.

REGION: NEA, NWA, SAM, PAN

Note: Regulated for conservation purposes; CITES Appendix II listed.

Plate 16e
Yellow-spotted River Turtle
Podocnemis unifilis

ID: Large (to 68 cm, 27 in; males much smaller than females, to only half maximum size); olive to brown, with slightly domed, fairly smooth shell; limbs and head uniformly olive to light brown, except for several yellow spots on head and snout; underside pale yellow.

HABITAT: Ponds, lakes, rivers, and swamps; diurnal; basks on logs in water.

REGION: NEA, NWA, SAM

Note: Regulated for conservation purposes; CITES Appendix II listed.

Plate 16   293

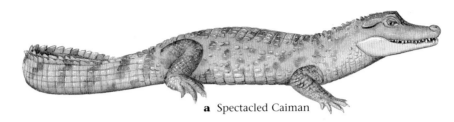

a Spectacled Caiman

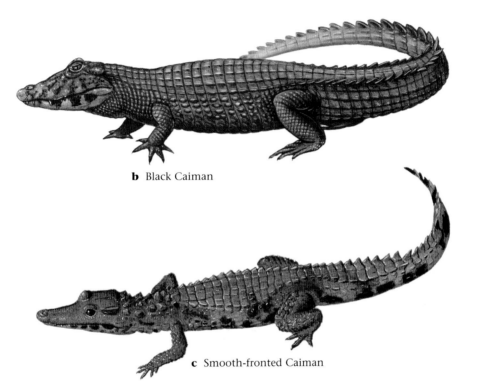

b Black Caiman

c Smooth-fronted Caiman

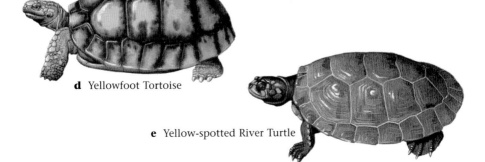

d Yellowfoot Tortoise

e Yellow-spotted River Turtle

Plate 17a
Twist-necked Turtle
Platemys platycephala
ID: Medium-sized (to 15 cm, 6 in); flat, with two ridges on upper shell; olive to dark brown upper shell; head bright yellow.

HABITAT: Forest streams, swamps, ponds; active by day; somewhat terrestrial.

REGION: NEA, NWA, SAM

Plate 17b
Matamata
Chelus fimbriatus
ID: Large (to 40 cm, 16 in); broad, upper shell flat with three longitudinal ridges; head broad, with fleshy proboscis on snout; snout and back part of head pale orange-tan; rest of head and limbs dark brown; upper shell dark brown with yellowish tan stripe running down center; shell often with thick layer of algae.

HABITAT: Rivers, creeks, oxbow lakes.

REGION: NEA, NWA, SAM

Plate 17c
Scorpion Mud Turtle
(also called Amazon Mud Turtle)
Kinosternon scorpioides
ID: Medium-sized (to 17 cm, 6.8 in); high-domed shell bearing three longitudinal keels (ridges); brown above, yellowish-brown below; often with orange or yellow spots on head; toes on front and hind legs webbed; males with sharp claw at tip of tail.

HABITAT: Aquatic, in forest; day-active.

REGION: NEA, NWA, SAM

Plate 17d
Ornate Thirst Snake
(also called Catesby's Snail-eater)
Dipsas catesbyi
ID: Small (to 70 cm, 28 in); reddish brown, fairly slender; large, paired, darker brown oval spots, each surrounded by white border, along sides; black head rounded with white line across blunt snout; white belly with irregular black markings; slightly larger row of scales runs along backbone.

HABITAT: Forest; on vegetation 1 to 4 m (3 to 13 ft) above ground; nocturnal.

REGION: NEA, NWA, SAM

Plate 17e
Big-headed Thirst Snake
(also called Amazon Snail-eater)
Dipsas indica
ID: Medium-sized (to 97 cm, 39 in); head blunt, brown with pale yellow and dark brown streaks; body gray or grayish brown with dark brown triangular-shaped blotches that are wider near the bottom; throat pale yellow, belly dark brown.

HABITAT: Arboreal, on branches or leaves in primary or secondary forest; nocturnal.

REGION: NEA, NWA, SAM

Plate 17 295

a Twist-necked Turtle

b Matamata

c Scorpion Mud Turtle

d Ornate Thirst Snake

e Big-headed Thirst Snake

Plate 18 (*See also*: Colubrid snakes, p. 105)

Plate 18a

Striped Sharpnose Snake
Xenoxybelis argenteus

ID: Medium-sized (to 1 m, 3.3 ft); slender, with pointed head and snout; dull green and tan stripes run lengthwise down body; green and white stripes run lengthwise on belly; body rounded (not flattened) in cross-section; tail long, often 70% of body length.

HABITAT: Arboreal in secondary primary forest; active during the day, usually in vegetation, but sometimes on ground; sleep on low vegetation at night.

REGION: NEA, NWA, SAM

Plate 18b

Brown Vinesnake
Oxybelis aeneus

ID: Long (to 2 m, 6.5 ft); very thin body, elongated head; color from gray to brown with indistinct markings of tiny black and white flecks; sides and underneath of head yellow or white; eyes yellow to beige.

HABITAT: Arboreal, often found in open situations; day-active.

REGION: NEA, NWA, SAM

Plate 18c

Common Cat-eyed Snake
Leptodeira annulata

ID: Small (to 75 cm, 30 in); tan to light brown or reddish brown, with zig-zag, wavy dark brown stripe running lengthwise along upper body; stripe usually broken into unconnected blotches on rear portion of body; creamy white to pinkish tan belly.

HABITAT: Arboreal in secondary and some primary forest; nocturnal.

REGION: NEA, NWA, SAM, PAN

Plate 18d

Blunt-headed Treesnake
Imantodes cenchoa

ID: Medium-sized (to 1.1 m, 3.6 ft) and slender with bulbous, blunt head and large eyes with elliptical (cat-like) pupils; body noticeably flattened from side-to-side, with larger row of scales running along backbone; body with alternating bands of dark chocolate brown and cream or tan; belly tan or cream with brown flecks.

HABITAT: Primary and secondary forest; on vegetation 1 to 4 m (3 to 13 ft) above ground; nocturnal.

REGION: NEA, NWA, SAM

Plate 18e

Olive Whipsnake
(also called Brown Sipo)
Chironius fuscus

ID: Medium-sized (to 1 m, 3.3 ft); juveniles tan or gray with brown blotches; adults brown above, yellow below. Small juveniles have white throat and chin; these areas become progressively more yellow with age; bright yellow in adults.

HABITAT: Mostly in secondary forest, but also in primary forest and forest edge; active by day; sleep on vegetation at night, at heights up to 4 m (13 ft).

REGION: NEA, NWA, SAM

Plate 18   297

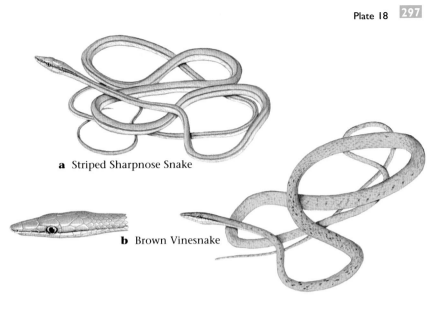

a Striped Sharpnose Snake

b Brown Vinesnake

c Common Cat-eyed Snake

d Blunt-headed Treesnake

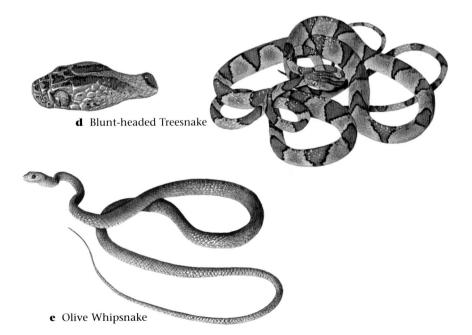

e Olive Whipsnake

Plate 19a
Common Mussurana
Clelia clelia
ID: Large and long (to 2+ m, 6.5+ ft); with large shiny scales; adults black with cream-colored belly; juveniles (up to 50 cm, 20 in) red (with black scale edges) with black snout and white neck-band.

HABITAT: Mostly in forests; terrestrial; day- and night-active.

REGION: NEA, NWA, SAM

Note: Regulated for conservation purposes; CITES Appendix II listed.

Plate 19b
Tropical Ratsnake
(also called Common Tiger Ratsnake)
Spilotes pullatus
ID: Large (to 2+ m, 6.5+ ft); large scales; irregular bands of black with yellow markings alternating with irregular yellow bands with black markings.

HABITAT: Mostly forests; terrestrial, but also found in low vegetation up to 3 m (10 ft) high; day-active.

REGION: NEA, NWA, SAM

Plate 19c
Common False Viper
Xenodon rabdocephalus
ID: Medium-sized (to 90 cm, 36 in); light brown to dark brown, with brown or black bands; some color forms closely resemble the venomous Fer-de-Lance.

HABITAT: Primary and secondary forest; terrestrial; active day and night.

REGION: NEA, NWA, SAM

Plate 19d
Common False Coralsnake
Erythrolamprus aesculapii
ID: Small (to 70 cm, 28 in); snout yellow-tan, followed by broad black band enclosing eyes, then yellow band; neck black; body pattern of red-black-yellow-black begins behind neck; colors extend onto belly; rear margins of the scales in the yellow and red rings are tipped with black.

HABITAT: Primary and secondary forests; terrestrial; day-active.

REGION: NEA, NWA, SAM

Plate 19e
South American Water Snake
Helicops angulatus
ID: Small (to 60 cm, 24 in) but fairly stout-bodied; alternating bands of light brown (or olive) and dark brown on upper body, darker bands being slightly wider; pale yellow, pink, or orange belly with brown to black markings extending from bands on upper surface; small eyes.

HABITAT: Small ponds, streams in forest, rivers; nocturnal.

REGION: NEA, NWA, SAM, PAN

IM

a Common Mussurana

b Tropical Ratsnake

c Common False Viper

d Common False Coralsnake

e South American Water Snake

Plate 20a
Brazilian False Water Cobra
Hydrodynastes gigas
ID: Large (to 2.5 m, 8.1 ft); thick-bodied; yellowish brown to bronze with black saddle-shaped markings on back (saddles on front half appear as paired black crossbands, often fused to form irregular rings or open saddles; on back half of body, centers of open saddles become progressively darker and eventually become wide black bands); conspicuous black bands along sides of head and neck; eyes relatively small.

HABITAT: Semi-aquatic, usually found in shallow, still water; nocturnal.

REGION: PAN

Plate 20b
Red-tailed Boa
(also called Boa Constrictor)
Boa constrictor
ID: Large (to 4 m, 13 ft, but most are much smaller); stout-bodied; tan to light brown upper body with dark brown transverse markings that outline oval-shaped tan markings; triangular head with wide, dark brown band running from nostril through eye and onto neck; cream-colored belly with scattered brown or black flecks and spots; tiny white bony spurs protrude from body near base of tail.

HABITAT: Forests; mostly terrestrial, sometimes found in trees; active day and night.

REGION: NEA, NWA, SAM, PAN

Note: Regulated for conservation purposes; CITES Appendix II listed.

Plate 20c
Amazon Tree Boa
Corallus hortulanus
ID: Medium-sized (to 1.25 m, 4 ft); body slightly flattened from side-to-side; gray or brown, usually with distinct dark brown circular or oval-shaped markings outlined with cream; some individuals solid yellow, pink, or red; cream to tan belly with scattered darker markings; scales on upper and lower lips have obvious, deep, heat-sensing pits.

HABITAT: Arboreal in primary but also secondary forest; often found along shores of creeks, small rivers, and oxbows; nocturnal.

REGION: NEA, CMF, NWA, SAM

Plate 20d
Rainbow Boa
Epicrates cenchria
ID: Medium-sized (to 2 m, 6.5 ft, but most are smaller); rounded body (in cross-section); three dark stripes on head; body brown to reddish brown or orange with roughly circular or oval pale tan, yellow, or orange markings, outlined in black; under strong light, scales reflect a rainbow of iridescence; creamy white belly.

HABITAT: Mostly terrestrial, somewhat arboreal in forest; mostly active by night, somewhat by day.

REGION: NEA, NWA, SAM

Note: Regulated for conservation purposes; CITES Appendix II listed.

Plate 20e
Common Anaconda
Eunectes murinus
ID: Very large (to 10+ m, 33+ ft, but most are much smaller); stout-bodied; gray, yellow, or tan, some with green tint, with alternating pairs of large dark brown or black blotches; lighter yellow or tan belly with scattered small dark markings; although the Common Anaconda ties with the Reticulated Python for being the largest snake on Earth, the anaconda is more massive.

HABITAT: Mostly aquatic in large lakes, rivers, and swamps, but sometimes on land near water.

REGION: NEA, CMF, NWA, SAM

Plate 20

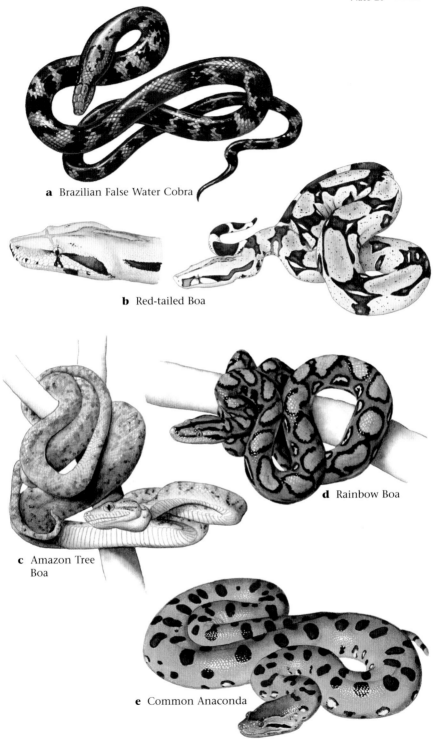

a Brazilian False Water Cobra

b Red-tailed Boa

c Amazon Tree Boa

d Rainbow Boa

e Common Anaconda

Plate 21a
South American Coralsnake
Micrurus lemniscatus
ID: Medium-sized (to 1.2 m, 3.9 ft); rings on body in triads: black-yellow-black-red-black-yellow-black beginning with black snout; red and black rings about equal in width, yellow rings narrower.

HABITAT: Terrestrial and fossorial (burrowing), found in primary and secondary forest and in open situations; active day and night.

REGION: NEA, NWA, SAM

Plate 21b
Neuwied's Lancehead
Bothrops neuwiedi
ID: Medium-sized (to 90 cm, 36 in, but most not more than 70 cm, 28 in); conspicuous dark band running from behind eye to corner of mouth; background color reddish brown, light brown, or gray; double row of dark brown markings (trapezoid-shaped) on back; front and back margins of trapezoids tan; two small brown blotches below each trapezoid; head flat; pit between eye and nostril.

HABITAT: Found both in forest and savannah in non-flooded areas; terrestrial; nocturnal.

REGION: SAM, PAN

Plate 21c
Fer-de-Lance
(also called South American Lancehead)
Bothrops atrox
ID: Medium-sized (to 2 m, 6.5 ft, but most are much smaller), medium-bodied; rough scales and distinctly lance-shaped head; dull olive, tan, or brown with pattern of irregular darker and lighter markings, which often form series of "X" shapes; dark bands extend from behind each eye to sides of head and neck; cream to yellow belly with irregular darker markings.

HABITAT: Forest, and often near human habitations; terrestrial; mostly active at night, somewhat by day.

REGION: NEA, NWA, SAM

Plate 21d
Amazon Bushmaster
Lachesis muta
ID: Large (to 3.6 m, 11.7 ft); rough-scaled, with lance-shaped head; light brown, pinkish tan, or golden tan, with diamond-shaped, dark brown or black markings outlined by light tan or cream; top of head brown; black stripe runs from behind eye to angle of jaw; lips tan; distinct raised ridge along backbone; cream-colored belly; longest viper on Earth.

HABITAT: Primary forest and forest edges; terrestrial; nocturnal.

REGION: NEA, NWA, SAM

Plate 21   303

a South American Coralsnake
(VENOMOUS)

b Neuwied's Lancehead
(VENOMOUS)

c Fer-de-Lance
(VENOMOUS)

d Amazon
Bushmaster
(VENOMOUS)

Plate 22a

Speckled Worm Lizard
Amphisbaena fuliginosa

ID: Long (to 37 cm, 14.8 in); worm-like with no legs; both ends of body blunt; eyes reduced to small spots; dull grayish white with slight pinkish or bluish tint in some individuals; black bars and spots, less conspicuous underneath.

HABITAT: Found in leaf litter and soil of primary forest; terrestrial; day-active.

REGION: NEA, NWA, SAM

Plate 22b

Amazon Streak Lizard
(also called Trinidad Gecko)
Gonatodes humeralis

ID: Small (snout–vent length to 4.2 cm, 1.7 in); vertical light bar just in front of front legs; tail banded gray and black; males salt and pepper mixture of yellow and black, with some red scales on head and back, half circle of cream on neck, and gray or yellow patches on head and neck; flank with or without red and/or black spots; females gray or olive-brown with black flecks.

HABITAT: Primary and secondary forest, and especially abundant in disturbed forests and edge situations; arboreal; day-active; usually found in shade, on tree trunks; at night sleep on leaves or small branches.

REGION: NEA, NWA, SAM

Plate 22c

Amazon Dwarf Gecko
(also called Amazon Pygmy Gecko)
Pseudogonatodes guianensis

ID: Tiny (snout–vent length to 3 cm, 1.2 in); covered with fine granular scales; fingers and toes short; color variable, ranging from grayish brown to dark brown; some with dark stripes running down length of body; conspicuous pale yellow to rust curved band behind head; tan, gray, or white belly.

HABITAT: Most often found in leaf litter in primary or secondary forest; frequently found near creeks or swampy areas; terrestrial; day-active.

REGION: NEA, NWA, SAM

Plate 22d

Common House Gecko
Hemidactylus mabouia

ID: Medium-sized (snout–vent length to 6.8 cm, 2.7 in); slender; long, fragile tail (breaks easily); large toe pads; large eyes; light to dark tan or gray, with darker tan or brown markings and bands on tail.

HABITAT: Commonly seen in and on outsides of houses, where they are attracted to insects coming to lights; nocturnal.

REGION: NEA, NWA, SAM

Plate 22e

Turnip-tailed Gecko
Thecadactylus rapicauda

ID: Medium-sized (snout–vent length to 12 cm, 4.8 in); large eyes; body robust, relatively flat; tail short and thick; color variable, usually gray or brown with irregular spots, blotches, and flecks; skin covered with granular scales; no eyelids; webbing between fingers and toes; greatly expanded tips of toes.

HABITAT: Primary or secondary forest, open areas, and inside houses near forest; arboreal; nocturnal; by day often found under loose flaps of bark, in hollow trees, or in fallen tree trunks.

REGION: NEA, NWA, SAM

Plate 22 305

a Speckled Worm Lizard

b Amazon Streak Lizard

c Amazon Dwarf Gecko

d Common House Gecko

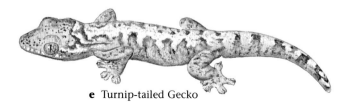

e Turnip-tailed Gecko

Plate 23a
Green Iguana
Iguana iguana
ID: Large (snout–vent length to 50 cm, 20 in); prominent head crest and throat fan (especially males); bright green to dull olive with irregular darker crossbands; tail banded, extremely long; distinctive, large round scale present just below ear opening; juveniles bright green, becoming darker with age.

HABITAT: Forest, especially along rivers; adults mostly arboreal but juveniles often found close to or on ground; day-active.

REGION: NEA, NWA, SAM, PAN

Note: Regulated for conservation purposes; CITES Appendix II listed.

Plate 23b
Slender Anole
Norops fuscoauratus
ID: Small (snout–vent length to 5 cm, 2 in); slender, long limbs and tail; snout relatively long and blunt; gray, brown, or tan; females often have pale tan lengthwise stripe running down center of body; chin, throat, belly pale gray with brown flecks; male dewlap (throat fan) large, variable in color (shades of red, yellow, olive, and gray, or often pale creamy yellow) with white scales and white border.

HABITAT: Primary and secondary forest, forest edges, and clearings; often found foraging on ground or on tree trunks by day; at night, sleep horizontally or head-down on vegetation usually less than 1 m (3 ft) above ground.

REGION: NEA, NWA, SAM

Plate 23c
Goldenscale Anole
Norops chrysolepis
ID: Medium-sized (snout–vent length to 8.6 cm, 3.4 in); large head, short snout; long tail; upper body tan or brown with darker markings of diagonal bars or semi-circles; usually males and occasionally females have narrow yellowish tan stripe running down center of back to base of tail; dark brown bar between eyes; male dewlap (throat fan) blue with white flecks, bordered by red.

HABITAT: Usually found on ground or on low vegetation such as tree trunks, in primary and secondary forest; day-active.

REGION: SAM

Plate 23d
Bark Anole
Norops ortonii
ID: Small (snout–vent length to 5.7 cm, 2.3 in); gray or brown, often marbled; some with tan stripe running down center of back; male dewlap (throat fan) orange with yellow spots; individuals change color from light to dark.

HABITAT: Most common in relatively open situations such as disturbed forest and edge areas, secondary growth, and cultivated areas; usually found on vegetation, but sometimes on ground; day-active.

REGION: NEA, NWA, SAM

Plate 23 **307**

a Green Iguana

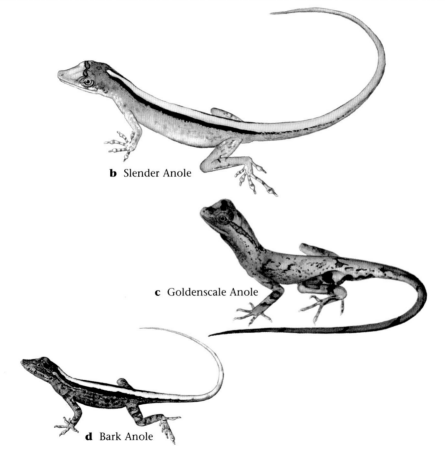

b Slender Anole

c Goldenscale Anole

d Bark Anole

Plate 24a

Collared Tree Lizard
Tropidurus plica

ID: Moderately large (snout–vent length to 18 cm, 7.2 in); predominantly green with black markings usually forming V-shaped bands on body; head may have salmon or olive-green color; black bands on limbs and tail.

HABITAT: Primary and secondary forest; day-active, arboreal, mostly found on large tree trunks; sleep on low vegetation at night.

REGION: NEA, NWA, SAM

Plate 24b

Blue-lipped Tree Lizard
Tropidurus umbra ochrocollaris

ID: Medium-sized (snout–vent length to 10 cm, 4 in); relatively small head and distinctive blue mouth lining; row of large spiny scales (crest) running down center of back; color of males highly variable, from bright green with small black spots to dull olive-green or olive tan, as in females; narrow black collar; tail long and slender.

HABITAT: Primary and secondary forest; day-active, arboreal, on tree trunks; sleep at night, on horizontal branches less than 1.5 m (4.5 ft) above ground.

REGION: NEA, NWA, SAM

Plate 24c

Black-striped Shade Lizard
Cercosaura ocellata

ID: Small (snout–vent length to 6.5 cm, 2.6 in); brown with black spots on back; usually with white spots bordered with black along side of body; often with cream stripes running down length of body; flanks ranging from orange to brown; tail long.

HABITAT: Most often found on ground, though occasionally on low vegetation, in primary and secondary forest; often found in sunny spots; day-active.

REGION: NEA, NWA, SAM

Plate 24d

Large-scaled Shade Lizard
Alopoglossus angulatus

ID: Small (snout–vent length to 6 cm, 2.4 in); upper surface of head amber or brown; upper surface of body brown with or without faint black spots, with or without amber or cinnamon stripe running partway down body from eye; underside of body cream; tail long.

HABITAT: Forests and open situations, usually near water; terrestrial; day-active.

REGION: NEA, NWA, SAM

Plate 24e

Elegant Eyed Lizard
Prionodactylus argulus

ID: Small (snout–vent length to 4.5 cm, 1.8 in); pointed snout; head and back brown, with reddish or brown stripes running along side of body; underside cream; tail bright orange to red; distinctive white spots bordered by black along side of body.

HABITAT: Forests, often found among leaf litter; terrestrial; day-active.

REGION: NEA, SAM

Plate 24   309

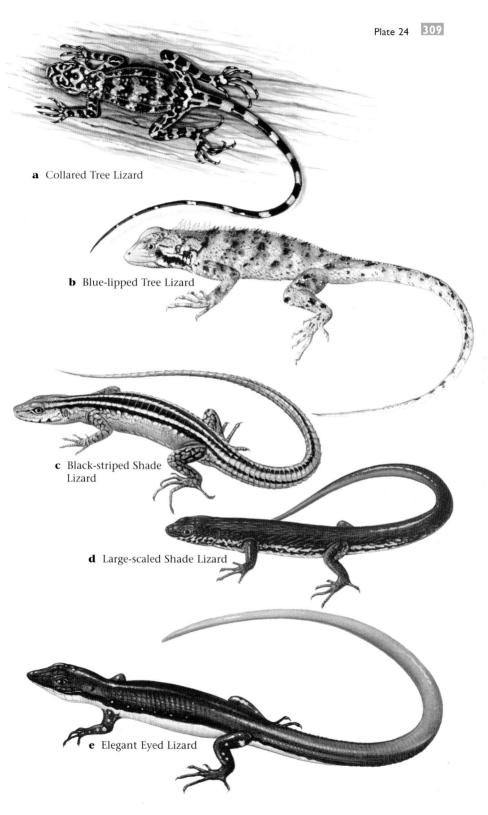

a Collared Tree Lizard

b Blue-lipped Tree Lizard

c Black-striped Shade Lizard

d Large-scaled Shade Lizard

e Elegant Eyed Lizard

Plate 25a

Amazon Racerunner
(also called Giant Ameiva)
Ameiva ameiva

ID: Moderately large (snout–vent length to 17 cm, 6.8 in); slender, with angular pointed head and snout; long tail; powerful jaws; color variable and changes with age; juveniles often completely brown or brown and green; adult body and sides patterned with bright green; light and dark stripes and spots run lengthwise along body; belly bluish white.

HABITAT: Terrestrial, basks in sun on ground in clearings, riverbanks, and forest edges; day-active.

REGION: NEA, NWA, SAM, PAN

Plate 25b

Spix's Kentropyx
Kentropyx calcarata

ID: Medium-sized (snout–vent length to 11 cm, 4.4 in); upper surface of head and neck black, back mahogany-red; or head brown, back cinnamon-brown to olive-brown; frequently with two rows of black spots running down length of sides of body; green stripe running down center of body, with yellow-green stripe on either side; large males often lack central stripe or have inconspicuous stripes.

HABITAT: Forests; usually in open, sunny areas such as treefall gaps, clearings, and forest edges; terrestrial; day-active.

REGION: NEA, SAM

Plate 25c

Golden Tegu
(also called Black Tegu)
Tupinambus teguixin

ID: Large (snout–vent length to 40 cm, 16 in); moderately elongate head, blunt snout; strong limbs; upper body black and either pale yellow, brown, or white; scales shiny; irregular crossbands on back become wider on tail; underside cream.

HABITAT: Found in forests and clearings; frequently seen near water; terrestrial; day-active; retreats into burrows at night.

REGION: NEA, NWA, SAM

Note: Regulated for conservation purposes; CITES Appendix II listed.

Plate 25d

Paraguay Caiman Lizard
Dracaena paraguayensis

ID: Large (total length to 1.2 m, 4 ft); semi-aquatic; tail similar to that of caiman, flattened and with double crest; head large; olive-brown, with darker transverse bars across body; indistinct crossbands on flanks; underside yellow, marbled brown.

HABITAT: Wetlands; terrestrial, but often found in water; day-active.

REGION: PAN

Note: Regulated for conservation purposes; CITES Appendix II listed.

Plate 25e

Black-spotted Skink
Mabuya nigropunctata

ID: Medium-sized (snout–vent length to 11.3 cm, 4.5 in); rather stocky; smooth, shiny scales; copper-brown or brown-gray with bronze sheen; black stripe running along each side of body; underside greenish white or bluish white.

HABITAT: Terrestrial and on logs, but also found on low tree branches; often seen sunning; most active during periods of sunshine; day-active.

REGION: NEA, NWA, SAM

Plate 25 311

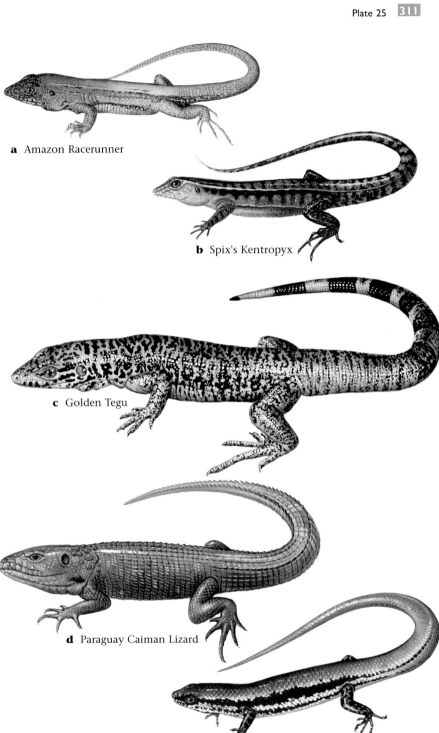

a Amazon Racerunner

b Spix's Kentropyx

c Golden Tegu

d Paraguay Caiman Lizard

e Black-spotted Skink

Plate 26a

Neotropic Cormorant
Phalacrocorax brasilianus
ID: Large (69 cm, 2.3 ft); all black; long neck.

HABITAT: Swimming duck-like in water, sitting upright on dead branches in or near the water, or flying in flocks of long lines or "V" formation on or over freshwater reservoirs, rivers and lakes and along the coast.

REGION: NEA, CMF, NWA, SAM, PAN

Plate 26b

Anhinga
Anhinga anhinga
ID: Large (84 cm, 2.8 ft); black with long straight bill and very long and slender neck; large silverish patches on upperwings of adults. Immature brownish.

HABITAT: Individuals or pairs on lakes or on vegetation along rivers and coastal mangroves. Occasionally soars on broad wings high overhead.

REGION: NEA, CMF, NWA, SAM, PAN

Plate 26c

Large-billed Tern
Phaetusa simplex
ID: Medium-sized (38 cm, 1.3 ft); black, white, and gray wings in flight; large greenish yellow bill.

HABITAT: Larger rivers and occasionally oxbow lakes of the Amazon and larger marshes in the Pantanal.

REGION: NEA, NWA, SAM, PAN

Plate 26d

Yellow-billed Tern
Sterna superciliaris
ID: Medium-sized (25 cm, 10 in); white wings with black tips; slender yellow bill.

HABITAT: Larger rivers and occasionally oxbow lakes of the Amazon and larger marshes in the Pantanal.

REGION: NEA, NWA, SAM, PAN

Plate 26e

Black Skimmer
Rynchops nigra
ID: Medium-sized (44 cm, 1.4 ft); black on top and white below with an immense red and black bill. Peculiar low flight over water's surface with lower part of bill "skimming" the water.

HABITAT: Coastal estuaries and larger inland rivers.

REGION: NEA, CMF, NWA, SAM, PAN

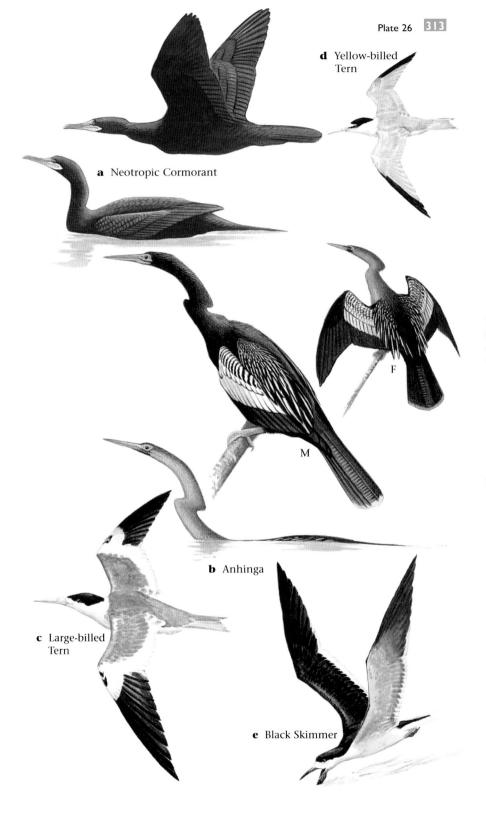

Plate 26 313

d Yellow-billed Tern

a Neotropic Cormorant

F

M

b Anhinga

c Large-billed Tern

e Black Skimmer

Plate 27a

Boat-billed Heron
Cochlearius cochlearius

ID: Large (49 cm, 1.6 ft); chunky, with monstrously wide bill.

HABITAT: Roosts by day in small group or alone in thick vegetation along water-courses; feeds at night on muddy shorelines, marshes and vegetated water edges.

REGION: NEA, NWA, SAM, PAN

Plate 27b

Black-crowned Night Heron
Nycticorax nycticorax

ID: Large (60 cm, 2 ft); bill relatively short but slender; adults with black crown and back; gray wings; whitish gray underparts; immature streaked brown and tan.

HABITAT: Coastal mangroves, river mouths, edges of lakes, marshes and rivers; usually roosts in dense vegetation near water during the daytime in small groups; most easily seen flying overhead at dusk and giving a loud and harsh squawk; mainly active at night.

REGION: NEA, CMF, NWA, SAM, PAN

Plate 27c

Snowy Egret
Egretta thula

ID: Large (61 cm, 2 ft); adults all white with black bill, legs and bright yellow feet.

HABITAT: Coastal estuaries, river mouths, lakes, marshes, and rivers; usually solitary.

REGION: NEA, CMF, NWA, SAM, PAN

Plate 27d

Cattle Egret
Bubulcus ibis

ID: Large (51 cm, 1.7 ft); adults all white with orange-yellow bill and greenish legs. During the breeding season the back becomes pinkish orange and the legs and bill reddish.

HABITAT: Marshes, pastures, and open areas along rivers and lakes, often in flocks and regularly associated with cattle and horses.

REGION: NEA, CMF, NWA, SAM, PAN

Plate 27e

Great Egret
(also called Common Egret)
Ardea alba

ID: Large (1 m, 3.3 ft); all white with yellow bill and black legs.

HABITAT: Coastal estuaries, river mouths, lakes, marshes, and rivers; usually solitary.

REGION: NEA, CMF, NWA, SAM, PAN

Plate 27 315

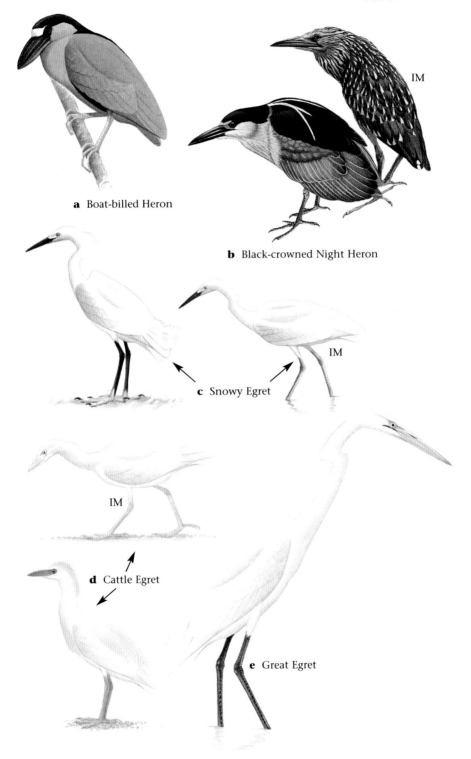

a Boat-billed Heron

IM

b Black-crowned Night Heron

IM

c Snowy Egret

IM

d Cattle Egret

e Great Egret

Plate 28a
Cocoi Heron
Ardea cocoi
ID: Large (1.2 m, 4 ft); white neck and throat, grayish body, top and sides of head all black.

HABITAT: Solitary in coastal estuaries, mangroves, and inland river banks, marshes, and oxbow lakes.

REGION: NEA, CMF, NWA, SAM, PAN

Plate 28b
Whistling Heron
Syrigma sibilatrix
ID: Large (55 cm, 1.8 ft); crown slaty gray; bare skin around eye blue; bill pinkish; throat and neck white; breast buffy; wings pinkish; back gray-blue.

HABITAT: Solitary or in pairs in small marshes, wet grassy areas and occasionally dry pastures; often flies with its neck outstretched.

REGION: PAN

Plate 28c
Rufescent Tiger-heron
Tigrisoma lineatum
ID: Large (70 cm, 2.3 ft); chunky; adult chestnut, black and white; immature buffy and white with barred back.

HABITAT: Solitary in thick vegetation along watercourses.

REGION: NEA, NWA, SAM, PAN

Plate 28d
Capped Heron
Pilherodius pileatus
ID: Large (60 cm, 2 ft); white body, cream-colored neck, black cap and bare blue skin on face.

HABITAT: Solitary in vegetation and shallow water along forested streams and lakes.

REGION: NEA, NWA, SAM, PAN

Plate 28e
Striated Heron
(also called Green-backed Heron)
Butorides striatus
ID: Medium-sized (40 cm, 1.3 ft); gray neck, greenish back. Gives loud high-pitched squawk when frightened into flight.

HABITAT: Solitary low in vegetation near water's surface of mangroves, swamps, small rivers and oxbow lakes.

REGION: NEA, CMF, NWA, SAM, PAN

Plate 28f
Little Blue Heron
Egretta caerulea
ID: Medium-sized (60 cm, 2 ft); slate blue body and dark purple head and neck; gray blue bill with black tip; immature white with black-tipped bill and often with small dark patches of feathers.

HABITAT: Solitary in vegetation near water's surface of mangroves, swamps, small rivers and oxbow lakes.

REGION: NEA, CMF, NWA, SAM

Plate 28　317

b Whistling Heron

a Cocoi Heron

c Rufescent
Tiger-heron

IM

d Capped Heron

e Striated Heron

f Little Blue Heron

Plate 29a

Jabiru Stork
Jabiru mycteria

ID: Huge (1.4 m, 4.6 ft); all white body, wings and tail; bare blackish head and thick neck with red collar; huge black bill upturned.

HABITAT: Solitary or in pairs during the wet season but often in large flocks during the dry season in marshes and swampy areas, ponds, and streams. Often soars high overhead on broad wings and with neck streched out. (Similar but smaller (95 cm, 3.1 ft), the white-bodied Wood Stork, *Mycteria americana*, has naked grayish brown head and down-turned bill; black wings and tail. It also occurs in marshy habitats but often in flocks.)

REGION: NEA, NWA, SAM, PAN

Plate 29b

Maguari Stork
Ciconia maguari

ID: Large (1.3 m, 4.3 ft) and heron-like; feathered white head, neck, and body; black back, wings, and tail; reddish legs and bare skin around eye; bill straight.

HABITAT: Solitary or small groups in swampy areas, ponds, and dry upland fields primarily in the Pantanal; often soars high overhead.

REGION: NEA, NWA, SAM, PAN

Plate 29c

Green Ibis
Mesembrinis cayennensis

ID: Large (71 cm, 2.3 ft); dark green, with greenish, down-curved bill.

HABITAT: Solitary in trees along the edge of swampy areas, ponds, and streams. (The similar shaped but smaller (60 cm, 1.9 ft) Scarlet Ibis, *Eudocimus ruber*, of the coastal magroves is bright scarlet except for its blackish wings. It often roosts in large flocks on coastal islands.)

REGION: NEA, NWA, SAM, PAN

Plate 29d

Plumbeous Ibis
Harpiprion caerulescens

ID: Large (73 cm, 2.4 ft); dark gray with shaggy crest on back of neck and small white forehead; black, down-curved bill; red legs.

HABITAT: Solitary in wooded marshes and ponds.

REGION: PAN

Plate 29e

Buff-necked Ibis
Theristicus caudatus hyperorius

ID: Large (74 cm, 2.4 ft); buffy-yellow head and neck; gray back and wings; black belly; black down-curved bill; red legs.

HABITAT: Solitary or small groups in savannah, marshes, and river edges. Common in the Pantanal but difficult to find in the Amazon.

REGION: NEA, NWA, SAM, PAN

Plate 29f

Bare-faced Ibis
Phimosus infuscatus

ID: Large (50 cm, 1.6 ft); dark green, with dull pink, down-curved bill, bare skin around eye, and legs.

HABITAT: Swampy areas, ponds, streams in savannah and forest primarily in the Pantanal. Often in flocks.

REGION: NEA, NWA, SAM, PAN

Plate 29 319

a Jabiru Stork

b Maguari Stork

c Green Ibis

d Plumbeous Ibis

e Buff-necked Ibis

f Bare-faced Ibis

Plate 30a
Limpkin
Aramus guarauna
ID: Large (66 cm, 2.2 ft); dark brown with small white spots on head, neck, and back; grayish brown bill with dark tip.

HABITAT: Forest swamps, marshes, river islands, and mangroves.

REGION: NEA, CMF, NWA, SAM, PAN

Plate 30b
Roseate Spoonbill
Ajaia ajaja
ID: Large (86 cm, 2.8 ft); pink wings, tail and breast, crimson shoulders; white neck and back; head bare; bizarre bill flat and widened at tip.

HABITAT: Feeds in shallow freshwater marshes and coastal saltwater estuaries by swishing its bill from side to side as it walks through the shallows; bill filters out invertebrates and plant material. Immature dusky white with a hint of pink.

REGION: NEA, CMF, NWA, SAM, PAN

Plate 30c
Horned Screamer
Anhima cornuta
ID: Very large (91 cm, 3 ft); dark back, white belly; white wing-patch in flight obvious; call a deep, throaty gulp heard far away.

HABITAT: Swamps, marshes, and nearby tree-tops; individuals or pairs often soar high on broad wings.

REGION: NEA, NWA, SAM, PAN

Plate 30d
Southern Screamer
Chauna torquata
ID: Very large (86 cm, 3 ft); gray with black crest on head; call a loud goose-like honking.

HABITAT: Swamps, marshes, and nearby tree-tops.

REGION: NEA, NWA, SAM, PAN

Plate 30e
Greater Rhea
Rhea americana
ID: Very large (1.8 m, 5.9 ft); flightless; long stout legs and neck; gray with white belly and neck; male with black chest.

HABITAT: Open grassy plains.

REGION: PAN

Plate 30   321

a Limpkin

IM

b Roseate Spoonbill

c Horned Screamer

d Southern Screamer

e Greater Rhea

Plate 31a
Wattled Jacana
Jacana jacana
ID: Medium-sized (25 cm, 10 in); adults with bright yellow bill, rusty-colored body, yellow-green wings in flight and extremely long toes; immatures with white breast and bold white eyeline.

HABITAT: Grassy edges and lily pads of freshwater swamps and marshes.

REGION: NEA, NWA, SAM, PAN

Plate 31b
Sunbittern
Eurypyga helias
ID: Medium-sized (47 cm, 1.5 ft); slender neck, small head with bold stripes; in flight or during display the spread wings have a distinctive "sunburst" pattern.

HABITAT: Along forested streams and lakes.

REGION: NEA, NWA, SAM, PAN

Plate 31c
Hoatzin
Opisthocomus hoazin
ID: Large (64 cm, 2.1 ft); rusty colored with buffy breast; crest on head, large wings, long tail.

HABITAT: In small family groups along forested swamps, oxbow lakes and small rivers.

REGION: NEA, NWA, SAM

Plate 31d
Purple Gallinule
Porphyrio martinicus
ID: Large (33 cm, 1 ft); small chicken-like; blue-purple head, neck, and breast; greenish blue back, wings, and tail; red, pointed bill with yellow tip; pale blue shield on forehead. Immature white below and pale brown above.

HABITAT: Marshes and vegetated lake edges.

REGION: NEA, NWA, SAM, PAN

Plate 31e
Gray-necked Wood-rail
Aramides cajanea
ID: Large (37 cm, 2.5 ft); bright red legs, long bill, gray neck contrasting with rusty breast. Loud, rollicking voice, often in duets at sundown and sunrise.

HABITAT: Forested swampy areas.

REGION: NEA, NWA, SAM, PAN

Plate 31 323

IM

a Wattled Jacana

b Sunbittern

c Hoatzin

d Purple Gallinule

e Gray-necked Wood-rail

Plate 32a

Muscovy Duck
Cairina moschata

ID: Large (84 cm, 2.8 ft); black with red bare face (male); large white wing patches obvious in flight.

HABITAT: Forested swamps, rivers, and oxbow lakes.

REGION: NEA, NWA, SAM, PAN

Plate 32b

Brazilian Duck
(also called Brazilian Teal)
Amazonetta brasiliensis

ID: Medium-sized (42 cm, 1.4 ft); all brown with black tail and wings, conspicuous white triangle on trailing edge of wing in flight; male with dark red bill and black crown; female with white spot above eye, brown crown, and gray bill.

HABITAT: Ponds and marshes.

REGION: NEA, NWA, SAM, PAN

Plate 32c

Black-bellied Whistling Duck
Dendrocygna autumnalis

ID: Medium-sized (42 cm, 1.4 ft); chestnut-brown with gray-brown face, black belly and tail; bright red-orange bill and legs; bold white stripe in wings obvious in flight. (The similar White-faced Whistling Duck, *Dendrocygna viduata*, occurs uncommonly in both the Amazon and Pantanal, but its bold white face, dark bill, and all-dark wings in flight readily distinguish it.)

HABITAT: Ponds, marshes, and wooded streams.

REGION: NEA, NWA, SAM, PAN

Plate 32d

Least Grebe
Tachybaptus (Podiceps) dominicus

ID: Medium-sized (20 cm, 7.8 in); duck-like with small unmarked and pointed bill and yellow eyes; gray with black crown, back of neck, and throat in breeding plumage (whitish throat in nonbreeding plumage).

HABITAT: Densely vegetated lakes and marshes.

REGION: NEA, NWA, SAM, PAN

Plate 32e

Sungrebe
Heliornis fulica

ID: Medium-sized (29 cm, 11 in); duck-like with bold white stripes on head and neck.

HABITAT: Swims under overhanging vegetation along lakes and small rivers; in the Pantanal, often in open marshes with many water hyacinths; escapes by flying low over water, often skittering along the surface with its running feet.

REGION: NEA, NWA, SAM, PAN

Plate 32   325

b Brazilian Duck

a Muscovy Duck

non-breeding

d Least Grebe

e Sungrebe

c Black-bellied Whistling-Duck

Plate 33a
Black-necked Stilt
Himantopus mexicanus
ID: Medium-sized (37 cm, 1.2 ft); tall, slender with striking black and white body and pinkish red legs.

HABITAT: Inland ponds, coastal estuaries and mangrove swamps.

REGION: NEA, NWA, SAM, PAN

Plate 33b
Spotted Sandpiper
Actitis macularia
ID: Small (18 cm, 7 in); pale-breasted; bobs up and down while walking or resting; in flight, a long, thin white stripe on upperwing surface; flies with a twittering, stiff-winged beat low over the water's surface; the breast spots appear only on individuals preparing (March to April) to migrate to nesting areas in North America.

HABITAT: Solitary on rocks, branches and sandy beaches along rivers and lakes; some individuals present throughout the year.

REGION: NEA, NWA, SAM, PAN

Plate 33c
Solitary Sandpiper
Tringa solitaria
ID: Medium-sized (18 cm, 7 in); gray with brown streaks; white eyering; white barring on tail in flight and no white in wings; olive-green legs. (The similar Lesser Yellowlegs, *Tringa flavipes*, has bright yellow legs, a faint eye-line but no eyering, and in flight has a distinct white rump.)

HABITAT: A northern migrant wintering in South America. Solitary on streamsides, forested swamps, and ponds. Often bounces up and down as it walks.

REGION: NEA, NWA, SAM, PAN

Plate 33d
Pied Lapwing
Vanellus cayanus
ID: Medium-sized (23 cm, 9 in); strikingly black and white-patterned with bright red legs.

HABITAT: Sandy beaches and islands on large rivers.

REGION: NEA, NWA, SAM

Plate 33e
Southern Lapwing
Vanellus chilensis
ID: Medium-sized (36 cm, 1.2 ft); black breast, throat and forehead; long black crest; metallic bronze-green back and wings; white breast and underwings (in flight); white tail with black band on end.

HABITAT: Resident of wet grassy areas and marsh edges. Easily located by its frequent and noisy calls.

REGION: NEA, SAM, PAN

Plate 33 327

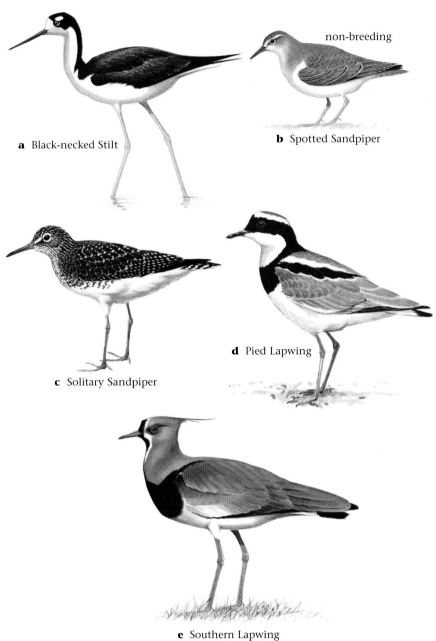

a Black-necked Stilt

non-breeding

b Spotted Sandpiper

c Solitary Sandpiper

d Pied Lapwing

e Southern Lapwing

Plate 34a
Chaco Chachalaca
Ortalis canicollis
ID: Large (53 cm, 1.7 ft); olive-brown; long tail; pheasant-like with gray head and neck; tan belly and bare red skin around eye and on chin. (It is replaced in northwestern and southern Amazon by the similar-sized Speckled Chachalaca, *Ortalis guttata*, which lacks the bare red patches around the eye and has distinct dark spots on the neck and breast; and in northeastern Amazon by the Little Chachalaca, *Ortalis motmot*, which has a chestnut head and a reddish breast without spots.)

HABITAT: Family groups in trees of forest edge and along watercourses; raucous calls between family groups at dawn.

REGION: PAN

Plate 34b
Spix's Guan
Penelope jacquacu
ID: Large (89 cm, 2.9 ft); long neck and tail, bare red skin on face and throat. (It is replaced in the Pantanal by the similar Chestnut-bellied Guan, *Penelope ochrogaster*, which has a reddish brown crown and bright chestnut underparts.)

HABITAT: Solitary or in pairs in upper levels of moist forest. Gives a wheezing whistle-like call when frightened and flies noisily through mid-levels of forest.

REGION: NWA, SAM

Plate 34c
Gray-winged Trumpeter
Psophia crepitans
ID: Large (53 cm, 1.7 ft); blackish; long legs; gray back.

HABITAT: Family groups of 5 to 15 on the floor of primary forest; fly to mid-level branches to escape danger and roost at night. (Replaced in the southeastern Amazon by the similar Dark-winged Trumpeter, *Psophia viridis,* and in the southwestern Amazon by the similar Pale-winged Trumpeter, *Psophia leucoptera.*)

REGION: NEA, NWA

Plate 34d
Blue-throated Piping-Guan
Pipile cumanensis
ID: Large (69 cm, 2.3 ft); blackish body; white top of head; whitish-blue bare throat and face; large white wing patch in flight. (Replaced in the southern Amazon and much of the Pantanal by the similar Red-throated Piping Guan, *Pipile cujubi*, which has red bare throat. The two species often hybridize in the Pantanal.)

HABITAT: Tops of forest trees, especially at forest edge or along rivers. Gives loud wing-whirring sounds that travel considerable distance.

REGION: NWA, PAN

Plate 34e
Undulated Tinamou
Crypturellus undulatus
ID: Medium-sized (28 cm, 11 in); whitish throat, distinctive barring on sides of belly.

HABITAT: Floor of flooded forest, and moist secondary forest. Gives low and melodic four-note whistle throughout the day, "ooh, oh-oh, ah," with last note rising up.

REGION: NEA, NWA, SAM, PAN

Plate 34f
Bare-faced Curassow
Crax fasciolata
ID: Large (76 cm, 2.5 ft); male all black except for white lower belly and tail tip; legs gray; bill yellow with black tip. Female black mottled and barred white with buffy belly; pink legs; black bill. (Replaced in terra firme forests of the southern Amazon by the similar Razor-billed Curassow, *Mitu mitu*, in which both sexes are black with a huge red bill, red legs, and a chestnut belly.)

HABITAT: Floor and lower branches of gallery forests along river edges. Low humming sounds given at dawn.

REGION: PAN, SAM

Plate 34   329

a Chaco Chachalaca

b Spix's Guan

c Gray-winged Trumpeter

d Blue-throated Piping-Guan

e Undulated Tinamou

f Bare-faced Curassow

Plate 35 (*See also*: Vultures, p. 142)

Plate 35a

Turkey Vulture
Cathartes aura

ID: Large (75 cm, 2.5 ft); blackish with silverish underwings, long tail, and bright red head; in flight, wings held in a broad "V," or *dihedral*, with little or no flapping (wingspan 1.8 m, 5.8 ft).

HABITAT: Solitary or in small groups soaring on rising warm air thermals in open country and secondary forest.

REGION: NEA, CMF, NWA, SAM, PAN

Plate 35b

Black Vulture
Coragyps atratus

ID: Large (62 cm, 2 ft); blackish with white patch on underside of wing, short tail, and all black head; in flight wings held flat and flap frequently (wingspan 1.4 m, 4.6 ft). On the ground, runs like a huge chicken.

HABITAT: Small to large groups soaring on thermals or sitting gathered around garbage or offal; almost always associated with human settlements.

REGION: NEA, CMF, NWA, SAM, PAN

Plate 35c

King Vulture
Sarcoramphus papa

ID: Large (80 cm, 2.6 ft); white with short, black tail and trailing edge of wings; colorful head is difficult to discern at a distance; soars with wings held flat (wingspan 2 m, 6.6 ft).

HABITAT: Solitary or in pairs over forest, usually away from human settlements.

REGION: NEA, NWA, SAM

Plate 35d

Greater Yellow-headed Vulture
Cathartes melambrotus

ID: Large (80 cm, 2.6 ft); similar to Turkey Vulture but with a bright yellow head. (The similar Lesser Yellow-headed Vulture, *Cathartes burrovianus*, occurs thoughout the Amazon and Pantanal regions but is usually confined to grassland and extensive marshy areas.)

HABITAT: Solitary or in pairs over primary forest in the Amazon.

REGION: NEA, NWA, SAM

Plate 35 331

a Turkey Vulture

b Black Vulture

c King Vulture

d Greater Yellow-headed
Vulture

Plate 36a

Crane Hawk
Geranospiza caerulescens
ID: Medium-sized (48 cm, 2.6 ft); gray with long yellowish orange legs; populations in the northern Amazon are uniformly slaty gray above and below; in the southern Amazon and Pantanal, populations are light gray with white barring on the breast and often on the upper wings; in all populations white crescents at the ends of the wings in flight are distinctive.

HABITAT: Solitary or in pairs in forest, often flapping and sailing from one forest patch to another.

REGION: NEA, NWA, SAM, PAN

Plate 36b

American Swallow-tailed Kite
Elanoides forficatus
ID: Large (60 cm, 2 ft), spectacular and beautiful; black and white with pointed wings and deeply forked tail; often soars in large groups.

HABITAT: Secondary and primary forests often near water.

REGION: NEA, NWA, SAM

Plate 36c

Double-toothed Kite
Harpagus bidentatus
ID: Medium-sized (35 cm, 1.1 ft); rusty colored breast, light throat with a dark center stripe.

HABITAT: Sits on branches in mid-level to canopy of secondary and primary forest; often in association with monkey troop, catching insects scared up by the troop.

REGION: NEA, NWA, SAM

Plate 36d

Snail Kite
Rostrhamus sociabilis
ID: Medium-sized (44 cm, 1.4 ft); male all gray with long squared tail, white rump, red bare skin on face; female similar but browner with streaked breast.

HABITAT: Always near or on extensive freshwater swamps, sitting on telephone wires or low bushes or flying low over marsh's surface.

REGION: NEA, NWA, SAM, PAN

Plate 36e

Plumbeous Kite
Ictinia plumbea
ID: Medium-sized (36 cm, 1.2 ft); all gray with long pointed wings, which in flight reveal extensive rusty colored tips.

HABITAT: Sits at top of tall dead trees; often soars alone or in pairs, especially along large rivers.

REGION: NEA, NWA, SAM, PAN

Plate 36   333

Amazon form

a Crane Hawk

Pantanal form

d Snail Kite

F

M

b American Swallow-tailed Kite

e Plumbeous Kite

c Double-toothed Kite

Plate 37 (*See also*: Hawks, Eagles, and Kites, p. 143; Falcons, p. 146)

Plate 37a
Bat Falcon
Falco rufigularis
ID: Medium-sized (25 cm, 10 in); dark body with white and rusty colored breast; flies with a rapid wingbeat on long, pointed wings; seldom soars.

HABITAT: Solitary or in pairs sitting at the top of tall, exposed trees.

REGION: NEA, NWA, SAM, PAN

Plate 37b
Aplomado Falcon
Falco femoralis
ID: Large (50 cm, 1.6 ft); slender bodied and pointed winged, light gray above with distinct buffy white line through eye; buffy white throat, black barred breast and rust-colored lower belly.

HABITAT: Generally perched prominently on trees or fence posts in dry sparsely treed habitats.

REGION: NEA, SAM, PAN

Plate 37c
American Kestrel
Falco sparverius
ID: Medium-sized (25 cm, 10 in); light-breasted with a blue-gray and rusty back and tail (male) or brownish back and tail (female). Males in the Pantanal tend to have grayer tails.

HABITAT: Generally perched prominently on telephone wires and isolated bushes in dry sparsely treed habitats.

REGION: PAN

Plate 37d
Black-collared Hawk
Busarellus nigricollis
ID: Large (47 cm, 1.5 ft); buffy white head; black band on throat; rest of body rusty brown; tail rusty brown with black bands.

HABITAT: Vegetated areas near open water and large marshy areas.

REGION: NEA, NWA, SAM, PAN

Plate 37e
Savanna Hawk
Heterospizias meridionalis
ID: Large (55 cm, 1.8 ft); head and underparts barred brown and buffy; upperparts reddish brown; tail black with white tip and prominent white band across middle.

HABITAT: Grassy savannah with some trees and open swamp lands.

REGION: NEA, NWA, SAM, PAN

Plate 37 335

a Bat Falcon

b Aplomado Falcon

M

F

c American Kestrel

d Black-collared Hawk

e Savanna Hawk

Plate 38 (*See also*: Hawks, Eagles, and Kites, p. 143; Osprey, p. 146)

Plate 38a

Roadside Hawk
Buteo magnirostris
ID: Medium-sized (35 cm, 1.1 ft); rusty-barred breast; in flight, a large rusty colored patch on tips of each wing.

HABITAT: Common sitting alone in bushes and small trees in open areas and secondary forest edge.

REGION: NEA, NWA, SAM, PAN

Plate 38b

Great Black Hawk
Buteogallus urubutinga
ID: Large (60 cm, 2 ft); completely black except for extensive white at base of tail and narrow white tip; yellow legs and base of bill.

HABITAT: Forest edge adjacent to water.

REGION: NEA, CMF, NWA, SAM, PAN

Plate 38c

Harpy Eagle
Harpia harpyja
ID: Very large (1 m, 3.3 ft); crest; black chest; short, rounded wings; long banded tail.

HABITAT: Remote primary forest.

REGION: NEA, NWA, SAM

Plate 38d

Ornate Hawk-eagle
Spizaetus ornatus
ID: Large (60 cm, 2 ft); rusty colored chest, face, and neck; black crest; in flight, soars to great heights and rounded wings are noticeably banded underneath; often calls while soaring, a loud series of whistles with every fifth one slurred up in pitch.

HABITAT: Primary and tall secondary forest.

REGION: NEA, NWA, SAM

Plate 38e

Osprey
Pandion haliaetus
ID: Large (60 cm, 2 ft); white underparts, dark upperparts; in flight, long, slender wings held with a peculiar bow in the middle.

HABITAT: Always associated with freshwater lakes and rivers or coastal estuaries and river mouths, where it hunts for fish. Nonbreeding in South America but some individuals present year-round.

REGION: NEA, CMF, NWA, SAM

Plate 38 **337**

a Roadside Hawk

b Great Black Hawk

c Harpy Eagle

d Ornate Hawk-eagle

e Osprey

Plate 39a
Black Caracara
Daptrius ater
ID: Medium-sized (45 cm, 1.4 ft); all black with bold white patch at base of tail; bare skin of face bright orange; noisy, with a harsh scream given frequently.

HABITAT: Seen in pairs in trees or on beaches of rivers and lakes.

REGION: NEA, NWA, SAM

Plate 39b
Red-throated Caracara
Daptrius americanus
ID: Large (51 cm, 1.7 ft); all black with white belly; red cheeks, bare throat and feet. Extremely loud, persistent and annoying alarm call given by pairs to warn the whole forest that you are in the vicinity, "ka ka ka KOW!"

HABITAT: Primary forest canopy and forest edge.

REGION: NEA, NWA, SAM

Plate 39c
Yellow-headed Caracara
Milvago chimachima
ID: Medium-sized (38 cm, 1.2 ft); buffy white head and underparts; brown back and wings; in flight, large white patch at end of each wing.

HABITAT: Open grassy areas, savannah, and agricultural fields.

REGION: NEA, NWA, SAM, PAN

Plate 39d
Crested Caracara
Polyborus plancus
ID: Large (57 cm, 1.9 ft); black crown with slight crest; buffy white neck and throat; black back and wings; breast distinctly barred black and white; orange bare skin on face; prominent white wing patches in flight.

HABITAT: Solitary or in pairs standing on the ground or perched in isolated trees of savannah and agricultural fields. Often scavenges dead animals and garbage sites fighting with Black Vultures (Plate 35).

REGION: NEA, NWA, SAM, PAN

Plate 39e
Laughing Falcon
Herpetotheres cachinnans
ID: Large (52 cm, 1.7 ft); chunky body; buffy white underparts; black mask; often gives its loud falsetto "laughing" call in morning and afternoon.

HABITAT: Sits solitarily in secondary forest and plantations.

REGION: NEA, NWA, SAM, PAN

Plate 39 339

a Black Caracara

b Red-throated Caracara

c Yellow-headed Caracara

d Crested Caracara

e Laughing Falcon

Plate 40a

Pale-vented Pigeon
Columba cayennensis

ID: Medium-sized (30 cm, 1 ft); rusty back; light gray rump patch in flight.

HABITAT: Single or in pairs perched on trees or shrubs at edge of swamps or flying over open wet areas.

REGION: NEA, NWA, SAM, PAN

Plate 40b

Ruddy Pigeon
Columba subvinacea

ID: Medium-sized (30 cm, 1 ft); dark brown with cinnamon-colored underwings evident in flight; best identified by its deep whistled and four-noted call, with the third note higher and lengthened. (The similar-looking Plumbeous Pigeon, *Columba plumbea*, occurs side by side with it and is best distinguished by its three-note whistle with emphasis on the first and last notes.)

HABITAT: Solitary or in pairs in mid-level to canopy of moist primary and tall secondary forest.

REGION: NEA, NWA, SAM, PAN

Plate 40c

White-tipped Dove
Leptotila verreauxi

ID: Medium-sized (28 cm, 11 in); rounded tail with broad white tips; no spots on back or head. (Replaced in open fields and gardens by the Eared Dove, *Zenaida auriculata*, which has a long pointed tail with white outer feathers and a pale gray back and wings with a few large black spots.)

HABITAT: On ground in secondary forests, scrubby vegetation, and forest edge.

REGION: NEA, NWA, SAM, PAN

Plate 40d

Picazuro Pigeon
Columba picazuro

ID: Medium-sized (36 cm, 1.2 ft); violet-gray head and underparts; white and black scaling on neck; back and wings gray; top of wing in flight with narrow white stripe.

HABITAT: Secondary forest, open fields surrounded by trees, and agricultural areas.

REGION: PAN

Plate 40e

Picui Ground-Dove
Columbina picui

ID: Small (18 cm, 7 in); gray-brown upperparts; light gray underparts; black and white wing stripe and white outer tail feathers.

HABITAT: On the ground or low bushes in vegetated fields, forest edge, savannah and gardens.

REGION: PAN

Plate 40f

Ruddy Ground-Dove
Columbina talpacoti

ID: Small (18 cm, 7 in); male reddish brown upperparts with pale head; underparts pinkish; female olive-brown upperparts and light brown underparts; both with 5 to 7 small black spots on upper wing.

HABITAT: On the ground or low bushes in drier open areas, such as vegetated fields, forest edge, savannah and gardens.

REGION: NEA, NWA, SAM, PAN

Plate 40 **341**

a Pale-vented Pigeon

b Ruddy Pigeon

c White-tipped Dove

d Picazuro Pigeon

e Picui Ground-Dove

F

f Ruddy Ground-Dove

M

Plate 41a
Scarlet Macaw
Ara macao
ID: Large (89 cm, 3 ft); bright red with yellow patches on upper wing; long tail; loud, harsh calls. (The similar Red-and-green Macaw, *Ara chloroptera*, has green rather than yellow patches on the upper wings. It occurs together with the more common Scarlet Macaw throughout the Amazon as well as into southern Mato Grosso, where the Scarlet Macaw is absent.)

HABITAT: In pairs or small flocks in moist forest.

REGION: NEA, NWA, SAM

Plate 41b
Blue-and-yellow Macaw
Ara ararauna
ID: Large (84 cm, 2.8 ft); blue upperparts, yellow lower parts, long tail; deep resonating calls.

HABITAT: In pairs or flocks of up to 20 in moist forest, Mauritia Palm swamps and flooded forest.

REGION: NEA, NWA, SAM

Plate 41c
Hyacinth Macaw
Anodorhynchus hyacinthinus
ID: Large (95 cm, 3.1 ft); completely violet-blue except for bare yellow skin around eye and base of lower bill; black underside of wings and long tail; huge bill; very loud croaking and screeching calls.

HABITAT: In pairs or small flocks in gallery forest and palm groves; feed mainly on palm fruits, primarily *Scheelia* and *Acrocomia* (pp. 28–29) palms in the Pantanal. Nest in cavities of Mauritia Palm in southeastern Amazonia and in large trees, such as *Sterculia* (p. 29), in the Pantanal.

REGION: SAM, PAN

Plate 41d
White-eyed Parakeet
Aratinga leucophthalmus
ID: Medium-sized (36 cm, 1.2 ft); all green with bright red and yellow patches on underwings; long pointed tail.

HABITAT: Large flocks of 20 to 100 flying high overhead or in treetops in moist forest and Mauritia Palm swamps.

REGION: NEA, NWA, SAM, PAN

Plate 41e
Chestnut-fronted Macaw
Ara severa
ID: Medium-sized (46 cm, 1.5 ft); green body; red underwings and undertail; whitish bare face patch; harsh voice carries long distances.

HABITAT: In pairs or small flocks in moist forest.

REGION: NWA, SAM

Plate 41f
Red-Bellied Macaw
Ara manilata
ID: Medium-sized (51 cm, 20 in); green body; bright yellow underwings and undertail; yellowish bare face patch; peculiar whining call in flight.

HABITAT: In flocks over moist forest, usually associated with Mauritia Palm swamps. (Replaced in the Pantanal by the similar-colored and sized Golden-collared Macaw, *Ara auricollis*, which has dull yellowish underwings, a bright yellow crescent on the back of the neck, orange base to upper tail, black forehead, and harsh shrieking calls in flight.)

REGION: NEA, NWA, SAM

Plate 41 343

b Blue-and-yellow Macaw

a Scarlet Macaw

c Hyacinth Macaw

d White-eyed Parakeet

e Chestnut-fronted Macaw

f Red-Bellied Macaw

Plate 42a
Cobalt-winged Parakeet
Brotogeris cyanoptera
ID: Medium-sized (20 cm, 8 in); green with short pointed tail.

HABITAT: Flocks of 5 to 50 in primary and secondary moist forest. The loud, shrill chattering of a flock can be heard long before it becomes visible flying high overhead.

REGION: NWA, SAM

Plate 42b
Canary-winged Parakeet
Brotogeris versicolorus
ID: Medium-sized (23 cm, 9 in); green with long pointed tail and large white and yellow stripes on upperwings in the northern Amazon. (The population in the southern Amazon and Pantanal has only a yellow stripe and is considered by some experts to be a separate species called the Golden-chevroned Parakeet, *Brotogeris chiriri*.)

HABITAT: Small flocks give shrill, metallic notes in flight. Common in a wide range of mostly open forested habitats, from river edges to city parks and savannahs.

REGION: NEA, NWA, SAM, PAN

Plate 42c
Black-headed Parrot
Pionites melanocephala
ID: Medium-sized (23 cm, 9 in); black crown; green back; cream-white breast; short tail; high-pitched squealing calls. (Population south of the Río Amazonas has a peach-colored crown instead of black and is considered by some experts to be a separate species called the White-bellied Parrot, *Pionites leucogaster*.)

HABITAT: In small flocks flying through the canopy of primary forest north of the Río Amazonas.

REGION: NEA, NWA, SAM

Plate 42d
Black-hooded Parakeet
Nandayus nenday
ID: Medium-sized (30 cm, 1 ft); green with coal black head, blue-black tail and trailing edge of wings. Close up its pale blue breast and red thighs are evident.

HABITAT: A Pantanal speciality, this parakeet moves in large flocks over open grassy areas and palm savannahs, often landing to feed on the ground or drink from the edge of a waterhole.

REGION: PAN

Plate 42e
Golden Parakeet
Aratinga (Guaruba) guarouba
ID: Medium-sized (34 cm, 1.2 ft); spectacular adult with bright yellow body and tail and green wings. Immature is dull olive-brown streaked with green.

HABITAT: Canopy of primary terra firme forest along the southeastern bank of the Río Amazonas and in Rondônia.

REGION: SAM

Plate 42 345

a Cobalt-winged Parakeet

b Canary-winged Parakeet

c Black-headed Parrot

d Black-hooded Parakeet

e Golden Parakeet

Plate 43a
Mealy Parrot
Amazona farinosa
ID: Medium-sized (41 cm, 1.3 ft); all green with large white eyering, small red wing patch, and a variably sized small yellow spot on crown; short tail with large yellow band on the end; "twittering" shallow wingbeats in flight.

HABITAT: Pairs seen in treetops or flying low over moist forest.

REGION: NEA, NWA, SAM

Plate 43b
Yellow-headed Parrot
Amazona ochracephala
ID: Medium-sized (36 cm, 1.2 ft); green body and head with yellow forehead variously extending back to cover most of the head in some populations (for instance on Marajó Island at the mouth of the Río Amazonas); large red wing patch; short all-green tail; "twittering" shallow wingbeats in flight.

HABITAT: Pairs and small flocks near swampy forests and oxbow lakes.

REGION: NEA, NWA, SAM

Plate 43c
Orange-winged Parrot
Amazona amazonica
ID: Medium-sized (32 cm, 1 ft); green with yellow face bisected by blue stripe; small orange wing patch; "twittering" shallow wingbeats in flight.

HABITAT: Secondary forest near water, agricultural clearings, varzea, and mangroves.

REGION: NEA, CMF, NWA, SAM

Plate 43d
Blue-headed Parrot
Pionus menstruus
ID: Medium-sized (25 cm, 10 in); green body with blue head and chest; red at base of short tail; deep wingbeats in flight; high-pitched call.

HABITAT: In small flocks flying high over moist forests, rivers and lakes.

REGION: NEA, NWA, SAM

Plate 43e
Short-tailed Parrot
Graydidascalus brachyurus
ID: Medium-sized (24 cm, 9.5 in); all green with extremely short square-ended tail; close up the dark gray bill and small red patches on the shoulder and at the base of each side of the tail are obvious. In flight the feathers of the upperwing have pale edges giving a mottled look. (Another similar-sized and -shaped parrot species confined to varzea, igapo, swampy forest, and river islands along the Río Amazonas and its main tributaries is the Festive Parrot, *Amazona festiva*, which is all green except for a bright red rump and a red forehead. Its "twittering" shallow wingbeats in flight readily distinguish it from the deeper wingbeats of the Short-tailed Parrot.)

HABITAT: Confined to varzea habitat along the Río Amazonas and some of its largest tributaries, where you can often see them flying noisily high overhead or feeding in the riverside forest canopy on *Cecropia* fruits (p. 28).

REGION: NEA, NWA, SAM

Plate 43f
Turquoise-fronted Parrot
Amazona aestiva
ID: Medium-sized (37 cm, 1.2 ft); green with yellow face, blue forehead and small white crown spot; yellow shoulder and large red wing patch; "twittering" shallow wingbeats in flight.

HABITAT: Open forest, savannah, and gallery forest, often close to human habitation. Often seen eating *Tabebuia* fruits (p. 29).

REGION: PAN

Plate 43 347

a Mealy Parrot

b Yellow-headed Parrot

c Orange-winged Parrot

d Blue-headed Parrot

e Short-tailed Parrot

f Turquoise-fronted Parrot

Plate 44a
Striped Cuckoo
Tapera naevia

ID: Medium-sized (29 cm, 11 in); buff and brown-streaked above with pale breast; often difficult to see but easily heard as it gives its monotonous and loud two-noted whistle (second note higher than the first) throughout the day.

HABITAT: Scrubby vegetation, grassy pastures, where it perches on fence posts or low bushes in early morning and skulks on the ground in dense cover the rest of the day.

REGION: NEA, NWA, SAM, PAN

Plate 44b
Squirrel Cuckoo
Piaya cayana

ID: Medium-sized (43 cm, 17 in); chestnut upperparts, gray underparts; extremely long tail with white spots at tip.

HABITAT: Solitary or in pairs; often runs along branches and hops or flies clumsily from tree to tree in mid-level and canopy of secondary and primary forests; frequently in mixed-species foraging flocks.

REGION: NEA, NWA, SAM, PAN

Plate 44c
Greater Ani
Crotophaga major

ID: Large (47 cm, 1.6 ft); all black with bluish sheen; white eye; long tail. Loud calls that can sound like a metal factory when an entire flock calls together.

HABITAT: Flocks in low vegetation along streams, lakes, and forested swamps.

REGION: NEA, NWA, SAM, PAN

Plate 44d
Smooth-billed Ani
Crotophaga ani

ID: Medium-sized (33 cm, 1.1 ft); all black; dark eye; large thin bill with high hump at base; long tail. Loose flight appears uncoordinated.

HABITAT: Family groups in open grassy areas, clearings, pastures, and along roads in Amazonia.

REGION: NEA, NWA, SAM, PAN

Plate 44e
Guira Cuckoo
Guira guira

ID: Medium-sized (40 cm, 1.3 ft); back and wings brown streaked buffy; head buffy white with brown streaks and orangish crest; buffy white breast; long black and white tail; yellowish bill and orange eye.

HABITAT: Pairs and small family groups obvious in open fields, brushy savannah, and gardens; frequently gives loud high-pitched calls.

REGION: PAN

Plate 44 349

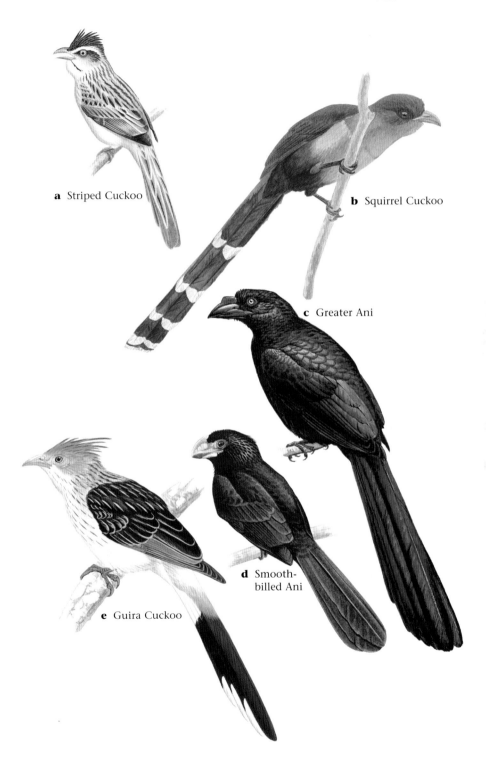

a Striped Cuckoo

b Squirrel Cuckoo

c Greater Ani

d Smooth-billed Ani

e Guira Cuckoo

Plate 45a

Tropical Screech-owl
Otus choliba

ID: Medium-sized (23 cm, 9 in); ear tufts; buffy white breast with dark streaks. Voice at night a rising quavery whistle ending with two quick but distinct pure notes.

HABITAT: Active at night in secondary forest, forest edge, plantations and gardens.

REGION: NEA, NWA, SAM, PAN

Plate 45b

Spectacled Owl
Pulsatrix perspicillata

ID: Large (48 cm, 1.6 ft); lacks ear tufts; deep brown back and chest contrasting with white facial markings and white, unstreaked breast. Voice at night a loud series of resonating hoots resembling someone shaking a large piece of metal sheeting.

HABITAT: Active at night in moist primary and secondary forest.

REGION: NEA, NWA, SAM

Plate 45c

Ferruginous Pygmy-owl
Glaucidium brasilianum

ID: Small (16 cm, 6 in); lacks ear tufts; relatively long tail; heavily streaked breast. Voice given commonly during day and night a series of high, whistled "whooks."

HABITAT: Active during day and night in secondary forest, forest edge and gardens.

REGION: NEA, NWA, SAM, PAN

Plate 45d

Black-banded Owl
Strix huhula

ID: Medium-sized (38 cm, 1.3 ft); black with narrow white bands; no ear tufts; voice given at night a loud scream ending with a distinctive but low hoot.

HABITAT: Active at night in mid-level and canopy of primary and secondary terra firme forest.

REGION: NEA, NWA, SAM

Plate 45e

Burrowing Owl
Speotyto cunicularia

ID: Medium-sized (23 cm, 9 in); soft brown with white spotting; long legs and short tail.

HABITAT: Stands on the ground "bobbing;" nests in burrows; often active during the day in open fields and treeless areas.

REGION: NEA, SAM, PAN

Plate 45 351

a Tropical Screech-owl

b Spectacled Owl

c Ferruginous
Pygmy-Owl

d Black-banded Owl

e Burrowing Owl

Plate 46a
Sand-colored Nighthawk
Chordeiles rupestris
ID: Medium-sized (22 cm, 9 in); buffy brown and white; in flight tail white except for black tip; long pointed wings white except for black tips and trailing edge. When disturbed from their roost during the day, they resemble a flock of flying terns.

HABITAT: Roosts during the day in flocks of 10 to 100 on sand bars of large rivers and in isolated trees in open flooded forest; night-active.

REGION: NWA, SAM

Plate 46b
Pauraque
Nyctidromus albicollis
ID: Medium-sized (28 cm, 11 in); mottled brown; usually seen in light of a flashlight when its orangish eyeshine reflects as it sits on the ground or in low vegetation along watercourses. In flight, rounded wings have a bold white (male) or buffy (female) band, and outer tail feathers are white. Voice commonly heard at night is a low, down-slurring whistle-hum.

HABITAT: Solitary on the ground in forest edge, pastures, river beaches, open secondary forest and gardens.

REGION: NEA, NWA, SAM, PAN

Plate 46c
Nacunda Nighthawk
Podager nacunda
ID: Medium-sized (30 cm, 1 ft); mottled brown and black with conspicuous white belly, underwings, and wing patches.

HABITAT: A showy and obvious species that flies like a huge moth before dusk and at night high over open grasslands and savannah, sometimes in large flocks.

REGION: NEA, NWA, SAM, PAN

Plate 46d
Common Potoo
Nyctibius griseus
ID: Medium-sized (40 cm, 1.3 ft); gray-brown; long tail. Sits on exposed trees during the day with its bill pointing up, resembling a broken branch. Most often noticed by its mournful song of low whistles that descend slowly but deliberately in pitch, step-wise ever lower, especially on moonlit nights.

HABITAT: Moist forest edge and along forested waterways.

REGION: NEA, NWA, SAM, PAN

Plate 46e
Great Potoo
Nyctibius grandis
ID: Large (51 cm, 20 in); entirely grayish white.

HABITAT: Perches high in trees during the day, usually at forest edge or along oxbow lakes and rivers. On moonlit nights gives a deep, growling call.

REGION: NEA, NWA, SAM

Plate 46 353

a Sand-colored Nighthawk

b Pauraque

c Nacunda Nighthawk

d Common Potoo

e Great Potoo

Plate 47a
White-collared Swift
Streptoprocne zonaris
ID: Medium-sized (20 cm, 8 in); black with bold white collar and slightly forked tail.

HABITAT: High overhead in swirling flocks of 10 to 200 individuals. Although they nest at mid-elevations, they often descend incredibly long distances to lower elevations for a few hours each day to catch insects.

REGION: NWA, SAM

Plate 47b
Short-tailed Swift
Chaetura brachyura
ID: Small (10 cm, 4 in); all black; pale gray rump; almost tailless appearance. (Four or five similar species of this genus occur over the lowlands of Amazonia, but they are difficult to separate in the field.)

HABITAT: In loose flocks overhead in forest and cleared areas, often in palm swamps; sometimes mixed with other species of swifts.

REGION: NEA, NWA, SAM

Plate 47c
Fork-tailed Palm-swift
Tachornis squamata
ID: Small (13 cm, 5 in); slender, gray-brown with distinctively long and deeply forked tail.

HABITAT: Low over the canopy of open forest or clearings, usually near Mauritia Palm stands, where they roost and nest; usually in small flocks of its own species or mixed with other swift species.

REGION: NEA, NWA, SAM

Plate 47d
White-banded Swallow
Atticora fasciata
ID: Small (15 cm, 6 in); completely bluish black with a bold white breast band; deeply forked tail.

HABITAT: Smaller forested rivers.

REGION: NEA, NWA, SAM

Plate 47e
Southern Rough-winged Swallow
Stelgidopteryx ruficollis
ID: Small (13 cm, 5 in); brownish back with pale rump patch; gray-brown breast with contrasting light rusty throat.

HABITAT: Over rivers and nearby cleared areas, where it roosts in small groups on exposed branches.

REGION: NEA, NWA, SAM, PAN

Plate 47   355

a White-collared Swift

b Short-tailed Swift

c Fork-tailed Palm-swift

d White-banded Swallow

e Southern Rough-winged Swallow

Plate 48a

Barn Swallow
Hirundo rustica

ID: Small (15 cm, 6 in); dark blue upperparts with rusty forehead; underparts pale buff (nonbreeding) to bright rusty (breeding); long tail deeply forked.

HABITAT: Northern migrant to South America but occasionally nests in northern Argentina. Usually seen flying low over open fields, water and grassy areas. At night often roosts in large numbers, especially in reed beds and cane fields.

REGION: NEA, CMF, NWA, SAM, PAN

Plate 48b

White-winged Swallow
Tachycineta albiventer

ID: Small (14 cm, 6 in); pure white underparts, blue-green upperparts; white patch on upperwing and on rump.

HABITAT: Perches on partially submerged poles and vegetation or flies low over lakes and larger rivers.

REGION: NEA, NWA, SAM, PAN

Plate 48c

Brown-chested Martin
Phaeoprogne tapera

ID: Small (17 cm, 7 in); larger than other swallows; gray-brown upperparts; white underparts with brown band across upper breast.

HABITAT: Savannah and open fields, often near water. Usually perched on exposed branches or flying low over open fields. Regularly take over hornero (Plate 59) nests for their own.

REGION: NEA, NWA, SAM, PAN

Plate 48d

Long-billed Starthroat
Heliomaster longirostris

ID: Small (12 cm, 4.9 in); long bill; upperparts bronzy green (crown of male blue); throat red, bordered on each side by white stripe.

HABITAT: Open woodlands and forest edge; commonly perches on prominent bare branches high over streams and rivers.

REGION: NEA, NWA, SAM

Plate 48e

White-necked Jacobin
Florisuga mellivora

ID: Small (10 cm, 4 in); white lower belly, tail and crescent on neck of male contrast with all-blue head and throat; scaly dark throat contrasts with the white lower belly of the female.

HABITAT: Undergrowth to canopy and subcanopy of moist secondary forest, forest edge and gardens.

REGION: NEA, NWA, SAM

Plate 48   357

a Barn Swallow

b White-winged Swallow

c Brown-chested Martin

d Long-billed Starthroat

e White-necked Jacobin

F

M

Plate 49a
Crimson Topaz
Topaza pella
ID: Small (19 cm, 7.5 in); upperparts glittering purple to gold; head black; throat golden green; underparts bright red and gold; long tail feathers crossed when perched. (The population in the northwestern Amazon is similar but has darker tail feathers and is considered by some to be a separate species, the Fiery Topaz, *Topaza pyra*.)

HABITAT: Usually in shrubs and trees along small to medium-sized forest streams.

REGION: NEA

Plate 49b
Swallow-tailed Hummingbird
Eupetomena macroura
ID: Small (15 cm, 6 in); entirely dark blue-green; long forked tail.

HABITAT: Brushy areas in savannah.

REGION: PAN

Plate 49c
Rufous-breasted Hermit
Glaucis hirsuta
ID: Small (10 cm, 4 in); green upperparts; buffy brown underparts; bill long and deeply down-curved; brownish tail with NO long white central tail feathers as in other hermits.

HABITAT: Common in moist undergrowth of secondary forest and riverine forests, especially near *Heliconia* (p. 27) or banana groves.

REGION: NEA, NWA, SAM

Plate 49d
Long-tailed Hermit
Phaethornis superciliosus
ID: Small (13 cm, 5 in); long bill strongly down-curved; brownish upperparts with contrasting buff rump; long dark tail with long white tip; buffy gray underparts; pale buffy head stripes and line down center of throat.

HABITAT: Moist secondary forest undergrowth; often in lecs.

REGION: NEA, NWA, SAM

Plate 49e
Black-eared Fairy
Heliothryx aurita
ID: Small (11 cm, 4.3 in); short bill; pure white underparts and prominent outer tail feathers; brilliant green upperparts; black mask.

HABITAT: At mid-levels and canopy in primary forest but lower at forest edges and in secondary forest.

REGION: NEA, NWA, SAM

Plate 49 359

a Crimson Topaz

b Swallow-tailed
Hummingbird

c Rufous-breasted
Hermit

d Long-tailed
Hermit

e Black-eared Fairy

Plate 50a
Glittering-throated Emerald
Amazilia fimbriata

ID: Small (8 cm, 3.1 in); glittering green upperparts and underparts except for white center of lower belly; red bill with black tip.

HABITAT: Secondary forest, shrubby grasslands, and savannah.

REGION: NEA, NWA, SAM, PAN

Plate 50b
Black-throated Mango
Anthracothorax nigricollis

ID: Small (10 cm, 4 in); male green above with black breast and maroon tail; female similar except breast white with black line running down the middle.

HABITAT: Gardens and scrubby forest.

REGION: NEA, NWA, SAM, PAN

Plate 50c
Versicolored Emerald
Amazilia versicolor

ID: Small (8 cm, 3.1 in); bronze-green upperparts; gray crown; underparts whitish with golden green spots becoming denser toward the sides; base of bill orange-red.

HABITAT: Forest edge, open secondary forest, and savannah.

REGION: NEA, NWA, SAM

Plate 50d
Racket-tailed Coquette
Discosura longicauda

ID: Small (10 cm, 4 in); upperparts shiny green with buff band across lower back; male underparts blackish with green throat and breast and long forked tail with two racquets at end; female underparts greenish with black throat and short tail.

HABITAT: Forest edge and secondary forest; in canopy of terra firme forest, where it is regularly seen from observation towers.

REGION: NEA

Plate 50e
Fork-tailed Woodnymph
Thalurania furcata

ID: Small (10 cm, 4 in); male with purple breast and green throat; gray-breasted female similar to several other species.

HABITAT: Undergrowth of moist lowland forest and forest edge.

REGION: NEA, NWA, SAM, PAN

Plate 50 361

a Glittering-throated Emerald

b Black-throated Mango

c Versicolored Emerald

F

M

d Racket-tailed Coquette

e Fork-tailed Woodnymph

Plate 51a
Pavonine Quetzal
Pharomachrus pavoninus
ID: Medium-sized (33 cm, 13 in); brilliant green upperparts; bright red breast; undertail black; male's bill bright orange.

HABITAT: Mid-levels of primary, moist terra firme forest and flooded forest. Male's song a distinct and descending whistle followed by a single low note ("Whuu-tok").

REGION: NWA, SAM

Plate 51b
White-tailed Trogon
Trogon viridis
ID: Medium-sized (28 cm, 11 in); male with metallic greenish back and dark-violet head and chest, bright yellow breast and mainly white undertail; female similar but with grayish head, chest and upperparts, black undertail with white barring, narrow but complete white eyering.

HABITAT: Mid-levels of humid primary and secondary forest; often associated with mixed-species foraging flocks.

REGION: NEA, NWA, SAM

Plate 51c
Blue-crowned Trogon
Trogon curucui
ID: Medium-sized (24 cm, 10 in); male with dark metallic green back, blue head and chest, and black face; red breast with white band across upper breast; black undertail with fine white barring; female with gray upperparts, head and chest; pinkish breast; undertail mainly black with some white bars.

HABITAT: Humid terra firme forest, tall secondary forest and flooded forest.

REGION: NWA, SAM, PAN

Plate 51d
Violaceous Trogon
Trogon violaceus
ID: Medium-sized (24 cm, 9.5 in); male with metallic green back, blue-violet head and chest, yellow breast, black undertail with fine white barring; female with gray upperparts and chest, yellow breast, black undertail with white barring and small spots, incomplete white eyering.

HABITAT: Open secondary forest, forest edge and occasionally forest interior.

REGION: NEA, NWA, SAM

Plate 51e
Collared Trogon
Trogon collaris
ID: Medium-sized (25 cm, 10 in); male with dark metallic green upperparts, head and chest, red breast, black undertail with broad white barring; female with brownish upperparts, head and chest, pinkish breast, grayish undertail, dark bill.

HABITAT: Mid-levels of humid secondary forest.

REGION: NEA, NWA, SAM

Plate 51 **363**

a Pavonine
Quetzal

M

F

b White-tailed
Trogon

M

F

c Blue-crowned
Trogon

M

F

e Collared
Trogon

M

F

M

F

d Violaceous
Trogon

Plate 52a
Ringed Kingfisher
Ceryle torquata
ID: Medium-sized (38 cm, 1.3 ft); blue-gray upperparts and white neck band; most of breast rusty (male) or blue-gray and rusty (female); crest on top of head.

HABITAT: Open vegetation along large rivers, lakes, and mangroves.

REGION: NEA, CMF, NWA, SAM, PAN

Plate 52b
Green Kingfisher
Chloroceryle americana
ID: Small (19 cm, 7.5 in); dark green upperparts; small white spots on upper wings; white underparts with single rusty colored breast band (male) or double green (female) breast bands.

HABITAT: Low in vegetation along small to medium-sized streams, lakes and mangrove estuaries.

REGION: NEA, CMF, NWA, SAM, PAN

Plate 52c
Green-and-rufous Kingfisher
Chloroceryle inda
ID: Medium-sized (22 cm, 9 in); dark green upperparts; small white spots on wings and tail; entirely rusty (male) underparts or with spotted green and white band on chest (female).

HABITAT: Low in dense vegetation along small to medium streams and flooded forest ponds.

REGION: NEA, NWA, SAM, PAN

Plate 52d
Amazon Kingfisher
Chloroceryle amazona
ID: Medium-sized (28 cm, 11 in); solid dark green upperparts; white underparts with rusty colored (male) or green (female) breast band.

HABITAT: Along open vegetation of large to medium-sized rivers and lakes.

REGION: NEA, NWA, SAM, PAN

Plate 52e
American Pygmy Kingfisher
Chloroceryle aenea
ID: Small (13 cm, 5 in); dark green upperparts; rusty colored chest (male) and white lower belly; narrow dark green chest band (female).

HABITAT: Low in dense vegetation of small streams and forest ponds.

REGION: NEA, NWA, SAM, PAN

Plate 52 365

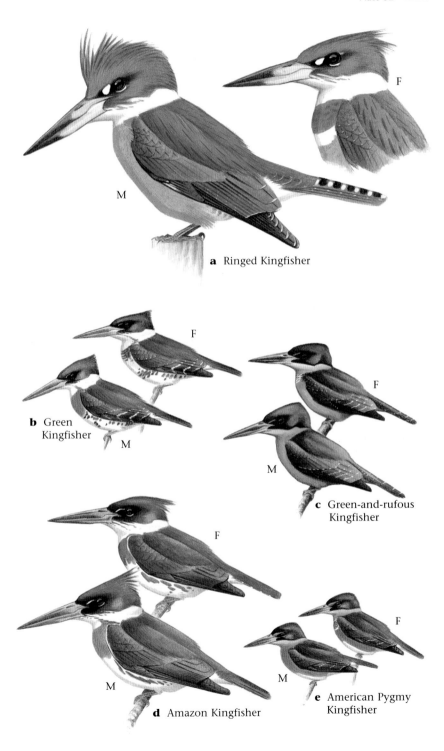

a Ringed Kingfisher

b Green Kingfisher

c Green-and-rufous Kingfisher

d Amazon Kingfisher

e American Pygmy Kingfisher

Plate 53a
Rufous-tailed Jacamar
Galbula ruficauda
ID: Medium-sized (23 cm, 9 in); metallic blue crown; metallic coppery green upperparts and chest; long bill; belly and undertail rusty colored.

HABITAT: Pairs seen in middle and lower parts of secondary forest and forest edge.

REGION: NWA, SAM, PAN

Plate 53b
Paradise Jacamar
Galbula dea
ID: Medium-sized (30 cm, 1 ft); all dark, with long thin tail and long pointed black bill; bold white throat.

HABITAT: Exposed branches in canopy of humid terra firme forest; often moves along with mixed species bird flocks.

REGION: NEA, NWA, SAM

Plate 53c
White-necked Puffbird
Notharchus macrorhynchos
ID: Medium-sized (25 cm, 10 in); black upperparts and white underparts except for black breast band; large heavy bill.

HABITAT: Solitary high on exposed branches of tall trees of primary and secondary forest.

REGION: NEA, NWA, SAM

Plate 53d
Black-fronted Nunbird
Monasa nigrifrons
ID: Medium-sized (25 cm, 10 in); dark gray; long bright red-orange bill; dark forehead. (Replaced in canopy and edge of Amazonian primary forest by similar White-fronted Nunbird, *Monasa morphoeus*, which has a white forehead.)

HABITAT: Secondary forest canopy and edge of river-associated forest.

REGION: NEA, NWA SAM, PAN

Plate 53e
Swallow-winged Puffbird
Chelidoptera tenebrosa
ID: Small (15 cm, 6 in); black upperparts, head and throat; rusty colored belly; short tail and white rump obvious only in flight.

HABITAT: Sits in open branches at top of small trees along rivers and forest edge looking like a husky swallow (both when perched and in its short sallying flights that usually return to the same perch).

REGION: NEA, NWA, SAM

Plate 53   367

a Rufous-tailed Jacamar

M

F

c White-necked Puffbird

b Paradise Jacamar

d Black-fronted Nunbird

e Swallow-winged Puffbird

Plate 54a
Toco Toucan
Ramphastos toco
ID: Large (66 cm, 2.2 ft); black body with white throat and lower back; huge yellow-orange bill with black spot on tip.

HABITAT: Forest edge, palm savannah and gardens.

REGION: NEA, SAM, PAN

Plate 54b
Cuvier's Toucan
Ramphastos cuvieri
ID: Large (61 cm, 2 ft); black body with white cheeks, throat and upper breast; large black bill with yellow ridge and base; loud yelping calls distinguish it from the almost identical but smaller Yellow-ridged Toucan, *Ramphastos culminatus*, which gives a low croaking call.

HABITAT: Canopy and tops of isolated trees of primary forest.

REGION: NEA, NWA, SAM

Plate 54c
Black-spotted Barbet
Capito niger
ID: Small (18 cm, 7 in); upperparts black with bright yellow spots and stripes; throat and upper breast clear orange-yellow (male) or orange with thick black streaks (female); call resembles deep, owl-like calls of Blue-crowned Motmot, but no hesitation between calls in a series, "BOO-boop, BOO-boop, BOO-boop ..." In the southern Amazon, males have red or orange throats and females have unspotted throats.

HABITAT: Canopy of moist primary and secondary forests, often in mixed-species foraging flocks.

REGION: NEA, NWA, SAM

Plate 54d
Blue-crowned Motmot
Momotus momota
ID: Medium-sized (39 cm, 15 in); head with blue and black mask, black crown, black breast and throat dull rusty colored; upperparts greenish blue; long tail with peculiar racquets at end often swung from side to side; bill large but not broad; voice a low "BOO-boop" usually heard in morning and afternoon.

HABITAT: Solitary or pairs in mid- to low levels of primary and secondary forest.

REGION: NEA, NWA, SAM

Plate 54e
Broad-billed Motmot
Electron platyrhynchum
ID: Medium-sized (33 cm, 1.1 ft); bright rusty head, throat and upper chest; black mask; green upperparts and lower belly extending fairly high up on the breast; long tail but lacks peculiar racquets at end; bill large and extremely broad; high-pitched nasal call given at dawn and late afternoon.

HABITAT: Dense undergrowth and mid-levels of secondary and moist primary forest.

REGION: NEA, NWA, SAM

Plate 54 369

a Toco Toucan

b Cuvier's Toucan

d Blue-crowned Motmot

e Broad-billed Motmot

M

F

c Black-spotted Barbet

Plate 55a
Spot-billed Toucanet
Selenidera maculirostris
ID: Medium-sized (33 cm, 1.1 ft); large pale green bill with black spots and bars; bare green face; dark green back, wings and tail; bright yellow and red spots on lower belly; black head and breast (male); dark rusty head and breast (female); voice sounds like a loud frog croaking.

HABITAT: Mid-levels and canopy of terra firme forest.

REGION: SAM

Plate 55b
Curl-crested Aracari
Pteroglossus beauharnaesii
ID: Medium-sized (38 cm, 1.3 ft); underparts yellow with red band across center of breast; cheeks and throat whitish; crown blackish with peculiar curled, plastic-like feathers.

HABITAT: Canopy and edge of primary forest.

REGION: SAM

Plate 55c
Lettered Aracari
Pteroglossus inscriptus
ID: Medium-sized (37 cm, 1.2 ft); underparts yellow with black throat but no breast bands; upper bill mostly yellowish white. (Replaced east of the Río Negro and north of the Río Amazonas by the similar Green Aracari, *Pteroglossus viridis*, which has a red and yellow upper bill.)

HABITAT: Primary terra firme forest canopy.

REGION: NWA, SAM

Plate 55d
Red-necked Aracari
Pteroglossus bitorquatus
ID: Medium-sized (36 cm, 1.2 ft); head chestnut with black crown; black and yellow bands on upper chest; breast, upper back and lower back red; upper bill mostly green.

HABITAT: Restricted to canopy of terra firme and river-edge forest of southeastern Amazon.

REGION: SAM

Plate 55e
Chestnut-eared Aracari
Pteroglossus castanotis
ID: Medium-sized (46 cm, 1.5 ft); underparts yellow with one broad red breast band; head chestnut except for black crown.

HABITAT: Canopy of moist secondary and primary forest and along rivers.

REGION: NWA, SAM, PAN

Plate 55   371

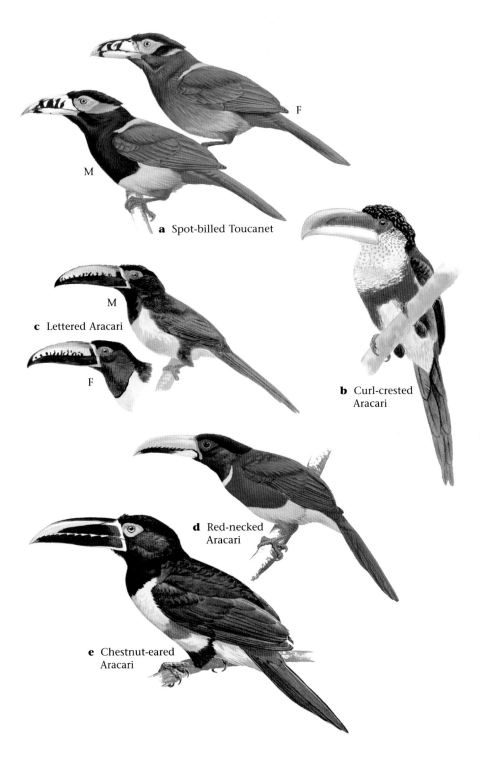

a Spot-billed Toucanet

c Lettered Aracari

b Curl-crested Aracari

d Red-necked Aracari

e Chestnut-eared Aracari

Plate 56a
White Woodpecker
Melanerpes candidus

ID: Medium-sized (24 cm, 9.5 in); head and underparts white; back, wings and tail black; bare yellow area around eye; male with prominent black stripe on side of head and neck; female without head stripe.

HABITAT: Small family groups in dry woodland, savannah, palm groves, gardens, and orchards, primarily in the Pantanal.

REGION: SAM, PAN

Plate 56b
Campo Flicker
Colaptes campestris

ID: Medium-sized (30 cm, 1 ft); golden head with black crown and throat; rest of upper and lower body barred buffy, white and brown; white patch on lower back obvious in flight; male with red moustachial streak.

HABITAT: In small family groups feeding on the ground, roads, and termite mounds of savannah and open fields; range spreading as forest is cleared.

REGION: SAM, PAN

Plate 56c
Lineated Woodpecker
Dryocopus lineatus

ID: Medium-sized (36 cm, 1.2 ft); crested; upperparts black with white lines on back forming an incomplete "V;" underparts barred brown and black.

HABITAT: Solitary or pairs in large trees in secondary forest or forest edge and mangroves.

REGION: NEA, CMF, NWA, SAM, PAN

Plate 56d
Red-necked Woodpecker
Campephilus rubricollis

ID: Medium-sized (36 cm, 1.2 ft); upperparts black with no stripes; head, neck and chest red; underparts rusty; female with white forehead and white line below eye.

HABITAT: Pairs seen on large tree trunks of primary forest, tall secondary forest, and varzea.

REGION: NEA, NWA, SAM

Plate 56e
Crimson-crested Woodpecker
Campephilus melanoleucos

ID: Medium-sized (36 cm, 1.2 ft); crested; upperparts black with white lines on back forming a complete "V," underparts barred brown and black; head of male red except for white and black cheek spot.

HABITAT: Pairs seen on large tree trunks of primary forest, tall secondary forest, varzea, savannah, and palm groves.

REGION: NEA, NWA, SAM, PAN

Plate 56

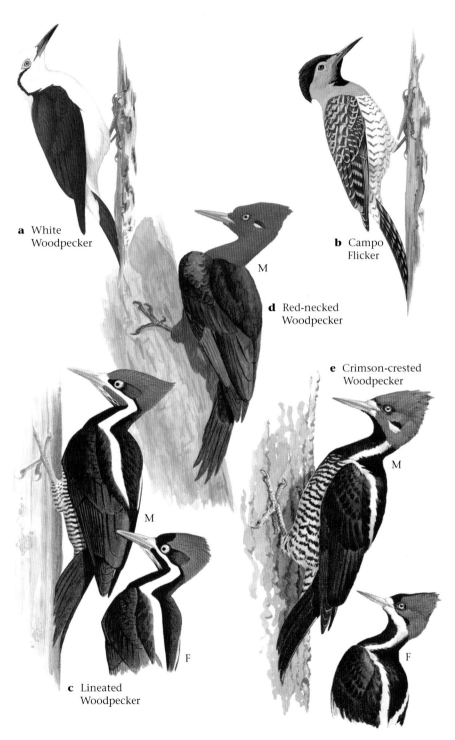

a White
Woodpecker

b Campo
Flicker

d Red-necked
Woodpecker

M

e Crimson-crested
Woodpecker

M

c Lineated
Woodpecker

M

F

M

F

Plate 57a
White-wedged Piculet
Picumnus albosquamatus
ID: Small (10 cm, 4 in); upperparts brownish with pale scalloping; underparts and neck white with dark scalloping; male crown black and red with whitish dots, female crown all black with whitish dots.

HABITAT: Small branches of mid-level and undergrowth of savannah woodland and gallery forests along rivers.

REGION: PAN

Plate 57b
Spot-breasted Woodpecker
Colaptes punctigula
ID: Medium-sized (20 cm, 8 in); yellow-green back with black bars; dotted black on breast; sides of head white.

HABITAT: Solitary on isolated trees in clearings and pastures, secondary forest edge, mangroves, palm groves, plantations, and gardens.

REGION: NEA, CMF, NWA, SAM

Plate 57c
Pale-crested Woodpecker
Celeus lugubris
ID: Medium-sized (23 cm, 9 in); pale buffy head with long crest (male with red moustache); underparts chestnut; upper back and wings black barred buffy white; large buffy white patch on lower back; tail black.

HABITAT: Pairs in trees of dry open woodlands and seasonally flooded gallery forest.

REGION: PAN

Plate 57d
Yellow-tufted Woodpecker
Melanerpes cruentatus
ID: Medium-sized (19 cm, 7.5 in); black body with yellow eyering and nape of neck; crown red (male) or black (female); belly and lower breast red. (In northeastern Brazil, many individuals have an all-black head.)

HABITAT: Family groups of 4 to 8 on dead branches high in canopy of primary forest and tall secondary forest; loud raucous calls obvious.

REGION: NEA, NWA, SAM

Plate 57e
Cream-colored Woodpecker
Celeus flavus
ID: Medium-sized (23 cm, 9 in); crested; cream-yellow body, rusty wings and black tail; male with bright red stripe on cheek.

HABITAT: Solitary or pairs in dense undergrowth vegetation of secondary forest, varzea, mangroves, and plantations.

REGION: NEA, CMF, NWA, SAM

Plate 57 375

a White-wedged
Piculet

b Spot-breasted
Woodpecker

c Pale-crested
Woodpecker

d Yellow-tufted
Woodpecker

e Cream-colored
Woodpecker

Plate 58a
Red-billed Scythebill
Campyloramphus trochilirostris
ID: Medium-sized (body 27 cm, 11 in; bill 8 cm, 3 in); extremely long and down-curved, reddish bill; brownish back, head and breast streaked buffy; rusty wings and tail.

HABITAT: Lower and mid-levels of primary, secondary, and gallery forest (mainly varzea in the Amazon), where it probes into crevices, bark, and bromeliads with its long bill.

REGION: NWA, SAM, PAN

Plate 58b
Wedge-billed Woodcreeper
Glyphorynchus spirurus
ID: Small (14 cm, 5.5 in); brown head and underparts with buffy eye-line and breast streaks; rusty back, wings, and tail; bill short and wedge-shaped.

HABITAT: Lower parts of small and medium tree trunks in primary terra firme and secondary forest; usually associated with mixed-species foraging flocks.

REGION: NEA, NWA, SAM

Plate 58c
Long-billed Woodcreeper
Nasica longirostris
ID: Medium-sized (36 cm, 14 in); extremely long, thin, straight bill (7 cm, 2.7 in); rusty back, wings and tail; white throat, bold black and white stripes on crown, nape of head, lower breast; loud, low whistles given frequently.

HABITAT: Pairs seen on larger tree trunks in varzea forest.

REGION: NEA, NWA, SAM

Plate 58d
Buff-throated Woodcreeper
Xiphorhynchus guttatus
ID: Medium-sized (23 cm, 9 in); thick, slightly down-curved bill; dark brown body with thin buffy streaks on upperparts and head; underparts brown with broad buffy white streaks coalescing into entirely buffy throat.

HABITAT: Lower trunks of terra firme primary forest, tall secondary forest, varzea and (in the Pantanal) gallery forest.

REGION: NEA, NWA, SAM, PAN

Plate 58e
Narrow-billed Woodcreeper
Lepidocolaptes angustirostris
ID: Medium-sized (20 cm, 8 in); pale bill; bold buffy-white eye-line; whitish underparts (with or without fine streaking); rusty back, wings and tail; crown brown with buffy streaks.

HABITAT: Alone or in pairs on trunks of scattered trees in gallery forest or margins of agricultural fields; often on fence posts.

REGION: PAN

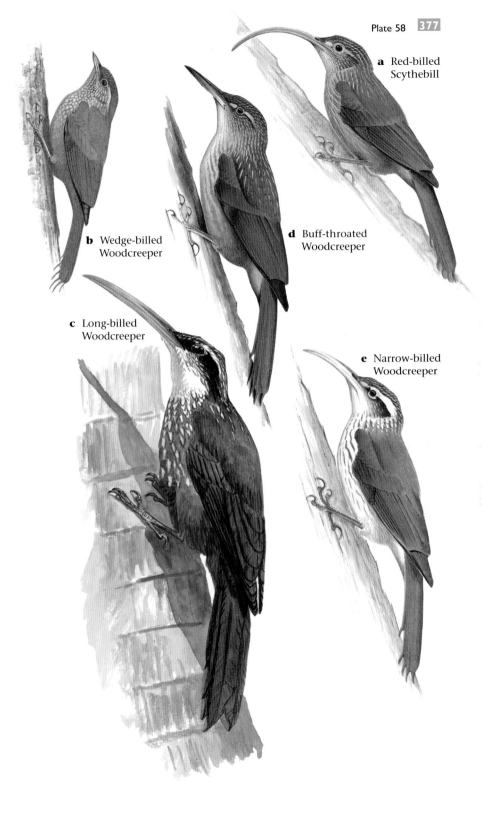

Plate 58 377

a Red-billed
Scythebill

b Wedge-billed
Woodcreeper

d Buff-throated
Woodcreeper

c Long-billed
Woodcreeper

e Narrow-billed
Woodcreeper

Plate 59a

Plain Xenops
Xenops minutus
ID: Small (12 cm, 4.7 in); drab brown body, buffy eye-line and bold silver-white moustache; wings and tail rusty with black feathers; bill short and upturned.

HABITAT: Lower branches and shrubs of primary and secondary forest; often in mixed-species foraging flocks of the understory.

REGION: NEA, NWA, SAM

Plate 59b

Rufous Cacholote
Pseudoseisura cristata
ID: Medium-sized (23 cm, 9 in); bright cinnamon with bushy crest and yellow eyes. Individuals in the Pantanal have somewhat grayer breasts and are considered a separate species by some experts.

HABITAT: Dry open woodlands, gallery forests and brushy margins of marshy areas; often staggers around on the ground, and in flight its slow wingbeat resembles that of a small jay.

REGION: PAN

Plate 59c

Great Antshrike
Taraba major
ID: Medium-sized (20 cm, 8 in); pure white underparts; black (male) or rusty colored (female) upperparts; red eye; voice commonly heard is an accelerating series of short whistled notes (bouncing ball) ending in a low growl.

HABITAT: Dense undergrowth and bushy secondary forest.

REGION: NEA, NWA, SAM, PAN

Plate 59d

Pale-legged Hornero
Furnarius leucopus
ID: Small (17 cm, 6.5 in); bright buffy color with gray crown and white eye-line; black wings with bright rusty colored patch obvious in flight; short tail and light-colored legs; loud ringing trills given throughout the day. (The similar-shaped and -behaving Rufous Hornero, *Furnarius rufus*, overlaps with the Pale-legged Hornero in the Pantanal, but is distinguished by its drab brown color and lack of eye-line; it is often confused for a thrush.)

HABITAT: Common on the ground in gallery forest, varzea, and forest edge where there are wet, swampy depressions; typically near water. Not as conspicuous as the Rufous Hornero, which occurs in open areas, secondary forest floor, city parks and along roads in pasturelands. Large spherical clay nests on fence posts, open tree branches, and buildings.

REGION: NWA, SAM, PAN

Plate 59e

Rufous-fronted Thornbird
(also called Common Thornbird)
Phacellodomus rufifrons
ID: Small (16 cm, 6 in); upperparts drab brown with rusty forehead and pale eye-line; underparts buffy white.

HABITAT: Pairs or small groups in trees of open woodlands and savannah. Most easily found by the distinct and large hanging nests made up of small sticks.

REGION: PAN

Plate 59 **379**

a Plain Xenops

c Great Antshrike

M

F

b Rufous Cacholote

d Pale-legged Hornero

oven-like nest

e Rufous-fronted Thornbird

hanging stick nest

Plate 60a

Black-spotted Bare-eye

Phlegopsis nigromaculata

ID: Small (18 cm, 7 in); bright red bare skin around eye; upperparts olive-brown with tear-shaped black spots on back; underparts black.

HABITAT: Near army ant columns in undergrowth of moist primary forest and varzea.

REGION: SAM

Plate 60b

Barred Antshrike

Thamnophilus doliatus

ID: Small (15 cm, 6 in); male black and white barred upper- and underparts; female rusty-colored upperparts and buffy underparts.

HABITAT: Thickets and secondary forest undergrowth.

REGION: NEA, SAM, PAN

Plate 60c

Mato Grosso Antbird

Cercomacra melanaria

ID: Small (16 cm, 6 in); male black with white spots on wings, back and tip of longish tail; female gray upperparts and light gray underparts with similarly placed white spots.

HABITAT: Pairs in brushy areas near water and gallery forest undergrowth.

REGION: PAN

Plate 60d

White-plumed Antbird

Pithys albifrons

ID: Small (13 cm, 5 in); spectacular white tufts on head and chin; rusty colored underparts.

HABITAT: Solitary in undergrowth of lowland moist primary and tall secondary forest.

REGION: NEA, NWA

Plate 60e

Thrush-like Antpitta

Myrmothera campanisona

ID: Small (15 cm, 6 in); brownish upperparts and whitish underparts with brown streaks; white throat and spot in back of eye; very short tail and long legs.

HABITAT: Pairs commonly heard calling from the ground of moist primary forest (terra firme and varzea), a series of bell-like hollow whistles.

REGION: NEA, NWA, SAM

Plate 60   381

a Black-spotted Bare-eye

F

M

b Barred Antshrike

c Mato Grosso Antbird

M

F

d White-plumed Antbird

e Thrush-like Antpitta

Plate 61a
Blue-crowned Manakin
Pipra coronata
ID: Small (9 cm, 3.5 in); males in northwestern Brazil are all black with bright blue crown; in central and southwestern Brazil they are bright greenish yellow with a light blue crown; female with bright green upperparts and grayish yellow underparts.

HABITAT: Undergrowth and lower levels of moist primary and tall secondary forest; fruiting trees.

REGION: NWA, SAM

Plate 61b
White-bearded Manakin
Manacus manacus
ID: Small (10 cm, 4 in); males with black back and cap, gray lower back and lower belly; white throat, breast and back of neck; female plain olive upperparts and grayish olive underparts; both sexes have bright orange legs.

HABITAT: Undergrowth and lower levels of brushy secondary forest; fruiting trees. Displaying males at a lec utter whistles, trills, and growls and snap their wings to produce loud popping sounds like small firecrackers.

REGION: NEA, NWA, SAM

Plate 61c
White-crowned Manakin
Pipra pipra
ID: Small (9 cm, 3.5 in); red eye; male black except for white crown and neck; female with olive-green upperparts, gray crown and sides of head, grayish olive underparts. Displaying males in lec give buzzing notes.

HABITAT: Undergrowth of moist forest.

REGION: NEA, NWA, SAM

Plate 61d
Golden-headed Manakin
Pipra erythrocephala
ID: Small (9 cm, 3.5 in); male black with bright golden head and white eye; female olive upperparts and grayish yellow underparts.

HABITAT: Lower parts of humid primary and tall secondary forest. Up to 10 males display in lecs where they give trills, buzzes, and chips to attract females (and curious ecotravellers).

REGION: NEA, NWA

Plate 61e
Helmeted Manakin
Antilophia galeata
ID: Small (14 cm, 5.5 in); male all-black except for scarlet upper back, crown and peculiar crest extending out over its bill; female yellow-olive with smaller but distinct crest.

HABITAT: Dense undergrowth of gallery forest and swampy woodlands.

REGION: PAN

Plate 61   383

F
a Blue-crowned
Manakin
M

F
b White-bearded
Manakin
M

F
e Helmeted
Manakin
M

F
c White-crowned
Manakin
M

F
d Golden-headed
Manakin
M

Plate 62a
Black-necked Red-Cotinga
Phoenicircus nigricollis
ID: Medium-sized (24 cm, 9.5 in); male brilliant red except for black face, back, wings and tail tip; female upperparts maroon to olive-brown, underparts pink.

HABITAT: Mid-level to canopy of moist terra firme forest; males in noisy lecs of 3 to 5.

REGION: NWA, SAM

Plate 62b
Plum-throated Cotinga
Cotinga maynana
ID: Medium-sized (20 cm, 8 in); male strikingly turquoise-blue with purple throat and yellow eye; female with gray upperparts and buffy underparts spotted gray. (Similar Spangled Cotinga, *Cotinga cayana*, more common in the eastern Amazon, is paler blue with extensive black spotting and a dark eye; females of the 2 species are difficult to distinguish.)

HABITAT: Canopy of moist primary and tall secondary forest and varzea; fruiting trees.

REGION: NWA, SAM

Plate 62c
Screaming Piha
Lipaugus vociferans
ID: Medium-sized (28 cm, 11 in); all gray; most often noticed by the ear-splitting whistle-screams of lecking males.

HABITAT: Mid-level to canopy of primary terra firme and varzea forest.

REGION: NEA, NWA, SAM

Plate 62d
Pompadour Cotinga
Xipholena punicea
ID: Medium-sized (20 cm, 8 in); male red-purple with white wings and pale eye; female gray with lighter breast and edges to wing feathers.

HABITAT: Often perches conspicuously in the canopy and on tall bare branches at the edge of forest, especially in sandy soils.

REGION: NEA, NWA, SAM

Plate 62e
Masked Tityra
Tityra semifasciata
ID: Medium-sized (20 cm, 8 in); bright red bill and bare area around eye; body white except for black wings and tail; male with black face; female with brown back, face and crown. (The similar Black-tailed Tityra, *Tityra cayana*, has an all-black crown, and the Black-crowned Tityra, *Tityra inquisitor*, has an all-black bill and no red around the eye.)

HABITAT: Tops of trees on forest edge, secondary and primary forest. Often noticed by its frog-like croaks and nasal grumbling.

REGION: NEA, NWA, SAM

Plate 62 **385**

b Plum-throated Cotinga

F

M

a Black-necked Red-Cotinga

M

F

c Screaming Piha

d Pompadour Cotinga

M

F

F

e Masked Tityra

M

Plate 63a

Amazonian Umbrellabird
Cephalopterus ornatus
ID: Large (51 cm, 1.6 ft); black with permanent crest and hanging wattle on throat; flies in an undulating up-and-down pattern reminiscent of a large, crested woodpecker; males at lecs give low mooing sounds.

HABITAT: Varzea forest and large river islands, usually associated with *Cecropia* trees.

REGION: NEA, NWA, SAM

Plate 63b

Purple-throated Fruitcrow
Querula purpurata
ID: Medium-sized (30 cm, 1 ft); all black; male with an indistinct purple throat; usually noticed by its noisy slurred whistles.

HABITAT: Family groups of 4 to 6 in the canopy of moist primary and tall secondary forest.

REGION: NEA, NWA, SAM

Plate 63c

Guianan Cock-of-the-Rock
Rupicola rupicola
ID: Medium-sized (32 cm, 1 ft); male bright orange with crest, gray and black wings; female dark brown with small crest; eyes of both sexes yellowish.

HABITAT: Middle and low levels of forest, especially near rocky outcroppings.

REGION: NEA, NWA

Plate 63d

Bare-necked Fruitcrow
Gymnoderus foetidus
ID: Medium-sized (34 cm, 1.2 ft); black and gray; small featherless head; in flight, the wide wings of the male flash black and silver.

HABITAT: Canopy of primary and secondary forest, varzea and isolated fruiting trees; flying high overhead along rivers.

REGION: NEA, NWA, SAM

Plate 63 387

a Amazonian Umbrellabird

M

F

b Purple-throated Fruitcrow

M

F

c Guianan Cock-of-the-Rock

M

F

d Bare-necked Fruitcrow

Plate 64a
White-headed Marsh-Tyrant
Arundinicola leucocephala
ID: Small (12 cm, 5 in); male all black with pure white head; female gray-brown with whitish forehead and underparts.

HABITAT: Perched conspicuously in marshes, moist grassland and islands in large rivers.

REGION: NEA, NWA, PAN

Plate 64b
Spotted Tody-Flycatcher
Todirostrum maculatum
ID: Small (10 cm, 4 in); long flat bill; gray head and olive-green back and tail; throat white and rest of underparts yellow; conspicuous black spotting on throat and upper chest; yellow eye.

HABITAT: Sits on open branches in undergrowth and mid-levels of secondary forest near water and in gardens.

REGION: NEA, NWA, SAM

Plate 64c
Cattle Tyrant
Machetornis rixosus
ID: Medium-sized (19 cm, 7.5 in); light gray head; olive-brown back, wings, and tail; throat white; rest of underparts bright yellow; looks like a Tropical Kingbird (Plate 66) but runs on the ground.

HABITAT: Open savannah, lawns, and agricultural fields – often near livestock.

REGION: PAN

Plate 64d
Vermilion Flycatcher
Pyrocephalus rubinus
ID: Small (14 cm, 5.5 in); flat black bill; male upperparts and eye-mask black, crown and underparts bright red; female upperparts pale brown and underparts whitish streaked pink on the sides.

HABITAT: Pairs on exposed branches in open areas; in Amazon present only as Austral migrants wintering in canopy and clearings (June to September); permanent resident in Pantanal in open savannah and brushy areas, often near water.

REGION: NEA, NWA, PAN

Plate 64e
Drab Water-Tyrant
Octhornis littoralis
ID: Small (13 cm, 5 in); drab and all brown with a black bill.

HABITAT: Single or in pairs perched low along edge of larger rivers of the Amazon – especially near open but shaded and vegetated vertical banks. Often fly repeatedly for short distances low over the water ahead of your boat or canoe.

REGION: NEA, NWA, SAM

Plate 64   389

a White-headed
Marsh-Tyrant

M

F

b Spotted
Tody-Flycatcher

c Cattle Tyrant

M

d Vermilion
Flycatcher

F

e Drab Water-Tyrant

Plate 65a
Eastern Kingbird
Tyrannus tyrannus
ID: Medium-sized (21 cm, 8 in); dark gray to black upperparts; white underparts with conspicuous white band on end of tail.

HABITAT: Wintering migrant from North America, often in large flocks at fruiting trees or moving along rivers.

REGION: NWA, SAM, PAN

Plate 65b
Fork-tailed Flycatcher
Tyrannus savana
ID: Medium-sized (40 cm, 1.3 ft); extremely long, black tail; black cap and wings; gray back; white underparts.

HABITAT: Nests primarily south of the Amazon in open agricultural areas and savannah where it perches conspicuously on fence wires and isolated trees. Migrant through the Amazon, usually along large rivers. In migration often in large flocks mixed in with Eastern Kingbirds.

REGION: NEA, CMF, NWA, SAM, PAN

Plate 65c
White-rumped Monjita
Xolmis velata
ID: Small (20 cm, 8 in); gray upperparts with white lower back and black tail tip; white breast, throat, and forehead; bold white wing stripe in flight.

HABITAT: Pairs perched conspicuously on fence posts, trees, and buildings in agricultural areas and open savannah, often near water.

REGION: PAN

Plate 65d
Sirystes
Sirystes sibilator
ID: Small (18 cm, 7 in); gray back; black cap, face and tail; black wings with white feather edgings; underparts light gray.

HABITAT: Canopy of primary and tall secondary forest in terra firme and varzea; often in pairs calling to each other, and most often seen from canopy towers.

REGION: NEA, SAM

Plate 65e
Black-backed Water-Tyrant
Fluvicola albiventer
ID: Small (14 cm, 5.5 in); black upperparts except for white forehead, face, spots on wings and tail tip; white underparts.

HABITAT: On or near ground in marshy areas, along lakes and rivers. Resident in the Pantanal and southeastern Amazon but a wintering migrant to southwestern Amazon.

REGION: SAM, PAN

Plate 65 **391**

a Eastern Kingbird

b Fork-tailed Flycatcher

c White-rumped Monjita

d Sirystes

e Black-backed Water-Tyrant

Plate 66a
Tropical Kingbird
Tyrannus melancholicus
ID: Medium-sized (22 cm, 8.5 in); gray head; olive back; brown tail with distinct notch; gray throat; olive-yellow upper breast, bright yellow lower breast.

HABITAT: Most common and easily seen flycatcher in open areas; perches alone on exposed branches and dead treetops in pastures, telephone wires, secondary forest edges and along rivers and lakes.

REGION: NEA, NWA, SAM, PAN

Plate 66b
Boat-billed Flycatcher
Megarhynchus pitangua
ID: Medium-sized (23 cm, 9 in); large replica of the more common Great Kiskadee, but with a much more massive bill; browner back, and less rusty in the wings; a long squeaking and nasal call.

HABITAT: Pairs in tops of tall secondary forest, varzea, dry wood lots and pasture edges often away from water.

REGION: NEA, NWA, SAM, PAN

Plate 66c
Great Kiskadee
Pitangus sulphuratus
ID: Medium-sized (22 cm, 8.5 in); chunky shape; black crown with bold white head band; brown back; rusty edges to wing feathers; bright yellow underparts; calls out its name in a loud voice throughout the day, "kis-ka-DEE."

HABITAT: High in secondary forest, forest edge, lake and river edges, gardens, city parks.

REGION: NEA, NWA, SAM, PAN

Plate 66d
Lesser Kiskadee
Pitangus lictor
ID: Small (18 cm, 7 in); smaller replica of the Great Kiskadee, but more slender, less rusty in the wings; a nasal, wheezing voice completely unlike that of the Great Kiskadee.

HABITAT: Pairs seen on low, exposed vegetation along the water's edge of oxbow lakes and small, slow streams.

REGION: NEA, NWA, SAM, PAN

Plate 66e
Social Flycatcher
Myiozetetes similis
ID: Small (17 cm, 6.5 in); olive-gray back, tail, and wings, with no rusty in wings; small black bill; yellow breast and contrasting white throat; harsh staccato calls. (Replaced in the Pantanal by the similar Rusty-margined Flycatcher, *Myiozetetes cayanensis*, which has rusty edgings to the wing and tail feathers.)

HABITAT: Pairs or small family groups perch together in mid to high levels of secondary forest, pasture edge and vegetation along watercourses.

REGION: NEA, NWA, SAM

Plate 66f
Piratic Flycatcher
Legatus leucophaius
ID: Small (15 cm, 6 in); dark brown upperparts; bold white eye-line, cheek patch and throat; yellowish underparts with faint dark streaking; no rusty color in wings or tail.

HABITAT: Alone perched high on exposed treetop or dead branch of secondary forest, forest edge and clearings with scattered tall trees in moist forest. Most easily noticed by their persistent, whining call notes often given from high in the canopy.

REGION: NEA, NWA, PAN

Plate 66

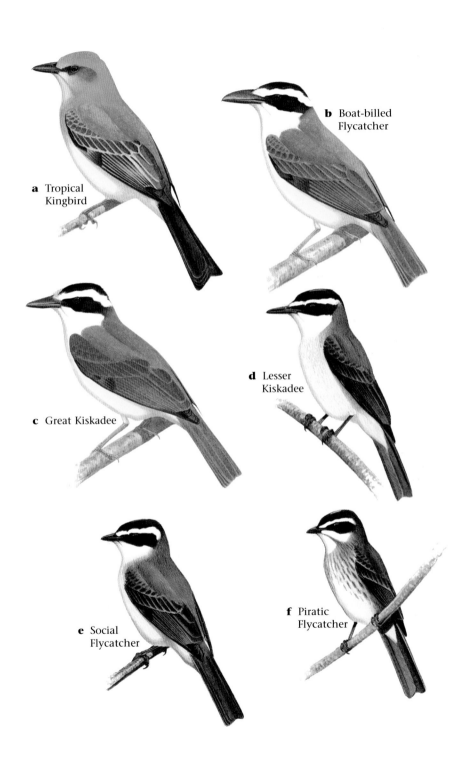

a Tropical Kingbird

b Boat-billed Flycatcher

c Great Kiskadee

d Lesser Kiskadee

e Social Flycatcher

f Piratic Flycatcher

Plate 67a
Thrush-like Wren
Campylorhynchus turdinus
ID: Medium-sized (21 cm, 8 in); Amazonian form with brownish gray upperparts; white underparts densely spotted; Pantanal form pale gray above with whitish unspotted breast; both forms with distinct eye-line and long tail.

HABITAT: Family groups in vine tangles, palm fronds and upper parts of forest edge, tall secondary forest, and varzea; explosive and rollicking songs obvious.

REGION: SAM, PAN

Plate 67b
Chalk-browed Mockingbird
Mimus saturninus
ID: Medium-sized (26 cm, 10 in); grayish brown upperparts, buffy white underparts; obvious white eye-line; bold white tail corners in flight. (During the Austral winter, the similar White-banded Mockingbird, *Mimus triurus*, also occurs in the Pantanal. It is distinguished by a white band on each wing in flight and outer sides of tail completely white.)

HABITAT: Savannah and secondary forest surrounding fields. Often feeds on the ground and perches in low bushes.

REGION: PAN

Plate 67c
Donacobius
(also called Black-capped Donacobius)
Donacobius atricapillus
ID: Medium-sized (22 cm, 9 in); brown back and wings; black tail, crown and cheeks; bright buffy underparts; long bill.

HABITAT: Family groups at the top of tall aquatic grass and low marsh vegetation; loud voices are obvious.

REGION: NEA, NWA, SAM, PAN

Plate 67d
Violaceous Jay
Cyanocorax violaceus
ID: Medium-sized (37 cm, 1.2 ft); pale blue-gray with black crown, face and upper breast; harsh, high-pitched calls.

HABITAT: Small family groups in moist forest edge, varzea and small clearings throughout the western Amazon.

REGION: NWA, SAM

Plate 67e
Purplish Jay
Cyanocorax cyanomelas
ID: Medium-sized (37 cm, 1.2 ft); dark purple with blackish head.

HABITAT: Small but noisy flocks in shrubby forest patches and gallery forest.

REGION: PAN

Plate 67 **395**

a Thrush-like Wren

Amazonian form

Pantanal form

b Chalk-browed Mockingbird

c Donacobius

d Violaceous Jay

e Purplish Jay

Plate 68a
Southern Nightingale Wren
Microcerculus marginatus
ID: Small (11 cm, 4 in); upperparts brown, underparts white; short tail.

HABITAT: Walks stealthily on the ground but usually in thick vegetation and vine tangles; difficult to see, but its single flute-like notes, each subsequent one lower in tone and with a longer interval of silence than the previous one, are a common sound of Amazonian forests.

REGION: NWA, SAM

Plate 68b
House Wren
Troglodytes aedon
ID: Small (11 cm, 4.5 in); brown upperparts, buffy underparts; buffy eyestripe; faint black barring on wings, tail.

HABITAT: Low vegetation and ground in clearings, dry open areas, and frequently near human habitation.

REGION: NEA, NWA, SAM, PAN

Plate 68c
Buff-breasted Wren
(also called Fawn-breasted Wren)
Thryothorus leucotis
ID: Small (14 cm, 5.5 in); rusty upperparts with black barring on tail and wings; white eye-line and black and white streaked cheeks; whitish throat and rusty breast. (The population in the Pantanal is similar in color but smaller and considered a separate species, Fawn-breasted Wren, *Thryothorus guarayanus*, by some experts.)

HABITAT: Thick undergrowth, forest edge, and mangroves.

REGION: NEA, CMF, NWA, SAM, PAN

Plate 68d
Long-billed Gnatwren
Ramphocaenus melanurus
ID: Small (12 cm, 5 in); long slender bill and relatively long slender blackish tail, often held cocked up over the back; upperparts brown; underparts grayish with buffy sides.

HABITAT: Low in thick undergrowth of secondary forests and forest edge, often in mixed-species foraging flocks.

REGION: NEA, NWA, SAM

Plate 68e
Masked Gnatcatcher
Polioptila dumicola
ID: Small (13 cm, 5 in); dark blue-gray with black mask bordered below by white line (male) or light gray mask (female); black tail with distinct white outer tail feathers; black wings with white edgings.

HABITAT: Usually in pairs in open forested areas and gallery forest, often with mixed-species foraging flocks.

REGION: PAN

Plate 68 **397**

a Southern Nightingale Wren

b House Wren

c Buff-breasted Wren

d Long-billed Gnatwren

e Masked Gnatcatcher

Plate 69a

Rufous-bellied Thrush
Turdus rufiventris
ID: Medium-sized (25 cm, 10 in); brown upperparts; yellowish bill; bare orange eyering; throat white streaked black; upper breast brown and lower breast rusty.

HABITAT: Running on ground in open woodland, forest edge, and gardens.

REGION: PAN

Plate 69b

Pale-breasted Thrush
Turdus leucomelas
ID: Medium-sized (23 cm, 9 in); brown back, wings, and tail; gray head; throat white with black streaks; breast buffy brown except for whitish center and lower belly; greenish bill.

HABITAT: Usually low or on the ground of forest edges, open woodland, savannah and gallery forest.

REGION: PAN

Plate 69c

Black-billed Thrush
Turdus ignobilis
ID: Medium-sized (24 cm, 9.5 in); brown upperparts; olive underparts with white lower belly; black bill.

HABITAT: Thick scrub and low secondary vegetation, often around human habitation.

REGION: NEA, NWA, SAM

Plate 69d

Lawrence's Thrush
Turdus lawrencii
ID: Medium-sized (23 cm, 9 in); gray-brown upperparts; olive underparts except for white lower belly and white throat with fine black streaks; bright yellow bill, eyering.

HABITAT: Feeds on ground and undergrowth of moist primary forest and varzea, but sings its flute-like songs that mimic other bird species from high in the canopy.

REGION: NWA, SAM

Plate 69e

Rufous-browed Peppershrike
Cyclarhis gujanensis
ID: Small (15 cm, 6 in); olive-green upperparts; gray head with broad rusty eye-line; yellow throat and upper breast; whitish lower breast; reddish eyes, pinkish legs.

HABITAT: Primary and tall secondary terra firme forest, varzea, and gallery forest.

REGION: NEA, SAM, PAN

Plate 69 **399**

a Rufous-bellied
Thrush

b Pale-breasted
Thrush

c Black-billed
Thrush

d Lawrence's
Thrush

e Rufous-browed
Peppershrike

Plate 70a

Slaty-capped Shrike-Vireo
Vireolanius leucotis
ID: Small (14 cm, 5.5 in); olive-green back, wings, and tail; gray head with bright yellow eye-line and forehead; underparts bright yellow; eyes yellow-green.

HABITAT: Canopy of humid primary and tall secondary forest; often in mixed-species foraging flocks.

REGION: NEA, NWA, SAM

Plate 70b

Red-eyed Vireo
Vireo olivaceus
ID: Small (15 cm, 6 in); olive-brown back, wings and tail; gray crown and bold white eye-line with narrow black line above it; underparts gray to pale yellow; eye bright red.

HABITAT: Often in mixed species flocks in mid-levels of primary forest, tall secondary forest, varzea, shrubby forest edge, and gardens. Resident population supplemented in western Amazonia (September to April) by migratory population that nests in North America.

REGION: NEA, NWA, SAM, PAN

Plate 70c

Chestnut-vented Conebill
Conirostrum speciosum
ID: Small (11 cm, 4 in); male grayish blue upperparts; pale gray underparts; rusty lower belly and bold white spot in wing; female with olive-green upperparts.

HABITAT: Open secondary forest, scrubby areas, gallery forest, and varzea; often in mixed species flocks.

REGION: SAM, PAN

Plate 70d

Flavescent Warbler
Basileuterus (Phaeothlypis) flaveolus
ID: Small (14 cm, 5.5 in); olive upperparts; yellow eyebrow; underparts yellow.

HABITAT: Pairs walking or hopping on or near the ground in shrubby clearings, forest edge, and gallery forest; spreads and fans its tail back and forth sideways while foraging; loud musical series of calls also make it obvious.

REGION: PAN

Plate 70e

Tropical Parula
Parula pitiayuma
ID: Small (11 cm, 4 in); dull blue upperparts, black mask, bright yellow-orange underparts.

HABITAT: Forest edge, gallery forest, and secondary forest; often in mixed-species foraging flocks of tanagers.

REGION: PAN

Plate 70f

Bananaquit
Coereba flaveola
ID: Small (10 cm, 4 in); black crown and cheek; white eye-line; gray throat; underparts and rump bright yellow; rest of upperparts gray; wing with a small white patch; short bill thin and curved down.

HABITAT: Active in pairs around flowering and fruiting trees, bushes and shrubs in open secondary forest, gardens and city parks; usually absent from primary forest areas.

REGION: NEA, SAM, PAN

Plate 70 **401**

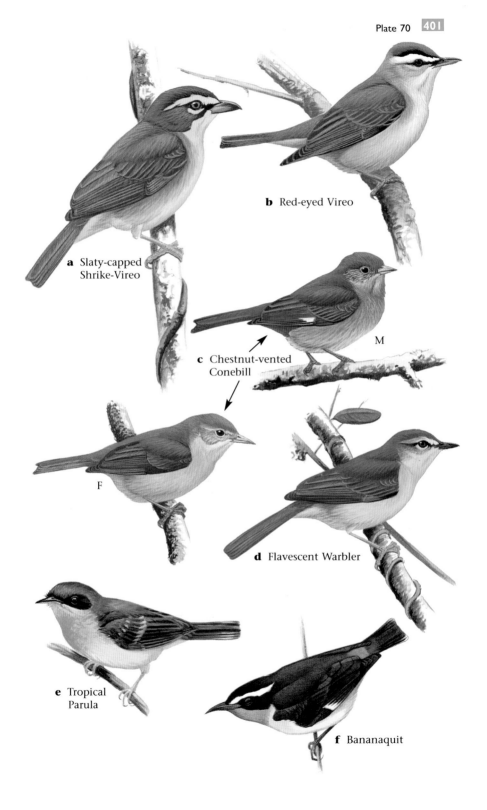

a Slaty-capped
Shrike-Vireo

b Red-eyed Vireo

c Chestnut-vented
Conebill

M

F

d Flavescent Warbler

e Tropical
Parula

f Bananaquit

Plate 71a
Green Honeycreeper
Chlorophanes spiza
ID: Small (14 cm, 5.5 in); male shiny green with black face and crown, red eye, and bright yellow bill; female yellow-green with dark eye.

HABITAT: Pairs forage in mid-level to canopy of moist primary, tall secondary forest, and varzea; often in large mixed-species foraging flocks.

REGION: NEA, NWA, SAM

Plate 71b
Blue Dacnis
Dacnis cayana
ID: Small (13 cm, 5 in); male bright turquoise-blue with small black throat patch, mainly black tail, wings; female green with blue-gray head.

HABITAT: Humid secondary forest, gallery forest and shrubby clearings, flowering and fruiting trees; often in mixed-species foraging flocks.

REGION: NEA, NWA, SAM

Plate 71c
Black-faced Dacnis
Dacnis lineata
ID: Small (11 cm, 4 in); eyes yellow; male bright turquoise with black mask, back of neck, back, wings, and tail; center of belly white; female olive upperparts, gray head and underparts.

HABITAT: Canopy of primary and tall secondary terra firme forest, varzea and forest edge; often in mixed-species foraging flocks.

REGION: NEA, NWA, SAM

Plate 71d
Yellow-bellied Dacnis
Dacnis flaviventer
ID: Small (13 cm, 5 in); male with bright yellow underparts with black throat, mask, back, wings, and tail; crown gray-green; female with pale brown-olive upperparts, buffy yellow underparts.

HABITAT: Pairs seen in mid-levels to canopy of terra firme, moist tall secondary forest, and varzea.

REGION: NWA, SAM

Plate 71e
Purple Honeycreeper
Cyanerpes caeruleus
ID: Small (11 cm, 4 in); long slender bill curved down; short tail; male glistening purple with black throat, wings, and tail, bright yellow legs; female with green upperparts, green to yellow underparts streaked white; legs dull yellow. (The similar Red-legged Honeycreeper, *Cyanerpes cyaneus*, occurs in the same areas and is distinguished by red legs in both sexes and a black back and blue crown in males.)

HABITAT: Canopy and upper levels of moist primary, tall secondary forest, and gardens; often in mixed-species foraging flocks.

REGION: NEA, NWA, SAM

Plate 71 403

a Green Honeycreeper

M

F

b Blue Dacnis

M

F

M

c Black-faced Dacnis

F

d Yellow-bellied Dacnis

F

M

e Purple Honeycreeper

F

M

Plate 72a
Yellow-backed Tanager
Hemithraupis flavicollis
ID: Small (13 cm, 5 in); male with black upperparts except bright yellow lower back; throat bright yellow and rest of underparts grayish white with yellow lower belly; female with dark olive upperparts and yellow edgings to wing feathers, yellow underparts.

HABITAT: Canopy of terra firme primary forest and varzea; usually in mixed-species foraging flocks.

REGION: NEA, NWA, SAM

Plate 72b
Guira Tanager
Hemithraupis guira
ID: Small (13 cm, 5 in); male with olive upperparts and bright orange lower back; yellow bill; black face surrounded by yellow above and orange breast patch below; rest of underparts yellowish gray; female olive upperparts and olive-yellow underparts.

HABITAT: Canopy of primary terra firme and tall secondary forest, open woodlands, and gallery forest, often in mixed-species foraging flocks.

REGION: NWA, SAM, PAN

Plate 72c
Hooded Tanager
Nemosia pileata
ID: Small (13 cm, 5 in); grayish blue upperparts; yellow eyes and legs; prominent white spot between eye and bill; white underparts; male with black cap and sides of head.

HABITAT: Secondary forest, shrubby forest edge, varzea, gallery forest, and gardens.

REGION: NEA, SAM, PAN

Plate 72d
Yellow-bellied Tanager
Tangara xanthogastra
ID: Small (12 cm, 5 in); bright green with small black spots on back, breast, and head; bright yellow belly unspotted.

HABITAT: Canopy of primary and tall secondary terra firme forest, varzea, and edge of forest clearings; often in mixed-species foraging flocks.

REGION: NWA, SAM

Plate 72e
Burnished-buff Tanager
Tangara cayana
ID: Small (14 cm, 5.5 in); light buff upperparts; blue wings and tail; male with black face and throat; rest of underparts light buff.

HABITAT: Pairs or small family groups in open woodlands, savannah, gallery forest, gardens, and forest edge.

REGION: NEA, SAM, PAN

Plate 72   405

a Yellow-backed Tanager

M

F

b Guira Tanager

M

F

c Hooded Tanager

d Yellow-bellied Tanager

e Burnished-buff Tanager

Plate 73a
Turquoise Tanager
Tangara mexicana
ID: Small (14 cm, 5.5 in); upperparts black with dark blue rump, forehead, face, and shoulders; underparts dark blue with bright yellow belly.

HABITAT: In mixed-species foraging flocks in secondary forest, forest edge, gardens, and varzea.

REGION: NEA, NWA, SAM

Plate 73b
Bay-headed Tanager
Tangara gyrola
ID: Small (14 cm, 5.5 in); bright rusty head; blue-green underparts and rump; bright green back, wings, and tail.

HABITAT: Canopy and mid-levels of primary, tall secondary forest, and forest edge; usually in mixed-species foraging flocks.

REGION: NWA, SAM

Plate 73c
Green-and-gold Tanager
Tangara schrankii
ID: Small (14 cm, 5.5 in); golden yellow crown, rump, and center of breast shading into bright green on underparts; black forehead and side of face; back streaked black.

HABITAT: Canopy of humid primary and tall secondary terra firme forest, varzea, and forest edge; usually in mixed-species foraging flocks.

REGION: NWA, SAM

Plate 73d
Paradise Tanager
Tangara chilensis
ID: Small (14 cm, 5.5 in); bright yellow-green head; bright red rump; blue-green underparts; black tail, wings, back, and lower belly.

HABITAT: Canopy of humid primary and tall secondary terra firme forest, varzea, and forest edge; usually in mixed-species foraging flocks.

REGION: NEA, NWA, SAM

Plate 73e
Opal-rumped Tanager
Tangara velia
ID: Small (14 cm, 5.5 in); crown and back black, rump and forehead whitish, tail and wings blue; underparts purplish blue with bright rusty lower belly.

HABITAT: Canopy of humid primary and tall secondary terra firme forest, flooded forest, and forest edge; usually in mixed-species foraging flocks.

REGION: NEA, NWA, SAM

Plate 73 407

a Turquoise Tanager

b Bay-headed Tanager

c Green-and-gold Tanager

d Paradise Tanager

e Opal-rumped Tanager

Plate 74a

Thick-billed Euphonia
Euphonia laniirostris

ID: Small (11 cm, 4 in); male with bright yellow underparts and crown, dark blue upperparts; female olive-green upperparts and gray-yellow underparts.

HABITAT: Open forest, dry secondary scrub, gardens, city parks; often in mixed-species foraging flocks.

REGION: SAM, PAN

Plate 74b

White-vented Euphonia
Euphonia minuta

ID: Small (10 cm, 4 in); male with bright yellow breast and crown, dark blue upperparts and throat, white lower belly and undertail; female olive upperparts, gray throat, olive-yellow breast and white lower belly. (In the Pantanal and the drier open areas along the Río Amazonas, the similar Purple-throated Euphonia, *Euphonia chlorotica*, has all-yellow underparts except for white undertail and a larger yellow cap.)

HABITAT: Canopy of moist primary and tall secondary terra firme forest and varzea.

REGION: NEA, NWA, SAM

Plate 74c

Chestnut-bellied Euphonia
Euphonia rufiventris

ID: Small (11 cm, 4 in); male with all dark blue head, chest, and upperparts; rest of underparts orange-yellow; female olive-gray upperparts and gray underparts except for buffy lower belly.

HABITAT: Canopy of humid primary and tall terra firme forest, varzea, and forest edge; often in mixed-species foraging flocks.

REGION: NWA, SAM

Plate 74d

White-lored Euphonia
Euphonia chrysopasta

ID: Small (11 cm, 4 in); male gray-olive upperparts, yellow-olive underparts; bold white area on chin and between eye and bill; female similar but grayer below.

HABITAT: Canopy of humid primary and tall terra firme forest, varzea, and forest edge; often in mixed-species foraging flocks.

REGION: NEA, NWA, SAM

Plate 74e

Swallow Tanager
Tersina viridis

ID: Small (15 cm, 6 in); male shiny turquoise with black mask, faint barring on sides of breast, white lower belly; female all grass-green with barring on sides of breast.

HABITAT: Small flocks or pairs perch high on exposed branches on the edge of humid forest, along rivers and gallery forest. Irregularly and often unpredictably common throughout much of the Amazon and Pantanal.

REGION: NEA, NWA, SAM, PAN

Plate 74 **409**

a Thick-billed Euphonia

M

F

b White-vented Euphonia

M

F

c Chestnut-bellied Euphonia

M

F

d White-lored Euphonia

e Swallow Tanager

M

F

Plate 75a
Gray-headed Tanager
Eucometis penicillata
ID: Small (18 cm, 7 in); gray head with inconspicuous crest (longer in the Pantanal); whitish throat; olive-yellow upperparts; yellow underparts.

HABITAT: Pairs or in mixed-species foraging flocks in undergrowth of moist secondary growth, forest edge, varzea, and gallery forest.

REGION: NEA, SAM, PAN

Plate 75b
Palm Tanager
Thraupis palmarum
ID: Small (18 cm, 7 in); olive-gray; blackish tail; wings in flight show contrasting black and bright olive pattern.

HABITAT: Pairs seen in isolated trees in open scrub and agricultural areas, secondary forest, parks, gardens; often near or in palms.

REGION: NEA, NWA, SAM, PAN

Plate 75c
Masked Crimson Tanager
Ramphocelus nigrogularis
ID: Small (19 cm, 7.5 in); bright crimson head, upper breast; black mask, back, wings, tail, and center of lower belly; silver-white lower part of bill.

HABITAT: Small groups in low vegetation and short trees along small rivers, oxbow lakes, and varzea.

REGION: NEA, NWA, SAM

Plate 75d
Silver-beaked Tanager
Ramphocelus carbo
ID: Small (18 cm, 7 in); male velvet black with deep red overtones, especially on head and upper breast; silver-white lower part of bill; female dark red-brown.

HABITAT: Noisy groups of 4 to 8 in scrubby areas, forest edge, and river edges.

REGION: NEA, NWA, SAM, PAN

Plate 75e
Blue-gray Tanager
Thraupis episcopus
ID: Small (17 cm, 7 in); pale blue-gray with white (south and western Amazon) to pale blue (north and eastern Amazon) shoulders. (Replaced in the Pantanal by the similar Sayaca Tanager, *Thraupis sayaca*, which is blue-green and lacks the pale shoulders.)

HABITAT: Pairs seen in open woodland, scrubby forest, secondary forest, gardens, and city parks.

REGION: NEA, NWA, SAM

Plate 75   411

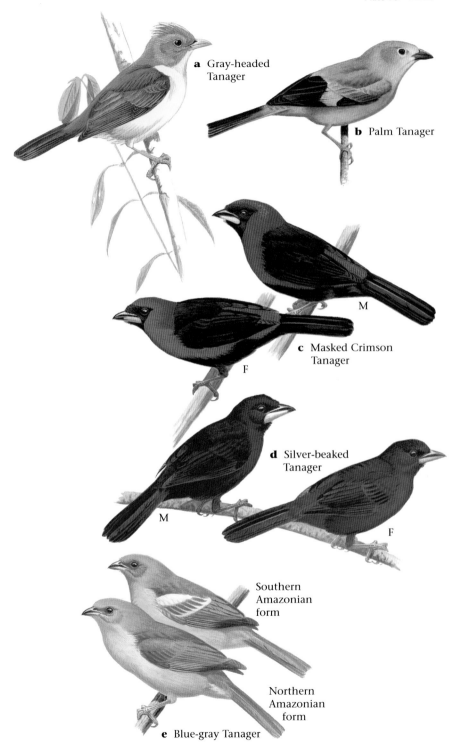

a Gray-headed Tanager

b Palm Tanager

c Masked Crimson Tanager

M

F

d Silver-beaked Tanager

M

F

Southern Amazonian form

Northern Amazonian form

e Blue-gray Tanager

Plate 76a
Flame-crested Tanager
Tachyphonus cristatus
ID: Small (16 cm, 6 in); male all-black except for bright orange crown and buffy yellow lower back and throat patch; female upperparts buffy brown and underparts yellowish buff.

HABITAT: Mid-levels and canopy of moist primary and secondary terra firme forest, forest edge, and varzea; frequently in mixed-species foraging flocks.

REGION: NEA, NWA, SAM

Plate 76b
White-shouldered Tanager
Tachyphonus luctuosus
ID: Small (13 cm, 5 in); male glossy black with large white shoulder patches; female with gray head, olive-green upperparts and bright yellow underparts.

HABITAT: Mid-levels and canopy of moist primary and secondary terra firme forest, forest edge, and varzea; frequently in mixed-species foraging flocks.

REGION: NEA, NWA, SAM

Plate 76c
Red-billed Pied Tanager
Lamprospiza melanoleuca
ID: Small (17 cm, 7 in); male upperparts and throat black; underparts white with a black line cutting across the corner of each side of the upper breast; bright red bill; female similar except back gray.

HABITAT: Canopy of terra firme forest, often in mixed-species foraging flocks.

REGION: NEA, SAM

Plate 76d
Fulvous Shrike-Tanager
Lanio fulvus
ID: Small (17 cm, 7 in); male bright buffy yellow with black wings, tail, head, and throat; brown patch on center of breast; female olive-brown with rusty lower back and grayish throat. (Replaced south of the Río Amazonas by the similar White-winged Shrike-Tanager, *Lanio versicolor*, in which the male has a large white patch on the wing and an olive crown and throat; female is yellowish brown with yellow center of belly.)

HABITAT: Canopy of terra firme forest; often in mixed-species foraging flocks.

REGION: NEA, NWA

Plate 76e
Magpie Tanager
Cissopis leveriana
ID: Medium-sized (28 cm, 11 in); conspicuous with its long tail and striking black and white pattern.

HABITAT: Pairs seen in secondary forest edge, shrubby areas, and vegetation along rivers and lakes.

REGION: NWA, SAM

Plate 76 413

M

a Flame-crested
Tanager

M

F

F

b White-shouldered
Tanager

c Red-billed Pied
Tanager

e Magpie Tanager

M

d Fulvous Shrike-
Tanager

F

Plate 77a
Red-breasted Blackbird
Sturnella militaris
ID: Medium-sized (19 cm, 7.5 in); male black with bright scarlet throat and upper breast; female brownish with black and buff steaks; buffy white eyestripe and crown. (Replaced in the Pantanal by the similar White-browed Blackbird, *Sturnella superciliaris*, in which the male has bold white line in back of the eye; females indistinguishable.)

HABITAT: Sitting on the ground, low bushes or on telephone wires of open pastures, grassy fields and irrigated areas.

REGION: NEA, SAM

Plate 77b
Giant Cowbird
Scaphidura oryzivora
ID: Medium-sized (37 cm, 1.2 ft); male glossy black with conspicuous ruff on neck; female smaller, duller black, and little or no ruff on neck.

HABITAT: In pairs or small groups walking on the ground or flying high overhead; often along river sand bars; usually near oropendola nests (the cowbirds lay their eggs in oropendola nests).

REGION: NEA, NWA, SAM, PAN

Plate 77c
Scarlet-headed Blackbird
Amblyramphus holosericeus
ID: Medium-sized (24 cm, 9.5 in); all-black with brilliant orange-red head, throat, and thighs.

HABITAT: Confined to extensive reed beds in marshes where they sit conspicuously in pairs at the tops of the reeds and sing loudly.

REGION: PAN

Plate 77d
Troupial
Icterus icterus
ID: Medium-sized (23 cm, 9 in); bright orange with black "bib" and face; black tail; black wings with small white patch; orange shoulder; its cheery song is a series of slow two- and three-noted loud piping whistles.

HABITAT: Moist forest edge and secondary vegetation along forested marshes and rivers.

REGION: NEA, SAM, PAN

Plate 77e
Oriole Blackbird
Gymnomystax mexicanus
ID: Medium-sized (28 cm, 11 in); black back, wings and tail contrasting with bright yellow head and underparts.

HABITAT: Pairs seen in top of small bushes in marshes and low, open vegetation along rivers, marshy areas and oxbow lakes on the Río Amazonas.

REGION: NEA, NWA, SAM

Plate 77 415

c Scarlet-headed
Blackbird

M

a Red-breasted
Blackbird

F

d Troupial

b Giant Cowbird

e Oriole
Blackbird

Plate 78a
Crested Oropendola
Psarocolius decumanus
ID: Medium-sized (47 cm, 1.5 ft); males are distinctly larger than females (37 cm, 1.2 ft) but both are glossy black with rusty rump and lower belly, bright yellow tail, and long, straight, whitish bills.

HABITAT: Large flocks in tall humid forest edges or flying high across open rivers and marshes to their roosts.

REGION: NEA, NWA, SAM, PAN

Plate 78b
Olive Oropendola
Psaracolius bifasciatus
ID: Large (50 cm, 20 in); olive-green head, neck, and chest; rest of body chestnut except for yellow tail; black bill tipped orange, bare pink patch on face.

HABITAT: High in canopy of terra firme forest.

REGION: NWA, SAM

Plate 78c
Yellow-rumped Cacique
Cacicus cela
ID: Medium-sized (30 cm, 1 ft); males are noticeably larger than females (23 cm, 9 in) but identical in their color pattern, black with yellow wing patch, rump, and base of tail.

HABITAT: Usually in flocks of 5 to 25 in tall vegetation along river and lake edges, varzea, open areas, and frequently near human habitation.

REGION: NEA, NWA, SAM, PAN

Plate 78d
Red-rumped Cacique
Cacicus haemorrhous
ID: Medium-sized (28 cm, 11 in); all-black with bright red lower back, whitish bill and pale blue eye (females similar but smaller).

HABITAT: Often in large family groups in the canopy and forest edge of terra firme forest.

REGION: NEA, NWA, SAM

Plate 78e
Epaulet Oriole
Icterus cayanensis
ID: Medium-sized (21 cm, 8 in); all-black with chestnut (southern Amazon and Pantanal) or yellow (northern Amazon) shoulders. (Replaced in northeastern Amazonia by the similar Moriche Oriole, *Icterus chrysocephalus*, which inhabits Moriche Palm swamps and has a bright yellow crown and rump as well as shoulders).

HABITAT: Forest edge, open secondary forest, varzea, and gallery forests.

REGION: NEA, SAM, PAN

Plate 78   417

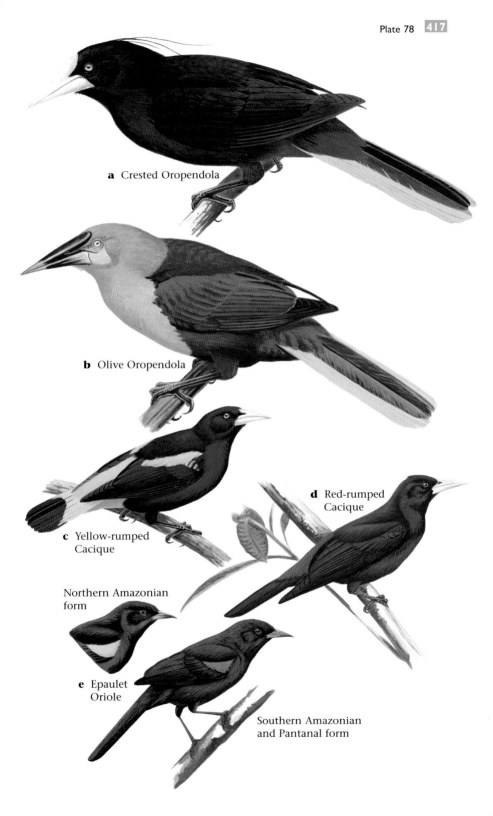

a Crested Oropendola

b Olive Oropendola

c Yellow-rumped Cacique

d Red-rumped Cacique

Northern Amazonian form

e Epaulet Oriole

Southern Amazonian and Pantanal form

Plate 79a
Buff-throated Saltator
Saltator maximus
ID: Medium-sized (21 cm, 8 in); green-olive back, wings and tail; gray head with short white line over eye; small white throat patch with black border; underparts buffy gray.

HABITAT: Shrubby undergrowth, forest edge, and low secondary forest.

REGION: NEA, NWA, SAM

Plate 79b
Slate-colored Grosbeak
Pitylus grossus
ID: Medium-sized (20 cm, 8 in); slate gray with thick red-orange bill and white throat patch.

HABITAT: Pairs in mid-level and canopy of moist primary and tall secondary forest.

REGION: NEA, NWA, SAM

Plate 79c
Red-crested Cardinal
Paroaria coronata
ID: Small (18 cm, 7 in); gray back, wings and tail; bright red head, throat, and prominent crest; white underparts extending up sides of neck.

HABITAT: Pairs or flocks in open shrubby areas and open woodlands, often feeds on the ground.

REGION: PAN

Plate 79d
Red-capped Cardinal
Paroaria gularis
ID: Small (17 cm, 7 in); bright red head; black upperparts and throat patch; white underparts; immature with brown head.

HABITAT: Low in vegetation bordering oxbow lakes and small rivers. (Replaced in the Pantanal by the similar Yellow-billed Cardinal, *Paroaria capitata*, which has a pinkish yellow bill.)

REGION: NEA, NWA, SAM

Plate 79e
Grayish Saltator
Saltator coerulescens
ID: Medium-sized (20 cm, 8 in); gray upperparts and head; white eye-line and throat patch; underparts grayish-white with buffy lower belly.

HABITAT: Dry shrubby areas, pastures, gardens, forest edge, and secondary forest along rivers.

REGION: NEA, NWA, SAM, PAN

Plate 79 419

a Buff-throated Saltator

b Slate-colored Grosbeak

c Red-crested
Cardinal

IM

d Red-capped
Cardinal

e Grayish Saltator

Plate 80a

Lesser Seed-finch
Oryzoborus angolensis
ID: Small (13 cm, 5 in); thick dark bill; male with black head and upperparts; underparts dark-rusty; underwings and small patch in upperwing white, obvious in flight; female all brown.

HABITAT: Pairs seen in moist grassy areas and shrubby forest edge.

REGION: NEA, NWA, SAM, PAN

Plate 80b

Blue-black Grassquit
Volatinia jacarina
ID: Small (11 cm, 4 in); male all blue-black except for white underwings; female brown upperparts, buffy white underparts streaked brown.

HABITAT: Open fields, agricultural areas, and low shrubby patches.

REGION: NEA, NWA, SAM, PAN

Plate 80c

Rusty-collared Seedeater
Sporophila collaris
ID: Small (12 cm, 5 in); male cinnamon-colored with black head, wings, tail, and breast band. White spot between eye and bill and another below eye; white throat, center of belly, and wing spot; female brown with two buffy wing bars and a whitish throat.

HABITAT: Pairs in moist grassy areas and marshes.

REGION: PAN

Plate 80d

Yellow-bellied Seedeater
Sporophila nigricollis
ID: Small (11 cm, 4 in); male olive-brown upperparts; black head, throat and upper breast; pale yellow underparts; female olive-brown upperparts, buffy underparts and dark bill.

HABITAT: Open fields and grassy areas with some bushes.

REGION: SAM, PAN

Plate 80e

White-bellied Seedeater
Sporophila leucoptera
ID: Small (12 cm, 5 in); male gray upperparts and white underparts; white spot in wing; pinkish-yellow bill; female olive-brown upperparts, pale brown underparts; pale bill.

HABITAT: Pairs in moist grassy areas, marshes, shrubs along rivers and lakes.

REGION: PAN

Plate 80   **421**

a Lesser Seed-finch

b Blue-black Grassquit

c Rusty-collared Seedeater

d Yellow-bellied Seedeater

e White-bellied Seedeater

Plate 81a
Blue-black Grosbeak
Cyanocompsa cyanoides
ID: Small (16 cm, 6 in); thick gray bill; male all dark blue with lighter blue forehead and eye-line; female all brown.

HABITAT: Undergrowth of humid primary and tall secondary forest and forest edge.

REGION: NEA, NWA, SAM

Plate 81b
Rufous-collared Sparrow
Zonotrichia capensis
ID: Small (15 cm, 6 in); upperparts brown with black streaks on back; rusty neck; gray head with prominent black lines; underparts whitish with black and rusty patch on side of upper breast.

HABITAT: Open areas including pastures, low shrubby areas, gardens and city parks.

REGION: NEA, PAN

Plate 81c
Yellow-browed Sparrow
Ammodramus aurifrons
ID: Small (13 cm, 5 in); upperparts brownish with black streaking; underparts grayish white; distinct yellow eyestripe and cheeks. (Replaced in tall grasslands of the Pantanal by the similar Grassland Sparrow, *Ammodramus humeralis*, which has a yellow shoulder and the yellow on the face restricted to the area between the bill and eye; also shier and harder to see.)

HABITAT: Open grassy areas in dry agricultural fields, along rivers, and cleared areas; easily located by its persistent, high buzzy song that sounds like an insect.

REGION: NEA, NWA, SAM

Plate 81d
Saffron Yellow-Finch
Sicalis flaveola
ID: Small (14 cm, 5.5 in); adult bright yellow with orange forehead; immature paler with light brown streaks.

HABITAT: Often in flocks in open areas with bushes and some trees, pastures, parks, and gardens in towns and cities.

REGION: PAN

Plate 81e
Chestnut-bellied Seedeater
Sporophila castaneiventris
ID: Small (10 cm, 4 in); male all blue-gray except for deep rusty colored center of throat, breast, and lower belly; female olive-brown upperparts, buffy underparts.

HABITAT: Open fields, grassy areas, floating vegetation along edges of oxbow lakes and small rivers.

REGION: NEA, NWA, SAM

Plate 81 423

a Blue-black Grosbeak

F

M

c Yellow-browed Sparrow

b Rufous-collared Sparrow

IM

d Saffron Yellow-Finch

adult

M

F

e Chestnut-bellied Seedeater

Plate 82a

Brown Four-eyed Opossum
Metachirus nudicaudatus

ID: Like a large brown rat (body length 27 cm, 10.5 in); distinctive buff spot above each eye; tail long (30 cm, 1 ft) and completely hairless.

HABITAT: Mature forests and tall secondary forests with undergrowth; forages both in the trees and on the ground for fruits, insects, and small vertebrates; active at night and shy.

REGION: NEA, NWA, SAM

Plate 82b

Common Opossum
Didelphis marsupialis

ID: Large (body length 40 cm, 1.3 ft); black in rain forests and gray in drier more open habitats; naked black ears and long, naked, black tail (40 cm, 15 in) with a white tip. (Replaced in the Pantanal by the similar White-eared Opposum, *Didelphis albiventris*, which has white, not black, ears.)

HABITAT: Common throughout the Amazon; around villages, secondary forests and river edge vegetation on the ground or in trees; night-active.

REGION: NEA, NWA, SAM

Plate 82c

Long-furred Woolly Mouse Opossum
Micoureus demerarae

ID: Small (body length 18 cm, 7 in); grayish brown; resembles more a rodent than a marsupial; long body fur; bicolored tail, black at base, whitish at end.

HABITAT: Primarily high above the ground in branches of trees in secondary and primary forests as well as in plantations and gardens in the eastern lowlands; occasionally forages on the ground and hisses if approached too closely; night-active.

REGION: NEA, NWA, SAM

Plate 82d

Silky (Pygmy) Anteater
Cyclopes didactylus

ID: Small (body length 18 cm, 7 in) with gray, brownish or yellowish dense, silky fur; darker on top; long (19 cm, 7.5 in), prehensile tail.

HABITAT: Moist primary and tall secondary terra firme forests, forest edge; nocturnal; arboreal, especially among vines and thin tree branches.

REGION: NEA, NWA, SAM

Plate 82e

Nine-banded Armadillo
Dasypus novemcinctus

ID: Medium-sized (body length 40 cm, 1.3 ft); long pointed tail (30 cm, 12 in); long nose; body armor plating covering the entire sides; 6 to 11 movable expansion bands across the back, most individuals with 9 bands. (In the Pantanal savannahs, the similar-sized Yellow Armadillo, *Euphractus sexcinctus*, is often active during the day. It has tiny ears, long hairs protruding from between the bands on its back, and a yellowish or tan color.)

HABITAT: Active day and night in forests, savannah and open areas.

REGION: NEA, NWA, SAM, PAN

Plate 82   425

a Brown Four-eyed Opossum

b Common Opossum

d Silky (Pygmy) Anteater

c Long-furred Woolly Mouse Opossum

e Nine-banded Armadillo

Plate 83a
Southern Two-toed Sloth
Choloepus didactylus
ID: Medium-sized (body length 65 cm, 2.2 ft); buffy colored on throat, chest, and back; long protruding snout; active mainly at night.

HABITAT: Restricted mainly to moist primary forest high in the canopy; nocturnal; uses its two sharp toes on front feet as effective weapons and can be quite aggressive when cornered.

REGION: NEA, NWA, SAM

Plate 83b
Brown-throated Three-toed Sloth
Bradypus variegatus
ID: Medium-sized (body length 60 cm, 2 ft); pale brown and gray but takes on distinctive green tinge during the rainy season when algae and fungi grow on the hairs; flat, black and white masked face and hooked claws. (Replaced in the northeastern Amazon by the similar Pale-throated Sloth, *Bradypus tridactylus*, which has a buffy-white throat.)

HABITAT: Restricted to moist primary and secondary forests, varzea, and gallery forest in drier areas. Most easily seen in open *Cecropia* forests along rivers; a docile and non-aggressive species active during the day.

REGION: NWA, SAM

Plate 83c
Giant Armadillo
Priodontes maximus
ID: Large (body length 90 cm, 3 ft) with long scaled tail (52 cm, 1.7 ft); incomplete armor plating; huge, curved central claw on the front feet.

HABITAT: Active at night in a wide range of habitats from primary forest floor to savannah and spends the daytime resting in large burrows dug into the forest floor.

REGION: NEA, NWA, SAM, PAN

Plate 83d
Giant Anteater
Myrmecophaga tridactyla
ID: Large (body length 1.6 m, 5 ft); striking, bold black, gray and white coloring; long, thin head and muzzle; long (75 cm, 2.5 ft), feather-like tail.

HABITAT: Active day or night, rare everywhere but most regularly found in primary forest and grassy savannah; found only on the ground; long claws on its front feet and a very aggressive nature when cornered can make it extremely dangerous.

REGION: NEA, NWA, SAM, PAN

Plate 83e
Southern Tamandua
Tamandua tetradactyla
ID: Medium-sized (body length 70 cm, 2.3 ft); distinct yellowish and black pattern; long (50 cm, 1.7 ft) furry tail is prehensile and used for climbing. An all-blonde form occasionally occurs.

HABITAT: Active both day and night either in trees or on ground of secondary and primary forest, and gallery forest in drier areas.

REGION: NEA, NWA, SAM, PAN

Plate 83 **427**

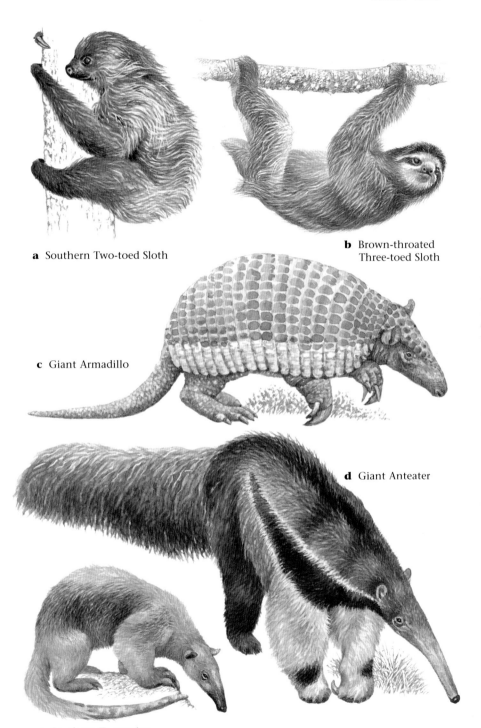

a Southern Two-toed Sloth

b Brown-throated
Three-toed Sloth

c Giant Armadillo

d Giant Anteater

e Southern Tamandua

Plate 84a
Greater Fishing Bat
(also called Bulldog Bat)
Noctilio leporinus
ID: Large (body length 9.7 cm, 4 in); brown to reddish brown with 60 cm (2 ft) wingspan; squared snout with no noseleaf.

HABITAT: Lakes, estuaries, rivers, pastures, and cleared areas; usually seen flying over water at night hunting for fish.

REGION: NEA, NWA, SAM, PAN

Plate 84b
Jamaican Fruit-eating Bat
Artibeus jamaicensis
ID: Large (body length 9 cm, 3.5 in; wingspan 40 cm, 16 in); brown to gray coloring; lack of a tail, prominent noseleaf and no white lines on the back are distinctive.

HABITAT: Wet and dry forests; feeds at night mainly on fruit, especially figs.

REGION: NEA, NWA, SAM, PAN

Plate 84c
Common Vampire Bat
Desmodus rotundus
ID: Medium-sized (body length 7.5 cm, 3 in); triangular-shaped ears; razor-sharp front teeth; "thumb" on the wing twice as long as that of any other species of bat.

HABITAT: Nocturnal in primary and secondary forests, gallery forest and clearings; most common in pastures and agricultural areas where there are large domestic animals to supply its blood meals.

REGION: NEA, NWA, SAM, PAN

Plate 84d
White-lined Sac-winged Bat
Saccopteryx bilineata
ID: Small (body length 5 cm, 2 in); dark brown with two bold white lines running the length of the back; sharp-pointed nose lacking a noseleaf.

HABITAT: Nocturnal in forest clearings and along forest paths, where they pursue insects.

REGION: NEA, NWA, SAM

Plate 84e
Hairy-legged Fruit Bat
Sturnira lilium
ID: Small (body length 6 cm, 2.4 in); relatively small rounded ears; triangular noseleaf; dark brown except for buffy yellow shoulder patch; no skin membrane connecting legs, which are covered with long dark hairs.

HABITAT: Exclusively frugivorous, this species often crawls on the ground to eat fallen fruits. Usually confined to clearings in moister habitats in primary and secondary forest, varzea, gallery forest, forest edge, and gardens.

REGION: NEA, NWA, SAM, PAN

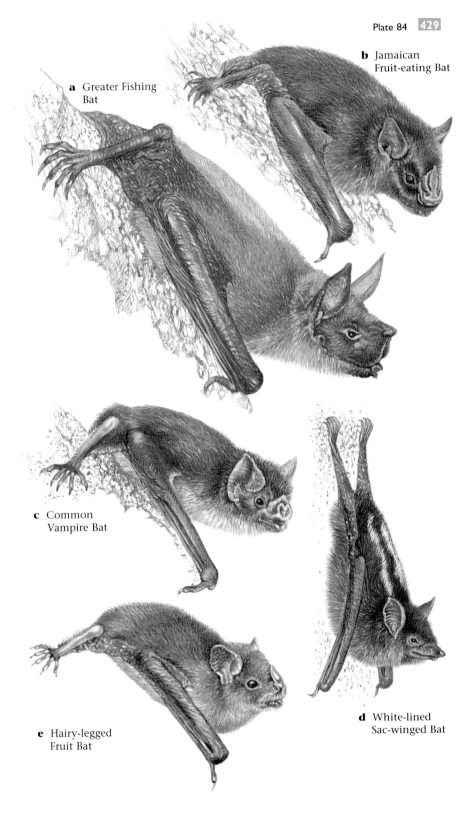

Plate 84 429

b Jamaican
Fruit-eating Bat

a Greater Fishing
Bat

c Common
Vampire Bat

d White-lined
Sac-winged Bat

e Hairy-legged
Fruit Bat

Plate 85a

Short-tailed Fruit Bat
Carollia perspicillata
ID: Small (body length 5.5 cm, 2 in); light brown; large noseleaf.

HABITAT: Forests of moist lowlands, gallery forest, and gardens; feed on the forest undergrowth fruits of *Piper* plants (p. 27), nectar, and occasionally insects sitting on leaves.

REGION: NEA, NWA, SAM, PAN

Plate 85b

Sucker-footed Bat
Thyroptera tricolor
ID: Small (body length 4 cm, 1.5 in); short muzzle lacking a noseleaf; silver-white breast contrasting with dark brown upperparts.

HABITAT: Moist forests, gardens, and banana plantations; feed nocturnally on insects along forested rivers and clearings. Unique suction cups on ankles and thumbs attach to leaf surfaces while roosting during the day, especially inside young *Heliconia* and banana leaves that are still rolled into tubes before opening as mature leaves.

REGION: NEA, NWA, SAM

Plate 85c

Common Long-tongued Bat
(also called Nectar Bat)
Glossophaga soricina
ID: Medium-sized (body length 5.5 cm, 2 in); long snout with small spear-shaped noseleaf.

HABITAT: Mainly found in moist forests but will go to flowering trees in agricultural fields and open areas; hovers while using its long tongue to reach flower nectar; also catches insects resting on plant leaves.

REGION: NEA, NWA, SAM

Plate 85d

Long-nosed Bat
Rhynchonycteris naso
ID: Small (body length 4 cm, 1.5 in); grizzly white; distinctively long pointed snout lacking noseleaf.

HABITAT: Always in moist areas near primary forest; hunts insects at night low over nearby water surfaces; several individuals roost together during the day on shaded logs along rivers and fly low over the water as a flock when frightened.

REGION: NEA, NWA, SAM

Plate 85e

Black Myotis
Myotis nigricans
ID: Small (body length 4 cm, 1.5 in); dark brown with a short nose and no noseleaf.

HABITAT: Common at night hawking for insects in the air over open areas of moist forest, savannah, agricultural fields, and near human habitation.

REGION: NEA, NWA, SAM, PAN, CMF

Plate 85 **431**

a Short-tailed
Fruit Bat

b Sucker-footed
Bat

c Common
Long-tongued
Bat

e Black Myotis

d Long-nosed Bat

Plate 86a
Black-chested Moustached Tamarin
Saguinus mystax
ID: Small body (26 cm, 10 in; tail 40 cm, 1.3 ft); blackish head, back, chest, legs and tail; bold white muzzle; rest of body dark brown.

HABITAT: Small family groups in primary and tall secondary terra firme forest; sometimes in mixed species troops with Saddle-backed Tamarin.

REGION: SAM

Plate 86b
Golden-handed Tamarin
Saguinus midas
ID: Small body (24 cm, 9.5 in; tail 33 cm, 1 ft); all blackish with dark muzzle and bright orange hands and feet north of the Río Amazonas; smaller with all-dark feet and hands south of the Río Amazonas.

HABITAT: Small family groups in primary and secondary terra firme forest.

REGION: NEA, SAM

Plate 86c
Saddle-backed Tamarin
Saguinus fuscicollis
ID: Small (body length 24 cm, 9 in; tail 33 cm, 1 ft); black head and feet; mostly chestnut body. The high chirping notes of the small family groups can easily be confused with sounds of a bird flock.

HABITAT: Active during the day in mid-levels of secondary and primary terra firme forest with dense tangles of vines and branches.

REGION: NWA, SAM

Plate 86d
Silvery Marmoset
Callithrix argentata
ID: Small (23 cm, 9 in; tail 32 cm, 1 ft); highly variable populations sometimes divided into as many as 5 species or subspecies, all occurring south of the Río Amazonas and east of the Río Madeira; ears without hair; body whitish to light gray or pale brown; tail dark brown to black, buffy or white.

HABITAT: Small troops in dense canopy of primary and secondary terra firme forest, forest edge, gallery forest, and more open deciduous forest, where they often descend from the trees to run like a large squirrel across the ground to the next grove.

REGION: SAM, PAN

Plate 86   433

a Black-chested Moustached Tamarin

b Golden-handed Tamarin

c Saddle-backed Tamarin

d Silvery Marmoset

Plate 87a
Dusky Titi Monkey
Callicebus moloch
ID: Small (body length 30 cm, 1 ft); long (40 cm, 1.3 ft) bushy tail; white forehead and rusty chest contrast with gray upperparts; often noticed by its whooping calls in early morning; moves little and is difficult to see when disturbed. Populations are variable in the amount of gray and rusty color on the body (and based on these differences, some experts divide it into as many as 10 different species).

HABITAT: Active only during the day in dense vegetation and vine tangles of moist secondary and primary forest, forest edge, bamboo, varzea, and gallery forest in drier parts of its range.

REGION: SAM

Plate 87b
Common Squirrel Monkey
Saimiri sciureus
ID: Medium-sized (body length 30 cm, 1 ft); long non-prehensile tail (40 cm, 1.3 ft); combination of black snout and white face and ears is unique. (The populations south of the Río Amazonas are considered by some experts as two separate species, *Samiri boliviensis* in the southwest and the naked-eared form, *Samiri ustus,* between the Río Purus and the Río Tapajos.)

HABITAT: Active during the day when its large, noisy troops move at mid- to upper levels of primary and secondary varzea forests; often in mixed species troops with capuchin monkeys.

REGION: NEA, NWA, SAM

Plate 87c
Brown Capuchin Monkey
Cebus apella
ID: Medium-sized (body length 42 cm, 1.4 ft); long (44 cm, 1.4 ft) prehensile tail usually carried coiled; buff brown with paler shoulders, black cap; vertical black line in front of each ear; blackish legs, feet, and tail.

HABITAT: Noisy troops in the mid- and lower levels of primary and secondary terra firme forest, varzea, and gallery forest, often in palm trees; frequently in mixed species troops with White-fronted Capuchin and Common Squirrel Monkeys where their ranges overlap.

REGION: NEA, NWA, SAM, PAN

Plate 87d
White-fronted Capuchin Monkey
Cebus albifrons
ID: Medium-sized (body length 40 cm, 1.4 ft); long (45 cm, 1.5 ft) prehensile tail usually carried coiled; combination of a dark cap and light-colored body and feet unique. (Replaced in northeastern Amazon by Wedge-capped Capuchin, *Cebus olivaceus*, which is all dark brown with a white face.)

HABITAT: Active during the day; large noisy troops move at all levels, from the ground to canopy, of primary and secondary forest.

REGION: NWA, SAM

Plate 87 435

a Dusky Titi Monkey

b Common
Squirrel
Monkey

c Brown Capuchin Monkey

d White-
fronted
Capuchin
Monkey

Plate 88a
Black Howler Monkey
Alouatta caraya
ID: Large (50 cm, 1.6 ft); long (60 cm, 2 ft) prehensile tail; male all black with dark brown back; female all buffy tan. (Replaced south of the Río Amazonas and east of the Río Madeira by the similar-sized Red-handed Howler Monkey, *Alouatta belzebul*, in which both males and females are all-black with orange hands, feet, and tail tip.)

HABITAT: Small family groups in gallery forest and deciduous forest stands of the Pantanal.

REGION: PAN

Plate 88b
Red Howler Monkey
Alouatta seniculus
ID: Large (body length 55 cm, 1.8 ft); bright rusty color, long prehensile tail (60 cm, 2 ft), and lion-like roars.

HABITAT: Small family groups sit quietly or move slowly during the day through the upper levels of primary forest and trees along rivers and lakes of northern and southwestern Amazon.

REGION: NEA, NWA, SAM

Plate 88c
Common Woolly Monkey
Lagothrix lagothricha
ID: Medium-sized (body length 40 cm, 1.3 ft); uniformly colored gray to brown; long prehensile tail (70 cm, 2.3 ft) carried coiled.

HABITAT: Travels during the day in noisy and often large troops through upper and mid-levels of primary terra firme forest and mature varzea.

REGION: NWA, SAM

Plate 88d
White-bellied Spider Monkey
Ateles belzebuth
ID: Large (body length 50 cm, 1.7 ft); all-dark except for a light chest; long arms, legs, and prehensile tail (78 cm, 2.6 ft); distinctive screaming calls. (Replaced north of the Río Amazonas and east of the Río Negro by the Black Spider Monkey, *Ateles paniscus*, which is all-black with a pink face.)

HABITAT: Active day and night; small to large troops forage mainly in the canopy of primary forest.

REGION: NWA, SAM

Plate 88 **437**

M

a Black Howler
Monkey

F

b Red Howler
Monkey

c Common Woolly Monkey

d White-bellied
Spider
Monkey

Plate 89a

Monk Saki Monkey
Pithecia monachus
ID: Large (body length 40 cm, 1.3 ft); shaggy gray and black body hair, naked face and long shaggy tail (45 cm, 1.5 ft). Along the western border of Brazil south of the Río Amazonas, another shaggy species, the Bald Uakari Monkey, *Cacajao calvus*, occurs. Its short and shaggy tail together with bright rusty fur and an all-red and bare head are distinctive.

HABITAT: Both sakis and uakaris are active during the day and occur in the upper levels of primary terra firme forest and occasionally varzea, the sakis in small family groups and the ukaris in large troops.

REGION: SAM

Plate 89b

Brown-bearded Saki Monkey
Chiropotes satanas
ID: Large (body length 40 cm, 1.3 ft); long (40 cm, 1.3 ft) non-prehensile tail with bushy end; all-black with rusty (north of the eastern Río Amazonas) or dark brown (south of the eastern Río Amazonas) back; distinctive large tuft at either side of the head and a "beard." Replaced in south-central Amazon by the similar White-nosed Bearded Saki Monkey, *Chiropotes albinasus*, which is entirely coal black with a white muzzle.)

HABITAT: Small troops walk along high branches of primary terra firme forest with fluffy tails held high and often arched over their backs.

REGION: NEA, SAM

Plate 89c

Guianan Saki Monkey
Pithecia pithecia
ID: Large (body length 40 cm, 1.3 ft); shaggy body hair and long non-prehensile, shaggy tail (45 cm, 1.5 ft); male coal black with pure white cheeks and forehead; female gray-brown with vertical buffy stripe on each side of the face.

HABITAT: Small family groups in middle and lower levels of primary terra firme forest and occasionally tall varzea.

REGION: NEA

Plate 89d

Black-headed Night Monkey
Aotus nigriceps
ID: Medium-sized (body length 33 cm, 1.1 ft); black and white face pattern, dark ears; long non-prehensile tail (30 cm, 1 ft) hanging straight down; often gives low owl-like hoots at night.

HABITAT: The small family groups rest during the day in dense vine tangles and forage at night in the upper canopy; occurs in southwestern Amazonian terra firme forest and varzea. Several other very similar night monkey species replace it in northwestern and southeastern Amazonian Brazil.

REGION: SAM

Plate 89   439

a Monk Saki Monkey

b Brown-bearded Saki Monkey

M

F

c Guianan Saki Monkey

d Black-headed Night Monkey

Plate 90a

Kinkajou
Potos flavus

ID: Medium-sized (body length 52 cm, 1.7 ft); large eyes, small ears, short hair and long, prehensile tail (48 cm, 2.4 ft); active only at night; bright eye-shine reflected from a flashlight is the best way to find it.

HABITAT: Moist forest, where it moves noisily through the upper levels of primary and secondary forest and even into plantations and gardens.

REGION: NEA, NWA, SAM

Plate 90b

Crab-eating Raccoon
Procyon cancrivorous

ID: Medium-sized (body length 60 cm, 2 ft); black mask, dark feet and legs, and prominently ringed tail (35 cm, 1.2 ft) carried low to the ground.

HABITAT: Active only at night on the shores of streams, lakes, and marshes.

REGION: NEA, NWA, SAM, PAN

Plate 90c

Crab-eating Fox
Cerdocyon thous

ID: Large (96 cm, 3.1 ft); body dark with short but grizzled gray, brown and black hairs throughout; belly in many individuals lighter gray.

HABITAT: Primarily nocturnal in pairs or alone in a wide range of habitats including savannah, gallery forest, and open woodlands. Eats mushrooms, fruits, small mammals, insects, lizards and, during the rainy season, crabs.

REGION: PAN

Plate 90d

South American Coati
Nasua nasua

ID: Medium-sized (body length 50 cm, 1.7 ft); long, tapered snout and long tail (48 cm, 1.6 ft) held up in the air.

HABITAT: Day-active; females travel in large groups on the ground and into the mid-levels of primary and secondary forest; males travel solitarily.

REGION: NEA, NWA, SAM, PAN

Plate 90e

Maned Wolf
Chrysocyon brachyurus

ID: Large (1.5 m, 5 ft long and 1 m, 3.3 ft high), buff and rusty body with black back of neck and black muzzle; large ears; long, black legs and white tail and throat.

HABITAT: Solitary in savannah grasslands and scrubby vegetation; often gives a loud, deep bark.

REGION: PAN

Plate 90 441

a Kinkajou

b Crab-eating Raccoon

LF

LH

d South American Coati

c Crab-eating Fox

LH

LF

Front

e Maned Wolf

Plate 91a

Giant Otter
Pteronura brasiliensis

ID: Large (body and tail together 1.5 m, 5 ft); dark fur with white-spotted throat and noisy calls; tail flattened at tip.

HABITAT: Family groups active during the day in remote rivers and oxbow lakes.

REGION: NEA, NWA, SAM, PAN

Plate 91b

Neotropical Otter
Lontra longicaudis

ID: Large (body and tail together 1 m, 3.3 ft); upperparts dark brown; cheeks, throat and entire belly creamy white (in northern Amazon) to partially brown (southern Amazon and Pantanal); tail rounded and tapered at tip.

HABITAT: Solitary or pairs in small, fast-flowing streams and clear lakes.

REGION: NEA, NWA, SAM, PAN

Plate 91c

Tayra
Eira barbara

ID: Large (body and tail 1 m, 3.3 ft); dark and short-legged; buffy throat and often an all-buffy head; bushy tail.

HABITAT: Solitary running on the ground or along branches of large trees, mainly during the day but occasionally during the night in moist and dry forests; primary and secondary forests, gallery forest, and in open areas near human habitation.

REGION: NEA, NWA, SAM, PAN

Plate 91d

Grison
Galictis vittata

ID: Medium-sized (body and tail 55 cm, 1.8 ft); distinctive black, gray, and white color pattern different than any other species in Amazonia.

HABITAT: Active at night, often in pairs, on the floor of primary and secondary forests.

REGION: NEA, NWA, SAM

Plate 91   443

a Giant Otter

b Neotropical Otter

c Tayra

d Grison

Plate 92a

Jaguarundi
Herpailurus yaguarondi

ID: Small (body length 60 cm, 2 ft); uniformly gray, brown, or reddish-brown; proportionately short legs; long tail (50 cm, 1.7 ft); can be mistaken for a small dog or otter.

HABITAT: Active mostly during the day, it is most often seen on the floor or clearings of primary and secondary forest but also hunts in swampy grasslands, deciduous forests, and thorn forest, sometimes near human habitation.

REGION: NEA, NWA, SAM, PAN

Plate 92b

Ocelot
Felis (Leopardus) pardalis

ID: Medium-sized (body length 80 cm, 2.7 ft); distinctive spotting and proportionately short tail (36 cm, 1.2 ft); most frequently noticed by its tracks.

HABITAT: Active day and night; occurs mainly on the ground in moist and dry forests, and gallery forests in drier parts of its range; often spends the day sleeping in trees.

REGION: NEA, NWA, SAM, PAN

Plate 92c

Margay
Felis (Leopardus) wiedii

ID: Smaller (body length 60 cm, 2 ft) than the similarly spotted Ocelot, but a longer tail (45 cm, 1.5 ft); very shy, it is most likely to be noticed by its tracks.

HABITAT: Primarily nocturnal, it spends most of its time in trees of secondary and primary moist forest and gallery forest in drier parts of its range.

REGION: NEA, NWA, SAM, PAN

Plate 92d

Jaguar
Panthera onca

ID: Largest (body length 1.5 m, 5 ft; tail 60 cm, 2 ft) spotted cat in the New World. Its presence is most likely to be noted by its huge tracks along river beaches or lake banks.

HABITAT: Solitary and active day and night in moist and dry forests and nearby savannah areas; usually stays on the ground except to flee danger, when it will climb trees.

REGION: NEA, NWA, SAM, PAN

Plate 92e

Puma
Puma concolor

ID: Large (body length 1 m, 3.3 ft); uniformly colored with a long black-tipped tail (80 cm, 2.7 ft); footprints smaller and different shape than Jaguar's.

HABITAT: Primarily on the ground in a wide range of habitats, from savannah scrub and dry forest to moist forest.

REGION: NEA, NWA, SAM, PAN

Plate 92   445

brown form

red form

a Jaguarundi

LF

LH

c Margay

LF

LH

b Ocelot

LF

LH

d Jaguar

LF

LH

e Puma

Plate 93a

Collared Peccary
Tayassu tajacu
ID: Smaller (body length 90 cm, 35 in) than the White-lipped Peccary; brown with a grizzled collar; occurs mainly in small family groups; a distinct smell lingers for several hours after the group has passed through an area.

HABITAT: Active during the day and night in moist and dry forests, thorn scrub, savannah and gallery forest.

REGION: NEA, NWA, SAM, PAN

Plate 93b

White-lipped Peccary
Tayassu pecari
ID: Larger (body length 1 m, 3.3 ft), darker, and lacks the collar of the Collared Peccary; often forages in herds of up to 100 or more individuals.

HABITAT: Active during the day in moist Amazon forest, dry scrub, and gallery forest; herds range over extremely large areas and their passing is often made obvious by their footprints and distinct smell.

REGION: NEA, NWA, SAM, PAN

Plate 93c

Pampas Deer
Ozotoceros bezoarticus
ID: Large (body length 1.2 m, 4 ft; height at shoulder 75 cm, 2.5 ft); longer-legged than brocket deer and smaller than the Marsh Deer, this species is best distinguished by its yellowish gray color, white eyering, and medium-sized antlers that usually have three points on each side.

HABITAT: Small groups grazing in moist and dry grasslands.

REGION: PAN

Note: Rare and endangered, CITES Appendix I listed.

Plate 93d

Red Brocket Deer
Mazama americana
ID: Medium-sized (body length 1.2 m, 4 ft; height at shoulder 65 cm, 2.1 ft); rusty color distinguishes it from the slightly smaller and darker Gray Brocket Deer, *Mazama gouazoubira*, which occurs in drier, more open areas.

HABITAT: Solitary and active night and day in moist and dry forests, swampy areas, secondary forests, gallery forest, and plantations.

REGION: NEA, NWA, SAM, PAN

Plate 93e

Marsh Deer
Blastocerus dichotomous
ID: Very large (body length 1.8 m, 6 ft; height at shoulder 1.2 m, 4 ft); reddish color with white belly; large ears; long black legs; multi-branched antlers.

HABITAT: Restricted to areas of standing water and dense vegetation, such as reeds and bunch grass; usually solitary, and active both during the day and night.

REGION: PAN

Plate 93 **447**

b White-lipped Peccary

a Collared Peccary

d Red Brocket Deer

c Pampas deer

e Marsh Deer

Plate 94a

Amazon Bamboo Rat
Dactylomys dactylinus

ID: Large (body length 30 cm, 12 in); squared snout and long, naked tail (40 cm, 16 in); loud staccato calls at night are the easiest way to notice it.

HABITAT: Active at night; usually associated with bamboo stands, thick river edge vegetation, or the canopy of moist forest.

REGION: NWA, SAM

Plate 94b

Spiny Tree Rat
Mesomys hispidus

ID: Medium-sized (body length 20 cm, 8 in); brown with conspicuous but short spines tipped buff on the back; ears short; thick tail (10 cm, 4 in, long) with spines and black tuft at tip.

HABITAT: Active at night from the ground and thick undergrowth to the canopy of primary and secondary forest and forest edge.

REGION: NEA, NWA, SAM

Plate 94c

Northern Amazon Red Squirrel
Sciurus igniventris

ID: Medium-sized (body length 27 cm, 11 in), noisy, brightly colored rusty and brown; large bushy tail longer (30 cm, 12 in) than its body.

HABITAT: Active during the day on the ground and lower branches of primary and secondary forest of the northwestern Amazon. (Replaced by the similar Southern Amazon Red Squirrel, *Sciurus spadiceus*, in the southwestern Amazon.)

REGION: NWA

Plate 94d

Amazon Dwarf Squirrel
Microsciurus flaviventer

ID: Small (body length 14 cm, 6 in); reddish brown with short ears and a short (10 cm, 4 in), bushy tail.

HABITAT: Day-active from the ground to canopy of moist forests.

REGION: NWA

Plate 94e

Guianan Squirrel
Sciurus aestuans

ID: Medium-sized (body length 20 cm, 8 in), noisy, dull-colored squirrel, olive-brown often with buffy breast and tail tip; slender bushy tail same color as its body and as long as or shorter (18 cm, 7 in) than the body.

HABITAT: Solitary or pairs active during the day from the tops of trees to the ground in primary and secondary forest, forest edge, gardens, and plantations; it is especially fond of palm fruits.

REGION: NEA, SAM

Plate 94 449

a Amazon Bamboo Rat

b Spiny Tree Rat

c Northern Amazon Red Squirrel

d Amazon Dwarf Squirrel

e Guianan Squirrel

Plate 95a

Brazilian Porcupine
Coendou prehensilis

ID: Medium-sized (body length 50 cm, 1.6 ft); covered with long, sharp spines that give a grizzled gray appearance; distinctive prehensile tail as long as or longer than the body.

HABITAT: Solitary at night in vine tangles at mid levels and canopy of primary and secondary forests.

REGION: NEA, NWA, SAM

Plate 95b

Green Acouchy
Myoprocta pratti

ID: Medium-sized (body length 34 cm, 1.1 ft); upperparts olive-brown with fine dark bands on the lower back; underparts and face rusty orange; short, thin tail with white tip; loud honking noises and squawks as it runs noisily from danger. (Replaced in northeastern Amazon by the similar Red Acouchy, *Myoprocta acouchy*, which has reddish brown upperparts and a dark rump with no banding.)

HABITAT: On the floor of terra firme forest with thick undergrowth.

REGION: NWA, SAM

Plate 95c

Red-rumped Agouti
Dasyprocta agouti

ID: Medium-sized (body length 55 cm, 1.8 ft); dark olive-brown with bright orange rump; virtually tailless; resembles a small peccary. (Replaced in the Pantanal by the smaller (50 cm, 1.6 ft) and more uniformly colored buffy gray Azara's Agouti, *Dasyprocta azarae*.)

HABITAT: Pairs seen during the day on the floor of primary and secondary forest, and swampy, deciduous, and gallery forests.

REGION: NEA, SAM

Plate 95d

Black Agouti
Dasyprocta fuliginosa

ID: Medium-sized (body length 60 cm, 2 ft); all dark and virtually tailless; resembles a small peccary.

HABITAT: Most often seen during the day foraging or running noisily through the forest undergrowth in western Amazon.

REGION: NWA, SAM

Plate 95e

Paca
Agouti paca

ID: Medium-sized (body length 70 cm, 2.3 ft); chestnut color with several rows of white spots on its sides and virtually tailless.

HABITAT: Active at night along the banks of rivers and lakes or the undergrowth of terra firme forests, varzea, gallery forest, mangroves, and gardens; frequently enters water to escape danger.

REGION: NEA, CMF, NWA, SAM, PAN

Plate 95　451

a Brazilian Porcupine

b Green Acouchy

c Red-rumped Agouti

d Black Agouti

e Paca

Plate 96a

Capybara

Hydrochaeris hydrochaeris

ID: Large (body length 1.2 m, 4 ft) brown rodent most likely to be confused with a pig.

HABITAT: Family groups active during the day or night almost always along lakes and rivers, into which they dive to escape danger; moist forest, scrub woodlands, flooded grasslands.

REGION: NEA, NWA, SAM, PAN

Plate 96b

Brazilian Tapir

Tapirus terrestris

ID: Large (body length 2 m, 6.5 ft); dark; long snout is diagnostic; its huge tracks in muddy areas are readily identified.

HABITAT: Primarily active at night, it is almost always associated with swampy and moist areas in forests but also occurs in terra firme forest, deciduous forest, and gallery forest.

REGION: NEA, NWA, SAM, PAN

Plate 96c

Gray Dolphin

Sotalia fluviatilis

ID: Large (body length 1.7 m, 5.6 ft); short snout and distinct triangular dorsal fin.

HABITAT: Small groups often leaping from the water of the Río Amazonas and its major tributaries; also in the ocean along the coast and in mangrove estuaries.

REGION: CMF, NWA, SAM

Plate 96d

Pink River Dolphin

Inia geoffrensis

ID: Large (body length 2.3 m, 7.5 ft); long snout and little or no dorsal fin.

HABITAT: Pairs restricted to rivers and oxbow lakes along the Río Amazonas and its major tributaries; small spout and loud snorts when surfacing but rarely leaps from the water.

REGION: NWA, SAM

Plate 96e

Amazonian Manatee

Trichechus inunguis

ID: Large (body length 2.5 m, 8 ft) and seal-like; grayish black; found only in freshwater, where it comes to the surface to breathe. Look for its round droppings floating on the water's surface. (Replaced in coastal estuaries and mangrove forests by the larger (3.2 m, 10.5 ft) West Indian Manatee, *Trichechus manatus*.)

HABITAT: Feeds underwater in rivers and oxbow lakes of the Río Amazonas and the lower reaches of its major tributaries, usually in areas of thick aquatic vegetation.

REGION: NEA, NWA, SAM

Plate 96 453

a Capybara

LF

LH

b Brazilian Tapir

LF

LH

c Gray Dolphin

d Pink River Dolphin

e Amazonian Manatee

Amazon Fish Text by Richard Francis

Note: Lengths given for fish are 'standard lengths,' the distance from the front of the mouth to the point where the tail appears to join the body; that is, tails are not included in the measurement.

Plate 97a

Tucunare
(also called Peacock Cichlid, Speckled Pavon)
Cichla temensis
A voracious predator, this large cichlid has a very large mouth, a bass-like body form, and mottled coloration. It favors the banks of main river channels and lagoons, where it preys mainly on fishes, especially characins. It is unique among Amazon fishes in being a pursuit-predator. If its prey escapes after the first strike, it does not give up like most fish predators; rather, it chases the prey until it is cornered or exhausted, then swallows it whole. This fish has long been a favored food fish among indigenous people, and it is fast becoming a prized sportsfish as well. (to 75 cm, 30 in)

Plate 97b

Acara-acu
Astronotus ocellatus
(also called Apaira, Oscar)
This cichlid will be familiar to many aquarists. It is moderately deep-bodied and has variably mottled coloration with a characteristic eyespot, or *ocellus*, at the base of the tail. Oscars prefer quiet shallow water, where they prey on small fish, crayfish, and other invertebrates. As is true of many cichlids, both parents guard the eggs and young. (to 40 cm, 16 in)

Plate 97c

Cara Bandeira
(also called Scalare, Scalare Angel)
Pterophyllum scalare
One of the most renowned of freshwater aquarium fishes, this distinctive cichlid has a flat diamond-shaped body with elongate dorsal and anal fins, and long filamentous pelvic fins. Its coloration is silvery with several black vertical bands. It generally can be found near the surface in quiet clear water, and especially under floating mats of vegetation. (to 15 cm, 6 in)

Plate 97d

Acara-morere
(also called Discus)
Symphysodon aquafasciata
Another aquarium favorite, this cichlid is named for its pancake body shape, which is accentuated by its symmetrical dorsal and anal fins. The body is typically tan, becoming bluish toward the perimeter, with numerous irregular dark lines, especially around the head. The eyes are frequently bright red. These fish can normally be found in schools but they pair up and become territorial during the breeding season. They feed primarily on insect larvae and plankton. (to 15 cm, 6 in)

Plate 97e

Acara Pixuna
(also called Saddle Cichlid)
Aequidens tetramerus
This is a very colorful cichlid, especially during the breeding season, and is therefore prized by aquarists. It prefers calm water over a substrate covered with organic (vegetative) debris. (to 25 cm, 10 in)

Plate 97f

Dwarf Cichlid
Apistogramma amoenum
The small cichlids of this genus are referred to as *dwarf cichlids*. Unlike most cichlids, dwarf cichlids have harems. A male maintains a large territory that includes several females. He does not participate in the care of the young. This species can be found in a variety of habitats, usually near the bottom. It feeds on worms and other invertebrates. (to 8 cm, 3 in)

Plate 97   455

a Tucunare (Peacock Cichlid)

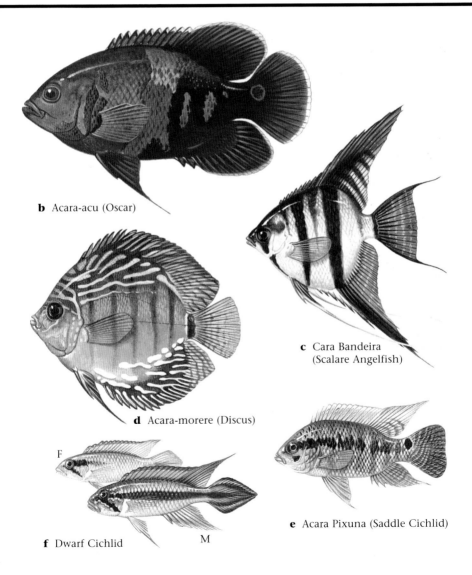

b Acara-acu (Oscar)

c Cara Bandeira
(Scalare Angelfish)

d Acara-morere (Discus)

e Acara Pixuna (Saddle Cichlid)

F

M

f Dwarf Cichlid

Plate 98a
Pirarucu
(also called Arapaima)
Arapaima gigas

This giant, perhaps the largest freshwater fish species on Earth, is for many a symbol of the Amazon, as much for its economic importance as its size. It reaches a length of over 4 m (13 ft) and a weight of 200 kg (440 lb). It was too large to be an important food fish for the Amazonian Indian groups, who preferred smaller species. The Portuguese, however, brought with them a taste for salt cod, for which the Pirarucu soon became a cheap substitute. It has been mostly downhill from there for this species. Traditionally, it has been speared during low water periods when it comes up to breathe; adults completely lack gills and must take regular gulps of air. The air bladder functions as a lung in this species, allowing it to exploit low oxygen environments. During the low

(continued on p. 466)

Plate 98b
Poraque
(also called Electric Eel)
Electrophorus electricus

This is not an eel at all but a member of the knifefish family (Gymnotidae). Most knifefishes are referred to as weakly-electric because they emit low voltage electrical pulses (from an electric organ) by means of which they detect their prey. This species has, in addition, a second, high voltage electrical organ that it uses to stun and kill its prey (fish and small mammals). The high voltage discharges serve to protect the eel against predators as well; the voltage is enough to stop a human heart, so this is not a fish you would want to grab. Like other electric fishes, it prefers turbid water. It can also thrive in very low

(continued on p. 466)

Plate 98c
Jacunda
(also called Pike Cichlid)
Crenicichla saxatilis

This formidable predator is named for its elongate pike-like body shape. The body coloration is typically brown with numerous small yellowish spots, with a darker brown patch behind the gills and numerous tiny white spots throughout. It prefers smaller creeks but can be found in larger tributaries during the dry season. It preys primarily on smaller fish and aquatic insects. The male alone cares for the eggs once they are laid. (to 50 cm, 20 in)

Plate 98d
Arawana
(also called Arowana)
Osteoglossum bicirrhosum

This smaller relative of the Pirarucu is known locally as the "water monkey" because of its penchant for leaping out of the water. These leaps are not expressions of joy but rather a means to snatch insects (especially large beetles) off nearby vegetation. This may be the largest species of fish in the world that feeds primarily on insects, but they will also take the occasional bird or bat. One was reported to have grabbed a newborn sloth off of its mother's back. The body is elongate and laterally-compressed, almost eel-like. It is silvery with a dramatically upturned mouth and two *barbels* projecting from the chin. The barbels are thought to be vibration detectors used for sensing prey; they may also help attract prey by functioning as lures. The Arawana swims at the surface; its unique horizontally divided eyes allow it to see both above and below the water's surface. Arawana are one of the flooded forest species that follows the rising water into the forest and the receding water back to the large channels (p. 243). The eggs of this fish are quite large and have abundant yolk. Upon fertilization,

(continued on p. 466)

Plate 98e
Carapo
(also called Banded Knifefish)
Gymnotus carapo

This knifefish emits only weak electric discharges, by means of which it senses its prey (primarily characins such as curimata) and communicates with other knifefish. Its laterally compressed body tapers into a long thin tail and is never bent as this would interfere with its electrical senses. It swims solely by means of undulations of its anal fins. It prefers slow-moving or standing turbid water, but it also thrives in home aquariums. (to 60 cm, 24 in)

Plate 98f
Acara-topete
(also called Pearl Cichlid)
Geophagus brasiliensis

Members of this genus are sometimes referred to as "earth-eaters" because in their search for benthic (bottom-dwelling) invertebrates, they dig and root around the bottom. This species has the elongate sloping head typical of the cichlid group. This species can be found in a variety of habitats, including brackish water. (to 28 cm, 11 in)

Plate 98 457

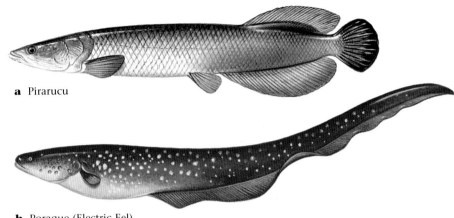

a Pirarucu

b Poraque (Electric Eel)

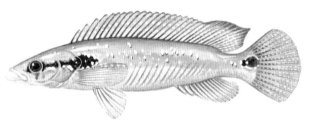

c Jacunda (Pike Cichlid)

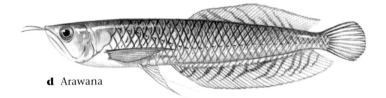

d Arawana

e Carapo (Banded Knifefish)

f Acara-topete (Pearl Cichlid)

Plate 99a
Traholto
(also called Four-eyed Fish)
Anableps anableps

The English name of this fish derives from the fact that, like the Arawana (Plate 98), its eyes are adapted – though in a different manner – to see both above and below the water surface. It can be found swimming along the water surface of the tidal mudflats of the lower Amazon, with its large protruding eyes half above and half below the water line. A flap-like extension of the iris divides the pupil into an upper and lower position. The upper part of the lens transmits light from the

(continued on p. 466)

Plate 99b
Red-bellied Piranha
(also called Red Piranha)
Pygocentrus nattereri

Of the approximately 25 species of piranhas in the Amazon, this is the most famous, because it is the most dangerous (though not nearly as dangerous as some horror films would suggest). There are no confirmed cases of humans killed by piranhas. They have inflicted numerous injuries but most of them occur out of the water (the fish biting a fisherman's toe, for example). Most reports of underwater bites occur during the low water season when the piranha are concentrated in floodplain lakes, so it is prudent to avoid swimming in them. This species has the sharpest teeth and the strongest jaws of any piranha, and it employs these weapons to bite out chunks of flesh like a cookie cutter. Part of its reputation also derives from the fact that, unlike other Amazon fish predators, it is a group hunter. Groups actively move in search of prey fish and the piranha tend to spread out once prey is located. Individual

(continued on p. 466)

Plate 99c
Tambaqui
Colossoma macropomum

Fortunately, this gigantic characin – a close relative of the bloodthirsty piranha – is a vegetarian, specializing on fruits and seeds. Its favorite food, in fact, is the seed of the Rubber Tree, truly a tough nut to crack. But strong jaws and molar-like teeth allow the Tambaqui to crush these seeds without much problem. Enough seeds survive, however, to make this fish an important dispersal agent for this and other forest trees. The Tambaqui also consumes vast amounts of fleshy

(continued on p. 466)

Plate 99d
Barboleto
(also called Silver Hatchet Fish)
Gasteroplecus levis

This characin derives its English name from its distinctive shape. The silvery body is extremely flattened, its wing-like pectoral fins are positioned very high on the body, and its small mouth is upturned, all of which suggests a surface feeder. You can find hatchet fish hanging out in groups under shelters in clear water. They are highly sought for the aquarium trade. (to 6 cm, 2.5 in)

Plate 99e
Neon Tetra
Paracheirodon innesi

This tiny beauty is perhaps the most famous of freshwater aquarium fishes. Its common name is extremely apt, as their red and blue-green bands fairly glow. A large school is a truly breathtaking sight. Neons and the closely related Cardinal Tetras of the Río Negro are blackwater fishes; they cannot tolerate any turbidity, but thrive in clear water over sandy bottoms. They are omnivorous, feeding on plants, small insects and worms. (to 4 cm, 1.6 in)

Plate 99f
Piratanta
(also called Splash Tetra)
Copella arnoldi

This tetra is celebrated more for its behavior than its appearance, though the males at least, have elaborate fins, somewhat like a guppy's. The males' hypertrophied dorsal, anal, and tail fins are mostly black with red and white highlights; and males alone have a white spot at the base of the dorsal fin. Females have less elaborate fins. Piratanta reproductive behavior is remarkable, not least because the eggs are deposited on objects (e.g. leaves) above the water surface. This feat requires the coordinated efforts of both sexes. The male and female partially lock their fins, then leap up to the underside of a leaf, where they use their fins to maintain suction for up to 10 seconds. About 5 to 10 eggs are deposited and fertilized on the leaf surface, before the adults fall back into the water. This procedure is repeated many times until the clutch size numbers in the hundreds. The male then keeps the eggs damp by spraying them with flicks of his tail. Once the eggs hatch, the fry fall into the water and are on their own. This species feeds on insects, worms and small crustaceans. (to 8 cm, 3 in)

Plate 99 459

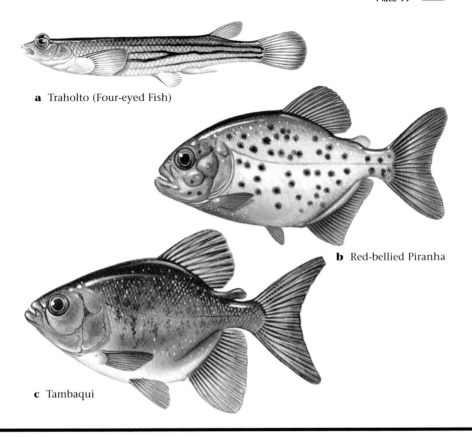

a Traholto (Four-eyed Fish)

b Red-bellied Piranha

c Tambaqui

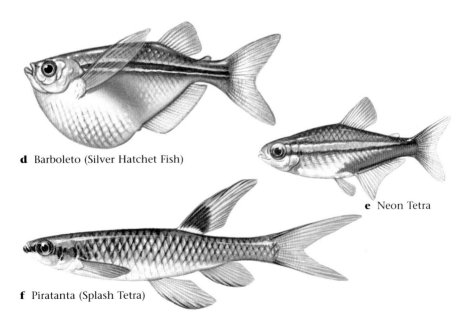

d Barboleto (Silver Hatchet Fish)

e Neon Tetra

f Piratanta (Splash Tetra)

Plate 100a

Madalena
(also called Humpback)
Roeboides meyersi

This parasite is the scourge of anything with scales. It rams its victim, dislodging the scales, then circles around gathering them up as they flutter to the bottom. In addition to the conical teeth inside the mouth, it has nipple-like protuberances on the outside surface of its jaws, which help to dislodge the scales. It hunts in groups, often accompanied by mimics of the genus *Charax*. These mimics are, not surprisingly, scaleless, and use the Madalena as protection from predators, which, also not surprisingly, avoid the scale-eaters. Madalena and other scale-eaters prefer water adjacent to sandy beaches and river banks. The Madalena's translucent body is deep near the head but rapidly tapers toward the tail. (to 15 cm, 6 in)

Plate 100b

Traira
(also called Snakehead)
Hoplias malabaricus

This nocturnal predator haunts rainforest streams. It is quite voracious and dramatically affects other fish populations, especially during the dry season, when it makes short work of fishes that have migrated into the forest in the high water season. It can be found in a wide variety of other habitats as well, resting under vegetation during the day. Its body is tubular and mottled grayish brown; its teeth are formidable. (to 50 cm, 20 in)

Plate 100c

Jaraqui
(also called Prochilodus)
Semaprochilodus varii

A herbivore with a carp-like body, this is one of the most important food fishes in the Amazon. Its coloration is silvery with striking black and yellow tail stripes. Like other members of the *curimata* group, it feeds on detritus but it specializes on the fine detritus covering submerged trees. Its thick fleshy lips can be turned inside-out to form a suction cup and they are endowed with hair-like teeth that function as a rasp. There is evidence that the trees on which it feeds release nutrients that enrich the detritus; the fish in turn release nutrients for the trees in their feces. After 2 to 3 months of feeding in the flooded forest the fish get very fat and they begin to form migratory schools just after the flood peaks. It is when they are migrating back into the main river channels that they are exploited by humans. When not in the forest they can be found swimming in rapids and areas of high current. (to 30 cm, 12 in)

Plate 100d

Aracu
(also called Many-banded Leporinus)
Leporinus affinis

This popular aquarium fish, in nature, prefers sand holes in fast-flowing streams and creeks, where it dines on fruits and other plant materials. It typically maintains a slightly head-down position into the current and belongs to a group of fishes known as *headstanders*. The body is elongate with a whitish-yellow background coloration and a number of broad black vertical bands; the throat area is deep red. There are a number of species of the headstander group (Leporinidae) in the Amazon. (to 25 cm, 10 in)

Plate 100e

Pirapoucou
(also called Golden Pike-characin)
Boulengerella lucius

Like the Jacunda (Pike Cichlid; Plate 98), this predatory characin has converged on the pike design. As is true of all pike-like predators, it makes quick short dashes at its prey, typically from an oblique angle. It bends its body like a bow; when the tension is suddenly released, it shoots itself like an arrow toward its victim, which it grabs with pincer-like jaws. Most of its attacks are near the water's surface, below which it lurks, motionless, often in small groups. It also lures prey with a fleshy orange-red appendage on the upper part of its beak-jaw. This species and other *pike characins* prefer water over sandy bottoms, especially near beaches. (to 60 cm, 24 in)

Plate 100   461

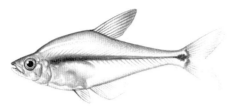

a Madalena (Humpback)

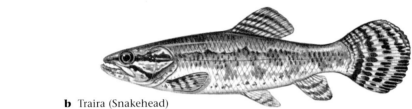

b Traira (Snakehead)

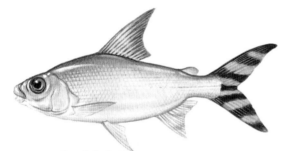

c Jaraqui (Prochilodus)

d Aracu (Many-banded Leporinus)

e Pirapoucou (Golden Pike-characin)

Plate 101a
Cuiu Cuiu
(also called Ripsaw Catfish)
Oxydoras niger
This cousin of the Bacu-pedra is the largest doradid ("talking catfish" family) catfish. It is heavily armored in a manner resembling some Paleozoic fossil fishes and possesses a huge mouth with giant lips, by means of which it creates suction to vacuum up detritus and organic ooze rich in bloodworms, insect larvae and other goodies. It prefers floodplain lakes with abundant floating meadows. (to 1.2 m, 4 ft)

Plate 101b
Piraiba
(also called Giant Catfish)
Brachyplatystoma filamentosum
Though very large, the Dourada is not the largest catfish in the Amazon; that distinction goes to its close relative, the Piraiba, also known as the Giant Catfish. The Piraiba is a more typical member of the long-whiskered catfish family in being a nocturnal bottom-feeder. It prefers the deep water (below 30 m, 100 ft) of the main river channels. In this dark muddy water vision is of little use; accordingly, its eyes are extremely small. Piraiba feed primarily on other fishes, but also a wide variety of other animals, including monkeys and even an occasional human. But far more often it is the humans who dine on Giant Catfish, as their flesh is quite tasty. (to 4 m, 13 ft; to 200 kg, 440 lb)

Plate 101c
Cochorhino
(also called Spotted Cochoro)
Acestrorhyncus falcatus
A formidable predator that preys exclusively on fishes, this species has a body shape intermediate to a bass and a pike. Its narrow jaws are packed with needle-sharp teeth, so once bitten, its victim seldom escapes. It is fairly ubiquitous but especially prefers water with moderate flow. Look for a characteristic black spot at the base of the tail. (to 30 cm, 12 in)

Plate 101d
Bacu-pedra
(also called Rock Bacu, Thorny Catfish)
Lithodoris dorsalis
This is one of the so-called "talking catfish" (family Doradidae), which make noises with their swimbladders. Talking catfishes are heavily armored and each lateral plate bears a hook or spine, from which they derive their other common name, "thorny catfish." This species is particularly blessed in that area and in addition it possesses formidable dorsal and pectoral fin spines that it wields like a spear to ward off

(continued on p. 467)

Plate 101e
Surubim
(also called Shovelnose Catfish, Tiger Flathead)
Pseudoplatystoma fasciatum
This is another commercially important foodfish, highly prized for its succulent yellow flesh. Its body is long and slender, built for speed; its gigantic head is flat and wide. Surubim forage at night along the bottom of the main river channels, primarily for fish prey. (to 90 cm, 35 in)

Plate 101f
Dourada
(also called Gilded Catfish)
Brachyplatystoma flavicans
This large predator exploits the entire length of the Amazon, from the Atlantic to the Andes. Its head is platinum, the rest of the body a shimmering golden color, one of the most beautiful fish anywhere in the world. It has recently become one of the most important game fish in the Amazon as well. Far more interesting to biologists, however, is its fascinating life history. Young Dourada exploit the nutrient-rich waters at the confluence of the Amazon and the Atlantic, where they grow rapidly on a diet of shrimp and smaller fishes. They begin to move upstream in large schools when they reach 50 to 75 cm (20 to 30 in) and begin to feed on characins and other catfish; as they grow they continue this westward migration, for 2 to 3 years, until they reach their spawning grounds at the base of the Andes, some 2500 miles (4000 km) from the Atlantic. In this journey they must surmount rapids and cataracts, which they negotiate like salmon and where they are gaffed by local fishermen. After spawning, and during the following flood stage, the young fry (and adult spawners) ride the swift current back down

(continued on p. 467)

Plate 101   463

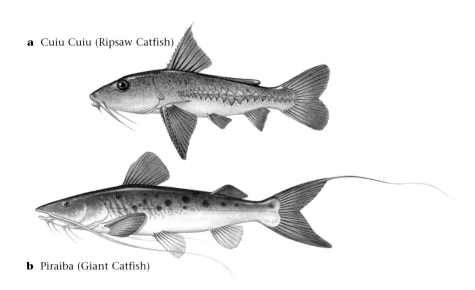

a Cuiu Cuiu (Ripsaw Catfish)

b Piraiba (Giant Catfish)

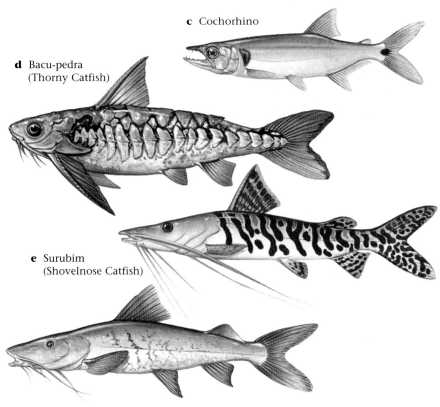

c Cochorhino

d Bacu-pedra
(Thorny Catfish)

e Surubim
(Shovelnose Catfish)

f Dourada (Gilded Catfish)

Plate 102a
Tabatinga
(also called Skunk Corydoras)
Corydoras arcuatus
The *smooth-armored catfish* (family Callichthyidae) are so called because their armor plates lack the prickles and spines present in the other two groups of armored catfish (Doradidae, Loricaridae). Many members of the genus *Corydoras* are imported for the aquarium trade, including this species; all are legendary for their complete lack of aggression, even among males in the breeding season. These diminutive catfish are also almost irresistibly cute, their moustache-like barbels somewhat droll. They are ideal citizens indeed for a community aquarium, where they busy themselves rooting around sand and gravel for bits of stuff eschewed by most other fishes. The body is silver-white with a prominent black band that runs down the dorsal surface; the fins are transparent. (to 5 cm, 2 in)

Plate 102b
Guitarita
(also called Banjo Catfish)
Dysichthys kneri
Members of the small family (Aspredinidae) of fish known as *banjo catfishes* are so called because of their body shape. The head region is very flat, and the tail relatively long and slender. This is a small catfish, as are most other members of the family. It frequents coastal areas including some brackish water environments. (to 8 cm, 3 in)

Plate 102c
Candiru
Vandella cirrhosa
There are actually two distinct groups of fish known as *candiru* in Brazil; the so-called "whale catfish" (because of their body shape), famous for the rapaciousness with which they attack hooked fish – much like piranhas – and bathers alike; and the much smaller, gill-dwelling catfish that have become legendary for swimming into unlikely human orifices (including the vagina, anus, nose, and ears). These needle-shaped fish are adapted to dwell in the gills of large catfishes, where they extract mucus and blood. Traditionally, menstruating Indian women avoid candiru-infested waters for fear their blood may attract these pests. According to native folklore, these fish are also attracted to urine, and they are reputed to be able to enter the penis of a man who is urinating by the side of a river, by

(continued on p. 467)

Plate 102d
Arraia
(also called Freshwater Stingray)
Potamotrygon motoro
This is one of several large stingray species in the Amazon. The sting, which is administered by a spine on the tail, is quite painful, though rarely lethal, and it easily penetrates rubber boots. Exert caution when walking along the shallow sandy areas that the stingrays frequent. They feed mainly at night on small bottom-dwelling fish and crustaceans. (to 1 m, 3.3 ft)

Plate 102e
Acari
(also called Sucker Mouth, Plecostomus)
Hypostomus plecostomus
This is a member of the *suckermouth armored catfish* group (family Loricaridae, also called *spiny armored catfish*), and a very popular fish in the aquarium trade. On a visit to any aquarium store, you will find it seemingly attached to the inside surface of the glass by its mouth. In nature it uses its powerful mouth suction to attach to rocks and other hard surfaces on which it grazes for algae. The lips are equipped with horny tooth-like protuberances that act as a rasp. The fins, particularly the dorsal, are large and fan-shaped; the background coloration is variable but both fins and body are always covered with small dark spots. This is but one of many species of algae-eating loricarids that inhabit the fast-moving streams of the Amazon region. (to 50 cm, 20 in)

Plate 102f
Bull Shark
Carcharhinus leucas
This marine predator frequently wanders up major rivers in tropical areas throughout the world. In the Amazon, it is most common in the estuary but it has been found all the way to the base of the Andes (5000 km, 3100 miles, upstream). It is more prone to attack humans than its more famous relatives, Great White and Tiger Sharks, and for whatever reason, it is more prone to these attacks in freshwater than saltwater; but the individuals that enter the Amazon are generally fairly small and few attacks have been recorded. (to 2.5 m, 8.2 ft, in the Amazon; to 3.4 m, 11 ft, offshore.)

Plate 102 465

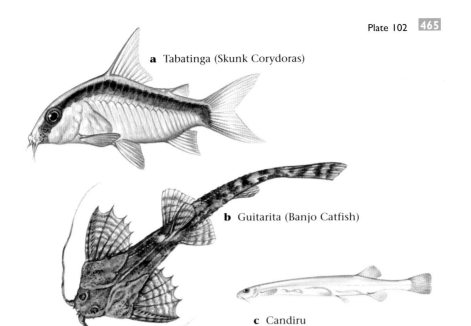

a Tabatinga (Skunk Corydoras)

b Guitarita (Banjo Catfish)

c Candiru

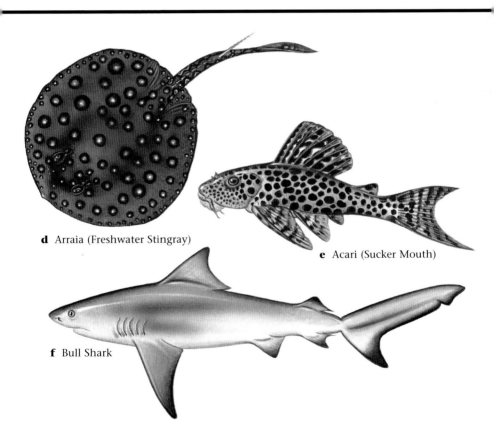

d Arraia (Freshwater Stingray)

e Acari (Sucker Mouth)

f Bull Shark

Plate 98a (continued from p. 456)

water period, when oxygen levels are lowest, many fishes reduce their activity or even become *torpid* (lower their metabolisms and sleep), which makes them easy prey for the air-breathing Pirarucu. Prey capture is facilitated by its tongue, which is armed with teeth and functions like a second set of jaws when pushed against the roof of the mouth. These tongues, dried, have been traditionally used as seed-graters. If you visit an area where Pirarucu are relatively abundant you may be able to see and hear them attacking their prey near the surface. (to 4.5 m, 14.5 ft)

Plate 98b (continued from p. 456)

oxygen environments because, like the Pirarucu, it is an airbreather. The mouth of the electric eel functions as a lung; it is full of highly vascularized protuberances in which oxygen is taken into the bloodstream. It has only vestigial gills that serve solely to eliminate carbon dioxide. The mouth lung would be easily damaged by fish spines and it is thought that the powerful electric discharges evolved primarily to protect it; the stunned prey is quickly swallowed and passed into the stomach so that it cannot damage the fragile mouth lining. (to 3 m, 10 ft)

Plate 98d (continued from p. 456)

the male takes them into his mouth, where they remain until they hatch and the yolk sacs are absorbed (2 to 3 weeks). The male then lets them out to forage but they return to his mouth whenever danger threatens. Like the Pirarucu, Arawanas are air breathers and thrive in low oxygen environments. (to 1.2 m, 4 ft)

Plate 99a (continued from p. 458)

aerial visual field, while the lower part transmits light from the aquatic visual field. To keep its upper eye from drying out it dips its head into the water every few minutes. It feeds primarily on insects in fairly brackish water, where it has little competition from salt-intolerant characins. Its aerial vision helps it escape wading and diving birds. Aside from the large eyes, this fish is rather nondescript; the elongate body is generally brownish; the dorsal fin is small and located far back toward the tail. (to 30 cm, 12 in)

Plate 99b (continued from p. 458)

piranha then dart in from all angles, taking bites, then dart away. Once a larger prey is disabled, a *feeding frenzy* may occur, attracting neighboring groups. Most of their prey is small but they will attack large species, including mammals. The Red-bellied Piranha feeds primarily at dusk and dawn. This species has a very blunt nose and a characteristic red belly. It prefers muddy rivers and floodplain lakes. It is replaced by the closely related Black Piranha in clearwater and blackwater areas. (to 33 cm, 13 in)

Plate 99c (continued from p. 458)

fruits that fall into the water, which it detects with its powerful olfactory sense. It feeds primarily during the high water season, when the forests are flooded, laying down fat reserves that sustain it through the lean low water season. Unfortunately for this fish, its flesh is among the tastiest, said to be delightfully fruity, and it is being severely overfished. The Tambaqui has a piranha-like saucer shaped body; it is generally black above but green to greenish yellow toward the belly. (to 1 m, 3.3 ft)

Plate 101d (continued from p. 462)

predators. Large adults frequent the flooded lowland forests, where they consume vast quantities of fruit. They migrate to the lower Amazon to spawn in the tidal flooded forest of the estuarine region. The young develop in this environment, following the tides into the forest and back, one of the few fruit-eating fish adapted to this environment. Bacu-pedra are important dispersal agents for several species of fruiting trees. In addition to the various fruits, bacu feed heavily on large arum (philodendron-like plants) leaves. (to 90 cm, 35 in)

Plate 101f (continued from p. 462)

to the Atlantic Ocean in a matter of weeks, completing one of the most epic journeys in the animal kingdom. Dourada differ from most catfish in a number of ways; they are not strictly nocturnal, nor are they primarily bottom feeders; they feed both day and night and they hunt from the surface to mid-depth. Though they belong to the family of so-called "long-whiskered" catfish (Pimelodidae), their own barbels (whiskers), by means of which most catfish "feel" around the bottom, are quite short; instead, Dourada rely heavily on vision. (to 2.5 m, 8.2 ft)

Plate 102c (continued from p. 464)

swimming up the urine stream. These reports are no doubt apocryphal. Candiru do, on occasion, however, enter the eurethra of both male and female bathers, perhaps attracted to their urine. However remote the likelihood of this unpleasant event, the mere prospect is sufficient to cause most would-be underwater micturaters to think twice, even the most skeptical. (to 2.5 cm, 1 in)

WCS Conservation Work in Latin America

The Conservation Challenge in Latin America

From Mexico to Tierra del Fuego, Latin America is a land of superlatives. Vast tropical rain forests, rivers comprising the largest freshwater systems on Earth, towering mountains and deep oceans are home to animals and plants found nowhere else in the world. Perhaps no other region on Earth presents such a variety of ecosystems and astonishing array of wildlife.

Latin American conservation efforts, however, face difficult social, economic, and environmental challenges. The region's human population has tripled since 1950. South America alone has lost almost a quarter of its forests, while more than 60 percent of Mexico's woodlands have fallen. Increased hunting, fishing, mining, and other natural resource exploitation threaten already stressed ecosystems.

Patagonia's elephant seals travel as far as the South Georgia Islands, staying at sea for up to 8 months. (Photograph with permission from William Conway and WCS.)

These problems, compounded by too few trained conservation professionals and a chronic lack of funding for natural resource management, have both pushed many species to the brink of extinction, and reduced the land's ability to support human life.

Working to reverse these trends, the Wildlife Conservation Society has supported conservation work in Latin America since 1909 with its landmark field studies in Trinidad, Venezuela, and the Galapagos Islands. Today WCS conservationists, working mainly through local projects run by nationals, are uniquely positioned to understand local conditions and conservation opportunities. WCS has developed hundreds of innovative conservation projects, from field studies of endangered species such as the Andean mountain tapir, to the protection of

WCS scientists conceived a network of protected areas in Central America called Paseo Pantera – the Meso-America biological corridor. By protecting these areas, the vast ecological diversity of the region will be preserved. Red-eyed treefrogs, tapirs and small hawksbill turtles are among the thousands of species found in the Paseo Pantera. (Photographs with permission from S. Matola, A. Meylan and WCS)

immense areas through the Patagonian Coastal Zone Management Plan and Central America's Paseo Pantera Project. Today, WCS operates more than 100 Latin American projects in 17 countries, from Mexico to Argentina.

All of these projects depend critically on scientific research. Field staff survey wildlife and assess biodiversity to determine how species interact with their habitats and their human neighbors. Projects lasting several years allow researchers to uncover trends and patterns not apparent in short-term research and to build relationships with local communities and governments. Local conservationists are trained to be responsible for the stewardship of their land and Government participation is encouraged.

Crossing Political Boundaries for Regional Conservation

The Biological Corridors of Paseo Pantera

Whether called panther, cougar, mountain lion, puma, or pantera, the New World's premier big cat ranges from Patagonia to northern Canada. The Central American Land Bridge joining North and South America, rose from the sea some three million years ago, allowing the panther and thousands of other species to expand their range and thrive in new territories. To protect this "biological highway," WCS has pioneered a conservation strategy called "Paseo Pantera" – Path of the Panther – to connect an unbroken corridor of parks and refuges throughout Central America.

The pumas and jaguars require huge expanses of unbroken habitat. Biological corridors in Central America are a key solution to preserving the range of these big cats along with many other threatened species. (Photographs with permission from A. Rabinowitz and WCS.)

Just a few decades ago, upland rainforests and dense vegetation covered much of Central America, and mangrove swamps and coral reefs lined its two coasts, forming a chain of natural areas between North and South America. Subsequent human development and population growth has pushed wildlife into dwindling, isolated patchworks of habitat. Working with all seven countries in the Paseo Pantera region, WCS seeks to improve management of existing parks and to restore degraded habitat for migratory wildlife. In Belize, WCS aims to establish new reserves along the Belize Barrier Reef. In reserves in the western Maya Mountains, researchers are developing guidelines to preserve biodiversity. WCS assists Guatemala in the management of the 3.1-million-acre Maya Biosphere Reserve. In Honduras, WCS musters resources to improve the management of protected coastal areas, including the Bay Islands and the Rio Platano Biosphere Reserve – one of the largest protected areas in Central America. In El Salvador, damaged areas are restored and in Nicaragua, plans have been developed to protect Bosawas, Miskito Cat, and the Si-A-Paz. WCS and several other organizations have helped Costa Rica expand Tortuguero National Park to four times its original size. And Panama is investing in conservation projects in the coastal bays of Bocas del Toro.

Manu Reserve in Perú contains incredible diversity of wildlife, including flocks of Scarlet Macaws, shown here at a lick. (Photograph with permission from C. Munn and E. Nycander.)

In 1994, all seven Central American countries signed an agreement affirming the Central American Biological Corridor as a conservation priority – Paseo Pantera will help sustain the region's unique mixture of wildlife well into the future.

Working with Nations to Protect Habitat

Bolivia Creates Two Massive Parks

When wildlife surveys in Bolivia revealed an extraordinary wealth of species in two diverse regions, WCS joined the Bolivian Government, local conservation organizations, and indigenous people to protect these areas. Two massive parks were declared in 1995 spanning 20,000 square miles – an area larger than Switzerland.

The first park, Kaa-Iya del Gran Chaco in southeast Bolivia, protects a vast 8.6 million acres of the Chaco – a unique dry forest and thorn-scrub habitat second only to the Amazon rainforest in size. Agricultural clearing has destroyed most

of the original Chaco, which once covered much of northern Argentina and Paraguay, leaving sparsely populated Bolivia with the last great expanse. Since 1984, WCS has cataloged 46 species of large mammals in Bolivia's Chaco, including giant armadillos, maned wolves, several big cat and primate species, and the rare Chacoan peccary, thought extinct until 1975.

The second park, Alto Madidi in northwest Bolivia, covers 4.7 million acres of glaciers, mountain and lowland rainforests, and Pampas del Heath savannahs. It could be the most biologically rich region in the world with almost 1,200 species of birds, Andean bears, jaguars, giant otters, anacondas, black caimans, and thousands of other animal and plant species.

Today, illegal hunting threatens wildlife. This jaguar skin was found in the Mamirauá Reserve. (Photograph with permission from J. Thorbjarnarson.)

Making these two parks a reality required several years of research and co-operation between the various interested parties. In the huge Chaco park, WCS is supporting the efforts of native peoples to develop management plans, foster eco-tourism possibilities and explore other economic incentives to local inhabitants. The Tacana Indians, who have long supported conservation efforts in the Madidi region, will similarly help manage their new park.

Stewardship Through Community Involvement

Mamirauá Lake Ecological Station

Amazonian Brazil boasts one of the most extraordinary, yet least studied ecosystems in the world – the seasonally flooded forest known as the varzea – an area larger than Florida. Rare uakari monkeys and umbrella birds forage in the canopy, while pink river dolphins, caimans, and Amazonian manatees swim among submerged trees. WCS has recorded over 200 species of fish, nearly 300 species of birds, and an exceptional diversity of trees in this unique environment.

In response to threats such as commercial logging and overfishing, WCS launched one of its most unique Latin American projects: the Mamirauá Lake Ecological Station, a 2.8-million-acre reserve. Brazilian and international scientists gather information and monitor the resource demands of the 2000 local inhabitants. Research projects include surveys of wildlife, plants, and fish; and measure the effects of timber extraction, fishing, and subsistence hunting.

Local people have provided crucial support to this initiative, protecting their livelihood from outside exploitation. Ultimately, local participation is the only way to insure future wise stewardship of this flooded Amazonian forest.

In 1995, $1 million was provided for the establishment of the "National Institute for the Varzea," to be built near the reserve in the town of Tefè, the first major Brazilian research institute in the upper Amazon region.

Long-term Commitments

Coastal Conservation in Patagonia

Spectacular concentrations of colonial seabirds and marine mammals flourish along Patagonia's rugged 2000-mile coastline. The plankton-filled Antarctic current supports southern right whales, elephant seals, Magellanic penguins, and one of the planet's most productive fisheries.

WCS has worked here for over 30 years, promoting the declaration of many coastal reserves, among them Punta Tombo and Punta Leon in Chubat Province.

To combat threats from burgeoning petroleum, shipping, fishing, and tourism developments, WCS has helped produce a Patagonian Coastal Zone Management Plan, a collaborative effort with local organizations to manage fast-growing industries while protecting the region's unique ecology.

WCS monitors Elephant seals and Magellanic penguins as indicator species of the southern Atlantic ecosystem. Chronic oil pollution has reduced penguin

Chronic oil pollution has caused a one-third decline in Magellanic penguin populations at Punta Tombo, Patagonia. WCS is working with Argentinean authorities to move oil tanker routes away from delicate breeding areas. WCS President and General Director William Conway pioneered WCS's work in Patagonia some 30 years ago. (Photograph with permission from William Conway.)

numbers by one-third in the past 15 years and WCS advocates that oil tanker routes be moved farther from the coast. Offshore, WCS examines the impact of whale-watching, which has grown 300 percent in 7 years, working with local governments and the whale-watching industry to insure that boats do not disturb the whales and their young. WCS monitors the impacts of commercial fishery "by-catch" – non-target fish species discarded overboard. Fisheries off Patagonia produce up to 50 to 70 percent by-catch, virtually all of which dies on the decks of the fishing vessels, reducing the food supplies of marine birds and mammals.

Conservation Through Training

WCS teaches scientific know-how to Latin American students and professionals, to create a core of conservationists, scientists, and decision-makers who will be able to protect the region's wildlife. Local people and park guards are taught how to census and monitor wildlife populations and conservation science is taught to university students and professionals. Since 1989, WCS has held courses in Colombia, Venezuela, Ecuador, and Perú.

The WCS Student Grants Program offers graduate and undergraduate conservationists much-needed funding for research projects to solve conservation problems in Latin America. Since 1987, this program has supported more than 140 projects in Perú, Ecuador, Colombia, Bolivia, and Venezuela.

The Scientific Challenge of Sustainable Use

"Sustainable use" – harvesting natural resources while preserving biodiversity – is often seen as the panacea to unite conflicting environmental and economic interests. However, the exploitation of natural resources, even on a sustainable basis, will inevitably involve some biodiversity loss, a problem under WCS scrutiny. WCS is investigating the effects of selective timber harvesting in Bolivia and Venezuela, for example, where some logging interests claim the practice is sustainable. In Ecuador, the Sustainable Utilization of Biological Resources (SUBIR) project monitors wildlife populations and works with local communities to develop economic alternatives to destroying habitats.

WCS trains park rangers and conservationists throughout Latin America. These Venezuelan park guards help protect world-renowned regions, including Angel Falls in Canaima National Park. (Photograph with permission from A. Grajal.)

You Can Make A Difference —
Your Membership Helps Save
Animals And Their Habitats

Join today! Your membership contribution supports our conservation projects around the world and here at home. For over 100 years, we've been dedicated to saving endangered species — including tigers, snow leopards, African and Asian elephants, gorillas and thousands of other animals.

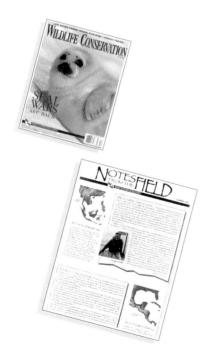

FOR A COMPLETE LIST OF
BENEFITS PLEASE TURN
THE PAGE ...

YES! I want to help save rare and endangered animals. Here is my membership contribution of:

☐ $25   ☐ $35   ☐ $75   ☐ $150

☐ I cannot join at this time but enclosed is my contribution of $ _____.

Full name (Adult #1) _____

Address _____

City _____ State _____ Zip _____ Daytime Phone (___) _____

For Family Plus and Conservation members only:

Full name Adult #2 _____

Full name Adult #3 _____ #Children ages 2–18 _____

Your employer may have a matching gift program that can double, even triple, your contribution. Be sure to check with your Personnel or Community Relations Office.

$25 ASSOCIATE

- One year of *Wildlife Conservation*, our award-winning magazine filled with breathtaking photographs and articles that will keep you up to date about our worldwide conservation initiatives.

$35 BASIC MEMBERSHIP

Wildlife Conservation magazine plus the benefits of *full membership* including:

- *Notes from the Field*, a quarterly newsletter with project reports from scientists in the field
- Opportunities to travel with WCS scientists
- A membership card that entitles one adult to unlimited admission for one year to all five of our wildlife parks in New York including the world famous Bronx Zoo, as well as passes for free parking where available.

$75 PLUS MEMBERSHIP

All the benefits of Basic and:

- *Passport to Adventure* ... Travel around the world learning about exotic animals without ever leaving home with this interactive, educational package of stickers, fun fact cards, a map and more. Great fun for the entire family!
- A membership card that entitles two additional adults (total of three) and children to unlimited admission for one year to all five of our wildlife parks.

$150 CONSERVATION SUPPORTER

All the benefits of Plus and:

- Limited edition sterling silver antelope pin.

JOIN NOW! Mail your membership contribution to:

WILDLIFE CONSERVATION SOCIETY
Membership Department
2300 Southern Boulevard
Bronx, NY 10460–1068, USA

Join using your credit card by calling
1–718–220–5111

or by visiting our website
www.wcs.org

TRAVEL WITH THE EXPERTS!

Wildlife Conservation Society tours take you to wild places with informed escorts who know the country, know the animals and care about wildlife. They have actively participated in establishing national parks or saving endangered species. You'll travel with experts who will share their excitement, wonder and love of wildlife conservation.

From the national parks of Kenya to the rain forest of Perú, WCS travel experts will make your trip an informative, educational and lively adventure.

For more information call or write:
WCS International Travel Program
830 Fifth Avenue
New York, NY 10021 USA
00 1 212–439–6507

Please clip this form and mail it with your gift to Wildlife Conservation Society/2300 Southern Blvd/Bronx, NY 10460–1068, USA.

IMPORTANT: Wildlife Conservation Society is a 401(c)3 organization. Non membership contributions are fully tax-deductible to the extent allowed by law. Membership dues are tax-deductible in excess of benefit value. Magazine is a $12 value, parking passes are an $8 value, *Passport to Adventure* is a $6 value. For a copy of our latest Annual Report you can write to us or to the Office of Charities Registration, 162 Washington Avenue, Albany NY 12231, USA. Your contribution to the Society will be used to support our general programs as described in the Annual Report.

Species Index

General Index

NOTES